Also by David Osborne and Peter Plastrik
Banishing Bureaucracy: The Five Strategies for Reinventing Government

Also by David Osborne
Reinventing Government (with Ted Gaebler)
Laboratories of Democracy

The Reinventor's Fieldbook

Tools for Transforming Your Government

David Osborne
Peter Plastrik

JOSSEY-BASS
A Wiley Company
San Francisco

Page 690 constitutes a continuation of the copyright page.

Printed in the United States of America.

Library of Congress Cataloging-in-Publication Data

Osborne, David (David E.)
The reinventor's fieldbook : tools for transforming your government / David Osborne, Peter Plastrik.— 1st ed.
p. cm.
Includes bibliographical references and index.
ISBN 0-7879-4332-0
1. Administrative agencies—Management. 2. Bureaucracy. 3. Government productivity. 4. Customer relations. 5. Entrepreneurship. I. Plastrik, Peter. II. Title.

JK421 .O724 2000
352.3—dc21

00-030373

FIRST EDITION
PB Printing 10 9 8 7 6 5 4 3 2 1

For my colleagues at the Public Strategies Group, with gratitude.
—D.O.

For Stanley and Simone Plastrik, my first teachers.
—P.P.

Contents

The Reinventor's Toolbox:

An Alphabetical Index of Approaches, Tools, and Competences

Acknowledgments

We have come to rely on a number of remarkable people to deepen our understanding of reinvention. Their thoughtful advice, constructive critiques, and cheerful patience improved this book and enrich our lives. Many of them are as close as family; all make themselves instantly available for conversations. They bring a sustained passion and a steady competence to the task of reinvention. In this, they inspire us.

Our close colleagues at the Public Strategies Group (PSG)—Babak Armajani, Camille Barnett, Lorraine Chang, Larry Grant, Rick Heydinger, Peter Hutchinson, Connie Nelson, Laurie Ohmann, Steve Struthers, and Jeff Zlonis—helped us in more ways than we can recount. They shared their wealth of experience and knowledge with us; they gave us feedback on ideas; they read and commented on drafts. They were our master consultants, as they have been for so many public organizations. We owe a particular debt to Babak, Connie, and Peter, who spent untold hours on the phone sharing their knowledge with us.

Bob Stone, a wise head with a wealth of stories, was enormously generous with his time and advice. When Bob retired recently as Vice President Gore's director of the National Partnership for Reinventing Government (NPR) to join PSG, he left the federal government a far better place. John Kamensky, deputy director of the NPR, was equally generous, enthusiastically answering our questions and constantly pointing us to the best resources available.

Tom Lewcock, former city manager of Sunnyvale, California, taught us an enormous amount about performance management, performance budgeting, and other tools he pioneered in that position. Ted Staton, city manager of East Lansing, Michigan, encouraged us to test ideas on his managers there and to listen to their real-world stories. Bob O'Leary shared his extensive war stories and helped us better understand the politics of clearing the decks and organizational empowerment. Mark Murray, a good friend who has worked at every level of state government, responded to our endless questions.

John Perry, John Gorczyk, and Lynne Walthers of the Vermont Corrections Department introduced us to an exciting use of reinvention in the criminal justice system. Duncan Wyse of the Oregon Business Council helped us understand and research the Oregon Benchmarks and Progress Board. Beverly Stein, the elected executive of Multnomah County, Oregon, shared her experience with strategic management throughout her tenure there.

Al Bilik, Jeremy Cowper, Tharon Greene, Tom Lewcock, Ron Oliver, David Riemer, and our colleagues at PSG reviewed drafts of chapters and helped us improve them.

We also called often on a number of people to respond to our need for expert information. In addition to those we have already thanked, Bob Behn, Jeremy Cowper, Gloria Craig, Derek Gill, Jim Flanagan, Michael Marsh, Adrian Moore, Adrian Montague, Mike Masterson, and Jeff Tryens rose to the occasion repeatedly, sending articles, suggesting contacts, pointing us to Web pages, and answering inquiries.

Hundreds of others shared their time and expertise with us in interviews as we did the research for this book. We thank them all, with deep gratitude for their help and their good work in the fields of government reinvention.

Our literary agent, Kristine Dahl, once again took us smoothly through the publishing industry's legal and financial white water. And our editors, Alan Shrader and Dorothy Hearst, encouraged us and provided good advice. Mary Garrett shepherded the book through production.

Can we ever thank our families enough? If they suffered from the long hours we put into the solitary acts of research and writing, they did not complain—at least not within our hearing. When they wondered why we decided to do a second book (an even longer one!) after the exhausting process of writing *Banishing Bureaucracy*, they never suggested we were too thick-skulled to learn.

Pete thanks his wife, Deb, for making room in the rest of their family's life for this intrusive project and for letting him commandeer the dining room table for a year. David thanks his wife, Rose, for letting him all but disappear for the final three-month sprint to the finish line. David and Pete both thank their children, who make it all worthwhile.

David Osborne
Essex, Massachusetts

Peter Plastrik
East Lansing, Michigan

Introduction

I can't understand why people are frightened by new ideas. I'm frightened of old ones.

JOHN CAGE

In 1992 *Reinventing Government* drew a map of a brave new world of public governance. It struck a nerve within American government, then within governments worldwide. Since it was published, we have spoken with hundreds of public sector groups about reinvention. Almost without exception, their most urgent questions boil down to this one: *How can we reinvent* ***our*** *bureaucracy?*

- *How do we get started?*
- *How do we deal with the unions?*
- *How do we get our political leaders to embrace change?*
- *How do we motivate our frontline employees?*
- *How do we get the money we need to invest in change?*

The passion behind these questions is remarkable. Many public leaders, managers, and employees are desperate for change, desperate to improve the bureaucratic systems in which they find themselves trapped. And yet, they find it extremely difficult to move their bureaucracies in any meaningful way—a difficulty we know all too well from our own work in and with governments. Their questions are often so urgent, and so heartfelt, that we feel a responsibility to respond. We have spent the last seven years doing so.

Our first response was our 1997 book *Banishing Bureaucracy: The Five Strategies for Reinventing Government.* Based on research in five countries, we laid out the fundamental strategies that have proven to have the most power to transform public bureaucracies into more flexible, innovative, entrepreneurial organizations and systems. We explained several different approaches possible under each strategy and briefly introduced many tools reinventors could use to implement those approaches. If *Reinventing Government* drew a rough map of the new world of governance emerging in the late 20th century, *Banishing Bureaucracy* began to put routes on the map, to help reinventors follow the pioneers and stake their own claims in the new world.

The Reinventor's Fieldbook begins to fill in the essential details on that map. Whereas *Banishing Bureaucracy* laid out the major routes (strategies), this book explains in detail the terrain you will encounter, the obstacles you will face, and the equipment and know-how (tools and competencies) you will need along the way.

Although this book includes dozens of case studies not included in *Banishing Bureaucracy,* it is based primarily on research in the same five countries: the U.S., Canada, Great Britain, Australia, and New Zealand. (We are aware of successful reinvention in non-English-speaking countries, and we have included some insights based on our reading about them, but our ability to do research in these countries was constrained by our limited language capacities.) We hope this fieldbook will be useful to practitioners in many countries; although conditions and governmental systems in the developed democracies vary, the problems encountered within their public bureaucracies are remarkably similar. The developing world has some different problems; reinventors there can use many of these strategies and approaches but must be careful in implementing the Control Strategy, a reality we discuss in Part Four.

We are confident that this fieldbook will be helpful to people throughout the public sector, whether they work in school districts, special districts, counties, cities, states or provinces, or national governments. Our research base includes all of these, and we have found an uncanny similarity between problems and solutions at one level and those at another. Though they are often unwilling to believe it, people in national governments can learn a great deal from their counterparts in provincial, state, and local governments—and vice versa.

Like any form of pioneering, reinvention is not for the faint of heart. It is hard work, it takes a long time, it requires genuine sacrifice, and it often fails. It requires people to give up the safety of the status quo and venture into the unknown, with no guarantee that things will end well. It is as frightening for many people in the public sector as it must have been for pioneer families to leave the safety of their homes in New England or Virginia and head west.

We wrote this book to make the journey easier. We thought that if people learned more about how to reinvent, they would be more successful at it. And success, we hope, will breed more success. This kind of snowballing is how innovations spread through society. It is how societies typically shift their basic paradigms—not all at once, but a little at a time. Big changes start out slowly, tentatively. Some efforts fail, but others lead to greater opportunities. Gradually, people spread the word. They share the best methods; they warn one another of mistakes to avoid; they exploit in one setting what worked in another. As the supply of change grows, it fuels demand for even more change.

JUST WHAT DO WE MEAN BY "REINVENTING GOVERNMENT"?

Before we move on to strategies and tools, perhaps we should revisit what we mean by "reinvention." *Reinventing Government* laid out a clear definition. But one price of popular success has been the loss of that clarity. Like "reengineering," the term "reinventing government" has been used so often by so many people to describe so many agendas that it has lost its meaning.

To make our definition clear, let us start by explaining what reinvention is *not.*

Reinventing government is not about change in the political system: campaign finance reform, legislative or parliamentary reform, term limits, and the like. In the United States, political reform is critical if we are to achieve significant policy and governance reform—but it is not what we mean by reinvention.

By reinvention we do not mean reorganization, either. Reinvention is not about moving boxes on an organizational chart. . . .

Nor is reinvention about cutting "waste, fraud, and abuse." It is not about efficiency reviews that generate a list of one-time changes to save money; it is about creating public organizations that *constantly* look for ways to become more efficient. It is not about weeding the garden; it is about creating a regime that *keeps* the garden free of weeds.

Perhaps most important, reinventing government is not synonymous with downsizing government. Some public organizations would be more effective with smaller budgets and staffs, some would not. We have never met a soul—liberal, conservative, or moderate—who thought we could improve our schools by cutting their budgets and laying off teachers. . . .

Nor is reinvention synonymous with privatization. Asset sales, contracting out, and other tools that fall under the heading of "privatization" are part of the reinventors' tool kit. But as *Reinventing Government* argued, it is competition and customer choice that force improvement, not simply private ownership. Shifting from a public monopoly to a private monopoly seldom leads to a happy ending.

> Reinventing government is also not a stand-in for simply making government more *efficient.* Part of the goal is efficiency, but more important is *effectiveness.* What is the point of making an organization or system more efficient, if it is completely ineffective? . . .
>
> Finally, reinvention is not simply a synonym for management reform—another way to say total quality management or business process reengineering. These are both tools that can help a reinventor succeed, if used in strategic ways. But they are not *sufficient.* . . .
>
> By "reinvention," we mean the fundamental transformation of public systems and organizations to create dramatic increases in their effectiveness, efficiency, adaptability, and capacity to innovate. This transformation is accomplished by changing their purpose, accountability, incentives, power structure, and culture.
>
> *Reinvention is about replacing bureaucratic organizations and behavior with entrepreneurial organizations and behavior. It is about creating public organizations and systems that habitually innovate, that continually improve their quality, without having to be pushed from outside. It is about creating a public sector that has a built-in drive to improve—what some call a "self-renewing system."*
>
> —From *Banishing Bureaucracy,* pp. 10–14

As we enter a new millennium, this wave of change is already building. Whatever you call the phenomenon—"reinvention," "postbureaucratic government," "the new public management," "entrepreneurial government," "high-performance organizations"—it is clearly here to stay. The contrast between 1992, when *Reinventing Government* was published, and today could hardly be greater. The changes sweeping through public institutions in the developed democracies are vast and deep. Ideas that were controversial in 1992—customer choice, competition, accountability for results—are now commonplace. Reinvention is well under way in a dozen different countries, from the U.S., Canada, the U.K., and Ireland to Australia, New Zealand, and Singapore; from Sweden, Norway, and Finland to Denmark, the Netherlands, and Germany. Even in developing democracies such as Chile, Argentina, Brazil, Costa Rica, South Africa, South Korea, Malaysia, Thailand, and the Phillippines, serious initiatives are under way. Consider just a few of the signs of change:

- Governments around the world have sold off more than $500 billion worth of assets since 1985.
- The U.S. government has trimmed its labor force by more than 300,000, creating the smallest federal workforce since John F. Kennedy was president.

- Canada's national government has driven its program spending, as a percentage of gross domestic product, back to the lowest level since 1950.
- Twenty-seven American states have adopted some form of statewide public school choice.
- In the U.S., nearly 1,700 charter schools—schools of choice created to be independent of school districts and exempt from most rules and regulations—enrolled some 350,000 students in 32 states and the District of Columbia during the 1999–2000 school year.
- In England, 20 percent of all high schools have seceded from their districts to operate independently, like charter schools in the U.S.
- Every state in the U.S., save one, has some systematic effort under way to measure performance, and a handful of states are operating performance budgeting systems.
- In a 1997 survey of city managers in American cities with more than 10,000 people, 80 percent said they trained employees in customer service, 75 percent said they recommended partnering with third parties to provide services, and 62 percent said they surveyed their citizens.

These changes are clearly bearing fruit. Many of these governments and education systems are demonstrably more efficient and effective than they were when the reforms began. Deficits are lower, workforces are leaner, and in the U.S., surveys show that public confidence in government at all three levels has begun to rebound.

In many developed democracies, the 1980s and 1990s will be remembered as a watershed period in the evolution of government. The last time we reinvented government—when we constructed the bureaucratic model (in the U.S., during the Progressive Era and the New Deal)—the effort spanned roughly 50 years, from the first stirrings in the late 1880s through about 1940. It may take just as long this time. If the first stirrings of the current reinvention were in the late 1970s, with the tax revolt in the U.S. and Margaret Thatcher's election in the U.K., the year 2000 finds us close to the halfway point. The new paradigm described in *Reinventing Government* is now fairly widely accepted, and a significant minority of governments in the U.S. and Canada (and a majority in centralized parliamentary nations such as the U.K. and New Zealand) are working hard to implement it. We have passed from the pioneering stage of the 1980s through an exploratory stage in the 1990s, during which the new paradigm was recognized, named, vigorously debated, and gradually accepted by more and more public leaders. Now, as we enter the 21st century, a third stage of serious implementation is well under way. The percentage of jurisdictions in the developed democracies that have succeeded in building postbureaucratic governments and public institutions may still be small, but the percentage that are working on the challenge is not.

HOW TO USE THIS FIELDBOOK

Banishing Bureaucracy laid out five strategies that have the most power to transform public organizations:

- The *Core Strategy* helps public systems clarify their fundamental purposes, eliminate functions that no longer serve those purposes, and organize their activities so that each organization is free to focus on its own well-defined mission or missions, all of which contribute to the system's overall purposes.
- The *Consequences Strategy* creates rewards for good organizational performance and penalties for poor performance.
- The *Customer Strategy* makes organizations accountable not only to their superiors in the hierarchy but also to their customers.
- The *Control Strategy* changes the locus and form of control in public systems; it frees organizations, managers, employees, and at times community members to improve performance by pushing significant decision-making power into their hands, while holding them accountable for results.
- The *Culture Strategy* changes the attitudes of public employees—their values, norms, assumptions, and expectations—by helping organizations change their employees' habits, hearts, and minds.

Reinventors can use a number of approaches to implement each of these strategies. For example, to create consequences for performance, reinventors can use enterprise management, which puts organizations into competitive markets and forces them to earn their revenues directly from their customers; managed competition, which forces public and private organizations to compete for contracts based on price and performance; and performance management, which sets performance targets for all units, measures how well they do, rewards those that succeed, and occasionally penalizes those that perform poorly.

The five parts of this handbook each focus on one of these strategies, with a chapter on each approach. (Part II also includes a chapter on a key competence, performance measurement.) New in the fieldbook are full dissections of each approach, dozens of new case studies to illustrate approaches and tools, and in-depth treatment of 74 tools you can use to implement the approaches (listed on pages xi–xii). Some will be of most use to elected officials and their appointees; others will be of most use to high-level managers; still others will be of most use to middle managers, supervisors, and frontline employees. Many will also be useful to civic reformers from the business world, foundations, and communities who pressure and work with public leaders to reinvent public institutions.

As *Banishing Bureaucracy* explained, these tools can be brought to bear at five different levels, outlined in the following box. The higher you go up this ladder, the more leverage you get to force change throughout the system.

THE HIERARCHY OF LEVERAGE

Level	*Examples*
1. Governing System	National, state, provincial, or city government; education system, health care system
2. Administrative System	Budget and finance, personnel, procurement, auditing, and planning systems
3. Organization	Municipal department of public works, state employment service, Social Security Administration
4. Work Processes	Benefit processing, permit processing, fire fighting, complaint handling
5. People	Manager, supervisor, road crew, police

The chapters in this fieldbook are not meant to be read in any particular order. The book was not designed to be read front to back; indeed, it would be hard to read it that way. It is designed as a toolkit, to be dipped into as you use various approaches and tools. *Banishing Bureaucracy* will give you the conceptual framework you need to decide which strategies and approaches to use, and when. *The Reinventor's Fieldbook* will help you decide which tools to use and when and how to use them. Once you've made those choices, it will help you implement your change effort. It is a how-to book, full of steps to take, lessons learned by those who have gone before you, pitfalls to avoid, do's and don'ts, and other pointers. We urge you to read the opening sections of each chapter whenever you read a tool section, because they include background and lessons that apply to all the tools in the chapter. But otherwise, we suggest that you delve into different tools as you need them. We hope the book will prove indispensable over time, like any good handbook—and that you will wear it out as you dip into section after section.

You will notice that the lists of tools for a few approaches have changed a bit since *Banishing Bureaucracy*. At times we have simply come up with better names for tools, consolidated two tools into one, or split one tool into two as we have come to understand them better. At other times, as in Chapter Twelve, our research has reshaped our understanding of certain tools. In addition, we had to drop a few tools to keep down the fieldbook's length. We plan to treat three of these—Total Quality Management, Business Process Reengineering, and WorkOuts—in a separate handbook on work process redesign.

You will also notice our battle to deal with the intimate link between this book and *Banishing Bureaucracy.* Since this fieldbook fleshes out the conceptual framework developed in *Banishing Bureaucracy,* certain themes have to be repeated to explain the approaches and to put the tools in context. We have tried to keep this repetition to a minimum, often signaling with a pointer in the margin that you will find more information in *Banishing Bureaucracy* or even *Reinventing Government,* as demonstrated here.

We also use pointers in the margin to let you know where in this book you can find additional information about a topic. At the end of each tool section we include a list of additional resources on the tool: books, articles, papers, Web sites, organizations, even videos. We indicate the best of these with a "blue ribbon" icon in the margin, as shown here. Finally, the most powerful tools are those that combine multiple strategies. We call these "metatools," and we indicate them with the symbol shown here.

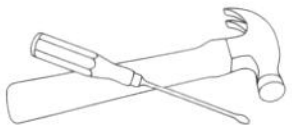

HIGH STAKES

In focusing on the nuts and bolts of reinvention, it is at times easy to forget the larger purpose of our work. In our view, reinvention is about nothing less than the future of democratic societies. The goal is to create public institutions capable of solving our most pressing problems.

Because some people think of reinvention simply as internal management reform, they believe it is of secondary importance. Some find it boring, fit only for bureaucrats. We think they are missing the point. Unlike management reform in the private sector, reinventing government is about helping entire communities and societies rise to meet their most important challenges.

Can we create public education systems vibrant enough to produce not only educated, skilled workforces but also responsible citizens capable of working together to strengthen democracy and revitalize their communities?

Can we create lifelong learning systems robust enough not only to help the poor and illiterate gain the skills they need to enter the economic mainstream but also to help every citizen keep his or her skills current in a rapidly changing economy?

Can we create a welfare system that is not only vital enough to give most recipients the helping hands they need to secure steady work at livable wages but also compassionate enough to support those who simply cannot support themselves?

Can we create a criminal justice system that is not only strong enough to keep the streets safe but also coherent enough that no suspect, criminal, or victim falls through the cracks between myriad court systems, police forces, probation programs, and juvenile justice systems?

These are the kinds of issues at stake in this quest to reinvent government, and we should not forget it. Policy decisions play a key role as well, but the strategies and tools we write about in this fieldbook are indispensable if we are to solve these problems. Reinvention on this scale leads to conflict, and conflict is rarely boring. It is difficult for public leaders, but it brings long-term solutions to fundamental problems. As former New Zealand finance minister Roger Douglas has written so eloquently:

> *Conventional politicians ignore structural reform because they think they are in power to please people, and pleasing people does not involve making them face up to hard questions.*
>
> *They use the latest polls to fine-tune their image and their policies, in order to achieve better results in the next poll. In other words, their aim is really to be in perpetual power.*
>
> *Their adherence to ad hoc short-term policies which focus on their own immediate problems, rather than the country's long-term opportunities, leads to accumulating difficulties over time.*
>
> *It becomes increasingly clear to people that the problems have not been solved, and the opportunities have been thrown away. So such governments end up being thrown out, neck and crop.*

In contrast, Douglas argues, "Genuine structural reform, carried right through fairly and without compromise, delivers larger gains in living standards and opportunity than those achievable by any other political route." When such reforms lead to conflict, Douglas advises, "Ask yourself: 'Why am I in politics?'"

> *Is it to gain a high income, two cars and the maximum available number of perks? Or can I do something that makes a real difference to the nation's future?*
>
> *At the end of the day, making that real difference matters more than anything else to the voting public.*

We hope this book will help public leaders, both elected and appointed, make a real difference. One definition of a handbook, according to the *American Heritage Dictionary,* is "a book in which off-track bets are recorded." In this handbook we have recorded the exploits of some of the world's most successful reinventors. Now we're betting on the rest of you.

Part I

The Core Strategy

Creating Clarity of Purpose

The Core Strategy is about steering, not rowing; it's about doing the right things, not doing things right. At the most fundamental level, it is about *creating clarity of purpose.* When everyone in a public organization or system is clear about its fundamental purpose or purposes, improving performance is far, far easier.

This no doubt seems very simple, and very obvious. Yet it is also very rare. Most public organizations have multiple purposes, some of which even conflict. Over the years, with the best of intentions, school boards, city and county councils, and state, provincial, and national legislatures have piled mission after mission onto public organizations. When this happens, employees gradually lose any sense of clarity about what's most important. When their leaders yell "Charge!" they all head off in different directions.

When the Public Strategies Group (PSG) was hired to act as superintendent of schools in Minneapolis, to turn the district around, the first thing it tried to do was create clarity of purpose. It held a retreat for key stakeholders and asked them to list the missions of the Minneapolis schools. People came up with dozens of goals, from improving test scores and enhancing discipline to developing good citizens, promoting racial integration, and feeding poor kids. Peter Hutchinson and Babak Armajani, who lead PSG, pushed and pushed to narrow the list. Ultimately, they decided on two core missions: improving student achievement and narrowing the achievement gap between white and minority students. For the next three years, they focused all their energies on strategies to achieve those two goals. They related every decision they made to those two purposes. They talked about them constantly. They measured progress toward them regularly, at every school. And gradually the message began to sink in. Scores began to improve, and the gap began to close. As we write this, two years after PSG's contract ended and the board returned to a traditional superintendent, professionals throughout the district—teachers, principals, and administrators—still gauge their success by how well their schools are doing on student achievement and narrowing the racial gap.

To achieve clarity, you must first define the system or organization's core purposes. Then you have to eliminate activities that no longer contribute to those purposes. And finally, you have to organize the system so that each unit is free to pursue its own piece of the core mission or missions. Often this means separating units that have fundamentally different purposes, such as service and compliance work, or "steering" and "rowing."

These are the three approaches of the Core Strategy, what we call *improving your aim, clearing the decks,* and *uncoupling.* There is no correct order among them; you should start where you have the most political will and the best opportunity to improve. You can come back to the other approaches once success has given you momentum.

We call this the Core Strategy because it helps you improve the most important role government plays—steering society toward better outcomes. It can leverage enormous activity, both within and outside government, by helping many different entities and communities align their efforts around common goals. But achieving clarity of purpose does not by itself improve the performance of public organizations; it only sets the stage. Improving your ability to steer, weeding out functions that are no longer necessary, and organizing your government or system around clear purposes get public organizations ready for improvement. You can then use the Consequences, Customer, Control, and Culture Strategies, which focus more on rowing, to create dramatic leaps in their performance. Once you have clarity of purpose, this is much easier. When you yell "Charge!" everyone marches in the same direction.

Because it focuses on steering, the Core Strategy is primarily the province of elected leaders, their appointees, and high-level civil servants—often working with leaders from the community and the private sector. But steering does not all take place at the top. Line managers can use these three approaches to align their rowing organizations. They can create outcome goals, mission statements, and strategies to align their organizations with the system's broader goals. They can clear their own decks, eliminating obsolete functions within their organizations. And they can uncouple their own internal units when multiple or conflicting purposes frustrate those units' ability to perform.

As you pursue these opportunities, we urge you to keep in mind these words of wisdom, often credited to the management sage Yogi Berra: "If you don't know where you're going, then any road will take you someplace else."

Chapter 1

Improving Your Aim

Using Strategic Management to Create Clarity of Direction

***Improving Your Aim*, often called strategic management, helps governments define their visions and core purposes—the outcome goals that are most important to them—and aim their entire systems at fulfilling them.**

In November 1990, after 15 years of frustration with rising property taxes, voters in Oregon passed a massive property tax cut, called Measure 5. Because it required state government to make up local governments' and school districts' revenue losses, it forced deep cuts in state spending. As Governor Barbara Roberts prepared her 1993–1995 budget, her staff told her she needed to cut *10 percent* from the general fund—$600 million out of a $6 billion budget. In the midst of the carnage, however, she proposed 21 new initiatives. And the legislature funded 18 of them, with $130 million.

Why spend new money while gutting the rest of state government? Were these pet programs? Was there a court mandate? No. The governor and the legislative leadership had simply reached agreement about the direction they wanted Oregon to go, and the new investments promised to help move things along. Why did the state's leaders have that clarity and consensus? Because of a remarkable innovation called the Oregon Benchmarks.

In the early 1980s, Oregon had experienced five years of wrenching economic pain. Employment in the state's lumber and wood products industries had collapsed—plunging from 83,000 in 1979 to 55,000 in 1982. By 1987, state wages and per capita income had fallen from the national average to 10 percent below it.

Neil Goldschmidt, a former Democratic mayor of Portland and U.S. secretary of transportation, campaigned for governor in 1986 on an economic platform he called "the Oregon Comeback." Once in office, he pulled 180 business, labor, government, and education leaders together to develop a vision and strategy. In a report called *Oregon Shines: An Economic Strategy for the Pacific Century*, they recommended three "strategic initiatives" for revitalizing the economy: Oregon should build a superior workforce, maintain an attractive quality of life, and develop a global outlook. They called for a new Oregon Progress Board to "serve as the long-term caretaker of Oregon's strategic vision, identify key activities that need to be undertaken, and then measure our progress over the next several decades." Appointed and chaired by the governor, it would have nine members.

Businesspeople from the governor's task force recommended that the Progress Board start by setting specific, quantifiable goals for the state. After conducting surveys and convening 12 community meetings around the state, the board proposed 158 outcome goals, which it dubbed the Oregon Benchmarks. It called 17 of them Lead Benchmarks, those related to urgent problems that required progress within five years, and 13 of them Key Benchmarks, the most important long-term goals for the state. Table 1.1 offers examples of the original Lead Benchmarks that focused on people, including historical data and quantifiable goals.

Table 1.1 Sample Lead Oregon Benchmarks

Lead Benchmarks for People	*1970*	*1980*	*1990*	*1995*	*2000*	*2010*
Teen Pregnancy. Pregnancy rate per 1,000 females ages 10–17		24.7	19.5	9.8	8	8
Drug-Free Babies. Percentage of infants whose mothers did not use illicit drugs during pregnancy			89%	95%	99%	100%
Drug-Free Teens. Percentage of 11th-grade students free of involvement with illicit drugs in the previous month			68.2%	85%	98%	99%
Job Skill Preparation. Percentage of high school students enrolled in vocational or technical education programs		7.3%	9%	18%	35%	55%

Source: Oregon Progress Board, *Oregon Benchmarks: Setting Measurable Standards for Progress. Report to 1991 Legislature* (Salem: Oregon Progress Board, 1991), p. 5.

Governor Goldschmidt's successor, Democrat Barbara Roberts, fully embraced the Progress Board and Benchmarks when she took office in 1991. Because *Oregon Shines* and the Benchmarks put a spotlight on education and workforce development, she and key legislators pushed through major reform legislation in both areas. As Measure 5 kicked in, Roberts decided to use the fiscal crisis as a lever, to get agencies to shift their spending to activities that would help achieve the Lead Benchmarks (now called Urgent Benchmarks). She asked them to begin preparing budgets with only 80 percent of their projected "current service level" spending, but she told them they could get more money if they could demonstrate that it would help achieve an Urgent Benchmark.

"The Benchmarks were our set of priorities," she explains.

> *We didn't have to invent them—they already existed. Nobody had apparently thought about linking the budget and the Benchmarks directly. But the Benchmarks literally came to life when I tied them to my budget. Agencies sat up and paid attention when I said the money is tied to the Benchmarks.*

Roberts also directed the agencies to develop performance measures consistent with the Benchmarks. Though not all followed through, the process spurred several key agencies to rethink their goals and strategies. For instance, *Oregon Shines* recommended a focus on industries critical to the state's future. So the Department of Economic Development convened meetings of leaders in those industries to talk about the challenges facing them and how to respond. Next it convened a Key Industry Benchmark Summit, in which leaders of 13 industries met in the same room—one table per industry—to hammer out benchmarks for their industry and a brief action plan.

"About 60 percent of it was education or workforce development," remembers department director Bill Scott.

> *So then [in 1994] we had a big meeting we called the Industry Education Summit. We brought in a team from all areas of education—K–12, community colleges, higher education—and we got a team from education assigned to each industry team. And they each came out with one project they were going to try to accomplish.*

When the state police developed 27 strategic performance measures tied to the Benchmarks, the process forced them to rethink many of their basic assumptions. One Key Benchmark was the rate of deaths due to "unintentional" (accidental) injuries. "The patrolmen could say, 'There's nothing about the traffic safety rate there, so that's not me,'" explains Major Lee Erickson.

> *Yet motor vehicle crashes drive this statistic for people up to age 45 or 47. So we said to the Highway Patrol: "You own the crash rate on state and federal highways; that piece of this benchmark is one of your strategic performance measures."*
>
> *Each patrol office then says, "OK, what's driving motor vehicle collisions in our areas?" They find the bad roads where accidents are happening. They come up with intermediate performance measures to help them decide whether they're being effective.*

But the only way to limit accidents was to get other players involved: the public, local police forces, and the state department of transportation. "For years the state police said, 'We don't handle all the problems there, therefore we can't be responsible,'" Erickson says. "The change is: 'You are responsible to go out and get some partners involved, identify your role, and then implement these things.'"

Outside state government, the Oregon Community Foundation and the Metropolitan Portland United Way both adopted the Benchmarks to guide their funding decisions. Six counties and five local communities created their own benchmarks, progress boards, or similar steering organizations. And a statewide consortium of hospitals, insurance companies, HMOs, and state and local health agencies decided to focus on the immunization benchmark, which aimed to raise the percentage of two-year-olds who were "adequately immunized" from 47 to 100 percent by the year 2000. With a combination of "immunization days," public education, and a massive database on immunization, they pushed the rate up to 81 percent by 1997.

Bumps in the Road

After the death of her husband, Governor Roberts chose not to run for reelection in 1994. Though a Democrat succeeded her, the Republicans swept the state legislature, just as they swept the U.S. Congress. Few of the new legislators were familiar with the Progress Board or the Benchmarks, and the Republican leadership had little use for an initiative sponsored by two Democratic governors. "The membership was somewhat hostile in 1995," says Representative Bob Repine, a Republican. By now there were also far too many Benchmarks, and data on many were either absent or questionable. (The number had expanded from 158 to 259 as the Progress Board refined and updated them every two years.) Legislators felt that "this thing was getting unruly," says Repine.

They decided to fire a shot across the Progress Board's bow—without sinking it. They let the authorizing legislation for the board expire, but allowed its appropriation to pass. The new governor, former state senator John Kitzhaber, reauthorized the board by executive order, hired a new director, and convened a 46–member task force, which included leaders from both legislative chambers, to reassess the entire process. After six months of meetings and public hearings, the task force voted almost unanimously, by secret ballot, to continue with the Benchmarks and Progress Board. They published a document called *Oregon Shines II*, which modified the original strategic initiatives and cut the number of Benchmarks to 92. Based on this work, the 1997 legislature overwhelmingly passed a bill making the Progress Board and Benchmarks a permanent part of state government.

Ten Years of Effort: How Much Impact?

By creating a steering organization and setting outcome goals, Oregon's leaders have changed the way a good deal of the public's business is done in their state. Throughout Oregon, the Benchmarks have acted as "magnets for collaboration," to use an oft-repeated phrase. On immunization, welfare reform, education reform, and a series of other issues, commitment to a benchmark has spurred public organizations, businesses, and community groups to come together and make dramatic changes. "What I see is an energizing of people to tackle really big problems that people in other places are viewing as hopeless," says Bill Scott.

> *There are so many times in political life where people say, "If we can afford to send a man to the moon, why can't we feed the children? We're rich enough to do this." The assumption is that there's somebody in a position of power, and if they only had the will, this would happen. The truth is, you need a whole lot of somebodies—you need a real collective. It takes a tremendous amount of shared responsibility, and to me the Benchmarks are a way of mobilizing that.*

It is now widely accepted by public leaders in Oregon that defining outcome goals should be the starting point of any initiative and that measuring performance against those goals should be standard operating procedure. When the legislature created the Oregon Commission on Families and Children to overcome the fragmentation of human service programs, for example, it defined 11 of the Oregon Benchmarks as its goals. When Governor Kitzhaber decided to do something about declining salmon stocks before the federal government stepped in and declared coho salmon an endangered species, he started with the existing Benchmarks for stream quality, stream flow, and wild salmon stocks.

There is much unfinished business, of course. To create an entire steering system, in which statewide outcome goals drive state government strategies—and therefore all agency missions, goals, and activities—Oregon will need other tools, particularly performance budgeting and strategic evaluation. But Oregon is the only state in the nation whose public and private leaders have agreed on a detailed vision, a set of strategic priorities, and a set of measurable outcome goals. That decision has clarified for many just what their priorities should be—leading to significant reforms in education, welfare, and job training; improvements in agencies as diverse as economic development and the state police; and public-private partnerships to increase immunization rates, prevent teen pregnancy, and the like. Ask yourself whether leaders in your own state or province have such shared vision and clarity of direction—as well as methods to measure their progress—and you will begin to understand how remarkable Oregon's achievements have been.

IMPROVING YOUR AIM: THE TOOLKIT

strategic management
visioning
steering org.
strategy development
mission statements
strategic evaluation

Improving your aim is about creating a system that helps your government stay focused on its most important goals, even as those goals change over time. The New Zealanders call it *strategic management.*

Think of reinvention as a voyage, a great crossing from the bureaucratic model characteristic of 20th-century governance to the entrepreneurial model necessary for successful 21st-century governance. *Visioning* helps your leaders, crew, and passengers get clear on where they want to go. (This is what *Oregon Shines* did.) *Outcome goals* (like the Oregon Benchmarks) give them targets to aim at and ways to measure their progress. *Steering organizations* (like the Oregon Progress Board) help them create their visions and goals, develop strategies to achieve them, fund those strategies, and measure progress. (By *strategies* here we do not mean the five strategies for reinvention, around which this book is organized; we mean strategies chosen to achieve particular policy goals, such as economic development strategies or education strategies.) *Strategy development* is the process of figuring out how you will achieve your vision and goals—how you will successfully complete your voyage. *Mission statements* help individual organizations—the various ships in your fleet—keep themselves headed in the right direction. *Performance budgets* help you shift your resources to the strategies you have chosen. *Long-term budget forecasting* helps you make those resource decisions with as much knowledge of likely future consequences as possible. And *strategic evaluation* helps you determine if you are drifting off course—and what to do about it.

Few governments use many of these tools—and when they do, they typically call what they are doing *strategic planning.* We prefer to avoid that term, for several reasons. First, it suggests that the key activity is creating a *plan*—which is hardly the case. Second, the business models of strategic planning normally imported into the public sector don't include most of these tools. And third, those models don't usually work very well in government.

Because strategic planning was developed to manage private organizations, not democratically elected governments, it subordinates politics to rationality, something that is usually impossible in government. It requires long, formal planning processes, which are difficult to sustain in public organizations. It creates plans that sometimes take on lives of their own, often acting as impediments to strategic thinking and action when circumstances change. And it rarely drives budgetary decisions, because those decisions are usually made quite separately and are shaped by political needs rather than strategic thinking. Hence funding rarely shifts to the strategies selected, rendering strategic planning relatively powerless.

Even in the business world, formal strategic planning has fallen into disrepute. In an influential *Harvard Business Review* article, Gary Hamel captured the problem with one sentence: "The essential problem in organizations today is a failure to distinguish *planning* from *strategizing*." He and others argue that strategic planning has become too static—too much about *planning* and not enough about strategic *thinking* and *acting*. Too often, strategic planning systems are overly formalized, complete with their own planning departments that impose annual planning cycles on all managers. They create formal plans that act as straitjackets, crowding out vision, flexibility, innovation, and real strategic thinking.

In government, strategic planning is usually a disembodied exercise to force managers to define their goals in the absence of management systems that do so. In contrast, strategic management builds systems that define purposes and outcome goals, create conscious strategies to achieve them, construct budgets to fund them, and use performance measures and evaluations to see how effective they are. Creating such systems will help you think, plan, and act strategically all the time—rather than going through the motions every time the deadline for a new strategic plan rolls around.

Why is strategic management so important today? In a world of rapid change, global markets, and technological revolution, governments must respond constantly to changes in their environment. "The ability to make consistently good decisions over time, enabling an organization to adapt quickly to changes in its environment, has become a critical determinant of success," explains New Zealand's State Services Commission. Indeed, a nation's, region's, or city's strategic capacity is now a key element of its competitive advantage or disadvantage.

Part of this competitive advantage is a government's ability to anticipate and prevent problems rather than trying to ameliorate them after they appear. In an age of global competition and fiscal limits, an ounce of prevention truly is worth a pound of cure. And strategic management holds the key to that ounce of prevention. A strategic management system gives leaders the ability to anticipate future trends, define the future they want, and bend their resources and staff to the task of creating that future. Without it, preventive government is impossible.

Strategic management is also critical because it eliminates the need for many rules, procedures, and internal controls in entrepreneurial organizations. When managers and employees are clear on the vision, mission, goals, and strategies chosen by their leaders, they require fewer rules to stay on course. These tools give leaders the leverage they need to steer effectively, without overly constraining the methods chosen by managers and employees to row the boat.

"The sense of purpose that strategic alignment provides can be unconscious," notes former New Zealand treasury secretary Graham Scott.

> *Many organisations that have it do not see it as particularly remarkable, unless they remember the times when it was missing. . . . People who know "why they are there" derive greater satisfaction from their work, and they are rarely cynical about it. Strong commitment to the job is a cultural norm, not a trait deserving great notice or reward. People stop playing power games and distorting information flows to enhance their position at the expense of the organisation's performance.*
>
> *An absence of strategic alignment can be recognised by the opposite characteristics: an internal focus on rules and procedures, conservatism about changing things, uncertainty about who has authority to make decisions and frequent referral upstairs, territorialism and patch [turf] protection, unwillingness to share information and cooperate or to accept peer review, detachment, resignation and blame shifting about inadequacies in performance, [and] refusal to take responsibility for results.*

Improving Your Aim: Lessons Learned

Getting clear on your vision and goals is the logical place to start a reinvention effort. But politics is rarely about logic. Strategic management requires political leaders to make decisions rationally and visibly, with a longer time frame than that defined by the next election—and that is not easy. In politics, short-term crises usually crowd out long-term thinking. Particularly when power is divided between multiple branches of government, as in many American systems, partisan politics often defeats rational efforts to reach consensus about goals.

The payoff for strategic management is also quite long-term. "You don't get to measure it in your term, while you're in office," says Governor Roberts. Hence few politicians put it high on their priority lists.

Some elected officials avoid clearly articulating outcome goals because they fear that if they fail to meet them, the voters might hold them accountable. Many also prefer to finesse political differences over goals rather than resolve them; at budget time, they split the difference. And some simply don't want their control over resources limited in any way. As Linda Loomis Shelly, then chief of staff to Florida governor Lawton Chiles, told *Governing* magazine, "The whole concept of accountability driving funding decisions is anathema to legislative types who want complete discretion as to what to spend money on. If you programmatically determine whether something is working, it limits the discretion of the legislature, and they don't like that."

Hence the biggest lesson about strategic management is that not all jurisdictions are ready for it. Before starting down this path, you should assess whether your elected leaders are willing to follow. Our first four lessons focus on these political realities. These and the other lessons articulated here apply to the entire approach—to all of its tools.

1. Focus on improving your steering capacity only after you have developed some momentum that builds faith in the effort.

pp. 44–46

It takes a long time to get results from this approach. Oregon has been at it since the late 1980s. Texas has been perfecting its performance budgeting system since 1991. Most reinvention efforts will require faster results to generate momentum. In many situations, then, we recommend starting with other approaches and strategies. Once people have faith that reinvention can yield important results, you can begin the long climb up the mountain of strategic management. The payoff can be huge, but it comes slowly.

Don Forbes, a successful reinventor during his tenure at the helm of the Oregon Department of Transportation, watched the Benchmarks' slow progress for years. But he didn't wait for it to reach his department; he started reinventing in other ways. "You've got to get the organization producing results for customers, day in and day out," he says.

> *Once we got our people to think in terms of customer and performance, I think we got the organization moving again. It's like redeveloping the muscles. Get the horse running again; don't put it in the Kentucky Derby right away. Once you develop a certain set of muscles, you can push it harder, toward longer-term efforts.*

2. The executive must take the lead in improving steering capacity, but he or she should involve the legislature, council, or board in the process.

If you don't have top-level leadership, you won't succeed in implementing this approach. By its nature, strategic management does not happen unless those who make the strategic decisions—elected officials and their advisers—buy in to these new tools. Without their commitment, you have lots of process work with no payoff, because they will continue to make decisions the old way.

Lip service does not cut it. What made the Oregon Progress Board work, in Governor Roberts's view, was her presence as chair at every monthly meeting. What made the Benchmarks come to life was her decision to use them to make budget decisions. Without visible gubernatorial support during her successor's first year, the Progress Board quickly foundered.

In most systems, executives have the greatest capacity to be strategic, whereas legislatures are more reactive. Hence it is far easier for an executive to lead this process than it is for a legislature. But as Michael Marsh, Roberts's former budget director, learned, "It does not work to complete the process and then say [to the legislature] 'Here it is.' You must work with the legislative branch in developing the process."

Representative John Watt, a legislative champion of the Benchmarks, is blunt about the issue:

> *People who serve in elected offices have to go through a certain ego thing. That's just the nature of the beast. So I would tell a new governor that you have to sell them ownership; convince them that this was their idea, or at least convince them that their input was absolutely essential. And to do that, I think you have to involve them up front a little bit more.*

Progress Board director Jeff Tryens cites four ways to get legislators to buy in: get them involved; listen to them and take their concerns seriously; show them how this approach can make a real difference in policy choices and spending decisions; and show them that it is meaningful to their constituencies. "If the legislative leaders aren't feeling this is having some effect on the way Oregonians view the world, they're going to wonder about it," he points out.

3. To get elected officials to take steering seriously, publish scorecards and help citizens and interest groups grapple with how to improve outcomes.

The $64,000 question in strategic management is whether elected officials will take it seriously. If they do not—if they care only about meeting the short-term needs of interest groups—their behavior will force top managers off any strategic focus and onto short-term issues. This is the norm in government. How do you break it?

In addition to educating, involving, and listening to elected officials, the key is to show them that improving outcomes is meaningful to their voters. If politicians are to focus on steering, they must be convinced that serving the collective interest is just as important to their future as serving special interests is. The only way we know to do this is to publish meaningful, digestible "report cards" that voters and interest groups will pay attention to, then get them involved in discussions about how to improve those outcomes. The media love to publish report cards and rankings—particularly when they come from a neutral, objective source.

pp. 210–213, 311–319

Publishing scorecards that include 92 different measures, like the current Oregon Benchmarks, is not terribly effective, however. They must be broken down into bite-size pieces the public can digest—for example, one scorecard for each of several basic policy areas (crime, children and families, education and training, environmental protection, and so on). And they must be presented in visual formats that make their implications clear.

Nor is publishing a visually arresting report enough. Beverly Stein, the elected executive of Multnomah County, discovered that her Benchmarks report had little impact because the city and county didn't quite know what to do with it—how to use it to engage the citizens. You need to create forums in which citizens and interest groups that care about the issues can discuss progress (or its absence) with their elected officials—and help them think through new strategies to improve outcomes.

4. *If you want politicians to take steering seriously, don't expect them to give up immediate constituent service.*

Having said all of the preceding, we must also share some more practical advice. In a democracy, one reality will never change: elected officials will always need to solve short-term problems for their constituents. If managers ask them to focus on steering and "leave the problem solving to us," elected officials will not be happy. A city manager who wants the city council to quit micromanaging and focus on steering, for example, must make sure there is a reliable system in place they can use when their constituents call with problems. When someone calls about a vacant lot filled with trash, or drug dealers on the corner, or drivers speeding through their neighborhoods, the manager must have some kind of quick response mechanism that will solve the problem. Otherwise the politicians are going to continue micromanaging. Managers should make a conscious deal with their elected officials: we will help you respond effectively to your constituents' needs, if you will help us create and use a strategic management system.

5. *Keep the steering process bipartisan.*

Governor Roberts went out of her way to make the Progress Board bipartisan; she even appointed the Republican she had defeated to the board. But by the time she left office, four years later, she had provided such active leadership that the board was closely identified with her. Its director was also one of her key aides. When the opposing party took control of the legislature, the combination spelled trouble. As Jeff Tryens told Congress in 1997, "A single champion or party affiliation can be deadly."

6. Build the whole strategic management system, not just a piece of it.

To quote Tryens again, "Benchmarks do not a system make." Oregon discovered what happens when you develop outcome goals without formally tying them to budgets and agency performance measures: some agencies take them seriously; some don't. Other governments have discovered what happens when you develop performance measures and budgets without getting clear on your long-term goals. In neither case do you propel departmental and agency managers to rethink what they do to accomplish the public's most important goals. You need them in the loop; otherwise the best steering in the world won't lead to different *actions.* Clarity of direction comes from using most or all of these tools—not just one or two.

7. Steering well is expensive; be prepared to pay the price.

Building a strategic management system takes a lot of time. You cannot expect busy staff to do it on top of everything else. You will need full-time staff dedicated to this process—and that costs money. If you're not prepared to invest serious money in gathering data and building steering organizations and converting your budget system, don't venture down this path. The secret is to finance your efforts through the savings you create—by using your outcome goals to help clear the decks and by eliminating line items, budget reports, and budget analysts as you convert to performance budgeting.

pp. 61–104

p. 51

8. Find powerful, high-level champions to drive this approach in both the executive and legislative branches.

"If you don't have somebody who's going to push this session after session, it's not going to happen," says Representative Henry Cuellar, who led Texas into performance budgeting. "You've got to have a legislative leader or leaders or a governor, depending upon your structure." If you don't, your efforts will stall and no one will be there to restart them.

Minnesota provides a perfect example. It has an excellent set of outcome goals, developed in 1991, called the Minnesota Milestones. But Governor Arne Carlson never made them a priority, and no other champion has emerged, so they have had little impact.

9. Get an early success—and then get some more.

"One of the things we learned was that you have to have an early success," says Governor Roberts. Oregon did that first by dramatically lowering workmen's compensation rates, second by dramatically increasing immunization rates. Both victories created significant enthusiasm for the Benchmarks process.

10. Be careful not to oversell the power of strategic management.

Strategic management will not change the fact that governing is a political process. Personalities will still play a big role. Partisan spats will still derail decisions. Constituencies will still fight to protect their interests at the expense of the common good. Strategic management will help you sort through all these pressures more rationally, but it will not eliminate them.

Nor will data and analysis answer every question. Outcome goals and performance budgeting are very useful, but they often point to the right questions rather than the right answers. Data simply cannot answer many of the most profound questions we have about public policy. Some issues are too complex

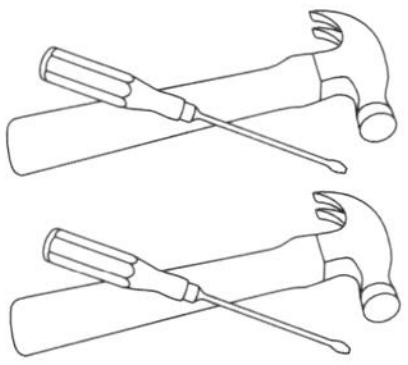

TOOLS FOR IMPROVING YOUR AIM

Visioning is a process for achieving agreement on the kind of future a community (neighborhood, town, city, county, region, state, province, or nation) wants to create for itself—and a shared commitment to creating that future. See p. 26.

Outcome Goals are the long-term results a jurisdiction needs to achieve to realize its vision. See p. 30.

Steering Organizations are boards, councils, departments, or other groups that create visions, set goals, choose (and often fund) strategies, and measure performance against those goals—or advise elected officials who do these things. See p. 35.

Strategy Development is the process of developing, choosing, and refining strategies to achieve outcome goals. See p. 39.

Mission Statements help everyone in an organization develop a shared understanding of its basic purpose. See p. 43.

Performance Budgets define the outcomes and outputs policymakers intend to buy with each sum they appropriate. See p. 43.

Long-Term Budget Forecasting projects current fiscal trends (spending, revenue, debt, and net worth) into the future, to indicate the long-term implications of today's decisions. It gives that information power by tying it directly to actual budget decisions and making it available to the press, the public, and decision makers. See p. 54.

Strategic Evaluation is the systematic analysis of the results produced by government strategies and programs. It goes beyond traditional program evaluation to include analysis of the cause-and-effect relationships between outputs and outcomes and between program outcomes and broader societal outcomes, extraction of lessons learned for future efforts, and recommendations for changes to produce improved outcomes. See p. 56.

for effective analysis, at least with the tools we now have at our disposal. Others come down to value choices, not data.

The danger is that champions of strategic management will, in their naïveté, promise more than they can deliver. And when the results do not materialize, elected officials will decide this approach is not worth what it costs. "What I've been consciously trying to do since we started is undersell," says Portland auditor Gary Blackmer, whose office audits performance against the Portland/Multnomah County benchmarks. "We need to make sure that we don't promise more than we can deliver on this."

VISIONING

***Visioning* is a process for achieving agreement on the kind of future a community (neighborhood, town, city, county, region, state, province, or nation) wants to create for itself—and a shared commitment to creating that future.**

The soul . . . never thinks without a picture.

ARISTOTLE

p. 13

When Neil Goldschmidt ran for governor, Oregonians were very unsure about their future. For decades, they had prided themselves on their quality of life, often contrasting their pristine state with California, which seemed to be turning into one big smog-ridden suburb. Yet by 1986 Oregon could no longer afford this insularity. The economic pain of the early 1980s made the old vision unsustainable; Oregonians now wanted jobs and growth. But how could they achieve them without ruining what they so valued about their state? To have both growth and a pristine environment, they would need a new vision.

When Goldschmidt brought 180 leaders together to work on *Oregon Shines*, they analyzed Oregon's economy, looked at international trends, figured out what the state would need to flourish in the global economy, and articulated a new vision. Although Oregonians' values would be preserved and their "quality of life would be undiminished," they said, the economy would have to diversify.

> *Industries requiring skilled, knowledgeable workers would abound, and Oregon would be a noted producer of products in microelectronics, computer software, biotechnology, specialty metals, and light manufacturing. Oregon's professional services would rank among the best in the country, and would be sought out by clients in other states and regions. . . . The work force would be Oregon's pride. . . . Quality would be the hallmark in all phases of Oregon life—quality jobs, workers, products, attractions, communities, environment, and overall quality of life. All these hallmarks of quality would be present alongside and within a dynamic, competitive, internationally oriented economy.*

Oregon Shines then listed six broad "goals that reflect this vision" and several strategic priorities. All in all, it was a classic example of visioning. It told everyone in the state where the governor and other state leaders wanted to go. And it left behind a new institution to carry the vision forward: the Oregon Progress Board.

p. 14

As this example demonstrates, visioning is about far more than painting a picture of the future a community wants to create. When visioning focuses not on one organization but on the future of an entire town, city, region, state, or nation, it must be informed by careful analysis. (For a treatment of organizational visioning, see p. 599.) It should involve community members, inspiring them while winning their allegiance. It needs to give some indication of how they can realize the vision—what priorities they must pursue—and thus act as a springboard for outcome goals and strategies. Unlike an organization, a community is not usually cohesive enough to be motivated and aligned by a vision alone. You have to start moving it toward action.

As Harrison Owen says in his eloquent book *Leadership Is,* "The equation of vision with a vision statement is at best weak, and at worst, a total perversion of what vision is all about."

All of this makes visioning a difficult tool to use effectively. On the rare occasions when it is used well, however, it has real power. It can:

- Help leaders step outside their current mind-set and think anew about their community's condition, potential, and strategic priorities.
- Help both leaders and community members internalize a new understanding of the challenges they face, a vision, and a new path to achieve that vision—a new "road map."
- Help leaders from different political parties, institutions, and sectors agree on a common vision and goals.
- Act as a "magnet for collaboration," inspiring thousands of people to work together to achieve a common purpose.
- Simplify thousands of decisions and avoid months of needless discussion by providing a guide that can help people figure out what to do and what no longer needs doing.
- Create a new vocabulary that can reshape public perceptions.

Do's and Don'ts of Successful Visioning

Make sure the right people launch the process. The call for visioning must come from people with significant power; otherwise, once the visioning is complete, no participant may have enough power to launch the necessary change efforts.

Create a leadership team. No matter how many people take part in a visioning process—and some have involved thousands—it needs a leadership team. That team should be broadly representative of those whose buy-in the leader hopes to secure. And it should include acknowledged leaders in the community, to build confidence in the process. Credibility comes from the involvement of institutions that have authority: chambers of commerce, universities, businesses, unions, and community organizations. Without support from some of these institutions, significant change is almost impossible—and every potential participant knows it.

Analyze the cards you've been dealt. "Although a good vision has a certain elegant simplicity," John Kotter points out in *Leading Change,* "the data and the syntheses required to produce it are usually anything but simple. A ten-foot stack of paperwork, reports, financials, and statistics are sometimes needed to help produce a one-page statement of future direction."

Kotter was writing about business, but this statement is just as relevant to the public sector. Many a community has painted a rosy vision of a robust high-tech economy, without any base from which to build that economy. In contrast, Oregon took the time to analyze its economic base. To develop a credible vision, it had to marry the past and future, describing a feasible path from its low-tech economy to a future that embraced technology, innovation, and quality.

Don't settle for plain vanilla. When visioning processes skip real research and analysis, the result is often a plain-vanilla statement acceptable to all and compelling to none. Such statements may be uplifting, but they do nothing to differentiate the community from others, define strategic priorities, or motivate action.

Communicate the vision. In a community of any size, a vision is only useful when it becomes widely shared. Once you have it written down, the hard work begins. You must take every opportunity you have—in speeches, meetings, videos, performance reviews, chance encounters, newsletters, and interviews—to communicate your basic vision, goals, and strategic priorities.

Tell a story. The more you can boil the challenges facing your community down to their essence—and communicate that essence with a story about where you have been and where you are going—the better you will communicate. In 1983 and 1984, Michigan produced a very sophisticated, analytical vision document called *The Path to Prosperity.* Yet it managed to boil the state's future down to three memorable choices: it could "get poor," by letting manufacturing wages fall to remain competitive; it could "get out" of manufacturing; or it could "get smart," by nurturing advanced manufacturing technologies like robotics and machine vision, making Michigan the place to go for cutting-edge manufacturing technology.

Create some structure to implement the vision. "Many community visioning efforts break down once the vision and strategic initiatives are identified," report David Chrislip and Carl Larson in their book *Collaborative Leadership.* To avoid this, you need to plan for further implementation. The executive or legislative body may take the lead, but often you need a structure more rooted in the community and more committed for the long haul. Perhaps the first big community visioning exercise, Goals for Dallas in the 1960s, created 12 "Goal Achievement Committees" to build public support and push both public and private institutions to work on the goals. The Phoenix Futures Forum left behind a Futures Forum Action Committee to oversee implementation for two years, organized into six action groups to mobilize partners who could help implement the recommendations. And, of course, Oregon created the Progress Board.

Don't forget to refresh your vision. Seven years after *Oregon Shines* was completed, Oregon's leaders discovered that they had to revisit their vision because conditions had changed. "The vision must act as a compass in a wild and stormy sea," Tom Peters writes, "and, like a compass, it loses its value if it's not adjusted to take account of its surroundings." Revisit your vision every five to seven years. By involving many others in the process, you can bring it back to life for those who have forgotten it.

pp. 16–17

CHARACTERISTICS OF AN EFFECTIVE VISION STATEMENT

An effective vision statement is:

- *Outcome-based.* The vision is stated in terms of end results.
- *Inclusive.* It resonates with a majority of its target community.
- *Vivid.* It creates a picture of the desired future.
- *Clear.* It is easily understood.
- *Communicable.* Kotter suggests this rule of thumb: it "can be successfully explained within five minutes."
- *Unique.* It differentiates your community from other communities.
- *Inspiring.* It appeals to the public spirit.
- *Challenging.* It includes audacious goals and has the power to motivate.
- *Realistic.* It does not require miracles; it builds on the cards you have been dealt.
- *Credible.* People believe they can bring it to life.
- *Focused.* It is specific enough to provide guidance in decision making.
- *Widely shared.* It is embraced across party lines and in the public, private, and nonprofit sectors.

RESOURCES ON VISIONING

Clement Bezold, ed. *Anticipatory Democracy: People in the Politics of the Future.* New York: Vintage Books, 1978. Though out of date, this is the best single text on community visioning. It includes useful case studies on several ambitious examples from the 1960s and 1970s.

David D. Chrislip and Carl E. Larson. *Collaborative Leadership: How Citizens and Civic Leaders Can Make a Difference.* San Francisco: Jossey-Bass, 1994. Although this study covers other forms of collaborative leadership as well, three of its six case studies began with community visioning, and many of its lessons apply to community visioning.

Merrelyn Emery and Ronald E. Pursur. *The Search Conference.* San Francisco: Jossey-Bass, 1996. A good description of search conferences: two- to three-day events involving 20 to 35 people who work together to develop a vision, goals, strategies, and action plans.

John P. Kotter. *Leading Change.* Boston: Harvard Business School Press, 1996. Although focused on private corporations, Kotter's chapters on developing and communicating a vision are among the best we have read.

Reinventing Courts for the 21st Century: Designing a Vision Process. Washington, D.C.: Institute for Alternative Futures, Hawaii Research Center for Futures Studies, and National Center for State Courts, 1993. Though written for court systems, this workbook has a great deal of clear, hands-on information about visioning in the public sector, including exercises, worksheets, and information on specific techniques. The Institute for Alternative Futures works with public organizations and communities and publishes useful material on this and other futures processes. Phone: (703) 684–5880. Fax: (703) 684–0640. Web: www.altfutures.com.

OUTCOME GOALS

***Outcome Goals* define the long-term results a jurisdiction needs to achieve to realize its vision.**

Definitions, pp. 249–250

Outcome goals are your compass: they tell you whether you are going in the direction you want to go in. (We are referring here to policy outcome goals, like the Oregon Benchmarks, not program outcome goals, which are specific to individual programs.) You can set out *without* an explicit vision; indeed, visions are often implicit. But if you don't articulate explicit outcome goals and measure your progress against them, you won't know whether you are on the right course. When Oregon set goals of raising per capita income to 101 percent of the national average by the year 2000, or lowering teen pregnancy rates from 19.5 to 8 per 1,000 girls age 10–17, it made it very easy to tell whether the state was on course.

In bureaucratic governments, policy is often made without a clear consensus about goals. The process is ad hoc and political, driven by elections, the balance of power in legislatures, media coverage, scandals, personalities, even accidents. Outcome goals do not eliminate these things, but they do provide some balance. They give elected officials a more rational framework within which to make their political decisions. And they give managers much clearer guidance about what elected leaders want to achieve. "They counter the instant gratification and fast-food policy making that we unfortunately have all too often," says Multnomah County executive Beverly Stein, a former state legislator.

Because the Oregon Benchmarks have received so much attention—and because they make such intuitive sense to most people—other states, cities, and counties have begun to copy them. Minnesota, Florida, Texas, Utah, and Vermont all have statewide outcome goals or indicators now, and many cities and counties in Oregon and Florida have followed suit. National governments are also beginning to use this tool. New Zealand and the U.K. have strategic management systems that begin with long-term outcome goals. The U.S. has set national goals for education and the war on drugs.

Unfortunately, *setting* outcome goals changes little. The key is *using* them to shift priorities and drive improvement throughout the system. By the late 1990s, very few governments had figured out how to do this in any systematic fashion. The U.K., New Zealand, Oregon, Texas, Florida, Alberta, Sunnyvale, California, Multnomah County, Oregon, and a few other jurisdictions were working on it.

One challenge they all face is elected officials' reluctance to hand their opponents a report card on their performance. In New Zealand, for example, the outcome goals (now called Strategic Priorities) set by the cabinet have been fairly general and nonquantifiable. (Typical examples: "achieve and sustain a prudent level of debt" and "ensure stable/predictable tax rates.") In contrast, output goals are specified for each department, and outputs are measured rigorously. So the government knows whether it is producing the outputs it wants, but it has little data to say whether those outputs are producing the desired outcomes. Lacking any requirement to focus on outcomes, some managers have fixated on producing their outputs at the expense of innovating to find ways of improving outcomes.

According to most observers with whom we have discussed the issue, the elected ministers' reluctance to measure outcomes stems from their desire to avoid the perception of failure. In 1996 New Zealand hired American public administration expert Allen Schick to review its reforms and make recommendations. In his report, Schick addressed this issue:

> *In my view, a system that would hold politicians accountable for conditions they only partly control invites loose definitions and evasions of responsibility. If outcomes were reported as the causal results of the outputs purchased by Ministers, politicians would be positioning themselves to be blamed for matters that are not truly their doing. In this situation, they are likely to devise expedient escape routes; one of the most popular is to define outcomes vaguely so that progress cannot be measured.*

One way to avoid the problem of elected officials' shying away from outcome measurement is to have a nonpolitical, community-based body like the Oregon Progress Board measure outcomes. If a neutral, respected body measures and reports on progress toward the outcome goals, elected officials will have little choice but to pay attention and push for improvement.

pp. 37–38

pp. 47–48

Another good solution, in our opinion, is to hold steering organizations—rather than elected officials—accountable for outcomes. We believe that elected officials should appropriate budgets to steering organizations to deliver specific outcomes. Those steering organizations should then purchase program outcomes and outputs from rowing organizations, both public and private. The directors of the steering organizations would be held accountable for achieving their assigned policy outcomes. With this system, it would not be politicians who were held accountable but high-level policy managers. A performance management system would then be built to hold operational managers and employees accountable for the specific program outcomes and outputs they produced to contribute to the policy outcome goals.

Using Outcome Goals: Do's and Don'ts

pp. 21–25

All ten lessons for improving your aim apply to this tool. In addition, we have compiled a list of "do's and don'ts" based on the experience of Oregon, New Zealand, Sunnyvale, Multnomah County, and other pioneers:

Sell outcome goals as a way to achieve things the public cares about, like better schools, more jobs, and less crime. If you sell them simply as "good government," you won't get far in most communities. The Oregon Benchmarks originally took hold because they grew out of Governor Goldschmidt's process for producing *Oregon Shines,* which focused on how to rebuild the Oregon economy. When you communicate about your outcome goals, don't sell the process, sell the *benefits* the public will experience.

Take a look at other jurisdictions' outcome goals as you craft your own, but don't copy them. You can learn from what others have done before you, but be careful to craft your own process and goals rather than copying another jurisdiction's. Shortcuts may save you time, but they may also help you avoid the work that is necessary to get stakeholders to buy in to the goal-setting process.

Set realistic goals. Enthusiasm is wonderful, but if goals cannot be reached, people will become discouraged with the process. The Oregon Progress Board originally set very ambitious goals: cutting teen pregnancy in half within five years, for example. In 1997, it reset many of its targets to more realistic levels. Sometimes the goal should simply be improvement, rather than an arbitrary number picked because it sounds good.

Measure not only how you're doing against your goals but also how comparable jurisdictions are faring. Otherwise, you often won't really know whether you are succeeding or failing. As Portland, Oregon, auditor Gary Blackmer points out, "If you find that all other places in the country have a 15 percent increase in teen pregnancy, and you only have 5 percent, then maybe you're doing the right things."

Check to confirm that citizens agree with the basic priorities and values expressed by your outcome goals. Otherwise your goals won't have power for long. In Oregon the Progress Board took its draft to 20 different communities around the state, using electronic voting at community meetings to get feedback. After the first version of the Benchmarks was published, the Oregon Business Council did a survey to see if they were on target—and found that they were.

Make the goals and indicator data readily accessible, in a user-friendly format. If people can't find or understand the data, it won't do much good. Publish progress reports periodically, distribute them to the media and the public, and put them on the World Wide Web. Vermont even televises an annual interactive program to report on its Community Profiles and statewide Well-Being Report, which has 51 indicators. When important and newsworthy pieces of data come in, send out press releases. And always try to present data graphically, using some form of charts.

Refresh your outcome goals periodically. "The Benchmarks were developed following the campaign of a guy who ran for governor using the slogan of 'the Oregon Comeback,'" says Representative Watt. "There's been a complete turnaround since then; now people are worried about managing the problems of rapid growth. So you have to constantly refresh and revise, and make sure the benchmarks continue to be relevant to current problems."

pp. 52–53

Tie your outcome goals to the budget process, to yoke your government to them. When you use performance budgeting to develop outcome goals for programs, strategies, or departments, make sure they contribute to your overall outcome goals. If you don't, your agencies may work harder and harder to achieve goals that have little to do with those your community cares most about.

Don't have too many outcome goals. For most jurisdictions, we recommend keeping the number of broad policy outcome goals under 15, so everyone in the community can focus on what is most important. The fewer you have, the better. If you have too many, none will have much power, because there will be so many of equal urgency—as Oregon discovered. Legislators' eyes will glaze over. It will be difficult to shift resources toward achieving your goals, because there won't be enough money for all of them. And so much measurement will be needed that the system may collapse under its own weight.

Experience suggests that there will always be pressure to have too many goals. If the process is taken seriously, every department and every interest group will want to come up with at least one key outcome goal. But if they all get an outcome goal, then no goals will stand out. Setting outcome goals is about picking the few critical outcomes the community wants to achieve over the next 10 to 20 years. It does not mean that nothing else should be done; it means nothing else is quite as important.

One solution to this conundrum is to create a hierarchy of goals. Multnomah County, Oregon's largest, offers a model here. The first time around, in 1994, its board of commissioners picked 85 Benchmarks—to make sure no division felt left out. Discovering its mistake, the board selected 12 of the 85 as "Urgent Benchmarks." But eventually it decided even that was too many. In 1996 it chose three high-priority long-term Benchmarks: increasing school completion rates, reducing the percentage of children living in poverty, and reducing crime. Then it developed a hierarchy, with other goals feeding into these three. From there, each department has adopted outcome and output goals that contribute, called Key Result Areas.

"I came to this reluctantly," says Beverly Stein, who chairs the board.

> *But I find this very useful, because I can now actually remember it. Whenever I speak, I say, we have three long-term Benchmarks, and we need the community to help with this. I think it's hard to remember more than three or four Benchmarks.*

We recommend deciding on the number of long-term outcome goals you want before you begin the process of choosing them. If you can agree in advance on a number, you'll have much better discipline—even if you decide in the end to exceed the number by two or three.

Don't ignore areas for which there is no data. Some of your goals will not be measurable, because no relevant data exist for those outcomes. For example, in Oregon and elsewhere, improving literacy rates is a crucial outcome goal. Yet no one measures literacy rates—and as Oregon discovered, doing so is quite expensive. In such cases, the temptation is to eliminate the goal. If you succumb to this temptation, however, you are letting the task of gathering data drive your goals, rather than the other way around. You will end up telling everyone to work hard to achieve certain goals simply because they are measurable, while ignoring others that are more important. We recommend that you keep the goals you want and work to convince decision makers to appropriate the money to measure them.

RESOURCES ON OUTCOME GOALS

Oregon Progress Board Web Site: www.econ.state.or.us./opb. This site includes the Oregon Benchmarks; semiannual reports on progress toward achieving the Benchmarks; papers on the Benchmarks, the history of the Progress Board, and other topics; and links to other relevant sites.

State Services Commission Web Site: www.ssc.govt.nz. New Zealand's State Services Commission (SSC) has produced the best work we have seen on this subject, including a series of papers by SSC staff and outside consultants and an evaluation of the New Zealand reforms authored by Allen Schick. All are available on the SSC Web site.

STEERING ORGANIZATIONS

Steering Organizations are boards, councils, departments, or other groups that create visions, set goals, choose (and often fund) strategies, and measure performance against those goals—or advise elected officials who do these things.

Steering is perhaps the most difficult work the public sector does. It takes a set of rare skills that few elected officials possess. Even those who do have some of these skills rarely have the expertise to set policy effectively in all the different arenas they face, from education to public safety to environmental protection. Most elected officials are simply too busy and too pressured by political demands to steer effectively.

As demands have escalated for dramatic improvement in areas like public safety, workforce development, and support for children and families, elected leaders have increasingly begun to create organizations designed to help with steering. Many are quasi-public organizations, at least partially insulated from political pressures. Some, like the Oregon Progress Board, are focused on the entire range of policy concerns in the community. Others, like workforce development councils and public safety coordinating councils, focus on one policy arena. Some are new organizations; others, like Sweden's small policy

p. 14

ministries or the U.S. Domestic Policy Council and National Security Council, have been around for decades—even (in the case of Sweden) centuries. Still others, particularly in the U.K. and New Zealand, are the remains of large departments that have been uncoupled from their rowing functions. In smaller local governments, mayors', city managers', and county executives' offices often act as steering organizations for the entire government.

pp. 110–117

The most important role of a steering organization is to purchase outputs and outcomes on behalf of citizens, whether through contracts, charters, vouchers, flexible performance frameworks, or other methods. When they do this, they act as the steering side of systems in which steering and rowing have been uncoupled, as we describe in Chapter Three.

In addition, steering organizations:

- Do research and analysis.
- Convene community leaders, particularly to do visioning, strategy development, and goal setting.
- Develop outcome goals.

p. 30

- Keep the vision and goals visible to the entire community.
- Educate elected officials and other policymakers about strategic issues, goals, and strategies.
- Develop and modify strategies.

p. 39

- Recommend policy changes to elected officials.
- Monitor the progress of strategies toward outcome goals.
- Evaluate why strategies are succeeding or failing.

p. 56

- Do research and development work on new strategies.
- Catalyze the creation of new initiatives or organizations.
- And coordinate the work of diverse organizations (public safety coordinating councils do this, for example).

How many of these roles a steering organization takes on depends on its mission, its level of political support, and its context. One size does not fit all situations. But in general, the more of these roles the organization can play, the more effective it will be at steering. Those that play only a few roles, such as research, analysis, and policy advice, tend to be quite weak. Those that control resources and fund strategies and operational organizations tend to be the strongest. When used in this way, steering organizations become the linchpins of strategic management.

Steering Organizations: Do's and Don'ts

pp. 21–25

All of the general lessons about improving your aim apply to steering organizations. In addition, we offer several pointers that are more specific to this tool:

Give steering organizations control over significant resources. Legislatures and county boards are increasingly authorizing steering organizations to shape entire service systems, such as workforce development or services to children and families. Unfortunately, they are seldom willing to face the storm of protest that would come from giving the steering organization real control over the resources in the system, so they give it control over a token amount of resources—and doom it to failure.

The Oregon legislature created the Commission on Children and Families to reshape the human services system, but gave it less than 1 percent of the resources in the system. The Massachusetts legislature created the Mass Jobs Council to steer the workforce development system, but gave it real control over only about 5 percent of the federal job training dollars in the state, which were already just a fraction of public workforce development spending. Both steering organizations tried to push operational agencies to change their priorities and fund new initiatives; soon they were as welcome in those departments as lepers. Since they controlled far fewer resources—and hence had far weaker constituencies—than those agencies, they inevitably lost the power struggles that ensued.

All too often, steering organizations don't have enough money even to field an adequate staff. The Progress Board has labored for years with only three staff members. Many counties in Oregon do not fund staffs for their public safety coordinating councils—and it is precisely those councils that are least effective.

Spread the involvement net as wide as necessary to achieve your mission. Some steering organizations have enough formal power that they do not need to involve a broad spectrum of citizens and stakeholders. But most don't. Because their authority rests largely on persuasion, they must bring many stakeholders together and build a consensus behind their goals and strategies.

Create accountability mechanisms for your steering organizations. This is very difficult, but it is important. Many steering organizations—particularly those that oversee a particular policy arena or group of agencies—should be able to negotiate with their authorizers (typically the elected officials who fund them) concerning which policy or program outcomes are most important to achieve. When a steering organization meets those goals, its members and staff should be rewarded. When it does not, the authorizers should explore what it needs to do better and try to provide it. If the organization still fails to achieve its outcome goals, the authorizers might want to replace its director or the membership of its board. Authorizers should do this with caution, however, because it often takes a long time for even the most effective strategies to produce outcomes.

For steering organizations without much formal power to influence outcomes, such as the Oregon Progress Board, different measures are necessary. The authorizers of such organizations might want to define their key customers, then survey them annually to determine their satisfaction with the organization. The board could in turn develop a performance contract with its staff director.

Select the members of a steering organization carefully, and then train them. Effective steering takes very rare skills. Members of a steering board or council need bold vision, a focus on results, and an ability to think strategically. They must also be able to work well with others and be patient. John Carver, in his excellent book *Boards That Make a Difference,* outlines a series of other qualities that apply to members of steering boards:

- "Commitment . . . to the specific mission."
- "Propensity to think in terms of systems and context"—to see the whole rather than just the parts.
- "Ability and eagerness to deal with values, vision, and the long term."
- "Ability to participate assertively in deliberation."
- "Willingness to delegate, to allow others to make decisions."

Anticipate and plan for succession problems. Few things are more destabilizing for steering organizations than political turnover. Executives, legislative leaders, department heads, and ministers all come and go. When this happens, steering organizations can quickly lose their base of support. Their leaders must anticipate such problems and plan for them—by including members of both political parties and both branches of government, by developing close relationships with key up-and-coming leaders on both sides of the partisan aisle, by developing powerful constituencies outside government, and by painstakingly educating legislators, their staffs, and key executive branch members about the organization's role and value.

Don't let steering organizations step over the line into operations. Their role is to set outcome goals, develop strategies, set direction for managers in operational agencies, measure those agencies' performance, and hold them accountable. But they must let managers develop and implement their own action plans to carry out those strategies and produce those outcomes. If they step across that line, they will get sucked into making operational deci-

pp. 110, 131–132

sions and lose their focus on steering, while undermining the authority and morale of managers.

Don't give providers seats at the table. If service providers sit on a steering board, they bring an inherent conflict of interest. When departments (or private entities) that act as service providers are represented on steering councils and boards, for example, their leaders tend to focus on protecting their interests. This can paralyze a steering organization, taking many strategic options—even topics of discussion—off the table. (The exception is a coordinating council, which must include those who are seeking to coordinate their efforts.)

Don't tie steering organizations' hands with categorical funding. Organizations that deal with children and families, for example, typically use funds from various departments and agencies, plus categorical grant funds from the federal government. If they cannot pool the money to finance their chosen strategies, their hands are often tied. Iowa invented "decategorization boards" to allow pooling of state funds. Made up of county government and community leaders, these are steering boards responsible for helping at-risk children. The state pools different departments' funds and then disburses the money to the counties to implement the boards' plans, so the boards can fund comprehensive strategies with categorical state money.

Don't promise too much too soon. It takes time to deliver improved results. First, a steering organization has to build an infrastructure of outcome goals, performance measures, and accountability. That task alone can take several years. Those who create and fund such organizations should understand that delivering improved outcomes will be a 5- to 10-year process, not a quick fix.

STRATEGY DEVELOPMENT

***Strategy Development* is the process of developing, choosing, and refining strategies to achieve outcome goals.**

Once you have created steering organizations and outcome goals, how do you develop strategies capable of meeting those goals? As *Oregon Shines II* says, "Identifying the Benchmark and target is only half the battle. Strategies are needed to achieve those targets."

This is a challenge most governments fail. They make strategies in ad hoc, highly political ways, with little data and less analysis. The biases and whims of key politicians and managers often play a dominant role, and the legislative process turns even well-thought-out strategies into sausage.

Every organization has a strategy or strategies, even if they are only implicit. Strategy development is about making those strategies explicit, then reexamining them and testing alternatives to see if there are better ways to achieve the desired outcomes.

As Henry Mintzberg explains in *The Rise and Fall of Strategic Planning,* the strategic planning literature is strangely silent on how the process of developing a strategy actually works. Based on his studies of business, Mintzberg believes that successful strategies are rarely planned; rather, they emerge from practice. Visionary, insightful, dogged individuals often play the greatest role in creating them, far from the rational disciplines of strategic planning. Hence the key to good strategy development is good *listening* and *observing.*

> *In general, we found strategy making to be a complex, interactive, and evolutionary process, best described as one of adaptive learning. . . . The process was often significantly emergent, especially when the organizations faced unpredicted shifts in the environment, and all kinds of people could be significantly involved in the creation of new strategies. Indeed, strategies appeared in all kinds of strange ways in the organizations studied. Many of the most important seemed to grow up from the "grass roots" (much as weeds that might appear in a garden are later found to bear useful fruit), rather than all having to be imposed from the top down, in "hothouse" style.*

If strategy development is "overmanaged," Mintzberg warns, it may lose its creativity. "To manage this process is not to preconceive strategies but to recognize their emergence and intervene when appropriate. . . . To manage in this context is to create the climate within which a wide variety of strategies can grow (to establish flexible structures, develop appropriate processes, encourage supporting cultures, and define guiding 'umbrella' strategies) and then to watch what does in fact come up."

In other words, organizations that are good at strategy development make a lot of room for learning. They play with different options and examine their possible results, piloting some to see what happens. Their leaders encourage the visionaries on staff to experiment and analyze, and then nurture continued conversation about what is working and what might work. They listen carefully to what their visionaries have to say. As Mintzberg argues, "An overemphasis on planning—in fact, a belief that strategies can be created through formal procedures—tends to drive out" both visionaries and organizational learning.

The trick is to create a forum in which strategy development can occur when opportunity strikes, without forcing everyone onto a strategic planning calendar. We have seen many forums used: steering organizations, policy staffs, subcabinets, temporary task forces, retreats, design labs, search conferences, and so on. All can be effective, if they are not overformalized. "The experience of governments shows that there is no intrinsically optimal way to organise the policy-making process," the Organization for Economic Cooperation and Development (OECD) concluded after studying the matter.

Do's and Don'ts of Strategy Development

Use both hard and soft data. You need all the quantitative, hard data you can get, but it will never be enough. As Mintzberg points out, "Hard information is often limited in scope, lacking richness and often failing to encompass important noneconomic and nonquantitative factors. . . . That is why a conversation with a single disgruntled customer can sometimes be worth more than a major marketing research report." Hard data also tends to arrive too late to be useful, and "a surprising amount of hard information is unreliable." Hence good strategists use both quantitative and nonquantitative data—and both analysis and intuition.

Find ways to get outside the box. Strategy development is most creative when participants drop their assumptions and think in new ways. Any number of techniques can help people do this:

- Bring in outside experts with a broader perspective, who can push people outside their boxes.
- Use a facilitator who is skilled at helping people look at things in new ways.
- Lead site visits to places that are using strategies your people have never considered, or bring people from those sites in to talk with your group.

pp. 592–596

- Use exercises: for example, have all members of the group define the givens in the relevant policy arena, then decide which ones they can discard.
- Use a checklist of alternative strategies, to see if you have considered all of the possibilities.

See *Banishing Bureaucracy* pp. 318–319

If possible, involve elected officials, policy staffs, and line managers. You will need the support of elected officials to implement many strategies, and the best way to get that support is to involve them in creating the strategies. Policy staffs should play a key role in managing any strategy development process. And line managers are the eyes and ears of the organization; they know what is actually happening on the front lines, what works, and what doesn't.

But don't expect elected officials to engage in lengthy strategy development processes. Very few politicians have the patience for this kind of process. If your authorizers don't, get your marching orders from them, round up an appropriate team, develop your strategies or strategic options, and present them to the elected officials. Involve them at the front and back ends, but don't expect them to sit on their rear ends through the middle.

Don't bother doing strategy development work on an issue unless at least one key leader feels a pressing need for it. If those who have the power to implement a strategy don't feel any need for it, they probably won't carry your water. Many policy offices have found their ideas falling on deaf ears because they have worked on issues the key executive or department head doesn't care about.

Don't fall into the ivory tower trap. Make sure your strategy development team is in touch with line agencies and the outside world. Keep their eyes and ears open through regular site visits, conferences, lunch discussions, e-mail networks, and the like.

Don't succumb to paralysis by analysis. You'll never have enough research or data; you'll always want more. At some point, you have to go with what you've got.

Don't invite all your stakeholders into your strategy development forum. Stakeholder councils can provide useful ideas and input, or feedback on proposed strategies, as a reality check. But if you bring them into your strategy development sessions, you run a real risk of getting watered-down, least-common-denominator solutions. Most will be in the room only to protect their constituents' interests. Once you have developed a strategy you'll need to get their reactions, their buy-in, and, hopefully, their help in implementing it. But don't expect them to help with your out-of-the-box thinking. Develop the strategy first; then try to build consensus around it.

Don't assume that strategy formulation means strategy adoption. The flip side of the previous advice is that you must consider the feasibility of implementation as you develop your strategies. If you come up with the most elegant conceptual approach in the world but every interest group hates it, you won't get far. That's one reason you'll need input from stakeholders—to test the feasibility of the ideas you are cooking up. You will also need to assign someone or some group to think through the politics of getting your strategy adopted.

Don't forget to link strategy development to budget decisions. Too often, new strategies are hatched but never funded because the strategy development process is so divorced from the budget process. You have to find a way to link them—an issue we will return to when we discuss performance budgeting.

RESOURCES ON STRATEGY DEVELOPMENT

John Bryson and Barbara Cosby. *Leadership for the Common Good: Tackling Problems in a Shared-Power World.* San Francisco: Jossey-Bass, 1992. A basic text on the wider topic of policy innovation, much of which is relevant to strategy development.

Henry Mintzberg. *The Rise and Fall of Strategic Planning.* New York: Free Press, 1994. A thorough dissection of the flaws of formal strategic planning, in which readers will find much wisdom about how strategies are actually developed and refined.

MISSION STATEMENTS

***Mission Statements* help everyone in an organization develop a shared understanding of its basic purpose.**

pp. 596–599

When one moves from the government-wide or system level to a specific organization, mission statements are an important strategic management tool. They help every employee in an organization (as well as external audiences) understand its purpose and how it fits within the goals of the larger system or government. Mission statements are covered in Chapter Fifteen.

PERFORMANCE BUDGETS

***Performance Budgets* define the outcomes and outputs policymakers intend to buy with each sum they appropriate.**

In government, the most important plan is the budget—and it is rarely strategic. Budgets are set through complex negotiations among program managers, executives and their budget offices, interest groups, and legislators. With a traditional budget process, the chances that an agency's budget will reflect its outcome goals and strategies are slim. When there is a conflict between the two, the budget will win every time. Performance budgeting is a tool that brings goals, strategies, and budgets into alignment: it helps you shift resources from past patterns to today's priorities.

A performance budget specifies what outcomes and outputs an agency, program, or strategy is expected to produce, at what price. This allows both the executive and the legislature to make their performance expectations clear, then track whether they are getting what they paid for. It also helps them learn whether the strategies and outputs they are funding are actually producing the outcomes they want. If not, they can ask for an evaluation to examine why—and what to do about it.

pp. 13–18

In Oregon, for example, performance budgeting is the logical next step. The state has set broad statewide outcome goals, and some departments have developed performance measures that align with those goals. But neither the governor nor the legislature constructs a budget structured around those goals and measures. As a result, the legislature has not systematically shifted resources to achieve the Benchmarks, other than in 1993 at Governor Roberts's urging. A performance budget would help Oregon do this.

See *Reinventing Government* pp. 142–145, 158

Quite a few local governments use performance budgets, led by Sunnyvale, California, which pioneered the tool in the 1980s. In 1993 the U.S. Congress passed the Government Performance and Results Act (GPRA), which required agencies to develop performance measures and launched pilots in performance budgeting at a handful of agencies. By 1993 Australia, New Zealand, and Sweden had already adopted performance budgeting, and after GPRA passed, many states followed suit. By 1997, fifteen states reported that they had performance budgeting initiatives under way—about two-thirds of them pilot projects, often in only a few departments. But Texas, Florida, Louisiana, North Carolina, Virginia, and Iowa were all building statewide systems.

Texas, whose legislature decided to convert to performance budgeting in 1991, is the furthest along. It has done for state government what Sunnyvale did for local government: proven that performance budgeting can work. As such, it offers a good illustration of the tool.

p. 14

Every two years, Texas's governor prepares a statewide vision and goals statement, called *Texas Tomorrow.* It includes goals and benchmarks, but not the kind of quantifiable targets Oregon sets (such as a teen pregnancy rate of 8 per 1,000 females age 10–17 by the year 2000). The powerful Legislative Budget Board, made up of five key leaders from each chamber, reviews and adopts the statement.

Agencies are required to use a strategic planning process to develop their biennial budget requests. Each agency must articulate a mission statement; values; general goals; quantifiable objectives (outcome goals), with targets and indicators; the strategies it will use to achieve those goals and objectives; output measures; efficiency measures; additional "explanatory measures" that are not used for performance accountability, such as demographic data or caseload data; and action plans for implementation of each strategy.

Agencies assign a cost to each strategy, which becomes a line item in the budget. For small agencies, all administrative overhead (or "indirect costs") are folded into that line item. Originally this was true for all agencies, but the legislature later decided it wanted to see administrative costs separately for large agencies. The agencies have considerable flexibility to move money between strategies.

The final appropriations act includes part of this data, as shown in Exhibit 1.1.

When they submit their budgets, agency boards and commissions prioritize their strategies, deciding which are most important to achieve their outcome goals. They list them in descending order, indicating the cumulative percentage of last year's budget as they go. The total can rise above 100 percent, suggesting what the agency thinks it could do with more money. This prioritization of strategies helps the legislature decide how to increase or cut an agency's budget.

The Legislative Budget Office staff negotiate the proposed budget with the governor's budget office and agency staff. This is where most of the work of reviewing the goals, strategies, outcomes, and outputs takes place. Once this is done, the Legislative Budget Board forwards a proposed budget to the appropriations committees, which complete the job, making adjustments as they see fit.

Exhibit 1.1 Texas Department of Commerce (TDOC) Appropriations Act: Excerpt

For the Years Ending	***Aug. 31, 1998***	***Aug. 31, 1999***
A. Goal: BUSINESS DEVELOPMENT		
To improve the state's economy by assisting businesses and communities to be globally competitive while strengthening the state as an economic region in a worldwide marketplace.		
Outcomes:		
Number of Job Opportunities Announced by Businesses That Receive TDOC Assistance	18,125	18,175
Number of Actual Jobs Created by Businesses That Receive TDOC Assistance	6,380	6,530
Number of Defense Dependent Communities That Implement Programs Enhancing Their Capabilities to Retain, Expand, and Create Globally Competitive Businesses or Defense Missions	12	18
A.1.1. Strategy: ASSIST BUSINESSES	$40,929,099	40,129,099
Assist business to create and retain jobs by increasing productivity; developing worker skills; diversifying customer base; and accessing finance.		
Outputs:		
Number of Smart Jobs Participants Trained for New Jobs	15,167	15,622
Number of Manufacturing Companies Assisted by TMAC with High Impact Project	325	399
Efficiencies:		
Average Cost per Smart Jobs Trainee Served	$1,265	$1,265

Source: The appropriations bill for fiscal years 1998 and 1999 is available at www.lbb.state.tx.us.

Using a computerized system, the agencies track and report output and efficiency measures quarterly and key outcome and explanatory measures annually. Agencies must explain to the Legislative Budget Board any variance of 5 percent or more from the established target for a key measure.

Since 1993, the legislature has added four pilots to test refinements:

1. A benchmarking pilot, which requires every agency to choose (or develop) a performance measure for each of its broad goals that can be used to compare its performance over time with that of other institutions, or with some objective standard.

2. An investment budgeting pilot, which involves a few agencies in an effort to do cost-benefit analyses of agency strategies.

pp. 382–388

3. A customer survey pilot, which requires 30 agencies to define their customers and survey them.

pp. 208–209

4. A pilot on activity-based costing, which requires a few agencies to determine the full cost of producing each output, to begin taking full-cost accounting down from the strategy to the output level.

The system has proven useful to state legislators—though not yet as useful as its designers had hoped. In a 1998 survey of state legislators, 53 percent of the respondents agreed that "performance measures are 'always' or 'almost always' useful in allocating the state's resources," according to a Texas Senate Finance Subcommittee report. The House has used performance information much more heavily than the Senate, whose 31 members are spread more thinly than the House's 150.

In the past, says Representative Robert Junell, chair of the House Appropriations Committee, legislators' impressions of agencies had more to do with what appeared in the newspapers or whether they liked the director than with performance. "I think this does give us an objective view of how an agency is doing and how they're supposed to be doing," he says. "In higher education it's helpful in comparing universities to one another, because you do have a way of comparing an apple to an apple."

Representative Henry Cuellar adds that legislators are far more willing to accede to agency requests for more money if the agencies have performed well. His subcommittee on performance-based budgeting reviews agency performance during the 18 of every 24 months that the legislature is out of session. It applauds those that are performing well, while inviting in those that are struggling for discussions on how to improve performance, often with knowledgeable people from the Legislative Budget Office and the State Auditors Office. The agencies are quite responsive to those sessions, he says.

But the legislature does not often use its performance information to make major decisions about which strategies to fund. "All these strategies have their own constituencies, which fight like heck to keep their money coming for their particular strategy," explains Junell. Strategic funding shifts do take place, argues Albert Hawkins, Governor George W. Bush's budget director, but the decisions are usually made by agency directors, not the legislature. Because the legislature has set higher performance standards for agencies, he explains, agency directors often have to change the way they do business—at times by shifting resources from one strategy to another, or shifting their mix of outputs within a strategy. Allen Schick, an expert on performance budgeting around the world, argues that this is typically the system's greatest benefit.

Output Versus Outcome Budgeting

Definitions, pp. 249–251

Perhaps the biggest debate among practitioners of performance budgeting is whether budgets should purchase outputs or outcomes. New Zealand's leaders chose outputs, for instance. Since departments did not have complete control over outcomes, they reasoned, it was unfair to hold them accountable for producing outcomes.

Output budgeting creates real pressure to increase efficiency, but it has several shortcomings. First, because the typical government produces so many discrete outputs, it leads to budgets almost as detailed and restrictive as traditional line item budgets. More important, citizens don't care about outputs; they want outcomes. They don't care how many people the police arrest or convict; they want lower crime rates and safer streets. They don't care how often the streets are swept; they want cleaner streets. This is why most governments that use performance budgeting, from Australia to Texas to Florida, focus more on outcomes than outputs.

Sunnyvale has experience with both systems. During the 1980s, it focused mainly on outputs, but in the mid-1990s, its leaders decided to shift to outcome budgeting. "That has a much stronger and more powerful capability to raise questions about policy setting, about strategies and tactics you use to achieve outcomes, and about fundamental organizational structure," explains former city manager Tom Lewcock. He cites police services as an example. Sunnyvale has nine outcome goals for the police, each given a weight of one to five to indicate how important it is. When the police began measuring these outcomes, they realized that domestic violence was producing 50 percent of the highly weighted crime. So the council quickly moved to spend more on dealing with domestic violence, and the Public Safety Department decided to reorganize internally so it could attack domestic violence more effectively. "This is taking the outcomes right back into the policy arena and using them as a frame," Lewcock concludes. "That wouldn't have happened with the old system."

Outcome budgeting has forced managers to think very hard about whether they are using the right strategies and producing the right outputs to achieve those outcomes. This in turn has forced them to look at whether their organizations are structured correctly and whether their internal rules are barriers to improvement. "It just *forces* people to take on those kind of issues," says Lewcock. "It has stimulated much more creative thinking by staff about strategic and tactical options—ways to do things differently to enhance the outcomes."

It is true that departments do not fully control outcomes. Sunnyvale's police are only one factor affecting violent crime rates. But most departments do *influence* outcomes. And if outcomes are what citizens want, a budget system—whose purpose, after all, should be to allocate resources to produce what citizens want—should focus on outcomes. If no one is actually held accountable for outcomes, as in New Zealand, no one will worry about how to improve them.

When you take the next step and create a performance management system—to *reward* performance—we suggest a different equation. It is clearly unfair to reward and punish people for outcomes they do not control. Hence, within a performance management system, a manager should be accountable primarily for what his or her organization can control. We suggest the following rules of thumb:

- A performance budget should include both outcomes and outputs but focus more on outcomes.
- A performance management system should include both outcomes and outputs but focus rewards more on outputs.

pp. 218–220

Getting the balance right is tricky, in both cases. Budget makers need to see some outputs as well as outcomes, to determine whether the expected cause-and-effect relationship actually appears to exist. If an organization is hitting all its output targets but is not producing the desired outcomes, it may be producing the wrong outputs. Policymakers need that information, to push agencies to reexamine their strategies.

Similarly, since departments have *some influence* over outcomes, they can be held accountable *to some degree* for producing them. If they are rewarded only for producing outputs, they will have a strong incentive to produce those outputs, but no incentive to examine whether they are the right outputs. Hence an agency or department manager's performance bonus should usually depend on a mixture of outputs and outcomes. The trick is to define program outcomes that are more under the organization's control than policy outcomes. The right mixture of outcomes and outputs will vary from one unit to another—and will depend in part on the degree of control the unit has over the outcomes in question. As you go down the organizational hierarchy, to lower level employees, performance rewards should focus more and more on outputs.

Definitions, pp. 249–252

pp. 218–220

The same debate has raged for years in the private sector: how much of a manager's reward should be based on the company's profit (the outcome desired), and how much should be based on the specific performance of the manager's unit (its ability to produce the outputs expected)? There is no right answer. Getting the most effective balance for each particular business is an art, not a science.

The Issue of Consequences

As this discussion suggests, performance budgeting and performance management serve different purposes. Performance budgeting is designed primarily to improve your ability to steer, performance management to improve your ability to row. When budgets give executives and legislatures good information about performance, of course, agencies often face consequences of some form: successful agencies often have smooth sailing when they ask for more funds; others are raked over the coals at budget hearings. However, elected officials should not use budget increases and reductions as direct rewards and penalties for performance. If a program or strategy is failing to achieve its goals, it might need more money, not less. (Imagine cutting the budget for every school whose students are doing poorly, and you quickly see the problem.)

Definitions, pp. 249–250

Though a performance budget should not be used to create consequences for performance, it should be aligned with a performance management system that does so. The two systems should support each other: the program outcomes and outputs rewarded in the performance management system should help achieve the policy outcome goals in the budget. But one should not be pressed into service to do the other's job.

Consider the issue of child abuse. A performance budget might include an outcome goal of reducing the rate of child abuse. Through the budget, in other words, a legislative body could make clear to a child welfare agency that this is the primary goal. But many factors influence the rate of child abuse, including economic conditions and the rate of alcohol and drug abuse. Hence it may be unfair to reward or punish agency managers for decreases or increases in the rate of child abuse. It might be wiser to evaluate their performance and assign consequences based on other goals, such as a reduction in the number of repeat incidents of child abuse.

When governments confuse the two systems, they create innumerable problems. When Minnesota began performance reporting, for example, it wasn't clear whether it was for legislative use or internal management use, so many departments were not sure what to measure. When legislators or city councilors talk about creating accountability for performance, managers typically throw up their best defenses. They worry that legislators will impose consequences without fully understanding why outcomes are stagnant or declining, or impose consequences for political reasons that have nothing to do with performance—that Republicans who hate taxes will use performance management to punish the revenue department, and Democrats who disagree with welfare reform will do the same to the welfare department.

These are very real dangers. We recommend that legislators stay away from making decisions about individual awards or pay. Instead, they should require the executive to create a performance management system—and change it through legislation if they are not satisfied with it.

Our Public Strategies Group colleague Peter Hutchinson, a former finance commissioner for the State of Minnesota, puts it this way: "If you believe that the executive proposes and the legislature disposes, then the role of the legislature is to say to the governor, 'When you deliver your budget proposal to us, we want that proposal to tell us what the results are going to be, how much it is going to cost, and what the consequences are going to be for success and failure in producing those results.'" If the legislature wants different consequences—higher bonuses, or fewer flexibilities, or more nonfinancial awards—it should amend the system. But it should then let that performance management system determine who gets rewarded.

Absent the power to refine and approve a performance management system, Hutchinson argues, "The legislature will exact consequences, but they'll do it on an ad hoc basis. They'll micromanage, they'll form oversight committees, they'll cut budgets, they'll torture people at budget hearings."

In sum, legislators should have the power to enact or approve a performance management system but not to administer it. If they try the latter, they will quickly destroy the value of both performance management and performance budgeting. Once the legislature starts imposing specific consequences on specific managers, those managers will find ways to make sure all performance targets are low, controllable, or irrelevant. Stretch goals will disappear, and everyone will concentrate on protecting themselves by gaming the system.

Other Lessons Learned About Performance Budgeting

pp. 21–25

pp. 247–271

All ten lessons about improving your aim apply to performance budgeting, along with much of what we present in Chapter Seven, on performance measurement. A few more lessons complete the picture:

1. Create a process that helps legislators trust the accuracy, honesty, and appropriateness of performance measures.

When the U.S. General Accounting Office (GAO) studied performance budgeting efforts in five states, it pinpointed distrust of agency measurement as one of the reasons why legislators did not use performance data. Where performance budgeting has worked—from Texas to Sunnyvale to Multnomah County to Sweden—someone has been assigned to audit each agency's measurement process for accuracy. Typically it is the auditor's office, which gives an audit opinion akin to its financial audit opinion, either certifying that the measures are accurate or reporting problems and requiring corrective action. The best auditors also help agencies learn how to measure accurately.

pp. 422–425

2. Create a forum outside the budget process for legislators to review agency or program performance and refine outcome and output goals.

"You can't do this stuff in the normal budget process," says Sunnyvale's Lewcock. "Budget development is a very intense period of time. You just don't have the time to focus on it." Every government that has tried performance budgeting has discovered this. The solution is to establish some other forum to handle this kind of review. In Texas, for example, the Legislative Budget Office does much of the review and refinement with agencies in the 18–month interim between legislative sessions, and Representative Henry Cuellar's subcommittee also holds review hearings between sessions.

3. Build in another forum outside the budget process for fundamental reexamination of programs and strategies.

If legislators are to view performance budgeting as something useful, they need to see it result in the elimination or redesign of programs that don't work and the expansion of those that do. The problem is, there is no time during the budget process to do this kind of fundamental review. Every government that has attempted to do it as part of the budget process has failed. In Chapter Two we present a tool for such reviews, a periodic options review.

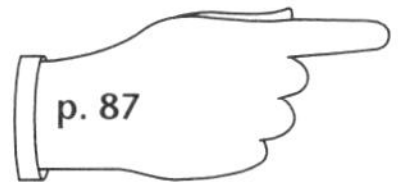

4. Don't just insert performance measures into an existing line item budget format; drop the line items.

Performance budgets should appropriate one lump sum for each program or strategy. The idea is to give managers flexibility to spend their funds in new ways to achieve the results expected by the legislature. Detailed line items, specifying categories on which money must be spent, deny managers this opportunity.

When the GAO studied performance budgeting efforts in five states, it found that when they left detailed line items in the budget, that's what legislators focused on. They were accustomed to using line items to control spending, so they kept right on doing so. Sweden made the same mistake.

Removing detailed line items also saves a great deal of energy, freeing people and money to do the measurement, oversight, and auditing required by performance budgeting. You can afford this new work if you stop doing much of the old work.

5. To make more time for performance budgeting, shift to biennial budgeting.

Performance budgeting makes it harder to finesse all the policy and political conflicts that go into budget decisions: it forces them out into the open and subjects them to rational analysis based on real data. In large governments this can slow the budget process down so much that legislators have a choice: either ignore the performance data and make decisions the old way, or adopt a longer budget cycle so they have more time. Some countries have even gone to three-year budget cycles to help address this problem.

Biennial budgeting is not a necessary precondition for performance budgeting, but it helps a great deal. Most participants in Texas agree that biennial budgeting has been instrumental in their success. Not every agency has to be on the same budget cycle. Arizona has adopted biennial appropriations for 88 state agencies, while preserving annual appropriations for the largest 14, which received more than 95 percent of total appropriations.

6. Put performance budgets and reports in useful, user-friendly formats.

"How you organize data and give it to the council is critical," says former Sunnyvale city manager Tom Lewcock. "You have to look at it from their perspective." Simple reports, using graphs and other visuals, are best.

7. Don't put too many performance goals and measures in the budget.

In their desire to make sure there are adequate measures for every unit, governments typically overwhelm their legislators. Until 1995, Australian budgets included as many as 5,000 pages of "program performance statements." Not surprisingly, Parliament ignored them. In Minnesota, managers worried that if their measures weren't in the budget somewhere, their unit would be considered dispensable—so they too overwhelmed the legislature with detail.

The key is to understand that performance budgeting is not the same thing as performance management. You may need thousands of measures for effective performance management—but they don't all have to go into the budget. Even those measures of value to the legislature do not all have to go into the budget; some can be published in supplements available to legislators who are interested in them. Arizona's budget includes a maximum of one page of key performance measures for each budget unit; a more comprehensive list of performance measures for every agency, program, and subprogram is published separately.

8. Build your performance budgeting system in manageable pieces, rather than all at once.

This is such a huge undertaking that it is virtually impossible to build a quality system all at once. Texas bit off a huge piece when it constructed its basic system in 18 months, after the 1991 legislative session. But it later began piloting additional pieces, such as customer surveys, activity-based costing, and investment budgeting. Sunnyvale is shifting to outcome budgeting in one policy area at a time.

pp. 45–46

9. Build down from jurisdiction-wide outcome goals, rather than up from agency or program goals.

pp. 13–18

When steering organizations articulate broad policy outcome goals like the Oregon Benchmarks, then look at what their agencies are actually doing, they inevitably discover a mismatch. Many agencies are hard at work on yesterday's priorities, not today's. It is not easy to cross this chasm—to align goals throughout the system. But when you start with broad policy outcomes, it is easier than when you start with program or strategy goals. If you can articulate your policy outcome goals first, you can then ask agencies to create program goals that—if achieved—will contribute directly to those policy goals. This usually requires some real change in priorities at the agency level, but that is exactly what strategic management is designed to produce. If agencies develop their goals first, you will have to ask them to completely redraft them after you have finally developed policy outcome goals—a difficult request to make, given the struggle most agencies go through to do this in the first place.

10. Don't try to do performance budgeting without automating your system.
"There is no way to do an adequate job of tracking measures if it is done manually," says Texas House Appropriations Committee chair Robert Junell. In the past, many attempts collapsed under the paperwork burden. Today, computers make possible what was impossible a few decades ago.

RESOURCES ON PERFORMANCE BUDGETING

The Florida Monitor (www.oppaga.state.fl.us) and *The Florida Government Accountability Report* (www.oppaga.state.fl.us/government), two Web pages posted by Florida's Office of Program Policy Analysis and Government Accountability. The former includes all policy analyses and performance reviews done by OPPAGA, plus information about Florida's performance-based program budgeting system; the latter has performance information on 400 state agencies and programs.

Instructions for Preparing and Submitting Agency Strategic Plans, Fiscal Years 1999–2003. Austin, Tex.: Governor's Office of Budget and Planning and Legislative Budget Board, January 1998. A useful "how-to" guide for agencies based on the Texas system. Available at www.lbb.state.tx.us.

Performance-Based Program Budgeting in Context: History and Comparison. Tallahassee, Fla.: Office of Program Policy Analysis and Government Accountability, April, 1997. A superb report on the history and practice of performance budgeting. Mail: P.O. Box 1735, Tallahassee, FL 32302. Phone: (800) 531–2477 or (850) 488 0021. Fax: (850) 487–3804. Web:www.oppaga.state.fl.us/ (click on "Performance-Based Program Budgeting," then scroll down to the report title).

Performance Budgeting. St. Paul, Minn.: Office of the Legislative Auditor, February 1994. Another excellent report on the history and practice of performance budgeting. Phone: (612) 296 4708.

Allen Schick. *Modern Budgeting.* Paris: Organization for Economic Cooperation and Development (www.oecd.org/puma/pubs/), 1997. A useful summary of budget reforms in New Zealand, Australia, Sweden, and the U.K.

LONG-TERM BUDGET FORECASTING

Long-Term Budget Forecasting **projects current fiscal trends (spending, revenue, debt, and net worth) into the future, to indicate the long-term implications of today's decisions. It gives that information power by tying it directly to actual budget decisions and making it available to the press, the public, and decision makers.**

To steer effectively, those at the helm need to be able to see what's coming. If the speed at which future events are approaching exceeds their ability to perceive change and react, they risk suffering the same fate as the *Titanic.*

One important tool to give public leaders future vision is long-term budget forecasting, which projects the future impact of all current budget decisions. In effect, forecasting acts an as early warning system, flagging potential problems beyond the one- or two-year horizon of most budgets. Some governments project out three years, some four or five, and a few 10 or more.

The key here is not simply to make projections, however; it is to integrate them into the decision-making process, by including them in the budget and making them visible to the press and the public. As *Reinventing Government* explained at length, when policymakers see the 10–year implications of spending decisions they are making in next year's budget, it changes their behavior. If they see that a program they want to create today for $5 million a year will cost $50 million in the fifth year, they will approach that decision with far greater care—particularly if the press has the same information.

See Reinventing Government pp. 236–241

Some U.S. states that use biennial budgeting project each spending decision into the second biennium, so they are in effect trying to balance budgets four years into the future. A number of countries have converted to three-year rolling budgets, which the OECD calls "medium-term budget frameworks." These are not multiyear appropriations, as biennial budgets are. They are, in the OECD's words, "rolling plans or forecasts of revenues and expenditures for future years that are updated periodically." Some do this only at the aggregate level; others do it at the agency or program level.

Twenty years ago, Sunnyvale, California, became one of the first governments to stretch this kind of system to 10 years, as *Reinventing Government* describes. Every time the city council is considering a new initiative or a change in service levels—or simply continuing a program at current levels—it sees the projected impact not for one year but for 10. These projections are not always accurate, of course, but they do flag potential problems and opportunities in plenty of time for the council to make corrections.

See Reinventing Government pp. 237–240

In 1994 New Zealand adopted a similar system, which requires the government to produce an annual budget policy statement three months before the budget deadline, to frame the budget debate; a fiscal strategy report, which compares the proposed budget and the actual economic and fiscal situation—

See *Banishing Bureaucracy* pp. 105–106

including 10-year projections of spending, revenue, debt, and net worth—with the intentions laid out in budget policy statement; and three-year fiscal and economic forecasts twice a year and roughly a month before any national election. "Too often in the past a short-term focus has been to our long-term cost," explained Ruth Richardson, the finance minister who pushed the Fiscal Responsibility Act through Parliament. "Experience shows that the future needs a voice. In this Bill, we are giving the future that voice."

The act has had a very real impact. After years of struggling with deficit spending, the government ran an operating surplus between 1994 and 1998, reducing its net debt from almost 50 percent of GDP in 1993 to less than 25 percent in 1998.

Long-Term Budget Forecasting: Do's and Don'ts

This is one of the easier tools in the reinventor's toolkit. Almost any government can do it, if it has the fiscal expertise or the financial wherewithal to hire a private forecasting firm.

Make long-term forecasts central to the budget process. Some governments produce long-term forecasts, only to watch legislators ignore them as they appropriate funds and pass budgets. To get value from this tool, you must find a way to force both executives and legislators to deal with the information, *as they make today's budget decisions.*

There are two ways to do this. Sunnyvale puts the actual forecasts in its budget documents. New Zealand requires the government to submit a fiscal strategy report, with forecasts, when it submits its budget to Parliament. Hence the government is exposing itself to ridicule if its projections show that it is submitting a budget with problems.

Publish the long-term frameworks, in user-friendly form, to encourage public scrutiny. The other way to make sure legislators pay attention to the information is to give it to the media and interest groups—who will in turn make sure the legislators know about it if there are any glaring problems.

Make sure your forecasters have credibility. If there is significant skepticism about the accuracy of forecasts, they are much easier to ignore. In a political situation, there will always be skepticism if the party in power controls the forecasting process. In Florida, budget staff from both legislative houses and the governor's office must agree on forecasts; otherwise, none can be made. In New Zealand, the Treasury Department uses an independent panel to review its forecasts. Some governments hire respected economic forecasting firms to prepare their forecasts.

Make the assumptions behind all forecasts clear. "Multi-year budget frameworks will always involve uncertainty and the appropriate assumptions to be used will be open to debate," the OECD explains. "It is therefore important to state clearly all underlying assumptions [about future economic growth, tax collection rates, demographic changes, interest rates, and the like], so that their appropriateness can be reviewed."

Don't use inflation-adjusted financial figures in projecting future spending. When the U.K. pioneered multiyear budget frameworks in the 1960s and 1970s, it used inflation-adjusted figures. When inflation accelerated, the system automatically adjusted spending forecasts upward, and agencies came to feel entitled to these increases. This made it much harder to cut spending and thus drove budget deficits upward. The U.K. and other countries have since solved this problem by using non-inflation-adjusted figures.

RESOURCES ON LONG-TERM BUDGET FORECASTING

Budgeting for the Future. Paris: Organization for Economic Cooperation and Development, 1997. Available at www.oecd.org/puma/online.htm. An excellent description of the multiyear budget frameworks in use in many countries.

Allen Schick. *Modern Budgeting.* Paris: Organization for Economic Cooperation and Development (www.oecd.org/puma/pubs/), 1997. A useful summary of budget reforms in New Zealand, Australia, Sweden, and the U.K., including long-term budget forecasting.

STRATEGIC EVALUATION

***Strategic Evaluation* is the systematic analysis of the results produced by government strategies and programs. It goes beyond traditional program evaluation to include analysis of the cause-and-effect relationships between outputs and outcomes and between program outcomes and broader societal outcomes, extraction of lessons learned for future efforts, and recommendations for changes to produce improved outcomes.**

Most practitioners who are at the cutting edge of strategic management have come to an interesting conclusion about performance measurement: it is necessary but not sufficient. Output and outcome data tell you whether your strategies are producing the results you want—*but not why.* When your organization is hitting its output goals but the outcomes you expect do not follow, what do you do? Sometimes you have a good sense of the reason, but often you have no idea.

At that point, you need a new tool: strategic evaluation. You need to analyze the performance data. Program evaluation, when done well, can tell you how effective and cost-effective your programs are, how they might be changed to improve the outcomes, and what alternative strategies might work better. But practitioners of strategic management need even more than this. They need to analyze why particular societal outcomes are occurring. Why are teen pregnancy rates falling? Why are teen smoking rates rising? What influences—from government, from the media, from social trends such as family dissolution—are contributing to produce those outcomes? And how could public and private leaders most effectively intervene, in multiple ways, to change those trends? This kind of evaluation does not examine the *program*; it examines the *policy outcome* desired.

A second challenge is to institutionalize evaluation as a normal part of strategic management. In most governments, evaluation is treated as an add-on: something to do occasionally for important programs but not a regular management practice. The trick is to institutionalize it without creating mandatory schedules (evaluation of every program every five years, for example), which—as Australia has learned—work no better for evaluation than they do for strategic planning. Obviously, this is not easy. It requires that evaluation work be given real status, by being funded at a serious level and taken seriously by top leadership. It also requires that managers face consequences for failing to commission evaluations and consider their recommendations.

We believe the key is to create accountability for outcomes. If steering organizations and agency managers face real consequences for their performance in achieving outcome goals, they will have to get serious about evaluation—because they will need to figure out which strategies work best to produce the desired outcomes.

We have found a number of other promising practices in Australia, Multnomah County, and elsewhere:

- Require that new programs always include the preconditions for successful evaluation: articulation of the intended strategy behind the program (its "theory of change"), outcome and output goals and indicators, a measurement system, an evaluation plan, and funding for evaluation.
- Gradually require the same of existing programs.
- Fund evaluation offices with enough staff, so the legislature does not have to appropriate money for each evaluation.
- Include action on evaluation recommendations as a responsibility of managers, in their performance agreements.
- Require periodic reports on implementation from program managers to senior management, to help them assess the managers' success in implementing evaluation recommendations.
- Create a prestigious awards program, and only allow programs that have been formally evaluated to apply.

Do's and Don'ts in Creating Evaluation Systems

This section is not a comprehensive how-to guide to program evaluation. (For that, we suggest you see our recommended resources.) Instead, it offers a few lessons about *evaluation systems*—how you can create an evaluation system that will be an effective, useful part of your steering system.

Design programs with evaluation in mind. When you create a new initiative, build evaluation in. The information you need for performance management will probably include some *but not all* of the information you will need to evaluate the impact of the program. Unless you collect both, it will be hard to do evaluations later. Hence, you should bring in an experienced evaluator at the beginning to help you decide what data to collect.

Involve evaluators throughout the program's life cycle. They can be useful not only in defining the data you will need but also in articulating the theory of change behind your program. As the program matures, evaluators can test that theory, help you refine the program to make it more effective, and—if it is working—help you defend it against attack. Evaluators, in other words, can be an integral part of your learning process.

Focus your evaluations on the high-leverage questions decision makers care about. "It's always difficult to put money into evaluation when there are pressing service needs, because we don't have enough money," says Multnomah County executive Beverly Stein. "So we have to be strategic and pick out areas we want to evaluate, and recognize that we can't do it all."

If you don't prioritize, adds her chief evaluator, Jim Carlson, "Evaluators will suck up your last dollar, and tell you the programs need more evaluation." The solution is to "be opportunistic"—focus your evaluation resources on key issues the decision makers care most about. If you spread those resources too thin, much of your evaluation work will wind up on the shelf.

Create separate evaluation tracks for separate purposes. Perhaps the biggest debate within the evaluation profession is whether evaluations should be controlled by "insiders" (managers) or "outsiders" (such as auditors or evaluators from a central finance department). The Australians, who have embraced "participatory evaluation," argue that if outsiders do the evaluations, program managers will rarely cooperate and even more rarely implement the recommendations. In contrast, legislators and others argue that internal evaluators will never ask the hard questions, such as whether the program should even exist. Both are correct. We suggest three different evaluation tracks: one for program learning and improvement, a second for program accountability, and a third for feedback to executives and legislators who make steering decisions. If the same staff does all three, its work will be suspect from all sides.

Don't get bogged down in a search for scientific exactitude. Don't let the desire for conclusive evaluation be the enemy of good evaluation. In the past, the evaluation profession has been too grandiose for the politicians—too focused on long, expensive studies. Today there is a shift under way toward more pragmatic evaluation. Don't expect scientific proof; it is rarely possible in public sector work—and when it is, it can be extremely expensive.

Don't separate evaluation from the rest of your steering system. Too often, evaluation is treated as a stand-alone function that has little interaction with the rest of an organization. Hence its only influence is through its evaluation reports. Most of the evaluators' intelligence and knowledge is wasted, because they do not interact regularly with managers to help them learn or with leaders to help them steer. This is a monumental waste of talent and work. Evaluators should rub elbows constantly with the other elements of the steering system; they should be intimately involved in the learning process that makes strategic management possible.

RESOURCES ON STRATEGIC EVALUATION

Improving Evaluation Practices and *Best Practice Guidelines for Evaluation.* Paris: Organization for Economic Cooperation and Development, 1999. Available at www.oecd.org/puma/online.htm. An excellent set of guidelines and best-practice lessons on program evaluation, with examples from Australia, Canada, Sweden, France, Finland, and the Netherlands.

Michael Quinn Patton. *Utilization-Focused Evaluation: The New Century Text.* 3rd ed. Thousand Oaks, Calif.: Sage, 1996. An update of the author's 1986 classic, this is a thorough (640 page) but readable how-to guide for evaluators bent on making their work useful to policymakers.

Michael Quinn Patton. *Qualitative Evaluation and Research Methods.* 2nd ed. Thousand Oaks, Calif.: Sage, 1990. A readable introduction and guide to qualitative evaluation methods, such as focus group interviews.

Joseph S. Wholey, Harry P. Hatry, and Kathryn E. Newcomer, eds. *Handbook of Practical Program Evaluation.* San Francisco: Jossey-Bass, 1994. A 600–page compendium of 25 essays from different authors on various aspects of program evaluation.

Chapter 2

Clearing the Decks

Eliminating Functions That No Longer Serve Core Purposes

We've got a hundred ways to skin a cat and no way to kill it.

U.S. REPRESENTATIVE RICHARD ARMEY

***Clearing the Decks* eliminates government functions and regulations that no longer contribute to core goals—by abandoning them, selling them, or moving them to a different level of government.**

Newt Gingrich tried in 1995 to eliminate three federal departments and hundreds of programs and subsidies. The Georgia Republican was regarded by some as the most powerful Speaker of the House since the beginning of the century; he controlled committee appointments, the drafting of legislation, and campaign funds for House Republicans. His party had won control of both chambers of Congress for the first time in 40 years. He had President Clinton on the ropes.

Gingrich and his lieutenants wasted no time. By the spring of 1995 the House had voted the largest budget "rescission" in American history: if passed by the Senate and signed by the president, it would cut some $16 billion from housing, job-training, home energy, and other programs approved the previous year by the then-Democratic Congress. Then they adopted a budget resolution for the next year that would kill more than 280 programs, as well as the Departments of Commerce, Education, and Energy.

The plan made good on a breathtaking hit list the Republicans had assembled after they won the 1994 elections. Targets included Amtrak, the Legal Services Corporation, the Maritime Administration, the Appalachian Regional Commission, the Corporation for Public Broadcasting, the National Endowment for the Arts, the National Endowment for the Humanities, the Direct Student Loan Program, the Student Loan Marketing Association, the College Construction Loan Insurance Association, the Summer Youth Employment and Training Program, the Low-Income Home Energy Assistance Program, the Office of the Surgeon General, the Goals 2000 education program, family planning programs, and housing programs. The House Republicans also wanted to sell off federal assets: power companies in Alaska and the Southeast, 40 or more ski areas on U.S. Forest Service land, and Governors Island in New York City. They planned to kill some $40 billion in subsidies and tax breaks for business while severely trimming crop subsidies and price supports for farmers. Gingrich had even dreamed up a fitting symbol for his revolution: he wanted to sell off a congressional office building, so it could be dismantled and sold in pieces to the public—just like the Berlin Wall.

But the building is still standing. So are the three departments, and so are most of the programs and subsidies the Republicans targeted. Within a year of its birth, Gingrich's bold plan to sweep clear the decks of the federal ship of state had sunk into oblivion.

It was drowned by resistance. Business interests fought successfully to keep their subsidies and tax breaks. "All too many of [the GOP's] friends—agriculture and ranching interests, logging and mining companies, export-oriented manufacturers—have come to expect a helping hand from Uncle Sam," observed conservative political analyst David Frum. Other interests, such as veterans, railroad employee unions, and mayors, withstood the attack on their own favorite services.

Back in their districts, Gingrich's conservatives heard from well-to-do Republicans unhappy about losing federal support for cultural programs, such as the National Endowment for the Arts, or social programs, such as family planning. This had a real impact on the lawmakers, noted one GOP leader: "They're country-club Republicans who wanted to be loved by the beautiful people [who are] the richest people on the contributor list, and that affects the vote count."

A majority of the voters thought the Republican plans went too far. Democrats bombarded the public with sound bites accusing the GOP of cutting programs for the poor to pay for tax cuts for the wealthy. Moderate Republican senators, who had never signed up for the Gingrich revolution, used their bargaining power to water down bills from the House. And much to Gingrich's surprise, a revived President Clinton vetoed most of the cuts Congress did pass. "To underestimate such a politician is a serious error," the Speaker later said, "and it is, I am afraid, an error we committed."

And finally, of course, the Republican revolutionaries tripped over their own feet. After they twice in confrontations with Clinton forced much of the federal government to shut down, public sentiment turned against them. What had started as a serious public debate over the role and size of the federal government had become "a silly, schoolyard brawl," as one analyst put it.

By the time Gingrich gaveled the first session of the 104th Congress to a close, on January 3, 1996, it had eliminated only one agency, the Interstate Commerce Commission (ICC). But the ICC had been on the ropes for years—even Clinton wanted to kill it. In the years that followed, the Republicans would score several domestic policy victories, including welfare reform and a plan to balance the budget. But when it came to clearing the decks of "unnecessary" federal functions, they failed.

STRIPPING THE BARNACLES FROM THE SHIP OF STATE

To everything there is a season, Ecclesiastes tells us—a time to be born and a time to die. Clearly, the author of that passage was not thinking of government.

In the public sector, programs rarely die. Civil servants gaze at politicians hell-bent on change and think to themselves, "I'll be here long after you're gone." And sure enough, after Gingrich resigned from the House in 1998, tens of thousands of federal employees were still performing the very functions he had tried to eliminate.

That is why clearing the decks is an important part of the Core Strategy. To use another nautical metaphor, when too many barnacles collect on the ship of state, they weigh it down. Part of steering well is stripping away those barnacles, to free up resources for better use elsewhere. Indeed, by clearing the decks, governments can free up substantial resources to invest in the other four strategies, to improve what remains.

Every government has functions that have become obsolete. More than a century ago, Congress decided there were serious problems with the quality of some imported teas. It set up a federal tea taster in an office in Brooklyn, New York, and for 100 years taxpayers subsidized the operation. After World War I, in which helium balloons were used to see behind enemy lines, Congress decided the federal government needed a helium reserve to ensure the supply of such a strategic material. By 1990 the government owned enough helium to serve its needs for 50 years—and the helium fund had built up a debt of $1.2 billion.

But not all obsolete functions are so major. When the Minnesota Department of Revenue put its divisions through a deck-clearing exercise in the late 1980s, it found that it still had three comptometer operators. A comptometer is a predecessor not to the computer, or even to the calculator, but to the adding machine. Three elderly women spent their days crunching numbers on these ancient machines. Department managers quickly got rid of the comptometers, retrained their operators, and reassigned them to more productive

p. 75

work. Managers can clear the decks within their own organizations, just as elected officials can clear the decks government-wide.

In today's world, activities become obsolete far more rapidly than they did in the days of comptometers. In 1982, after President Reagan fired all air traffic controllers who had gone out on strike, the Federal Aviation Administration faced a desperate shortage of controllers. So it launched a program to improve postsecondary training in aviation, to produce more graduates who could be hired and trained as controllers. Within a decade it had spent about $50 million and solved the problem. In 1993, President Clinton's National Performance Review (NPR) recommended that the program be eliminated.

In the late 1980s, Arizona—like many states—experienced a sudden spike in the price of medical malpractice insurance. So its legislature created a program to subsidize malpractice insurance for physicians. By 1996, when the state carried out its first Program Authorization Review, the crisis was already over. The review recommended killing the program, and the legislature agreed.

Sometimes programs aren't obsolete; they simply don't work. Arizona's first review also examined a dropout prevention program in the Department of Education. The program addressed a serious problem, but there was no evidence that it was working—so the review suggested eliminating it.

Clearing the decks will not improve the programs and agencies that remain. This fact is sometimes lost in the ideological warfare over the role of government, but it is nevertheless a fact. Partisans of shrinking government sometimes talk as if it is all we need to solve our public sector problems. Clearing the decks is certainly a good place to start, because it keeps reinventors from wasting their energy trying to improve programs and agencies that no longer serve any core purpose. But unless they follow up by using the other four reinvention strategies and the other core approaches, unresponsive, inefficient bureaucracy will remain the norm.

The Challenge of Interest Group Resistance

Why is it so difficult to clear the decks? Why did even the determined Republican House conservatives fail to achieve this, one of their most cherished goals?

One answer is that the GOP bit off much more than it could chew. Looking back on the wreckage of his strategy, Gingrich argued that the country wasn't ready for such huge changes. "Trying to get a free people to freely decide in the absence of a depression or a war to make decisive changes is incredibly hard," he said.

But even ending one program, agency, or regulation—whether it's a military base in California, an economic development unit that helps entrepreneurs write business plans, an underused post office, or a state police post—can require enormous effort. And the effort often fails.

Everything government does has a beneficiary, someone or some group that benefits. Individuals, organizations, or communities benefit directly; elected officials benefit when those groups support them with votes, campaign contributions, or publicity; government employees and contractors benefit because they get jobs and revenues. It's natural for beneficiaries to support functions that meet their needs; they have their "piece of the pie," and they're not interested in letting go of it. "Behind every inefficiency and goofy thing government does," says John Sharp, former comptroller of Texas, "there's always a special interest group that knows it's inefficient, knows it's goofy, and would not have it any other way."

This interest group paralysis is not an exclusive problem of government. Corporate bureaucracies face similar pressures: managers, employees, and unions fight to preserve obsolete work units and product lines that provide them with jobs or status. But business leaders can usually point to their company's bottom line to cut through the resistance; if changes aren't made, the company may fail. In government, the bottom line is unclear and debatable, organizations don't go bankrupt, and most decisions are made democratically.

That is why it is easier to clear the decks when you have a crisis, such as the economic or fiscal collapse of a city, state, or country. A crisis creates the equivalent of a bottom line for government; elected officials must act decisively and quickly or face electoral consequences.

When Canada's Liberal Party won control of Parliament in 1993, for instance, the federal deficit had been so large for so long that almost 30 cents of every tax dollar went to pay interest on the debt. The public was so worried about the problem—and had given the Liberals such a huge majority—that the prime minister launched a disciplined drive to kill corporate subsidies, sell off government assets, and devolve functions to provincial and local governments. In New Zealand a decade earlier, public anxieties about deteriorating economic conditions paved the way for the Labor Party to eliminate subsidies and sell off billions in publicly owned businesses. In Texas in 1991, the state faced a budget deficit estimated at $5–6 billion. Many political leaders were reconciled to imposing the state's first income tax, but they wanted to come up with at least $200 million in budget cuts as well. They asked State Comptroller John Sharp to lead a review to find the savings. When he proposed $4.2 billion in spending cuts and delays, increases in fees and federal aid, and shifts among state funds, they were in no position to resist. "The press asked [legislators], 'Why pass a tax increase when you can do these things?'" says Sharp. "So that's what the legislators were hearing when they were going home. They were coming back to me saying, 'Hey, can you go into my district and say I'm being cooperative?'"

See *Banishing Bureaucracy* pp. 75–82

But even when elected officials must fix a problem that is widely acknowledged and serious, parochial interests often prevent them—because the process of making governmental decisions is highly susceptible to pressures from narrow-interest champions. A legislative committee chairman has considerable sway over which bills will advance or die, for instance; that's why Gingrich installed loyal lieutenants as the chairs of three key committees, bypassing the traditional seniority system. Or a champion may have a seat on an appropriations committee and therefore be in a position to horse-trade with other legislators: "Support my program, and I'll support yours." In 1995, Senate Republicans only had a two-vote majority on the Senate Appropriations Committee, which made it easy for moderate Republicans to trade their votes to save programs they favored. In addition, the U.S. Senate's procedural rules, which require 60 votes to end a filibuster, give narrow interests even more power to block action. At one point during negotiations over the budget rescission, Senate Majority Leader Bob Dole had to put $800 million back into the bill to attract enough Democratic votes to end debate and allow the bill to advance. And, of course, American executives can usually veto deck-clearing bills—and normally it takes a two-thirds vote to override their vetoes.

Government managers can also defend parochial interests. Perhaps the most powerful tool at their disposal is their ability to manipulate information elected officials use to make judgments. "They may mount an aggressive defense, or passive resistance, or try to co-opt you," explains Mark Murray, Michigan state treasurer and former budget director. "If I ask what a unit is doing, they say they're doing great things, and all of a sudden I'll start getting calls from people about the great things they're doing."

Champions outside government, such as businesspeople, labor leaders, and editorial writers, have the power to provide or deny what decision makers need to get elected: campaign funds, campaign workers, and publicity. Business interests used their financial might to help blunt GOP deck clearing in 1995, according to Frum, the conservative analyst. They "learned to pay their protection money to Republicans rather than Democrats," he observed, "and the well-rewarded House committee chairmen of the 104th Congress in return are transfusing cash from the taxpayers to favored industries and firms almost as enthusiastically as the committee chairmen of the 103rd."

Special interests "are usually well-organised," points out Roger Douglas, who as finance minister led the deck-clearing charge in New Zealand. "They are capable of mobilising quite powerful opposition against reform." At the same time, the benefits of taking them on—of representing the general interest—are hard to reap. "The cost of protection is relatively small per person per item, widely dispersed across the rest of the economy, and often invisible to the people paying the bill. At best they are weak and disorganised allies of reform."

Aligning Political Will and Political Mastery

Triumph over special interests requires two things above all else: political will and political mastery. "At some point in eliminating things," says Michigan's Murray, "it comes down to personal leadership by public officials." First, they must decide what to eliminate. Then, they must damn the torpedoes and lead a flat-out assault to overcome opposition.

To be successful, they need political mastery. Gingrich, after all, had plenty of will and withstood many political scaldings in his 1995 effort—but he still failed. Eliminating government functions requires a strategy for beating the special interests when the votes are counted. Murray recalls the example of a failing community college in Highland Park, Michigan. "It had few students and poor performance; there were other community colleges nearby with available space, and the local tax base supporting the college had diminished," he says. Governor John Engler recommended shutting it down, but there was some resistance in the legislature. A face-saving deal was worked out. Legislators approved two appropriations for the college: one was its usual annual budget, the other a transitional budget to allow it to operate for only a short time before closing. Then the governor signed the transition budget and vetoed the full appropriation. "That allowed the legislature to make its statement" in support of the college, Murray explains, while also allowing the governor to kill it.

In a parliamentary system, clearing the decks is much easier, because the prime minister and his cabinet are also the legislative leaders, and party discipline is usually enforced. When the cabinet proposes something, Parliament passes it. If not, the failure triggers a vote of confidence. If the prime minister loses that vote, he or she has to call a new parliamentary election—so parliaments rarely buck their prime ministers.

In an American system, where the executive and legislature are elected separately—and are often controlled by different parties—majority votes are much more difficult to assemble. At the federal and state levels, all legislatures but one have two coequal branches, which must both pass any reform. Our forefathers designed our governmental systems to ensure that no one would gain too much power, and they were quite successful. It is extremely difficult to pass controversial reforms in these systems, particularly when party discipline is weak. To clear the decks, the political stars—fiscal crisis, party dominance, and the like—must be aligned. And this occurs only rarely. That is why some reinventors try to improve the odds by creating special processes that help the general interest triumph over special interests. Oddly enough, the search for a better clearing-the-decks mousetrap leads back to the 104th Congress.

Clearing the Bases

At exactly the moment that the Gingrich revolution began to falter, in 1995, Congress performed an extraordinary act of deck clearing. That summer, it approved plans to shut down 79 U.S. military installations and scale back 26 others, for a projected savings of $19.3 billion over 20 years. It was the fourth time since 1988 that Congress had shut bases, using a process specially designed to prevent special interests from derailing decisions. According to a 1999 report by the General Accounting Office, the process has been a huge success: base closings have saved $2–3 billion a year, and the affected communities have recovered most of the jobs they lost within two years.

This was not deck clearing on the scale that the Gingrich Republicans had attempted, and it built on a clear political consensus that America needed fewer military bases in the post–Cold War era. But the base closings still had to overcome strong resistance. More than 200 congressmen complained on behalf of their districts, because of the local economic importance of the bases. President Clinton complained openly about the hit list, which eliminated bases with more than 40,000 jobs in politically important California and Texas. Yet in the end the base closings became law—approved by the president and supported by a huge bipartisan majority in Congress.

The process for determining which bases to close contained several features that helped the general interest triumph over the parochial interests of congressmen, communities, and the president. Designed in the mid-1980s, it was the brainchild of Richard Armey, then a junior congressman in the Republican minority. "The Pentagon fought against it," recalls Bob Stone, then a deputy assistant secretary of defense, "because we fought against anything that wasn't our idea."

But the military brass wanted to close bases too, and they had been unable to do so since the early 1970s, when Congress passed the National Environmental Protection Act (NEPA). Under NEPA, the Defense Department had to announce its base-closing plans before it took action, and it had to hold public hearings on them. That meant, Stone says, that "everyone who wanted to keep a base open knew they had to mobilize and had time to mobilize." Communities could—and did—create an uproar. Congressmen could—and did—lean on the Pentagon to save a base, by threatening to hold up an appropriations bill or other legislation the military wanted. "Instead of the odds being in favor of what we wanted to do," Stone says, "the odds favored total inaction."

Armey's plan created a powerful, independent advocate for the public interest and reduced the power of parochial interests to thwart or twist the decision-making process. The advocate for the general interest was an eight-member base-closing commission, nominated by the president and approved by the Senate. The 1995 commission included a former senator, an airline executive, a banker, a retired general, and a utility CEO. The commission had its own staff, which reviewed the Pentagon's recommendations for base closings and held public hearings. Then the commission issued its own recommendations, which it sent to the president. In 1995, the commission made significant, controversial changes in the Pentagon's original list. It initially added 29 bases to the Pentagon's list for possible closure, and it ultimately agreed with only 84 percent of the Pentagon's proposed list.

Armey's process also used several devices to thwart parochial interests. One required the president and Congress to take it or leave it; they could accept or reject the commission's recommendations, but they could not amend them. This made it extremely difficult, perhaps impossible, for champions to shield their projects from death. To do so, they would have to get a majority of both chambers of Congress to turn down the whole package, which was highly unlikely. As Armey had foreseen, there were always enough votes (congressmen without targeted bases in their districts) for the general interest to beat the parochial interests.

A second device forced the decision on base closings into one vote, instead of spreading it across many bills. This allowed champions of the general interest to focus their energy, and it made legislators' decisions on the issue quite visible to the public. It didn't prevent politicking, but it kept it under control. When President Clinton objected to base closings in California and Texas, he did not reject the entire list, which would have caused a political uproar. Instead, he approved it and then announced measures to ease the economic impacts in those states.

A third provision set a deadline for decision making: if Congress did not pass legislation blocking the commission's plan within 45 days after receiving it from the president, it would automatically become law. Delay was not possible.

DECK CLEARING: LESSONS LEARNED

Armey's base-closing process offers many lessons about how to overcome resistance from narrow interests and successfully shut down obsolete government functions:

1. Create a powerful, independent advocate for the general interest.

Other governments use independent boards in much the same way that Armey did. In many states, for instance, a sunset commission makes recommendations about whether or not an agency or program should be reauthorized. Canada chose a different method: the prime minister appointed a special "minister for public renewal." Unlike other members of the cabinet, he was not responsible for oversight of government departments, so he had no narrow interests to represent. "He had no turf," says Jocelyn Bourgon, then deputy secretary to the cabinet, "and he was not the keeper of the money," a finance or budget director. Instead, his assignment was to guide the program review process, to represent the general interest of improving government.

Whatever form you choose, the general-interest advocate must have the staff, expertise, and time to carry out and publicize its analyses of government functions. It must also be able to stand up to political pressures—which brings us to Lesson 2.

2. *Create a process that reduces the power of parochial interests to thwart decision making.*

Again, the base-closing process demonstrated several ways to do this. By giving legislators only one vote on the commission's entire package, and no chances to amend it, the process protected the general interest from being nibbled away in dozens of subcommittees and hundreds of barely noticed votes. Similarly, the do-or-die deadline took away the special interests' opportunity to win by stalling. Deadlines force action. "That's why the tough issues usually get worked on at four in the morning on the last day of the legislative session, when there's no time left," notes Mark Murray, Michigan's treasurer. In Canada, the deadline for preparing the annual budget helped to drive the process of proposing spending reductions. In Texas, after John Sharp issued his first performance review, the legislature had only 30 days in special session to act; there was little time for special interests to mobilize. A deadline helps spring the mousetrap shut.

3. *Distribute the pain as fairly as possible, by goring many oxen at once.*

It is sometimes easier to clear the decks when you take on a great many interests all at the same time than it is to do so one by one. "Big packages can neutralise" interest groups, says New Zealand's Roger Douglas, because when many groups are potential losers, it is harder for any one group to complain about the damage it is suffering. Each group also has an interest in seeing that other groups don't escape the pain. And, Douglas adds, "whatever their own losses, each individual group also [has] a vested interest in the success of the reforms being imposed on all of the other groups in the room."

When Sharp prepared the first Texas Performance Review (TPR), he used a similar approach. "We kept the lobbyists at bay until the very last minute," he explains, "and then we threw so many recommendations at them, there weren't enough lobbyists to go around."

Gingrich seemed to be trying to use this tactic in his deck-clearing effort. "One of my key decisions in November of 1994 was to launch a revolutionary rather than a reformist effort," he said.

> *A revolutionary launches sixty battles. Two things happen: each battle attracts its particular group, so you can increase your total energy level enormously, and you spread the opposition—the establishment, the decaying old order. You spread their attention so they can't focus. They can beat you on any five things. They can't beat you on sixty.*

But the Gingrich revolutionaries caved in to their own special interests—which destroyed their image of fairness. They might have fared better had they heeded this caution from Douglas: "The public will take short-term pain on the chin, if the gains are spelt out convincingly, and the costs and benefits have been shared with visible fairness across the community as a whole. If insufficient consideration is given to these balances, the reactions of aggrieved people forced to take more than their share of the costs will end up tearing the reform process apart."

4. Make sure to have high-level leadership visibly driving the process.

Unless you have a highly structured process like Armey's base-closing procedure, deck clearing is impossible without full commitment from the top leader: the president, governor, prime minister, mayor, county executive, or city manager. Leaders must get their political allies and appointees on board, and they must stick with their agenda. In Massachusetts, Governor William Weld unveiled a full-blown review with numerous deck-clearing proposals, then announced, within a month or two, that he was going to run for the U.S. Senate. With the leader exiting, so did the leverage.

The political leader must visibly demonstrate deep personal interest in the success of the initiative. "The reason we were so successful was that John Sharp was the biggest champion of what we did, and he pushed us beyond our limits," says Andrea Cowan, a former TPR director. "You need someone who is that focused."

President Clinton tried to demonstrate his support by putting his vice president, Al Gore, in charge of reinventing government. After Gore issued the NPR report in 1993, Clinton said:

> *Here's the most important reason why this report is different from earlier ones on government reform. When Herbert Hoover finished the Hoover Commission, he went back to Stanford. When Peter Grace finished the Grace Commission, he went back to New York City. But when the Vice President finished his report, he had to go back to his office—20 feet from mine—and go back to working to turn the recommendations into reality.*

Initially, this visible support had a real impact. But as the president's attention moved to issues he cared about more, such as health care, he lost his visibility in the reinvention battle. As a result, Congress never took it very seriously, and too many of Clinton's political appointees shrugged it off as well. Gore worked hard to build support, but a vice president has only a fraction of the clout a president wields.

5. Create a stage in the process for professional analysis, using performance data, before political pressures come into play.

Ultimately, elected officials must decide whether or not to abandon or sell public functions, so political objectives will always be part of the calculation. Ideology often plays a role as well; elected officials may differ sharply over what role government should play in society. But clearing the decks is more likely to be successful if you build in a more analytical stage in whatever process you construct. "Privatization for the sake of privatization may meet some perceived ideological need, but may not make good business sense in all cases," says John Kost, who directed Governor Engler's deck-clearing process in Michigan. "Sound business judgment requires a sound analytical process, conducted by people with no vested interest in a particular outcome."

In the base-closing process, there were four stages. First, the military services offered up their suggestions for bases to close. Then a team under Bob Stone, the deputy assistant secretary for installations, subjected those lists to rational analysis, using eight criteria established in Armey's legislation. Once the Pentagon forwarded its final list, the independent commission staff analyzed it using the same criteria. They made recommendations to the commissioners, who held hearings and made the final decision. The process was remarkably free of political pressures. Stone recalls recommendations in 1993 that "basically closed everything" the U.S. Navy had in the San Francisco area. "If anybody was doing a political calculation, they wouldn't have done that. Instead, it was driven by technical and cost considerations."

In the late 1980s, Stone remembers, he built time into the process for Defense Secretary Richard Cheney to review his recommendations. Cheney declined. "He said, 'All I need is 30 seconds to sign my name,' implying he wasn't going to put bases on or take then off the list." Another time, the commission staff gave Cheney a political briefing:

> *They showed a graphic showing who the senators and congressmen were from the places they proposed to close. Cheney just blew up. He said, "This is not political. I don't even want to see those calculations; that's not part of the game."*

When you make room in the process for nonpolitical, technical analysis, you will want to examine data on performance: just what results is each function, program, organization, or regulation producing, and at what cost? This analysis can build a case for elimination that does not depend on ideology. It may expose the fact that a function provides little value or value only for very narrow interests, and it may do so in a way that has credibility with the public and some politicians.

Criteria for assessing performance vary. The eight criteria used in Armey's base-closing process included each base's military value, its return on investment, and its economic, community, and environmental impacts. The Canadian Program Review identified six key questions. The Texas Sunset Advisory Commission uses 13 standards for review, ranging from an agency's efficiency to its achievement of statutory objectives.

p. 80

One caution is in order here, however. By demanding too much performance data, a deck-clearing process runs the risk of getting bogged down in numbers. This happened to Governor Engler's review process in Michigan (called PERM, because programs could be privatized, eliminated, retained, or modified). It established a sophisticated analytical process, but "the level of work required meant you could only do a few of these reviews at a time," says Mark Murray. "Sometimes the 50–cent answer does as well for you as the $50 answer."

6. *Bring both the legislative and the executive branch into the game.*

In parliamentary systems, such as Canada's, the same people control both branches. And in council-manager systems at the local level, the executive is a nonelected appointee of the legislative body. But in governments where the executive and legislature are elected separately, it takes two to tango. A different political party may control each branch, and even if both are run by the same party, each branch will jealously guard its power. Unless the chief executive commands a very loyal majority in the legislature, it will take collaboration to get the decks cleared.

Typically, however, one branch decides to go it alone. Once its recommendations are complete, it tries to sell them to the other branch. This is a recipe for failure. If joint ownership is established at the outset, credit for results can be shared. With both branches having something to gain, the odds increase that the legislature will enact the reforms and the executive will implement them.

President Clinton needed Congress to clear any decks, for example, but he decided against legislative proposals for a joint commission to do the job. This cost him dearly when he tried to get the NPR's recommendations passed.

Two years later, Newt Gingrich figured he could roll the president, but he was equally wrong.

"You have to have collaboration with the legislative branch," says Michigan treasurer Murray—"but at the right points in time." Though the precise form of collaboration will differ for different political structures and contexts, two points seem most critical. The first is at the beginning: if you're going to build a powerful mousetrap, you will need joint ownership of the effort. The second is when you announce the recommendations—when politicians can start taking credit.

In between these points, it's best to insulate the process from elected officials. As noted earlier, you need a professional staff that is able to do its work without too much political interference. If you had collaboration in this phase—if a review were staffed by both executive and legislative aides, for instance—every controversial idea would leak to the media, and the interest groups would immediately mobilize to start beating them down. Political leaders are usually in on the final decisions, but involving political staff in the analysis phase will usually compromise the process.

7. Give the bureaucracy a chance to contribute—and incentives to do so.

It is natural to assume that civil servants will not help to abolish their own work. Why should they? They have few, if any, incentives to offer up savings, and they may not be protected from negative consequences such as losing their jobs.

Yet government managers and employees often know the most about government functions. If you leave them out of the process, you lose an extremely valuable resource. Civil servants have been involved in some of the most effective deck-clearing exercises we have seen. "You need the two perspectives: political judgment and professional judgment," Canada's Jocelyne Bourgon explains. "People with great political courage but with no knowledge about government's activities will fail, even if they are brave. If you have great policy knowledge, but you are without political mastery, you will fail too."

The trick, then, is to provide civil servants with incentives and job security, so they will reveal their judgments without feeling they have to protect themselves. This can be difficult when they perceive that politicians are eagerly hunting for cuts, either for ideological or financial reasons. At these moments, the bureaucracy tends to batten down the hatches to wait out the assault.

Two incentives may promote different behavior. One is the simple pride involved in helping government perform better. It is easy to discount the power this has among high-level civil servants, but that is a cynical view. Many senior managers have a natural desire to be part of the solution, not part of the problem. If you handpick those you involve, you cannot find a better resource.

The other incentive is the potential to gain some of the funds saved by eliminating unnecessary functions. This is how it works in the U.S. military: savings achieved through deck clearing or other means are normally returned to the military budget. "There's a widespread understanding that any money we can stop wasting can go to pay for vital needs that are not being met," says Bob Stone. Even if only half the savings are returned to an agency, this "shared savings" incentive can be quite powerful.

p. 241

DECK CLEARING FOR MANAGERS

Clearing the decks, like the rest of the Core Strategy, is mainly about steering. It is an approach for use by those who have the power to steer: elected officials, their appointees, and high-level civil servants.

But managers within line organizations can also use this approach. Most public organizations have at least a few functions that are obsolete, and efforts to weed them out are an important part of a manager's job.

Managers can conduct their own, smaller, versions of a program review, periodic options review, asset sale, or privatization initiative. They can weed out obsolete programs, processes, assets, and regulations. They will need agreement from their authorizers—the executive and perhaps a legislative committee or two—to make big changes. But they will find many things that they can eliminate without permission. Conditions change so fast in today's world that some degree of obsolescence is almost guaranteed.

Try the following tools:

- ***Divesting to invest:*** Have your customers rank your activities in value. Use those rankings to find the 10 percent of functions that are least valuable to your customers, and see which of those 10 percent you can abandon. (This is a modified zero-based budgeting technique, but it can be used within or outside the budget process.) Use the savings to invest in improving what customers do value or to increase value through new initiatives.

p. 241

- ***Shared savings:*** Before you start divesting, work out a deal with your authorizers that allows your organization to keep all or part of its savings. Otherwise there is limited incentive to eliminate the obsolete, because you risk having the money taken away before you can invest it.

p. 237

- ***Gainsharing***: Get permission to share the savings with employees. If they can benefit financially from reducing spending, they will turn into an army of cost cutters. Suddenly, they will look at everything the organization does with new eyes: Do we need to use such expensive paper? Can't we reuse our file folders? Couldn't we use cheaper sand on the roads in winter?

8. *Win the battle for public credibility.*

Many deck-clearing efforts come down to a fight for the public's approval, since elected officials pay attention to what the voters say. And the more controversial the proposal, the more important it is to get voters on your side. "If you don't come up with something that the public is interested in," observes John Sharp, "you're going to have a hell of a time explaining the rest of that stuff to a reluctant group of legislators who deep in their hearts don't want to change any of it anyway." As comptroller in Texas, Sharp was a master at translating his proposals into something that television viewers could understand. The key, he believed, was to emphasize how much money would be saved. "There have been so many studies and so many reports through the years that most people don't know and don't care," he says. "But I can assure you that Bubba knew the scope and importance of our study by the time it was published."

Sharp and his deputies brought this approach to the National Performance Review (NPR), which they helped run. The management team at the NPR fought hard to make sure that their recommendations would add up to savings of more than $100 billion—the magic number they thought necessary to establish credibility with the press and the public.

But saving money is not the only thing people care about, as Gingrich's failure demonstrated. You also have to establish the basic necessity and fairness of your deck-clearing proposals. The key here, says former TPR staff member Alan Pollock, is how you present your case: "Our background material, and the way we characterized problems and inefficiencies—everyone agreed we were right on the money. And that's where our credibility came from."

Making your case in the media, the main source of information for most people, is critical. Sharp knew he would get into fights over his recommendations, so he actively cultivated the press. "We went to the press at the very beginning," he says, "and begged them for this. We said, 'If somebody says something bad about one of our recommendations, before you print it we want a chance to respond.' That was critically important, because once you miss that first response, it's out there and it's over."

Sharp thought it important to respond to every attack. When officials at a state university held a press conference to charge that some of his recommendations would kill indigent care programs, Sharp retaliated immediately. "I was there that afternoon," he recalls, "saying something to the effect that these high-paid bureaucrats are 'a handful of gimme and a mouthful of bull,' some ridiculous quote like that. There weren't any more of those kinds of press conferences."

See *Banishing Bureaucracy* pp. 132–135

9. *Mitigate the shock of death.*

When eliminating government functions, it is important to manage the transition humanely, as we recommended in *Banishing Bureaucracy.* Unless your government is under severe fiscal stress, you can use attrition, early retirement incentives, and other methods to downsize without resorting to layoffs. You can even find ways to send positive signals to other government employees. When the British sold government businesses, for instance, they sometimes helped employees purchase discounted stock in the private firms. "If the people who move out of activities that you are killing prosper, that's a powerful message to the rest of the organization," says Mark Murray.

pp. 199–200

p. 98

This lesson also applies to the interests of government's customers. For instance, when the Canadian government wanted to eliminate transportation subsidies for grain growers, it offered several years of transitional funding. Similarly, when Governor Engler in Michigan eliminated a community college, he provided a transition budget that allowed some nursing students to finish their program.

10. Getting government right is an ongoing problem, so set up an ongoing process to address it.

The base-closing process involved four separate rounds, over seven years. In Texas, after the success of the comptroller's first performance review, the legislature authorized reviews every two years. In Canada, the 1994 Program Review led to a continuing process for examining the necessity of government functions.

Each of these examples was a response to a practical consideration: the need to spread the deck-clearing process out over several years. Trying to judge every aspect of government all at once is simply too enormous and complex a job. "It is much too intense, too difficult," says Canada's Jocelyne Bourgon.

To build the habit of deck clearing into the fabric of government, you can create targeted reviews that bite off one piece at a time. In general, we think these "periodic options reviews" provide more value, over time, than do one-shot program reviews. (If you attach a do-or-die deadline to the review, by requiring the legislature to reauthorize the program to keep it alive, you have what is widely known as a sunset review.)

pp. 88–89

One option besides abandoning the function is to turn it over to the private or the nonprofit sector. You can do this either through an asset sale or by using a quasi-privatization tool, such as a 50-year lease or an agreement by which the private sector builds the asset and operates it but ultimately transfers ownership to the public sector.

TOOLS FOR CLEARING THE DECKS

Program Reviews provide comprehensive, in-depth analyses of the results, costs, and necessity of specific government functions and regulations, with recommendations to maintain, eliminate, or improve them. See p. 78.

Periodic Options Reviews establish regularly scheduled examinations of agencies and their functions to determine whether they should be abandoned, sold, devolved, or otherwise reformed. See p. 87.

Asset Sales move government assets, such as publicly owned businesses, corporations and pieces of physical infrastructure (airports, dams, railroads) to private ownership. In most countries this is synonymous with the word *privatization,* although in the U.S. that term is also used to describe contracting out. See p. 93.

Quasi-Privatization Methods let the private sector lease or build physical assets, such as prisons, hospitals, and highways, and use them to deliver services governments want. The asset may be owned by government or may shift to public ownership at a specified future date. See p. 102.

PROGRAM REVIEWS

On February 27, 1995, a prominent North American politician declared that progress toward a balanced budget "can only happen if we redesign the very role and structure of government itself." The country, he said, needed "a new vision of the role of government in the economy. In many cases that means smaller government."

> *We are dramatically reducing subsidies to business. We are changing our support systems for agriculture. We are putting government activities on a commercial basis wherever that is practical and productive. . . . In creating this budget, no activity of government has gone unexamined. Nothing less than a complete rethink has been required—top to bottom.*

The country in question was not the U.S., but Canada. The speaker was not an acolyte of Newt Gingrich, he was the Canadian finance minister. He was not a rabid conservative, but a leader of the Liberal Party, the Canadian equivalent of the Democrats. Paul Martin was unveiling his party's 1995 budget proposal in Ottawa.

The Liberals had swept into power in late 1993, gaining an enormous majority in Parliament. Their first priority was to reduce the federal deficit, which was significantly higher than the U.S. deficit, both as a percentage of spending and as a percentage of gross domestic product (GDP). Previous Canadian governments had tried across-the-board budget cuts—14 times in eight years. While failing to tame the deficit, this hurt all programs indiscriminately. "Cutting everything across the board leads to incompetence across the board," observed Jocelyne Bourgon, then secretary of the cabinet.

See *Banishing Bureaucracy* p. 92

The Liberals tried a different tool. As we reported in *Banishing Bureaucracy,* they conducted what they called a Program Review, a comprehensive examination of spending in every federal department. Instead of cutting across the board, the Liberal government decided to make choices and eliminate lower-priority programs.

The first phase of the review produced recommendations that would save $17 billion over three years, cutting roughly 10 percent of departmental spending and eliminating 14 percent of federal jobs. A second phase identified an additional $2.2 billion in potential savings. Overall, the Liberals shrunk spending on all federal programs to the lowest level since 1950, as a percentage of GDP. Economic programs such as corporate and transportation subsidies took the biggest hits, whereas social programs expanded their share of the dwindling pie.

Perhaps the most radical overhaul took place in Canada's transportation sector. The Liberal government decided to:

- Sell the Canadian National Railway System to stockholders.
- Transfer ownership and operation of most smaller airports to interests in local communities.
- Turn over the Air Navigation System and the operations of the St. Lawrence Seaway to private, not-for-profit corporations.
- Transfer regional and local ports to provincial and local governments or community organizations.
- Largely end transportation subsidies for business interests and reduce those supporting passenger railways and ferries.
- And abolish subsidy payments to railways for grain transport.

The Canadians carefully organized the Program Review to get the nation's political leaders working hand in glove with the civil service's top managers. They started by developing six criteria for judging the value of each program (see the box on p. 80). Then, in each of the 25 federal departments, the elected minister and the deputy minister (the top civil servant) used those criteria to develop proposals for changes. They relied not on outsiders but on themselves and their staff of civil servants.

These proposals then went to a special review committee made up of six handpicked, top-level civil servants with deep knowledge of the 25 departments. As the cabinet's secretary, Bourgon chaired the group. "The membership was carefully selected," she says. "Collectively, the six of us had been in every department."

CANADA'S DECK-CLEARING CRITERIA

The Program Review asked departments to review and assess their activities and programs against the following six criteria:

1. *Public interest test.* Does the program area or activity continue to serve a public interest?
2. *Role of government test.* Is there a legitimate and necessary role for government in this program area or activity?
3. *Federalism test.* Is the current role of the federal government appropriate, or is the program a candidate for realignment with the provinces?
4. *Partnership test.* What activities or programs should or could be transferred in whole or in part to the private/voluntary sector?
5. *Efficiency test.* If the program or activity continues, how could its efficiency be improved?
6. *Affordability test.* Is the resultant package of programs and activities affordable within the fiscal constraint? If not, what programs or activities would be abandoned?

The committee raised questions about the proposals and made suggestions. But, says Bourgon, "We were not to instruct the departments and were not to force them to change the proposal. *They* were accountable—not us." To ensure that departments paid attention to its advice, the committee wrote up its assessments and passed them on to a special committee of elected ministers, the next stop for the departments' plans. This group had also been handpicked by the prime minister. "Assume you are a deputy minister," says Bourgon. "You would want to take on board as much advice as possible because you want your minister to have clear sailing in that next meeting."

Only two departments disregarded the criticisms and took their proposals unchanged to the ministers' group. "They went ahead, and they failed," Bourgon says. "That sent a huge signal to the others."

Once the committee of elected ministers approved proposals for every department, the cabinet examined the whole puzzle they had been assembling. "I remember telling them at the beginning [of the process], 'You may hate this camel at the end,'" Bourgon says. The cabinet took several two-day retreats to look over the pieces and decide if the package as a whole was politically feasible. Bourgon says they looked at the impact of the reductions in various ways: effects on regions of the country, on the economy, on the nation's fiscal deficit, and so on. "At the end of the day, let's be honest, it is a subjective judgment," she explains. "It's mainly a political judgment: Can you marshal support? Do you have the political will?"

Prospecting for Gold

Canada's Liberals were not the first to use this kind of review. During and after the long recession of the early 1990s, many American states did some kind of review, whether they called it a performance review, as Texas did; a PERM review, as Michigan did; or a performance audit, as North Carolina did. Many local governments did the same thing. And, of course, the Clinton administration launched its National Performance Review, which came up with nearly 300 recommendations to save $108 billion over five years; reduce the federal payroll by 252,000 positions; reform the budget, personnel, and procurement systems; and make many other improvements.

We call this kind of review a program review rather than a performance review because it typically focuses less on how well programs are performing than on whether they should be abolished, reformed, or restructured. In six or nine months, it is impossible to do a true "performance review" of more than a small slice of a typical government. But by whatever name, prospecting government-wide for inefficiencies and obsolescence often uncovers mother lodes of gold. Not all of the savings come from eliminating functions; typically, most result from improvements in management.

Some governments use this tool to eliminate regulations as well as programs. Indianapolis created a Regulatory Study Commission to help eliminate outdated and unneeded rules. In California, Governor Pete Wilson's Office of Planning and Research held six regional roundtables to gather recommendations for regulatory streamlining; it identified 3,100 regulations for abolition. New York governor George Pataki created the Governor's Office of Regulatory Reform, which claimed to have reduced operating costs to individuals, businesses, nonprofits, and local governments by more than $1.6 billion in its first two years of reviews.

The basic components of a program review are deceptively simple:

- You need a mandate that describes the scope of the review. Will it cover all departments? Will it review administrative systems? Regulations?
- You need to assemble a team to conduct the review.
- The team needs to lay out and implement an analytical process, including data gathering, assessment, and options development.
- The team should establish a timetable, with specific deadlines along the way.
- And finally, the review should produce a set of recommendations and sell them to decision makers.

In reality, the exhaustive, in-depth nature of program reviews creates many complications in implementation. And the fact that a program review lives—or dies—in a political environment adds even more. There is no "right" way to conduct a program review, but past experience does suggest some lessons. For starters, all 11 of the general deck-clearing lessons outlined previously apply to program reviews—in spades.

pp. 69–77

Program Reviews: Lessons Learned

1. Don't try a program review unless the political stars are aligned.

Though powerful, a program review "is a tool that only works when the stars are in alignment," says Richard Paton, a veteran of Canada's two reviews. In Canada and in Texas, they were. Fiscal crises forced action, political majorities had enough power to pass tough measures, and public opinion supported dramatic change. But in many other cases, when the stars have not been so well aligned, even herculean efforts have failed. The NPR, for instance, led to significant reforms and significant downsizing but few votes to eliminate programs. Clearing the decks is just too difficult unless political will, political mastery, and the political stars all line up behind it.

See *Banishing Bureaucracy* pp. 92–93

2. Use fiscal targets to drive the process.

An undertaking as massive as a program review needs a powerful lever to gain the attention and cooperation of politicians and civil servants. Improved efficiency and effectiveness may be enough to generate enthusiasm in some governments, but not in most. Experience shows that a financial bottom line—money saved—has the most power to attract political support, stimulate the creativity of agencies, and keep the public interested.

In Canada there was a strenuous debate over the use of fiscal targets in the Program Review process. Although the Liberal government had an overall target for reducing the federal deficit, some officials felt it was unwise to set department-by-department targets for savings, because the targets could become de facto ceilings on savings. What if an agency could do even better? Others felt it was essential to have targets so departments would know what they had to accomplish. In the end the cabinet decided to use targets, but it called them "advisory," says Richard Paton, then an official with the Treasury Board.

Although we believe that an overall fiscal target is almost always useful, the utility of departmental targets depends a great deal on the situation. If civil servant employees of a department or agency are doing the review, for example, a challenging fiscal target is probably necessary to force them outside the box—outside their usual view of change as incremental. If outsiders are doing the review, however, departmental targets may be less necessary.

If you do choose to set departmental targets, make sure they are not arbitrary. When a new administration comes in, there is a danger that it will launch a program review and set half-baked targets based on the anecdotal impressions of a few recently elected or appointed leaders. To have any credibility, departmental targets should be set by people who are well informed about realities inside the departments, such as Canada's deputy ministers.

Of one thing we are sure: don't set the same target for every department. Program reviews are about making choices and setting priorities, not about making across-the-board cuts.

3. *Articulate a clear and feasible scope for the review; don't try to bite off more than you can chew.*

In any large government, it is impossible to review all functions overnight—or even in six months, which was how long the NPR was given to get the job done. Clinton and Gore bit off too much for a six-month review; the short time span precluded doing true in-depth analysis in some departments. And in the rush, Gore's team did not have time to develop an implementation strategy. Predictably, Clinton and Gore launched a second review two years later.

In Texas, John Sharp had only five months to complete his first performance review—enough time to generate nearly 1,000 recommendations, but not enough time for a thorough review of the entire state government. Every two years, Sharp came back with another report—and hundreds of new recommendations. In North Carolina, the government-wide performance audit took 18 months.

The appropriate length of time for a review depends on its scope. For shorter reviews, you can narrow the focus—for example, to the most costly and troubled programs. The Canadians left out of their Program Review several very hot issues, including federal transfer payments to the provinces and major entitlement programs such as unemployment insurance. These required a very different sort of analysis than the Program Review did of the departments' service and compliance programs, says Bourgon. The North Carolina audit looked not only at government programs but also at administrative control systems, such as procurement and personnel, and at health care costs. It divided the vast terrain into separate major reports, which were issued sequentially rather than all at one time.

If the review's focus is unclear, it will hamper the team's effectiveness. Because Clinton's mandate for the NPR was fuzzy, for example, different NPR work teams sometimes operated on different assumptions. No one was quite sure just how bold the president wanted to be, and different people gave the teams different advice. As a result, some teams were timid, while others spent time generating lists of programs for the chopping block that were ultimately rejected by the White House because they would upset Congress.

4. Create a team that combines expertise with a willingness to think outside the box.

Conventional wisdom suggests that civil servants will never develop bold proposals to clear the decks—that for truly innovative thinking you need outsiders, such as businesspeople. But conventional wisdom is wrong. Reviews dominated by outsiders, such as the Reagan administration's Grace Commission, typically offend the insiders so profoundly that they stonewall any action. Reviews done by insiders, such as Canada's Program Review, usually get much further.

But the real question is not whether to use insiders or outsiders; it is how to assemble a team that has deep knowledge of what government does, expertise about possible alternatives, and the courage to suggest bold new ideas. This is difficult to orchestrate, especially if you're in a hurry.

One way to get insiders involved is to borrow them. For the first TPR, Sharp's office borrowed staffers from various agencies, then set them loose on other agencies to find improvements. This way, says Sharp, they had the advantage of not being captives of the agencies' "spheres of influence"—and they could go back to their agencies without fear after the review. Sharp's deputies used the same technique when they staffed the NPR's teams that examined federal departments. The disadvantage, of course, was that the temporary staffers knew very little about the terrain they were invading. And it is very hard to make bold recommendations when you feel you are on shaky ground. With just a few months to pull together their recommendations, some of the NPR's departmental teams were remarkably timid. (In Texas, after the legislature authorized Sharp to conduct repeated performance reviews, he greatly increased the permanent staff in his office to handle the task, and he sometimes contracted with outside experts to review particular programs or systems.)

The NPR staffed the other half of its teams—those examining administrative systems and structures—by handpicking both insiders and outsiders who had real expertise in their subjects. This nonrandom method worked far better than selecting staffers from agencies indiscriminately, and the mix of insiders and outsiders was more effective than relying only on insiders.

In North Carolina, the performance audit team obtained an outside perspective by hiring a consulting firm, Peat Marwick. The outsiders "brought no predisposition to the table," says Curtis Clark, then manager of the state's performance audit division. "They were not hesitant to trample on sacred ground."

Yet in Canada, no outsiders were involved in the Program Review. Instead, a heavy burden fell on the deputy ministers, the highest-ranking civil servants in the system. Canada's method worked because the elected officials set a bold fiscal target and made it very clear that they wanted the decks swept clean—

and because the deputy ministers brought deep knowledge and years of experience to the table. In general, however, we believe program reviews are most effective when done by a handpicked combination of insiders and outsiders. The right insiders bring the deep knowledge of government; the right outsiders bring knowledge of potential alternatives and a greater ability to think outside the box.

5. *Use a variety of methods to gather information and ideas.*

When Sharp launched the first TPR, he did what any good politician would instinctively do: he held public hearings around the state and publicized a hotline (1–800–BEAT-WASTE) to generate ideas. The hotline received 2,600 calls. These efforts fit well with Sharp's combative approach, which treated the review as an incursion into the agencies' turf. They also generated great press. But they didn't produce many useful ideas. The TPR staff learned that public hearings "are a huge waste of money, especially when you have to do them statewide," says Mary Buckley, then a special assistant to Sharp.

> *The first time we put up the hotline we got over 2,000 recommendations, and maybe 5 or 10 of them were worthwhile. Now, one of them was a $500,000 savings, but those were few and far between. It was a great PR tool. But we did it for school district performance reviews also, and we never got anything useful.*

Over the years, Sharp, Buckley, and their colleagues learned to use five different sources of information: an environmental scan, agency employees, experts, customers, and the general public. They found the first two to be the most useful and the public to make the least useful contributions.

- ***Environmental scanning.*** Both the TPR and the NPR told their staffs to begin by reading every existing report they could find on the agency or program in question. This usually surfaced an enormous amount of valuable information, while also orienting the staff to their topic. As the Internet matured, it became an extremely useful tool for this kind of scanning. "We found a lot of good ideas from other states, or the private sector," says Andrea Cowan, a former TPR director. You have to be willing to read "everything you can get your hands on. A lot of our ideas didn't come from experts—they came from scanning the globe, seeing what others were doing."
- ***Public employees.*** Civil servants often know the most about how programs really work and how they can be improved. Occasionally, says Sharp, these employees "were disgruntled folks that we found out about."

But a lot of times there were very low-level people within the agency that always knew something was screwed up but never could get their ideas past the first tier of management. We took their ideas and we did something they could never do. We took them to the top.

"Talking to them one-on-one was best," adds Cowan, "because sometimes in a group they would get nervous, and not want to criticize the agency." Once they learned to trust the TPR, agency employees would sometimes hand over legislative proposals that their directors wouldn't take forward, says Cowan. "We probably got the best ideas that way."

- ***Experts.*** Academics and consultants with particular expertise in an area are often helpful in outlining alternatives to current practice. They weren't usually very familiar with the actual process being examined, Buckley notes, but they knew other models and had opinions about which were best. Both the TPR and the NPR routinely invited experts in and picked their brains. Occasionally the TPR even organized day-long policy roundtables, involving a few experts, a few agency managers, and a few legislative staff members, to delve into an issue.
- ***Customers.*** Surveys, focus groups, and other methods for listening to the customer were also somewhat helpful—although as we explain later, they help less with deck clearing than with performance improvement. Mary Buckley says she learned the most by actually walking through a process—such as welfare intake—as a customer.

p. 89
p. 542

- ***The public.*** Hotlines and e-mail generate a lot of heat but not much light. Most citizens know what makes them angry, but they don't know enough about the inner workings of the bureaucracy to suggest useful solutions. Public hearings tend to attract special interest groups, who are there to defend their self-interest, and cranks. The TPR had much greater success with "charettes": day-long (8 A.M. to 8 P.M.) forums that citizens could drop in on when it was convenient, to register their views. Rather than using a hearing format, TPR simply set up numerous tables, each manned by a staff member and focused on a particular kind of issue. Citizens could talk with the staff member, or if they were too timid or too hurried to do that, they could simply write their comments on poster boards mounted on the walls. This didn't result in great insights, Buckley and Cowan found, but it did give them a sense of what most concerned people.

6. Develop an implementation strategy before you issue recommendations.

Unfortunately, a recommendation made is not a recommendation implemented. Many proposals offered in a program review will have to run the legislative gauntlet, where they will be attacked by various interest groups. As with any major piece of legislation, before the process begins, you should have a plan for succeeding.

pp. 73–74

At the outset, it is critical to line up as much political support as you can—by sharing the credit for the review with the other branch of government, for instance. You must also carefully package and broadcast the report's unveiling so that it will build positive public and media support. President Clinton and Vice President Gore unveiled their report on the White House lawn, in front of forklifts piled high with volumes of government red tape. They then blitzed the country for several days, even taking their show onto late night television. Gore constantly used visual props, like the ashtray he smashed on David Letterman's television show to satirize the government's bureaucratic procurement specifications.

One common mistake in the marketing of program reviews is overselling. "In order to push governmental reform proposals through the many veto points in the American system," observes R. Kent Weaver, a senior fellow at the Brookings Institution, "political executives need to promise greater returns than are likely to be achieved." If opponents can point to a specific claim that is inflated, they may be able to discredit much of the report.

But implementation is not just about winning political and media wars over recommendations. It is also about winning support within the bureaucracy, which must do most of the actual implementing. To do this you will need a high-level, government-wide steering group of appointees and senior civil servants to develop strategies, clear away obstacles, and monitor progress.

RESOURCE ON PROGRAM REVIEWS

Andrea F. Cowan. *Performance Review: Streamlining Government Operations and Management.* Austin, Tex.: Sheshunoff Information Services, 2000. Written by a former manager of the Texas Performance Review, this looseleaf manual and CD provide guidance on implementing a program review, based on experience in Texas and elsewhere. Available for $345. Phone: (512) 305–6658. Web: www.sheshunoff.com.

PERIODIC OPTIONS REVIEWS

***Periodic Options Reviews* establish regularly scheduled examinations of agencies and their functions to determine whether they should be abandoned, sold, devolved, or otherwise reformed.**

A program review usually generates savings and modernizes government operations. It also inevitably leaves some stones unturned. So why not try it again? Like John Sharp in Texas, many reinventors decide that once is not enough; they want a process that is done regularly and constantly.

pp. 77–80

When Canada wrapped up its first Program Review, officials realized that the process was too massive to use regularly. "You have to allow people to breathe," says Jocelyne Bourgon, then secretary to the cabinet. They decided not to institutionalize the Review's focus on efficiency and savings, only its focus on the proper role of government. "Our view was that efficiency gains are marginal improvements only. What really matters the most is to focus on what should be the role of government."

pp. 110–113

The British created periodic reviews as the heart of their Next Steps reforms. Every five years, British departments review the executive agencies under their purview to examine their roles and decide if all or part of their functions should be abolished, sold, contracted out, merged with other agencies, or restructured. Two central organizations, the Treasury Department and the Next Steps Team, monitor the process to make sure it is thorough. Based on the reviews' results, the departments negotiate a "framework document" with each agency, specifying its mission, role, and performance criteria for the next five years. In their first five years, the British reviews resulted in decisions to privatize about a dozen organizations.

The state of Arizona created its own version of this tool in the mid–1990s, first called Program Authorization Reviews, then renamed Strategic Program Area Reviews. They begin by asking the selected agency to do a self-assessment of a particular program it administers. Then, to engage both the executive and the legislative branch, evaluations are prepared by both the Governor's Office of Strategic Planning and Budgeting and the Joint Legislative Budget Committee staff. Each staff makes recommendations on whether to retain, eliminate, or modify the program. When both staffs agree on a recommendation, it has more credibility with the legislature.

In our view, periodic options reviews, when done well, have far greater value than one-time program reviews. Why? Because they institutionalize the habit of examining whether functions are still needed and, if they are, how to improve them. Since agency managers know the reviews are coming, they keep a critical eye on these core questions. The first two Texas Performance Reviews "accomplished some short-term things; they saved some money," says Mary Buckley, then a special assistant to the comptroller.

> *But I think in the long term they have done a lot to change the way people think about how they do business. Managers ask themselves, "How could we save? How could we do it better?" To the extent someone does it on an ongoing basis, not as a one-shot deal, people know it's out there and they've got to be thinking about it. They know they're going to have go through a review, and so they keep an internal process of rethinking going on.*

Periodic options reviews also:

- Allow governments to sequence their reviews, so they can cover the entire waterfront over time, rather than trying to do it all at once.
- Encourage leaders to reinvent for the sake of reinventing, not just to cut budgets.
- Give government officials a regular opportunity to engage in public dialogue about the proper role of government, which prompts them to explore the issues related to each function in depth.
- Require government leaders to develop and maintain an ongoing capacity to perform this work, in special units and within departments, rather than building that capacity from scratch sporadically.

Periodic Options Reviews: Lessons Learned

pp. 69–77, 83–87

All of the general lessons about clearing the decks are relevant to this tool. And all but the first two lessons on program reviews apply to periodic reviews as well. In addition, we offer the following advice, gleaned from experience in Texas, Canada, Arizona, and the U.K.

1. If you don't have the performance information and evaluation capacity necessary to make informed judgments about programs, don't try to use this tool.

Because periodic options reviews examine smaller slices of government than program reviews, they allow for greater focus on performance. And because they are repeated, they tend over time to weed out most of the functions that no longer serve a core public purpose—leaving the question of how to reform existing functions even more prominent. Hence they require good data on performance and, at times, evaluation to understand what the data means. If you don't have these capacities, you are probably not ready to use this tool.

pp. 56–59, 247–271

2. Build consultation with customers and other stakeholders into the review process.

Decisions about clearing the decks can be informed by input from customers and stakeholders, but ultimately they are made in the interests of government's "owners"—the citizens—by their elected representatives. They have less to do with how customers feel about a service function than with whether its owners feel it still needs to be performed by the public institution in question. Customers may want the service to continue, for example, even though the owners feel it is not worth continuing, given fiscal constraints, or could be better handled by the private sector. But because periodic options reviews get beyond clearing the decks and into performance issues, customer feedback becomes much more important. A review process should build in a variety of ways to get input from customers and other stakeholders.

pp. 382–388

3. In an American system of separately elected legislative and executive branches, special efforts are necessary to ensure buy-in and action by both branches.

A periodic options review is much more difficult in a system that separately elects the legislative and executive branches than in a parliamentary system, particularly in these days of weak party discipline. In parliamentary systems, legislators in the majority rarely object publicly when the prime minister, their party's leader, proposes to abolish, sell, or devolve a function. In most American systems, however, no such proposal can be implemented without legislation, and most are hotly debated.

Arizona dealt with this problem by having both the executive budget office and the legislative budget staff review programs and recommend whether to retain, eliminate, or modify them. This two-branch process "is half the genius of this thing," says Peter Burns, former director of the Office of Management and Budget. "With the joint things going, you boil down to what are the facts, and you get opinion out of the way—because sometimes we have wildly different opinions on something." When there are disagreements, Burns says, it forces the two offices to discuss their views and negotiate. "If both of us agree, people assume it to be true."

Even with both branches involved, however, the Arizona legislature gradually lost its sense of urgency about the reviews. The Texas legislature also lost much of the sense of urgency it felt early in the 1990s about TPR recommendations. These realities suggest that some jurisdictions would be wise to create a version of the federal base-closing process described earlier. For example, a legislative body could require that each government agency or program undergo a thorough review every five years—whether it is conducted by two offices, as in Arizona; by an independent office, like the Texas comptroller; or by an ongoing, independent commission, selected by the executive and legislative branches. That office or commission would be authorized to recommend whether to abolish, sell off, devolve, or in some other way reform the agency. Its recommendations could become law within two, three, or four months, unless the legislature voted against them or the chief executive vetoed them. In this way, the normal inertia of the legislative process could not kill a recommendation; only deliberate action by either branch could do so.

pp. 68–69

Such a process would clearly have to be handcrafted to fit the political realities of the government involved. And like any periodic options review, it would need strong champions in both branches—and probably in both houses of a bicameral legislature.

4. *Review all organizations working in the same policy arena at the same time.*

Jeremy Cowper, who ran the U.K.'s Next Steps Team from 1994 to 1997, suggests performing reviews for all agencies related to a particular policy area, such as criminal justice or employment and training, at the same time. In this way, the government can examine its overall policy, set new directions, and make sure all agencies in that area are aligned with the new direction. Problems that fall between agencies, conflicts between agencies, and duplication or overlap among agencies can also be addressed. Agencies that need to work more closely together can be directed to do so.

Arizona learned this lesson in its first review. "We set [Program Authorization reviews] up to examine a program in isolation," explained State Senator Carol Springer. "We should be trying to examine programs that overlap or duplicate. We would have a better chance of eliminating a program if it could be absorbed into another program." In the second round, Arizona began reviewing similar programs together.

5. *Tie the timing of reviews to the business planning cycle used by the organizations being reviewed.*

One critical issue in institutionalizing a review process is how often to review each agency or program. In the U.K., each review is followed by the negotiation of a new framework document between the department and agency, which clarifies the agency's mission, role, and key performance criteria for the next five years. The Canadians decided to follow suit, timing their review cycle to the business planning cycle they require each department to use, either a three-or a five-year span. "Every time a department or large organization produces a business plan," explains Bourgon, "their first step is to pause, look ahead, and think of the future and what their role should be."

Large governments tend to gravitate toward a five-or six-year cycle, because they have so many agencies. (The Swedes, for example, use a six-year cycle.) Smaller governments, particularly local governments, often want a shorter cycle. But in either case, they should tie the review to a strategic management cycle, as the British and Canadians do. An annual or biennial budget cycle is usually too short, and a 12–year cycle, like the Texas sunset review process, is disconnected from the agencies' planning horizon.

6. *Reduce the natural defensiveness of organizations being reviewed by asking them to begin with a self-assessment.*

In Arizona, the review begins with a self-assessment of the program by its agency. "This gets the people in the agencies involved, which puts them in a less defensive posture," says Ted Ferris, former director of the Joint Legislative

Budget Committee staff, which evaluates the assessments. The next stage is performed by outside offices, to give the review some real discipline.

pp. 77–80

This is similar to the method Canada used for its Program Review. In the U.K., agency managers and employees also have opportunities to give their views to the departmental reviewers. This kind of involvement is crucial in creating a mentality of self-examination within the agencies. "The greatest benefit of the self-assessment is that by responding to a series of questions about their history, performance, and management, staff figure out for themselves what is working and what needs to be fixed in their programs," says Rebecka Derr, the strategic management analyst in the Arizona Governor's Office of Strategic Planning and Budgeting.

> *In fact, by the time we get the self-assessment, most programs have already started to take corrective action on identified problem areas.*
>
> *Untold numbers of hours go into these reports, and at first, most of these programs are not real thrilled to be part of the process. But without question, every program that has gone through a review has revealed to the budget office staff that this is one of the best processes they have been through. In fact, positive comments by programs that have undergone a PAR have resulted in agencies adopting the PAR self-assessment to informally evaluate their programs on their own.*

7. Don't underestimate the time and capacity required to do periodic options reviews.

As Derr points out, serious reviews take an enormous commitment of time and energy. In the U.K., reviews are supposed to take about nine months. Initially, they were to be done every three years. But with elected ministers sometimes pushing for privatization, civil servants often disagreeing, and Treasury Department officials sometimes challenging the reviews' conclusions, the process bogged down. By 1994, some reviews were taking two years or more. The government finally decided to extend its timetable from every three years to every five.

8. If you don't have enough staff capacity, contract out pieces of the review.

The TPR often contracted with consulting firms or academic experts to review particular functions or programs if the comptroller's staff did not have the time or expertise required. Generally this worked well, says Mary Buckley. But "it was critical that someone stayed on top of the consultants, so you didn't get recommendations that weren't useful near the end, when you didn't have time to get them fixed. You have to monitor the consultant; you have to stay in touch."

> **RESOURCE ON PERIODIC OPTIONS REVIEWS**
>
> United Kingdom. Cabinet Office. *Guidance on Agency Reviews,* December 1995. A brief document laying out basic guidelines for an agency review in the U.K.

ASSET SALES

***Asset Sales* move government assets, such as publicly owned businesses, corporations and pieces of physical infrastructure (airports, dams, railroads) to private ownership. In most countries this is synonymous with the word *privatization*, although in the U.S. that term is also used to describe contracting out.**

By 1995, roughly 100 countries had programs to divest their public enterprises, according to the Reason Foundation, a nonprofit advocate of privatization. Some 16,000 state-owned enterprises had been sold in the previous decade; estimates of their value range from $388 billion to $445 billion. Though Latin American and Asian nations led the early charge, these numbers were boosted by sales in formerly communist nations, where government-owned businesses had accounted for the vast majority of economic activity.

Sales have included anything under the sun that might attract a profit-seeking buyer, including airlines, airports, telephone companies, oil companies, ports, sewage treatment plants, water systems, toll roads, bridges, tunnels, prisons, off-track betting operations, hospitals, convention halls, stadiums, parking garages, electric and gas utilities, waste-to-energy plants, telecommunications systems, and dams. In December 1994, Australia conducted the world's first stock-market sale of shares in a toll road. In 1995, New York City initiated the sale of its radio and television stations. In 1997, the U.S. government sold its 17,000–acre oil and gas reserve in California for $3.65 billion, the largest price ever paid for a public asset in the U.S. And in 1998, the *Wall Street Journal* reported that competition by firms around the globe to acquire and construct the infrastructure for water systems was the new frontier of privatization.

Asset sales usually involve the service functions of government—unloading either "hard" assets, such as physical infrastructure, or "business" assets, such as a steel company or electric utility. In general, this tool doesn't work for eliminating policymaking, regulatory, or compliance functions, since these don't normally have commercial value. In some cases, however, a regulatory or compliance organization sells an asset, such as its database or information technology operation, and then contracts with the buyer for services.

Definitions, p. 119

As E. S. Savas points out, governments can also give away assets to employees, the public, or customers. They can abandon them as well, by simply getting out of a business. Usually, though, governments sell their assets; like private investors, they seek to recoup the cost of developing them. The sale may be to a private buyer, by auction, sealed bid, or negotiation; to the public, by sale of shares; to government managers or employees; or to users or customers.

Why Sell?

In the U.K., when Margaret Thatcher kicked off the global trend toward asset sales, she firmly believed that the government's extensive ownership of enterprises was ruining the economy and had to be reversed. "The state should not be in business," she wrote.

> *State ownership effectively removes—or at least radically reduces—the threat of bankruptcy which is a discipline on privately owned firms. Investment in state-owned industries is regarded as just another call on the Exchequer, competing for money with schools or roads. As a result, decisions about investment are made according to criteria quite different from those which would apply to a business in the private sector.*

A second purpose of asset sales is to get the government out of activities that the private market can perform better. Though public enterprises sometimes perform as well or better than private ones, businesses often have advantages. As Wilbur Ross, senior managing director of Rothschild, Inc., points out, private companies tend to have fewer high-paid managers, they can more readily adopt labor-saving technology, they often enjoy economies of scale, they are unencumbered by the procurement and personnel procedures of government, and they are more effective at marketing and collecting receivables. As a result, shifting businesses into private markets tends to result in lower costs to consumers. "We know of no privatized entity in the entire world whose costs were higher after privatization than before it," Ross says. "Hundreds lowered their costs dramatically, with reductions of 20 percent to 40 percent not at all unusual."

As consumers benefit, so typically do taxpayers, because selling public assets not only earns revenues, it often eliminates money-losing operations. It also frees up resources and people for other, more essential public work. In the early 1990s, for instance, Mexico's finance minister calculated that what it cost the Mexican government to upgrade the fleet of its national airline, which served only 2 percent of the Mexican people, could have been used to pave more than half of the country's unpaved roads.

Perhaps the most important reason to sell assets, in this era of global markets, is to increase the competitiveness of a nation's economy. Asset sales can unleash substantial business investment and innovation, since private owners have more incentives to invest and innovate than public officials do. According to Per Westburg, then Sweden's minister of industry and commerce, when Sweden decided in the early 1990s to put 35 state-owned businesses on the market, one of its goals was to make the firms more competitive.

Asset sales also affect a country's economy by spreading the ownership of economic assets. When the sale is to a company or a single bidder, this impact is not necessarily substantial. But some reinventors, including Thatcher, have insisted that some public assets be sold to the public through stock sales. "Privatization was not for the fat cats," explains Geoffrey Bell, a prominent British businessman. "It was absolutely made clear to the merchant banks that distribution of the shares of U.K. companies that were privatized had to go to the small investor." This brought "a whole new range of investors" into company ownership, Bell says, and had a political benefit as well: "If we have a change in government . . . then you're not going to get a renationalization of those companies that were made private. Why? Because people like having shares." In 1986, more than 4.5 million individuals applied for shares in British Gas.

Does It Work?

Asset sales have a strong track record of producing the expected benefits. There are many well-known success stories, such as British Airways, once a chronic money loser under government ownership but now a world-class airline. An authoritative study by the World Bank in 1992 that examined 12 sales of government assets in the U.K., Malaysia, Mexico, and Chile found that 11 of the privatized firms became more efficient. As a result, their shareholders made more money. In addition, workers were offered opportunities to buy stock at discounted prices and to receive severance payments. And in some cases, the new private companies increased employment. In the Mexican auto parts industry, for instance, privatized companies increased employment by 30 percent.

Government assets can be sold, and their activities thus left to markets to perform, when three conditions are met:

1. They are commercially feasible, and therefore the market can provide them. This requires that buyers will purchase their goods and services and nonpayers can be excluded from enjoying them.
2. They are "private goods" that mainly benefit individuals or groups of individuals, rather than society as a whole.
3. There is no requirement in the community that everyone have access to them.

Assets sales are not without controversy, however. Sometimes people object because they believe the public interest will be jeopardized if a government business is made private. For instance, efforts to privatize postal services in the U.K., New Zealand, and elsewhere are routinely opposed for fear that they will lead to the end of service to rural areas. Other objections are motivated purely by self-interest: for example, legislators may fear the loss of power over government resources, or public employees may fear the loss of their jobs. Privatization of enormous government businesses in New Zealand, Argentina, and the former East Germany led to massive unemployment when the new companies cut jobs to become competitive. When Germany's Treuhandstalt, an organization created to handle the massive privatization effort, began to sell thousands of government businesses, it triggered widespread social unrest. Detlev Rohwedder, its director, was assassinated. (As explained elsewhere in this book, there are many ways to mitigate the unemployment problem, and reinventors should use them whenever possible.)

pp. 76–77, 199–200

Sometimes assets sales do go wrong, due to mistakes in the sales process, misjudgment of market conditions, corruption, or other problems. These problems are discussed in the following section.

Selling Assets: Lessons Learned

1. Make sure you have the stomach to withstand political controversy.

"No one should underestimate the extent to which political will, commitment, and single-mindedness was needed to implement the British privatization program," says Brian Pomeroy, a partner in Touche Ross U.K. "There was considerable risk-resistance by the industries that were to be privatized; considerable resistance initially on the part of employees and the labour force; and even within government there were considerable tensions and differences as to how individual enterprises should be privatized."

This is how asset sales often play out politically. Therefore, political leaders must anticipate the opposition and figure out how to deal with it. They must believe that whatever the controversies in the short term, there will be a payoff for consumers, investors, the public interest—and perhaps also employees—once the asset has been sold.

2. Prepare the assets for sale.

A great many government-owned businesses aren't performing well enough to attract a good price; in financial terms, they are underperforming assets. This doesn't necessarily scare away bidders, since some buyers look to buy low and then turn the business around. But in some cases it may chill the market for the asset. Either way, the government's potential for revenues is reduced.

See Banishing Bureaucracy pp. 75–82

pp. 164–169

The key to getting full value for an asset is to get it in shape for the sale. In New Zealand, the government first "corporatized" a number of state-owned enterprises, forcing them to operate in competitive markets without subsidies; then, when they had demonstrated business viability, it put them up for sale. Using this tactic gives public enterprises as much exposure to the commercial market as possible without actually changing their ownership. It encourages them to strengthen their management teams, introduce new working practices, change their capital structures, and provide clear, accurate accounting information, using business standards such as accrual accounting. It also creates the track record necessary to justify a decent price.

If your government-owned entity is losing money, turn it around before you sell it, if at all possible. Another option is to sell only the profitable parts of the entity, advises Rothschild's Wilbur Ross. The rest can be sold later, after you have turned it around.

3. *Ensure private competition for the asset.*

A basic rule is that competition among potential buyers will get you a better price. The World Bank's Mary Shirley provides an example: "The price offered for a steel mill in a Latin American country went from about $5 million to $33 million—well above the minimum asking price—thanks just to the threat of competition."

When selling a public business that has enjoyed monopoly status, it may be necessary to break the asset up into multiple businesses, the way a judge split AT&T into the "Baby Bells" in the U.S. The British, for instance, split National Bus into more than 60 separate businesses before putting them up for sale, to stimulate competition among bus operators.

If potential bidders are scarce, consider letting public managers or public employees in on the bidding.

4. *Get the regulatory framework right.*

Some asset sales involve government monopolies, such as telecommunications systems or railroads, for which no regulatory framework exists. In such cases you will have to develop one, to promote competition and protect consumers. Designing such frameworks is complex work that requires knowledge of specific markets and business practices within those markets. At the heart of any framework is some sort of regulatory body, with the power to monitor business activities and change the pertinent regulations. In creating the regulatory framework, however, you don't have to buy in to the bureaucratic model. There is now ample experience to draw on with postbureaucratic regulatory and compliance models.

pp. 334–338

In addition to rules, the framework you develop may need to include public subsidies to ensure desired levels of service or universal access to services. You can directly subsidize businesses, in the form of grants or tax incentives, or consumers, in the form of vouchers or tax breaks.

5. *Protect the public interest.*

When the British sold Rolls Royce and British Aerospace to private investors, they limited ownership in them by foreign investors, because both companies were deemed important to the national defense. There are several reasons to maintain public values and limited control over an asset after it is sold: national security, the desire to ensure certain service levels or standards, the desire to give former public managers time to adjust to the private sector, and the need to prevent the embarrassment caused by quick resales of the asset for high profit. "The task," observes Wilbur Ross, "is to balance government's need to protect the citizenry on the one hand, and the entrepreneurs' premiums for freedom of action on the other."

p. 100

Other ways for the government to exercise postsale influence include:

- Maintaining partial government ownership of the asset, with veto power over certain major decisions.
- Retaining control over a number of board seats, and requiring a super-majority vote of the board on important issues.
- Executing a long-term performance contract between the government and the buyer, with provisions spelling out behaviors required by the government.
- And selling only a "limited duration franchise" to use the asset, renewable only if the government so desires.

6. *Make employees winners.*

See Banishing Bureaucracy pp. 132–135

Perhaps the most common barrier to selling public assets is resistance from public employees and their unions. As noted earlier in this chapter and in *Banishing Bureaucracy*, one important solution to this problem is to manage the transition to private status humanely.

But you can do even more: you can make employees winners. The British did this several times by letting employees purchase discounted shares in businesses that were being privatized, so they would have a financial stake in the success of the private companies. According to Robert Poole, president of the Reason Foundation, "earmarking for workers and managers a meaningful fraction (e.g., 10 percent or more) of the shares in a firm being privatized has become routine around the world, especially for large firms and especially for those which are labor-intensive."

Some governments have also sold public businesses to public employees—a public sector version of the employee buyouts seen in the private sector. Both Canada and the U.S. have approved employee-takeover policies. The first U.S. agency to try this was the Office of Federal Investigations, the unit that investigates the personal histories of applicants for federal jobs. In August 1996, USIS, Inc., incorporated and hired nearly 700 former employees of the federal office the day after they were voluntarily separated from federal service. They became employee-owners, just like the millions of employee-owners of thousands of companies in the U.S., including Avis and United Airlines. USIS matched their federal base salaries and gave them comparable health benefits and leave entitlements. Its revenues quickly climbed, and the case backlog it inherited from the government was eliminated.

Other methods for managing the transition include:

- Buying out employees who are no longer needed, by offering them lump-sum payments to leave their jobs.
- Offering early retirement incentives.
- Limiting employment cuts to attrition and retirement.
- Paying the remaining staff a bonus for taking on an increased workload.
- Encouraging the employees' union to set up a new local as the bargaining agent for the private company, and requiring the buyer to recognize it and accept a prenegotiated contract.

7. Use expert help.

Assets sales are not for amateurs. Few people in government have much experience in this field. You will need advice about financial and legal matters, such as setting a value on the assets and structuring sales agreements, and expertise about the businesses and markets in question. You can buy this knowledge from the private sector, where asset sales are a well-understood business tool.

8. Use a savvy champion inside government to manage the sale.

Outside experts can only do part of the job. You also need at least one savvy insider—a top manager or political appointee—to guide each sale through the government's unavoidable administrative processes and the likely political minefields. In short, you need a committed champion who can drive the process and close the deal. The champion should create a detailed work plan that lays out every step, a timetable, and strategies for dealing with the political dynamics.

9. *Create incentives for your public organizations to sell their assets.* Private sector advisers will build incentives for performance into their fee structures. But you should consider ways to provide incentives to your government sales team as well. When Canada set up a privatization process in the mid–1980s, its leaders decided that no revenues from sales could go to departments or crown corporations, so ministers and managers lost interest in the process. The U.K., by contrast, allows its departments to capture some of the financial rewards of what they sell—so they have been fairly aggressive about selling assets. The principle is the same one that makes shared savings and gainsharing so powerful: if you share cost savings or revenue increases with organizations or employees, they are far more likely to produce them.

pp. 237–243

Pitfalls to Avoid

Avoid quick-profit embarrassment. "Woe to the public official who privatizes something only to have the buyer flip it quickly at a large profit," observes Rothschild's Wilbur Ross. The best protection against this danger is to get a fair price for the asset you are selling. If you can't be sure of that, one remedy is to sell only part of the equity in the business initially, then sell more later to capture any increases in value. You can also include in the sales agreement a provision giving the government part of any future profits or revenues from the resale of the asset. And as Ross points out, you can prohibit resale of the asset for a specified period of time, or require government approval within the first few years after the sale. Finally, the government can offer shares in the privatized business to employees and citizens, so if the value goes way up, they will benefit.

Avoid selling to monopolies. Selling public assets to a monopoly is often a mistake, because it jeopardizes service improvements. Mexico, for instance, sold its telephone system to a monopoly, which didn't act quickly to improve service. In 1996, the British government sold the tracks of its national railway system to a private monopoly, Railtrack, which then charged fees to private rail service operators using the tracks. Railtrack began to generate substantial profits, and the value of its stock soared. But so did customer complaints about the quality of rail service. In mid–1998, they rose 39 percent in a three-month period, while complaints about late trains jumped by 88 percent. Under fire, newly private railway operators, who operate rail lines on franchises, complained that Railtrack's exorbitant access fees were keeping them from expanding service capacity.

Some services are natural monopolies. But many former monopoly industries, including telecommunications and electric utilities, are rapidly becoming competitive. If faced with a monopoly situation, you can sometimes deregulate the industry, allow competition, and then sell the asset. If you must

p. 97

maintain monopoly status, you should regulate the new business, as discussed previously, while also examining ways to create a competitive marketplace. Sometimes it makes more sense to sell the monopoly to its users; an example would be the conversion of a public utility into a user-owned cooperative. In the U.K., for example, it might have made sense to sell the rail tracks to a co-operative made up of the private operators of rail lines. In such cases, if the monopoly charges too much, its users get the money back in profits, because they own it.

Avoid ineffective buyers. When selling government assets, it pays to look carefully at the experience and financial strength of the bidders. Don't sell to inexperienced, capital-thin buyers. Mexico has had serious problems with this.

RESOURCES ON ASSET SALES

Robert W. Poole Jr. *A Federal Privatization Agenda.* Los Angeles: Reason Foundation, 1995. Available for $2.50 from the Reason Foundation, this testimony before the U.S. Senate reviews federal assets that could be sold.

The Reason Foundation (www.reason.org). A national public policy research organization in Los Angeles that focuses on privatization. Its Web site contains a myriad of useful papers, from how-to guides to studies of privatization in particular sectors (railroads, airports, water systems, and so on) and comprehensive reviews of the status of privatization around the world. Telephone: (310) 391–2245.

Wilbur L. Ross Jr. "Privatization: An Important Tool for Government." Unpublished manuscript. An excellent summary of practical, how-to knowledge from a veteran of asset sales, the senior managing director of Rothschild, Inc., in New York City. Available from Ross at 212-403-3500.

E. S. Savas. *Privatization: The Key to Better Government.* Chatham, N.J.: Chatham House, 1987. A useful, comprehensive primer on all varieties of privatization.

E. S. Savas. *Privatization and Public-Private Partnerships.* Chatham, N.J.: Chatham House/Seven Bridges Press, 1999. An updated primer on both privatization and partnerships.

United Kingdom. Her Majesty's Treasury. *Privatisation—Sharing the U.K Experience.* London: Her Majesty's Treasury. An excellent brief summary of key lessons in asset sales, with examples from the British experience. Available from the Public Enquiries Unit, Room 110/2, Treasury Chambers, Parliament St., London SW1P3A6. Phone: 0171 270 4558. Fax: 0171 270 5244.

It sold government banks to Mexican investors who didn't have deep enough pockets when a financial crisis hit in December 1994. It also sold two airlines to owners with little experience and insufficient capital; within a few years, they were on the brink of bankruptcy. Mexico's program for private road construction flopped when the highway builders set tolls so high that few working people could afford to pay. In 1997, the government announced a $7.5 billion bailout to renationalize 23 of the private highways and two of the bridges.[111]

Avoid fraud. As in any business deal, greed may be a factor. If you detect a problem, immediately stop the sale. Openness and transparency are important in any privatization process, and due diligence—that is, careful examination of potential buyers—is critical. A watchdog organization should be appointed to oversee all sales and investigate any hints or charges of corruption.

QUASI-PRIVATIZATION METHODS

Quasi-Privatization Methods **let the private sector lease or build physical assets, such as prisons, hospitals, and highways, and use them to deliver services governments want. The asset may be owned by government or may shift to public ownership at a specified future date.**

Although asset sales have become an enormously popular tool with reinventors, governments have other ways of getting value out of their physical assets short of selling them off. Quasi-privatization methods can save governments money, end construction cost overruns and delays, and improve public service delivery.

Public organizations can *lease* their assets to businesses—giving them permission to use the assets under certain conditions. The asset remains publicly owned, preserving it for future generations. In 1994, for example, Australia's national government offered 50–year leases on all 23 of its major airports—allowing private operation but ensuring their preservation as airports. Austin, Texas, leased its hospital to a health care business for 30 years. Such lease agreements usually involve long terms, because this makes the business opportunity more attractive. They specify what services the private entity must provide and at what levels.

A variation of the lease is a *joint operating agreement*, in which the public organization also retains the power to appoint part of the board of directors of the company that will use the asset. When Oklahoma transferred operation of its teaching hospitals to a private company in 1998, it created a joint venture—and appointed half of the directors. The state-appointed directors had the right to unilaterally fire the CEO if he did not maintain a certain level of spending on operations.

Increasingly, governments also create *incentives for private firms to build assets that provide public services.* Usually the incentive is a long-term government contract to use the asset to provide public services. In Australia, for example, the state of Victoria signed 20–year contracts for three new privately owned and operated prisons. Another incentive is access to a unique market opportunity. California leased the right of way in the median of the Riverside Freeway to a private company to build a toll road, called "91 Express Lanes." More than 90,000 motorists pay to use the road every week, which relieves congestion on the freeway.

If the government wants such an asset to convert to public ownership at some point, it can negotiate a *build-operate-transfer agreement.* This gives a business the right to build and operate an asset but ensures that it will at some point become a public asset.

In the U.K., the Private Finance Initiative (PFI), launched by the Conservative Party but continued by the Labor Party, had by 1999 stimulated the private sector to construct and maintain ownership of an estimated $18 billion in assets the government wanted built. The PFI encourages the private sector to design, build, finance, own, and operate assets necessary to provide services the government desires. The government never owns the assets; instead, it uses the incentive of a long-term contract for services to convince businesses to build and operate them. A PFI contract, which typically spans 15 to 25 years, covers what normally would involve three separate contracts—for design, construction, and operations. This method has been used to create rolling stock for the London Underground, a national insurance records system, a new hospital wing and patient hotel, a rail link, a bridge, an armory, prisons, roads, and schools.

Normally, the government gives the private sector great latitude to get the job done. The PFI involves "the art of defining the end without specifying the means," says Adrian Montague, chief executive of a U.K. Treasury Department task force. When it comes to asset building, he explains, government should "ask, 'What is to be provided?' not 'How is it to be provided?'"

A benefit of this approach, according to Treasury Department officials, is that private sector partners have much stronger incentives than government managers to invest carefully and manage efficiently. Because their own money is at stake, they try to manage the asset productively after they build it. In addition, they get paid by the government only if the asset performs to specified levels.

The U.K. Treasury Department was so enamored of the tool that in 1996 it required all proposals for public capital projects to be examined for their PFI potential.

Negotiating Quasi-Privatization Agreements: Lessons Learned

pp. 96–101

Many asset sales lessons pertain to quasi-privatization as well, particularly the need to protect the public interest in the arrangement and to avoid the common pitfalls of dealing with the private market. In addition, the somewhat different nature of quasi-privatization leads to several other lessons:

1. *Negotiate performance-based service contracts.*

Governments that make use of quasi-privatization usually end up contracting for services from the businesses that operate the assets developed. To ensure quality services, they should include performance incentives in their contracts with these businesses. When the Victoria, Australia, government signed long-term contracts for private prisons, for example, it tied a portion of future payments to performance indicators such as escapes, deaths in custody, and assaults on inmates and staff.

pp. 191–195

2. *Ensure that private companies maintain or—better yet—increase current government service levels.*

Typically, elected officials and others are nervous that private companies operating public assets will try to increase their profits by reducing services or investments in the upkeep of the asset. To reassure them, negotiate contracts that call for increases in service and investment levels.

3. *Share the financial risks with private operators.*

It takes money to build an asset, which means there is always a risk of not recovering financial outlays or not making a profit on the investment. When the quasi-privatization agreement is negotiated, therefore, it is essential to be clear about which party bears which risks. "Risks should be allocated to the party best able to manage them," advises Adrian Montague. In particular, he says, businesses should take the risk of securing planning permission, designing and constructing the asset efficiently and effectively, operating the asset properly, and obtaining project financing. Governments should share with businesses the risk of insufficient service demand.

RESOURCE ON QUASI-PRIVATIZATION METHODS

United Kingdom. Her Majesty's Treasury. Web site on the Private Finance Initiative: www.treasury-projects-taskforce.gov.uk. This site contains a variety of resources, including papers that describe the initiative, evaluate it, provide examples, and give readers a step-by-step guide to implementing a PFI project.

Chapter 3

Uncoupling

Creating Clarity of Role by Separating Steering and Rowing

Definitions, p. 119

***Uncoupling* separates policymaking and regulatory roles (steering) from service delivery and compliance roles (rowing), while also separating service delivery functions from compliance functions. This helps steering organizations concentrate on setting direction and frees rowing organizations to concentrate on achieving one or two clear missions.**

The U.S. Federal Aviation Administration (FAA) faces one of the most complex tasks of any government agency in the world. With 352 air traffic control (ATC) towers, hundreds of radar facilities, and 36,500 employees, it handles 200,000 aircraft takeoffs and landings every day. It has more than 30,000 technological systems, uses more than 40,000 aeronautical radio frequencies, and conducts more than 11,000 flight inspections every year. It regulates an aviation industry that produces 6 percent of the nation's GDP. The lives of millions of Americans—and foreigners—depend on its performance.

Yet the FAA is a troubled organization. A vast computer modernization program begun in 1981 is more than 10 years behind schedule. While other nations import sophisticated American computer technology for their own ATC systems, the FAA still imports vacuum tubes for use in a few of its ancient computers. "Antiquated backup systems cannot be expected to provide needed safety assurance as communication and radar failures become a more frequent occurrence," warned a December 1997 report by the National Civil Aviation Review Commission, chaired by former congressman Norman Mineta. "Just between 1992 and 1996, the number of hours of unscheduled outages more than doubled."

Because of such equipment failures, airline delays forced by the ATC system are increasing. By 1997 they were costing the airlines more than $2.5 billion a year, according to the commission. Yet FAA investments in technology are shrinking: "Between 1992 and 1997, the effective buying power of the FAA's capital budget has decreased nearly 40 percent."

The FAA's problems have been studied repeatedly for at least 15 years; indeed, the FAA has been "commissioned" to death. There is significant consensus about the basic problem: air traffic control is a massive, complex, technology-intensive service business operating within a conventional U.S. government bureaucracy. "The FAA is unique for a government agency in that it provides around-the-clock, 365–days-a-year air traffic control services—a linchpin of our nation's economic well-being," the Mineta Commission explained. "However, the FAA is funded and budgeted like other government agencies, most of which do not have this type of operating responsibility." It is a bit like putting a Ferarri engine into a dump truck body and still expecting it to win races.

Until 1996, the FAA operated within exactly the same constraints as every other federal organization. Bureaucratic procurement rules frustrated its efforts to modernize its massive computer systems, and arcane personnel rules so limited its flexibility to move, pay, and promote people that some of its busiest centers were chronically understaffed. Federal budget rules made it difficult to move money where it was most needed as problems emerged, and federal budget caps made it impossible to spend billions of dollars sitting in the Airport and Airway Trust Fund, all of it raised by taxes and fees on airline passengers, shippers, and operators. As a result, the agency had to "forgo capital development programs in order to keep the day-to-day operations adequately staffed," the Mineta Commission reported.

On top of all this, the FAA has long suffered from having dual, conflicting missions: promoting commercial aviation through service functions like ATC and airport grants, while also enforcing compliance with safety rules. Both missions were intended to create a safe system, but one requires FAA managers to support the airline industry, whereas the other requires them to police it. Whenever a commercial airplane crashes, critics charge that the agency is doing too much promoting at the expense of enforcement and safety.

The FAA's ATC division operates the air traffic control system, writes the rules (such as how far apart airplanes must be during takeoff, landing, and flight), and enforces compliance with those rules by its own employees. This form of self-regulation has been questioned for years. As the Aviation Safety Commission said in 1988, "Both safety and public confidence in the safety of the system might be enhanced if greater separation existed between the functions of regulating the ATC system and operating it."

Indiana University professor Clinton Oster Jr. explains the basic problem:

> *FAA has two goals in operating the air traffic control system and these goals can often pull in different directions. One goal is to operate the air traffic control system safely. The other goal is to provide enough capacity to avoid excessive and persistent delays.... [Some] capacity-related decisions such as aircraft separation standards and the conditions under which various runway configurations are used can pose a tradeoff between safety and capacity that FAA must make.... With the current form of self-regulation, these tradeoffs are made internally, without any meaningful review from outside the organization and without a public forum in which the regulatory decisions are reviewed and justified.*

Oster offers the FAA's policies on overtime work as an example of how self-regulation can lead to different treatment than regulation by an external body. "While FAA carefully regulates the amount of time pilots can fly within specified periods and does not allow the airlines exceptions to these duty time regulations," he points out, "FAA allows, and in the past has even mandated, considerable overtime for air traffic controllers."

Oster recommends uncoupling ATC operations from ATC regulation. He notes that Canada, New Zealand, Australia, Portugal, South Africa, Singapore, the Czech Republic, and Latvia have all done this over the past decade. Most have created public corporations to handle ATC operation, while leaving regulation of the ATC system and enforcement of compliance in the hands of a normal agency.

In 1993, the National Commission to Ensure a Strong Competitive Airline Industry, chaired by former Virginia governor Gerald Baliles, recommended moving ATC operations into a public corporation, to accomplish the same separation. Later that year, the Clinton administration's National Performance Review (NPR) seconded the proposal. This solution would have taken the service business of ATC out of its bureaucratic straitjacket, the NPR argued, leaving the rest of the FAA to "focus on regulating safety"—thus giving each separate entity a much simpler, clearer purpose.

The Clinton administration pressed the case on Congress, but there was little support within the Democratic leadership for fundamental change. By 1996, however, air traffic problems were so acute that Congress exempted the FAA from normal personnel and procurement rules and attempted to remove the inherent conflict between promoting commercial aviation and enforcing safety rules by removing the word *promoting* from the FAA's authorizing legislation.

But ATC remained within the FAA, and the agency still combined its service, regulation, and compliance functions in one division. Meanwhile, budget restrictions kept one arm tied behind the agency's back.

Understanding that Congress had already rejected a public corporation, Mineta and his colleagues recommended another way to separate air traffic control from the larger FAA. They suggested uncoupling ATC operations from policy and regulation by turning ATC functions into a performance-based organization (PBO), an organizational model championed by Vice President Gore.

See *Banishing Bureaucracy* pp. 23–30

Gore had modeled his PBO proposals on the Next Steps initiative in the U.K., which by 1998 had created 138 uncoupled agencies. These "executive agencies" were uncoupled from their policy-focused departments; given clear purposes; awarded significant budget, personnel, and procurement flexibility; and made accountable for their performance against quantifiable targets. Under Gore's scheme, functions that had clear service or compliance missions, measurable activities, and proven capacity to measure their performance would be set up as PBOs, just like Britain's executive agencies. They would have flexibility to manage their own personnel, procurement, budget, real estate, and other operational issues—within very broad civil service, procurement, and budget parameters. They would be managed by chief executives hired through a competitive search, paid a base salary of $150,000, and eligible for up to $150,000 more in performance bonuses. They would focus on carrying out their service or compliance functions, leaving most policy decisions to the departments that oversaw them. And they would negotiate three-to five-year agreements with their mother department, spelling out their performance targets, flexibilities, and consequences for performance.

The Mineta Commission recommended that an air traffic PBO be removed from federal budget caps, funded exclusively from fees paid by those who used the system, and given the power to borrow. "The ultimate goal," it said, "is to create an executive structure where broad policy issues are determined by policy officials and operational and financial issues are managed by the Chief Operating Officer" of the new PBO.

Organizing for Clarity

The FAA is a classic example of why uncoupling is necessary to achieve clarity of purpose in so many government organizations. Particularly in larger governments, multiple functions with different purposes often cohabit in the same organization. All are managed in the same way, using the same administrative systems and rules and subject to the same constraints. The same organization is often involved in policy work, service delivery, and sometimes even compliance work. Inevitably, some of these functions suffer, because they can't operate well within the constraints of the larger organization. Sometimes two different functions, such as service and compliance, conflict with each other: the same organization is supposed to serve its customers (such as airlines) while also regulating them and enforcing the rules they must follow. Meanwhile, the lengthy chains of command so often found in the public sector make it hard for managers of discrete functions to get decisions ratified. And the reality of having too many bosses means the organization is pushed this way and that, with no one person ultimately able to make decisions and be held accountable for them. With so many interest groups pushing on elected policymakers, legislators tend to pile on ever more missions, creating less and less clarity of purpose.

This problem is epidemic in the public sector. Congress asks the national forests to serve mining interests, timber interests, recreational interests, and local community interests—all at the same time. Since it formed the Agency for International Development (AID) in 1961, Congress has given it nearly 40 different missions—everything from promoting rural development, education, and agriculture to protecting human rights and endangered species. Some of these missions conflict, and taken together, they offer AID managers what the General Accounting Office has called "a complicated and incoherent set of objectives with no clear priorities." State and local organizations often house service and compliance functions side by side, telling one set of employees to meet their customers' needs while their colleagues enforce regulatory rules on them. Even school districts, which would seem to have fairly obvious purposes, get saddled with mission after mission: educating students, combating segregation, feeding the poor, inoculating children, delivering social services, operating day-care facilities, and on down the list.

Uncoupling is meant to sort out these multiple missions by separating steering from rowing and placing different rowing functions into different organizations, each with one or two clear missions. *Banishing Bureaucracy* described at length how both the British and the New Zealanders did this. New Zealand took many of its large departments apart, leaving policymaking ministries separate from service and compliance departments. The British, through their Next Steps reforms, kept the uncoupled agencies within their departments, but gave them an arms-length relationship outlined in a five-year "framework document."

See *Banishing Bureaucracy* pp. 23–30, 82–85

In the U.S., Canada, and other countries, national, state, provincial, and local governments have also begun uncoupling. The exercise creates certain costs: performance agreements must be negotiated, performance must be measured, and periodic reviews must be conducted. But these transaction costs are the price one must pay for clarity about role and direction and accountability for performance. In return, uncoupling can create enormous value.

At the simplest level, it allows each organization to concentrate on a clear mission. It helps elected officials and their top political appointees focus on steering—on policy issues—while freeing managers to focus on running their operations. Peter Drucker long ago noted that successful organizations separate top management from operations, so as to allow "top management to concentrate on decision making and direction." Operations, Drucker said, should be run by separate staffs, "each with its own mission and goals, and with its own sphere of action and autonomy." Otherwise, top managers will be distracted by operational tasks, and basic steering decisions will not get made.

In government, the danger is even greater, because the temperaments required to succeed at governing and managing are so different. "I always say, management is about the head, government is about the heart," explains Terrence Musgrave, chief executive in the London borough of Bexley. Good politicians don't usually make good managers, and vice versa. And "if politicians spend their time managing, then who the hell is minding government, making long-term decisions, setting priorities? Managing a provider function can be a massive diversion from your primary role of figuring out what those people out there need."

The British Model

In 1988, Margaret Thatcher's Efficiency Unit released a seminal report: *Improving Management in Government: The Next Steps.* It recommended carving operational agencies out of the U.K.'s large departments and giving each one a clear mission, an accountable chief executive, quantifiable performance targets, and significant management flexibility. Thatcher backed this plan to the hilt, and today more than 75 percent of civil servants in the British national government work in these uncoupled agencies.

As it worked out in practice, the reform:

- Separated departments' service delivery and compliance functions into discrete units called executive agencies.
- Gave those agencies much more control over their budgets, personnel systems, and other management practices.
- Installed chief executives for the agencies, normally hired through a competitive search process open to the private sector (a radical break with past practice).
- Paid chief executives whatever it took to get the talent needed, including performance bonuses of up to 20 percent of their salaries, but denied them the normal lifetime tenure of a civil service job and required them to compete for their jobs every five years.
- Required chief executives to negotiate with their departments five-year "framework documents" specifying the general results their agencies would achieve and the flexibilities they would be granted; draft annual business

plans with objectives, performance targets, and planned investments; and produce three-to five-year corporate plans spelling out their longer-term business strategies.

- And put agencies on trial for their lives every five years through "prior options reviews," which asked whether the agency or its individual functions should be abolished, sold to private owners, merged with another agency, or restructured.

The first executive agency was the Vehicle Inspectorate, carved out of the Department of Transport. A compliance organization, it keeps the roads safe by performing annual tests on heavy-goods and public service vehicles; oversees the annual testing of automobiles, motorcycles, and light-goods vehicles by private garages; and enforces the laws on roadworthiness, vehicle weight, and commercial drivers' hours, primarily through roadside inspections. It came first because the department had almost privatized several of these functions. After choosing not to privatize, departmental officials decided to restructure the functions on a more businesslike basis. When the Next Steps white paper was released, the division's director, Ron Oliver, jumped at the opportunity it presented to deepen the change process he had already launched.

As a guinea pig, the Vehicle Inspectorate was the first organization to negotiate a framework document—to put down on paper its mission, its responsibilities, its accountabilities, and its flexibilities. "What I was responsible for and accountable for had never been in any way described to me," Oliver remembers.

> *It was a very vague situation. In a sense the whole civil service was very vague, because that's how it operated. Now for the very first time I knew exactly what I was responsible and accountable for. That was the single biggest change: suddenly I felt I was responsible and accountable.*

It wasn't just Oliver who thought accountability had been too vague; departmental leaders agreed. "Under the old regime responsibility was diffuse," Permanent Secretary A. P. Brown told Parliament in 1991. "It is no longer diffuse."

> *Mr. Oliver and all who work with him are now absolutely clear as to what their objectives are, what is required of them. . . . It also has efficiency targets which are probably much more explicit than they were in the old days. . . . They do have a clarity which allows them as managers . . . to go on with the job without interference from the Department, without always having to ask senior officials or occasionally Ministers for decisions on things which really are managerial rather than policy.*

In addition, the agency got a few management flexibilities, including the right to purchase several internal services from private vendors rather than the department, and the right to create a gainsharing program. If the organization exceeded its annual efficiency target, 50 percent of the excess savings went to the staff.

pp. 237–241

Later, as the Next Steps reform process deepened, Oliver won significantly greater flexibilities: the right to operate as an enterprise fund, which gave him financial flexibilities such as the right to borrow from the department and the right to carry funds forward from one year to the next; authority to redesign the personnel rules, including the pay and grading system, for all but senior executives; and the authority to do all bargaining concerning pay with the unions.

Oliver and his team used their new framework to restructure the way the entire organization carried out its business. They started with "the relatively easy changes, the structural changes," Oliver remembers. "We cut the whole of the country up into 53 accountable management areas." Each one had a team. "We brought in all the systems to measure their performance and compare their performance from one district to another."

They worked with 100 managers from across the organization to prepare a mission statement, which included a vision statement and four basic goals. They removed a tier of regional directors from the management structure. They devolved more responsibility to the districts and worked to get more employees involved in decision making. They competitively bid out, or "market-tested," a number of services. And after the department merged another function into the agency in 1991, they trimmed their staff by 20 percent over four years.

pp. 200–207

Oliver and his staff worked out an efficiency measure based on unit costs, called the Aggregate Cost Efficiency (ACE) Index. The department set aggressive targets for annual increases in efficiency, and year after year the agency exceeded them, averaging 4.5 percent a year over the first eight years. (These results were audited and confirmed annually by the National Audit Office.) During the agency's first three years, employees took home gainsharing bonuses of up to £213 (about $350) a year.

On the quality front, Oliver and his team opened test centers on Saturdays; published information about the contents of the tests for the first time; instituted prefunded accounts for transport businesses, so they would not have to pay each time one of their fleet was inspected; increased the number of privately run testing facilities available to vehicle operators; and dramatically increased staff training. By 1991, a customer survey commissioned by the National Audit Office showed that 91 percent of heavy-goods and public service vehicle operators and private inspection garage owners considered the inspectorate's overall service either fairly good or very good. More than 40 percent thought it had improved over the preceding three years, whereas very few thought it had grown worse.

pp. 346–359

Oliver and his agency went on to commission their own customer surveys, create customer service standards, train employees to analyze and solve problems using Total Quality Management methods, create an advisory board broadly representative of the various compliers with which they dealt, and develop a "balanced scorecard" of performance targets at all levels of the organization, which included measures of customer satisfaction; agency quality, effectiveness, and efficiency; return on capital; contributions to road safety; and the long-term development of the inspectorate.

In April 1990, the Department of Transport set up three more executive agencies, which began to produce similarly dramatic improvements. In 1992 it created a fifth, which it sold. In 1994 it created three more; in 1998 it merged two of them; and in 1999 it announced plans for a seventh executive agency.

The Advantages of Uncoupling

As the Vehicle Inspectorate example illustrates, uncoupling is really very simple. It separates the steering functions of setting policy goals and deciding how to achieve them from the rowing functions of providing services and enforcing compliance. When these roles are separated, each organization's mission becomes much clearer. And when that happens, it becomes much easier to measure how well those missions are being accomplished and to hold managers accountable for their organizations' performance.

Before uncoupling, the typical organization looks like the illustration in Figure 3.1. If this organization were a state commerce department, for example, the director and his or her deputies would be responsible for steering: carrying out the policy goals of the executive and the legislature, measuring whether the department's activities were achieving those goals, evaluating why or why not, and recommending appropriate policy changes. But they would also be responsible for managing the department. They might have nine divisions, agencies, and the like, some focused on regulating the business community, others providing services such as small business development centers, loan funds, a venture capital fund, and a grant program for municipalities. There would also be a personnel office, a budget office, a procurement office, and perhaps an equal opportunity office. All of these activities would be run by employees of the department. Hence the director and his or her deputies would both manage these employees and evaluate whether their units should continue to exist. Not surprisingly, few directors would ever recommend closing down a unit because an alternative outside the department might work better.

After uncoupling, the department might look like the one in Figure 3.2. Now the department would be much smaller: it would consist of a director, a few deputies, a policy staff, a contracting unit to negotiate performance contracts with other organizations, a performance measurement and evaluation unit, and a small administrative services unit that would deal with budget, personnel, procurement, and other administrative issues. The department would be a true steering organization: it would decide what strategies to use and which organizations, if any, to contract with to execute those strategies. But it would not implement any strategies itself. As the figure makes clear, it might contract with three state agencies, two private nonprofit organizations, and two for-profit firms to implement different strategies. It might also provide vouchers to small businesses, to buy management assistance, and grants to municipalities for community development work. The department's performance measurement and evaluation unit would monitor how well each strategy and organization was achieving its mission and goals, and why. It would recommend to departmental leaders when to reexamine or change strategies or hire different contractors.

pp. 35–39

Figure 3.1. Typical Public Department Before Uncoupling

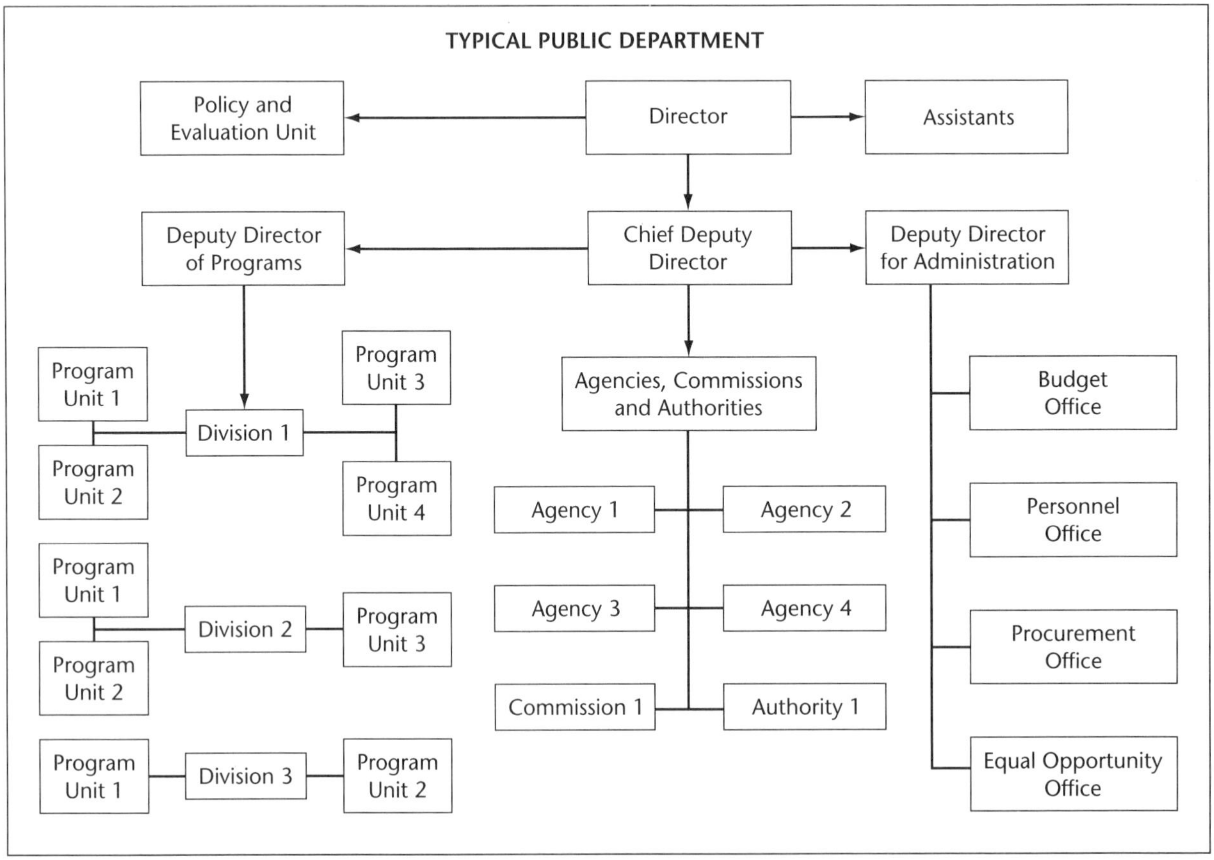

pp. 43–53

The governor would recommend the department's budget and the legislature would appropriate it. The budget document would list the outcomes the department was expected to produce. But it would be the department's job to decide what to buy with that money: which strategies to fund and which organizations to hire to execute them. This uncoupling of funding from operations is known in the British Commonwealth countries as *separating purchasing from providing.* It is not always done; sometimes the steering organization simply advises the executive and legislative body, and they appropriate directly to the rowing organizations. But a legislature would get far more leverage to improve outcomes by appropriating money only to the steering organization—because that would leave the steering organization free to choose whatever combination of strategies and organizations it believed would most effectively deliver those outcomes.

Figure 3.2. Public Department After Uncoupling

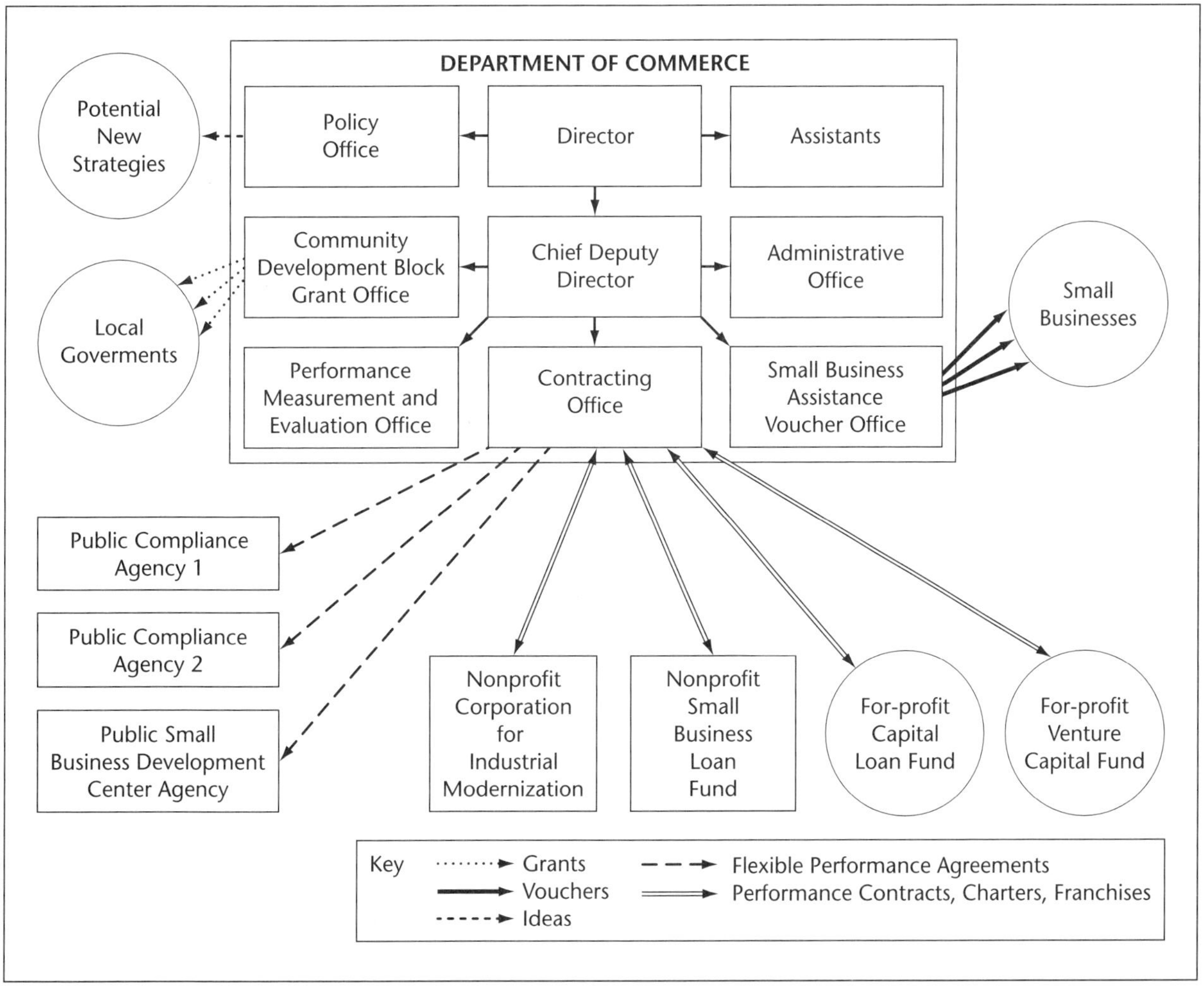

See Reinventing Government pp. 290–298, 332–342

Reinventing Government described 36 different options such a steering organization could use to achieve its desired outcomes, including the following:

pp. 188–200

pp. 164–169

- Contracting with a private nonprofit or for-profit organization.
- Contracting with another government.
- Creating a public corporation funded by its customers.
- Franchising private providers.
- Taking regulatory action.
- Creating tax incentives or disincentives.
- Providing subsidies to private producers (grants, loans, equity investments, favorable procurement policies, favorable investment policies).
- Offering subsidies to consumers (vouchers, tax credits).
- Sharing risk with private producers (insurance, loan guarantees).
- Catalyzing voluntary community action.

pp. 308–310

We describe how to use several of these options in other chapters of this book, as indicated by the pointers in the margin above.

By giving steering organizations the freedom to choose different strategies, separating purchasing from providing breaks the monopoly most public organizations enjoy. It gives policymakers the freedom to look elsewhere for solutions. The British, Australians, and New Zealanders call this "contestability." In the words of former British minister William Waldegrave, contestability "ends potential conflicts of interest and allows the purchaser—health authority, council, local education authority or whatever—to become the advocate of the consumer, rather than the defender of the producer."

Consider the case of an elected school board that employs all of its district's administrators, teachers, custodians, bus drivers, and aides. Its job is supposed to be to run the system in the best interests of the students. But when those interests conflict with the interests of employees, as they sometimes do, school board members know which of the two constituencies is unionized, which organizes at election time, and which votes. Indeed, district employees typically vote at much higher rates in school board elections—which often have very low turnouts—than does the rest of the community. So when conflicts between students' and employees' needs surface, the employees usually win. If schools were uncoupled, however—if districts contracted with a variety of organizations to run schools rather than employing their staffs directly—the balance of power would shift. Most policy changes would produce both losers and winners among the service providers hired by the district; hence, they would tend to balance each other in the political process. (A decision to contract with more Montessori programs would be seen as a threat by traditional programs but a boon to Montessori schools and teachers, for example.) In addition, providers would be less willing to oppose school board members at election time, for fear of antagonizing them and jeopardizing future contracts.

In 1999, the Education Commission of the States proposed this model as a serious alternative for school boards to consider. Boards would negotiate three-to five-year charters with organizations to operate schools, rather than owning their own schools. Milwaukee, the nation's 12th largest district, now has not only charters but also contracts and vouchers, while the board also operates many of its own schools.

pp. 279–284

Uncoupling purchasing and providing also "forces both sides to define the nature of the service and the standards of quality which are to be provided," as Waldegrave explains. It then helps those doing the steering demand better performance from rowers and back it up with consequences, both positive and negative. "The greater the distance between Ministers and managers, the more independent and demanding the government can be as a purchaser of outputs and enforcer of accountability," notes American public administration expert Allen Schick, in his exhaustive evaluation of New Zealand's reforms.

Uncoupling also helps minimize political interference and corruption in public services. William Eggers described in *Government Executive* magazine what happened in New Zealand after uncoupling:

> *Lobbyists used to line up outside New Zealand Cabinet meetings to wait for their opportunity to ply ministers for special privileges. This doesn't happen anymore. . . . Because the chief executives [who are appointed by a neutral body, the State Services Commission, not by elected officials] have complete control over the mix of inputs they use to produce outputs, from road construction to science spending, the mix of projects funded is determined solely on a cost-benefit analysis, by the relevant agencies. "With our system, there is no political interference on where the money goes for roads," says Stuart Milne, the chief executive of the Ministry of Transport.*
>
> *"I couldn't imagine having people coming through this office all day lobbying for special favors," says Simon Upton, a member of Parliament. "Our new system is a good security against corruption in politics."*

In sum, by funding steering organizations to achieve outcomes and letting them choose which strategies and rowing operations to engage, governments make it far easier to steer effectively. The legislature's role shifts to defining the outcomes it wants and appropriating money to steering organizations, which are responsible for achieving them. Although this takes management decisions out of the hands of elected officials, it makes it far easier for them to use the steering tools described in Chapter One. It has many other advantages as well, as described in *Reinventing Government* and *Banishing Bureaucracy*.

OTHER ADVANTAGES OF UNCOUPLING

- "Freeing policy managers to shop around for the most effective and efficient service providers helps them squeeze more bang out of every buck."
- "It allows them to use competition between service providers."
- "It preserves maximum flexibility to respond to changing circumstances."
- "Steering organizations that shop around can also use specialized service providers with unique skills to deal with difficult populations."
- They "can even promote experimentation and learn from success."
- Finally, they "can provide more comprehensive solutions, attacking the roots of the problem. They can define the problem in its entirety—whether it is drug use, crime, or poor performance in school—then use many different organizations to attack it."

—From *Reinventing Government*, pp. 35–36.

- Uncoupling also creates "smaller, more focused organizations 'with short chains of command.'"
- "'Focused units have the advantage of being able to provide much more clear information about their resource use, as the separation forces the allocation of assets to specific activities. It is thereby easier to generate information about the real costs of services.'" (Quoting New Zealand reformer Graham Scott.)

—From *Banishing Bureaucracy*, pp. 98–99.

Uncoupling Within Rowing Organizations

Uncoupling can actually take place at several levels. We have discussed how it works at the highest levels, by separating steering from rowing and service from compliance functions. But at the next level, each service or compliance organization can also uncouple its role as a purchaser from its role as a provider. It can use other mechanisms to get services provided, including vouchers and contracts with private organizations. Many "rowing" organizations contract out distinct functions—maintenance, data processing, groundskeeping, printing, and the like—to cut costs. In the U.K., "Parts of Agencies are increasingly being

pp. 188–200, 308–310

contracted out to private firms, often for long periods," according to a survey done by Price Waterhouse. Rowing organizations can even set some of their functions up as internal enterprises, using the enterprise management approach.

pp. 174–182

Often service organizations contain small compliance functions, or vice versa. In such cases, they can set up small pieces of their organization as distinct units, operating on performance contracts much like the flexible performance frameworks discussed later in this chapter. A tax collection agency might create a distinct unit to handle a service function such as providing telephone assistance for taxpayers, for example. A police department might do the same for the service unit that handles its 911 calls.

Similarly, when large organizations cannot uncouple, for political or other reasons, they can still separate distinct service and compliance functions into different divisions, to give each division more clarity of purpose. British leaders decided not to set up their tax collection organization, Inland Revenue, as an executive agency, for example. But Inland Revenue's managers liked the Next Steps model, so they reorganized into 30 units, all structured as if they were executive agencies but all still within Inland Revenue. In New Zealand as well, reports Allen Schick, "When conglomerate departments remain intact, the preferred practice has been to restructure their components (including the policy unit) into separate business units, each with its own objectives, performance targets, business manager, and operating budget."

Many managers do versions of this on an informal basis. A department head may negotiate informal agreements with his or her division managers. Or an enterprising division manager may propose a deal to his department head: "I will agree to produce a quantum leap in performance, as measured by these indicators, if you will let me run my own business—and give me waivers to *x*, *y*, and *z*. If I haven't produced a quantum leap in two or three years, let me go." But such informal agreements don't uncouple purchasing and providing; they don't give department heads the easy option of going elsewhere for the service in question. They also work only for those managers who have the organizational savvy to create and manage such a relationship. And they force even those managers to put a lot of wasted energy into circumventing budget offices and personnel rules. As we argue later in this chapter, creating a formal, written agreement to uncouple has many advantages.

pp. 132–133

Uncoupling Regulatory and Compliance Functions

See Banishing Bureaucracy p. 46

Few people make a distinction between regulatory and compliance functions, but as we argued in *Banishing Bureaucracy,* the distinction is just as useful as that between setting policy and delivering services. We define regulatory organizations as those that write the rules society must obey (a steering function), whereas compliance organizations enforce those rules (a rowing function). Just as it is wise to separate policymaking from service delivery, it is also usually wise to separate writing the rules from enforcing them.

The easy example is law enforcement. If society let the police write some of its laws, it might soon experience problems. Because police spend much of their time dealing with criminals, they often develop rather dark views of humanity. And because their job is to catch criminals and help the courts convict them, they desire laws that make that job easier—even if they impinge on individuals' rights. Most would agree that we are all safer if neutral bodies that can reflect all of society's interests—such as legislatures—write the laws.

Some areas are so technical that legislators write relatively broad laws and leave it to regulatory agencies to draft the regulations that flesh them out. This is true in environmental policy, where the Environmental Protection Agency and its state counterparts play a significant rule-making role, and in regulation of the financial markets, where the Securities and Exchange Commission and other bodies write many regulations. In such areas, society is also better off if rule making is separated from enforcement. Even in reinvented compliance agencies that have embraced a strategy of winning voluntary compliance, the perspective of agency staff will reflect their experience and desires, not the totality of society's interests. Consider an Occupational Safety and Health Administration officer who wants to make life better for industry by changing a rule regarding a chemical that has been proven safe in the workplace. Will that officer know whether the chemical is safe once it gets into the groundwater? We think it is better to have a neutral regulatory body that can hear all sides of every question write the rules, while a separate body enforces them. When one organization both writes the rules and enforces them, as the FAA does for air traffic control operations, there is too much room for institutional bias to creep into the decisions.

pp. 334–338

(Admittedly, there are gray areas here. It will often make sense for a regulatory body to give a compliance organization some discretion to write minor regulations or interpret its rules differently in different areas, for example. But in our opinion it is best if that discretion is spelled out clearly and publicly by a separate regulatory body, rather than being worked out behind closed doors within one agency.)

There is a price to pay for separation, of course. Unless compliance agencies keep the rule makers well informed about what is happening on the front lines, the rule makers will not be able to write effective rules. The greater the distance between the two types of organizations, the more likely the rule makers are to write rules that are too rigid, too black and white. When that happens, compliers will become angry, voluntary compliance will plummet, and compliance organizations will have great difficulty enforcing the laws. The solution is to create mechanisms to ensure continuous, significant communica-

p. 139

tion between regulatory and compliance bodies. We return to this topic later in this chapter.

The Challenge of Steering Well

The greatest challenge in uncoupling steering and rowing is getting the steering side to do its job. Virtually every government that has tried uncoupling has run into this problem. Steering is hard work, and for most public sector leaders, it is new work. Few city managers, county executives, governors, department heads, steering board directors, or ministers have either the skills or the desire to steer effectively. The strategic management tools discussed in this chapter and in Chapter One—defining outcome and output goals, examining alternative strategies to achieve them, negotiating performance agreements with rowing organizations to produce them, and monitoring and evaluating performance—are not easy to use. Even when organizations are created specifically to steer a public system, their leaders typically don't know how to use these tools, aren't given training to learn them, and don't have enough staff even if they were trained.

Consider New Zealand. "Separated from departmental resources, most Ministers are weak policy makers, despite their nominal control of appropriated funds and their contracting powers," Allen Schick concluded after his in-depth look at its reforms. "Most have only a few aides who assist on Cabinet and Parliamentary work and typically spend little time on departmental matters."

Both Sweden and the U.K. have experienced similar problems. To facilitate better steering, "Many Ministers have advisory boards to assist them with setting targets, to advise on the monitoring of agencies' performance and to act as a link between the Minister and the agency," explains a British government paper on the reforms. "These advisory boards typically consist of a mixture of civil servants, who are familiar with the work carried out by the agency, and outsiders who bring business expertise or knowledge of the market in which the agency operates." In a 1994 survey, agency executives expressed great enthusiasm about the contributions of these boards.

p. 30

Still, most departments and advisory boards have lacked an essential element of effective steering: outcome goals. The British government did not create departmental outcome goals until 1998. Before this, the departments knew how to push their uncoupled agencies to become more efficient and effective at what they already did, but few examined whether they were achieving the right outcomes. "They've created the agencies, and they've all done very well in a very narrow sense, to deliver process and service improvements," Ron Oliver told us in 1999. But because the departments told them what to do, not what outcomes to achieve, few had much room to rethink the strategies they used. Some departments even slid back into business as usual, no longer taking very seriously the evaluation of agencies during their five-year reviews or the negotiation of framework documents and annual targets.

The Department of Transport took the negotiations seriously, Oliver says, but resisted any focus on outcome goals, such as reducing the number of highway accidents and deaths. It also focused on the parts, not the whole. "Unless you have a strategy applying to transport as a whole," Oliver points out, "you may miss service improvements, process improvements, and so on." Should people really have to take a driver's test from one agency but receive their license and registration from another, for instance?

> *You may also do something in one agency that works against another agency's objectives. You need a very high-level set of objectives and a vision and strategy. . . . None of that exists, and it became clear a couple of years ago that without it we weren't going to be able to meet our real potential.*

With each agency so focused on its own performance targets, it was difficult to develop new cross-agency strategies. And the department never stepped in to force collaboration between agencies—or even to include it in agency goals.

Frustrated by the lack of strategic leadership from the department, Oliver finally left the agency and civil service in 1998. About that time the new Labor government began to focus on the problem, and the department (now merged into a new Department of the Environment, Transport, and the Regions) launched a review to examine ways to improve the delivery of services by five different transport agencies. It recommended (and the ministers agreed to create) a "strategy board" to "set the direction for the five organisations and drive change across the area."

Meanwhile, the Labor Government negotiated public service agreements (PSAs) with each department specifying departmental outcome and output goals, performance measures, resources, key policy initiatives, and plans to improve productivity. The government promised that its departments would renegotiate their agencies' "objectives and targets" to make sure "that they are better focussed on ensuring that the targets set out in the PSAs are met." If so, this will push the departments to rethink what they want from their agencies. If the elected ministers now hold their top departmental civil servants accountable for achieving the PSA outcome goals (and keep them in their positions longer than the two to three years that is now common), those civil servants should begin to take a more strategic view with the agencies. All of this will require, of course, that the British government get as serious about leadership and accountability at the steering (departmental) level as it has at the rowing (executive agency) level.

As this example demonstrates, to get effective steering someone must be held accountable for thinking strategically about improving outcomes. This is yet another reason why we encourage governments to create distinct steering organizations when they uncouple steering and rowing. Few elected officials are capable of actually evaluating competing strategies and negotiating good performance agreements with rowing agencies. They should delegate that job to steering organizations, fund them sufficiently to purchase the outcomes the elected officials desire, and hold them accountable for doing so effectively. (See Chapter One for a thorough discussion of how to do all of this.) The elected officials should focus their best energies on the most important steering questions: "What outcomes do we want to deliver for our citizens? How can we best achieve them? And how much are we willing to pay for them?"

p. 32

pp. 35–59

Uncoupling: Other Lessons Learned

1. Clear the decks before uncoupling.

This is simple common sense. In the process of uncoupling large departments, it makes sense to review whether each function still needs to be performed. There is nothing quite as wasteful as working hard to improve an organization that should no longer exist (unless it is necessary to uncouple and restructure a function to raise its value before trying to sell it). We recommend a periodic options review to make these decisions, as outlined in Chapter Two.

pp. 87–93

2. If you want real results, combine uncoupling with the Consequences and Control Strategies.

Parts II & III

In both the U.K. and New Zealand, uncoupled organizations were given performance targets, consequences, and significant new flexibilities. The act of uncoupling separate functions will spur improvement, but the dramatic results seen in the U.K. and New Zealand come from using all three strategies together. When Canada copied the Next Steps reforms, it failed to provide significant consequences or flexibility to most of its new special operating agencies (SOAs). The results were disappointing—except in SOAs set up as enterprise funds (called revolving funds in Canada) and deprived of their monopolies. Once their customers could go elsewhere, they faced direct consequences.

3. Reform your administrative systems to take control away from central agencies and hand it to uncoupled organizations.

pp. 404–426

See *Banishing Bureaucracy* pp. 82–86

Unless you simplify and decentralize your budget, personnel, and procurement systems, uncoupled organizations will not have the flexibility they need to maximize their performance. New Zealand gave its uncoupled organizations virtually full control over their money, people, and purchasing, with very positive results. In contrast, Canada required its SOAs to ask for waivers. Because this led to so little real decentralization of control, a 1994 evaluation of the reform recommended that the Treasury Board create a standard package of flexibilities for all SOAs.

As you reform your administrative systems, you also need to change the behavior of the personnel in any remaining central budget, personnel, and procurement offices. When administrative systems are reformed, those who run them typically keep holding tight to the reins. They do so out of habit and from a sincere belief that managers cannot be trusted with too much flexibility. You need a process to help them adjust to their more limited roles and, in many cases, downsize their staffs.

FLEXIBLE PERFORMANCE FRAMEWORKS

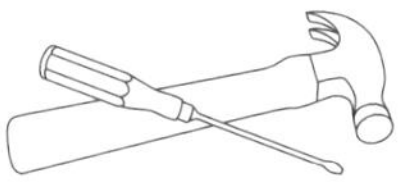

The *Flexible Performance Framework* is a metatool that uncouples steering and rowing, separates rowing functions with clearly different missions and places them in different organizations, then uses written agreements to spell out those organizations' purposes, expected results, performance consequences, and management flexibilities.

The basic model invented by the British and the New Zealanders, which we have labeled a flexible performance framework, has been highly successful in both countries. In the U.K., where most of the 138 executive agencies have significantly improved their performance, few would argue with Parliament's view, expressed in 1994, that it has been "the single most successful Civil Service reform programme of recent decades." The Labor Party certainly didn't; after it took power in 1997, it not only embraced the Next Steps reforms but extended their basic principles to the departments.

The model has been equally powerful in New Zealand, and it has spread to other countries rapidly. In 1989 the Canadian government sent a delegation to London to learn about the Next Steps process, then decided to imitate it. The effort never got the high-level attention it received in the U.K., however, and by 1998 there were only 19 SOAs, covering only a small percentage of the federal civil service. Meanwhile, however, the province of Manitoba had created 16 SOAs, and Quebec was not far behind.

The Netherlands also copied the U.K.'s Next Steps reform, beginning in 1994, and the Australian state of Victoria launched an initiative in 1997. In the U.S., after three years of effort, the Clinton administration finally secured congressional approval of its first PBO in 1998, to run the Education Department's student aid programs.

The Swedes have had uncoupled agencies for 200 years, but they put performance management and organizational empowerment into play only in the 1990s. They have 13 small policy ministries and some 300 fairly independent agencies. Agencies prepare annual performance reports, income statements, balance sheets, and budget and financial analyses. They are subject to in-depth reviews at least every six years, and their "director generals" are hired for six-year terms.

Even local governments have experimented with the model. Richmond, Virginia, negotiated flexible performance agreements with many of its departments in 1998. In Canada, Winnipeg and Toronto have piloted initiatives modeled after SOAs. Other jurisdictions invented the model anew, without ever hearing about the British or New Zealand reforms—simply because it made so much sense. Beginning in 1993, for example, Catawba County in North Carolina created a kind of flexible performance framework for a number of its departments, complete with lump-sum budgets, negotiated outcome and output measures, enhanced authority over personnel positions, and the right to roll over unexpended funds at the end of the fiscal year for departments that met at least 90 percent of their performance targets.

Elements of a Flexible Performance Framework

A flexible performance framework combines at least three strategies: Core, Consequences, and Control. The components of all three are spelled out in what we call a flexible performance agreement (FPA)—a written agreement that articulates the steering organization's expectations, the rowing organization's goals and freedoms, how performance will be reported, and how that data will be used to trigger consequences, both positive and negative. Ideally, FPAs cover three to five years, although we have helped local governments experiment with two-year FPAs. The possible elements of a flexible performance framework can perhaps best be described in terms of the three strategies.

Core Strategy

• ***Uncoupling:*** An FPA separates different functions within a large organization into several different, smaller organizations. Ideally, each smaller organization is given one clear mission—or at most two or three related missions. In a national or state government, four to eight different rowing organizations are typically carved out of a large department. While operating at arm's length, they can be set up as subunits of the department, as in the U.K., or independent organizations, as in New Zealand.

In most local governments, departments are not terribly large, and most steering is done by the elected executive's office or the city or county manager's office. Some cities and counties—such as Richmond and Catawba County—have negotiated flexible performance agreements between the city or county manager and each department. The process of doing this can flush out specific functions that should be uncoupled from the department, because it forces into the open cases in which departments have multiple or conflicting missions. Large departments can always turn around and negotiate FPAs with their divisions, if those divisions have distinct missions.

pp. 35–39

• ***Improving Your Aim.*** After uncoupling, the steering side concentrates on developing policy, setting outcome goals, buying services and compliance work from uncoupled agencies, evaluating performance, and using other strategies, such as vouchers and performance contracts with private organizations, to achieve its goals. It gives direction to agencies by negotiating FPAs that define their most important outcome and output goals for the term of the agreement.

pp. 87–93

• ***Clearing the Decks.*** Every three to six years the status of the organization should be reviewed, as the British do through their options reviews. This periodic options review should include a reappraisal of the strategies the uncoupled agency is using to achieve the outcome goals set by the steering organization—and of whether those strategies and outcome goals are contributing as expected to the government's long-term outcome goals. The following options should be considered: abandoning part or all of the function; privatizing, through an asset sale, part or all of the function; devolving part or all of the function to a lower level of government; shifting to other strategies, such as vouchers or tax incentives; contracting out part or all of the function to another organization; merging part or all of the agency with another agency; restructuring the agency to improve performance; or continuing the agency's current status. If either of the last two options is chosen, the steering organization needs to decide whether the chief executive should be rehired, released, or required to compete for the position in an open job search.

Consequences Strategy

pp. 215–246

A flexible performance framework uses several key performance management methods to create real consequences for performance:

• ***Performance targets.*** The FPA should spell out ten or fewer key outcome and output goals for the uncoupled organization. Typically, specific targets and indicators for each of these goals are then negotiated each year. For example, an outcome goal for a police department might be a reduction in the rate of violent crime. Each year a specific percentage reduction would be negotiated, based on both past trends and what the city manager and police chief think is possible in the coming year. (As we explain in Chapter Six, the best approach is often to avoid arbitrary numerical targets and simply set a goal of overall improvement.) Ideally, some outcome and output goals will remain stable over the three-to six-year life of the agreement, to allow comparisons over

pp. 221–224

time. But as performance improves and priorities change, specific targets and indicators will change, emphasizing different aspects of performance (quality versus efficiency, for example.)

pp. 243–246

• ***Performance contracts.*** Although an FPA is signed by an agency's chief executive, it is an agreement about the purpose, performance accountability, and flexibilities of the *entire agency.* It is not a personal performance contract, with the kind of legal standing such documents have. In larger governments, the steering organization typically develops such a personal performance contract, carrying the same length term as the FPA, with the chief executive of the uncoupled agency. In local governments with city or county managers, the FPA is often the only written agreement. The difference is politics. Chief executives of uncoupled agencies should not be fired because a new administration has come into office—a new president, minister, governor, mayor, or county executive. They should be removable for cause or performance, but not for political reasons. If a government consistently violates this principle, it will find it impossible to recruit the quality managerial candidates it needs, and its chief executives will become typical political appointees. Agency executives already have this protection in most city or county manager systems; hence they don't usually need special contracts. In other systems, they need the contract to protect them from political removal.

pp. 232–237

• ***Performance bonuses.*** The agency director is typically eligible for a financial bonus, based on the organization's performance against its annual targets. Many directors also negotiate the right to institute performance bonuses for some or all of their employees. To create commitment and teamwork among all employees, we recommend including bonuses for as many employees as possible in the FPA. Although local governments with which we have worked have started with 10 percent bonuses for CEOs, to keep the stakes from being too high in the first year, Vice President Gore proposed bonuses of up to 100 percent of salary for chief operating officers of PBOs. In the U.K. bonuses can range up to 20 percent, though most are less than 10 percent.

Though the formula to determine how much of the potential bonus the chief executive gets should rest primarily on objective performance levels, we suggest you also include some element of subjective judgment by the steering organization. This is to compensate for external events, such as particularly bad winters that drive up snow-plowing costs for a public works department, or sharp recessions that hurt a job placement agency's ability to find people jobs.

pp. 224–225

• ***Periodic performance reviews.*** The agency's and chief executive's performance should be reviewed by the steering organization at least once a year, to assess progress, provide feedback, and stimulate learning from experience. We recommend doing this more than once a year, to maximize learning, although in large governments this is sometimes difficult. Formal reports on performance should be submitted by the agency annually. After the annual report and review, any performance bonuses should be calculated, and new annual performance targets should be negotiated.

• ***Other consequences.*** There are innumerable other consequences that can be included in flexible performance agreements, such as customer redress, increased or decreased flexibilities for the organization, increased or decreased privileges for the chief executive or other employees, and increased or decreased rewards for employees. Although financial consequences are important, "psychic pay" is equally important. Steering organizations should put particular emphasis on publicly recognizing high performers.

pp. 362–368

pp. 224, 231–232

Control Strategy

• ***Organizational empowerment.*** Flexible performance frameworks produce dramatically better results only if they give uncoupled agencies enough freedom to initiate serious innovation. We recommend negotiating agreements of three to six years, to give uncoupled organizations long enough that they feel free to undertake major efforts to change what they do and how they work. If their budget and expectations keep changing every year, they will feel that it is risky to start a change process that may take several years to bear fruit, because it could easily be disrupted in midstream. To produce fundamental improvement, uncoupled agencies need both flexibility and *time.*

Organizational empowerment should come in two other ways: from systemwide reforms in budget and finance, personnel, and procurement systems, to give all uncoupled agencies significant flexibility; and from additional flexibilities granted to particular agencies in their FPAs. We have found that it is often difficult for managers to define the flexibilities they need. Like fish who don't understand the water in which they swim because it is all they know, they often accept restrictions as simply the way things are. Hence it helps to give them a checklist of possible flexibilities they can use, such as those described in the box on the following pages.

pp. 404–426

Designing Flexible Performance Frameworks: Lessons Learned

1. Make sure the initiative has high-level political support.

In New Zealand and the U.K., uncoupling had strong support from the prime minister and other key ministers. Without such support, departments often go through the motions of creating uncoupled agencies but don't fundamentally change they way they deal with them. They don't take the negotiation of FPAs seriously, they don't give agencies significant flexibility, they don't shift from a hierarchical to a contractual relationship, and they don't stop telling agencies what to do and start telling them what results to produce. After a few years, the uncoupled agencies look much like the rest of the department, despite their new trappings. This is precisely what happened to many of Canada's SOAs.

POTENTIAL FLEXIBILITIES FOR UNCOUPLED ORGANIZATIONS

pp. 407–411

Budget Flexibilities

- Shared savings, in which agencies are allowed to keep part or all of any operating money they do not spend during a fiscal year
- Shared earnings, in which they are allowed to keep part or all of any new funds they earn
- Lump-sum operating budgets, or lump sums for each division or program's operating expenses
- Freedom to move money between accounts or line items without approval from above
- Freedom to borrow a certain amount against next year's appropriation
- Access to an innovation fund, from which the organization can borrow to finance investments that will improve its performance

pp. 411–415

Personnel Flexibilities

- Simplification of job classification systems—preferably down to a dozen or fewer basic job classifications (clerical, technical, professional, managerial, and so on)
- Use of three to five broad pay bands for each broad job classification
- Power to recruit and hire people on their own, within broad guidelines—and to use commercial firms to help
- Streamlined hiring and firing processes: changes to probationary periods, doing away with some written exams, different methods to rank applicants, streamlined appeals processes for firing, and so on
- Changes in procedures to deal with poor performers, short of firing
- Authority to develop new dispute resolution or grievance procedures for employees
- Changes in compensation: lump-sum payments or special pay rates to recruit or retain talent, incentives to encourage early retirement, team-based pay, skill-based pay, and so on
- Authority to create performance appraisal systems and set rewards (both financial and nonfinancial)
- Authority and funding to award employee performance bonuses

pp. 232–237

pp. 237–241

- Authority to create gainsharing for employees
- Freedom to create nonpermanent positions and to use part-time employees, temporary employees, and commercial temporary help services
- Authority and funding to provide any necessary training for employees, using any training providers

pp. 199–200

- Authority to retrain redundant employees and place them in other agencies through a job bank
- Freedom from ceilings or floors on numbers of personnel

pp. 415–422

Procurement Flexibilities

- Credit cards for managers, for purchases up to a set dollar amount
- Increased authority for managers to purchase off-the-shelf commercial products
- Higher purchase floors before procurement regulations kick in
- Simplification of purchasing rules and processes
- Authority to use simplified processes to deal with protests from vendors
- Freedom to substitute best-value for lowest-cost purchasing
- Authority to prequalify bidders in complex contracting processes
- Authority to use past performance as criteria in selecting suppliers, vendors, and consultants
- Authority to use multiple award contracts and quick, informal competitions between the awardees

Support Service Flexibilities

- More flexible travel and reimbursement rules
- Freedom to use nonpublic office space, leasing arrangements, and property management services

pp. 174–182

- Freedom to purchase some support services (such as vehicles, office space, building management, travel services, printing, and maintenance) wherever the agency can get the best deal, combined with control over funding for those support services

pp. 380–382

- Authority to negotiate service agreements with support service providers that maintain their monopolies

"Throughout the study," the 1994 evaluation concluded, "respondents stressed the need for political support, yet it has been evident that ministers and other parliamentarians have not been seriously seized with the SOA initiative and influenced its evolution."

2. Choose a unit outside the central administrative agencies (budget, personnel, planning) but close to the executive to run the initiative.

Normally, administrative agencies resist creating true flexible performance frameworks, because they think accountability means tying everyone down with rules and restrictions. If the budget office is leading the reinvention charge, as happened in New Zealand, the FPF team can operate out of that office. But in most situations, because the budget office is an obstacle, it is best to set up an independent unit. To earn the trust of agencies and departments, the reform unit must be perceived as neutral and fair—another reason not to use an administrative agency like a budget office, which is never perceived as neutral. To earn the respect of agencies and departments, the reform unit must have significant power; hence it should be close to the executive (president, prime minister, governor, mayor, county executive, or city manager). In the U.K., Thatcher put the Next Steps Team in her Cabinet Office and staffed it with bright young civil servants seconded from their departments.

Canada's experience demonstrated the pitfalls of relying on a budget office—in this case the Treasury Board Secretariat. Canada's 1994 evaluation recommended designating a high-level champion from outside the Treasury Board Secretariat to take over the initiative. "Many participants felt that the operational responsibilities and role of the Secretariat overwhelmed the more discretionary activities related to the SOA reform initiative," it reported, tactfully. "Some even felt that they conflicted."

In addition to launching the initiative, the reform unit should be responsible for monitoring and evaluating it. Creating flexible performance frameworks is not easy. Results are always uneven: some agencies use their new flexibility and accountability to perform miracles; others make few changes. Some elements of the reform work; others get bogged down. And over time, some organizations inevitably sink back into business as usual, going through the motions required by the new arrangements but not taking them seriously. Hence every government needs to monitor and evaluate its flexible performance frameworks—and intervene every few years to shake things up where they aren't working.

3. Force those doing the steering (departments, ministers, city managers, and so on) to let go of their power to micromanage.

Steering organizations must not keep their uncoupled agencies on too short a leash. The New Zealanders avoided this problem by removing every function save policymaking and oversight from the policy ministries. But in the U.K., where departments remained sizable, "the dead hand of the parent department" remained heavy, as one agency chief executive put it in a 1993 survey. William Waldegrave, then the minister in charge of government reform, told us in 1994, "The departments are still hankering after micromanagement of the agencies and are still retaining people with skills in micromanagement of the agencies."

Even after the uncoupling process was complete, in 1998, some departments still held their agencies too close for maximum effectiveness. Too many departmental staffers went along with the structural reforms—because they had no choice—but continued to act much as they had before agencies were uncoupled. In Canada the problem was even worse. We conclude from this experience that New Zealand's approach is preferable: make the agencies independent organizations whose relationship with their steering organizations is purely a contractual one.

Where this approach is impractical, consider the following potential solutions:

- Use a reform office close to the executive to push the departments to let go.
- Create a council of departmental chief operating officers, like the President's Management Council in the U.S. government, and use it to keep the pressure on departments to let go.
- Require departments to create clear written statements of the responsibilities of each of their remaining units (particularly budget, personnel, and procurement offices), to help them understand where those responsibilities now end.
- Create a process to help the departments adapt to the new situation by eliminating what is no longer necessary. The U.K. used a round of fundamental expenditure reviews (FERs), through which it examined how the departments should be organized for effective steering and reduced their operating budgets.

4. Express the new relationship in a written agreement that forces the steering organizations to guarantee specific flexibilities and the rowing organizations to commit to delivering specific results.

Written agreements help force issues out into the open. In the U.K., the task of writing the initial framework document made visible many of the problems that had to be dealt with to improve performance. A permanent secretary in the Department of Social Security put it this way, referring to the Resettlement Agency:

Defining its objectives and writing its framework document of responsibilities and its first annual business plan proved a major task, since it brought out starkly the inconsistencies in policies and practices with which it had been operating for many years. If the main objective was to resettle its "customers" back into society, where were the targets or the information on how many had been successfully resettled? What counted as "successful" resettlement? Not returning to one of our resettlement centres within a specified period? For how long?

Written agreements also help expose situations in which the steering side is not allowing agencies the flexibilities it had promised. Agencies can use them to resist when steering organizations trample on their management freedoms. In the same way, steering organizations can use them to demand improvement when agencies fail to meet their written performance targets.

5. Make sure steering organizations provide regular feedback to rowing organizations on their performance.

Rowing organizations will take their performance goals seriously to the extent that their steering organization takes them seriously. If the steering organization does a perfunctory annual review before slightly adjusting the targets, the rowing organization will realize its performance is not terribly important to that organization, and it will relax. But if the steering organization reviews performance quarterly or every six months and takes the process of setting annual targets seriously, the rowing organization is likely to put great effort into improving its performance.

Feedback is also critical for organizational learning. The more often feedback is provided, the more often the rowing organization can learn from it. This is particularly true with feedback that goes beyond a review of the numbers to a discussion of what is behind them. Why are key outcomes not improving, even though the organization is hitting its output targets? Why is customer satisfaction low? Is the organization sacrificing quality to increase efficiency? Is this what the steering organization wants? And which of the targets are most important to the steering organization? The more these conversations take place, the more both sides will learn, and the more performance will align with the steering organization's goals.

6. Give uncoupled organizations budget continuity beyond one year, through biennial or three-year rolling budgets.

If uncoupled organizations are to take advantage of their three-to six-year frameworks to strive for fundamental improvements, they need to know at least the rough outlines of their budget for more than one year. Many governments

pp. 54–56

now use multiyear budget frameworks, which not only give organizations their budget for the current year but also project it for two or three extra years. These projections can be adjusted, but those adjustments should usually be minor.

Multiyear budget frameworks tend not to work well during times of fiscal crisis, when deficits force repeated budget cuts that defy the out-year projections. Hence we recommend combining them with biennial budgets. The ideal approach might be a biennial budget within a four-year budget framework, coupled with a four-year flexible performance agreement. This would appropriate an agency's budget for two years and project its likely budget for the following two years.

7. Use a mix of output and outcome goals to hold uncoupled organizations accountable.

pp. 47–50

Both New Zealand and the U.K. hold uncoupled agencies accountable for producing only outputs, not outcomes. As we argue in Chapter One, a good strategic management system should hold organizations accountable for producing a mix of outputs *and* outcomes.

8. Create accountability to customers through customer boards, customer service standards, customer involvement in setting performance targets, and other customer quality assurance tools.

pp. 323–388

Flexible performance frameworks make rowing organizations more accountable vertically, up the chain of command. For compliance organizations, whose customers are usually elected officials (representing citizens), this vertical accountability also means accountability to their customers. But for service organizations it does not. Steering organizations can make their service agencies accountable to their customers, however, by giving those customers power. For example, steering organizations can create customer boards to oversee rowing organizations. They can involve an agency's customers in creating performance targets for the agency. They can require agencies to survey their customers and use the results to create customer service standards. And for agencies that can charge their customers for services, steering organizations can use enterprise management to make the agencies dependent on their customers for their revenues.

pp. 153–182

9. Create a process for resolving problems that arise between steering and rowing organizations.

Even with the clearest FPAs, problems may emerge. The steering organization or executive may suddenly decide that they need the agency to do something new that is not in its FPA. Or the agency may take an action that is within its rights but creates an unexpected embarrassment for elected officials, such as closing branch offices in their districts. When problems arise, the steering and rowing organizations need a process to iron them out. In the U.K., ministers appoint one high-level civil servant within the department to be a liaison with each agency. This person keeps an eye on the agency, and if a problem emerges, he and the agency chief executive know they can contact each other. Another option would be to create a mediation process for differences that cannot be easily worked out.

10. Create a risk management process to deal with serious failures.

In 1995, a cantilevered deck built by New Zealand's Department of Conservation collapsed, killing 14 people. An investigation blamed departmental personnel for constructing it with nails rather than bolts. In the U.K., the Prison Service suffered high-profile escapes in both 1994 and 1995. How do steering organizations minimize the risks of such big, costly mistakes by their rowing organizations? First, they make sure the rowing organizations use risk management techniques: anticipating potential risks and developing procedures to reduce or eliminate them, developing information systems that give them early warnings, purchasing insurance when appropriate, and creating cultures in which identifying problems is encouraged and rewarded. Second, they make sure the rowing organizations have options in place in case problems begin to emerge, such as switching to another service provider.

11. Don't create new reporting requirements without eliminating old ones that are no longer necessary.

When agencies negotiate FPAs, they typically agree to measure performance against up to 10 key outcome and output goals and to report the results quarterly or semiannually. They often agree to provide business plans and annual financial reports as well. Yet most agencies are already suffering under a load of reporting requirements. Consider what the National Performance Review found when it looked at reports required by Congress:

> *On August 31 of each year, the Chief Financial Officers (CFO) Act requires that agencies file a five-year financial plan and a CFO annual report. On September 1, budget exhibits for financial management activities and high-risk areas are due. On November 30, IG reports are expected, along with reports required by the Prompt Payment Act. On January 31, reports under the Federal Civil Penalties Inflation Report Adjustment Act of 1990 come due. On March 31, financial statements are due and on May 1 annual single-audit reports must be filed. On May 31 another round of IG reports are due. At the end of July and December, "high-risk" reports are filed. On August 31, it all begins again. And these are just the major reports!*

Rather than add to that load, we recommend eliminating many current reporting requirements, so agency staff have the time to concentrate on performance reports, business plans, and financial reports. Typically, a large percentage of required reports are little more than fossils of forgotten initiatives. Often, no one even reads them.

12. Take very seriously the challenge of recruiting quality chief executives for the uncoupled organizations.

In all three countries we have studied, New Zealand, the U.K., and Canada, the quality of the chief executives appointed to run uncoupled agencies has been a critical success factor. Not surprisingly, strong leaders use their new agency status to push for dramatic improvements. As the Canadian evaluation put it, "People, and particularly the agency head, make the difference."

Pitfalls to Avoid

Some problems emerge so often they can almost be predicted. Among the most common are the following.

1. Lack of clarity about the ground rules.

In both the U.K. and Canada, those running uncoupled agencies received mixed messages about the reform. Part of this had to do with different understandings: reformers expected arm's-length separation and genuine negotiations between departments and agencies, but some departmental leaders expected business as usual. (Because it legally separated its uncoupled agencies, New Zealand did not have this problem—a strong argument in favor of its approach.)

See Banishing Bureaucracy p. 301

The U.K. also suffered from misunderstandings about whether agencies could later be privatized. When it began creating agencies, the Next Steps Team told their leaders that once their agencies were created, they would be given a number of years to "settle down" before the issue of privatization was raised again. Then, in 1991, John Major's government released "Competing for Quality," a white paper announcing that sale of each agency would be considered during each subsequent three-year review. The new policy also required agencies to "market test" roughly 15 percent of their activities every year, by creating managed competition between agency staff and private bidders. This shift toward privatization infuriated and demoralized many in the agencies, who saw it as a betrayal.

If at all possible, the ground rules governing flexible performance frameworks should be spelled out clearly, fully, and repeatedly as the initiative is launched. In any change process of this magnitude, fear and uncertainty will be widespread. "Will my agency remain public or will it be privatized?" "Will we have significant independence or will our superiors hold us on a short leash?" "Will our job classifications and pay scales remain the same?" And most important, "Will I profit or suffer from these changes?"

Any confusion or mixed messages will simply heighten the uncertainty, anxiety, and resistance. The media often further muddles things by misunderstanding the government's intentions—equating uncoupling with privatization, for example.

2. *Lack of clarity about accountability for things that go wrong.*

When the deck collapsed in New Zealand, killing 14 people, there was great confusion about who should shoulder the blame. Should it be the minister overseeing the department in question, as it would have been before the reforms? Or was it now the chief executive of that department? Or perhaps the head of the unit that built the deck using nails rather than bolts? The traditional impulse was to find a scapegoat and demand a resignation. But whose?

This kind of confusion is inevitable, unless the government clarifies when it launches flexible performance frameworks who will be held accountable for problems. Commonwealth countries have held on to their constitutional tradition that ministers are accountable for everything that happens in their departments, a tradition that may have made sense when they had a few dozen or a few hundred people working for them, but does not make sense when they oversee tens of thousands of employees. Clearly, an elected minister cannot be expected to know if workers are using nails or bolts—and if he is expected to know these things, he will hold the reins very tightly. We recommend that governments adopt an explicit doctrine that the person who manages a unit is responsible for problems that occur in that unit. Accountability and responsibility should be at the same level, in other words. In a political world, of course, mistakes that have extremely serious consequences are often going to cost an agency executive his or her job. Because this is true, FPAs should spell out as clearly as possible what kinds of mistakes the chief executive will be held responsible for—which risks he or she cannot delegate.

We are not suggesting that you include long lists of potential mistakes for which you will hold the chief executive responsible. An FPA is not a contract, and the last thing you want to do is involve lawyers in the negotiations. But if you know in advance that certain events would have serious consequences for the chief executive—such as a jail break, or the death of a client, or a major case of embezzlement—it is best to make that clear.

3. *Loss of the collective interest.*

When flexible performance frameworks are effective, the uncoupled agencies become almost obsessively focused on meeting their goals. As a consequence, they have less time and energy for collaboration with other organizations around goals that are not in their FPAs. If governments do not counteract this tendency, they lose something valuable: the willing collaboration of all managers in solving problems beyond their own organization's turf. By heightening vertical accountability for results, in other words, flexible performance frameworks can lessen horizontal cooperation between agencies.

The British and New Zealanders talk about this challenge as one of protecting the government's interests as an "owner" of uncoupled agencies, not just as a purchaser of their services. Its ownership interests include collaboration between agencies to meet common challenges; contributions to discussions about policy (for example, a job training agency's contribution to government-wide discussions about welfare reform); and maintenance of the long-term value of government assets, including buildings, equipment, and people. By negotiating only for the best service or compliance work at the lowest possible price, governments risk sacrificing these interests.

New Zealand has confronted this problem directly. Ministers now expect that in negotiating purchase and performance agreements, chief executives will identify for them the potential impact of different options on the government's ownership interests, such as the quality of the workforce or the maintenance of infrastructure assets. They also require chief executives to develop one or more key result areas (program goals) concerned with ownership interests.

This is one good solution: put at least one specific goal related to ownership interests in the FPA. If you want collaboration, make it a performance target. For example, the city manager of Hartford, Connecticut, put a goal of collaboration with selected other departments into each FPA, with performance to be measured by a survey of those other department heads. Other reinventors have included goals related to staff training, to make sure the uncoupled organization maintained a skilled workforce.

A second option is to put one or two government-wide policy outcome goals into each FPA. When Robert Bobb was city manager of Richmond, Virginia, he announced that every department head's new FPA would include a goal of reducing the city's crime rate. He wanted every department to work together to reduce crime.

A third option is to make sure that the outcome goals put into FPAs are those that will contribute to a jurisdiction's government-wide outcome goals. For example, if a state decides that reducing teen pregnancy and increasing the high school graduation rate are statewide outcome goals (as Oregon did), the governor's office could negotiate an FPA with the welfare agency that included the goals of reducing the teen pregnancy rate and increasing the high school graduation rate for teenagers whose families were on welfare.

pp. 13–18

These three options are not mutually exclusive, of course. Indeed, we urge you to use all three. In addition, we suggest that a central management agency periodically review whether departments are maintaining their ownership interests, as New Zealand's State Services Commission does.

4. *The Ivory Tower Syndrome.*

When rowing is uncoupled from steering, policymakers sometimes lose touch with those working where the rubber actually meets the road. Those who know the most about service delivery or compliance work are no longer involved in policymaking discussions. (In many organizations, of course, they never were.) This problem, which has surfaced in New Zealand, the U.K., and Sweden, can be extremely serious.

One useful remedy is to rotate people between policy organizations and operational agencies. Another is to require that uncoupled agencies play a role in the policy development process. In the U.K., for example, some agency chief executives have specific roles in the formulation of departmental policy. "We had an agreement in our framework document that neither party could put a policy submission up without consulting the other, and the other party could put a counterproposal up," Ron Oliver explains. "This forced us to reach agreement before submission. It forced us to try to find solutions before we took policy recommendations to the politicians."

A third remedy is to give uncoupled agencies a role in evaluating policymaking officials' performance—so those officials will realize it is in their self-interest to reach out to agencies as they do policy work. Again, we suggest using all three remedies, because this problem is so common.

5. *Lack of shared information in a balkanized system.*

"One of the risks of splitting up agencies is that each one builds their own information collection system," explain New Zealanders Judith Johnson, Katrina Casey, and Tony Crewdson in a paper on interagency cooperation and information management. The obvious solution, they suggest, is to build information systems that cross agency lines. In a world of rapid change, which requires different organizations to work together on a myriad of shifting problems, this becomes an absolute necessity. Information must flow easily throughout a 21st-century government if its various organizations are going to be able to collaborate effectively. We have seen governments of all shapes and sizes struggling with this problem. To provide just one example, local police departments, state police departments, the FBI, the various court systems, juvenile justice systems, prison systems, and parole programs are struggling to build systems that help information on accused or convicted criminals flow between them. Johnson, Casey, and Crewdson provide one case study of such a cross-agency information system, in the criminal justice sector in New Zealand.

Tips on Negotiating Flexible Performance Agreements

Negotiating an FPA is a new experience for most people in government. We have found that some approach it with a bureaucratic mind-set—as an exercise in which the boss tells the manager what he or she wants. They tend to spell out activities they want performed, rather than results they want produced. And they have trouble even identifying flexibilities that might help the manager. Hence without some guidance, department heads, mayors, city or county managers, and their deputies can easily turn FPAs into one more exercise in top-down micromanagement.

We have also found that everyone underestimates how long it takes to negotiate an FPA. Done correctly, an FPA raises the most profound questions one can raise about an organization: What is its core purpose? What strategies should it use to achieve that purpose? What outcomes and outputs is it most important for the organization to produce? How can it measure those outcomes and outputs? What level of performance is acceptable? What flexibilities does it need to be effective? And what consequences should management face for their performance? To think that these issues can all be discussed and resolved in a month or two is usually a fantasy, particularly the first time around.

We suggest the following rules of thumb in negotiating FPAs.

Make sure those negotiating FPAs from the steering end buy in to the basic idea. Sometimes executives delegate the negotiation to deputies who don't quite understand or believe in the concept. In our experience, such individuals can quickly turn FPAs into instruments of increased hierarchical control rather than increased clarity, accountability, and flexibility.

Make sure the process is a true negotiation, with plenty of room for give-and-take. Instinctively, many people accustomed to working in a bureaucracy approach the negotiation of an FPA as an occasion for the boss to tell the agency head what's what. When the two sides disagree about performance targets, both sides expect the boss to prevail. This attitude undermines the purpose of a flexible performance framework. If agency managers feel FPAs have been jammed down their throats, they will not buy in to the goal of dramatic improvement. Some will go through the motions and try their best to fudge the performance data—or better yet, make sure it's never collected.

Others will look for another job. But few will dedicate themselves to profound improvement.

When the two sides disagree, it is important for the agency head to feel free to push back as hard as necessary to get a fair agreement. It is up to the executive negotiating the agreement to make sure all agency heads understand and believe they are expected to push back—and that there will be no negative consequences if they do.

A neutral referee can be useful. One of the best ways to ensure that the negotiation is a two-way street is to have a neutral referee who can help both sides understand the ground rules, tell them when they are out of bounds, and mediate when they cannot agree. This is another reason you need a respected, neutral office to drive the uncoupling process, like the Next Steps Team in the U.K.

p. 131

Coaches for both sides of the negotiation can also be useful. Particularly the first time people negotiate an FPA, they can benefit enormously from having coaches, who can walk them through the process, help them with first drafts, and help them decide what to push for in negotiations. Either internal or external consultants can play this role.

Executives (the steering side) should indicate what outcomes, strategies, and outputs are most important to them at the beginning of the negotiation process. If they don't do this, some agency heads will prepare draft FPAs that bear little resemblance to what the executive wants. When the executive then says, "I'm not interested in much of what you have prepared; here's what I want," it can quickly feel like another top-down exercise. But if the executive communicates the core of what he or she wants in an FPA up front—and gives the agency head a chance to discuss it—such misunderstandings can be avoided.

pp. 254, 261

Don't overwhelm the agency with too many performance targets; keep the number under 10. FPAs are not meant to list everything an agency must do; they are meant to pinpoint the most important results it should achieve. If you give agency managers too many priorities, they will be forced to spread themselves so thin it will be hard to achieve significant improvement in any area. They may also feel that the entire exercise is simply one more opportunity for their superiors to harass them.

A British government review of best practices in executive agencies recommended setting only four to seven performance targets per year. Given that it also said, "Target packages should reflect cost, quality, time and output measures," each performance target might have more than one indicator. But we agree wholeheartedly with the basic principle: "Targets should be sufficiently few in number to ensure the right degree of focus from managers."

Don't make the stakes too high in the first year or two if the agency has no performance track record to go by. If an agency is new or has no real track record, it is difficult to tell what level of performance it can achieve. You can either pick targets out of the air during the first year or simply use the first year to establish a baseline from which to set targets in the future. (We normally recommend the latter.) Either way, it doesn't make sense to create high stakes for the agency manager—such as large performance bonuses or major penalties—during that first year. If you do, agency managers may feel the process is unfair, and those who do poorly may resent those who did well, concluding that favoritism was at play.

pp. 221–222

Don't be overly prescriptive in the FPA about how work should be done. For those accustomed to working in bureaucracies, the instinct is usually to tell managers what to do. FPAs are meant to break that pattern: to tell managers what results to produce while giving them the flexibility to find or invent the best methods to produce them.

Specify in the FPA where the executive or department head can intervene and where he or she cannot. After signing an FPA, agency directors should expect to be free from micromanagement. Yet because governments operate in a political world, there will come a time when the executive needs to overrule an agency head's decision or intervene to ask him or her to do something not in the FPA.

To avoid bad feelings, it is wise to be as explicit as possible in the FPA about this. To the degree that he or she can foresee such actions, the executive should spell out the situations in which he or she reserves the right to overrule an agency head's decision or otherwise intervene. As Price Waterhouse advised new Labor Party ministers in the U.K., they should try to distinguish "the many situations about which you need to be informed from the few circumstances in which you need to intervene."

Assume that the negotiation process will require a minimum of two drafts. We suggest roughly the following approach:

- The executive or department head tells the agency manager what outcomes and outputs are most important to produce, providing some opportunity for discussion, clarification, and modification.
- Using a general format provided for all FPAs (see the accompanying example), and working with a coach, the agency head prepares a first draft and submits it.
- The executive and agency head meet, with a neutral referee (and coaches if desired), to discuss the draft. The executive suggests changes, and after a discussion, presents them (as shaped by that discussion) in written form.
- Again working with a coach, the agency head prepares a second draft.

pp. 144–145

- The executive and agency head meet again to discuss the second draft and try to reach a final agreement. If they are successful, the referee prepares the final draft.
- If they cannot reach a final agreement, the referee mediates a final meeting, pushes them to responsible compromises, and if they still cannot agree on an item, imposes a solution.

Set a deadline for first drafts and a deadline for completion of the final draft. This process is difficult enough for most people that it can drag on forever. Often it is easier for both sides to let time pass than to do the hard work necessary to resolve tough issues. Deadlines are indispensable.

When the negotiations pinpoint policies that need to be changed to allow more flexibility, make those changes. If you pay attention, the agency heads' requests for flexibility will show you where your budget, personnel, procurement, and other rules need to be changed. This is one of the side benefits of the process. In most governments, changing these rules is difficult. If you do nothing to reform them, however, agency directors will quickly conclude that the promised flexibility—their biggest upside in the deal—is a sham. Sometimes the executive won't be able to change the rule in time to grant the flexibility outlined in the FPA, but he or she should at least promise, in writing, to pursue the necessary reforms.

RESOURCES ON FLEXIBLE PERFORMANCE FRAMEWORKS

Next Steps Team. *The Strategic Management of Agencies: Models for Management.* London: Her Majesty's Stationery Office, September 1995. A look at how departments can best steer executive agencies, including very specific recommendations on best and worst practices.

Performance-Based Organizations. Web page: www.npr.gov/initiati/21cent/index.html. A description of the U.S. government's proposed flexible performance frameworks, along with model legislation, sample position descriptions for PBO chief operating officers, and a list of potential flexibilities in personnel, procurement, and administrative services.

Allen Schick. *Modern Budgeting.* Paris: Organization for Economic Cooperation and Development, 1998. An excellent book on budget and finance system reform in developed countries. Includes material on uncoupled agencies in Sweden, New Zealand, and the U.K.

A MODEL FLEXIBLE PERFORMANCE AGREEMENT

I. The Organization's "Statement of Purpose" (Mission Statement)

II. The Organization's Basic Responsibilities

III. Resources

pp. 133–134

- A. The budget to be provided, preferably over the term of the FPA.
- B. Anything related to other resources, such as the workforce or the capital budget.
- C. The financial accounting, auditing, and reporting system to be used.

IV. Expected Results

- A. Half a dozen key outcome and output goals for the organization.
- B. One or two citywide, countywide, statewide, or nationwide outcome goals to which the agency is expected to contribute.
- C. The agency's expected role in providing policy advice to the executive, and how its performance in doing so will be measured.
- D. Individual objectives for the agency director, such as leadership training or development of increased skills in a particular area.
- E. How performance will be measured and reported.
- F. How performance measurement will be audited to make sure it is accurate and fair.

V. Flexibilities

pp. 129–130

- A. Budget flexibilities to be allowed.
- B. Personnel flexibilities to be allowed.
- C. Procurement flexibilities to be allowed.
- D. Support service flexibilities to be allowed.
- E. Other flexibilities.

VI. Special Conditions

This section can be used by either side to indicate conditions that must be met for it to fulfill what the FPA requires. For example, the agency director might say that unless the purchasing rules are changed in a particular way, the agency will not be held accountable for meeting one of its efficiency targets. The steering organization might say that unless the agency achieves a certain performance level or uses an approach such as managed competition, personnel ceilings will be reestablished.

VII. Expectations of the Steering Executive

This is where the executive can lay out his or her expectations of the agency director beyond results to be produced. For example: "When you bring me a problem, it is your responsibility to bring with it options for solutions and your recommended solution." Or: "When problems occur, I want to hear about it first." Or: "I will hold you personally responsible for the death of a client."

VIII. Responsibilities of the Steering Executive

A. How the executive will play an oversight role: for example, who the executive will delegate oversight duties to, if anyone; how often that person will meet with the agency director to review performance; and how available he or she will be to the agency director for meetings on other issues.

p. 142

B. Definition of areas in which the executive can intervene or override the agency director and areas where he or she cannot do so.

IX. Consequences

A. Financial consequences for performance, such as bonuses. Typically this section would define the formula used to calculate a performance bonus for the agency director and perhaps other agency employees. For example: if 80 percent of performance targets are met, the bonus will be 10 percent of salary; if 90 percent are met, the bonus will be 20 percent of salary.

pp. 346–368

B. Redress to customers. If some of the performance targets are in the form of customer service standards, the FPA could spell out how the agency will make it up to customers if and when it fails to meet those standards.

C. Other consequences. These might be positive or negative or both. They could include increased or decreased flexibilities, increased or decreased privileges (such as use of a car, or extra professional development time), or even increased or decreased investments in training, technology, or office space.

X. Term of the Agreement

Ideally, the term of the FPA will be three to six years, though performance targets may be adjusted more often than that.

XI. Amendment Procedures

Typical FPAs state that they can be amended by mutual written agreement of the executive and agency director at any time.

SAMPLE FLEXIBLE PERFORMANCE AGREEMENT FOR A POLICE DEPARTMENT

I. Mission Statement
Improve public safety through collaboration, problem solving, and equitable and fair enforcement of the law.

II. The Organization's Basic Responsibilities
A. Prevent crime through community policing.
B. Investigate crimes and apprehend criminals.
C. Work with prosecutors and the courts to achieve convictions.

III. Resources
The budget over the term of this agreement will be $31.2 million in Year One, $32 million in Year Two, and $32.4 million in Year Three.

IV. Expected Results
A. Departmental Outcome and Output Goals
1. Reduce the rate of violent crime: murder, rape, robbery, aggravated assault, and domestic assault.
2. Increase the number of firearms confiscated by 10 percent a year.
3. Improve the clearance rate of homicides to 80 percent within eight months of the crime.
4. Achieve a positive customer satisfaction rating from 70 percent of citizens surveyed.
5. Respond to all action line requests and complaints within five business days.
6. Achieve at least a "satisfactory" rating by neighborhood organizations on a survey of their members' satisfaction with departmental responsiveness to their concerns.

B. Citywide Outcome Goals
1. Increase the percentage of positive ratings on a citywide citizen satisfaction survey each year.

C. Individual Objectives
1. Participate in at least one week (five days) of leadership development training per year.

D. Performance Measurement, Reporting, and Auditing
1. Performance on these goals will be measured by the measurement unit within the police department and reported to the city manager quarterly.
2. The city auditor's office will audit the measurement system through periodic spot checks.

V. Flexibilities

A. Budget flexibilities. The Police Chief is free to transfer funds within the department as needed, without permission, with the exception of spending on hiring additional personnel.

B. Personnel flexibilities. Authority is granted to provide gainsharing and performance bonuses to employees and to hire civilian (nonpolice) personnel for clerical positions.

C. Procurement flexibilities. Authority is granted to make purchasing decisions below $2,000 free of normal procurement processes.

D. Support service flexibilities. Authority is granted to have departmental vehicles serviced at any repair shop designated by the police chief.

VI. Special Conditions

This agreement assumes that no major catastrophe, such as a civil disturbance, a gang war, or a natural disaster, occurs. Should such an event occur, this agreement will be renegotiated.

VII. Expectations of the City Manager

A. I expect you to anticipate problems and opportunities and act on them, rather than waiting to be told what to do by the city manager's office.

B. I expect deadlines set by the city manager's office to be met. If you cannot meet a deadline, I expect an explanation in advance.

C. I expect all police officers to receive diversity training during their first year on the job.

VIII. Responsibilities of the City Manager

A. The police chief will report to Deputy City Manager Ford, who will meet with the police chief quarterly to review agency performance.

B. In the event of a civil disturbance in response to police behavior, the city manager and her deputy reserve the right to intervene and override decisions of the police chief.

IX. Consequences

A. Financial consequences. If all performance goals are met, the police chief will receive a bonus of 20 percent of his salary; if eight or more are met, including Goal 1, the bonus will be 15 percent; if eight or more are met, not including Goal 1, the bonus will be 10 percent; if seven are met, the bonus will be 5 percent.

B. Other consequences. If the police department fails to meet five or more of the performance goals, the city manager will impose one of the following consequences:

1. A monthly meeting to review performance.
2. Limits on travel until performance improves.
3. Probation for a specific period of time.

X. Term of the Agreement
This agreement will be valid for fiscal years 2000, 2001, and 2002. Specific performance targets will be renegotiated at the beginning of each fiscal year.

XI. Amendment Procedures
This agreement may be amended at any time through mutual agreement of the city manager and the police chief.

Part II

The Consequences Strategy

Introducing Consequences for Performance

The Consequences Strategy gives public employees powerful incentives—risks and rewards—to improve their performance. It breaks up public monopolies, hallmarks of bureaucratic government that unnecessarily shield government employees from the pressure to meet customer needs. Some government functions should be monopolies—for example, policy and regulatory functions; some compliance functions, such as the courts; and a few services, such as the military. But the bureaucratic model has left us with far more monopolies than necessary.

When reinventors cannot eliminate a public monopoly, they use the Consequences Strategy to shatter the status quo by measuring performance, rewarding improvement and excellence, and refusing to tolerate persistent failure. This can be done in any government organization.

There are three approaches to introducing consequences. *Enterprise management* thrusts public service delivery organizations into the private marketplace, where they must function as business enterprises with financial bottom lines. There, they survive and prosper—or fail and wither—by selling products and services to customers. This is the most powerful approach, but it is only appropriate for services that can be charged to their customers. It is not appropriate for policy, regulatory, or compliance functions.

Managed competition is the second most powerful approach. It forces potential service providers—whether private businesses, public agencies, or both—to compete against one another for contracts, based on performance and cost. Managed competition is appropriate for any service or compliance function. However, when concerns about safety, national security, privacy, or due process make the public uncomfortable with private providers, only public agencies should be permitted to compete.

See *Banishing Bureaucracy* pp. 111–112

When neither enterprise management nor managed competition is appropriate or possible—due to political or other resistance or because the activity in question is a policy or regulatory function—reinventors can turn to *performance management.* This approach uses performance targets, rewards, and penalties to motivate public organizations and employees. It is not usually as powerful as the other two approaches, because the rewards and penalties it imposes are rarely as compelling or unavoidable as the consequences of competition. They come in two basic forms: *financial* incentives, such as cash bonuses and gainsharing from budget savings; and *psychological* incentives, such as awards and days off. Reinventors use both; the key is always to tie them to performance.

These three approaches are not mutually exclusive. Public organizations that compete for contracts normally use performance management to maximize their ability to compete. Indeed, we advise every public organization to use performance management, whether it is a public monopoly, a competitive enterprise, or a competitor for contracts.

This puts a premium on measuring performance. Because performance measurement is a core competence that makes the Consequences Strategy (as well as other strategies) possible, we have devoted an entire chapter to it.

Whichever approach is used, it is likely to stir fear in public employees and their unions, at least initially. They will worry about layoffs: Will their organization fail in the marketplace? Will private businesses win contracts to deliver the services they provide? Will they need to trim costs to win competitive bids? As we said in *Banishing Bureaucracy,* handling these concerns is one of the most important issues that reinventors face. We believe that governments should protect employees from the threat of unemployment, unless they are in a fiscal crisis so serious they can't afford to. As we discuss in subsequent chapters, governments can adopt no-layoff policies and take other actions to relieve employee anxiety and resistance.

See *Banishing Bureaucracy* pp. 132–135

pp. 199–200

pp. 279–322

The Consequences Strategy is extremely powerful, particularly when used in combination with other reinvention strategies. Coupled with customer choice, it creates *competitive* customer choice, which puts significant pressure on public organizations, such as schools, to respond to their customers' demands. Linked to the Control Strategy, it strengthens the motivation of empowered employees to improve their performance. Using flexible perfor-

pp. 124–148

mance frameworks, for example, governments can set performance goals for organizations, give their managers the freedom they need to achieve the goals, and create consequences for doing so. This is one of the most basic trade-offs found in reinvention: more flexibility in return for greater accountability for performance.

Chapter 4

Enterprise Management

Using Markets to Create Consequences

***Enterprise Management* forces public organizations to function as business enterprises, with financial bottom lines. They remain publicly owned, but they must earn their budgets by selling services to their customers—citizens or other public organizations. Their success as enterprises depends on how well they meet those customers' needs.**

Sunnyvale, California, began to phase out taxpayer support for recreational programs in 1991. Like many cities, it decided that "leisure services" were not a high enough priority to spend so many taxpayers' dollars on them. Unlike many communities, however, Sunnyvale did not abandon its recreational programs; it turned them into a public enterprise. Instead of living almost entirely off tax revenues, the enterprise would have to rely increasingly on its sales to customers. It would have to compete with businesses also chasing the recreation dollar.

Several years earlier, reinventors in New Zealand used a similar approach to shake up their bureaucracies. Government departments there produced aviation, rail, mail, communications, hotel, banking, insurance, shipping, and weather forecasting services, plus electricity, coal, and forest products. The departments were rarely as efficient as private businesses. Some were notorious monuments to waste: many lost money year after year. Beginning in 1987, the government made them state-owned enterprises (SOEs): it withdrew monopoly status from all but two, and it forced all of them to earn their keep from sales to customers.

pp. 164–167

At about the same time, the U.S. Congress did much the same thing to the General Service Administration's Federal Supply Service (FSS), a mammoth internal provider of office supplies. It took away FSS's monopoly and its appropriation, giving its customers—other government agencies—credit cards they could use to buy from FSS or from its private competitors. It even turned over one FSS region to a private office supply company to serve as a competitive benchmark for the rest of the organization. "When suddenly forced to confront head-to-head competition with the giant national office supply discounters, there was a rude awakening," remembers Gerald Turetsky, then assistant regional administrator for Region 2 in New York. "It was like being thrown into an ice-cold shower with your clothes on."

Call it the shock of the marketplace. That's what Turetsky's FSS, Sunnyvale's Leisure Services unit, and New Zealand's SOEs experienced: the "ice-cold" impact of having their survival depend for the first time on pleasing customers and besting competitors. Just like a business, some might say. Yes, but not exactly.

Like businesses, public enterprises have markets and customers, prices and profits, and financial bottom lines. This is an enormous change for government managers accustomed to operating in a bureaucratic environment. The rules are entirely different; customers are powerful, and financial performance is a life-and-death issue. That's why New Zealand's SOEs laid off half their workers; to compete, they had to cut costs. It's why Sunnyvale's recreation department invested in research about its customers. And it's why the FSS began to compare its services with Fortune 100 companies, killed off unprofitable product lines, and negotiated long-term agreements with its contractors. It's also why public enterprises often hire top managers from the private sector.

But some things about public enterprises don't change. Most important, the government still owns them; their assets and income are public property. As a result, they remain under the ultimate control of elected officials. The degree of direct control that politicians exercise may vary greatly, from *laissez faire* to constant intrusions—an issue we will return to shortly.

WHEN TO USE ENTERPRISE MANAGEMENT

Most government organizations that produce services that can be sold to their customers can be subjected to enterprise management. It can be applied to agencies, such as Sunnyvale's recreation department, that serve external customers, as well as to government's "internal" providers: agencies that supply other public organizations with printing, vehicle maintenance and fleets, data processing, and other products and services.

Definitions, p. 119

But because it relies so heavily on markets, enterprise management is not appropriate for every public activity. Policy, compliance, and regulatory functions exist to benefit the citizenry as a whole, not to provide goods and services to specific consumers. They should not be charged to paying customers, nor held to market tests.

In addition, there are some services that should not be operated as enterprises funded by customers. This is true if:

- A service serves the public interest more than any specific internal or external customers (examples include national defense, public health services, and fire prevention).
- A service cannot be charged to customers, because nonpayers cannot be excluded (a municipal park without gates, for instance).
- Some customers who use the service cannot afford it, officials want the service to be available to all, and the only efficient or effective way to accomplish this is to provide it free or at a discount for all.

Some services are "natural monopolies," because they are more efficiently provided by one central source than by many. Sewer and water services are examples. These can still be organized as enterprises, but as regulated monopolies, like private utilities, rather than competitive businesses. They can be made accountable to their customers by placing customer representatives on their boards of directors, or through regulation by public commissions.

THE POWER OF ENTERPRISE MANAGEMENT

Forcing public agencies into a competitive marketplace changes their behavior almost overnight, because they *must* please their customers to survive. Suddenly, they have entirely new challenges: finding out what customers want, learning what competitors are offering, and reducing costs so their prices will be competitive. But this is just the tip of the iceberg: public enterprises eventually take on most of the management characteristics of businesses. Sunnyvale's Leisure Services unit invented new recreation services, marketed them to customers, and entered into business partnerships with the school district. The FSS developed a business plan and an activity-based accounting system to track costs. New Zealand's enterprises sold assets and borrowed money.

When the FSS was thrown into the marketplace after more than four decades as a monopoly, some observers thought it was a dead duck. "The folks on [Capitol] Hill said we'd soon be out of business," remembers FSS commissioner Frank Pugliese. "But we set out to prove them wrong." By 1996, the organization was selling products and services for 30 percent less than its competitors, on average. Annual sales were $13 billion. Year after year, customers of Turetsky's Region 2 rated its services a 10 on a scale of 1 to 10.

Before Sunnyvale's Leisure Services unit had to compete in the marketplace for its funds, about 75 percent of its money came from tax dollars. By

2000, taxpayers provided only about 20 percent; sales to customers brought in the rest. The reduction had saved the city millions of dollars.

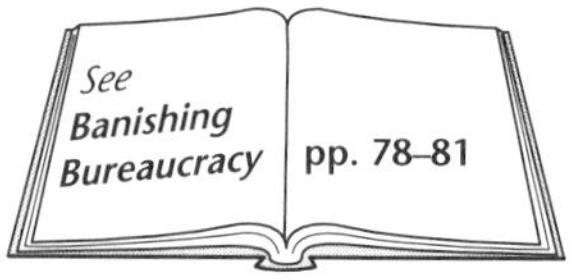

In New Zealand, as we reported in *Banishing Bureaucracy*, the SOEs increased their revenues by 15 percent and quadrupled their profits in their first five years in existence. In 1992, they paid roughly $1 billion in dividends and taxes to the government.

Enterprise management is so powerful because it combines four strategies: Core, Consequences, Customer, and Control. It uncouples public organizations, creates consequences for their financial performance, makes them

OTHER ADVANTAGES OF ENTERPRISE MANAGEMENT

- ***Enterprise management makes agencies directly accountable to their customers.*** A public enterprise's success or failure depends on its customers' decisions. . . . In contrast, managed competition and performance management rely on decisions by government officials.
- ***Enterprise management forces continual improvement, because the competition is constant; it doesn't just happen at contract or review time.*** Agencies that compete for contracts have to beat the competition—but only once every few years. Agencies that must meet performance standards also face only periodic reviews. . . .
- ***Enterprise management empowers public enterprises to make the long-term financial decisions necessary to maximize value for their customers. . . .*** Because they retain part of their earnings, depreciate assets, and borrow money, they can make the long-term investments in technology, training, and productivity improvements that are so difficult in the public sector.
- ***Enterprise management saves money because it is simple to administer.*** It creates competition without creating a time-consuming bidding process to administer.
- ***Finally, enterprise management radically simplifies the politics of improving performance.*** No one has to vote to eliminate or privatize an enterprise activity that is not performing well; the competitive market takes care of it. . . . No one has to choose which bid wins a contract; no one has to defend the contracting process from cries of favoritism; and no one has to withstand a lobbying assault from disappointed contractors. Customers decide who offers the best deal, not administrators and politicians.

—From *Banishing Bureaucracy*, pp. 138–139

accountable to their customers, and gives them control over their own operations, typically exempting them from bureaucratic administrative controls. This gives it enormous advantages over the other two consequences approaches.

PITFALLS TO AVOID: WHY SOME PUBLIC ENTERPRISES HAVE A POOR TRACK RECORD

Not all public enterprises have been as successful as those in Sunnyvale and New Zealand. Often, organizations are called public corporations but are protected from real consequences and are not given the freedom and flexibility they need to succeed. To benefit from the power of enterprise management, you need to use all four of the strategies it draws on. The following flaws in implementation are all too common.

- ***Government enterprises often face minimal or no competitive pressure.*** Many public enterprises are designed as statutory monopolies and therefore do not face competition. Even when they are not explicit monopolies, they often enjoy such substantial regulatory advantages that no competitors can emerge to take them on; the barriers to entry are too high. Before New Zealand's reforms, for example, the government's railway freight services benefited from the high rates that regulators imposed on its competitors, the private trucking companies. Public businesses also enjoy financial advantages: they pay no taxes and obtain free capital from the government.
- ***Government businesses are not always held accountable for their performance.*** Most public enterprises collect very little data that can be used to analyze their commercial performance. In New Zealand, as former finance minister Roger Douglas points out, their "information systems were designed to help government ration the annual resources voted to State-owned enterprises, not measure the value of what they were producing." In addition, most public businesses blend together the costs and benefits of their commercial and social activities. "This," says Robert Anderson, a consultant for the World Bank, "inevitably leads to a complex monitoring system that is not likely to produce clear, unambiguous measures of performance." Finally, the private sector has no reason to monitor the performance of public enterprises the way it does that of private firms offering stock or seeking to borrow funds.

  It is also difficult to assign accountability to government managers if they have little control over the resources they use. Central agencies often control personnel, purchasing, and budgeting decisions. As Douglas found, "The authority delegated to managers of State businesses was therefore extremely limited. They were quite fairly able to evade all responsibility for the success or failure of the enterprises they were supposed to be running."
- ***Government businesses seldom offer effective performance incentives to managers and employees.*** Government bureaucracies do not usually reward managers or employees for improving performance. Managers have

reasons to spend more money and hire more staff, not to increase efficiency. Their "status and personal advancement," says Douglas, are "directly dependent on the number of employees working under them in their departments."

• ***Government businesses usually are required to pursue social as well as commercial goals.*** Elected officials ask them to provide services that cannot meet market tests, such as delivering a letter anywhere from Maine to Hawaii for 33 cents. These mandates send conflicting signals to the organizations' managers, who wonder whether succeeding as a business is really a priority. They end up not focusing exclusively on economic efficiency and financial performance. And when they have financial problems they have an easy scapegoat: they blame their social obligations.

Often the conflict between commercial and social goals leads the government business to distort its prices. Some "cross-subsidize," overcharging one customer to cover the cost of undercharging another. For example, rural postal services cost more than services to denser urban areas, so urban customers subsidize rural customers. Postal services rarely calculate or make public the true costs of each service, so no one can tell if the social objective can be achieved more efficiently some other way.

• ***Government businesses often face intervention from elected officials who want to override market signals.*** Most politicians take a "hands-on" approach to public enterprises. "Over the years," writes Douglas, state businesses "had often been required to hold prices below cost for favoured political constituencies. Successive governments had targeted capital expenditures to politically sensitive regions."

The railroads "were run partly as an employment agency," adds Richard Prebble, one of his colleagues in the cabinet.

> *Every election year the general manager of the New Zealand Railways got a call from the minister. He was told he was going to hire people. He was given the number and told where.*

Enterprise management, when properly used, changes these realities. It makes public organizations accountable to their customers, lets them focus on their commercial goals, and insulates them from most political pressures. This last task is a constant struggle, however.

MANAGING ENTERPRISES: FOR PROFITS OR POLITICS?

Public business enterprises live—squirm, really—on the horns of a dilemma. On the one hand, they are supposed to make money. On the other hand, the politicians who govern them sometimes impose other priorities on them. In short, they are caught between profits and politics.

See *Banishing Bureaucracy* pp. 139–141

In *Banishing Bureaucracy* we described this fundamental, perpetual tension in implementing the enterprise management approach. It boils down to deciding who will control a public enterprise—its managers or elected officials—and how completely to thrust the enterprise into the marketplace. Decisions about these issues vary case by case, and they often are the subject of continuing political tussles.

A closer look at the history of the U.S. Postal Service, the nation's largest government-owned business, illuminates some of the critical choices to be made in balancing profits and politics. Since it was made a public enterprise in 1971, it has been trapped in an ongoing identity crisis. Sometimes it has been a cumbersome, rule-bound, politicized federal bureaucracy. At other times it has been an aggressive business competitor that is—with $56 billion in revenues in 1996—bigger than many Fortune 500 firms.

The postal service's political face shows in ways that give it competitive advantages and disadvantages. The enterprise continues to have a monopoly over regular, "nonurgent" first-class mail. Indeed, poachers in this market are subject to criminal penalties. This advantage is the basis of the service's financial success. However, the service is required to meet noncommercial objectives. It must provide six-day-a-week delivery to every mailbox in the country at the same price. It must operate thousands of branches, many of them in rural areas, that steadily lose money. It also subsidizes the cost of delivering third-class advertising mail out of revenues from first-class mail.

In competitive markets, the postal service has had a rough time. Competition from private companies has steadily increased. In 1970, package deliveries by United Parcel Service exceeded parcel post deliveries by the post office for the first time. In 1981, Federal Express took leadership in the overnight delivery market. By 1986, private competitors were dominating two-day delivery service. By the early 1990s, UPS was delivering 10 times the volume of parcels the postal service was delivering. By 1997, private companies claimed 96 percent of the overnight delivery market. At the same time, growth in faxes, e-mail, long-distance telephone calls, and computerized billing had completely transformed the postal service's marketplace.

In recent years, the postal service has fought back. In 1996, it went after a larger portion of the $7 billion market for two-and three-day deliveries by advertising its Priority Mail service. Its $20 million television ad campaign attacked competitors Federal Express and UPS—an unprecedented act by a federal agency. Federal Express and the National Advertising Division of the Council of Better Business Bureaus filed lawsuits, claiming false advertising and unfair competition. Meanwhile, the ads helped boost Priority Mail volume by 20 percent.

But there was a price to pay. Loren Smith, the postal service vice president who championed the advertising, was forced to resign by the service's governing board, because he overspent the agency's advertising budget. Smith denounced his critics as people wedded to postal service traditions.

In 1997, Postmaster Marvin Runyon asked the governing board of presidential appointees to give him greater price flexibility and to allow him to develop new products, such as mail packing services and an electronic "postmark" as proof of an e-mail delivery. His requests touched off a furor. Congressmen warned that the service should not compete with businesses, such as Mail Boxes, Etc., that offer packing services. The American Postal Workers Union expressed anxiety about changes that might affect its workers' bargaining power and job security. Business competitors argued that the postal service would never compete successfully in markets that increasingly rely on sophisticated technology.

As this story shows, there are many choices on the path from inefficient government bureaucracy to money-making public enterprise. You must decide exactly what you will put into the marketplace—an entire organization with many product and service lines, or just a specific product or service? You must determine how far the organization or service will be thrust into the competitive environment; will it have any government protections and advantages? You must judge how soon you expect the enterprise to become financially self-sufficient—quickly or over the long run? Finally, you must choose the degree of direct political control you want over the enterprise. In some cases, elected officials handcuff managers. As a World Bank study found, "Some governments have refused to give SOE managers the power to react to the new environment of heightened competition and hard budgets with appropriate measures, which may include laying off excess workers, seeking out cheaper suppliers, eliminating money-losing services or seeking new markets."

In using the tools of enterprise management, these choices are unavoidable. When elected officials create public enterprises, they lose some control over their operation. They have to decide just how much they can let go. In return, they get genuine financial and performance accountability and genuine savings. But they can no longer micromanage these organizations; indeed, they no longer even appropriate their budgets. They often experience this as a serious loss of control and are reluctant to let it happen.

The solution is to convince officeholders that in addition to saving them money, enterprise management will increase the real accountability of public organizations. Although legislative committees will no longer tell public enterprises how much to spend or what to spend it on, they can be sure those organizations will have powerful incentives to provide what their customers want at the lowest possible prices.

ENTERPRISE MANAGEMENT: LESSONS LEARNED

1. Give enterprises the flexibility to manage in a businesslike way.

Rigid rules and restrictions will quickly kill most public enterprises, because they must compete with private firms. (They won't kill monopolies, but they will hobble their efforts to improve quality and lower costs.) To capture the benefits of enterprise management, legislative committees, budget offices, and personnel agencies must eliminate things like appropriation limits, personnel ceilings, slow hiring processes, and restrictions on carrying funds over from one year to the next. They must allow enterprise funds to invest their resources themselves, retain some of their profits, and take some losses. They must have faith that competition and rate negotiations will control costs for them.

When Karen Sorber and Ronald Straight published an analysis of the barriers to internal enterprise management in the federal government, they reported that budget, finance, and personnel rules were the worst obstacles. Similarly, the Australian Finance Department concluded that the government's personnel system hindered progress toward commercialization:

> *It needs to be recognized that for some public sector service providers, their capacity to operate fully in commercial mode is limited because they are still required to follow APS [Australian Public Service] pay, conditions and practices. This can have a couple of adverse implications. One is that the organisation cannot compete on an equal footing. The second is that they may lose skilled staff to the private sector because of a lack of flexibility in remuneration levels.*

2. Give enterprises full control over their businesses.

When you make something like a recreation department an enterprise, don't leave functions like maintenance in the hands of other public agencies. Former Indianapolis mayor Stephen Goldsmith tells a story about his city's golf courses that illustrates the problem:

> *The golf pros, who were closest to the customers, supposedly oversaw golf operations. But that did not mean much when the greens were mowed by the same parks employees who painted playground equipment, and the golf carts were maintained by the same people who repaired garbage trucks. During one walk-through I asked the pro at the city's premium course how he could let the restrooms slip into such awful condition. His response brought it all home. "The restrooms," he noted sardonically, "are maintained by* ***your*** *parks employees."*

3. Make sure the legislature or council understands enterprise management and buys in to the basic "deal"—more accountability in return for more flexibility.

Because they no longer appropriate the budgets of public enterprises, elected officials often feel that they have lost control. Using the example of internal enterprise management in Minnesota, Michael Barzelay explains:

pp. 174–182

> *Legislators were notoriously suspicious of revolving funds. During budget hearings, revolving funds were discussed only briefly since appropriations were not made to them. . . .*
>
> *For some legislators, in fact, the spectre of converting more operations to revolving funds intensified their existing sense of powerlessness to influence the operation of state government. Revolving fund financing of DOA [Department of Administration] activities meant that the legislature could not control what state government spent as a whole on computing services or printing, for instance. Moreover, because state agencies were granted some discretion in shifting funds among budgeted line items, an agency might choose to purchase large quantities of some DOA products without obtaining specific legislative approval, and DOA would have every incentive to meet the "consumer demand." Many legislators worried that an increased utilization of revolving funds would reduce legislative oversight on all fronts.*

The solution was to convince legislators that enterprise management would both save them money and increase the real accountability of enterprise units. Legislative committees still exercise oversight over enterprise funds, but the tools they use change. Instead of passing annual line-item appropriations, they review profit-and-loss statements, quarterly financial statements, and business plans. These are far superior tools for assessing the value public service entities are creating for customers and taxpayers.

4. Create authentic mechanisms to ensure that public enterprises are financially accountable.

These include accrual accounting, activity-based costing, profit-and-loss statements, quarterly financial statements, business plans, interest charges on loans, and in-lieu-of-tax payments. Unless you can prove that enterprises have real financial integrity, it will be difficult to survive the inevitable political pressures that arise. Private vendors will charge that public enterprises are not including all their overhead costs in their prices, for example. Others will argue that public agencies are given free credit by the government. To withstand the resulting assault in the legislature or council, you must prove that the playing field is level.

pp. 208–210

The shift to activity-based costing can be difficult. It often requires a private consultant and up to a year of work. Minnesota short-circuited this process by simply using the "indirect cost plan" the federal government required states to develop when they received federal grants. Because this method of calculating indirect costs was familiar to the finance office and the legislature—and because the federal government used it to audit grant spending—it quickly passed muster.

5. *Secure buy-in from the budget office as well as from elected officials.*

Enterprise management changes the financial oversight role of the budget office (or finance department or treasury). It takes away that office's authority to control public enterprises' spending, for example. But the trade-off—dramatic spending reductions and performance improvements without privatization—can be quite attractive to budget offices, once they understand it.

pp. 382–388

6. *Help public enterprises listen to their customers.*

The most important skill that ensures survival is the ability to understand what customers want. This is foreign territory to many public organizations. When he joined the Minnesota Department of Administration as deputy commissioner, Babak Armajani remembers, "I'd ask many people in DOA who their customer was. Many had no idea." So he began requiring the managers of each service unit to meet with their customers. They heard an earful. The process was painful, but it began to wake people up to the needs of their customers.

Jim Masch, the fleet manager in Sunnyvale, did something similar. "When I arrived in 1982," he remembers, "there was some conflict between our guys and the customers." Employees were thinking more about "knocking down the complaints" than about listening to their customers. "It just became the shop pointing at the users and the users yelling at the shop."

So Masch immediately set up liaison meetings with the shop's customers. "Every manager who is a support manager has a fear of getting all his customers together," he admits. But Masch did it once a month for years. When his customers had complaints, he and two of his supervisors would verbally commit to a date when the problem would be solved.

Today Masch makes it a point to see all his customers—about a dozen people—daily. The shop also does a regular customer survey. He would still be holding the monthly meetings, he says, but the daily communication has become so good that there aren't any big issues left to deal with at the end of the month.

7. *Never forget that even when elected officials are no longer your customers, they remain important stakeholders.*

Accountability to those elected by the citizens will always remain an important part of the management equation. Public enterprises must give elected officials—both legislators and executives—the information they need to be sure the public interest is being served. The tools may change from line item budgets to profit-and-loss statements, but the need remains.

TOOLS FOR ENTERPRISE MANAGEMENT

Corporatization turns government organizations into publicly owned businesses that are semi-independent from government. Public corporations focus on business goals, such as generating profits and returns on investments. Usually they have nongovernment directors and top managers who set the organization's direction and policies and are accountable for its performance. Often they operate outside of the government's budget, personnel, planning, and procurement systems. See below.

Enterprise Funds, also known as *revolving funds, trading funds,* or *enterprise centers,* are government-owned business activities funded with customer revenues rather than tax dollars. However, enterprise funds are not converted into public corporations with independent governance. See p. 169.

Internal Enterprise Management is the use of enterprise management to make internal service units accountable to their customers, the line agencies they serve. See p. 174.

CORPORATIZATION

In the mid-1980s, New Zealand's post office, with 40,000 employees, was the nation's largest employer. It delivered the mail, provided and serviced all of the country's telephones, and ran a savings bank. When Richard Prebble became a cabinet minister for the Labor Party, the post office was in his portfolio, so he took a look at its operations.

"I was absolutely horrified by what I found," Prebble remembers. "It was so inefficient that it was crippling the country." The Postbank was bankrupt. The mail service was losing nearly $40 million a year in New Zealand dollars, which were worth 50–70 percent of U.S. dollars in the late 1980s. And the telephone service was worse. It took an average of six weeks to get a phone installed. The post office had bought so much phone equipment that most of it was obsolete before it could be installed.

Prebble surveyed business leaders, and a large majority of them said the telephone system was holding their businesses back. "That was a bit of a shock," he recalls. "We asked the post office what was wrong and they said there was nothing that a billion dollars couldn't fix." Then the Post Office Department asked Prebble to approve a large public expenditure for new equipment and facilities. Although it would strain the government budget, he was inclined to agree with the request—until he asked the department managers how many employees they had.

"They couldn't answer the question," Prebble remembers. "I said, 'Give us figures next week.'" The numbers stunned him: the department employed 1,100 more people than the management plan authorized by ministers just three months earlier. Prebble concluded that "this monster was out of control."

Prebble and his Labor Party colleagues decided that the nation's troubled economy could no longer tolerate the chronically poor performance of its post office and other government businesses. Taken together, they produced one-eighth of the nation's economic output. Their inefficiency was a drag on New Zealand's overall economic performance. Labor was not prepared to sell these public businesses into private hands, but it did want to tackle the main reasons they performed so poorly. So its leaders decided to create public corporations that would be truly commercial. The government would provide them with initial capital—equity and short-term loans—and would expect a market rate of return on its investment. At the outset, these SOEs would be wholly owned by the government. They would be governed by independent boards that, along with their top managers, would control all of their operational decisions.

Labor also designed the SOEs to overcome or at least minimize the factors that cause government businesses to perform so badly. To end the debilitating conflict between social and commercial goals, Finance Minister Roger Douglas insisted that SOEs pursue only commercial ends. Labor separated government's commercial from its noncommercial activities. For example, it created an SOE to run the government's television network, but a separate Broadcasting Commission funded television programs that promoted the nation's identity and culture. The SOE law, passed in 1986, required SOEs to try to be as efficient and profitable as comparable businesses. It also forced the government to pay for any noncommercial activities it asked SOEs to undertake.

To ensure that SOEs would face competition, Labor ended statutory monopolies, removed regulatory barriers to competition, and stripped SOEs of unfair business advantages. The new entities had to pay taxes and had to borrow money from commercial lenders rather than receiving taxpayer funds.

To minimize attempts to influence the actions of SOEs politically, Labor assigned all relationships with SOEs to just two ministers, rather than spreading them across the cabinet. The minister for state-owned enterprises and the minister of finance had no responsibility for social issues; their role was to advance the commercial success of the new entities. These "shareholding ministers" negotiated with each SOE board an annual statement of corporate intent that specified the corporation's business activities, its financial and other performance targets, and the dividend the government expected from it. It did not deal with operational issues, including prices and investments; these were left up to the boards. In addition, Labor kept politicians off the SOE boards; instead, it appointed businesspeople with the expertise necessary to monitor their performance.

To give SOEs flexibility, Labor exempted them from government administrative systems. Their boards were free to hire and fire top managers. These executives were free of government's civil service and personnel systems, procurement policies, and budgeting systems; they had full control over their organization's resources. To stimulate private sector scrutiny of SOE operations, the law allowed the government to sell nonvoting stock in SOEs.

Lastly, to provide managers with performance incentives, Labor permitted the SOEs to tie financial rewards for managers to their organization's performance.

The Results of Corporatization in New Zealand

Until February 8, 1988, local post offices in New Zealand seemed to be immortal. Before then, no politician had either a reason or the nerve to close any of these cherished institutions. But on that date, Richard Prebble signed a death warrant for more than a third of the nation's 1,200 post offices. He even closed half of the post offices in his own parliamentary district.

The simultaneous demise of these post offices, most of them in rural areas, resulted directly from the passage of the SOE Act less than a year earlier. Labor had separated the Post Office Department into three government-owned corporations: one each for mail, telecommunications, and banking. In the new postal SOE's effort to become profitable, it had identified 600 post offices that were losing money; they accounted for only 5 percent of its total business. The SOE directors had announced that without a subsidy they would close 432 of them, so the government had agreed to provide about $30 million (U.S.) to keep them open for a year, while it decided if they met an indispensable social need.

In late 1987, Labor decided not to provide additional funds. Making the real cost of the subsidy visible had forced Parliament to decide if this was really the best use for the money. They decided it wasn't, so Prebble closed the offices.

While the post office still provided some delivery services and community mailboxes, private stamp retailers opened up in the 432 rural areas. Still, Prebble recalls, "There was considerable public outrage at the closures. Many people have still not forgiven me." But a parliamentary study found that no community had been adversely affected by the change, and many were getting better service.

Within a year, the postal service was registering solid financial gains. It moved from an annual loss of more than $25 million to a profit of more than

$50 million. It cut staffing by 20 percent, from 12,000 to 9,800. It began a new, next-day delivery service. It improved on-time delivery of high-priority mail from 80 percent to more than 95 percent. By 1992, it had cut staffing by 30 percent and paid about $125 million in taxes and dividends to the national treasury.

In similar fashion, the Postbank SOE cut staffing by 30 percent, reduced retail outlets by 40 percent, and turned an expected loss into a profit. The telephone SOE, which gradually lost its monopoly over phone equipment and services, cut overall prices by 20 percent. The average wait for telephone installation dropped from six weeks to two days.

These improvements were comparable to those registered by the other SOEs. "The gains in efficiency brought about by these structural changes dumbfounded even the most skeptical opponents," says Douglas.

Encouraged by this enormous success, Labor continued creating SOEs—and when the National Party came to power in 1990, it followed suit.

Corporatization: Lessons Learned

New Zealand pushed corporatization at a breakneck pace—much more aggressively than most governments do. It demonstrated that government businesses can accomplish leaps in productivity and quality of service—when they are allowed to focus exclusively on business outcomes and abandon bureaucratic ways. In the process, its leaders learned some important lessons.

1. The success of public enterprises depends on getting very good people to govern and manage them.

"Quality outcomes start with quality people," says Douglas. "Getting the policies right will not be enough unless you also get quality people into all the strategic positions at the right time." By avoiding tokenism and the test of party affiliation, he adds, Labor recruited "some of the country's most dynamic and experienced business people as directors."

2. The price of corporatization is usually significant cuts in public employment.

Many public employees lost their jobs as New Zealand's government businesses sought competitiveness and profitability. From 1987 to 1992 the seven larger SOEs cut their staffs by 53 percent. In Australia, government businesses reduced their payrolls significantly as well.

With so many public employees involved, New Zealand could not absorb them into vacancies in the rest of government. It provided laid-off workers with severance payments. As we discuss in Chapter Five, there are other ways to soften the blow when workers lose their jobs—including retraining and placement in private jobs.

pp. 199–200

3. *You can't always keep the politicians' hands off of the business.*

Labor tried to minimize the potential for political interference in SOE decisions, but it was not always successful—even within it own ranks. The Labor-controlled parliament balked at further reductions in money-losing rural mail services. When the postal SOE's board of directors decided to raise the price of rural delivery, the National Party, which had taken power in 1990 and represented a large rural constituency, immediately attacked it. "All hell broke loose within the government, which was trailing in the polls," observed Douglas. The price increase, he wrote, was "a heaven-sent opportunity to win electoral credit by attacking the avarice of the company."

When the electricity SOE also raised prices, National Party leaders attacked the SOE model and threatened to fire the company's managers. Overall, Douglas observes, the political environment for SOEs became highly charged under the National Party Government.

> *State corporations were subjected to annual investigation by parliamentary select committees with the power to ask questions about any detail of operations, well beyond the limits allowed [for private companies]. . . . Information was sought with the sole intention of turning it to discredit the SOE. An atmosphere of confrontation was deliberately fomented by the government to deter SOEs from taking politically difficult decisions.*

In 1992 the chairman of the postal SOE, Michael Morris, warned that the political skirmishing would lead the company and the government to sacrifice "economic efficiencies and sales proceeds which would otherwise have been available to improve the nation's competitive position."

pp. 93–101

4. *Corporatization is not as powerful a remedy for inefficiency as is the sale of government's business assets.*

Corporatization does not shift public businesses fully into the marketplace, as we have seen. In addition to suffering political interference, their directors and managers are immune from the threat of takeover, which so influences private corporate behavior. Nor do they have shares on the market and private investment analysts who aggressively track and assess their performance. Public corporations are unlikely to slide into bankruptcy, since elected officials who want to avoid the embarrassment of market failures are all too willing to bail them out at taxpayer expense. Thus, says Douglas, they "are under significantly less pressure than private sector companies to maintain competitive levels of performance."

Douglas and his Labor Party allies concluded that state-owned enterprises should serve mostly as a "halfway house" to privatization. By wringing inefficiencies out of government operations, SOEs paved the way for selling public assets to the private sector. In 1988, the Labor Government began to sell some of its SOEs to the highest bidders.

RESOURCES FOR CORPORATIZATION

Roger Douglas. *Unfinished Business.* Auckland, New Zealand: Random House New Zealand, 1993. See Chapter Eight, "SOEs—A Half-way House." In this excellent analysis of New Zealand's reinvention in the 1980s, Douglas tells how he—a Labor Party minister—came to recognize the importance of enterprise management and designed New Zealand's state-owned enterprise strategy.

World Bank. *Bureaucrats in Business: The Economics and Politics of Government Ownership.* New York: Oxford University Press, 1995. An insightful study on the track record of public corporations around the globe.

ENTERPRISE FUNDS

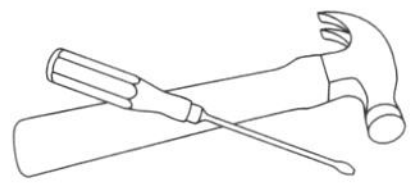

***Enterprise Funds*, also known as *revolving funds*, *trading funds*, or *enterprise centers*, are government-owned business activities funded with customer revenues rather than tax dollars. However, enterprise funds are not converted into public corporations with independent governance.**

When Sunnyvale turned its Leisure Services unit into an enterprise fund, as we described earlier, it saved the taxpayers millions of dollars. But cutting the city budget's support for the agency was only part of the story. Although its tax support declined, the Leisure Services unit grew rapidly—by increasing its base of paying customers. "A lot of cities have been cutting recreation services and loading on new fees," said then–city manager Tom Lewcock. "They find they end up doing less. We've been doing the opposite—we're growing the programs."

It took a "huge amount of market research," new service offerings and "smart pricing" to increase the organization's market share, Lewcock said. "We are competing with zillions of businesses for the recreation dollar, but we offer things that others don't."

The key was listening closely to the customers. Shortly after Parks and Recreation Director John Christian arrived in Sunnyvale, he sent a team of managers, frontline employees, and professionals to Disney's customer service training program. He then made them an internal customer service training team. He also began sending similar teams on benchmarking trips, to learn from other cities and counties.

One of the first innovations to result was a customer satisfaction guarantee. Christian described it this way: "No matter what we do, if you're not satisfied, you get your money back." They also shifted from offering programs on a quarterly basis, with three-week breaks in between, to continuous programming. And rather than forcing people to come in and reregister for a continuing program, they now assume people will continue in the next session. "We'll assume you're registered, and we'll bill you," said Christian. "If you want to continue, just send it in."

Because the schools were in a fiscal squeeze and were cutting back on things like music and art, Leisure Services developed a series of high-quality after-school classes for middle and high school students. Acting as a broker, it recruited dozens of other organizations—from community colleges to music schools to dance studios—to run the programs. "The parents—our customers—say, 'Don't you dare take those away,'" said Lewcock.

Leisure Services also cut business deals with the schools. One lets the city use school playing fields for its programs for 25 years, in exchange for maintaining and redeveloping the land. Another involves the school's indoor facilities. Whenever the gyms, auditoriums, and multipurpose rooms are not reserved for school use, the city can rent the space out to the public. The schools get 20 percent of the fees collected by the city. The arrangement not only increases use of school facilities, it provides citizens with one-stop shopping for facilities.

Christian credited all these innovations to the fact that Leisure Services had to sell programs to its customers to generate 80 percent of its revenues. "That has changed our way of operating," he said.

> *We have found ways to do business differently, particularly with partnerships. We're forced to look at the bottom line. People talk about bottom-line stuff, people talk about being market driven, people talk about being customer service driven.*

The city's success with its Leisure Services enterprise prompted it to develop another public business in 1996: selling services to people who are researching patents. The city's patent library decided to install a video link to the Patent and Trademark Office in Washington, which provides powerful new computers and services such as teleconferences with Washington experts. As Sunnyvale's patent library becomes the most advanced in its region, it plans to phase out tax subsidies and expand services to paying customers.

Local governments have long used enterprise funds to finance operations at convention centers, golf courses, airports, and the like. They institute user fees, segregate the accounting of those revenues from the government's general fund, and use the customer revenue to support the services. By shifting costs to service users, the tool allows governments to undertake activities their budgets won't support. Often, however, governments use the tool simply to shift costs. They neither force the enterprise funds to raise all their own revenue nor free them to respond to their customers' needs.

Sunnyvale's enterprise funds are designed to become virtually self-sufficient, and their costs are fully accounted for. They cannot escape the discipline of the marketplace. They are also free to change their day-to-day operations. Christian told Lewcock that he would have to "organize like a business, not a traditional public recreation department,'" Lewcock recalls. "I said, 'John, you can do most anything you want to do. We're going to focus our attention on your bottom line."

Sunnyvale uses enterprise funds mainly to make existing government employees more customer-oriented, cost-conscious, and business-minded. Reinventors also use the tool to start up new activities the government cannot fund by itself. This allows public agencies to create exciting opportunities for public entrepreneurs, as Fox Valley Technical College in Appleton, Wisconsin, discovered.

In the late 1980s, Fox Valley's president, Stanley J. Spanbauer, noticed his calendar was filling up with educators who wanted to learn how his institution was implementing Total Quality Management. "It began to drain our resources, because they were coming in and taking my time and a lot of people's time," he recalls. But Spanbauer had an entrepreneurial bent. Perhaps, he thought, the demand signaled a money-making opportunity for the college. So he created the Quality Institute—a college-sponsored business designed to serve customers from outside the college's enrollment boundary—and signed up two faculty members to run it.

By 1994, as many as 50 Fox Valley staffers were working at least part-time for the institute, conducting seminars, workshops, and training sessions. That year, according to Spanbauer, the institute generated $650,000 in contract fees—enough to cover its costs and return a $28,000 profit to the college.

By the time Spanbauer retired from Fox Valley in 1994, entrepreneurial faculty members had created 16 enterprise centers. Each was a separate business, complete with a business plan and monthly income statements. Each was managed by faculty who controlled their operations. None cost the taxpayer a dime.

Enterprise Funds Versus Corporatization

Unlike public corporations, enterprise funds remain under the control of elected officials and government administrators and stay within the government's traditional institutional framework. Because enterprise funds do not require a separate institutional structure with a governing board and new administrative systems, they can be set up and dismantled with relative ease and speed. However, they can also become the victims of bureaucratic controls that reduce their flexibility, effectiveness, and incentives. In addition, they are more susceptible than public corporations are to intervention by elected officials, who are inevitably tempted to set their prices. In Sunnyvale and many other communities, for example, setting greens fees for public golf courses involves interminable political maneuvering, since elected officials do not want to offend senior citizen golfers.

In general, corporatization is the better tool. But if elected officials swear off controlling prices or services—and if you use business accounting and financing procedures—an enterprise fund will give you most of the advantages of a public corporation.

We have identified only three situations in which we would recommend an enterprise fund over a corporation:

1. *When it is politically impractical to create a corporation.*

2. *When there are public interests at stake that conflict with the bottom line.* For example, in creating an enterprise to operate a park such as Yosemite or Yellowstone, stewardship of the land, water, and wildlife to protect it for future generations would be more important than generating a return on investment. The recent return of wolves to Yellowstone provides a classic example: a public corporation driven to break even would rarely spend the money to do such a thing; hence its decisions might sacrifice the quality of the park for future generations.

For this reason, elected officials might want to keep some control over park policy, while sacrificing efficiency and return on their investment. This would be perfectly appropriate. It could also be done by having elected officials control the board of the corporation and by providing subsidies for stewardship purposes. But the inevitable tensions might be easier to manage if the park remained an enterprise fund.

3. *When important synergies would be lost by moving the activity into a corporation.* Enterprise funds operate inside public agencies or departments and report to their directors. Hence it is easier to ensure that their strategies are congruent with those of the rest of the organization than it would be if they were corporatized. A state might want to make sure that its telecommunications network used hardware and software standards that were compatible with other technologies used by state agencies, for instance. Public corporations

would care far less about such issues than about their bottom lines, so resolving them would require extensive negotiations and formal contracts or partnerships. Collaboration with enterprise funds would normally be far easier.

Using Enterprise Funds: Do's and Don'ts

pp. 161–164

All the general lessons outlined earlier apply to enterprise funds. The following "do's and don'ts" round out the picture.

Create a business plan with measurable objectives. "You must know what your markets are and put a business strategy together with customer input," says Lewcock. The plan must be clear about what the enterprise is supposed to accomplish. The best way to do this is to articulate measurable objectives such as return on investment, percentage of operating costs that must come from customer revenues, and customer satisfaction levels. In addition, Lewcock says, set high targets for the fund's service levels, so it cannot make a profit by cutting back on its services—particularly if it is not in a very competitive market. Demand for golf courses so far exceeds supply in many places, for instance, that a public golf course could maximize profits by cutting its staff and letting the quality of the course suffer.

Change organizational structures, processes, and administrative systems to fit the business you're in. Government's control systems impede commercial behaviors. If you want enterprise funds to succeed in the marketplace, you have to change those systems. In the process, give them powerful incentives to improve their performance. Let them keep all or a portion of their profits to invest in equipment, training, and gainsharing bonuses.

pp. 404–426

pp. 237–243

Don't plunge into enterprise funds; do careful market research first. Playing hunches will more than likely backfire. Starting a new business—even a public enterprise—is risky; most private business start-ups actually fail. Initial success depends in large part on how well you understand the market you are getting into. Take the time to do your homework.

Don't underestimate the anxiety your managers and employees will feel. People in public organizations often resist the change to a commercial basis. Many worry that they will fail. Some argue that the organization is losing its public purpose. They will need help making the transition—strong leaders willing to change the way the organization operates and its basic culture.

Don't shoot for instant success; build the business deliberately. "Do not attempt to move from your present business environment to the new one overnight," cautions Lewcock. "People need time to understand how to change the organization, and to begin to work with customers." Some enterprise funds, such as golf courses, can turn a profit their first year. Others may take more time. Some may need generous start-up loans; others may not.

Don't let elected officials set the prices enterprise funds charge. Many enterprise funds are, in effect, controlled by elected officials, who approve all fee levels and increases, all new services offered, and the like. This destroys the most important value of creating an enterprise fund: its accountability to its customers. The beauty of an enterprise fund is that it can respond to what its customers want, charge what they will pay, and quickly change its service offerings and fees if its customers indicate dissatisfaction. The minute elected officials control new service creation and fee increases, that responsiveness is gone.

In addition, an enterprise fund that can't set its own prices cannot be held accountable for its performance. Rather than being required to prove its value to its customers by making a profit, it can—rightly—blame the council or legislature for its financial problems. As we said earlier in discussing public corporations, if elected officials want to subsidize an activity, they should do so explicitly—not by forcing the entity to keep its prices below its costs.

If an enterprise fund has a monopoly on services, elected officials should set up a mechanism to regulate its prices, just as they would with a private utility. The fund's customers should be part of the process. We suggest a way to do this later in the chapter when we discuss the treatment of monopolies under internal enterprise management.

pp. 177–178

Don't make enterprise funds pay for customers who can't afford the service they are offering. You can always decide to subsidize some customers' access to public services, even when those services are provided on a commercial basis. For example, Sunnyvale offers discounts to senior citizens who use city golf courses, and it waives service fees for "dependent" parents who want their children to attend after-school recreational programs. However, do not make an enterprise fund cover the cost of such subsidies. That would lead to cross-subsidizing, which distorts the fund's pricing, causing it to overcharge some customers to cover the costs of those who don't pay their way. Instead, make the subsidy part of an explicit government appropriation.

INTERNAL ENTERPRISE MANAGEMENT

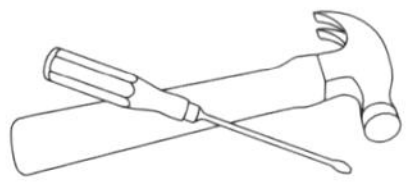

***Internal Enterprise Management* is the use of enterprise management to make internal service units accountable to their customers, the line agencies they serve.**

Government's internal service monopolies—its print shops, personnel offices, information technology offices, maintenance shops, even its vehicle fleets—are notoriously insensitive to their customers' needs. Line managers often detest them. Over the past decade, reinventors at every level of government—from cities like Milwaukee to the national governments of Australia, the U.K., and New Zealand—have used enterprise management to solve this problem.

Reinventing Government told the story of Minnesota's Department of Administration, which pioneered the development of this tool during the 1980s.

See *Reinventing Government* pp. 90–92

Led by Commissioner Sandra Hale and Deputy Commissioner Babak Armajani, the department took ideas that were already in some use, both in Minnesota and elsewhere, refined them, and knit them into a coherent whole they called enterprise management.

Definitions, p. 119

As with external enterprise management, the first step in implementing this tool is borrowed from the Core Strategy: uncoupling steering and rowing. Many internal staff units combine policy, compliance, and service functions. In Minnesota, for example, the same organization that sold agencies time on its mainframe computer also told them whether they could buy their own computers. The conflict of interest was obvious, and most Minnesota agencies resented it. Many suspected that the Information Management Bureau denied purchase requests to make sure it could sell enough mainframe time to meet its budget.

Armajani and his staff solved the problem by dividing the organization. They put the policy and compliance function in a new Information Policy Office, which set standards for computer systems and reviewed agency purchase requests. They put mainframe and other information technology services in a separate InterTechnologies Group.

They called policy and compliance functions "leadership activities." These benefited the citizens of Minnesota more than individual state agencies—by providing standards that would guarantee the best value for the dollar, for example. Their real customer was the public at large, represented by the governor and legislature. So Minnesota financed them from the general fund, and both the commissioner of administration and the appropriate legislative committees oversaw their operations. As we argued earlier, policy and compliance functions should not be managed as enterprises operating in markets.

Marketplace Services

Armajani and his colleagues put most internal services into enterprise funds. Armajani wanted to corporatize them, but the administration and legislature were not ready to go that far. (Technically, under generally accepted accounting principles, internal enterprise funds are called internal service funds. Both these and "external" enterprise funds are subsets of a category called "revolving funds." We have chosen to stay with the phrase *enterprise fund,* however, to make it clear that when we talk about internal enterprise funds, we mean organizations that operate on the same principles as external enterprise funds.)

They divided the internal enterprise funds into two groups: those that should face competition from private firms and those that should remain monopolies. The former group, which they labeled "marketplace services," included copy centers, data entry, computer programming, electronic equipment rental, micro graphics, voice mail, electronic mail, internal management consulting, printing,

Central Stores, the motor pool, and some training functions. They made a series of changes to force true market discipline on these funds:

- They allowed state agencies—the customers—to buy these services wherever they chose, from public or private sources.
- They shifted funding for the services from the internal service agencies to the customer agencies and made the former earn all of their revenues from sales to the latter.
- They required marketplace service units to pay the state for all of their overhead, including rent, utilities, and a share of statewide overhead, such as the governor's salary and the attorney general's budget.
- They allowed marketplace units to set their prices, because they were now in competitive markets. If market conditions allowed high profits on some services and kept profits low on others, that was fine.
- They required marketplace units to return a portion of their profits to the general fund, based on an annual business plan negotiated with the department and reviewed by the legislature. These units could invest the rest of their profits in productivity improvements—new equipment, performance rewards, or anything else—as long as they followed guidelines spelled out in their business plans.
- They allowed marketplace units to borrow from the state treasury to make further investments. The Finance Department charged interest and demanded proof that the returns on these investments would be adequate to repay the loans, as any bank would.
- Finally, they allowed marketplace units to carry over all unexpended funds into the next fiscal year. (Since these units now used accrual accounting, their cash balances at the end of a fiscal year were different from their profits or losses.) Previously, managers of these units had joined in the traditional end-of-the-year spending rush—getting rid of all excess cash before the Finance Department could take it back.

The legislature still performed an oversight function, but it no longer controlled marketplace units as it did others—through the appropriations process. Indeed, these units received no appropriations; they made their money by selling to their customers. Nor did the legislature regulate inputs—their prices, staff levels, or investments. Instead, it relied on market competition to ensure that they were providing the best value possible for the dollar. They were free to manage their own operations, to get maximum productivity out of their staff and resources, without interference. If they did a poor job, the consequences were clear: their customers would go elsewhere, and they would shrink or die.

Internal "Utilities"

For some services, monopolies are more efficient than competition. In the private sector these are called utilities, and they have traditionally been used them to operate local telephone and cable television systems and provide water, gas, and electricity. Armajani and his colleagues decided to use the word *utility* to describe internal government services that are more efficiently provided by monopolies. They believed that telephone service for state agencies would be cheaper as a monopoly, for example, because the state could negotiate bigger discounts with private phone companies if everyone were on the same system. In other areas, such as the State Records Center, they wanted to ensure standardization—to make sure all records would be available in the same place, in the same form.

These internal utilities operated under rules similar to those governing marketplace services, but without customer choice of service providers. The legislature shifted appropriations to the customer agencies, leaving the internal utilities as enterprise funds. The agencies could choose what volume of services to buy from utilities but not where to buy them. Instead, Minnesota gave customer agencies a voice in setting prices. Specifically:

- The commissioners of finance and administration set utility prices annually, in negotiation with each utility, after getting advice from customer panels. These panels—normally made up of executives from customer agencies—compared the utilities' rates to those of other public and private providers of similar services and advised the commissioners. They also advised the administration and finance departments on the types of services each utility should produce, the service levels their customers required, and the wisdom of proposed utility investments in new technologies and the like.
- The commissioners exercised control over rates, types of service, and investments by negotiating annual rate packages and reviewing quarterly financial statements. Otherwise, they left the utilities free to manage as they saw fit. The legislature exercised oversight on the same basis.
- The utilities negotiated service contracts with each of their customer departments or agencies, specifying the estimated volume of services each agency would buy, the quality to be delivered, and the price. These contracts let the utilities estimate their projected volume, which in turn helped them know where to set rates.

Utilities retained their profits. Decisions on how to use them—whether to lower rates, invest in productivity improvements, give rebates to customers, or do some combination of all three—were made during negotiations on future rate packages. When a utility showed a loss, it had to raise rates the following year to make up for the deficit.

Like marketplace units, utilities were allowed to roll over all unexpended funds at the end of the fiscal year, to eliminate the spend-it-or-lose-it incentive.

Internal Franchises

In Minnesota, the Department of Administration (DOA) had only one provider for each internal service. But in some governments there are multiple internal providers. In the U.S. government, for example, most departments have multiple personnel, procurement, and travel offices.

In 1993, the Clinton administration's National Performance Review (NPR) suggested a new wrinkle on the internal enterprise management model, in which marketplace services in one agency could compete to sell their services to other departments and agencies. The result would be competition among both internal service units (dubbed "franchises" by the NPR) and private businesses. One model was the Federal Systems Integration and Management Center, which has helped more than 50 different agencies acquire and manage information technology since 1972.

The NPR suggested that internal franchising could be applied to many different services, including budget, finance, personnel, procurement, payroll, information technology, engineering, facility management, quality assurance, alternative dispute resolution, training, travel, workmen's compensation, security, and printing services. The NPR convened a franchise planning committee, and Congress authorized the Office of Management and Budget to designate six "franchise fund pilot programs."

In 1996, the selected agencies launched three-year pilots. Among them were the Veterans Affairs Department's automation center in Austin, Texas, which provides data processing services, and the Interior Department's payroll and personnel processing and accounting services. About a year later, the Department of Agriculture (DOA) computer center in Kansas City, Missouri, surprised four computer companies, including IBM, by outbidding them to operate the Federal Aviation Administration's computer system. The DOA center's bid was nearly 15 percent lower than those of the private firms.

Advantages of Internal Enterprise Management

See *Banishing Bureaucracy* p. 137

Internal enterprise management typically saves those who use it a significant amount of money. More important, it forces their internal service units to continuously improve their services. It is "funny how clearly focused the condemned prisoner becomes when he walks up those steps to the gallows and the hangman's noose comes into view," says the General Service Administration's Gerald Turetsky.

Internal enterprises have to respond quickly to their customers' needs. In Minnesota, for example, Armajani reports that the purchasing office responded to competition by stocking dozens of items it had long ignored.

The documents division liquidated obsolete titles and began to stock many new books about Minnesota or by Minnesota authors. . . . Plant management experimented with differentiating its product into three different levels of service quality and cost. The printing operation began to offer quick-turnaround photocopying services at locations near its customers.

Internal service enterprises also become more accountable for their performance. The Minnesota Department of Administration shut down several operations that could not break even, including typewriter repair and computer programming. Other units shrank dramatically.

At the same time, internal enterprises are freed to make the long-term financial decisions necessary to maximize value for their customers. Because they retain part of their earnings, use accrual accounting, depreciate assets, and can borrow money, they can invest in technology, training, and other productivity improvements.

The vehicle fleet in Sunnyvale, which operates as an internal utility, offers a good example. Managers project their spending needs out 20 years, to cover all vehicle replacement costs. Out of an annual budget of $2.7 million, all funded by rental fees paid by other agencies, roughly $1 million goes into a vehicle replacement fund. Fleet Manager Jim Masch describes Burbank, California, where he formerly worked:

The fleet manager didn't control the fund, so you'd save up a couple million dollars, and they'd end up using it to renovate a park. I meet with other fleet managers, and some of them don't even have a replacement fund. They go to council every year and beg for police cars. I can't imagine managing like that.

Internal enterprise management also has a profound impact on the behavior of line agencies, because it forces them to pay for internal services. Under the traditional approach, public agencies don't have any idea how much their employees are spending on telephone service, car rentals, print shops, and other internal services. They have every incentive to use these services, because they are free. When enterprise management changes that, line agencies suddenly become cost-conscious. As Australian reinventors put it, the new "price signals" influence the agencies' "consumption patterns." When Minnesota made government telecommunications services an internal utility that charged its customers, for example, usage dropped by 50 percent. Suddenly, everyone became a cost cutter—rather than leaving that job to the administration and finance departments.

When customer panels help set utility rates, they not only become more careful about their own costs, they become more vigilant about everyone's costs. Customer panels ensure that utilities are managed for the collective interest. They push to keep rates low, and they make decisions based on the customers' interests, not the utilities'. At one point, for instance, the Minnesota Department of Natural Resources (DNR) asked the government's telecommunications utility to put a special voice and data line into its research facility in the northwest corner of the state. The utility did a cost analysis and reported the results to its customer panel. "At that point," says Armajani, "everybody turned to the utility manager and said, 'What are you going to do about this?' He turned back to them and said, 'What are you going to do about it? You set the rates.'"

They scheduled a special meeting to consider the issue. The utility's larger customers didn't like the idea of paying for the DNR's special line. After some debate, they worked out a deal: DNR would pay most of the cost, and the utility would pay the rest. "It was negotiated between the customers, in the true fashion of a cooperative," says Armajani. "The Finance Department and the utility really didn't get involved in deciding, 'Yes, there should be a special line, or no, there shouldn't.'"

Even the powerful Finance Department lost out at times. At one point, it wanted the mainframe computer center to buy a particular database program. The customer panel told the department it should use the software everyone else used. But the finance commissioner was adamant—so the customer panel made Finance pay for the special software itself. "You got much tougher discussions, much stronger oversight than would have been provided under the old system," says Armajani, "because the customers knew more about this stuff and had a strong interest in keeping rates low."

Internal Enterprise Management: Lessons Learned

The pioneers of internal enterprise management have learned a great deal, often the hard way, about what it takes to use this tool successfully. The general lessons on enterprise management all apply to this tool, and the following lessons add a few more relevant points.

pp. 161–164

1. Be prepared to close down internal enterprises that can't compete.

To prove to elected officials and finance departments that internal enterprise management is serious, you must be willing to let competition take its course. In Minnesota the legislative appropriations committees were suspicious of enterprise management until the department proved it would allow the ultimate consequence—business failure. "We had a typewriter business," says Armajani.

> *No one believed that it was really going to go out of business. It was doing poorly, and we gave it all kinds of support, hired consultants, and so on. We went a year, and we couldn't fix it. So we actually put it out of business, laid off employees, shut it down, and took responsibility for the red ink on the books. People at Harvard, from their interviews, say we got an enormous amount of credibility from this—that this was serious. It was after that, in the next legislative session, that they agreed to support the strategy more extensively.*

2. *In deciding which units should be leadership activities, which should be marketplace units, and which should be utilities, be pragmatic.*

Compromise is sometimes necessary. A perfect example is building maintenance in Minnesota, which became a utility. When legislators realized that

WHEN TO CREATE AN INTERNAL SERVICE ENTERPRISE: RULES OF THUMB

p. 155

Policy and compliance functions should always be classified as leadership activities, rather than enterprises. But not all services can be run as enterprises. As we noted earlier, those that serve the general interest, rather than specific interests, should not be charged to specific customers. Specifically, internal services should not be placed in enterprises if any of the following are true:

- They serve a broad public purpose distinct from the interests of the agencies that actually consume the service (for example, central procurement offices, which work to prevent fraud and secure the best value for the taxpayers, in addition to meeting individual agencies' needs).
- Legal requirements such as laws, court orders, or privacy issues give agencies no choice but to use them.
- There is no practical way to measure the service in finite units, making it impossible to attribute charges directly to specific users of the service.

If services do benefit specific customers and can be charged to them but are more efficiently provided by one central source than by many sources, then they should be classified as utilities.

All others services should be classified as marketplace activities. (See pp. 172–173 for a discussion of when to structure them as enterprise funds and when to structure them as public corporations.) One useful test to use before putting an internal service into a competitive market is to ask, "Would we be willing to let this unit go out of business?" If the answer is no, it should not be made a marketplace enterprise.

the charges for offices in the capitol building would be quite high—because it was marble, with fancy grounds and lots of ceremonial space—they rebelled. So the department agreed that since the capitol and its grounds were "the front door of Minnesota," their maintenance should become a leadership service, financed by the general fund.

3. Keep reexamining your classification of leadership functions, utilities, and marketplace activities over time.

Sometimes circumstances change over time—particularly when technology advances. Thirty years ago, for example, both computers and copying machines were quite expensive, so most jurisdictions required central approval for any purchases of either item. Today you can buy a serviceable copy machine or computer for $1,000, so central control no longer makes sense.

RESOURCES ON INTERNAL ENTERPRISE MANAGEMENT

Michael Barzelay. "Introducing Marketplace Dynamics in Minnesota State Government, A & B." Case studies prepared for the John F. Kennedy School of Government at Harvard University, 1988. The story of enterprise management as it unfolded in Minnesota.

Michael Barzelay and Babak Armajani. *Breaking Through Bureaucracy.* Berkeley and Los Angeles: University of California Press, 1992. The best primer on internal enterprise management, based on the Minnesota reforms. See especially Appendix 1, pp. 137–160.

The National Academy for Restructuring School Districts, a part of the National Center on Education and the Economy. This organization collects information on school districts that use internal enterprise management, such as Edmonton, Alberta. The director of its high-performance management program, Michael Strembitsky, was Edmonton's superintendent of schools for 22 years. The National Center can be reached in Washington, D.C., at (202) 783–3668 or by fax at (202) 783–3672.

The Public Strategies Group, a consulting firm specializing in the reinvention of government. Babak Armajani is chief executive officer of the firm, several of his former colleagues from the Department of Administration also work for the firm, and David Osborne is a partner in the company. They can be reached at 275 E. 4th St., Suite 710, St. Paul, MN 55101. Phone: (651) 227–9774. Fax: (651) 292–1482. Web: www.psgrp.com. E-mail: reinvent@psgrp.com.

Chapter 5

Managed Competition

Using Competitive Contracts and Benchmarks to Create Consequences

> *It is better for the public to procure at the market whatever the market can supply; because there it is by competition kept up in its quality, and reduced to its minimum price.*
>
> THOMAS JEFFERSON

***Managed Competition* makes potential providers of government services—whether private firms or public agencies—compete against one another to win government work. The contests create economic or psychological incentives that stimulate performance.**

When the subject of cutting government costs comes up, as it persistently does, many a public manager's fancy turns to contracting out services. More than likely, they know a story or two about the millions saved when a lean business, driven by the fabled *bottom line,* took over a public bureaucracy's work.

See *Banishing Bureaucracy* pp. 120–124

Ted Staton, the city manager of East Lansing, Michigan, had heard a good one: how Indianapolis mayor Steve Goldsmith had saved $65 million over five years by contracting out management of the city's wastewater treatment facility. "I'd had lunch with Goldsmith," says Staton. "I'd read the Indianapolis story and heard about the gains in efficiency at the plant."

Staton was relatively new in his position. A self-styled reinventor, he'd been hired in 1995 to shake up a traditional bureaucracy. From the beginning, he'd also been hunting for savings. The city budget had been bleeding slightly red year after year, because growth in property taxes, the city's main revenue source, consistently ran lower than growth in costs. So in 1996 Staton drew a bead on the city's wastewater treatment operation. With 26 employees, it cost about $3 million a year to run. "I had a gut sense that perhaps our wastewater operation wasn't as efficient as it might be," he recalls.

Staton's judgment was not shared by the unit's managers and employees. "They were pretty defensive," he says. "You know: they couldn't get more efficient; they were already the envy of all of Michigan." The facility was exceeding state standards for effluents, but Staton still thought contracting out the work might save money.

Staton saw an unexpected opportunity in a flier that came across his desk announcing a conference about contracting out wastewater operations. He ordered the director of public works, Pete Eberz, to attend.

The conference had an unexpected impact on Eberz, a veteran administrator. He came away impressed by a speaker who argued that government-operated wastewater facilities could run at the same or lower cost as privately managed plants—if they adopted the operational practices of private firms. Eberz told Staton not to contract out the work, but to give the workers a chance to show they could match the private sector.

The first step was to compare the city's performance with what businesses could do. "We needed a comparison to tell how far out of line we were," Eberz explains. "Maybe we were so bad that we ought to privatize, or maybe we were very competitive. We didn't know." If there was a cost gap with the private sector, the city could develop a plan for closing it.

In April 1997, the city hired EMA Services to conduct a comprehensive "optimization" study that compared East Lansing's performance with that of 120 other privately and publicly managed wastewater facilities. During the next five months, EMA reviewed the plant's technology, operations, maintenance, consumption of energy, chemicals, materials, staffing plans, barriers to efficient staffing, job descriptions and lines of responsibilities, and employee training and performance incentives.

Then EMA officials came to East Lansing to share their findings with the city manager and wastewater unit employees. "I knew it would be a tense meeting," says Staton.

"There was a lot of fear," recalls Antoinette Imhoff, a laboratory technician with more than 20 years on the job, "especially among those close to retirement."

Rumors swirled about possible layoffs. "I tried to stop all cooperation with the process," says Ed Mahaney, a lab technician who served as steward for the employees' union. The union refused to cooperate unless it was assured in writing that there would be no layoffs.

Other employees thought the study would be beneficial. Before he was hired into the maintenance unit, Dennis Smith had worked on the construction crew that built the plant, 20 years earlier. Now a shift supervisor, he had helped select EMA to conduct the study. "I was optimistic about the study," says Smith. "I'd always felt like we were overstaffed and underworked. Of course, to a lot of people I was a bad guy for even going to the meetings."

Staton recognized that employees were divided. "Some thought it was a reasonable approach and privatization might become a reality unless they did it. They felt pressured by the threat of the competition, and they understood the pressures facing government." Others, he says, "thought if employees stuck together, they could keep this from happening."

EMA officials delivered the good news first: the plant had an excellent track record, they said. Then they talked about improvements that could be made and new equipment the city should invest in. Finally came the news few employees wanted to hear: the plant could operate 20 percent more efficiently and save $614,000 a year. Much of the savings would come from eliminating eight of the 26 jobs.

Some employees reacted bitterly. "There was denial," says Eberz. "People said, 'We don't believe you.' And there was fear—'you're taking my job away.'"

Even Smith, an enthusiast for improvements, was startled. "I never dreamt we could cut as far as they proposed. I stood up and said, 'Cut it less.'"

The consultants said that outsourcing would not be necessary—the city's staff could achieve the savings. The next step, they suggested, was for employees to join with management in developing and implementing a cost-saving improvement plan.

When Eberz tried to form a planning committee, it wasn't clear that employees would participate.

> *I said, "Look, we're either going to improve or privatize. Right or wrong, the cat's out of the bag; the numbers are out there. We can't just ignore it. With you or without you, we're going to follow the council's directive to be cost-competitive."*

Mahaney, the union steward, pressed Staton on the key issue: What about the jobs? "The only person there who could answer that question was me," Staton says. "I stood up and said, 'You have my word: we will do this through attrition.'"

"I think he actually said it three times," says Mahaney.

The employees' mood changed quickly. "From that point forward," says Staton, "the extremely reluctant employees started to become more cooperative. They actually built a plan that we presented to the city council." The six-year plan included the staff reductions and an additional incentive for employees: a "gainsharing" provision to give them 25 percent of the savings, minus the cost of new equipment. When the council approved the plan in October 1997, it pledged that staff reductions "will be obtained through attrition and retirement."

In the first two years, the wastewater treatment unit met its savings targets with little difficulty.

USING MANAGED COMPETITION

The threat of competition forced East Lansing's wastewater treatment workers to cut costs. Managers and employees had to agree to meet the competition's "price," a stunning 20 percent below their existing costs, or face the possible loss of their jobs through contracting out.

Competition is a powerful force for improving government's performance. It breaks down the traditional monopoly that government employees have over their work, forcing them to compete for work just like businesses in a marketplace. To illustrate the negative impact of public monopolies, former Indianapolis mayor Steve Goldsmith, a great champion of managed competition, describes what would happen if fast food businesses did not face serious competition. "They're always competing in terms of price, food quality, and service," he says.

> *No one says they're perfect. But imagine what they would be like if there were only one fast food chain. If people had no choice, if there were no competition, if fast food were a monopoly, two things would definitely happen. Prices would go up, and quality would go down.*
>
> *Most of government is run that way.*

"Competition is the driving force of excellence," adds Ron Jensen, the former public works director in Phoenix who invented public-private competition for municipal services. "Would Roger Bannister have broken the four minute mile barrier without the competition of other runners? Our national commitment to land on the moon was spurred on by the fact that the Russians had the first satellite in space."

We call this approach *managed* competition because it is not a cutthroat contest to drive down prices but a carefully directed use of market forces. It requires potential providers of government services, whether they are private firms or government agencies, to compete against one another for government work on the basis of their performance.

Reinventors use two tools to create managed competition. The strongest, competitive bidding, forces organizations to compete with one another to provide public goods and services. The second, competitive benchmarking, is what East Lansing used. Rather than contract out or create a formal public-private bid, Staton and Eberz created a competitive standard, based on a study of private sector performance, and asked their employees to meet that benchmark. If they had conducted a bid, they might have found a bidder who proposed to cut costs by more than 20 percent. Instead, competitive benchmarking allowed them to avoid the time and cost of a bidding process and, more important, avert a confrontation with the employees' union. Had the treatment unit's employees failed to close the cost gap the consultants identified, the city still could have contracted out the work.

Competitions create winners and losers—and then the winners have to deliver. When government agencies award contracts to private bidders, they must carefully monitor the contractors' performance. But when a public sector provider wins, much more than contract management is necessary: government employees have to learn how to improve their organizations.

Indianapolis's garbage collection crews redesigned their work processes to win their bids. "My guys figured out how to go from 800 homes per day on each trash route to 1,200," explains Michael Stayton, then the city's public works director. The crews reconfigured the daily pickup routes and, Stayton says, created "a nifty shuttle system for the garbage trucks. When a truck gets full, instead of taking it back, emptying it, and going back out, now an empty truck comes out, the crew gets on it, and the full truck is taken back to the station." As a result, the city team's bid was about 25 percent less than those of private competitors, without reducing workers' wages and benefits.

In East Lansing, implementation of the cost-cutting plan was slow and difficult. Dick Hansen, a maintenance mechanic who chaired an implementation group of employees, says they came across many barriers. Sometimes, facility managers ignored their recommendations or made decisions that contradicted the plan. Sometimes employee anxiety got out of hand, because "[employees] just don't trust management." The city's personnel system also stood in the way, since it was not designed to support bonuses and gainsharing incentives. And some managers signaled that the facility might not have to reach its $650,000 cost-cutting target. "They [would] say, 'All we have to do is come close,'" explains Hansen.

These difficulties are all part of trying a new way of doing business. "We're just starting down this path," says City Manager Staton, well aware that he and his top managers are on the hook for delivering the results they promised to the city council. The hook was created by managed competition.

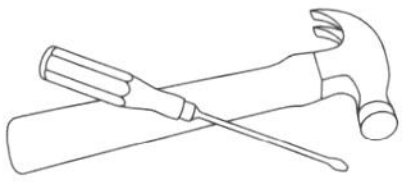

TOOLS FOR MANAGED COMPETITION

Competitive Bidding forces organizations to compete to provide goods and services paid for by the public sector. There are three basic variations: private-versus-private competition (known as *contracting out* or *outsourcing*); public-versus-private competition; and public-versus-public competition, in which only public organizations are allowed to bid. See p. 188.

Competitive Benchmarking measures and compares the performance of public and private organizations. It publicizes the results in "report cards," "performance tables," and other types of scorecards. This creates psychological competition between organizations, appealing to their members' pride and desire to excel. It can also be used as the basis for financial rewards. See p. 210.

COMPETITIVE BIDDING

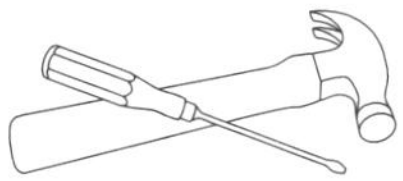

Of the three ways to use competitive bidding, contracting out is the most familiar and widely used among government officials. Also known as outsourcing, it makes private organizations compete to provide goods and services to government. These services may be for government's own use, such as copying and printing, or for use by its customers, such as road repairs and school lunch service. Rather than hire workers to perform these activities, agencies invite private organizations to bid for contracts that specify the scope of work and other conditions. After contracts are signed, government employees monitor contract compliance and enforce contract provisions.

Public-versus-private competition uses the same bidding mechanisms as contracting out, but it changes the pool of bidders. It allows public providers—departmental units, teams of managers, teams of employees—to compete with private providers for the right to keep performing their work. In public-versus-public competition, bidding for work is restricted to public organizations.

The Basics of Contracting Out

Contracting out is a well-tested tool in both the public and private sectors, and in recent years governments have increased its use. In the process, they are expanding its application to public functions that were previously off limits, such as the management of public schools and prisons.

These trends began in the late 1970s and are strong at the local, state, and national levels. Between 1987 and 1995, more than half of the 82 American cities surveyed by the Mercer Group outsourced solid waste management services, janitorial services, construction projects, and food services at public facilities. Taylorsville, Utah, an edge city near Salt Lake City with a population of 60,000, has only 12 municipal employees, including the mayor; everything but planning and permitting is contracted out or shared with another government. Similar growth in outsourcing is occurring at the state and federal levels, as well as in Australia, New Zealand, and the U.K. By 1991, outsourcing accounted for nearly a third of Australia's federal outlays.

Contracting out has spread to many new arenas. Defense departments are contracting for services that have been handled in-house for decades. The Australian military, for example, hired a private contractor to completely manage one of its bases. In 1993, the Minneapolis board of education contracted with a consulting firm, the Public Strategies Group, to provide leadership services, including a superintendent. Other school districts have contracted out other management functions. And Wyoming, Arizona, Indiana, and Wisconsin have put major pieces of their welfare systems in contractors' hands.

The main reason for this trend is that contracting usually saves money. Private companies tend to have fewer layers of management, they adopt cost-saving technologies more rapidly, and they use their personnel more flexibly. This helps makes them more efficient than most public bureaucracies.

Labor unions often charge that private contractors cost less because they pay workers less. For low-skilled jobs such as custodial work, this is often true. But after a careful study, the Council of State Governments concluded that in many cases "private providers can provide services at low cost without lowering wages." It attributed the private sector's lower costs to a variety of management factors: "private firms give fewer days off with full pay, use more part-time workers, have greater managerial authority to hire and reward good workers, and, if necessary, to discipline or fire unsatisfactory ones [and] have clearer job definitions and greater accountability."

Saving money is not the only benefit of contracting out; it can also improve performance. State administrators told the council that they use the tool to meet demands for increased personnel, to reduce red tape, to increase flexibility in hiring personnel, and to achieve speedy implementation and high-quality services. In other words, public managers find that private businesses can be easier to deal with than their own bureaucracies.

The Limits to Contracting Out

There is no simple formula for drawing the line between private and public production of government services. It is theoretically possible to contract out any government service or compliance function that can be quantified and is available from private organizations. But decisions about which public services to deliver through contractors are subject to the traditions, histories, ideologies, and public values of a particular nation, state, or community.

Sometimes, no one even realizes that a crucial government function is being performed by a private firm. For example, during the Persian Gulf War, a defense facility in Australia used satellites to track SCUD missiles launched by Iraq. "What is not well known," points out Gary Sturgess, an Australian state government reinventor, "is that the individuals who actually monitored the launches were employees of a private contractor, Serco Australia." Serco, he continues, is a wholly owned subsidiary of a British company that for 30 years has run the U.K.'s early warning system against air attacks.

Former Indianapolis mayor Steve Goldsmith declares that "with very few exceptions, virtually every aspect of government" can be competitively bid. But the devil is in the exceptions. Experiences around the world suggest several reasons to keep some government functions out of private vendors' hands:

- ***Don't contract out when doing so might jeopardize important public policy goals, such as safeguarding due process rights or providing security.*** Goldsmith, a former county prosecutor, exempted most police and other safety functions from competition. "The more you depend on due process, the less likely [you are] to compete it," he says. Law enforcement, criminal justice services, and other compliance functions must be conducted in ways that ensure fairness, privacy, and other legal rights. To some degree they are inherently inefficient. They are also extremely sensitive; leaders cannot risk their being abused for private gain. The closest most governments come to outsourcing these functions is contracting for the operation of low-security prisons.

Security is often a concern. When the U.S. Justice Department considered contracting out management of some federal prisons, its biggest concern was the potential for a strike by contractors' employees. In the end it decided it could not afford to take that risk.

• ***Don't contract out when doing so will create a private monopoly.*** In many rural or smaller suburban settings, there may not be enough private firms to generate competitive bidding. As the Council of State Governments cautions, "Without true competition, 'government monopoly' could be replaced by 'private monopoly.'" If this happens, the benefits of competition will not be realized. One way to avoid this problem is to use public-versus-private bidding, which allows public employees to compete as well.

• ***Don't contract out when critical public capabilities must be maintained.*** Few risks terrify local government officials more than the thought of a snowstorm that paralyzes their city. If the snow is not removed quickly, angry citizens may remove the mayor or city manager. Clearing the streets after a large snowfall requires a massive mobilization of people and equipment. In many cities, sanitation workers are called out to do this work. But if government contracts out trash collection to private firms, who will show up to work, around the clock and in miserable conditions, to remove mountains of snow? Not the private firms—unless it's in their contracts. And if it is, can a mayor be sure they will deliver?

"Once the city employees are gone, you have to pay top dollar for emergencies," says Steve Fantauzzo, a public employee union leader in Indianapolis. He uses the blizzard scenario to argue that governments should "maintain a flexible workforce to deal with emergencies: snowfall, water main breaks," and the like. (Of course, Indianapolis also pays top dollar for overtime for its own employees. Either way, emergencies are expensive.)

Other emergencies may arise when private contractors fail to perform essential services satisfactorily. When this happens—and it does—governments do not usually have workers of their own to throw into the breach. To avoid this scenario, some governments wisely limit how much of a crucial service may be contracted out. Indianapolis, for example, exposed only 10 of its 11 garbage collection districts to competition; the protected district remained in the hands of city employees. That way, says Mayor Goldsmith, "the city always has the capacity to collect trash in case problems arise with our private sector vendors."

Another way to prevent a calamity is to break up service contracts into smaller parcels so that a number of businesses get the work. Then if one provider fails, another can take over.

• ***Don't contract out when doing so would violate the public's strongly held values.*** Contracting out places a premium on the cost and quality of services. Sometimes, however, other community values should have priority. In Hampton, Virginia, for instance, a surprising number of community residents told the city council that they wanted their garbage picked up by city workers, even though a private firm had offered to do the work for less money. Citizens were willing to pay more to provide workers with better health insurance and retirement benefits than private businesses were offering, according to then–city manager Bob O'Neill. They said that "it's okay for the city to be a better employer," he recalls. The city council decided not to contract out the work.

A community's values usually clash with the prospect of having a private company make money by running the police department. Other functions, such as handling nuclear waste or guarding violent criminals, are sensitive enough that many citizens are anxious about having the profit motive involved (although for-profit firms manufacture nuclear weapons and operate nuclear plants).

Of course, public values are often hard to assess, and they are subject to change. They should be probed, and conclusions about them should be challenged. Public officials should be skeptical of claims that citizens won't tolerate contracting out a particular function. For instance, the former commissioner of the U.S. Internal Revenue Service, Margaret Milner, argued against using private tax collectors, as suggested by Republican congressmen. She said it raised concerns about privacy and would damage public perceptions of the agency's fairness. However, as the *New York Times* reported, the idea was first proposed by the Clinton administration, more than a dozen states made some use of outsiders to collect from delinquent taxpayers, and at least one state, Pennsylvania, already used private firms to collect current taxes.

Steps in Contracting: Avoiding the Pitfalls

Most government agencies do some contracting, but many do not do it well. Whether it is done with private firms, public organizations, or both, it involves a series of discrete steps. In what follows we provide a detailed description of each step, pointing out some serious pitfalls to avoid along the way.

1. Decide the purpose of the contract.

At the outset, a public agency must describe its objectives for the proposed contract. Unfortunately, agencies often do a poor job of figuring out exactly what their demands and expectations are—especially when they are purchasing services for someone else, such as food services for students. This can lead to costly amendments after a contract has been signed. The remedy is to start by asking the customers what they really want.

2. *Design the contract specifications.*

The organization must specify what the contractor will provide. This is spelled out in terms of:

- *Outcomes:* what results the contractor will produce.
- *Outputs:* what services customers will receive.
- *Processes:* which activities the contractor must undertake.
- *Inputs:* what resources the contractor must use.

Public agencies should emphasize the first two and avoid specifying processes and inputs as much as possible. But most are weak when it comes to detailing outcomes and outputs; instead, they write contracts that stipulate the use of the very inputs and processes they use to run their own organization. This causes several problems. It builds the inefficiencies of government work processes into the contract. It results in inflexible contracts, which are likely to require changes when inputs vary. And it increases the cost of contract administration, because monitoring input and process compliance is typically more labor-intensive than tracking outputs and outcomes. To overcome these difficulties, organizations must learn the art of performance measurement.

pp. 247–271

3. *Design the contract conditions.*

Organizations must be clear about starting and end dates, payment conditions, dispute resolution procedures, and other arrangements with the contractor. Contracts must also be specific about what constitutes a performance failure by the contractors and what remedies are available to the government if one occurs.

One concern is poor service quality. Contracts can address this by using customer quality assurance tools, such as customer service standards and redress mechanisms. Contracts should also require providers to resolve customer complaints within a specific amount of time and to document any problems that arise. Contracts should always include rewards and penalties related to quality of service.

pp. 346–377

Another major concern is service disruption. The agency should have contingency plans in place in case of failure—another provider or public employees who can fill the gap. The contract should provide a means for the agency to recover funds it spends dealing with service disruptions. To handle chronic problems, the contract should detail an escalating series of penalties, concluding in termination. Agencies can also insist on performance bonds or parent company guarantees to insure against failure, though this may prevent smaller contractors from bidding on work.

4. Qualify potential bidders (optional).

pp. 415–422

Governments that have modernized their procurement systems often build in a step before requesting bids: they invite interest from potential bidders, then choose those who are qualified to bid. Particularly on complex projects or services, this gives them a chance to weed out bidders they don't feel have the expertise, track record, or capability to handle the job, before those bidders go to the trouble of assembling a bid. It also gives the contracting agency an opportunity to talk with potential bidders, to get feedback on its contract specifications and conditions before finalizing them. Entrepreneurial governments have learned that they can improve their bid processes enormously by soliciting potential bidders' ideas for improving work processes, contract specifications, and the like.

5. Request bids.

pp. 415–422

Organizations must invite bids, publicizing the specifications and conditions of the contract. Fairness is critical throughout the bidding process—all bidders must be treated equally. That means keeping politics out of the process. (It does not mean sticking with the traditional procurement processes, however; by all means, reinvent procurement.) Sometimes public agencies and elected officials try to steer contracts to favored businesses or away from firms that have angered them in some way. To prevent these behaviors, governments should give control over the bidding process to a neutral party—for example, a civil servant auditor or purchasing chief. They should also establish an oversight board or ombudsman to investigate complaints about the bid process.

Governments must treat bidders well if they want to maximize competition. Agencies should provide potential bidders with clear information and stick to the timetables they announce for taking and evaluating bids and awarding contracts. In Phoenix, the city holds a prebidding conference at which vendors can critique draft specifications.

6. Evaluate competing bids.

The neutral body that evaluates the bids and chooses the winner must look at much more than the prices bid. Indeed, most experts warn against taking the lowest bid. Because you want to maximize value, not just minimize costs, you should look for the bid that will give you the best value for your money. This is often the lowest-priced *quality* bid.

The Government's Guide to Market Testing, produced by the U.K.'s Efficiency Unit, recommends that agencies make four assessments in addition to considering cost:

- ***A capability assessment.*** Does the bidder have the capacity—the experience, qualifications, and ability—to deliver the service? How has the company performed for other clients? Does it have solid personnel practices and policies?
- ***A technical assessment.*** Does the bid "meet the detailed requirements set out in the specification"?
- ***A quality assessment.*** Can the bidder deliver the service to the specified quality standards? Does it have relevant quality certifications?
- ***A financial assessment.*** Are all relevant costs included in the bid? Is it realistic, or is it unrealistically low? Does it include anything that might spark significant cost overruns during the contract?

Losing bidders should be briefed so that they can learn why they lost and how to compete more effectively next time. As the *Government's Guide to Market Testing* puts it, "Unless suppliers are convinced that the evaluation has been fair potential tenderers [contractors] will be less willing to bid for future contracts and services."

7. Negotiate and award the contract.

Once you have selected the best bids, you can often ask the bidders to sweeten their offers. Even after you have selected a winner, you can still negotiate many points.

8. Monitor the contract.

There are many ways to monitor performance: for example, customer satisfaction surveys, on-site inspections, complaint logs, and examination of contractors' documentation. Usually government units want to keep their monitoring costs down, however.

Some governments achieve economies of scale by centralizing contract monitoring in a single agency. Others use random inspections to cut costs but keep contractors on their toes. For example, the Oxfordshire County Council has computerized the inspection of 500 sites in which contractors clean buildings or provide food services. The computer generates a random sample of inspection visits, but it steers away from sites with continuously high performance and targets those known to have problems. The British Audit Commission reported that this method has helped keep the county's costs of inspection relatively low in comparison to those of other counties.

It is essential that agencies follow up vigorously on complaints about service. They should also report on contractor performance to elected officials, senior managers, and customers. Ideally, these reports should educate customers and elected officials about how performance can improve, how they can raise complaints, and how they can act as intelligent customers and overseers.

9. *Administer the contract.*

The hiring agency must pay its contractors, make decisions about any contract variations that providers request or that the agency thinks are needed, communicate effectively with the contractor, and design future contract bids. Effective contract administration depends largely on the relationship that the agency builds with the contractor. If it is based on trust and open, honest communication, problems that arise can usually be settled to both parties' satisfaction. The British government recommends that agencies appoint one person to handle relations with each contractor.

No matter how good the relationship, government organizations should have a strong bias against simply renewing contracts with providers. They should rebid contracts as much as possible, because competition helps to drive down costs and boost quality.

Choosing Public Services for Competition

Whether they include public competitors, private competitors, or both, public leaders have to decide what services will face competition. We have seen six different processes for doing this—only three of them effective. Some organizations use a combination of these methods:

- ***Asking public organizations to identify targets.*** This only works when government has unusually entrepreneurial managers. Few government employees will make recommendations that might put themselves—or their employees—out of work. In 1986 Brian Mulroney's Progressive Conservative Government in Canada announced a voluntary "make-or-buy" policy, under which federal departments were invited to identify bureaucratic functions that could be bid out. Not surprisingly, the initiative yielded little, and in 1990 the government quietly dropped it. In 1987, Texas adopted a law requiring some state agencies to contract with private vendors to provide goods or services if costs were at least 10 percent less than those of the government. Six years later, the state comptroller found that *not one service* had been outsourced as a result.

• ***Asking private providers to identify targets.*** Intuitively, most people would expect this to work. But when Texas's Council on Competitive Government, a body of elected officials, asked businesses to identify services they could do a better job of providing, potential vendors were reluctant to come forward. They were wary of disclosing in public their costs and other proprietary information, says Andrea Cowan, then a council staff member. And they were afraid that if they appeared to be raiding the state's services, they would be blackballed by vengeful state agencies. Such concern about revenge is a powerful deterrent. As former Indianapolis deputy mayor Skip Stitt put it, private vendors realize that "the people they're putting out of business are going to be their contract managers." (This is less of a problem with big national firms, which often lobby for outsourcing if the potential contract looks big enough. They have less at risk and more to gain than smaller local firms.)

• ***Letting a group of elected officials identify targets.*** This politicizes the selection process. It heightens the anxiety of public employees and union leaders, who often believe that politicians only want to outsource and downsize, not to give them a chance to compete. And it creates concerns among private vendors and citizens about whether the bidding process will be tainted by political favoritism.

This structure also has practical problems, which became apparent in the Texas Council's first years. Most elected officials don't sustain the attention and energy required to guide a large-scale competitive process. They just don't have the time, and in many cases, they don't stay interested for very long. Turnover is also fairly frequent and, therefore, disruptive. When Governor George W. Bush was first elected in 1994, for instance, he had no commitment to the council's work and only gradually warmed to the effort.

See Banishing Bureaucracy pp. 115–128

• ***Setting up a nongovernmental commission to select targets.*** This worked well in Indianapolis, as we described in *Banishing Bureaucracy.* Local entrepreneurs and business leaders selected by the mayor formed the Service, Efficiency, and Lower Taxes for Indianapolis Commission (SELTIC) and scrutinized every city agency. They focused on taking action, not issuing reports, and they designed their activities to help educate the public about the managed competition approach.

"We told them at the beginning that we didn't want reports," says Mayor Goldsmith. "We wanted transactions that could be debated in the public domain." By handing the process over to the commission, Goldsmith also helped keep the taint of politicization out of the process.

SELTIC was linked to the city government by a full-time liaison, Skip Stitt, then an assistant to the mayor. And the commission had politically savvy leadership. Its chairman, Mitch Daniels, was a vice president of one of the city's biggest firms and a former political director in the Reagan White House. He developed the SELTIC tactic of building success by first going after relatively easy targets and then taking on bigger, more controversial activities.

• ***Requiring each organization to competitively bid a certain amount of services each year***. This is the method the British Conservative Government used to "market test" national services. It required every department and agency to seek bids—often from both public and private bidders—for services accounting for roughly 15 percent of its operating costs each year. It allowed the chief executive to select which services would be market tested and asked him or her to assign someone to be in charge of the process. Activities could be nominated by top managers, line managers, or Consultancy, Inspection and Review staff.

Once targets were selected, the organization usually appointed a project manager to conduct each market test and a separate leader to take charge of preparing the in-house bid. (He or she could hire external consultants when necessary.) Their respective teams were kept separate from one another. The project manager put together a team to evaluate bids, which reported to senior line management and got their approval before awarding the contract. When a private bidder won, the project manager typically became the "contact control officer" in charge of managing the contract.

This process led to a significant amount of market testing. It appears to have had one flaw, however: it allowed for considerable bias. Top management often leaned toward the ministers' preference for outsourcing; hence more services were outsourced without public competition than with it. But once the decision had been made to use public-versus-private bidding, some of the market-testing teams appeared to lean the other way. "I am suspicious as to the amount of in-house work that's been won," William Waldegrave, then the minister in charge of public sector reform, told us in 1994. "I think quite a lot of it is that we're specifying contracts in ways that are very hard for outsiders to win."

• ***Making competitive bidding compulsory.*** The British government's other method was to require local authorities to "competitively tender" a long list of services, with public providers bidding against private ones. Its Audit Commission required an annual audit of each local authority, and if the auditors found that an authority had not bid out a required service—or had not done so by the rules—it could levy financial penalties such as the loss of government funds. The government did so in some cases, although Audit Commission officials believed many local authorities found plenty of ways to rig the bidding in favor of their own units.

There are pros and cons to compulsory competitive bidding. On the positive side, in Britain it forced massive changes in local government. It acted like antitrust policy, forcing competition in areas that would otherwise have been locked up by monopolies. On the negative side, it stirred up enormous resentment at the local level. And because such a blatant use of central authority contradicted the Conservative Party's stated belief in decentralization, it sowed cynicism among local officials. When the Conservative Party lost power, it was the one major reform the Labor Government abandoned.

In the U.S., of course, it is hard to imagine one level of government ordering another to competitively bid a series of services. Hence this is simply not a practical alternative. On balance, we would not recommend such a heavy-handed approach, even in countries that are more like the U.K. than the U.S.

The most important lesson that emerges from this review is the value of using a neutral, independent body like SELTIC to decide which activities should be bid competitively. There are undoubtedly alternatives to a strictly private sector body, such as a public-private commission or a politically independent auditor's office. If you use an auditor's office, however, you will have to abandon any hope of using it to help agencies benchmark and improve their performance, because agencies will not willingly share information with it. Whoever is vested with the power to pick services for competitive bidding will inevitably be treated as a potential executioner by most agencies. The best solution might be to set up two different auditing bodies, one to be the bad cop, the other to be the good cop.

Competitive Bidding: Other Lessons Learned

In addition to all we have said so far about competitive bidding, government officials have learned much about how to strengthen the effects of this tool. Four lessons in particular stand out:

1. Generate increased competition—and then generate even more.

The more competition you create, the more value for the dollar providers will deliver. Research the potential providers, find out what will attract them to bid, and advertise aggressively. Then structure contract incentives in ways that appeal to many businesses.

The size of the contract you offer bidders will often determine who bids. If you cut it up too small, major national firms will not bid. If you make it too large, small, local firms may not be able to compete. Decide what type of firms you want, talk with them, and create contracts that will attract them. (If you want small businesses, minority-owned businesses, or businesses owned by women to have a better chance, cut your contract into smaller segments that they can more easily handle.)

Similarly, if your contracts are for too short a duration, some firms will not compete. In some service areas, governments set contracts to coincide with the life of the equipment to be used. For instance, Phoenix bids out its garbage districts for as many years as the garbage trucks are expected to last—usually five to seven—so the winner can buy new equipment and use it for the life of the contract.

If your contracts are long, on the other hand, contractors will not feel enough competitive pressure to continuously improve their operations. As the British Efficiency Unit points out, several things may happen during a long contract: "technology may improve," "new suppliers may enter the market," and prices may fall. When any of these happen, you may not want to be stuck with a long-term contract.

To enhance the attractiveness of the contract, minimize the documentation contractors have to produce and make sure the bidding process does not drag out too long. Lastly, when potential bidders drop out of the process, find out why and redesign future contracts to lure them back.

2. *Build the customers into the process.*

When defining a contract's purpose and specifications, be sure to consult with the intended customers to see what they value. To find out how well contracted work is being performed, once again, ask your customers. As the British Audit Commission advises: "Empowering consumers to act as monitors of service delivery by contractors will almost always be more effective and cheaper than employing an army of authority inspectors." Newspapers, for instance, track customer complaints about late deliveries to monitor performance by the agencies they contract with for delivery.

3. *To overcome managers' resistance to contracting out, tie their compensation to their organizations' performance, not to the size of their empires.*

Contracting out threatens managers in bureaucratic systems, because their status and compensation depend on the size of their budgets and staff. They have a powerful reason to oppose handing resources to the private sector. The solution is to pay managers instead for how well they contribute to the organization's goals. That way, they will focus on effectively using resources, rather than on empire building.

pp. 215–246

4. *Minimize negative impacts on employees.*

See *Banishing Bureaucracy* pp. 132–135

In *Banishing Bureaucracy* we discussed what public organizations should do when the use of managed competition and other reinvention approaches means they will need fewer employees. Agencies should protect their workers from the threat of joblessness, unless they are in such a deep fiscal crisis that they can't afford to. We recommend that agencies adopt a no-layoff policy, as East Lansing's Ted Staton did, then use a menu of options for helping employees whose jobs disappear. This is not as difficult as it sounds. A U.S.

Department of Labor study in 1989 examined dozens of examples of contracting out that each affected more than 2,000 employees. It found that, on average, only 7 percent of those employees were eventually laid off. Some 58 percent went to work for the contractor, 24 percent shifted to other government jobs, and 7 percent retired.

Your options to help dislocated workers include the following:

- Require firms that win contracts to hire them before anyone else.
- Keep those who are close to becoming vested with pensions on the public payroll, but make the private contractor pick up the cost.
- Retrain them and place them in other government jobs.
- Use a "job bank" to keep open some jobs that can be made available to them.
- Offer them severance packages or early retirement incentives.
- Provide them with outplacement services to find private sector jobs.
- Protect the benefit levels of those who go to work for contractors, by providing any benefits necessary to keep pace with those they would have received in public service, or by requiring the contractor to do so.

Public-Versus-Private Competitive Bidding

pp. 191–200

The lessons and pitfalls discussed so far apply as well to public-versus-private bidding. Letting public employees into the bidding creates some new wrinkles in implementation, however.

Why let government employees compete with private businesses to keep their own work? Why not just contract out the work? One reason is fairness. "Before we let entrepreneurs provide government services, let's allow government service providers to become entrepreneurs," says Mayor Goldsmith. After all, public employees did not create the inefficient systems in which they work.

Another reason is political pragmatism. By using this tool instead of simply contracting out, Goldsmith avoided increased strains with unions representing about 20 percent of his workforce. Too often political leaders underestimate the difficulty of contracting out if unions can rally elected officials and the public to their side. Massachusetts governor William Weld made this mistake, and the state legislature put the brakes on his effort to institute competition. Reflecting on his experience, Weld advised incoming governors to use the word *competition* instead of *privatization*.

p. 190

A third reason is to maintain some public capacity you can use in emergencies or to step in when private contractors fail, as we discussed earlier. In addition, some organizations decide that they need to preserve some in-house service delivery so they won't lose the hands-on knowledge necessary to act as an intelligent buyer or to offer useful advice to policymakers.

But the most compelling reason to let public providers compete is to maximize competition. As Goldsmith and others have discovered, when public employees face competition they often figure out how to slash costs below those of private competitors. They give the taxpayers a better deal.

In Indianapolis, government bidders won 37 of the first 86 competitive bids after Goldsmith launched managed competition. When the Australian Department of Defense initiated public-versus-private competition for 51 military projects worth about $500 million, government workers won 16 times. In Phoenix, where public-private competition began in 1979, city employees won 22 of the first 56 contests. And in the U.K., national government agencies won about two-thirds of the first "market tests" in which they competed directly with the private sector. No matter which side won, savings were typically 20–25 percent the first time a service was bid out—and more in subsequent rounds.

How does the lowly public sector win? By radically changing the way work is done. But public organizations also enjoy some financial advantages. Steve Fantauzzo, the AFSCME leader in Indianapolis, says his workers' costs are nearly one-third lower than those of private firms, because they pay no business taxes, make no profit, and don't pay sales taxes when purchasing items such as fuel. "If we still can't compete," says Fantauzzo, "shame on us."

Why Public Organizations Lose Competitive Bids

Unfortunately, most public organizations also face some real disadvantages, which must be addressed if they are to have a shot at winning. For example:

- ***They have excessive management overhead costs.*** Public employee unions frequently point to this factor. Mayor Goldsmith agrees: "The jobs that are often at risk are the middle-manager jobs. . . . [because governments] piled up levels and levels of control and supervision. To be competitive, we have to get rid of these." Delayering of management helps address this problem.

pp. 462–463

- ***They lack technological expertise and advanced equipment.*** Government typically lags far behind business in adopting new technologies. Businesses invest in new technology because gaining a technological advantage can generate profits for them. In contrast, public officials view technology as a cost, not an investment that will pay for itself. "We have a lot of the wrong technology and we don't stay current," says Stitt, former deputy mayor of Indianapolis. As a result, business usually wins technology-intensive work, whereas public employees compete most successfully for "low-tech" work such as pothole filling and trash pickup.

• ***They are saddled with high-cost, low-quality "internal services."*** Public bidders are usually the "captives" of inefficient internal service monopolies that provide them with facilities, equipment, information technology, personnel, and other services. The solution to this problem is internal enterprise management.

pp. 174–182

• ***They have higher labor costs.*** Public-private wage differences vary greatly. Business executives usually earn more than government's top managers, but some lower-level public employees earn more than their private sector counterparts. Increasingly, a big driver of government's higher labor costs is the health and retirement benefits it provides. To deal with these cost disparities, public officials can require private bidders to offer their workers wage and benefit packages comparable to what the public sector provides.

• ***They can't achieve significant economies of scale.*** Companies that operate in large markets are able to generate economies of scale that reduce their bidding costs. They can buy equipment in bulk, at discount prices. They can afford to invest in the development of new technologies. Most government organizations, in contrast, are limited to bidding on local work—and therefore cannot generate the volume that helps reduce marginal costs.

• ***Their rigid personnel, budget, and procurement systems deny them the flexibility they need.*** Private companies can usually hire faster, fire faster, use more part-time employees, move employees around as their needs change, and reward extra effort by employees. They can also purchase what they need when they need it and move funds between budget accounts when necessary. Until they reform their systems, public organizations can do little of this. Hence they are often slower and less efficient than their private competitors.

pp. 404–426

Public-Versus-Private Competition: Other Lessons Learned

pp. 198–200

In addition to the lessons presented earlier, most of which apply here, the following lessons apply specifically to public-versus-private bidding.

1. Tone down the political rhetoric.

The inflated rhetoric that politicians use aggravates the hair-trigger anxieties of public employees. Beating up faceless bureaucrats on behalf of taxpayers scores easy political points, but it reinforces the wariness public employees feel toward elected officials. And it antagonizes their unions, which turn to their political allies and the public to stop the competition.

Old political dogs must therefore learn some new tricks. Goldsmith did. Six months after running for mayor on a privatization platform, he went out of his way to defend public employees. "Contrary to their undeserved poor public image most civil servants are hard-working and talented, and they know a lot more about how to do their jobs well than mayors or union presidents," the mayor wrote in a letter published by the *Indianapolis News*. "The problem is that [workers] historically have been trapped in a system that punishes initiative, ignores efficiency and rewards big spenders."

See *Banishing Bureaucracy* pp. 115–128

His approach, Goldsmith concluded, would "free [employees] from the shackles of bureaucracy." That was very different from trying to "free" them from their jobs. And it paid off. Goldsmith managed the minor miracle of staying friendly with AFSCME while phasing out 45 percent of non–public-safety jobs.

2. *Create a level playing field.*

Governments should build competitive bidding systems with two objectives in mind: to maximize value for the taxpayers and customers and to make sure all bidders are treated fairly. This means both public and private bidders should be asked to calculate their costs in the same fashion—including overhead costs and capital costs. And all financial advantages should be neutralized. Public bids should include pension costs, capital costs, in-lieu-of-tax charges, interest charges on capital depreciation, and all overhead charges—and private bids should too.

3. *Help public employees become more competitive.*

Government employees don't always know how to develop a bid, cut costs, or improve quality, so smart reinventors help them learn how. They provide consultants and training, and they remove obstacles that get in the employees' way.

In Indianapolis, Michael Stayton paid consultants to help his wastewater division managers design their bid. That got them over a key technical barrier. "We do what we can to eliminate legal and purchasing barriers," says former deputy mayor Stitt. "If they need accounting help, more training—we do it."

In Charlotte, North Carolina, when the mayor and city council decided to make city employees compete with private providers, they initiated "Competition 101" workshops to prepare in-house units.

4. *Create a bidding process everyone can trust.*

See *Banishing Bureaucracy* pp. 142–144

We discussed this at length in *Banishing Bureaucracy*. Give control of the process to a neutral, nonpolitical party—a civil servant auditor or purchasing chief, for example. Check up on performance and costs after a winning bidder has established a track record. And create an oversight body that can investigate complaints.

5. *Make competition a two-way street.*

This lesson raises one of the most intriguing issues in the design of public-private competition. The basic question is this: Should public workers be limited to bidding only on services they currently perform? Elected officials, who don't want local businesspeople on their backs, usually answer yes. But that answer has serious implications.

It means that when city workers lose competitions, they permanently lose the work. They cannot compete for it again, and they cannot compete for additional work. As Fantauzzo puts it, this creates a one-way street. Competition leads inevitably to increased contracting out with private vendors and reduced public employment. Fantauzzo argues that this approach is anticompetitive.

Instead, he believes, public workers should be allowed to bid for new work the government wants done, for work they previously lost or never had, and for work in other government jurisdictions or even the private sector. "The competitive ax has to swing both ways," he insists.

We agree with the underlying principle Fantauzzo invokes: government is best served by maximizing the competition to provide public services. By creating a one-way street, governments undermine competition in three ways:

- They gradually take public competitors out of the picture, making it more tempting for private competitors to divide up the market and rig their bids.
- They make it impossible for some public organizations to minimize their costs, because they don't allow them to achieve economies of scale. When owning expensive equipment provides a competitive edge, providers who can spread the costs of buying that equipment over as large a base of services as possible will win most of the bids.
- Finally, they undermine any sense among public employees that they are being treated fairly. This makes it much more likely that unions will work to elect politicians who will end competitive bidding altogether.

We have seen many situations in which public organizations are not allowed to bid for services they do not already deliver. But we have also seen situations in which public organizations do bid for other *public sector* work—in Indianapolis; in New York City, where the Sanitation Department's Bureau of Motor Equipment created a "contracting in" program and went after repair work on other city fleets; and in Los Angeles County, where many municipalities contract with the county or other municipalities to provide dozens of services, including entire police and fire departments.

When public organizations go after work done by private businesses, however, the situation becomes far trickier. Local business leaders quickly get up in arms when they see government poaching on their turf. They immediately invoke the traditional ideology: government should not compete with business.

In reality, governments have competed with businesses for hundreds of years. But public leaders who use this approach should recognize that the minute they cross the line into services formerly provided only by businesses, they will run into a hornet's nest of opposition. If they choose to take the risk, we would advise them to do so with great care—*after* they have lined up the politics. When he was city manager of Visalia, California, Ted Gaebler learned to follow a rule laid down by one of his city councilors, Bonnell Pryor: They could go into any business that had no current local competitor. As Gaebler said, "If nobody else is operating a baseball team, whose toes are you stepping on, locally?"

Even when public organizations begin competing on turf formerly controlled by other public organizations, the politics can get difficult. But there is another issue to consider. When public organizations bid on work they do not currently perform, how can anyone be sure they will be able to perform it? What if they fail—after they have hired new employees and purchased new equipment?

Our answer is that public organizations that choose to expand into new markets should be treated just like private ones. They should be required to sign performance contracts with incentives and penalties, and in extreme cases they should be required to post performance bonds. The new employees they bring on to do the work should not receive lifetime tenure or seniority protection. Finally, when they win new contracts, they should drop their no-layoff policies for employees who work on those contracts. If they expand their market share, hire employees, and then lose a big contract, a no-layoff policy will cost the taxpayers money. We believe these expenditures are justifiable to protect regular employees whose organizations have lost traditional public sector work. But when organizations become entrepreneurial and move into new markets, we think they should bear the same risks private companies do. Ideally, such units should be required to form public corporations and operate under the same rules as businesses.

pp. 164–169

6. *Let the chips fall where they may.*

The point of using public-private competition is to create greater value for the citizens and customers. It doesn't matter whether the public agency or the private provider wins. That's a tough pill for partisans of either side to swallow. Privatization ideologues don't want public employees to win; public sector unions don't want private firms to win. But public officials who implement public-private competition shouldn't have a preference. They shouldn't set targets for how much of the contracting private providers should win. They must be willing to "let the chips fall as they may," as Ron Jensen puts it. Otherwise, no one will trust the process.

7. Try to make sure both public and private bidders win some early competitions.

If you can do this without tilting the playing field, it is a pragmatic way to build trust in the competitive process. If the private sector wins all of the early bids, public employees will complain that privatization, not competition, is the goal. If public providers win the early contests, private bidders will think the process is rigged against them. The answer is to share the wealth, by carefully selecting and sequencing the services bid out in the early rounds. There is a good chance that public employees can win certain kinds of bids—for example, trash collection. Similarly, private firms are likely to win services that rely on technological expertise or large-scale efficiencies. By mixing the contests up, you have a good chance of allowing both sides some early victories.

8. Phase in competition; start with services that are easier to bid out.

Once a government has decided to use private-public competition, it has to decide where to start, since it can't put all services out to bid at once. You need a plan for phasing in the bidding. In something as complex and contentious as public-versus-private competition, it helps to start with the low-hanging fruit, as Indianapolis did. That might include low-cost, low-employment services such as courier services and pothole repair, or services that could be easily automated, such as sewer or water billing. If you start small, you can take your organization up the learning curve while the risks are still low. You can score early victories that build public support for the bigger challenges. And you can avoid big fights before you have proof that competition works. It's much harder to defeat a competitive initiative if it has already been proven to save 25 percent of the cost of services.

The British did this with compulsory competitive tendering when they imposed it on local authorities. In 1980, Margaret Thatcher ordered it for all highway and building construction—one of the easiest areas to try, because the outputs were so tangible and there were many experienced private providers. In 1988, she added refuse collection, street cleaning, building cleaning, food services, grounds maintenance, vehicle maintenance, and recreation services. In 1992, the government added many white-collar services, including architectural, engineering, property management, legal, information technology, and personnel services—but allowed local authorities to phase in competition for each one.

Phasing in helped local authorities learn how to manage competitive bidding a step at a time. It also gave the private sector time to develop new capacities as new markets opened. And it made it difficult for local authorities to say the policy was unrealistic, because each time the government expanded the list of services, it could point to the success of competition in those that had gone before.

9. Deal with government bidders that fail to live up to their bids.

Sometimes government agencies exceed the costs of their bids. Sometimes they fall short on service levels or quality. If you catch these problems early enough, says Indianapolis's Stitt, you can get the agency to make a course correction. That's why it is important to continuously track the project's finances and results, especially customer satisfaction.

If you cannot correct the problem in time, you can take the work away from the organization and give it to a private firm—say, the next best bidder. If this is not an option, you can exclude the agency from future competitions, or at a minimum make sure that its next proposal reflects the real history of its performance.

What doesn't seem to exist yet is a way to make public agencies financially guarantee that they will meet the terms of the contract. Sometimes private firms are required to put up performance bonds or guarantees in case of a default on the contract. This is not done with public bidders, to our knowledge. But it could be.

10. Take action to ease unions' anxieties about competing.

Unions' typical first response to public-private competition is to attack. Thus the first thing most reinventors must do is win a political battle with public sector unions. To help build public support in Indianapolis, Goldsmith pledged that savings generated by competition would be reinvested in inner-city neighborhoods. Competition, he added, was an alternative to raising taxes. In Philadelphia, Mayor Ed Rendell enlisted private sector unions as important allies in forcing public employees to compete. He gave them fact sheets comparing city employees' pay and benefits with those in the private sector. "Guys would listen to this," says Rendell, "and say, 'Yeah, bingo! Privatize. Turn it over.' "

It helps diminish union opposition if you pledge that union workers will not be laid off as a result of competition. This was critical in Indianapolis. But you can also offer public employees real incentives for bidding. A good one is gainsharing, also an important part of the Indianapolis success story. If employees win a bid and come in under the contract's cost, let them keep a portion of the savings.

pp. 237–241

Public-Versus-Public Competition

pp. 189–191

It's not appropriate to put some public services into the hands of private businesses, as we discussed earlier. For example, governments are unlikely to contract out policing to businesses, because citizens would not stand for it. It is still possible, however, to bring the power of competition into play by using public-versus-public bidding. In Los Angeles County, local governments use such contests to cut costs and boost the performance of law enforcement services. Many municipalities bid out their police work every few years. The county sheriff's department and other local police departments compete for the work.

Because public-versus-public competition is at heart a contract bidding process, the lessons about contracting out and competitive bidding apply.

pp. 191–207

Activity-Based Costing (ABC): A New Competence

Everyone complains about how much government spends, but almost no one knows how much it actually costs government to do anything—fill potholes, collect garbage, deliver the mail, or operate a bus line. Governments rarely know because knowing has rarely mattered; in the absence of real demand to improve costs, they have had no reason to collect data about costs. Governments typically budget by organization, not by activity. And those organizational budgets rarely include overhead costs, such as employee benefits, central management, and internal support services.

In 1992, Mitch Roob, then Indianapolis's transportation director, decided to let his employees compete with private businesses for a street repair contract. Right away he ran into an accounting roadblock: "We didn't know how much it cost to put a ton of asphalt down into potholes." Without that information, Roob's employees couldn't put together a bid.

See *Banishing Bureaucracy* pp. 115–117

The solution was activity-based costing (ABC), an accounting technique that has been used in the private sector for years. It allows an organization to specify what it actually costs to perform each of its activities. It not only helps in preparing bids for contracts, it also helps organizations discover their hidden costs and compare their costs over time.

p. 426

In a case study for the John F. Kennedy School of Government at Harvard, Howard Husock described how Indianapolis developed its ABC system. It started with potholes: a team of transportation workers and a consultant began by identifying *direct costs*, such as labor and materials. They found in the city budget the pay and fringe benefit rates of workers. But figuring out how much it cost for a repair crew to perform a typical day's worth of street repairs was tricky. Because of seniority policies, not all the laborers were paid the same. And no one was sure how much time was spent on the repairs.

The consultant looked at the workers' time sheets, interviewed the workers, and then estimated how long it took a crew to repair a typical block. Then the team investigated the market price of materials, mainly asphalt.

With direct costs accounted for, they turned to *indirect costs*—support for the street crews. Some, such as heating and lighting the workers' garage and offices, were easy. Others were not. The deterioration of city buildings and vehicles had never been counted as an expense, as it would have been in a business's accounting system. The team decided to use the cost of annual upkeep and repairs rather than any depreciation formula.

The city's central fleet maintenance shop took care of the repair crews' trucks. Those costs could be tracked, but everyone believed they were much higher than those of private garages. The team decided it had to count the city's real maintenance costs, even though they would put the city employees at a disadvantage.

Finally, there was the indirect cost of management. Roob had already cut this in half by laying off 18 supervisors. But should some portion of Roob's salary be included as a cost? And what about counting part of the mayor's salary, too? Roob decided not to include the cost of upper management, reasoning that no matter who provided the service, top management would be needed to request proposals and monitor performance.

With all the financial data in, the team concluded it cost $407 per ton of asphalt to repair Indianapolis's streets. That was too high, they decided. As employees developed ideas to cut costs, they tested them by plugging different numbers into the ABC formula. They drove their costs down to $301 per ton—a winning bid.

To develop your own ABC accounting system, we recommend that you do as Indianapolis did: hire a consultant. Have that consultant teach your own accountants the new system, so you will develop the in-house competence to apply it throughout your government.

RESOURCES FOR COMPETITIVE BIDDING

The Reason Foundation. This nonprofit public policy research and educational organization in Los Angeles offers a catalog of publications, how-to guides, and studies concerning privatization. The foundation holds conferences, issues an annual report that examines international trends in privatization, and has a Web site chock full of information: www.reason.org. The foundation is located at 3415 S. Sepulveda Blvd., Suite 400, Los Angeles, CA 90034–6064. Telephone: (310) 391–2245.

United Kingdom Audit Commission. *Realising the Benefits of Competition: The Client Role for Contracted Services.* Local Government Report No. 4. London: Her Majesty's Stationery Office, 1993. An excellent guide to contracting, available for £8.50 from Audit Commission Publications, Bookpoint Ltd., 39 Milton Park, Abingdon, Oxon OX14 4TD, or by telephone at 0800 502030.

United Kingdom. Cabinet Office. *Better Quality Services.* A comprehensive handbook on contracting out and public-versus-private bidding. Available on the Web at www.servicefirst.gov.uk/index/publications.htm (scroll down to "Quality Awards/Schemes and Tools").

The Carnegie Council Privatization Project. The Carnegie Council is a non-profit research and education institution that conducts and publishes a set of excellent briefings on privatization worldwide. The briefings are free. To order them, write to the Carnegie Council Privatization Project, 170 East 64th Street, New York, NY 10021.

City of Indianapolis. *The Indianapolis Experience: A Small Government Prescription for Big City Problems.* A summary of the city's managed competition approach. Includes case studies and details on technical issues. Contact Enterprise Development Office, City-County Building, Suite 2460, 200 East Washington Street, Indianapolis, IN 46204.

Ron Jensen. "Managed Competition: A Tool for Achieving Excellence in Government." Washington, D.C.: Alliance for Redesigning Government, 1995. An excellent article on public-versus-private bidding, available on the Web at www.alliance.napawash.org.

Jim Flanagan and Susan Perkins. *Public/Private Competition in the City of Phoenix, Arizona.* Government Finance Review, June 1995. A strong discussion of the challenges of and methods for implementing public-private competition, by leading pioneers in using this tool.

COMPETITIVE BENCHMARKING

Competitive Benchmarking **measures and compares the performance of public and private organizations. It publicizes the results in "report cards," "performance tables," and other types of scorecards. This creates psychological competition between organizations, appealing to their members' pride and desire to excel. It can also be used as the basis for financial rewards.**

The British Employment Service periodically publishes comparisons of its regions' performance. Former chief executive Michael Fogden held four meetings a year in which, he said, regional managers "had to account to their peers. If there was one that was holding up the organization, his or her colleagues may very well have wanted to know what was going on."

The comparisons had a big impact on Martin Raff, who ran one of the regions. "I certainly was humiliated when for three years we had the worst record," he told us. "It was very humiliating, and it was a strong motivator." Several years and many reforms later—including the widespread adoption of Total Quality Management—Raff's region reached the top ranks of performance.

The Employment Service was using competitive benchmarking to prod its regions to improve. Later it applied the tool to local offices, posting comparisons of each local office's performance with that of neighboring offices.

"When performance is measured, it improves," says Bill Creech, who used competitive benchmarking in the U.S. Tactical Air Command (TAC). "When performance is measured and compared, it improves further."

The psychological consequences of competitive benchmarking are not as powerful as the economic consequences created by competitive bidding. But you can use competitive benchmarking when these other tools are not an option—and you can combine it with performance rewards. As Creech goes on to say, "When performance is measured, compared, and appropriately recognized and rewarded, it improves even more—dramatically more."

pp. 231–237

Competitive benchmarking works best in organizations that have many similar units—service organizations with many local outlets or local school districts with many schools, for example. But cities increasingly benchmark against other cities. The International City and County Management Association is benchmarking fire, police, neighborhood, youth, and internal business services in 120 large cities and counties. Some organizations, including the U.S. Air Combat Command (ACC), even benchmark against private firms. That's what East Lansing did with its wastewater treatment operation.

p. 213

pp. 183–185

This tool can also be used by those *outside* an organization, to create pressure for improvement. For example, some U.S. states issue annual report cards on the performance of their public schools. In Australia, the federal Industry Commission publishes comparative performance information on 12 services in eight states. Under the Citizen's Charter, the British Audit Commission and other entities measure performance and publicize comparisons of five separate services: local government services, hospitals, police forces, fire brigades, and schools. They compare them within "families"—London boroughs against London boroughs, cities against cities, rural areas against rural areas. Their annual reports receive massive coverage in the media, with major newspapers often devoting several pages to the results and reprinting some of the charts. Although officially titled *Performance Indicators,* the press has dubbed these reports "league tables"—the British name for league standings in professional sports.

The power of this tool is that it reveals variations in performance between similar organizations. Suddenly citizens, customers, elected officials, and managers can understand how their organizations' performance stacks up. They talk about it, analyze it, complain about it, defend it—and in the process create real pressure for improvement. As Wisconsin governor Tommy Thompson told the *Washington Post,* "Nothing drives a governor faster than a report that says you don't measure up."

In the U.K., the *Local Authority Performance Indicators* have caused an enormous stir. When the Audit Commission had a public opinion survey done, 80 percent of the public said they supported publication of the comparisons. Simply because they knew the comparisons would be embarrassing, the worst-performing councils made dramatic improvements in the year leading up to publication of the first *Performance Indicators.* Hospitals and schools have also improved significantly since comparative data on their performance was published—though it is of course impossible to isolate the impact of the comparisons, given all the other reforms taking place simultaneously.

Clearly, however, the annual publicity creates very real pressure on elected officials and their top managers to pay attention to actual performance—something they don't always do. "This exercise is very much in the public interest," says Audit Commission controller Andrew Foster, "because it makes politicians deal in facts rather than assertions."

Using Competitive Benchmarking to Improve Your Organization

We recommend Chapter Seven, on performance measurement, and the Customer Information Systems tool in Chapter Eight for anyone planning to use benchmarking. A few high points of those discussions follow:

pp. 247–271, 311–319

1. In choosing what measures to benchmark, be sure you ask customers what is most important to them.

Organizations that skip this step often find themselves comparing how efficient and effective they are in doing things their customers don't particularly care about—while ignoring the big issues. Hence they may get better and better at doing the wrong things.

2. Make the information a focus of discussions within the organization.

It's not enough to distribute the information and leave it at that. Take a page out of Michael Fogden's book: make your managers deal with the comparative data and identify causes of weak performance. This increases the psychological stakes for them. General Loh of the ACC also used competitive benchmarking to spread best practices. When he assembled managers to review performance data, he prodded those running low-performance units to learn from those that were doing better.

In the U.K., the Audit Commission assists local governments that want to improve their performance. It holds conferences and seminars and issues management guides about improving particular public services.

3. Publicizing the performance data outside the organization increases the pressure it creates.

The point is to get many people talking about the information—analyzing it, debating it, figuring out how to make sure it's better next time. One way to build awareness of the data is to get the media to use it in news reports. Another is to publish and distribute the information yourself.

pp. 311–319

pp. 215–237

4. Enhance the power of competitive benchmarking by rewarding high performance.

Some organizations use psychological and economic rewards to further spur competition. For example, they recognize units that rank at the top of comparisons—honoring them at an awards ceremony, publicizing their accomplishments in internal newsletters. Or, more rarely, they provide financial bonuses to top competitors.

Awards for competition must be carefully tailored to support collaboration among employees and to avoid stimulating the wrong behavior, such as hoarding of information about successful innovations. This problem can be avoided if competition is managed properly. First, reward teams of employees, not individuals, because this promotes the cooperative behaviors that are part of teamwork. Then carefully select benchmarks that promote collaboration. For example, Inland Revenue, the giant tax agency in the U.K., rewards local tax offices for working well with other offices with whom they share clients.

Some organizations reward teams that show the most improvement over previous performance levels. Others have teams compete to exceed a specified performance standard—such as an efficiency target. This gives every team a chance to succeed; the number of winners is unlimited. Such competitions help identify which teams are doing best and give weaker performers an incentive to learn how they do it, without encouraging high-performing teams to hoard their secrets.

RESOURCES FOR COMPETITIVE BENCHMARKING

Bill Creech. *The Five Pillars of TQM: How to Make Total Quality Management Work For You.* New York: Truman Talley Books/Dutton, 1994. Creech explains the power of psychological competition to spur improvement and describes his successful use of competitive benchmarking at the Tactical Air Command.

Comparative Performance Measurement: FY 1998 Data Report. Washington, D.C.: International City/County Management Association, December 1999. This is the fourth annual report of the ICMA Center for Performance Measurement, which offers comparative data on 15 services in 120 American and Canadian cities and counties (with pilots in New Zealand and Australia). It is updated every year. This and other ICMA titles related to performance measurement are available at www.bookstore.icma.org (type *performance measurement* in the search engine).

Steering Committee for the Review of Commonwealth/State Services Provision. *Commonwealth/State Services Provision.* Melbourne, Australia: Productivity Commission. An annual two-volume report offering comparative data on Australian state government services. Available for download at www.indcom.gov.au/service/gsppubs.html, or in printed form from AusInfo, at www.pc.gov.au/ausinfo.html (catalog number 9812 595).

United Kingdom. Audit Commission. *Local Authority Performance Indicators; Using Your Indicators; Watching Their Figures: A Guide to the Citizen's Charter Indicators; How Is Your Council Performing*? London: Her Majesty's Stationery Office, published annually. The annual *Local Authority Performance Indicators* and other Audit Commission publications are available on the Web at www.audit-commission.gov.uk (click on "National Reports," then "Online Catalogue") or from Her Majesty's Stationary Office Publications Centre, P.O. Box 276, London, SW8 5DT. Phone: 0170 873 9090. Fax: 0171 873 8200. The others are available directly from the Audit Commission at 1 Vincent Square, London, SW1P 2PN. Phone: 0171 828 1212. Fax: 0171 976 6187.

Also see the resources on performance measurement (pp. 269–271) and customer information systems (pp. 311–319).

Chapter 6

Performance Management

Using Rewards to Create Consequences

Using *Performance Management*, organizations measure results, establish standards or targets, reward good performance (financially, psychologically, or both), and penalize poor performance.

In 1996, the 304 county employees who clean up Greater Seattle's wastewater scrimped and saved every dime they could. Some cut back on the use of chemicals in the process of "decaking" the waste. Machinists made spare parts rather than purchase new ones. A facilities team recycled lumber. "We have people who wash their own gloves, because they don't want to spend the money on new gloves," says John Kruse, a senior operator in one treatment facility.

At year's end, the wastewater division returned more than $513,000 of its budget to King County. It was the fourth year in a row that it had given money back, without reducing service levels or effluent quality. The savings amounted to $2.4 million.

Until a few years earlier, the division had acted like most public agencies: it spent every dollar in its budget. If it didn't, its managers feared, they would get less money the following year. The pattern changed when management agreed to let employees take home half the savings they generated for the agency. This is called *gainsharing,* and like profit sharing in the private sector, it has an enormous impact on employees' behavior.

Before employees could pocket a share of savings, they had no reason to improve their efficiency. Performance had no impact on pay. "We were 'command stupid,'" says Kruse. "We did what we were told, no more, no less. Our initiative was not valued."

Then management and labor began to focus on performance, because private firms were winning bids to take over wastewater treatment in other places. First they cooperated to empower employees, giving workers better training and more authority to make improvements. Then, in 1993, they adopted gainsharing.

"We wanted a way to compensate workers for continuously improving things," recalls Kruse, then president of Service Employees International Union Local 6. There was no guarantee that gainsharing would pay off, but the union agreed to substitute it for an automatic 50–cents-an-hour pay increase. One mechanic, skeptical that he'd ever see a nickel, sold the right to his first gainsharing check to a coworker for $50.

But once financial incentives were introduced, workers had no trouble rooting out waste. "There was a lot of fat in the budget to cut," says Kruse. "So the first check"—for $732 apiece—"was easy to achieve." Once employees saw those checks, he adds, "everyone started talking about how to save money."

Bill Burwell, a division operations manager, saw a rapid change in employees' attitudes. Suddenly, he says, they were thinking, "It's my money out there. How can I save it?"

In March 1997, when the fourth-year gainsharing checks went out, the average check for yearlong, full-time employees was $1,061. Over four years, workers pocketed an average of $4,100 apiece—more than $1.2 million in all.

That is about 9 cents per hour better than the 50–cents-an-hour raise the union left at the bargaining table, according to Burwell. And employees gained more than money, says Kruse. "The people here are very proud of the work they do. We can point to what we did to earn the extra money."

LINKING PERFORMANCE TO REWARDS

Gainsharing gave King County's wastewater treatment workers a powerful incentive to improve their performance. It made clear what outcome was desired: reduced costs without reduced quality. And it made clear what the reward would be: half of the savings. Measurable performance outcomes linked to rewards—this is the heart of performance management. In addition to gainsharing, other performance management tools include awards, psychic pay, bonuses, shared savings, and performance contracts and agreements.

pp. 231–246

Reinventors use performance management when they cannot or should not create consequences for performance by using managed competition or enterprise management. Like these other two approaches, it upends the traditional bureaucratic paradigm, which offers public employees few if any rewards for above-average performance and imposes few if any penalties for below-average performance. Almost nobody in government gets bonuses or raises based on performance, and almost nobody is demoted or fired. In most

pp. 153–182, 183–214

organizations, seniority is a better protection against being laid off than high performance is.

This reality is a legacy of bureaucratic assumptions. Industrial-era bureaucracies control workers by specifying their tasks in detail. They assume that those who qualify for a job—because of educational credentials, work experience, or their performance on tests—are interchangeable: they all can and will perform the required duties. Therefore, employees in similar jobs should all be paid the same. Each civil service position is part of a class of jobs with similar duties. Each classification has a pay range that contains a number of salary steps from top to bottom. Employees advance up the steps, usually on the basis of longevity: another year, another step. Typically, civil servants also receive cost-of-living increases, across-the-board general raises, and annual longevity bonuses—none of which depend on their performance.

The system offers employees an implicit deal: if you do as you're told by management, you won't suffer negative consequences (such as firing), and your status and compensation will improve steadily.

Often a manager must certify that an employee's performance has been satisfactory. But most of the time, managers trivialize this process. They do not want the burden of giving an employee a bad rating; it means hassles with the employee and the unwelcome job of documenting and justifying the decision. Nor do they want to anger most of their employees by singling out a few for superior ratings. It is easier just to bless the performance of all but the absolutely worst employees. Thus, in most public organizations, the vast majority of employees receive positive performance ratings. In the first year of Australia's bonus pay program, for instance, 94.4 percent of the eligible senior officials got a bonus. This was also the norm in the U.S. and Canada, where most managers spread merit pay increases equally. Public management expert Robert Behn calls this the "Lake Wobegon syndrome," after Garrison Keillor's mythical town where "all the children are above average."

Although the bureaucratic personnel system is known as the "merit system," merit has little to do with it. Because it rewards marginal and superior employees equally, it promotes mediocrity and waste. Superior performers become demoralized when they are treated the same as marginal performers. When their organizations undervalue their contributions, people have trouble sustaining their commitment. They become cynical and either reduce their efforts or leave.

"Everyone wants to *matter*," says General Bill Creech, who initiated many of the incentives used by the U.S. Air Combat Command (ACC). "Policies that in effect tell people they don't matter are a big turnoff. . . . Conversely, those that make people believe they do matter inspire loyalty and commitment in return."

Performance management, a response to these and other ills, gives public employees a stake in their organization's results. It sends them unmistakable signals about which results matter, and it rewards employees who produce those results. Elected officials and top managers spell out what they want public organizations to accomplish, then create incentives to "pull" employees' behavior toward achieving those goals.

Performance management also creates pressure to change bureaucratic organizational cultures and administrative control systems. When employees start caring about boosting efficiency and effectiveness, they inevitably find that government's centralized purchasing, budgeting, and personnel systems stand in their way—and they begin demanding reform.

The Fine Art of Setting Performance Goals

To use performance management, organizations must decide which achievements they will reward. Incentives for performance must be linked to some measure of performance: "if you produce *that,* you will get *this.*" Usually, bureaucracies measure the wrong *that:* whether or not employees comply with management requirements. In performance management, you must measure the *results* that government organizations and people produce.

As we explain in Chapter Seven, on performance measurement (where we define all the terms used here in detail), reinventors can tie incentives to five kinds of results:

pp. 252–256

- Increases in the *quantity* of outputs produced.
- Increases in *efficiency,* which reduce the cost of work performed.
- Improvement in the *quality* of services produced, such as their timeliness, responsiveness, and accessibility.
- Improvement in the impact of an organization's work—its *effectiveness.*
- Reductions in the cost of producing that level of effectiveness, or *cost-effectiveness.*

In Chapter Seven we also explain that you can measure these factors at several steps in the process of producing results. You can target your incentives on improvement in:

pp. 249–252

- *Processes:* the activities or production methods of employees, such as street sweeping.
- *Outputs:* the products of that work, such as miles of streets swept.
- *Strategy or program outcomes:* the direct results of the strategy or program used, such as the cleanliness of streets just after they have been swept.
- *Policy outcomes:* the longer-term results that citizens care about, such as clean streets, clean air, and low crime rates.

The key is to hold the right team or organization accountable for the right results. Some frontline teams may have little control over outputs but significant control over processes, for example. Consider the unit that controls the process of determining clients' eligibility for benefits. Other units may have to complete other processes before the basic output—payment of benefits—can take place. So the first unit should be held accountable only for the quality and efficiency of the process it controls.

Further up the chain, the welfare department may have some control over its program outcomes, such as how many recipients it places in jobs. But it may have little control over other program outcomes, such as how long those recipients keep the jobs and remain off welfare. And it probably has very little control over the broader policy outcomes, such as how much of the population is on welfare in the first place. Typically, that depends largely on the state of the economy and the welfare rules put in place by legislators.

The important thing is to build incentives around results a unit can significantly influence or control. If you ask frontline employees to become accountable for outcomes, you will only frustrate and confuse them. If you ask most operating ("rowing") organizations to be accountable for policy outcomes, they will object. They will rightly feel that they are at the mercy of events beyond their control, and they will become cynical about the entire performance measurement process.

At the same time, you want to motivate managers to look for new strategies that will produce better outcomes. If they have no responsibility for outcomes, most will not do this. They will concentrate on what earns them rewards. They may work harder, but they will have little incentive to come up with better strategies and work processes. They will improve, but they may not innovate.

p. 47

What happened in Sunnyvale, California, the American pioneer of performance management, illustrates both the problem and its solution. Until 1994, Sunnyvale's system focused primarily on outputs and efficiency, as opposed to outcomes and effectiveness. It was powerful enough to produce 6 percent annual productivity increases. But managers complained that it drove people to focus on producing the desired numbers, regardless of whether they contributed to the overall result their departments wanted. Employees worked very hard—but at fairly traditional public service jobs. The one place where we found tremendous innovation—including a rethinking of the basic way the organization achieved its goals—was in the Leisure Services unit, which was reinvented as an enterprise fund. Because it depended on its customers for its revenues and faced real competition for their recreation dollars, this unit constantly dreamed up new ways to meet their needs. Its staff not only worked harder, they worked smarter.

pp. 169–170

City Manager Tom Lewcock and his department heads recognized the problem and developed a solution they called *outcome management*, which shifted the key targets toward effective outcomes. With their businesses tied to improvement in outcomes, managers had a powerful incentive to rethink the basic strategies their organizations used.

p. 47

There is a real dilemma here. On the one hand, if you go so far in this direction that managers feel their targets are unfair, they will run and hide. They will develop easy targets or vague targets; they will make sure no real measurement takes place; and some may even falsify data. Evaluation expert Michael Quinn Patton offers an equation that sums up the danger nicely:

Demand to produce outcome
− control over outcomes
+ high stakes
= corruption of indicators

On the other hand, if you don't go far enough, everyone will work hard to improve what they already do, but no one will question whether other strategies would be more effective.

pp. 47–50

As we said in Chapter One, a performance budgeting system should focus more on outcomes than a performance management system does. Performance budgeting is about setting direction, telling everyone in the system the results policymakers want. Performance management is about creating consequences for performance, so people will produce those results. But as we explained in Chapter One, if you try to combine the two systems, neither will work. You cannot hold everyone accountable for outcomes that are far out of their control. Top managers must translate the broad policy outcomes policymakers want into appropriate program outcome, output, and process goals at each level of the organization.

The challenge is to figure out which results you can reasonably ask each level of your system to produce. With the caveat that every situation is different, we suggest the following very rough guidelines:

Who Should Be Accountable?	***For What?***
Elected officials, city and county managers	Policy outcomes
Department heads (for example, cabinet members)	Program or strategy outcomes
Operating agency executives	Program or strategy outcomes and outputs
Agency units and their managers	Unit outputs
Work teams	Processes and their outputs

Setting Target Levels

Your next challenge is to set the levels above which performance will be rewarded. W. Edwards Deming, the widely revered pioneer of Total Quality Management, railed against using numerical targets. Among his famous 14 Points, the tenth is "Eliminate slogans, exhortations, and numerical targets." Deming felt strongly about the matter, and as Creech notes, "Many of his disciples are holier than the Pope on the same subject."

Deming argued that you can know how much better performance can be only *after* you have improved your work processes. Hence, he reasoned, all targets are arbitrary. He also stressed the negative impacts targets can have. Arbitrary targets create cynicism among the workforce. When workers fail to reach targets that were set too high, for example, they are unfairly blamed. If they exceed targets, they are praised and rewarded—regardless of how difficult or easy the improvements were to achieve. In other words, when targets are pulled out of the air and incentives are tied to them, the results are often unfair. Thus, rather than building productivity, they can undermine morale.

We agree with much of Deming's analysis, but we believe he went too far when he railed against *all* performance targets. We doubt that the businesses he worked with eliminated all performance targets. They still measured profit and loss, market share, return on investment, net worth, customer satisfaction, and the like—and no doubt had performance targets for some. And they experienced real consequences if they succeeded or failed to hit their targets. Deming may have been right to say that they did not need performance targets for individual employees (although many high-performing corporations reject this advice). But that is not the same as saying that they did not need objective targets for their organizations—the entire corporation and its individual units.

This is an example of the danger of importing business management wisdom into the public sector without any translation. Most public agencies don't have to compete and don't measure any bottom lines. They need performance targets that are consequential—the equivalent of profit-and-loss, return-on-investment, and customer satisfaction measures in business.

The best solution to this apparent conundrum, in our view, is the one pioneered by Sunnyvale and other local governments. In most cases, these governments simply measure current performance and create incentives for managers and (in some cases) employees to improve those levels significantly. Managers in Sunnyvale whose units demonstrate significant improvement are eligible for raises and bonuses of up to 10 percent of their salaries. But the performance level they have achieved becomes their expected target from then on. If they fall too far below that level, they can receive up to a 5 percent pay cut. This system creates a powerful incentive for continuous improvement.

This approach has a number of advantages over setting specific performance improvement targets. First, it takes arbitrary judgment out of the process, and thus it minimizes employee cynicism. Second, it saves the time and energy that otherwise has to go into choosing and negotiating over performance targets. Third, it creates a process that gradually squeezes out the fat and forces the organization to stretch its capacity. This does not all happen immediately; but over time, it does happen. After three or four years, organizations can no longer game the system by setting easy targets. Finally, this approach avoids making central management set targets about activities it doesn't know much about—something that breeds cynicism among line employees.

This approach is insufficient in two situations, however. The first is when an organization is creating new activities, because there will be no "current level" of performance. In such cases we suggest that organizations set targets but wait to tie incentives to them until they develop enough experience to make sure the targets are realistic. This may take two or three years.

The second situation is when leaders want a quantum jump in performance—when they are not satisfied with 5 percent improvement per year. When reinventing a dysfunctional bureaucracy, it often makes sense to demand 25 or 50 percent increases in performance. The same is true when redesigning a program or reengineering a process.

A "stretch target," which sets a target just beyond the reach of easy improvement, forces employees to look for new ways to best performance. In New Zealand, for example, George Hickton, general manager of the Income Support Service, set a daunting target for his managers. In 1993, it took his agency an average of six days to decide if an applicant was eligible for welfare benefits. Hickton told his managers he wanted the average period down to one day, within a year. They couldn't believe it; they told him it was an impossible target. But he insisted that if they made radical changes, they could do it. One year later—without staffing or budget increases—it took *less than a day* to process applications.

These kinds of stories are becoming common. But setting targets this way is an art, not a science—and it does not always work. Derek Volker, the former secretary of the Australian social security department, recalls what happened when he tried to cut the target for how much time it took to answer the phone from three minutes to 30 seconds. "We'd say, you go and be on the phone and see how long three minutes is, see how long two minutes is, see how long one minute is," he remembers. "*A minute is a hell of a long time when you're waiting for some public servant to answer the phone.*" When the union resisted, arguing that it would take more resources to hit the target, Volker simply mandated that employees pick up the phone within three rings. But that didn't work: "They were picking up the phone and saying good day and then putting it down." So finally he compromised: he set a new target of one minute but agreed that only 85 percent of all calls had to be answered in that time—as long as 98 percent of all calls were answered within two minutes.

Negotiating Performance Goals

pp. 377–380

The process of setting performance goals should ideally involve at least three parties: the organization in question; a neutral agency committed to performance improvement, such as the U.K.'s Cabinet Office; and something like a customer council or board. Many managers already use feedback from customers as they develop performance targets; we're talking about going a step further, by giving customers a place at the table as goals are developed. If possible, all those involved in working out performance goals should have information about the performance of comparable organizations, including those in other cities, counties, states, or countries.

Negotiating an organization's goals requires a great deal of give-and-take, especially on the part of central agencies accustomed to dictating to other organizations. In the U.K., for example, executive agencies now operate on the basis of five-year "framework" agreements, which include key performance goals, and annual business plans, which include annual targets. The framework agreements are negotiated between the agency, its department, the Next Steps Team (in the Office of Public Service), and the Treasury Department. The Treasury acts as a kind of gatekeeper: the agreements are not finalized until it is satisfied. Later the Next Steps Team reviews the annual targets.

pp. 264–265

The danger is that this central control will go too far. The U.K. has a good balance: "We don't give ourselves the power to parachute in and say, here are some better targets, do them now," Sonia Phippard, who ran the Next Steps Team during the mid-1990s, told us. "We feel it is very important for the agency to own the [performance measurement] process." Instead, the team conducts informal conversations with the agencies to build their confidence to take on more aggressive targets.

Organizations can circumvent some of this work if (in all but new or special cases) they simply define the target as "improvement" and create incentives to reward it, as Sunnyvale does.

Whichever approach they use, they should also make certain that they structure the incentives so the target does not become a ceiling. Whatever the target, incentives should encourage employees to go far beyond it. In Sunnyvale, managers' bonuses increase as their performance increases. In Indianapolis, employees can earn more money by cutting costs more.

Finally, you need to understand that occasionally, elected officials will decide that the quality of a service or compliance activity has been improved enough. Once they are satisfied with the quality, they may prefer that all further improvements focus on cutting the cost, so they can free up resources for other priorities. In such cases, managers simply announce that rewards will now go exclusively for efficiency and productivity improvements—and that the quality and effectiveness goals will remain at current levels.

PERFORMANCE MANAGEMENT: OTHER LESSONS LEARNED

In *Banishing Bureaucracy* we spelled out several other lessons that bear repeating here, in briefer form. In addition, we offer a few new lessons.

See Banishing Bureaucracy pp. 145–147

1. Don't underestimate the power of psychological incentives.

Money matters, but so do psychological rewards such as recognition and increased responsibility. In the ACC, the generals can't use cash incentives, so they offer other rewards for performance. Top-achieving airplane mechanics get a ride in the back seat of the two-seat F–15 fighter jets they maintain, for example. "Those rides go a long way in convincing our young folks of how important they are," says Brigadier General Gregory Martin. The organization also gives out trophies, plaques, and certificates of recognition to teams that win ACC competitions in gunnery, aircraft maintenance, and the like. The military agency's biggest incentive is a three-day weekend. Each month, every ACC squadron—big teams of employees—can win a long weekend by meeting the organization's tough standards for performance.

See Banishing Bureaucracy pp. 147–148

2. Magnify the power of incentives by applying them to groups as well as individuals.

Most results are produced by groups of people working together, not by a single individual. So you should use collective rewards for performance. For example, schools and school districts in more than half the states in the U.S. can win rewards on the basis of student performance on tests, according to *Education Week*.

See Banishing Bureaucracy p. 150

3. Tie financial incentives to objective measures of performance, not to subjective appraisals.

Using measures on cost savings, program effectiveness, customer satisfaction, and the like avoids the concern that subjective measures, such as employee appraisals by managers, are inconsistent and possibly unfair. We offer one caveat here, however: you need to allow some room for adjustment to compensate for realities outside the organization's control. If there is a bad winter, for example, snowplowing crews may do a heroic job, but their numbers may look bad. Conversely, if there is little snow, they will almost inevitably look good. Within a system focused on objective measures, top managers must have some leeway to adjust for such circumstances, using common sense. This may open you up to employee cynicism, admits Tom Lewcock, former city manager of Sunnyvale and an expert on performance management. But if you don't adjust for common sense realities, you'll encounter even more cynicism.

4. Be careful what you target—you might get it.

Because performance incentives have a powerful effect on employees, you must carefully select which results you reward. If your goals are all short-term, then short-term improvements are all people will work on. If you emphasize productivity but not effectiveness, then that's all you'll get. We recommend a "balanced scorecard" approach: a mix of targets that promote longer-term results, including the quality of outputs and the effectiveness of outcomes.

"The wrong measure of performance can be—and has been—more harmful than no measure," says Roger Vaughan, a veteran consultant to state and local reinventors. "Most program administrators will do whatever they can to generate good numbers."

Consider the elementary school that set itself stretch targets and met them. To do so, it had to squeeze out art, music, storytelling, and virtually everything else the students enjoyed. The result, says Harvard's Patricia Rogers, is that "most of the students hate school and have lost interest in learning, and most of the teachers are wanting to leave."

A striking example of unbalanced targets occurred at the Internal Revenue Service. In January 1998, an internal audit revealed that the agency routinely measured employees' performance on the basis of how much money they collected. Evaluations of agency managers were tied to how well they achieved these goals. And the IRS's 33 districts were ranked by how well they did on meeting collection targets. These practices, auditors said, pressured employees in ways that placed "taxpayer rights at risk in the collection process"—leading to congressional hearings in which politicians painted the entire affair as a scandal. The IRS's new top official, Commissioner Charles Rossotti, ended this narrow targeting and adopted a balanced scorecard that includes business results, customer satisfaction, and employee satisfaction.

5. Work hard to create a culture of learning, not fear.

If you push too hard to achieve narrow results, you will create enormous anxiety and fear. People will concentrate on reaching their goals at all cost, regardless of whether that makes sense for the rest of the organization or system. This is the opposite of what you want. To use a manufacturing metaphor, factories will meet their quotas even it means shipping junk.

pp. 219–220

pp. 531–614

The solutions include focusing on outcomes, using rewards far more than penalties, and rewarding innovation and experimentation. Most important, mold a culture of learning, not blame. "Put ten good professionals in a room and they will devise your outputs and outcomes," says Sylvie Trosa, a veteran reinventor who has worked in France, the U.K., and Australia.

> *But what they won't devise is the rules of the game with your staff, and how confident your staff are not to hide bad results, not to cheat on . . . targets, and to talk about problems. Are you in a culture of fear, or a culture of trust? . . .*
>
> *At some stage there must be something like a trust contract where basically you reward more those people who have the courage to talk about problems than those who hide them.*

6. Don't assume the numbers alone will tell you why you are or are not getting the results you want.

pp. 56–59

As we explain in Chapter One, you may need evaluation to discover what is behind the numbers. At the least, you need some written explanation to go with the performance report, from those who understand the numbers. You also need to train your managers and elected officials about the limitations of the data: why they cannot always draw conclusions without knowing more.

"If an agency or organization is small enough, then performance monitoring will be supplemented by on-the-spot discussions, meetings," and so on, points out Jerome A. Winston, director of the Program for Public Sector Evaluation at the Royal Melbourne Institute of Technology. "The measures will not be misinterpreted because their context is well understood. The risks associated with performance monitoring appear to be greatest when used to report simplistic measures 'up the line', where they are used by people who are quite distant from the activities that give meaning to the measures."

7. Overcome resistance to paying for performance by starting with rewards for saving money.

Elected officials and citizens are often reluctant to use financial incentives. They wonder why they should pay *more* to get better results—aren't public employees already being paid to do well? The simple answer is that incentives work. "You get significantly better performance," notes Bill Burwell, the King County wastewater manager. "Do you want better performance or rhetoric?"

(The tougher question is how to get elected officials to care about performance in general. For this discussion, see Chapter One.)

pp. 22–23, 32

The best way to address concerns about offering incentives is to start by rewarding increases in productivity, as King County's wastewater division did. That way, the incentives pay for themselves, out of savings generated from improvements. After the politicians and the public become accustomed to this, you can move on to other forms of performance bonuses.

Hampton, Virginia, offers a good example. First, reinventors there sold the city council on bonuses for employees who came up with money-saving ideas. "That was not a hard sell," says Michael Monteith, a former assistant city manager who runs the city's information systems. "The council saw that first there had to be some hard savings; it was truly an incentive to do business differently."

Several years later, the council agreed to try a one-year experiment with shared savings: letting departments keep part of budgeted funds they didn't spend. Elected officials liked the results—they got 30 percent of the money departments saved. So they adopted the incentive permanently. Then the city manager asked the council to approve an incentive that did not yield financial savings: a bonus for every employee if citizen satisfaction hit a certain level annually. This time, says Monteith, the pitch was different. "We had a major emphasis on restructuring city government. We said we needed this incentive so employees would pay attention to what we thought was important, citizen satisfaction." The council, already convinced that incentives worked, adopted the bonus plan, which costs several hundred thousand dollars a year.

pp. 241–243

Often there is a backlash after prominent officials get performance bonuses. In Houston several years ago, when scores in the school district went up by a larger margin than the average improvement in the state, it triggered a performance bonus for Superintendent Rod Paige. When he accepted the $25,000 award, equivalent to 16 percent of his salary, he also took some heat. Teachers wrote letters to the newspapers complaining that they were only getting a 2–3 percent raise. The president of the Houston Federation of Teachers, Gayle Fallon, griped that Paige got "$25,000 for raising test scores, but I don't recall a single student that Rod Paige taught. I fail to see where he earned it."

Paige and the school board defended the bonus, as they should have. The superintendent said that he deserved some credit for the district's improving test scores and observed that some teachers were also getting bonuses. "We should reward people who can and will get the job done," Paige said.

8. Overcome union opposition by rewarding large teams, not individuals.

Labor leaders typically oppose certain kinds of financial incentives, but not all of them. Usually, they don't want their members to be paid differently for performing similar work. They fear that such differentials will erode the workers' shared economic interests and, therefore, their need for a union. They also oppose giving managers discretion over how much money individual workers earn, because they don't want managers to have the power to play favorites or to get workers to compete with one another.

These concerns can be addressed. To have a shot at union support, use incentives for groups or teams of workers, not individuals. And use objective performance measures; don't leave performance evaluation in the hands of managers. In King County, the union blessed gainsharing because it provided incentives to teams and used an objective measure, dollars saved by teams.

The Delicate Matter of Negative Consequences

Performance management giveth and, yes, it taketh away; with rewards come risks. It is the *combination* of possible rewards and sanctions, not just the potential upside, that motivates performance. Without both, a performance management system often lacks credibility with elected officials. But the right balance is difficult to achieve in practice. When the World Bank studied the issue, it found that when governments made performance contracts with managers, they "rarely imposed any negative consequences [for] inadequate performance." Of course, poor performers won't get bonuses or other rewards. This is hardly trivial, but it does not have the same bite as the imposition of sanctions or penalties.

Several types of negative consequences can be designed into performance agreements:

• ***Negative Publicity.*** Most people don't want the world to know they are failing. In Kentucky, where the state offers substantial cash bonuses to schools that meet improvement targets, educators say they are more motivated by the fear of negative publicity about their school's performance than by the bonuses. Poor performance damages their standing in the community and their professional pride.

pp. 210–214, 311–319

The trick, then, is to ensure full public disclosure of performance results. In Michigan, one way this is done is through an annual school accreditation report, which rates every school on several performance standards. This sends loud signals to school staff—and to parents. One year, Kimberly Gonzalez, a parent in Lansing, learned that the lowest rating had been given to Grand River Elementary School, where she had three children. "I was over at the school in a half hour when I heard about it," she says. "I was worried. I wanted to know why."

• ***Loss of Privileges.*** Performance agreements can specify that if performance falls below certain levels, managers will lose certain privileges—a city-owned car, the right to travel on the job, the right to waive certain regulations, and so on—until it improves.

• ***Loss of Autonomy.*** When organizations fail to perform, you can take away the managers' control over their budgets. This inevitably gets their attention. If you then provide the coaching or training they need, things sometimes turn around.

• ***Loss of Income.*** In general, we don't suggest using financial penalties for poor performance for most employees, because they trigger fierce resentment and resistance. They also curb innovation, because they make managers afraid to try new things, for fear they will not work and performance will suffer. But when it comes to the top manager in an organization—a city or county manager, a school superintendent, a cabinet member in a state or national government—financial penalties signal that there is accountability for performance at the very top of the organization. The message is "that we're deeply committed to a hard-edged accountability system that will hold my feet up to the fire," says David Hornbeck, who risked losing up to 5 percent of his salary as superintendent of schools in Philadelphia, if he missed his performance targets.

• ***Intervention from Above.*** In education, it is now common for school districts, states—even national governments—to threaten to intervene if schools fall below standards. In 1996, for example, Chicago's school board put 109 of the city's lowest-scoring schools (20 percent of the district) on probation because fewer than 15 percent of the students performed at grade level on national reading tests. The board sent a team of experts into each school to develop improvement plans. If the schools then failed to improve, the board could replace principals and teachers. As a last resort, it could close the schools.

This can be a big stick, if the stick holder has the nerve to use it. In the mid-1990s Kentucky's education department targeted 53 schools for failing to improve performance. The state assigned a "distinguished educator" to help the principal and teachers in each school. Within a year, all of the schools showed measurable improvements. This tactic has also been effective in the U.K.

• ***Takeover.*** This is a favored tool of politicians, particularly in education. In many American states, if students in a school or district perform poorly enough for long enough, the state government can take over. Although such laws make politicians look tough, they unfortunately do little for children.

First, they offer few consequences and little help until things are desperate. They are like safety systems for the space shuttle that only kick in after a shuttle blows up. Second, they are difficult to impose, because local politicians usually fight them. Hence they are applied only in the worst cases. This leads to the third problem: they help very few schools. Finally, takeovers offer no guarantee that the new management will be able to improve performance—and no consequences if they don't!

By takeover time, things are usually almost beyond repair. In New Jersey, the state has run the Jersey City schools since 1989 and the Patterson schools since 1991. By 1996, neither showed improvement in student test scores. But the governor was stuck with them. By now, it has no doubt occurred to the governor that "owning" sick school districts is a no-win proposition.

pp. 279–322, 183–214

As the list above indicates, however, there are alternatives to takeovers. In addition, elected officials can create powerful consequences for every school (or organization) through competitive customer choice and managed competition—making every school, in effect, a charter school. They can use the threat of regular takeovers—by competitors—to force continual improvement. Why wait until things are desperate?

• ***Loss of Employment.*** This is the ultimate sanction: firing people who consistently fail to perform, even after coaching and training. For years, governments have been notoriously reluctant to do this, but that is changing. Increasingly, managers at the top of government agencies, including school principals, are being given fixed-term contracts rather than lifetime tenure. If they don't work out, their contracts are either not renewed or, in some cases, cut short. In some schools, it's also getting easier to oust incompetent teachers, who traditionally have been protected by tenure systems.

THE PERFORMANCE MANAGEMENT TOOLKIT

Performance Awards provide employees with nonfinancial recognition for their achievements. This lets workers know their performance is appreciated, respected, and valued. See p. 231.

Psychic Pay provides employees, teams, or organizations with quasi-financial benefits of real value, such as paid time off or new equipment, to reward them for high performance. See p. 232.

Performance Bonuses are one-time cash awards provided in addition to salaries. They go to individuals or teams that achieve specified performance targets. They do not become part of an employee's compensation base. See p. 232.

Gainsharing gives employees a guaranteed portion of financial savings their organization achieves while continuing to meet specified service levels and quality. It gives workers a clear economic stake in increasing productivity. See p. 237.

Shared Savings is gainsharing for organizations. It allows them to keep a portion of the funds they save during the fiscal year (or biennium) to use in the future. It creates an organizational incentive to save money. See p. 241.

Performance Contracts and Agreements put managers and their organizations on the hook for performance. They build in rewards and penalties, and they give public leaders the freedom to get rid of top managers—or entire organizations—that do not deliver the desired results. See p. 243.

PERFORMANCE AWARDS

In the mid-1980s, the director of the Michigan Department of Commerce, Doug Ross, started buying advertising space in a monthly statewide business magazine. The full-page ads didn't contain the usual pitch to businesses about why they should invest more money in the state. Instead, each ad told a story about department employees—"associates," they were called—who had helped businesses solve their problems. The message tried to persuade companies that the department was on their side. But Ross was also sending a message to his employees: he valued their achievements. To underscore the point, he had a copy of each ad framed and presented to the employees at an awards ceremony. Then he hung the framed ads in the agency's main hallway.

Most of the civil servants, Ross says, were surprised that he was willing to spend money—even small amounts—on making them feel good. "It didn't cost much, but to them it was a meaningful form of affection," he recalls. And by recognizing his employees' accomplishments, Ross's ads reinforced the behaviors that he valued.

Performance awards have this double effect: they show employees that they are valued, and they signal what kind of behavior and achievement matters. Very small sums can go a very long way with people. "There is no limit on plaques, parties and pictures," notes public management scholar Robert Behn.

Awards can be made by outside entities too. In Texas, for instance, the state comptroller's office started issuing "Breaking the Mold" awards in 1992 to state agencies that had reinvented themselves. Since 1985, the Ford Foundation has given Innovation Awards to 10 government programs every year, each worth $100,000, plus far more in prestige and publicity.

POSSIBLE PERFORMANCE AWARDS

1. Awards ceremonies for employees
2. Plaques
3. Certificates of achievement
4. Photos and stories in organization newsletters
5. News stories about achievements
6. Breakfast, lunch, or dinner with the CEO
7. Lapel pins
8. Engraved objects like nameplates and coffee mugs
9. Employee of the Month awards
10. Vouchers, gift certificates, or tickets for cultural or sporting events

pp. 564–566

Here are some tips for using performance awards:

- Make celebrating success a big part of the organization's culture.
- Recognize teams as well as individuals.
- Make awards ceremonies exciting.
- Publicize performance achievements in the local media.
- Use peer-to-peer awards, in which an employee can instantly call attention to another employee's "beyond the call" performance.
- Don't feel you have to spend a lot of money on awards. It's more important to make the award meaningful than to make it expensive. It's the thought that counts.
- Make department-to-department awards. Honor the performance of agencies that share responsibilities with yours or that you depend on for support.
- If the success of the organization or system depends on the effort customers make (as in schools, training programs, economic development programs, and welfare programs), give awards to outstanding customers, too.

PSYCHIC PAY

***Psychic Pay* provides employees, teams, or organizations with quasi-financial benefits of real value, such as paid time off or new equipment, to reward them for high performance.**

When government managers cannot offer additional income as a reward, they can turn to popular substitutes that also have economic value. The ACC, for instance, uses paid time off for units that perform above targets. "It's a big incentive, a very big incentive," says General Michael Loh, the former ACC commander.

Other quasi-economic incentives include throwing parties, buying new office equipment, refurbishing facilities, and paying for people to take college or graduate school classes or attend conferences or workshops.

Psychic pay can go to organizations, too. In 1984, South Carolina began giving cash awards to schools that exceeded student achievement standards and teacher and student attendance standards. The money—$15,000 to $20,000 per school in 1995—can't go into anyone's pocket, only into things that will improve school performance, such as new equipment or materials.

PERFORMANCE BONUSES

***Performance Bonuses* are one-time cash awards provided in addition to salaries. They go to individuals or teams that achieve specified performance targets. They do not become part of an employee's compensation base.**

In the late 1970s, public organizations began borrowing the idea of performance pay from the private sector. The U.S. and Canadian federal governments both tried it. By 1995, ten state governments reported tying at least some employees' pay to performance. School districts and states began experimenting with merit pay for teachers. In 1995, Cincinnati became the first U.S. school district to link raises for all central office managers to student test scores, dropout rates, and other objectives.

In short, the days of automatic pay raises are over in an increasing number of public organizations. Unfortunately, these performance pay systems fail more often than they succeed. We have already identified some of the problems: most performance pay systems use subjective ratings of employee performance, and most reward individuals, not teams. Most managers are afraid to use the tool, and those that do find themselves sowing envy, resentment, and jealousy in their ranks.

p. 224

See Banishing Bureaucracy pp. 147–150

Most systems also use salary increases rather than bonuses to reward performance. This often becomes expensive, because the salary increase costs money not just for one year but for every year thereafter. Legislatures, councils, school boards, and budget offices usually get nervous about escalating personnel costs and push to keep both the number of performance pay increases and the dollar amounts low, which undermines the value of the tool. In addition, if an outstanding employee earns several performance pay increases, he or she often hits the top of the salary range—and the tool becomes useless, because further salary increases are impossible. When that happens, good employees often begin looking for other jobs that pay more—an unintended consequence of the worst kind.

The solution is to use bonuses, which avoid many of these problems. In our opinion, salaries should be determined by market conditions: what it takes in your labor market to attract and keep the talent you need. They should be adjusted for groups as inflation rises and market conditions change, and for individuals when necessary to keep a valuable employee. (To do this, you need a broad-band pay system, as we describe in Chapter Ten.)

pp. 411–414

After an exhaustive study of performance pay plans in public education, performance management expert Harry Hatry and his colleagues at the Urban Institute also concluded that bonuses work better. They are becoming quite common. In 1995, Kentucky handed out $26 million in bonuses to teachers in 38 percent of the state's public schools—those that had improved student performance by more than 10 percent over two years on key measures targeted by the state. Their 13,500 teachers decided how to use the money, sometimes sharing it with other school employees or investing it in their schools.

Since 1990, Dallas teachers and principals whose students' test scores have improved have won $1,000 each, with $500 going to each of the schools' other staff members. In the U.K. and New Zealand, chief executives are eligible for bonuses as large as 20 percent of their salaries. And more than a dozen British executive agencies have used group bonus schemes, some awarding as much as £500 (about $825) to each staff member. A few government organizations even use "lightning bonuses"—on-the-spot cash awards that managers give to employees who do something of extraordinary merit.

Money is a powerful incentive. It is not "the most important driver" of behavior, says former Sunnyvale city manager Tom Lewcock. "But it's important enough that when a person's income is contingent upon how well they've achieved certain outcomes—not things like maintaining their turf or getting at least as much money as last year—their behavior changes." In 1980, Sunnyvale announced that managers could get up to a 10 percent bonus for exceeding their performance targets or up to a 5 percent pay cut for falling short.

> *That's when it started to get real serious. All of the traditional ways bureaucracies cover their butts flew out the window as a result of that shift. Lots of folks started looking at the world in a different way. That catalyst was a giant step forward—the consequences were absolutely powerful.*

This is true not only for managers; it works just as well with the lowest-paid public employees. In 1991, then governor Lawton Chiles convinced the Florida legislature to turn the Revenue Department and the Division of Worker's Compensation free from civil service and line item budget restrictions, as an experiment. For years, the division had been plagued by a backlog that multiplied its expenses, because workers whose claims lay dormant often filed suit. Labor Secretary Frank Scruggs used his new freedom to eliminate 20 middle management jobs and put the savings into a monthly bonus program for 500 line employees who processed the claims—some of whom were paid so little that they qualified for food stamps. If they increased their productivity significantly, they got an extra check.

In the first month alone, productivity shot up 30 percent in one unit, 50 percent in another, and 60 percent in a third. By the third month, 265 employees were earning bonus checks, and the backlog was gone. At its former productivity rate, the division would have had to hire 52 new employees to achieve the same increase in output.

"A dollar for a good deed works," said Scruggs.

> *I remember handing a check to one of our employees. She quivered when she took the check. She said, "It's real." That's the goal—to be able to communicate that there will be a reward.*

Using Performance Bonuses: Lessons Learned

Because bonuses are add-ons to compensation, you don't need to change the entire compensation system to use this tool. They are relatively simple to design, quick to implement, and easy to eliminate. As with any financial incentive, they usually work best if they are based on objective measures of performance, not managers' appraisals. Our research found several other keys to their effective use:

pp. 224–227

1. When outputs are produced by teams, use your system to reward teams.

Unless individual workers' activities lead directly to outputs you can measure—as in the case of the keypunch operators and claims processors in Florida's Division of Worker's Compensation—you are better off giving performance pay increases to teams than to individuals. Why? Team-based bonuses reinforce all the virtues of teams that we describe in Chapter Eleven. They bind people to the collective purpose. They give employees a powerful reason to make sure each team member pulls his or her own weight—by pressuring laggards to improve. And they drive employees toward job flexibility: people quit caring whether something is in their job description and start caring about producing results.

pp. 478–486

This works best, of course, if employee teams have real control over their work. Can they get rid of a bad apple? Can they change their work processes? Can they hold staff agencies—their internal suppliers—accountable for their performance? If they can do these things, they can usually improve their performance dramatically.

2. Don't limit bonuses to managers; push them down into the ranks.

Introducing bonuses for managers can drive improvement, but not as much as making all employees eligible can. In Sunnyvale, managers and employees alike report that managers-only bonuses fuel divisions between them. "It causes me more problems than it's worth," says Robert Walker, director of parks and recreation. "All you get from employees is, every time you start improving the product, they understand the system well enough to say, 'Oh, I see, so *you* can get a raise.'" One manager was so concerned about the problem that he used any bonus he received to throw a barbecue for his employees.

(Sunnyvale's leaders did try to negotiate a performance pay system with the union for six years during the 1980s, but they failed each time. The key sticking points were fear of subjective ratings and negative financial consequences. The union wanted nothing similar to management's potential 5 percent pay cut for poor performance, and City Manager Tom Lewcock felt employees should share the same risks as managers. This experience is one reason we suggest you avoid imposing negative financial consequences.)

More important than the resentment the managers-only system creates is the fact that it fails to motivate employees to improve performance and cut costs. When we last visited Sunnyvale, its employees worked very hard, but they didn't actively look for savings and process improvements the way employees eligible for gainsharing in, say, Indianapolis did. "We are not tapping into a real important part of the organization to get new ideas and real breakthroughs," Assistant City Manager Ed James told us. "Most of the breakthroughs have been in management, not [among] line employees."

3. Create winners, not losers.

Some bonus programs limit how many eligible employees can actually win. They allocate less money than it would take to pay out bonuses to everyone. This creates competition for bonuses. It turns some employees into losers—even though they are improving their performance. We agree with Robert Behn, who argues that creating losers this way is a bad idea. As we discussed earlier, it's much better to tie bonuses to improvement over past performance. Those who improve *more* than others can get bigger bonuses. That way, people compete against themselves, rather than each other.

pp. 221–222

4. Give organizations the flexibility to tailor their bonus programs.

When instituting bonuses throughout a government system, allow organizations to adapt the plan to their own cultures and structures. No single model will be best for every agency.

5. Involve all key parties in designing and implementing performance bonuses.

Because bonuses can be controversial, you need to develop buy-in among those who will be affected.

6. Don't make your system too complex.

The temptation—to make sure the system is fair—is to measure all possible objectives, then weight each of them according to their importance. If you do this, the result will be a Rube Goldberg contraption no one can understand. Make it fair, but try to keep it simple.

7. Make bonuses big enough to get people's attention.

You need bonuses large enough to capture your employees' imaginations. We recommend a minimum of $500 per employee—and at least $1,000 for highly paid employees.

RESOURCES ON PERFORMANCE BONUSES

Harry P. Hatry, John M. Greiner, and Brenda G. Ashford. *Issues and Case Studies in Teacher Incentive Plans.* 2nd ed. Washington, D.C.: Urban Institute Press, 1994. A careful review of these issues in public education.

Carolyn Kelley, Allan Odden, Anthony Milanowski, and Herbert Heneman III. "The Motivational Effects of School-Based Performance Awards." *CPRE Policy Briefs.* February 2000. Useful research on what makes bonuses work, from the Consortium for Policy Research in Education (www.upenn.edu/gse/cpre).

GAINSHARING

***Gainsharing* gives employees a guaranteed portion of financial savings their organization achieves while continuing to meet specified service levels and quality. It gives workers a clear economic stake in increasing productivity.**

pp. 215–216

The King County wastewater division is not alone in giving workers a financial stake in increasing their productivity. In Indianapolis, garbage collectors saved more than $2.1 million in 1995, taking home gainsharing checks of $1,750 each. As word spread, other union locals negotiated similar deals. In 1996, the fleet services team split $75,659—one-quarter of what it saved in the previous year.

As a result, workers "are looking to save every dime," says Steve Fantauzzo, the city employee union leader who helped design the gainsharing agreements. "They figure a piece of the pie is going into their pocket."

Workers responsible for sealing cracks in roads wondered why the city spent $22 for a gallon of vulcanized rubber for sealing. They said, "If we go to the local junkyard, we can get tires and melt them down for 30 cents a gallon, and it's ecologically more sound," according to Fantauzzo.

They also started questioning the performance of their suppliers. For instance, the private business that repaired transmissions on Indianapolis's city vehicles took two weeks to do each job. It felt no hurry, since the city was always slow in paying the company's invoices. So the fleet service workers got their union leaders to meet with the company and work out a more rapid response. Then they persuaded the city to arrange for backup suppliers in case performance did not improve. "We did all the troubleshooting," Fantauzzo says.

The fleet service workers even realized they couldn't perform some of their work as efficiently as the private sector could. So in areas like auto body repairs, they suggested outsourcing their work. When public union members push to contract work out to private companies, the bureaucratic model has been turned on its head.

In Portland, Maine, public works department employees get $100 each when they reduce a construction project's cost by 10 percent, and $250 for a 25 percent cut. In New York City, the Sanitation Department gave the union gainsharing in return for a shift from three workers per truck to two.

In Michigan, the state used gainsharing to reduce the cost of employee health benefits. It calculated the average cost of health benefits in the preceding seven years, then offered to give employees half of the savings if they drove costs below that average. In the 1997 fiscal year, the state saved about $40 million. Half of it went to 36,000 employees, whose checks averaged $555. "By working with employee groups, we cut costs and increased wages," says Mark Murray, the state treasurer.

The Benefits of Gainsharing

Gainsharing encourages employees to demand a role in rooting out systemic waste. Because they can gain financially, workers begin to question costs and come up with new, less expensive ways of doing things. They become less willing to let others—managers and central administrative agencies—make decisions that drive costs. As Fantauzzo says, employees take more ownership of their jobs.

Gainsharing promotes a collaborative, results-oriented culture. Gainsharing is a team sport; since everyone shares in the gains, it promotes employee collaboration.

Gainsharing can be used to defuse tension over downsizing and to encourage unions to work with management. Because it relies on positive group incentives and objective performance standards, gainsharing often appeals to unions. They don't have to worry about workers competing with one another for bonuses handed out by managers. Sometimes they oppose gainsharing because they don't want one group getting higher bonuses than another. But this flies in the face of their members' self-interest, so it is a difficult position to defend.

When leaders of the New York City Probation Department sought to reengineer and automate work processes, tensions developed with employees and their union, a local of the United Probation Officers Association. Management eased the conflict—even while slashing budgets and staff—by agreeing to share a third of the savings with union members, as cash bonuses. Pittsburg, California, dealt with resistance by making its gainsharing program voluntary.

Gainsharing avoids the problem of subjective appraisals of performance. As we discussed earlier, subject appraisals create many problems. With gainsharing, employee performance is rewarded based on something very objective: how many dollars they have saved.

pp. 217, 224

Finally, gainsharing saves money. This is the bottom line: workers only gain when they cut costs, and they only get to keep a portion of what they save. The organization—and the taxpayers—keep the rest. The process doesn't cost them a dime.

Gainsharing: Lessons Learned

Gainsharing is a flexible tool that can be tailored to fit most organizations. To use it, you must first decide who will gain and how much they can gain.

1. ***Use gainsharing to reward teams, not individuals.***

   Although a big part of gainsharing's appeal is that it works as a team incentive, the tool can be—and often is—used with individuals. For instance, a few organizations have employee suggestion programs that share with employees a portion—usually 10 percent—of the savings their ideas generate. This is definitely worth doing. But it usually generates one-time innovations by individual employees rather than a steady stream of cost-saving reforms by groups of workers. And typically it leaves managers in control of decisions. Hence it has far less impact on the organizational culture.

2. ***Reward units that feel mutual ownership of an identifiable type of work.***

   To reward teams, you have to decide what size unit makes the most sense. Indianapolis started with work units involving 75 to 150 employees, such as sanitation and fleet services. Fantauzzo predicts that future gainsharing agreements will cover larger groups of employees, however—perhaps even entire departments. One reason is that few work teams are really self-sufficient; they depend on people in support services and on other work teams. Yet those people rarely get to share in the rewards.

3. ***Let employees keep enough of the savings to motivate them.***

   The gainsharing split between the organization and the employees is negotiable. Indianapolis's sanitation workers negotiated 10 percent of savings, but its fleet service workers negotiated 25 percent in the first year and 30 percent in each of the following two years. New York City's probation officers got 33 percent, whereas workers in the U.S. Air Force PACER SHARE project received 50 percent. The rate does not have to be fixed forever. In Indianapolis, Fantauzzo anticipates that his union will negotiate for larger shares as the amounts of potential savings decline.

4. ***Let the employees in each unit decide how to divide up the money.***

   Sometimes the workers split the gains in equal shares. Sometimes they take other factors into account. For example, the Indianapolis fleet service team allocated gains according to how many hours each member of the team had put in during the year. People who worked overtime received bigger bonuses.

We recommend letting the employees decide how they will split the money. The point is to engage them in the process as fully as possible. Letting them divide the savings reinforces the message that they are empowered to make more of their own decisions.

5. *Specify required service levels and quality even as costs are being cut.*

This prevents corner cutting to boost financial gains. King County's wastewater workers, for example, had to meet the same requirements for effluents that existed before gainsharing.

6. *Guarantee that employees will not lose their jobs because they improve productivity.*

When organizations make their work processes more efficient, they usually end up needing fewer workers. But employees won't make changes that will cost them their jobs. And their unions usually want some type of assurance that workers will not be laid off as a result of productivity increases due to gainsharing. So it's best to adopt a no-layoff policy and use natural attrition to downsize, or move employees into other government jobs when theirs become obsolete. Neither King County nor Indianapolis put their policies in writing, but both adopted a no-layoff approach. This is a critical ingredient in Indianapolis, says AFSCME's Fantauzzo. Workers there know that even if they cut staffing levels, they will be retrained and relocated to other government jobs. Research about gainsharing confirms the importance of providing workers with job security, as well as a voice in workplace decisions, if you want them to push for increased productivity.

7. *Be flexible when extraneous events change costs.*

Gainsharing should apply only to costs that are under the employees' control. In King County, for instance, a supplier's cut in the cost of chemicals for wastewater treatment did not count as savings, since it was not due to employee efforts. When a problem on a construction site that was not caused by employees boosted costs, the increase was not counted against the employees.

8. *Don't create other conditions for receiving the gainsharing bonus.*

If there are too many conditions, employees will become skeptical that they will ever get the bonus—and their motivation to save money will vanish. For example, the most common temptation is to say, "Gainsharing bonuses will only be paid if the budget ends the year in balance or surplus." This immediately makes most employees cynical. They assume that even if they work hard to save money, they'll never get their bonuses; instead, the savings will be used to bail the government (or school district) out of a deficit. Yet gainsharing, by definition, never contributes to a deficit, because it is only paid if a unit has not spent all of its budget. We recommend that governments always honor gainsharing bonuses. After all, when a unit earns a gainsharing bonus, it has already helped balance the budget, because part of the savings reverts to the general fund. To cope with deficits, we recommend that governments use the same methods they would use if gainsharing did not exist, rather than raiding employees' gainsharing bonuses and thereby destroying any incentive to save.

9. Once employees embrace financial incentives, look for ways to reward more than efficiency.

John Kruse says his colleagues began to worry that they would run out of new, big cost reductions. "In some things, you get as efficient as you can," he says. That may look like a problem, but it's actually an opportunity. Once employees buy into rewards for performance, why limit them to improving efficiency? When efficiency gains slow up, negotiate bonuses for improving quality and effectiveness.

After all, the whole point is to motivate every employee to commit to improving performance. Gainsharing is probably the single fastest way to create a culture of continuous improvement, and bonuses based on quality are the logical next step. Once employees realize it's in their self-interest to improve their organization's performance, the battle is half won.

SHARED SAVINGS

***Shared Savings* is gainsharing for organizations. It allows them to keep a portion of the funds they save during the fiscal year (or biennium) to use in the future. It creates an organizational incentive to save money.**

In the closing month of a government fiscal year, many public agencies engage in a senseless spending frenzy. They quickly spend money on low priorities—before their authority to use the funds expires. If they don't use it, they lose it. What's worse, they may get less in the next budget cycle. Edwin G. Fleming, an Internal Revenue Service district manager, described the perversity of the system in a letter to the National Performance Review. "Every manager has saved money, only to have his allocation reduced in the subsequent year," he wrote. "This usually happens only once, when the manager becomes a spender rather than a planner."

In this way, traditional government budget systems encourage every manager to waste money. We have asked tens of thousands of public employees whether they agree with this statement. Very few have disagreed.

The solution is relatively simple: let organizations keep some of what they don't spend. In the U.K., Australia, Canada, Sweden, and an increasing number of state and local governments in the U.S., this is now the norm. Unless the legislature adopts a policy change requiring more or less of a service, each organization gets to roll over at least part of what it doesn't spend into a future budget cycle. The percentage varies from organization to organization. But as long as it is enough to motivate managers and employees to look for savings, it works.

There are three basic ways to do this. You can let organizations keep all or part of what they save, as local government pioneers such as Fairfield, California, did. You can force everyone to reduce spending a set amount and let them keep all of what they save beyond this, as Visalia, California, the U.K., and Australia did. Or you can cut spending across the board and let agencies compete to get some of the money back by proposing specific investments in productivity improvement, as Florida did under Governor Lawton Chiles.

There are several keys to making shared savings work:

Let agencies spend their savings as they see fit. Don't prescribe how agencies can use money they save. The point is to create a powerful incentive to eliminate unneeded spending. The more you limit what agencies can do with their savings, the more you weaken the incentive. Let them give gainsharing bonuses, buy technology, refurbish their offices, or throw a party to celebrate their success—whatever they prefer. As long as you have consequences for their performance, you needn't worry about how they spend every penny.

Require that they maintain or improve their performance levels. As in gainsharing, you don't want to reward agencies that save money by cutting back on customer service or their volume of production. If their performance falls, they should not receive the shared savings (unless the decline results directly from factors outside their control, such as a recession).

Minimize retroactive raids on their savings. If you let agencies carry over some of their year-end savings but then give them less money in the next budget cycle because they saved money in the last cycle, you will destroy their incentive to save. Hence shared savings programs must erect protections against this impulse. At the same time, they must recognize that elected officials—who face constituencies demanding that they spend money on new priorities—will not stand by forever and watch agencies accumulate large reserves.

There are at least two ways to walk this tightrope. In Fairfield and Visalia, the council agreed that it would not cut departmental budgets unless it also cut their workloads. Every five years or so, however, the city manager would examine accumulated savings and departmental efficiency increases and recommend adjustments in budget levels to the council. Departments that had begun the process "fat"—and had thus been able to save a great amount—found their budgets cut more than departments that had begun the process "lean." This satisfied the council, without doing undue damage to the departmental incentive to avoid unnecessary spending.

The second approach is to give agencies two-year budgets. This gives managers some assurance that retroactive raids will come, at most, every second year.

Convert your budget or finance officers and key appropriations committees. Shared savings is simple common sense, but it flies in the face of years of conditioning of budget officers and appropriators. From where they sit, there is never enough money. They face so many competing demands for funding—many of them not only legitimate but also urgent—that they feel compelled to reallocate any savings. You may be able to convince them that if they let agencies keep 50 percent of their savings, everyone will benefit, because half of something is better than all of nothing. But given the urgency of the demands they face, they will find it very hard to leave that other 50 percent on the table. They are like the greedy monkeys who reach into a jar for a handful of sweets and find themselves caught because they cannot remove their fist when it is full. They may know that if they let go of the sweets they can get free, but the temptation to hold on is too great.

If you cannot win the argument with sweet reason, try a pilot project. Get your budget office or appropriations committees to allow one or two agencies to keep part of what they don't spend. Let them see the savings that result—and let them learn firsthand how gratifying it is to get 50 percent of something rather than all of nothing. Once they have experienced the benefits, it will be easier for them to let go of the sweets.

RESOURCE ON SHARED SAVINGS

David Osborne and Ted Gaebler. *Reinventing Government.* Reading, Mass.: Addison-Wesley, 1992. See pages 118–121 for a full picture of the Fairfield-Visalia version of this tool.

PERFORMANCE CONTRACTS AND AGREEMENTS

***Performance Contracts and Agreements* put managers and their organizations on the hook for performance. They build in rewards and penalties, and they give public leaders the freedom to get rid of top managers—or entire organizations—that do not deliver the desired results.**

Public school principals in Chicago have something in common with public executives in New Zealand and the U.K. Reinventors have stripped them of traditional job tenure—guaranteed employment—and forced them to work on performance contracts of no more than a few years duration. If the organization's performance lags, they can be shown the door.

In Chicago, changes in state law ended tenure in 1989 and forced principals to apply for their jobs. The shift contributed to a mass exodus of principals. Some retired early or left the system; others were not rehired. Within several years, about half of the approximately 540 principals were newcomers. By 1996, turnover had increased to roughly *80 percent,* according to John Easton, district director of standards, assessment, and research.

pp. 188–200

pp. 124–148

The most common form of organizational performance contract is a contract with a service provider, whether a public agency, a private firm, or a nonprofit organization. The flexible performance framework metatool we described in Chapter Three is an organizational performance agreement, often accompanied by a performance contract with the chief executive. In the U.K., for example, departments negotiate five-year "framework documents" with executive agencies. Agency chief executives then sign individual performance contracts that typically include a bonus for delivering on their targets. The contracts are good for five years—at which point the executives must compete for their jobs. "That concentrates the mind a bit," says Michael Fogden, former head of the Employment Service. The U.S. General Accounting Office agrees. It found that Britain's "chief executives were acutely aware of their visible personal responsibility and accountability for the success of their agencies."

See *Banishing Bureaucracy* pp. 84–85

New Zealand also put its chief executives on performance contracts. By 1995, only 6 of the 33 in place when it began the practice in 1988 were still employed as chief executives. Even Costa Rica has negotiated performance contracts between its president and his department heads.

U.S. school boards have traditionally contracted with superintendents—but usually without specifying the results they wanted. This is changing in some districts, because superintendents are asking for performance contracts. In others, school boards are turning to performance contracts to hold superintendents' feet to the fire.

In Swanton, Ohio, Superintendent Roger Barnes announced in 1994 that he would resign if the district did not achieve a 10 percent increase in the number of ninth graders passing all four sections of the Ohio proficiency exam. Barnes had just signed a five-year contract. He says his unusual move led "my colleagues in the superintendency [to] wonder what would inspire me to make such a commitment. They feel I am either crazy or bored with my current position."

In reality, Barnes was neither crazy nor bored. He was concerned. His school district's scores on state tests were the lowest in the county, he says.

I realized I had to make a statement to indicate to the community that we were maintaining our strong commitment to academic improvement. By holding myself ultimately accountable for the continued progress of student performance, I sent a crucial message.

Some of Barnes's staff told him his announcement put "undue pressure" on them, he reports. For others, his goal became a focal point for renewed efforts to improve student performance. And that is precisely the point of performance contracting. When top managers are accountable for producing specific results, they are more likely to lead their organization to produce them.

Performance Contracting: Pitfalls to Avoid

pp. 128–148, 191–207

pp. 218–230

Chapters Three and Five offer numerous lessons about performance contracts with both public and private organizations. Performance contracting with individual managers is not quite as challenging, but it has its share of potential pitfalls. The general lessons on performance management offered earlier cover many of these. We discuss a few more pitfalls—and how to avoid them—in the paragraphs that follow.

Elected officials may not follow up on their commitment to performance contracts. In the U.S., for example, Vice President Al Gore's National Performance Review drew on overseas experiences to recommend in 1993 that the president develop written performance agreements with department and agency heads. Two and a half years later, only a handful had been completed. Similarly, the Labor Government in New Zealand was slow to follow up after it required performance contracts with department executives.

Part of the problem is that politicians get distracted by more pressing issues. Some, however, don't really believe in the tool, because they don't want the public to have information about the performance of their government. Clinton's Office of Management and Budget fought to wipe out all quantifiable elements of performance agreements with cabinet secretaries, to prevent failures that might embarrass the president. The only solution to this obstacle is to send a clear message from the top—something that requires courage.

p. 121

Another barrier is that elected officials often don't know how to use performance contracts. They have trouble specifying what they want agencies to accomplish, in measurable terms. In other words, they have trouble steering. In New Zealand, for example, elected ministers had great difficulty figuring out what to put into their contracts with agency chief executives.

pp. 247–271

To ensure effective implementation of performance contracts, managers must help elected officials with performance measurement. To create pressure to secure agreements, we suggest that you tie agency budgets to the presence of a performance agreement: no agreement, no budget.

Performance contracts may only contain vague measures. If you do not nail down specific performance measures, you may not be able to tell at the end of the contract how well the manager performed. For any measure under consideration, ask yourself if the data will really help you judge the quality of performance.

The pool of talent from which top managers is selected may be too small. Performance contracts are only as good as the people who sign them. A number of governments—including New Zealand and the U.K.—have used the shift to performance contracting as an opportunity to break the civil servant monopoly on top public management positions. They have changed the rules to allow private sector managers to compete for the jobs.

Chapter 7

Performance Measurement

The Critical Competence

They say that figures rule the world. I do not know if this is true, but I do know that figures tell us if it is well or poorly ruled.

GOETHE

***Performance Measurement* creates information about the results of public activities. This enables officials to hold organizations accountable and to introduce consequences for performance. It helps citizens and customers judge the value that government creates for them. And it provides managers and employees with the data they need to improve their performance.**

Is government performing well or poorly? Performance measurement answers that question by creating information about the results produced by departments or agencies, programs, work teams, and even individual employees. This information is indispensable if you want to use the Consequences Strategy to transform government. If you do not measure performance, you cannot manage for it, reward it, contract for it, or even identify the bottom lines for which public organizations will be held accountable. In short, if you cannot measure performance, you cannot tie incentives to it.

Performance measurement is also a core competence needed to implement the other four strategies. To use the Core Strategy, you need information about how well both steering policies and rowing institutions are working. A performance measurement system allows legislators and elected executives to specify the results they want and to determine which organizations are delivering those results.

To use the Customer Strategy, you need information about how well an organization's performance satisfies its customers. With that information, customers can make informed choices about which organization to use; thus, organizations become more accountable to them.

To use the Control Strategy, you need to replace traditional hierarchical control systems with a new form of control: accountability for results. Decentralization of authority without reliable performance information can quickly lead to problems.

Finally, performance information helps immensely in changing an organization's culture. In the words of Duke professor Robert Behn, it helps everyone use "the same definition of winning." It helps employees understand how their work contributes to the organization's success. And it helps reinforce the values of improvement and innovation.

Clearly, performance measurement plays a central role in the process of reinvention. By itself, however, it is insufficient. It creates awareness but not always action. In the 1970s, New York City began generating a thick volume of performance data about city agencies every year. But until the Giuliani administration began using this information to manage performance, it mostly gathered dust. Few managers and no elected officials used it to make decisions about budgets or personnel—so most public employees ignored it.

In short, performance measurement points the way, but it doesn't necessarily move anyone's feet—particularly when there are bureaucratic and political brick walls standing in the way of change. This is why we call performance measurement a *core competence* of government rather than a tool that activates people. To force significant changes in organizational behavior, you need incentives that give employees a reason to respond to performance data. "Without the consequences," says Don Forbes, former director of the Oregon Department of Transportation, "you shouldn't bother measuring performance."

UNDERSTANDING THE ARCHITECTURE OF PERFORMANCE MEASUREMENT

Governments measure all kinds of things. They typically drown themselves in information. But almost all of it concerns *inputs.* In the past, real information about outputs and outcomes was rare.

Fortunately, this is changing rapidly. Beginning in the 1980s, entire nations, states, and local governments have committed themselves to measuring performance, including New Zealand; the U.K. (both the national government and many local authorities); Australia; U.S. states such as Oregon, Florida, Texas, North Carolina, Minnesota, Iowa, and Arizona; and dozens of cities and counties. The U.S. government took the pledge in 1993, when Congress passed the Government Performance and Results Act (GPRA), originally drafted by John Mercer, a former mayor of Sunnyvale, California, who had gone to work for the U.S. Senate Governmental Affairs Committee.

The GPRA experience demonstrates just how difficult performance measurement is, particularly at the beginning. In early 1994, twenty-one federal agencies became GPRA pilots. They were on their own; they received no additional resources and—by design—no assistance from the Office of Management and Budget. They had four months to produce their plans for performance measurement.

When they submitted their plans, a panel of experts convened by the National Academy of Public Administration (NAPA) examined them. It found that many were still confused about what performance measurement was, even after months of trying to understand it. For most, the subject was completely new—as it is for most public organizations. To make matters worse, experts offer different and sometimes conflicting explanations and definitions. "Around the world," writes NAPA fellow Donald Kettl, "measuring government performance is like the weather. Everyone talks about it. . . . But there is no consensus on how to do it."

The first step to cut through this confusion is to define a "conceptual architecture" that explains what you want to measure and how you will measure it. Our examination of performance measurement systems suggests that this architecture has five linked components:

Component	***Examples***
Policy Outcomes	Unemployment rate, water quality, literacy rate
Program or Strategy Outcomes	Job training participants hired, reduction in industrial water pollution, increase in reading levels at fourth grade
Outputs	Unemployed people trained, water pollution permits granted, students taught in after-school reading program
Processes	Recruitment, registration, training classes; educating businesses, intake, permit processing; selection of students, instruction, self-paced learning with software
Inputs	Employees, budgets, equipment, contractors

The first component is called *policy outcomes.* These indicate the effectiveness of government policies in achieving the basic goals of a nation; a state, province, region, or county; or a community. For example, economic policy outcomes include unemployment rates, inflation rates, poverty levels, and trade balances. Environmental policy outcomes include public health, air and water pollution levels, soil erosion, and the like.

Typically, policy outcome goals come in two varieties: long-term (10–20 year) outcome goals, and intermediate (2–5 year) outcome goals, which are intended to contribute to achieving the long-term goals. For example, a long-term outcome goal might be to stabilize global warming; related intermediate goals might be to decrease oil consumption and to decrease the total number of miles driven by automobiles. Meeting these intermediate goals is not sufficient, because other things may be happening to intensify the problem. But unless we measure them—and others—we won't have a short-term handle on whether we are progressing toward the long-term goal.

Citizens judge politicians' performance, at least to some extent, by looking at how well they deliver these policy outcomes: Is the economy good or getting better? What is happening to the crime rate? How clean is the air we breathe?

Policy outcomes are shaped by many factors, some of which are outside the control of government. Public leaders try to affect them by creating *program and strategy outcomes,* the next component in the measurement architecture. Program and strategy outcomes indicate the effectiveness of government programs, strategies, regulations, or other activities at achieving the desired policy outcomes. (These don't necessarily correspond to organizations: they may involve several organizations; one organization may house several programs; and one program may involve multiple strategies.) One program outcome goal, for example, might be to place 80 percent of all participants in a government training program in jobs. If that goal is achieved, it will contribute to the policy outcome goal of lowering unemployment.

A public organization's success in creating program outcomes depends on the *strategies* it uses. For example, street sweeping is one strategy for producing clean streets; an antilittering campaign would be a different strategy. A sanitation department can measure the outcome of each strategy: how clean the streets are just after the department sweeps them and how clean they are at other times. In some organizations, it is useful to measure both program and strategy outcomes, because they are so distinct. In others, they are essentially the same, so it makes sense to measure only one. Even when they are distinct, measuring both may introduce too much complexity. This is why we treat program and strategy outcomes as one component of the architecture.

An organization's success in creating positive strategy and program outcomes depends on its *outputs*—the actual work products it produces. Sanitation departments produce outputs like miles of streets swept and numbers of household garbage pickups. The Social Security Administration produces benefits checks. Environmental agencies produce regulations, inspections, and fines. Police and fire departments produce emergency responses, arrests, traffic tickets, and the like. These outputs lead to program and strategy outcomes.

Agencies can usually measure the quantity and cost of their outputs and the efficiency with which they are produced. They can also measure their quality (for example, their accuracy and timeliness) and their effectiveness (the degree to which they produce the desired outcomes). Government agencies usually have substantial control over outputs. But often they provide grants to other levels of government or contracts to private organizations to produce outputs. In such cases, they depend on these other organizations to produce services of a certain quantity, cost, quality, and so on.

Outputs are created by *processes,* or activities. (Some jurisdictions distinguish between activities, which they define broadly, and processes, which are sub-elements of the activities.) These are the production methods of government, the work that is actually performed. Social Security Administration employees determine applicants' eligibility for benefits, establish benefit levels, process and deliver payments, and check for fraud. Sanitation workers set up collection routes and schedules, pick up trash, and haul it off to landfills. Law enforcement officers patrol communities, respond to complaints, subdue perpetrators, read them their rights, take them in to be booked, file reports, and testify in court. Performance measures for processes include efficiency (how much they cost to perform), quality (for example, how much time they take), and effectiveness (how often they produce the right output).

Processes depend on *inputs*—the resources that are required to create them. Employees, salaries, information, offices, computers, money, garbage trucks, uniforms, guns, and prisons are all examples of inputs. Here quantity, cost, efficiency, and quality can be measured.

The five components of performance measurement are connected one after another and work together, like a production line: inputs create processes, which create outputs, which determine strategy and program outcomes, which impact policy outcomes.

Inputs → Processes → Outputs → Strategy/Program Outcomes → Policy Outcomes

pp. 52–53

Performance measurement systems should start by defining policy outcome goals and then work their way down—as we explained in Chapter One. Few governments have developed systems that link each of these components. Those that do refine this architecture in different ways and use different terms to describe it. In New Zealand, for instance, the government now uses a framework of long-term "goals" (policy outcomes), "strategic priorities" (the most important intermediate policy outcomes for the next three to five years), "key result areas" (ideally, each department's most important program and strategy outcomes), and "outputs." Sunnyvale uses "program outcomes," but calls outputs "products" and calls processes "activities" and "subactivities." You should use whatever language works best for you; if your employees intuitively grasp what a product is but not an output, call them products.

It is the focus on results rather than activities that is most important. We stay away from the traditional management-by-objective phrase "goals and objectives," for example, because so many organizations use this language to measure activities rather than results. We purposefully use language—such as *output goals* and *outcome goals*—that highlights the difference between means and ends.

When people ask how well government is performing, typically they want to know what impact it is having: what are the policy and program outcomes? But when people want to improve program outcomes, they must turn to government's strategies and outputs. Is it using the best strategies? Are they producing the right outputs? Would different outputs and strategies lead to better outcomes?

When people want to change or improve government's outputs, they must change its processes and activities. Unless activities and processes change, outputs remain the same.

Finally, new processes often require new inputs, and improved processes often require improved inputs—or better use of existing inputs.

The other critical architecture question is what to measure about each of these elements. Your specific measures, often called indicators, can gauge the quantity, efficiency, effectiveness, quality, or cost-effectiveness of an outcome, output, or process. Unfortunately, few people have ever carefully defined what each of these terms means. Yet lack of precision can quickly lead to confusion. It can also create blind spots: areas no one measures because there is no label for them in the measurement system.

There is no final arbiter of the meaning of these terms, no *Webster's Dictionary* of performance measurement. However, we offer below our best effort to define them in a way that focuses each term on a distinct issue—and thus gives you the broadest possible set of terms with which to measure your processes, outputs, and outcomes.

Quantity: How much of an output you produce: how many people are trained, how many permits are processed, and so on. This is the least important element on our list.

Efficiency: The cost per unit of process or output: that is, the ratio of inputs to outputs or processes. Most processes produce outputs, so measuring the cost of those outputs is, in effect, the same as measuring the cost of the process. But sometimes it takes multiple processes to produce a single output. In welfare offices, for example, eligibility workers may need to complete several different processes to produce an output, such as a determination of eligibility. Thus to improve their overall efficiency they might want to measure the efficiency of each process. (*Productivity*, the ratio of inputs to outputs—that is, how many outputs you can produce for how many dollars—is a subset of efficiency.)

Effectiveness: How successful inputs and processes are at producing desired outputs, outputs are at producing desired program or strategy outcomes, and programs or strategies are at producing desired policy outcomes. You can do a splendid job of hitting output goals—such as a certain number of people graduating from a training program, or a certain number of students passing a course—while failing completely to produce the outcomes you want, such as people finding jobs or acquiring skills. Effectiveness is the most important thing you can measure. If a program or process is not effective, why worry about how efficient it is?

Quality: How well an activity or process is performed or an output is produced. This is not quite synonymous with effectiveness, because one can measure the quality of a process or output without measuring its effectiveness. For example, one can measure the quality of telephone service delivered by an office: how quickly they answer the phone, how helpful they are, how satisfied the people on the other end of the conversation are. This won't necessarily tell you how *effective* their phone service is, however. In fact, you can provide high-quality services that are not effective at achieving your desired outcomes. For example, a welfare eligibility office could offer customer service of such high quality that welfare applicants

The British Treasury's publication *Executive Agencies: A Guide to Setting Targets and Measuring Performance* provides useful lists of aspects of quality you can measure. They include the following:

Quality of Outputs

- Accuracy (for example, the error rate).
- Did the output meet technical specifications and standards?
- Clarity of information or advice.
- Response to errors, complaints, or failures.
- Customer rating of general quality.

Quality of Processes

- Timeliness (for example, waiting times, turnaround times, and processing times).
- Backlogs.
- Responsiveness (for example, timely feedback to customers).
- Pleasantness, helpfulness of staff.
- Accessibility of services to customers.
- Availability of products, such as documents and forms.

and recipients find it appealing to remain on welfare—frustrating the desired outcome of moving people into jobs.

Cost-effectiveness: The ratio of inputs to outcomes—that is, what level of outcomes can you achieve for the dollars you spend? This is what the British mean by "value for money." It answers the question "How effective is your spending?" It measures not how many outputs you can produce for your dollar but how much value you produce. As with effectiveness, you can measure the cost-effectiveness of *strategies, programs,* and *policies.*

Table 7.1 provides examples of these categories, applied to each level of the performance measurement architecture. This is quite a complete framework, which should help you see all the particular elements you could include in your measurement system. *But don't assume that you should use all of it.* Pick and choose what is most important for your organization to measure; otherwise your staff will be overwhelmed. You may only want to measure process data when you're trying to redesign a process, for example. You may even need to minimize how much output data you collect, except where you see outcomes faltering. Information is only worth something if people use it, and if they're drowning in it, they won't use it.

p. 261

Some people use the metaphor of a dashboard to explain this idea. When you drive a car, you need to know a few key things: How fast are you going? How much gas do you have left? Is the engine overheating? And do you have enough oil pressure? You don't need to know what the pressure is in each cylinder or what the air pressure is in each tire. You wouldn't want to drive without a dashboard—but if it were as complex as an airplane's dashboard, you'd probably never use it. At each level of your system, you want people to have a dashboard that works for them.

Measures of →	*Quantity*	*Efficiency*	*Effectiveness*	*Quality*	*Cost-effectiveness*
Policy Outcome Goals:					
Clean Air	NA (Not Applicable)	NA	Air pollution level	NA	Air pollution level ÷ cost
Low crime rates			Crime rate		Crime rate ÷ cost
Skilled workforce			Percentage of workforce with high school and college degrees		Degree percentage ÷ cost
Programs/Strategy Outcome Goals:					
Environmental Protection Agency: Reduction in industrial pollution	NA	NA	Volume of industrial emissions	NA	Industrial emissions volume ÷ cost
Police Department: Reduction in violent crime rate			Violent crime rate		Violent crime rate reduction ÷ cost
State Colleges: Increase in percentage of college entrants who graduate			Percentage of college entrants who graduate in X years		Percentage of college entrants who graduate in X years ÷ cost
Outputs:					
Air pollution permits processed	Number of permits processed	Cost per permit processed	Volume of industrial emissions	Percentage of permits processed by deadline	NA
Arrests made	Number of arrests	Cost per arrest	Percentage of convictions	Percentage of arrests thrown out by courts	
Students graduated	Number of graduates	Cost per graduate	Percentage of college entrants who graduate in X years	Satisfaction level of graduates, on survey	
Processes:					
Educating businesses; intake; permit review	Number of businesses advised; number of permits reviewed	Cost per business advised; cost per permit review	Percentage of businesses that complete permit application properly; percentage of permit decisions overturned on appeal	Satisfaction of businesses with advising process; number of complaints; average time required for permit review	NA

Table 7.1. Performance Measurement Matrix

Measures of →	*Quantity*	*Efficiency*	*Effectiveness*	*Quality*	*Cost-effectiveness*
Processes:					
Investigation; arrest; booking	Number of investigations, arrests, bookings	Cost per investigation, arrest, bookings	Percentage of investigations that lead to arrest	Error rate in booking	
Registration; courses; advising	Number of courses; number of advising hours	Cost per course; cost per student advised	Percentage of students registered in classes desired; student ratings of courses	Student ratings of registration staff, faculty, advisors; percentage of students registered on time	
Inputs:					
Employees, salaries, equipment, overhead	Number of employees; cost of salaries, equipment and overhead	Cost per employee; percentage of indirect (overhead) costs to direct costs	Percentage of employees who have mastered required skills; percentage of equipment downtime	Employee satisfaction level; average rating of employees in 360 degree evaluation; employee ratings of equipment quality	NA

Table 7.1. Performance Measurement Matrix, cont'd.

IMPLEMENTING PERFORMANCE MEASUREMENT: LESSONS LEARNED

Performance measurement is not easy. It typically takes about three years to develop an adequate set of performance measures. The first time around, most agencies find themselves measuring inputs and processes, not outputs and outcomes. They often go through several iterations—nudged along by a neutral body that has authority to approve their measures—before they get the focus squarely on results.

Performance measurement requires a combination of technical, managerial, and political savvy. Because it employs highly rational, scientific observation and analysis, it demands technical expertise. Because it must be implemented in a messy, changing environment, it requires managerial skill. And because it influences public perceptions of elected officials—as well as elected officials' decisions about policy and budgets—it requires political sensitivity.

See *Reinventing Government* pp. 349–359

Reinventing Government addressed some of the most important challenges in an appendix, "The Art of Performance Measurement." It contained a glossary of terms and a list of books from which you could learn more. It also provided advice to practitioners, including the first four lessons on our list. For a few additional pointers, also see pp. 314-319 in this book.

IMPLEMENTING PERFORMANCE MEASUREMENT: LESSONS LEARNED

1. Measure qualitatively, not quantitatively.
2. Anticipate powerful resistance to performance measurement.
3. Keep the measurement function politically independent and impartial.
4. Watch out for perverse incentives.
5. Begin with policy outcome goals and work downward.
6. Don't just measure efficiency.
7. Measure customer satisfaction.
8. Involve your customers in choosing performance indicators.
9. Watch out for overkill: don't try to measure everything.
10. To get a full picture, create a balanced scorecard.
11. Phase in the new system gradually.
12. Continuously improve your system.
13. Don't attach consequences to performance too soon.
14. Standardize, but don't centralize.
15. Build a quality gatekeeper into your system without taking too much control away from the agencies.
16. Use experts in the design stage.
17. Top managers have to get their hands dirty.
18. Communicate with the unions.
19. Train, train, train.
20. Automate the system.
21. Make performance data usable and visible.
22. Beware of tempting measurement shortcuts.
23. Expect setbacks.
24. If you're not going to use performance data to make decisions, don't bother collecting it.

1. *Measure qualitatively, not just quantitatively.*

Some results are impossible or impractical to quantify and should be measured qualitatively. Don't just go by the numbers; use on-site observations, peer review, professional evaluations, employee interviews, customer focus groups, and other methods of gathering information.

2. *Anticipate powerful resistance to performance measurement.*

Performance information can be extremely threatening to service providers—contractors, grantees, or public employees—who worry about how well they will perform. They will mobilize political opposition to the process. Bringing them in to help design the measurement system can help address their concerns and defuse their hostility.

3. *Keep the measurement function politically independent and impartial.*

Performance data must be trustworthy; it must be free from political or bureaucratic taint. It is important to maintain the integrity of the data gathering and analysis processes. Organizations should collect most data themselves, so they get quick feedback and can learn from it. But make sure an independent unit, such as a city auditor, audits the data for accuracy.

4. *Watch out for perverse incentives.*

Sometimes using the wrong performance measures leads organizations to do the wrong things. For instance, if a police department is measured on the number of arrests it makes every month, its officers may make hasty arrests and work hard on cases that are easy to solve. To avoid perverse incentives, test them first for problems.

5. *Begin with policy outcome goals and work downward.*

"You can't measure for results if you don't know where you are going," notes Camille Barnett, former city manager of Austin, Texas. Hence you should begin the measurement process at the top, with your overall mission and policy outcome goals. Once you have done this, define missions and outcome goals for your steering organizations. Then move to the operational agency level. Define each agency's mission: just what is it supposed to accomplish? Then begin defining key outcome goals for each of the agency's programs and/or strategies. (Don't try to do this for the agency as a whole, unless it is very small. When large agencies try to define agency-wide outcome goals, they often discover that it doesn't work, because the agency is really an agglomeration of disparate programs and strategies.)

pp. 30–39

pp. 596–599

Although starting at the top may seem obvious, many organizations learn it the hard way. The Oregon State Police provide a perfect example. Its top managers started by drafting about 270 measures. When they asked field staff for feedback, it was negative: employees couldn't connect the measures to the agency's priorities. Management stopped the process, realizing that it had to begin with a clear understanding of the department's goals. "We have to clarify some organizational goals and values as early as possible, and it has to come from the top," Major Lee Erickson told us.

> *Otherwise there is no sense of direction. It's kind of like a bunch of horses milling around the infield. If you get them hitched up and pulling in the same direction, there's real power. But we don't have clarity of purpose.*

Most of the U.S. GPRA pilot agencies experienced a similar problem: NAPA found that their measures were unrelated to their missions.

Once you have program and/or strategy outcome goals, you can build down through the organization, measuring outputs, processes, units, teams, and—if appropriate—individuals. If you try to build up from units, teams, and individuals, you will probably discover at some point that your measures have little to do with the outcomes you're after.

6. *Don't just measure efficiency.*

Often finance agencies—treasury departments and offices of management and budget—lead the charge on performance measurement. This was the case, for example, in Australia, the U.K., and New Zealand. Quite naturally, their focus was on the cost and efficiency of government outputs.

Unfortunately, this approach ignores quality, effectiveness, and cost-effectiveness. As we asked earlier, what good does it do to make services more efficient if they are ineffective—if they are not achieving the desired outcomes?

This problem is quite common. After almost 15 years of performance measurement, Sunnyvale decided it was too focused on productivity—often to the exclusion of effectiveness. So it revamped its system, which it now calls "outcome management." In Australia, a review of performance reporting found that, after nearly a decade of finance-driven efforts, agencies collected little data on outcomes. The same thing happened in the U.K.

p. 219

Focusing only on financial measures can also generate resistance among employees and managers. Employees are typically suspicious of efforts to improve "productivity," because they assume that means making them work harder—or cutbacks and layoffs. In contrast, they usually like efforts to improve "quality" or "effectiveness," because many of them want to improve service to their customers.

7. Measure customer satisfaction.

Perhaps the most difficult step for many organizations is finding quantifiable measures of their effectiveness. Education officials endlessly debate the value of standardized tests and search for alternatives. Police departments debate whether the crime rate is the key measure of their effectiveness—or whether it is response time, or something else. Often, we have found, the best way to cut through such debates is to focus on customer satisfaction. How safe do the citizens feel? How satisfied are parents, students, and employers with the schools? For much of what government does, former Sunnyvale city manager Tom Lewcock points out, "A satisfied customer is the ultimate performance measure." Sunnyvale now requires every city service to measure its customer satisfaction, including satisfaction with the timeliness, convenience, and accuracy of the service.

A classic example occurred during a seminar David Osborne conducted in Brazil. The director of a state industrial development corporation said he was having trouble figuring out how to measure the performance of his recruiting teams, whose job was to convince foreign companies to open plants in his state. Usually the companies chose their locations based on factors outside the control of these teams, like the cost of land, labor, and taxes, so success or failure was not a very good indicator of the teams' performance. He was perplexed about what to measure. Osborne suggested that he ask the foreign firms to rate his teams' performance. As it often does, the simplicity of this solution opened up a whole new vista for him. By the next day he had decided to use customer feedback to benchmark against his competition—and to build a financial reward system based on the results.

Customer satisfaction is not the only useful measure of effectiveness: you will need to measure other things. But it is often the most important one. It is also an attention grabber. Elected officials, public employees, and the public will pay attention to customer ratings. Customer feedback will not only help people understand the value of a performance measurement system, it will build support for developing one.

8. Involve your customers in choosing performance indicators.

Customers often understand better than anyone what else you should measure—because they know what is important to them and what isn't. Unless customers are involved, says Camille Barnett, performance measurement becomes little more than "professionals and bureaucrats deciding what is best for the public."

In Phoenix, City Auditor Jim Flanagan persuaded five departments to meet with their customers to develop measures. "We sat down in a room with people who run these agencies and people who are customers and simply discussed what quality is and what the indicators of success are," he explains. "These were some of the best conversations ever held in Phoenix." Other organizations create ongoing customer councils or boards to help with tasks like this.

pp. 377–380

9. *Watch out for overkill: don't try to measure everything.*

Don't measure what you won't use, and stop measuring what you don't need. Otherwise you will end up creating an enormous, unwelcome burden for your organization. "Perhaps our most glaring mistake was getting lost in the data," confesses Craig Gerhart, who spearheaded the performance measurement effort in Prince William County, Virginia. "We overcounted; we overmeasured. We measured a lot of things because they were countable, and we mistook that for progress."

The point is not to measure everything. As officials from Atlantic Richfield told the U.S. federal government, measurement should be "a vehicle for focusing people's attention on the factors *critical* to the success of the organization."

The British Next Steps Team makes the same argument. Based on the experience of executive agencies, it recommends four to seven key measures for any particular unit. Certainly you should avoid having any unit target more than 10 measures, or it will lose sight of what is most important.

One way to restrain "measurement creep"—the endless demands for more and more measures—is to identify the cost of measuring things. That way, when a legislator or manager willy-nilly orders up a new measure, you can ask how to pay for the additional effort, or which existing measures should be dropped.

It's also important to keep the measurement system from getting too complex. If people can't understand it, they won't use it. The Oregon Department of Transportation developed a system to weight the importance of different indicators and calculate a weighted average for each activity—a system we loved when we first saw it, because it was so sophisticated. But after several years, department officials abandoned it. It turned out that employees didn't use it, because they were befuddled by its complexity.

You have to find the right balance between too few measures and too many measures and between reporting systems that are too simple and those that are too complex. This is an art, not a science. You have to find the dashboards that work for your agency, your customers, and your funders.

p. 254

10. *To get a full picture, create a balanced scorecard.*

As the British Treasury explains, "Any one measure or indicator, taken in isolation, may give a misleading picture. To form a complete understanding of what is happening, you need to look at the measures and indicators as a whole." Some targets will drive you to achieve one objective at the expense of another:

increased efficiency, for example, at the expense of a higher error rate. "Timeliness, quality and cost are always in contention with each other, and the impact of improving any one or two must be weighed in relation to the expense to the third," adds the U.S. Treasury.

The solution is what many call a "balanced scorecard," which touches all the important bases without creating so many measures that its complexity overwhelms people. For a look at all the elements you can choose from, see Table 7.1.

pp. 255–256

11. Phase in the new system gradually.

Don't try to put an entire performance measurement system in place across your whole organization all at once. Pick a few programs to start with. "We didn't do this, but I wish we had," says Craig Gerhart, Prince William County's budget director. When you try to tackle everything at once, the process may collapse under its own weight. Looking back at the collapse of the U.S. government's complex Program Planning and Budgeting System in the early 1970s, experts in the U.S. Office of Management and Budget developed a carefully phased implementation for the 1993 Government Performance Results Act.

Implementing in stages allows you to show people how the new system will work and what it will be used for. You can use volunteer agencies to get the bugs out early on and build some successes. Phasing in also allows you to give employees a greater sense of control over the system; they can critique the early efforts and improve them.

12. Continuously improve your system.

Because performance measurement systems are technical and complex, it is tempting to try to get the design perfect at the beginning. In reality, that is impossible.

"You have to go through several cycles to get good measures," cautions Craig Holt, formerly a top manager in the Oregon Transportation Department. "We have our people check them and redo them after about six months." Holt learned this the hard way; after the department "locked in" in some measures, he found out they weren't the right ones. Typically, organizations go through three or four cycles before they are comfortable with their measures—and then they keep refining them periodically. As Sylvie Trosa concluded after her analysis of the Next Steps program, "Experience shows that implementing a good target setting process shared by all staff (a management culture), needs at least three years."

Even when you develop appropriate performance measures, the data you gather may throw you a curve ball. For example, a sanitation department may find that a ticker-tape parade or spells of bad weather will throw their data off. The water department in Portland, Oregon, was rated highly until suddenly, in 1992, only 30 percent of citizens said they were satisfied with it. The reason: the previous summer's drought had led to severe restrictions on water use. "People could not water their lawns or wash their cars, so when they got the survey, they said, 'That damned water department!' and gave it bad ratings," explains Richard Tracy, director of city government audits.

All of this means that getting performance measurement "right" is an evolving process filled with constant adjustments—a process that never ends. When Sunnyvale began in 1980, City Manager Tom Lewcock advised his staff not to expect the system to be perfect—just to get it started and then improve it. They began by focusing on efficiency, then in the 1990s discovered the need to measure customer satisfaction. In 1995, they added a focus on outcome measures.

Over those 15 years, Sunnyvale learned a related lesson: Don't let your system get too rigid. When John Christian took over the Parks and Recreation Department in the early 1990s, he brought a focus on customer satisfaction with him. Yet the performance system forced him to concentrate on producing specific outputs—specific recreation programs and courses—regardless of what customers wanted. He found it difficult to change those targets—and impossible to do it quickly. As another manager put it, "We need to use the performance system as a tool, but it's become a straitjacket."

"We change our quality performance measures constantly," says General Michael Loh of the Air Combat Command (ACC). "Every time we review them—every quarter—we go back and change them and make sure we're measuring the right outputs and outcomes." Between 1990 and 1995, he says, the ACC changed about 50 percent of its measures to reflect changes in its basic mission.

But be careful not to change too much. You will want to be able to compare performance over time, and you can do this only if you have a core set of measures that remain unchanged.

13. *Don't attach consequences to performance too soon.*

Although it is crucial to tie performance to consequences, there are several reasons to wait until the bugs have been worked out of the measurement system. We suggest that you build consequences in *after* the typical two-or three-year start-up period.

If you build consequences in too soon, people will argue endlessly about the validity of measures and data, because the stakes are so high. They will also fear that the system will be used to cut agency budgets and staffing—and thus resist it.

There is also a good chance that an agency will discover that its performance is not very good. This is exactly what everyone needs to know, so that improvement can begin. But finding out poses risks. Everyone else—elected officials, the media, customers, the public—may find out, too. Then the blaming will start, particularly if the groundwork for understanding and using performance measurement has not been well laid. Attaching consequences early on only exacerbates this tendency.

14. Standardize, but don't centralize.

"Do not create a bureaucracy to administer or monitor a performance measurement program." This warning—from officials of Boeing who were responding to a federal government survey on implementing performance measurement—is important. Every experience we have studied teaches the same lesson: if you centralize control of performance measurement—in a budget unit or departmental headquarters, for instance—those who must collect and use the data may never come to "own" it. Instead of welcoming performance measurement as a way of improving their work, they will resent it. They will view it as another administrative control imposed on them from above, and ignore or resist it. When his Oregon State Police made this mistake, says Major Lee Erickson, they ran into a wall of passive resistance. The attitude was, "It's just one more thing headquarters needs; they're cranking out numbers." To get employee buy-in, get employees involved in creating the system, and let them run the system.

At the same time, you can't let each agency or unit go its own way on performance measurement. There have to be some basic standards, to ensure both quality and consistency. Otherwise, the information will become a Tower of Babel: many languages, no communication.

This is precisely what happened, initially, in Oregon. Budget Director Michael Marsh invited agencies to volunteer to create performance measurement systems. When they responded, he allowed them to invent their own systems. Different agencies built very different systems for tracking performance and reporting it. That made it difficult to aggregate data and report it as a whole, and it confused legislators.

The solution, Marsh decided, was to get agencies to agree on a basic framework—a set of standards—for what would be measured. A neutral agency such as a budget office or auditor's office can take responsibility for developing the framework and for helping other organizations use it. But it should be flexible: agencies should be free to vary what they measure, when appropriate.

Marsh found that to make performance measurement work, he needed both a commitment from key central agencies and leadership within the line agencies. To get the latter, he convinced agencies to create steering committees made up of the key champions of measurement: high-level managers; budget, personnel, and information systems staff; and a performance coordinator who became the in-house expert. The coordinator, who quarterbacked the implementation and training, had to have access to the agency director.

15. Build a quality gatekeeper into your system without taking too much control away from the agencies.

If you want useful measures that focus on the right things, you will need to put ownership of the measures in agency hands without abandoning quality control. In Prince William County, for example, Budget Director Craig Gerhart asked middle managers to get together with employees and customers and design appropriate performance measures—but no one had to approve their measures. "With this approach," Gerhart says, "You are going to get a lot of bathwater with the babies. We acquired some really bad measures, and [several years later] we still have some."

The best solution is to ask agency leadership to drive the process, but have a central team with expertise act as a coach and gatekeeper—helping agencies develop measures, pushing them to improve, and signing off when they have finally developed a useful set of measures. The gatekeeper should require that both agency employees and customers participate in developing the measures.

pp. 260–261

It should require agencies to evaluate their measures periodically, with the help of a coach and a customer group. And it should ensure that someone audits the performance data that agencies produce—just as one would with financial data.

16. Use experts in the design stage.

Experts—consultants or practitioners with experience in performance measurement—can help you avoid many pitfalls. They can help you understand what developing a performance measurement system is all about, and they can help you solve technical measurement problems. But don't let them hand you an off-the-shelf system; make sure your system is customized to meet your needs.

17. Top managers have to get their hands dirty.

If top managers are not firmly committed to performance measurement, it will not work. But commitment is not enough. Executives have to get their hands dirty building the system. In many of the federal GPRA pilot agencies, NAPA found that top managers were largely absent from the process. This deprived the design teams of critical knowledge about the agencies' missions and objectives—the foundation of performance measurement.

When top managers don't participate in the process, they also miss a critical learning experience. They don't learn how difficult measurement is, nor why patience is required. They don't recognize that they are not the only users of the system, that other potential users—legislators, the budget office, top executives, employees, customers, partners, and interest groups—are interested in different kinds of information. If top managers fail to understand these realities, they are likely to underinvest in the development process.

18. Communicate with the unions.

Public employee unions often resist performance measurement, for fear that it will lead to performance pay. This would break a fundamental union precept—"the same pay for the same work."

Most organizations don't use performance measurement to appraise individual workers—only individual *managers*. They do use it, however, to measure the performance of units and work teams. This does not usually cause problems with unions, unless it leads to performance pay.

The solution is to communicate clearly with the unions about your intentions, from the beginning. If you intend to create a performance bonus system, ask the union to participate in the design process. If it refuses, involve employees.

19. Train, train, train.

As we keep saying, performance measurement is difficult. If you don't educate your people in how to do it, it will be even more difficult. "In the majority of pilot plans," NAPA reports, "the program people did not appear to have a full understanding of outcome measurement, the need to identify the various categories of their customers, [or] how to identify service quality and outcome indicators."

In Oregon, training began with a small group of volunteers from state agencies. It took about five months, after which the graduates became mentors for a second group. Doing it that way helped make the training feel like working with "a sister agency," says Mike Marsh.

20. Automate the system.

Recognize that performance measurement is an *information* system. Unless you use information technology to run it, its care and feeding will be extremely labor-intensive. Practitioners advise that as you design your performance measurement system, you should automate the data collection and reporting processes as much as possible.

21. Make performance data usable and visible.

Communicating about performance measurement is like telling a story. To keep the audience interested, you need to make the story both entertaining and relevant to their needs. This is true whether the audience is employees, managers, central agencies, elected officials, the press, or the public. There are a number of useful rules of thumb for doing this:

- ***Make sure the performance information is accurate.*** It has to be "viewed as valid, reliable, and objective, not public relations," cautions Richard Tracy, audit director for Portland, Oregon.
- ***Explain the context of the performance information.*** Recognize that most citizens and many elected officials don't know the history of government programs and agencies. Therefore, you must often provide them with brief background summaries of programs, the rationale for using particular measures, historical data trends, and other explanatory information.
- ***Tailor publication of performance reports to specific audiences.*** Because different audiences care about different measures, one size does not fit all. For example, since the public cares about results, it will pay attention to outcome measures but rarely to process measures. Yet employees need process measures to figure out how to improve their organization's performance. Gauge your audiences' needs and tailor your reports for them. Don't make them wade through a sea of information to find what they care about.

Every year, Portland's city auditor, an elected official, produces a report on the city's performance. It contains information about the city's nine largest services, covering at least 80 percent of its staff and budget. Each service gets its own chapter, which describes its mission and background; reports on its process, output, and outcome measures; and gives the results of citizen satisfaction surveys. The city auditor presents the report to the city council, holds a press conference, and sends it to neighborhood associations, community groups, and libraries.

In 1995 and 1997, City Auditor Barbara Clark mailed residents a four-page, tabloid-size "Report to Citizens." Much shorter than the detailed annual report, it contained easy-to-understand charts, maps, and information about the city's spending, financial condition, and service results. It was not just a "good news" document: the 1995 version noted that the condition of the city's streets had declined in 1994 and that city spending for fire, police, and sewer services was above the average of six comparable cities.

The idea was to increase citizen interest in the city's performance, explains Richard Tracy, the audit director. "It's a document the city can use to communicate with all sorts of people: citizens, outsiders, downtown businesses. We can give this to anyone and say, here's what's happening."

Local authorities in the U.K. go a step further. They publish similar documents but include comparative data supplied by the Audit Commission, which shows how local services compare in cost and quality to those of all other localities in their region.

pp. 211–212

22. *Beware of tempting measurement shortcuts.*

Because developing a performance measurement system is difficult and time-consuming, you will be tempted to make things easier, quicker, or less costly. Here are some temptations to avoid:

- ***"Let's just use the data we already have."*** Wrong! Much of it probably is not relevant; most of it is only about inputs and processes. The right thing to do is to stop gathering data that isn't useful, so you will have time to gather data that is. This may require that the legislature and central administrative agencies eliminate some of their reporting requirements.
- ***"Let's just use year-end measures."*** Wrong! Managers need feedback more frequently than that. Some data is affected by seasonal variations or other factors that occur more often than once a year. And getting data more often will provide early warning signals and other important insights. Many agencies review performance data quarterly.
- ***"Let's not disaggregate the data too much."*** Wrong! Data should be disaggregated to the level of the unit responsible for performing the work, so it can be used to create consequences and improve performance. It should also be cut up by customer categories, by geographic area, and by any other categories that will illuminate the reasons behind different results.

23. *Expect setbacks.*

You will select some bad performance measures. Employees will resist collecting the data, and some managers will resist using it. People will complain about how much time it takes to develop and use the system. These problems are inherent in trying to develop a new organizational competence. Over time, you can work through them. Be patient. Acceptance will grow and flaws will fade. The one thing everyone who measures performance has discovered is that it is, to a degree, a self-correcting system: when you use the wrong measures, you immediately generate pressure to improve them.

24. *If you're not going to use performance data to make decisions, don't bother collecting it.*

If you're not going to use performance data to reward employees and organizations, improve work processes, and allocate resources, don't bother gathering it. It will become an expensive, time-consuming paper chase—one that builds cynicism rather than performance.

MEASURING PERFORMANCE: CHECKING YOUR ORGANIZATION'S PROGRESS

- Do people understand what performance measurement is and how it is used?
- Do people like the process that is being used to develop performance measurement?
- Do people believe that the measures used are valid?
- Does everyone in the organization receive performance measurement reports?
- Is the measurement data reliable and accurate?
- Do people think the report format is user-friendly?
- Is staff using the performance data to make management decisions?
- Is the data being used in budgeting?
- Is the data being used for determining the objectives of contracts and grants?
- Is the data being used to reward high performance by work groups?

—Adapted from the Oregon Department of Transportation

RESOURCES ON PERFORMANCE MEASUREMENT

David N. Ammons. *Municipal Benchmarks: Assessing Local Performance and Establishing Community Standards.* Thousand Oaks, Calif.: Sage Publications, 1996. A comprehensive guide to measurement in local government, with thousands of specific measures used by cities.

Balancing Measures: Best Practices in Performance Management. Washington, D.C.: National Partnership for Reinventing Government (NPR), 1999. Available at www.npr.gov/library/papers/bkgrd/balmeasure.html, this is a comprehensive guide to creating a well-balanced set of performance measures, complete with dozens of case studies, resources, and links to useful Web pages.

Robert D. Behn. *Bottom-Line Government.* Durham, N.C.: The Governors Center at Duke University, 1994. Telephone: 919–613–7374. A thoughtful monograph on why governments need to measure their "bottom lines" and on the many challenges they encounter in doing so.

Jack A. Brizius and Michael D. Campbell. *Getting Results: A Guide for Government Accountability.* Washington, D.C.: Council of Governors' Policy Advisors, 1991. A basic guide to performance measurement at the state level, available from the National Governors Association in Washington, D.C. Phone: (202) 624–5300.

City of Portland Service Efforts and Accomplishments. Portland, Ore.: Office of the City Auditor, published annually. The city began issuing these performance reports, described on p. 267, in 1992. They are available at www.ci.portland.or.us/auditor/pdxaudit.htm. Telephone: (503) 823–4005.

The Governmental Accounting Standards Board Web site: www.gasb.org. An excellent and comprehensive collection of information on performance measurement in government.

Harry P. Hatry et al. *How Effective Are Your Community Services? Procedures for Measuring Their Quality.* 2nd ed. Washington, D.C.: Urban Institute and International City and County Management Association, 1992. An excellent how-to guidebook on measuring local government performance, chock full of specifics.

Harry P. Hatry et al. *Service Efforts and Accomplishments Reporting: Its Time Has Come, An Overview.* Norwalk, Conn.: Government Accounting Standards Board, 1990. An overview of performance measurement in many different services, at different levels of government.

The ICMA Center for Performance Measurement (www.icma.org/performance) offers a comprehensive program in comparative performance measurement for cities and counties. Components include on-site training for new participants, statistical data cleaning, and a private Web site that facilitates discussion among participating jurisdictions about best practices and innovative management techniques. The program brings together 120 jurisdictions in the U.S. and Canada (plus two pilots in Australia and New Zealand) to analyze performance in 15 different service areas. ICMA publications related to performance measurement, including an annual volume of comparative data on these services (*Comparative Performance Measurement: FY 1998 Data Report*) and *Accountability for Performance: Measurement and Monitoring in Local Government,* are available at www.bookstore.icma.org (type *performance measurement* in the search engine) or by calling (800) 745–8780.

Robert S. Kaplan and David P. Norton. *The Balanced Scorecard: Translating Strategy into Action.* Boston: Harvard Business School Press, 1996. A comprehensive introduction to the concept of balanced scorecards, based on business examples.

United Kingdom. Her Majesty's Treasury. *Executive Agencies: A Guide to Setting Targets and Measuring Performance.* London: Her Majesty's Stationery Office, 1992. An excellent nuts-and-bolts guide, which can be ordered from the Stationery Office at www.itsofficial.net (use the search function to search for the title).

Jonathan Walters. *Measuring Up: Governing's Guide to Performance Measurement for Geniuses (and Other Public Managers).* Washington, D.C.: Governing Books, 1998. An entertaining and enlightening guide to the challenges and pitfalls of performance measurement, published by *Governing* magazine. To order call (800) 638–1710.

Part III

The Customer Strategy

Putting the Customer in the Driver's Seat

The Customer Strategy makes public organizations accountable to their customers. Most organizations are accountable only up the chain of command, to their superiors in their hierarchy (and, ultimately, to elected officials). In systems and organizations that use the Customer Strategy, however, the customers have power: if the organization does not please its customers, it faces consequences. This does not eliminate accountability up the chain of command; it simply augments it. Such organizations are both "vertically" accountable, to their superiors, and "horizontally" accountable, to their customers.

Why isn't vertical accountability, using the Consequences Strategy, enough? Because a public organization or system that creates consequences to boost its performance may still be missing the boat. A public transit system that uses managed competition to cut its costs by 25 percent may still have riders who are intensely frustrated by slow, unreliable buses or desperate for air conditioning. A recreation department that doubles the number of programs it offers may still have many customers who want different programs altogether. A school district that pulls its test scores up dramatically may still have parents deeply frustrated by the rote-learning approach taken in the classrooms or by a paucity of elective courses. Virtually every organization we have studied that has made dramatic gains using managed competition or performance management has at some point realized that it needs a customer strategy as well. These two approaches are powerful, but they don't tell you whether

you're producing what your customers value, nor what they think of your quality. (Enterprise management is the exception, because it includes competitive customer choice.)

As we discussed in *Banishing Bureaucracy,* the Customer Strategy makes public organizations somewhat like private businesses that are accountable both to their owners and to their customers. In the public sector, elected officials—who represent the public, the true "owners"—define the basic parameters and rules of the system. While operating within those parameters, reinvented organizations must also please their customers. This works best when elected officials and their appointees can include customer satisfaction in the goals they set for each organization, thus aligning accountability to customers with accountability to elected officials. When conflicts between the two occur—when customers want something elected officials don't want—elected officials should have the final say, just as the owners of a business have the final say. Often service customers want more service than the elected officials are willing to fund, for example—smaller classes, more buses, bigger parks. Sometimes customers want things elected officials (or the courts) have ruled to be illegal. In such cases, vertical accountability to elected officials should trump horizontal accountability to customers. In the public sector, the customer is not always king.

We define the primary customers of a public function as its *principal intended beneficiaries*—those individuals or groups that the work is primarily designed to benefit. Secondary customers are others that the work is designed to benefit who are less important than the primary group. For example, the primary customers of schools are students and their parents; secondary customers would include employers, who want skilled employees.

In functions whose principal product is compliance, not service—such as police departments, environmental protection agencies, and tax collection agencies—the primary customer is usually the community at large. The people the agency deals with day after day, such as suspected criminals, polluters, and taxpayers, are *not* its primary customers. They are important, but they are not the principal intended beneficiaries. To distinguish them from customers, we call them *compliers.* Many reinventors call them customers, because they want compliance agencies to treat them better. We share this goal, but in our experience, the employees of these agencies know that suspected criminals, polluters, and taxpayers are not their customers. They know that pleasing these people could even compromise their mission. (They could please polluting businesses but ruin the environment, for example.) As a result, they quit listening the minute some outside expert starts talking about "customers" and "customer service."

Banishing Bureaucracy defined three approaches under the Customer Strategy. *Customer choice* gives customers a choice of providers; this makes sense for most service and compliance functions but not for steering (policy and regulatory) functions.

Definitions, p. 119

Competitive choice adds a dimension of consequences by letting the customers take public resources to their provider of choice. In an education system using competitive choice, for example, the public dollars supporting each student go to the school the student attends. Because this automatically rewards or punishes service providers by giving them (or denying them) funds, it is much more powerful than choice alone. But it is not appropriate for compliance or steering functions—or even for all service functions.

The third approach, *customer quality assurance,* sets customer service standards, rewards organizations that do a good job of meeting them, and penalizes those that don't. Though not as powerful as competitive choice, it can be used for any function, whether customers have choices or not.

Customer choice without consequences is certainly better than no choice at all, in most cases. It gives customers access to different kinds of services—different kinds of schools, different kinds of day care, different kinds of health providers. Customers who choose their service providers are also more committed customers: researchers have found that students who choose their schools are more committed to education, for example.

See Reinventing Government pp. 166–194

Reinventing Government discusses at length the advantages of customer choice and the wonderful things public organizations can do for their customers. (The list grows every year, from one-stop shopping to on-line service to electronic commerce to mobile service centers.) In this book, we address how to motivate public organizations to *habitually* do these wonderful things. And as a motivator, choice without consequences has limits. If service providers are not rewarded for attracting more customers and punished for losing them, choice has less power to change their behavior. The main thing at stake is pride, and pride is not always enough to overcome union resistance, political resistance, red tape, and the inertia built into large public systems.

Therefore, we recommend using competitive choice to improve service systems, whenever possible. When this is impossible, for political or other reasons, we suggest combining choice with performance management or managed competition, to create the consequences needed to drive improvement. Because of this, we have combined our discussion of customer choice and competitive choice into one chapter, which we call "Competitive Customer Choice." Much of what we say in Chapter Eight about systems of competitive choice applies to customer choice systems in which money does not follow customers, as well.

pp. 183–246

pp. 279–308

In policy and regulatory work, allowing for even simple choices is rarely appropriate; customer quality assurance is the only viable option. It makes no sense to create two or three institutions to write the rules covering some kind of behavior, and then let people choose which set they prefer to obey. The U.S. has long had two sets of rules for banks: they can apply for state charters and be regulated by their state, or they can apply for national charters and be regulated by federal institutions. This allows them to shop for the weakest regulator, undermining government's ability to prevent abuses in the banking system.

In compliance work, offering choices often makes sense, but competitive choice does not. A tax agency or permitting department can give compliers choices: to file taxes by mail, by phone, or electronically, for example, or to use different permitting offices. Some environmental protection agencies allow polluters a choice of responses: they can clean up their pollution, buy pollution credits, or use a combination of these strategies to meet the required standards. In Vermont, corrections reforms have dramatically expanded the choices given judges and community reparative boards—which represent the primary customer, the public—in sentencing criminals.

pp. 489–494

If compliance offices were funded according to the number of people or businesses they served, however—if the money followed the complier—they might have an incentive to overlook problems. A permitting agency would have an incentive to approve permits, when its real job is to protect public safety and standards by approving only those construction projects that meet those standards. An auto emissions inspection station would have an incentive to attract more customers by overlooking pollution and safety problems in autos, rather than forcing their owners to fix the problems. This is why competitive choice is not appropriate for compliance functions

Where Each Customer Approach Is Appropriate

Approach	Function		
	Policy & Regulatory	*Service*	*Compliance*
Customer choice		X	X
Competitive customer choice		X	
Customer quality assurance	X	X	X

Listening to one's customers is a critical competence necessary to use the Customer Strategy. We call it a competence rather than an approach because we seldom find it is enough, by itself, to force public organizations to break through the resistance and radically improve their customer service. In Chapter Nine we discuss the many methods organizations can use to listen to their customers, in the section on *customer voice.* But knowing what your customers want and delivering it are two different things. Knowledge does not force organizations to change in the way that consequences can.

pp. 382–388

See *Banishing Bureaucracy* pp. 157–202

For a full discussion of all these issues, we suggest you read Chapter Six of *Banishing Bureaucracy.* In the meantime, one final observation: because the Customer Strategy makes organizations directly accountable to their customers, it takes significant political will to implement it. It is rarely successful without full and active support from the executive: the president, the governor, the mayor, the city or county manager, or the superintendent. (In some departments, in some governments, aggressive support from a department head is enough.) If you are going to force public organizations to compete for their customers and dollars—or if you are going to force them to set customer service standards and offer redress when they fail to meet them—you will encounter serious resistance. Without the political muscle of the executive behind you, you will probably fail.

This suggests a good rule of thumb. Before you launch a customer strategy, ask the following question: Is your executive personally willing to fight for its success? If the answer is no, your chances of success are not good.

Chapter 8

Competitive Customer Choice

Making Customers Powerful Through Choice and Competition

Competitive Customer Choice gives customers a choice of service providers and allows funding to follow the customer, forcing providers to compete for both their customers and their money.

With 209 schools and more than 100,000 students, Milwaukee has the nation's 12th largest school district. Though well funded, with relatively good facilities and well-paid teachers, it has long had many of the problems associated with large urban districts. Although its white and Asian students have performed as well as students elsewhere in the state, African Americans, Hispanics, and Native Americans—who make up about three of every four students in the district—have not.

"By any measure of academic achievement, MPS is a failing system," former superintendent Howard Fuller declared soon after he was hired in 1991.

> *Only 40 percent of our freshmen graduate from high school. The grade point average for high school students is D+. Our next report card will show yet another overall decline in standardized test scores.*
>
> *The public knows we are failing. A 1990 MPS survey of Milwaukee parents and taxpayers showed that 72 percent believe their children would get a better education elsewhere. . . .*
>
> *As an organization, we lack incentives for high performance and consequences for failure. Despite the unacceptable outcomes cited above, our schools continue to operate and our funding goes up. . . . Everyone is protected except the children.*

A combination of bureaucratic gridlock and union power perpetuated the status quo. The Milwaukee Teachers' Education Association (MTEA) had enormous power to block change, because it could elect or defeat most school board candidates. The principals—who were theoretically responsible for creating good schools—could not even hire or fire teachers. In 12 years as a public school principal, former principal Allen Nuhlicek told *Education Week*, he had been allowed to hire only two of the teachers who worked for him— and then only because of a bureaucratic loophole.

By the late 1980s, inner-city parents had pushed and pushed and pushed again for improvement, with little success. A legislative drive to create a separate, minority district for the inner city had failed. In desperation, two African American Democratic state legislators, Representative Annette "Polly" Williams and Senator Gary George, introduced a bill to let up to 1 percent of the system's students take public vouchers to private, non-religious schools. They forged an unusual coalition with the Republican governor, Republican legislators, and maverick Democrats, and in 1990 they passed the nation's first voucher program. To qualify, students' family incomes had to be under 175 percent of the poverty line—$23,000, at the time, for a family of four. The voucher was worth about $2,500, roughly what the state gave districts per pupil.

The voucher program was small enough that it cost the district only $3.8 million over its first three years, but it attracted enormous publicity. Williams's idea was to prod the public system to improve, by providing competition for it. "It's not that I think the public school system can't be changed, but I don't think we have to sacrifice the lives of our children while waiting on that system," she said.

> *Because the system just won't turn over and do right. The teachers' union will fight any kind of change that will reduce its power. So we shouldn't wait. After all, these people getting the big paychecks [teachers and administrators] have already moved their children out of the public schools. Yet they're having a fit because our parents are doing what they've already done—leaving.*

Frustrated by their inability to improve the schools, the MPS board hired an African American activist as superintendent in 1991. Howard Fuller, then director of the county Department of Health and Human Services, had made his name as a militant community leader in Milwaukee. He quickly proposed radical reinvention:

- Decentralizing key decisions to the schools.
- Changing union contracts to give real hiring and firing authority to principals.

- Contracting with nonprofit organizations to run alternative schools.
- Aggressively expanding Milwaukee's limited public choice system, with dollars to follow children to their families' schools of choice.
- And closing failing schools and, in their place, contracting "with public and private groups to open schools free of current restrictions that impede effective management."

Over the next three years Fuller succeeded in pushing a bit of this through the board: some decentralization, some contracting with outside groups to run alternative schools, performance measurement and improvement plans in schools, and creation of a few Afrocentric immersion schools and other programs designed to help minority students. But the union blocked the rest of his agenda. When he proposed contracting with the Edison Project, a for-profit company, to manage a Milwaukee public school, the union erupted. Union leaders mobilized and won four of the five school board seats up for election in April 1995. (John Gardner, a reform activist, won the fifth, the only at-large seat on the nine-member board.) Two weeks later Fuller resigned in frustration, publicly blaming the union and its school board members for blocking his reform efforts.

That spring, however, the state legislature passed a bill to expand the voucher program to 15,000 students. It was pushed through by a broad but frustrated reform coalition that included Milwaukee mayor John Norquist, a New Democrat; Republican and Democratic state legislators from the city; business leaders; religious leaders; private schools; and Milwaukee's minority communities and parents. Under the new law, parents could use the vouchers at secular or religious schools—adding 93 private schools to the eligibility list. The bill had been carefully crafted to avoid unconstitutionality: the voucher checks went to parents, not schools, and participating schools had to agree not to require any voucher student to participate in religious training, indoctrination, or education.

Suddenly the district stood to lose as much as $48 million a year—a healthy chunk of its $785 million budget. When the state opened enrollment in the new program in August, more than 5,000 students applied. Though the Wisconsin Supreme Court issued an injunction blocking the program's expansion in late August, the school board, prodded by Gardner and one other reformer, took the threat very seriously. From the moment it became clear that the expanded voucher bill would pass, it began working to compete for those 15,000 students:

- It opened seven new "Innovative Schools."
- It expanded the district's limited public school choice system.

- It voted to close and reconstitute ten schools, despite protests from 300 outraged MTEA members.
- It passed what Gardner calls "the nation's most stringent graduation requirements." Beginning in 2004, graduating seniors will have to pass exams in math and oral and written communication, take a minimum number of courses in science and the social sciences, write and defend a research paper, and do at least one community service project.
- It established procedures to authorize charter schools: new public schools of choice, free of most regulations and red tape, that compete with existing schools for students and funds. (See Chapter Ten for an in-depth look at chartering.)

pp. 434–443

- It authorized the MPS's first charter school.
- It voted to dramatically expand three programs that had long waiting lists: early childhood education, before-and after-school child care, and alternative schools for students who did not do well in MPS schools.
- It added eight new schools or programs in other areas with waiting lists: language immersion, Montessori programs, and high school programs for the college bound.
- It embraced decentralization, giving schools more power to determine the grade levels they would offer, their calendars and schedules, the nature of their governance councils, and their curricula.
- It negotiated memoranda of understanding with the teachers' union authorizing exemptions to its labor contracts in seven schools, so those schools could hire teachers and teaching assistants without regard to seniority.
- Finally, it negotiated with the teachers' union two reforms related to teacher performance. The first kept new teachers on probation for two years, before they achieved tenure. The second created a teacher evaluation unit, jointly appointed by the board and the MTEA, that could terminate any teacher who performed poorly and did not demonstrably improve after intervention and help.

In March 1996, after almost a year of breakneck reform, Wisconsin Circuit Court judge Paul Higgenbothom ruled the 1995 voucher law unconstitutional. MPS principals, teachers, and union officials "breathed grateful sighs of fatigued relief," in Gardner's words. The decision was appealed, but for now, the pressure was off.

Suddenly, the teacher's union changed its stance. It refused to approve any more memoranda of understanding—or even extend existing agreements when they expired. In August, it filed suit to block implementation of the board's charter school and contracting policies.

Faced with a hostile union, the board quit closing schools and creating Innovative Schools. It suspended the process for opening charter schools. It quit contracting for alternative programs. It slowed down its expansion of early childhood programs—missing its goal by more than 300 seats. And it pulled back its decentralization initiatives.

"Some efforts, that generate no internal opposition, have gone forward," Gardner wrote in a 1997 article. "But the burst of entrepreneurial effort, the sudden coalescence of internal collaboration, the political will to respond, and the managerial impetus to implement, have effectively dissolved. Without the general environment and specific threat of losing students and losing money, revolutionary reform has all but died."

In April 1997, the coalition got a third reformer, Bruce Thompson, elected to the board. The three managed to cobble together a majority for a few more contracted schools and a bit more decentralization. The reform coalition also pushed an amendment to the state's charter school law through the legislature, giving the city and two public universities the power to charter schools in Milwaukee.

But the real turning point came in 1998, when the Wisconsin Supreme Court ruled the voucher law constitutional and the U.S. Supreme Court declined to review the case. At about the same time, the reformers put together a slate of four new candidates to take on the four union-sponsored board members in the April 1999 election.

Suddenly, the union and its board members changed course again. "They got real scared about losing this election," says Bruce Thompson. They were also worried about losing more students to vouchers. "And it looked like their suits against charter schools would lose."

In January 1999 they negotiated a new union contract—six months early. "The teacher's union was afraid of losing control of the board, and they wanted to negotiate with a board they controlled," says Gardner. In addition, "their own board members were asking them for concessions to protect themselves" at the polls.

The union gave up the seniority system for assigning teachers, allowing school governance councils (made up primarily of elected parents and teachers) and principals to interview and hire the teachers they wanted. It agreed to new language on school reconstitution, under which 50 percent of the teachers in a reconstituted school could be reassigned. And it settled its suits against the district's charter school, contracting, and reconstitution policies, on terms favorable to the reformers.

But it was too late. Running on a unified "Compete Don't Complain" platform, the reformers swept all seats. The *Milwaukee Journal Sentinel* called it "an electoral setback perhaps unprecedented for the Milwaukee Teachers' Education Association" and "a sensational victory . . . for advocates of change in the Milwaukee Public Schools."

The new board quickly bought out the superintendent's contract and hired the system's most entrepreneurial principal to take his place. It voted to let six public schools become charter schools, while the city and the University of Wisconsin in Milwaukee chartered four more schools. It let white Milwaukee parents use open enrollment to send their kids to suburban public schools for the first time, and it contracted with two private schools to bring them into the MPS system as public schools (which gives them more money per student and allows free tuition for all their students). It also required the creation of school-based cost accounting, in preparation for a budget system in which dollars would follow children to their schools of choice. The tide had clearly turned.

"The momentum to create a system where parents' choices for their children determine what schools are available and what schools provide—the momentum to strip the power away from the bureaucracy and give it to the parents—is like a mighty river now," said David Riemer, Mayor Norquist's director of administration and a key player in school reform. "I think we've reached a point where it's so powerful it's going to sweep away the old system."

THE POWER TO FORCE HARD DECISIONS

As Milwaukee's story demonstrates, once a monopoly has to compete for its customers and money, it will embrace changes it would never otherwise have entertained. Without that threat, "there is tremendous built-in resistance to giving up centralized power," Bruce Thompson explains, "and tremendous opposition to real accountability for the schools."

See *Banishing Bureaucracy* pp. 157–173

It is not that those who run the monopoly—in this case, the school board, the superintendent, and the central administration—are bad people. Most of the time, they want to do what is best for the children. But often, doing that is simply too risky. Ted Kolderie, the Minnesota school reformer who helped bring public school choice and charter schools to America, explains the dynamic very well.

> *As they consider proposals for change, the superintendent, board, principal, union and teachers weigh the potential benefits to the kids against the risk of creating "internal stress." They want to help the kids. But upsetting people might create controversy. It might produce a grievance. It might lose an election. It might cause a strike. It might damage a career.*

So they don't make the changes.

In Milwaukee, John Gardner points out, many of the reforms he and his allies accomplished had been on the table for a decade or more. But without the threat of competition, the system found them too difficult to enact. "Reforms, including those with clear merit and without vigorous opposition, died because one of many parties—the board, superintendent, central administration, teachers' or administrators' union, principals, or teachers—could effectively veto them. Lining up all internal vested interests for the same thing, at the same time, generally proved more than anyone could do."

In contrast, choice and competition force decision makers to fight through the inertia and resistance and do what is best for their customers. "School choice is making MPS begin treating poor children of all races as valued customers, in large part because, for the first time, they are," says Gardner. What helps poor children "is the same thing that improves public education and government schools: clear, accountable choices and consequences for school districts that everyone understands—money following students to where they are best served."

See *Banishing Bureaucracy* pp. 157–173

Studies of other competitive choice systems support this argument. We wrote at length about the impact of competitive public school choice in Minnesota in *Banishing Bureaucracy*. Soon after that book was published, the Pioneer Institute studied the impact of interdistrict choice in Massachusetts. Its researchers, David J. Armor and Brett M. Peiser, conducted detailed surveys and interviews in 9 of the 10 Massachusetts school districts that had lost the most students to other districts. Their findings confirmed what common sense would suggest: those that lost the most students (5 to 6 percent) and felt the most financial pain made the most changes to improve their competitiveness; those that felt the least financial pain did nothing in response.

The three districts that lost 5 to 6 percent of their students made enough changes to bounce back, cutting their losses sharply. Ten of the 12 staff members interviewed in those districts "believed that the ultimate effects of choice were positive in that they led to increased resources and/or enhancements in specific program areas, especially the number of teachers and course offerings." None thought choice had a negative impact.

"I think the fact that a lot of kids left and continue to stay out had the effect of being an academic wake-up call to our faculty," said one administrator.

"We now offer full-day, part-day, and a two-year kindergarten," added another, from a second district. "Now we have a technology guru on staff who spends $100,000 to $200,000 a year putting technology in certain locations. It's been a big change, a big increase."

Initially "some people felt betrayed," said a third. "There was a lot of anger and disenchantment because . . . most of the ones who left weren't long-time residents [and] didn't have loyalty." Things began to change, however, when the district convened a retreat.

Key stakeholders . . . got off-site for a couple of days with a good facilitator and identified a vision statement [and a] mission statement. . . . One of the common visions was a first-rate educational system, a first-rate educational plant. . . . The last three years we've averaged 11 percent increase in our operating budget. . . . And then the capital expenditure, an elementary school [had] a $7 million rehab and addition . . . [and] a $9 million rehab and addition to the middle-high school. So there has been a renaissance, a reawakening, a revitalization.

A 1998 study of the impact of charter schools on public school districts reported similar effects. Conducted by doctoral candidate Eric Rofes for Policy Analysis for California Education, an independent research unit of the University of California-Berkeley, it looked at 25 school districts in eight states and the District of Columbia. Charter schools have performance contracts with their authorizing body, which may be a local school board, a state board of education, or in some states even a university. They are schools of choice, and their funding normally comes with the students who choose them, from the districts those students have left.

pp. 434–443

Rofes found that the districts that made the most changes were those in which charter schools had taken away a significant percentage of students and dollars. Within the first few years, six districts "responded energetically to the advent of charters and significantly altered their educational programs." Another six exhibited what Rofes called a "moderate" response—including Boston, which responded by creating nine charter school–like "pilot schools," and Grand Rapids, Michigan, which opened a new school focused on environmental education and had plans for additional thematic schools.

Overall, districts "which had experienced high levels of impact usually exhibited responses to charters, though not necessarily at a high level; districts which had experienced low levels of impact generally exhibited low levels of response or no response at all." Perhaps the biggest factor motivating change was financial loss, but strong leadership was also critical.

The day after a charter was awarded in one Massachusetts town, the superintendent walked into an administrators' meeting, tossed a copy of David Halberstam's book *The Reckoning* on the table, and asked, "Who do you want to be—Honda or General Motors?"

Our middle school, which is the school at which the charter school is aimed, was by any rational standard the least successful school in the district. . . . Its test scores were mediocre. . . . It had a faculty that was defensive and complacent.

The charter school was a wake-up call, like it or not. The fact is that the parents of more than 100 kids said, "We want our kids out." . . . Charter schools served notice to everybody that complacency wasn't an option. . . . With no competition, people show up to work, do what they consider to be their jobs, go home feeling tired, satisfied, fulfilled—you pick it. The unfortunate reality, perhaps, is that the competition forced us to look in a mirror and ask who we were, who we wanted to be, why these people had chosen to leave us, and what we were gonna do about it.

Forcing Innovation, Improving Outcomes

Do the changes districts are making in response to competition lead to improved outcomes for students? That, after all, is one of the foremost reasons to create choice and charter schools. In Milwaukee and Massachusetts it's too early to tell; statewide exams were first conducted in Massachusetts in 1998, and Milwaukee changed its exams in 1997. There is one place, however, that has enough data over enough years to support a very clear hypothesis: England. Beginning in 1988, the British government pushed through a series of reforms that created a system of competitive choice, in which at least 80 percent of the money in the system must be delegated to schools—and most of it follows children to the schools of their choice. Schools can opt out of their district if they find it too restrictive (and more than 1,100 have done so, including nearly 20 percent of all secondary schools). Schools control their own budgets. Hundreds of specialized alternative schools have been created, and new competitors, much like charter schools, can enter the market as well. The government measures progress carefully, through both national exams and qualitative inspections. It publishes the results in annual "performance tables" and inspection reports, both of which help parents compare schools.

p. 306

Choice and competition have not been the only reforms in the British system, but they have been central. No one can prove a cause-and-effect relationship between competition and performance with scientific certainty, but on virtually every indicator, student achievement has soared since the reforms began. In 1986–87, less than 25 percent of 15-year-olds received satisfactory scores (A, B, or C) on the key exam (the General Certificate of Secondary Education). For more than a decade the percentage has steadily increased, until 46.3 percent did in 1997–98. (Meanwhile, real spending on secondary education has declined and teacher-student ratios have grown worse—though the percentage of time teachers actually teach has increased, thanks to pressures from reform.)

Education is compulsory in England to age 16. Since the reforms began, the participation of 16-to 18–year-olds in education has doubled, to roughly 50 percent. Student participation in higher education has increased from 17 percent in 1989–90 to more than 30 percent in 1997–98.

Test scores for younger children, though only published for the last few years, are also marching upward. Although these results don't prove anything, rigorous qualitative evaluations of each school, begun in 1993 and now required at least once every six years, suggest that the reforms are responsible. In its 1999 report, the Office of Standards in Education (OFSTED) reported that "the performance of teachers and pupils stands in sharp contrast to that of four years ago.

pp. 313–314

> *Teachers are now teaching better, and pupils, as a consequence, are learning more. . . .*
>
> *The statistics this year speak for themselves. In 1993/94 the quality of teaching was judged to be less than satisfactory in 25 per cent, 30 per cent, 19 per cent and 17 per cent of lessons in Key Stages 1, 2, 3 and 4 respectively. [Each stage is several grade levels.] This year the comparable figures have fallen to 8 per cent, 8 per cent, 10 per cent and 7 per cent. Teaching is now deemed to be good in over half of the lessons observed in each key stage. . . .*
>
> *Evidence from the re-inspection of secondary schools shows that the overwhelming majority of schools are actively trying to raise standards, often in response to performance tables and OFSTED inspection. Seven in ten of the schools inspected in 1997/98 showed an upward trend in results since their previous inspection.*

"Nobody now questions the need to raise standards," OFSTED's Chief Inspector concluded.

> *Fewer take refuge in socio-economic explanations of school failure. Most within the profession accept that the beliefs about education and teaching which have dominated practice for the last forty years must be, at the least, questioned. The culture is now less self-indulgent. We have a new and rigorous focus on what actually works.*

Beyond Education

Competitive customer choice is beginning to transform more than just public education: it has had an impact in many other arenas as well. This approach has been used to provide child care, job training, adult education, higher education (Pell Grants and the G.I. Bill), services for alcohol and drug abusers, health care, and food stamps. Some of these programs use vouchers (or their modern equivalent, benefit cards that permit electronic payment), some reimburse providers for their services, and some simply develop a financial system that sends public money to the provider chosen by the citizen.

Sometimes the customer is unable to make the choice by himself or herself. Parents choose schools for children, for example, and sometimes social workers or therapists choose treatment for patients with mental or behavioral problems. In the mid–1980s, Minnesota consolidated a myriad of funding sources for alcohol and drug treatment, distributed the money to counties and Indian reservations, and let their assessment centers pick the best treatment providers, with the money following the client. Under the state's new Consolidated Chemical Dependency Treatment Fund, many clients received more appropriate treatment for their needs. Meanwhile, by forcing providers to compete and by using less in-hospital treatment, the state saved enough money that it could serve 33 percent more people.

pp. 275–276

Customer choice without competition is even more common. As we discuss in the introduction to Part III, customer choice makes sense in compliance work but is a weak agent of change in service systems. Milwaukee gave families a choice of different public schools in the 1970s, in an effort to promote racial integration, but it did not create a situation in which schools competed for students and dollars. During the next two decades, choice helped some students and parents, but it did little to force the district or its schools to change. It had no power to force the teachers' union to put students' interests above teachers'. It had no power to force school board members and school administrators to make tough, controversial decisions—like closing schools that performed poorly or firing language teachers who could not speak the language they were teaching. And it gave parents no power to force schools to give their children what they needed. If few parents chose a school because they thought it was unsafe or had poor teachers, the district still filled it up. Choice did not bring many consequences.

pp. 434–443

In this chapter we present four basic tools you can use to create a successful system of competitive customer choice. The first is a *competitive public choice system,* which encourages customers to choose between different public providers and lets public dollars follow customers to the providers. This is what Minnesota, Massachusetts, and many other states have done in public education. (Charter schools, which we discuss in Chapter Ten, are one way to create more choices within such a system.) The second is a *voucher system* or *reimbursement program,* which gives designated customers the resources to purchase services themselves, from whomever they choose, or reimburses providers when customers choose them. This tool is different from the first primarily because it gives people access to private providers (although public providers can be included as well.) The third is a *customer information system,* which gives customers information about the quality and cost of each provider, so they can make informed decisions. And the fourth is a system of *brokers*—akin to real estate agents or stockbrokers in the private sector—who help customers sort through that information and make good choices.

These tools are not mutually exclusive; you could use all four together. Indeed, when you create a competitive public choice system or a voucher or reimbursement program, a customer information system is often indispensable, and in complex markets brokers are necessary as well. Because these tools are so often used together, most of the lessons in this chapter focus on the entire approach rather than on one tool.

OVERCOMING POLITICAL HURDLES

The single biggest obstacle to competitive choice is politics. By definition, creating a system of competitive choice denies established institutions their monopolies—or, at minimum, their privileged positions. Predictably, they object. And they are rarely shy about sharing their objections with elected officials.

In Milwaukee, the teachers' union put up a decade-long fight against vouchers, contracting, and charter schools. Many of the system's administrators resisted as well, though more through bureaucratic inertia than through political activism. In Minnesota, the teachers' unions, principals' association, and superintendents' association resisted public school choice, as we described in *Banishing Bureaucracy.* Also in Minnesota, the legislature defeated the governor's first proposal to create a Consolidated Chemical Dependency Treatment Fund because state hospital employee unions opposed it. They knew that their hospitals would lose patients to cheaper halfway houses and outpatient treatment centers if they had to compete.

See *Banishing Bureaucracy* pp. 157–173

Reinventors must have the courage to take on special interests. They also need the street smarts to beat them in the political arena. Based on our study of a dozen different transitions to competitive choice—from public education to job training to drug treatment to child care—we offer the following tips for winning the political wars.

1. Show the public how little the emperor is wearing.

"Someone must announce that the emperor has no clothes," says Curtis Johnson, a leader in the fight for public school choice in Minnesota. "Someone or some group of some standing must say the current system doesn't work." Johnson led his organization, the Citizens League, to do so in the early 1980s, with a groundbreaking report on the quality of the public school system. The Minnesota Business Partnership, made up of the leaders of the Twin Cities' 80 largest corporations, followed with its own study. Finally, leaders in the state began to realize that their public education system—long the pride of the state—was not all it was cracked up to be.

The lesson is very simple: if you cannot convince people that the existing system is broken, they will not endure the political pain necessary to fix it. To convince them, you will need data. It is no accident that Howard Fuller began his first report to the Milwaukee school board with a recitation of the sorry statistics of student achievement in Milwaukee.

p. 279

2. *Articulate the general interest.*

Interest groups will always defend their own interests: their jobs, their salaries, their power. To defeat them, you must focus public attention on the *general interest:* better schools, cheaper health care, increased opportunity for job training or child care. Interest groups will bring to bear all the pressure they can on elected officials. Often, a threat to field and fund an opponent at election time is daunting, because elections for school boards, city or county councils, and state legislatures don't get a lot of media attention or stimulate high voter turnout. In quiet elections, well-organized interest groups can often defeat incumbents. If you want to overcome this kind of pressure, you have to make the issue very public and focus it on the general interest. In a back-room political battle, the special interests will win every time.

3. *Seize the high ground.*

In Milwaukee, opponents of vouchers accused the reformers of trying to destroy the public schools. They painted them as elitists who didn't care about the children who would be left behind when better students jumped ship with vouchers. The reformers refused to bite; instead, *they* seized the moral high ground. Mayor Norquist pointed out that the choice program "offers poor and working-class families in the city something wealthier Americans have always had: the power to choose their children's school."

"What the opponents of school choice are really saying is that they just don't trust you to decide which school is best for your child," Bradley Foundation president Michael Joyce told a group of black parents.

"I have yet to meet an opponent of school choice who didn't already have it," added John Gardner.

In Minnesota several years earlier, reformers made it very clear to the teachers' unions that if they fought the governor's proposal for public school choice, equity would be the central issue. "If you have a lot of money, you have a lot of choice," Verne Johnson pointed out. "If you don't have a lot of money, you don't have a lot of choice." If they opposed choice, unions made up primarily of white, middle-class teachers would be accused of denying equal opportunity to poor and working families.

Once the reformers seized that ground, the unions realized they couldn't win—not with the governor leading the fight for reform. After the reformers laid down the gauntlet on equal opportunity, Ted Kolderie remembers, "I think it became clear to the unions for the first time how vulnerable they were."

4. *Keep your message simple.*

Few issues are more complex than mental health funding. When Minnesota created its Consolidated Chemical Dependency Treatment Fund, the reform was hopelessly complex. So the reformers boiled it down to a simple idea: "The dollars follow the client." It "helps to have a simple overall concept to explain what may be a fairly complex policy change," they counseled others in their application for an Innovations in State and Local Government award.

5. *Communicate in terms people understand and feel comfortable with.*

Abstractions like "restructuring schools" or "outcome-based education" won't get you very far, says Joe Nathan, a Minnesota education reformer who runs the Center for School Change at the University of Minnesota.

> *I never talk about restructuring schools. I go around and tell stories. I was trained by Alinsky, and one of his central rules was you've got to talk within the framework that people understand. When I would go around the state and talk about school choice, I would talk about opportunity, not about competition, because there are a whole lot of people in this state who don't believe in competition.*

When Nathan works in rural communities to help them restructure their schools, he says to people, "'We'd like to provide your kids an opportunity to do hands-on things like they're doing in Little Falls, or in *X, Y,* or *Z.*' One good story is worth about 100 pages of strategies. We've worked in 35 communities, and in not one have we had resistance."

6. *Sell results, not a process.*

Too often, reformers try to engage the public in a discussion of the *process* they are trying to create: how the new system of competitive choice will work. On some occasions, this is appropriate. But to win a political battle, you must sell the public on the *results* you want to deliver. If the reform will save money, give people choices, or force providers to improve, then focus on those goals. Most people don't care how you get there, but they do care about results.

Once you begin to produce results, you must measure and document them and publish your data. In Milwaukee, for example, a careful study by Harvard University political scientist Paul Peterson and two colleagues showed that by the third and fourth year in a private school, students who received vouchers had made significant academic gains compared with those who had applied unsuccessfully for vouchers and remained in public schools.

7. *Use polls to prove your support.*

If politicians pay attention to anything, they pay attention to polls. In Milwaukee, strong support for vouchers among minority parents, proven in poll after poll, helped the program survive. When interest groups oppose a reform that is supported by a broad majority of the public, everyone suddenly understands that the groups are defending their own narrow self-interest, not the general interest.

8. *Sell your side of the story to the media.*

Too often, reformers wait for the media to come to them. This is a mistake; you need to take your story to the media. This requires more than just presenting your arguments. It means backing them up with data—and most important, dramatizing them with stories of real-life people and conflicts. "We're not content to issue press releases; we don't wait for journalists to call us," says Nathan. "We constantly sit down with journalists and tell them what's going on."

But the media won't report most things "unless you make it a good story," Nathan has learned. During the battle for school choice, he constantly fed stories to the media. One involved a young woman in an inner suburb who had a three-year-old and a five-year-old, he remembers. She was a secretary at 3M. "The three-year-old had some disabilities, and she found somebody near 3M who not only did day care but did physical therapy, who could help her kid. In order to make this work, she needed to have her other kid go to kindergarten nearby, because it was half-day, and the kid needed to be dropped off before school and after school at day care."

She asked her district to let her send her child to kindergarten in a different district. They refused, because the superintendent thought it was another case of a parent who just wanted convenience. "We found some young working women at the two newspapers and told them about this," Nathan smiles.

> *We found a producer at one of the local TV stations who was a working mother. Day after day after day, there were stories about this situation: Mother appeals to school district, is turned down. Mother appeals to school board, is turned down. The superintendent wouldn't budge.*

It went on for eight weeks before the school board finally gave in.

9. *Organize constituencies that will benefit from reform.*

In most situations, the potential losers from choice and competition—existing providers—are already well organized. Reformers have to organize those who would benefit from competition: both customers and providers who do not yet have access to those customers. State hospitals and their unions feared the competition from Minnesota's Consolidated Fund, but other providers of care welcomed it. So after its first bill failed, the Perpich administration put together an advisory commission of stakeholders, including the other providers, to develop the final legislation.

Minnesota's education reformers consciously built a series of constituencies. They started by convincing the Citizens League to endorse school choice. Then they recruited the Minnesota Business Partnership. Next they reached out to minority communities, where parents felt particularly captive of the public school monopoly because they couldn't afford private schools. Later they organized students and parents from the first school choice program into a potent constituency.

See *Banishing Bureaucracy* pp. 162–163

10. Develop champions in both parties.

Reforms can quickly become politicized, with one party opposing them simply because the other party supports them. But if only one party supports a change, reformers run a risk that the executive or legislative branch will fall into the opposition's hands and kill the reform. The solution is to develop solid backers in both parties. In Minnesota, for example, most of the pioneering school choice reformers were Democrats. Early on, they recruited the former Republican governor, Al Quie, to their cause. Next they went after the sitting Democratic governor, Rudy Perpich. Once he signed on, the reform coalition was solidly bipartisan.

11. Don't take on too many opponents at once.

Sometimes wisdom is the better part of valor. When the Perpich administration was working to pass legislation to create the Consolidated Chemical Dependency Treatment Fund, it faced opposition from public hospitals, their unions, and even some private hospitals, which also feared losing business to new competitors. In addition, the counties did not want the Community Social Service Act funds they controlled to go into the Consolidated Fund. So the reformers decided not to take on that battle.

12. Make a deal with the special interests.

Often the best way to soften opposition is to protect the interest groups from their worst fears. If you can make a deal with one or two key interest groups, you can divide the opposition. Unions can be guaranteed that their workers will not be laid off; if their units lose customers, as they almost inevitably will, surplus employees can be retrained and placed in other public sector jobs. Monopoly providers can be guaranteed a slow transition to full competition, to soften the blow. When Texas converted its day-care funding to competitive choice, for example, it gave providers who had local monopolies guarantees of gradually decreasing enrollments, along with training in marketing techniques.

pp. 199–200

13. Get the new system in place before the next election.

Shifts from monopoly systems to competitive choice are almost always controversial. And politicians hate controversy at election time—particularly when angry interest groups are involved. So if possible, get the new system in place before the next major election. A system already in place is hard to undo, but a transition just begun can easily be halted.

14. Be prepared for lawsuits.

When they lose something as important as the job security that comes with monopoly status, providers and their interest groups often pull out all the stops to block the change—including filing lawsuits. Reformers need to anticipate this and have a way to fund an aggressive defense.

15. Stay on offense.

Opponents will always attack reforms that take away their monopolies, but the best defense is a good offense. If you keep pushing forward, expanding the reforms, you can force your opponents to play defense. "Once you start the momentum rolling, never let it stop until you have completed the total programme," says Roger Douglas, the former Labor Party finance minister who led New Zealand's dramatic reinvention efforts. "The fire of opponents is much less accurate if they have to shoot at a rapidly moving target. If you take your next decision while they are still struggling to mobilise against the last one, you will continually capture the high ground of national interest and force them to fight uphill."

See *Banishing Bureaucracy* pp. 75–90

See *Banishing Bureaucracy* pp. 157–173

In Minnesota, as we described in *Banishing Bureaucracy,* public school choice reformers pushed through one advance after another over 10 years. "Traditional educators were kept so busy on redesign issues that they had little time to develop initiatives of their own," academics Nancy Roberts and Paula King reported in their study of the process. "They were forced into a reactive mode as redesign proponents took the initiative, framed the issues, and eventually convinced many educators that public school choice had merit."

"You only score when you have the ball," says Curt Johnson, a leader of the Minnesota effort. "You have to keep playing offense all the time, or the people who want to block you will prevail. You can't stop when you're winning."

16. Don't compromise the fundamentals.

This is perhaps the most important advice we can give. Competitive choice systems are very powerful; they provide enormous leverage to change behavior, because they force all providers in the system to work very hard to satisfy their customers. But they do not work if the customers' choice or the providers' competition is diluted too much.

Though reformers sometimes have to compromise with interest groups, it is a mistake to compromise on choice or competition. Indeed, it is wiser to wait for a better moment than to pass legislation that compromises the fundamentals. This is one of the basic rules passed on by Curt Johnson, Ted Kolderie, and their band of Minnesota reformers. Roger Douglas agrees. "The problem with compromise policies is simple," he says. "They do not produce the right outcome for the public at the end of the day. So they come back to haunt the politicians responsible for them."

CALMING LEGISLATORS' NERVES

The political struggle for systems of competitive choice almost always takes place in a legislative body, whether a school board, a city or county council, or a state, provincial, or national legislature. Elected executives often support choice and competition, because they represent all the people and can afford to uphold the general interest. Legislators face very different incentives: they get little credit for big changes like school choice, but they get tremendous heat from interest groups at election time if they support those changes. As a result, they find the hard work of breaking monopolies very risky.

There are a number of ways to help legislators cope with this risk. The best one, quite obviously, is to organize constituencies to push legislators for reform just as hard as the interest groups are pushing against it. In addition, you can use a number of other techniques to lessen legislators' anxiety:

- ***Provide quid pro quos.*** Give legislators something they need politically, such as savings to balance the budget or support for a project they want, in return for their support.
- ***Provide "letters of comfort."*** The late Bill Donaldson, a legendary city manager in Cincinnati, Tacoma, and Scottsdale, Arizona, counseled other reformers to find ways to reassure legislators that reforms would not blow up in their faces. He compared this to the letters borrowers secure for bankers, testifying to their good character and creditworthiness. For example, one could take legislators to another area that has created choice or charter schools and show them how the controversy quickly died down and teachers accepted the reforms—or bring teachers from elsewhere in to explain the same thing.
- ***Find credible partners.*** Often, legislators will be reassured if the business community is active in a reform coalition. Community organizations also have credibility in many environments. Even better, if any unions support the reforms, they can quiet fears about opposition from other unions.

See *Banishing Bureaucracy* pp. 162–163

• ***Deliver early victories.*** Nothing succeeds like success. If you can prove that choice and competition work—and create happy constituents—you can win over many legislators. In Minnesota, the Postsecondary Options program, which slipped through unnoticed while the unions were blocking a broader choice bill, proved how popular and effective it was to give juniors and seniors a real choice and make high schools compete with colleges for their students and dollars. When the interest groups tried to repeal it, the outpouring of support from parents and students was eye-opening for the legislature.

• ***Share credit with legislators.*** When results come in, let legislators who back the reforms release the data and take the credit. This produces the currency that counts with elected officials: good press. If they get to bask in the glow of success, they will be more likely to take a risk next time.

THE EQUITY ISSUE

The most serious issue opponents raise about systems of competitive choice is that they will benefit the affluent and educated, who will know how to get what they want as customers, but hurt the poor and uneducated, who will not. For example, middle-class parents will work hard to get their children into the best schools, but poor, uneducated parents will leave their kids in schools that will spiral downhill as their best students leave. A related issue has to do with race: in the U.S., critics argue, whites will use choice to flee schools with significant numbers of minorities, undermining attempts to integrate the schools and leaving minority students in poor, failing inner-city schools.

The truth is that under traditional systems, many white families have done just that—moved to the suburbs or sent their children to private schools. After forced busing was implemented to integrate U.S. schools, so many whites fled the cities that many urban districts became 90 percent or more "minority." Low-income students are also trapped in failing inner-city schools as the middle class flees to private schools or the suburbs.

But the fact that past systems were flawed does not excuse similar flaws in reformed systems. The equity issues are all too real. A pure voucher system, in which all students received a voucher worth the same amount, would probably produce an education system with even less racial and socioeconomic integration than exists today. Parents would add their own money to the vouchers to buy their children the best education they could afford. Then, like any other market, the education marketplace would stratify by price: it would produce \$20,000 schools, \$15,000 schools, \$12,000 schools, \$10,000 schools, \$8,000 schools, and schools that charged only the price of the voucher.

This would be a mistake, in our view. Public schools exist to educate children, but they also play a role in socializing them, in developing them into constructive citizens of a multiracial, multicultural democracy. If students don't go to school with kids from different walks of life, they will grow into adults who don't understand people who are different from them. Some will fear those who are different; others will simply never discover that beneath their skin color and income level, most people are pretty much alike. Before long, our society will lose some of its empathy, some of its commitment to caring for people who need help. We will become less a community and more a collection of individuals.

In addition, the quality of other students is a big factor in a child's educational experience. If low-end voucher schools end up with only poor children, few of whose parents have attended college, those children will never benefit from exposure to children who have broader horizons—children who read a great deal at home, use computers often, and strive to do well so they can attend good colleges. This would inevitably widen the achievement gap between poor children and affluent children.

Voucher systems can certainly be structured to promote equity—by limiting vouchers to those below certain income levels; by using a sliding scale, with higher-income families receiving vouchers of lesser value; or by forbidding schools that accept vouchers from charging parents any amount above the voucher. But in a democracy, it would be very hard to sustain any of these alternatives. The middle class would inevitably demand its right to equal vouchers and to spend any amount above the voucher's value. And in a developed democracy, what the middle class demands, the middle class usually gets.

Another approach would require all schools accepting vouchers to enroll at least a set proportion of low-income or minority students. But in the U.S., given recent court rulings on affirmative action, race-based admissions would face insurmountable legal obstacles. Income-based admissions would also face immediate legal challenges, as well as determined political opposition. These realities lead us to conclude that we are better off with highly competitive systems of public choice, using vouchers only for limited populations—such as low-income students or those in failing schools.

But even in competitive public choice systems, the equity issues are real. We must think of a "social market," not a "free market," when we create such systems. Michael Alves, an education consultant who has helped design numerous choice systems, says it well:

> *After implementing controlled choice in fourteen districts around the country, we feel confident that there is no conflict between choice and integration, if you control for it. And we are equally confident that if you don't control for race and social class, then choice will have no positive effect [on integration]. If anything, history shows that uncontrolled choice will make things worse. So you need to design the ground rules of choice programs very carefully.*

This careful design should include, at minimum:

- A system in which dollars follow the child, to create real financial pressure on districts to improve the schools people are deserting, so kids whose parents leave them in those schools will no longer be trapped in declining institutions.
- A requirement that districts close and "reconstitute"—that is, reopen under a new principal, with many new teachers—shrinking schools that fail to improve after two years.
- Programs to create new schools specifically designed to foster socioeconomic and racial integration, such as charter schools and magnet schools.
- Subsidized transportation to their school of choice for low-income students.

Some states and districts use racial quotas, in one form or another, to promote integration. In some states, for example, students cannot move from one district to another if doing so will make the system less integrated; this typically keeps white students from leaving districts with large minority populations. (Many of them leave for private schools or move to the suburbs, however, defeating the purpose of such a rule.) Some districts that use "controlled choice" to integrate have numerical targets for racial minorities in each school, to ensure that all schools are fairly balanced. These approaches may be necessary in some situations, but they undercut the competition between schools of choice, because they restrict so many decisions. Also, they are gradually being ruled unconstitutional by the courts. We recommend that reinventors exhaust other methods first, before resorting to such restrictions. Options include:

- Requirements that schools actively try to recruit minorities and low-income students.
- Financial bonuses to schools that are integrated racially and economically, so schools have incentives to recruit kids that differ from their norm.
- Special programs to promote integration, such as METCO, which helps minority students in Boston attend schools in the suburbs that are otherwise hard to access through the choice program.

By carefully working to promote racial and socioeconomic integration, we believe, public systems of competitive choice can actually increase equity in our schools. By creating many high-quality alternatives, for example, they can bring white middle-class families back to the cities. The more good schools there are in the cities, and the more school choice, the less residential segregation there will be. But we must acknowledge that an unfettered market would increase segregation by income levels. If we want to reach all our collective goals—high performance by students, equal opportunity for all students, and the democratic values reinforced by mixing races and classes—then we must carefully structure that market to maximize choice, competition, and equity.

DESIGNING COMPETITIVE CHOICE: LESSONS LEARNED

Banishing Bureaucracy presented other important lessons (pp. 187–191) that apply to competitive choice systems, on which we elaborate in the following.

1. ***There must be enough suppliers to give customers real choices.***

If a particular service is a natural monopoly—if it is far more efficient to have one provider—choice is the wrong approach. If there are only two or three suppliers, the government may need to catalyze the creation of new suppliers, depending on the situation. Two or three accessible suppliers of child care may be all one can expect in a rural area, for example, but it would hardly be enough in a city or suburb.

There are many ways to do this. One can establish new public institutions; in education, for example, one can create charter schools, magnet schools, schools-within-schools, and so on. (We recommend charter schools, because they have the flexibility and accountability needed to succeed.) Or one can spur new private providers into existence, through public-private partnerships; subsidies such as grants, loans, and tax credits; or funding for customers via vouchers or reimbursement programs.

pp. 434–443

pp. 308–310

2. ***Customers must have sufficient resources to access quality service providers.***

If low-income customers don't have enough income to buy quality services, governments may need to subsidize them, through vouchers, reimbursement mechanisms, or public systems in which dollars follow the customer. In creating systems of private day-care providers, for example, some states subsidize families on a sliding scale, depending on their income.

3. ***Customers need useful, reliable, accessible information about the quality and cost of different service providers.***

Services intended to promote human development, such as education, training, day care, and health care, are particularly difficult for customers to judge. Any parent who has shopped for the best school for his or her children—or anyone who has tried to pick the best college for himself or herself—understands the problem. Public systems can provide a range of information about quality, customer satisfaction, outcomes, timeliness, responsiveness, cost, and other factors, so customers can weigh them and decide what is most important to them. Many customers will also need people they can talk to about the data, to sort through their choices. We discuss ways to do this using customer information systems and brokers later in this chapter.

pp. 311–322

In some cases, customers aren't even aware they have choices. Eight years after Massachusetts launched its interdistrict choice program, we were still meeting parents who didn't know that it existed. Often, the first thing a public system needs to do is to advertise the fact that choice exists and where to get information about available choices.

4. Governments need to structure the rules of the marketplace carefully, then enforce those rules.

As *Reinventing Government* argued, the only truly "free" markets—if that means free of government intervention—are black markets. And as everyone knows, black markets are ruled through force and racked by violence. To function smoothly, any market needs rules, and government must enforce those rules. This is just as true of social markets created within public systems as it is of private markets.

Consider what happened when Arizona passed the nation's most wide open charter school law, in 1994. Within four years, 400 charter schools enrolled 50,000 students, 6 percent of the state's public school population. According to the *Wall Street Journal,* the founder of one school "hired her sister to keep the books, her mother to teach etiquette, another sister to teach science, her brother to head security and her brother-in-law to work as a guard." She paid herself $89,000 a year and her sister $79,000, and they both received $350–a-month car allowances. In 1996, state auditors found their financial controls "practically nonexistent," and the school filed for bankruptcy. Revoking its charter, the state accused the school of inflating its enrollment by 100 students to get excess state aid.

5. Systems of competitive choice must guard against "creaming"—the tendency of providers to select the best or easiest customers.

If providers are paid according to how many people they serve, they will have a powerful incentive to recruit those who are easiest to serve. Health maintenance organizations will recruit young, healthy people, not the elderly. Job training and placement organizations will recruit those who have the most education or work experience and are easiest to train and place in jobs. Schools will recruit students whose presence will attract other students: those who behave well, score high on tests, star in athletics, and get into top-flight colleges.

This is natural behavior, and governments must anticipate it. If they want to preserve equal opportunity in their systems of competitive choice, they must establish rules that minimize creaming. For example, job training and placement organizations can be paid more for training and placing individuals with low skill levels than those with high skill levels, to ensure that the former get served. Many public school choice systems require that schools with more applicants than they can accept use lotteries to decide who gets in, so schools cannot favor gifted or well-behaved students.

This is a trade-off, of course. There are good reasons to let public schools choose their students, if one wants to create schools that excel in particular areas. It is harder to create an excellent performing arts school or math and science school if one has to admit students by lottery. If a district can create enough specialized schools to meet the demand—so no one is denied the opportunity to attend one—then selective admissions can be justified. But those setting the rules should be very careful to trade away as little equal opportunity as possible in their quest for excellence.

6. Systems of competitive choice must guard against deceptive marketing.

The more competition they face, the better public institutions will get at marketing themselves. In the process, some will inevitably distort reality and deceive prospective customers. Some private providers, such as for-profit vocational training schools, are already notorious for their deceptive advertising. To combat this, governments must crack down on such practices and provide the objective information customers need to make informed decisions.

TOOLS FOR COMPETITIVE CUSTOMER CHOICE

Competitive Public Choice Systems encourage customers to choose their providers and let public dollars follow the customer to the provider. See p. 303.

Vouchers give designated customers the resources to purchase services themselves, wherever they choose; ***Reimbursement Programs*** reimburse providers when customers choose their services. See p. 308.

Customer Information Systems give customers who are choosing service providers—with public resources, their own resources, or a combination—information about the quality and cost of each provider, so they can make informed decisions. See p. 311.

Brokers help customers find and evaluate information about different providers and choose which one would be best for them. See p. 320.

COMPETITIVE PUBLIC CHOICE SYSTEMS

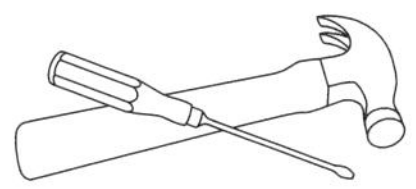

When schools, day-care centers, or other public service providers have to attract and keep customers to get their funding, most of them do what is necessary to please those customers. Competitive public choice systems harness much of the power of competitive markets while allowing public leaders to structure those markets to enhance public values such as diversity, fairness, and equal opportunity. Unlike enterprise management, which creates true competitive markets, this approach creates "social markets"—markets that can be managed to deliver public goods and preserve collective values.

Enterprise management is preferable for private goods, which primarily benefit those who use them. It gives providers maximum flexibility but makes them directly accountable to their customers, normally in a competitive market. But many services are public goods, or combinations of private and public goods. Public education and public health are combinations, for example: in addition to the obvious individual benefits, society benefits by having everyone educated and immunized. Enterprise management is not appropriate for such services, because they should not be charged to individuals. Society has a clear interest in making sure that they are available to all, regardless of their ability to pay.

All the lessons and tips articulated earlier apply to competitive public choice systems as well. The following "do's and don'ts" round out the picture.

Don't assign any customers; make all customers choose. In many public school choice systems, students are assigned to schools, but their parents can choose a different school from among those that have room. Inertia takes over, and only a small percentage of families choose their school. Assigning customers in this way minimizes competition rather than maximizing it, regardless of the service in question.

In such situations, many schools retain the character of their neighborhood: some are affluent suburban schools, for example; others are white, blue-collar suburban schools; others are heavily minority urban schools. Those students who choose to change schools must fit into a school with a particular socioeconomic character—which may be different from their own. This inevitably dampens the number of people who exercise their right to choose. As education consultant Michael Alves points out, "If your schools are segregated by race and income, what you ask people to do in these plans is to come into somebody else's school, where they may not feel they are going to have equal status."

In addition, the evidence shows that better-educated, affluent parents will be more aggressive about making choices in this situation than will those with less education and income. Hence their children will have greater opportunities for improvement than less advantaged children, widening the opportunity gap. If there are no assigned schools, however, every family will have to make a choice. Educated, affluent parents may still be more aggressive, but the gap should not be as wide.

Allow providers open entry into the market, to spur innovation and maximize choice and competition. In the private marketplace, much of the innovation in any industry comes from new businesses, which are often started by entrepreneurs inspired by an innovative idea—a new product, a new service, or a new way of manufacturing something. Existing firms are weighed down by their current products or services, their current organizational structures, and their current habits. The few large firms that are highly innovative structure themselves so that employees can launch the equivalent of new businesses, without leaving the company.

This reality is even more true in the public sector, where there is more red tape, more inertia, more internal politics, and more resistance to change. Public systems need a constant supply of new start-ups to produce the innovations that will allow them to continually improve their quality and lower their costs. This is precisely what Minnesota senator Ember Reichgott-Junge had in mind when she authored the nation's first charter school bill:

> *In Minnesota, one of our major employers is the 3M Company, and I think they are one of the most visionary companies we have, because when they project their revenues in ten years, they project that 50 percent of their revenues are going to come from products that haven't even been invented yet. And then they invest money in small groups within the company to go out and invent products and be creative.*
>
> *What if 50 percent of the learning methods in education haven't been invented yet? We need to find a way to allow that innovation to occur. I think charter schools are the way to do that. And those methods then can be transferred to the entire system, to jump-start the entire system.*

New providers are also necessary to maximize the choices available to customers—and to maximize competition. In many school systems, there are so few empty seats that although parents have choices in theory, most of the schools they would choose don't have room. In a closed market such as this, schools face very little real competition for their dollars. But if new schools are springing up all the time, creating excess capacity in the system, the competition will increase dramatically. As new schools arise, other schools will shrink, losing money. Only when they lose enough to feel the pain, as we have seen, will they begin making changes to win back their customers.

pp. 284–287

To create real open entry in a public market, where start-up capital is not available, you may have to provide it. The biggest obstacle faced by those starting charter schools has been the absence of start-up money to help them lease or build a facility. In Chapter Ten we suggest several different ways that governments can meet this challenge.

pp. 434–443

Don't protect service providers; let them feel the pain of failure. In many statewide interdistrict choice programs, districts that lose large numbers of students are protected from financial consequences, so they have little financial incentive to win back market share. In Massachusetts, during the first two years of interdistrict choice, losing districts paid a large price: they had to send tuition payments to the receiving districts, based on *those* districts' per-pupil spending levels. Sometimes these were far higher than the per-pupil spending levels of the losing districts. This caused so much protest that the legislature changed the funding formulas, blunting the cost of losing students, particularly for poor districts. Districts that lost 5 to 6 percent of their students still felt financial pain—and continued working to solve their problems and lure students back. But the three districts in Armor and Peiser's research sample that lost 2 percent of their students experienced no financial pain, because of the state formulas. Not surprisingly, they did nothing to respond.

pp. 285–286

If you want choice to motivate providers to make improvements, you have to make sure they experience the consequences of losing customers. The formula must be fair, however. Otherwise the political backlash may drive the legislature to remove the sting of failure—and thus the incentive for providers to improve.

Close down failing providers. As schools or other service providers lose volume, the system must intervene. If not, those providers may continue to spiral downward, trapping customers who aren't paying attention (or whose parents aren't paying attention) in a shrinking, failing program. As Jersey City teacher Jerri O'Brien-Cass told the *New York Times Magazine*, "If my best students, my Schnelle and my Phillip, are going off to charter schools, God bless them—let them go if it gives them better lives. But that makes us like a prison. We'll be the Last Stop Incarceration Public School."

According to the British Office of Standards in Education (OFSTED), this dynamic has occurred in some English schools:

> *Some secondary schools have become locked into a vicious circle. The fact that their examination results are modest has meant that few parents outside their immediate catchment area indicated a preference for them. As a consequence they have unfilled places and have been regularly confronted with the demand that they admit difficult pupils. The difficulty of assimilating such pupils has rendered some schools even more unpopular with parents.*

The solution is to put failing providers on notice, with a deadline for improvement. If they fail to meet minimum standards by the deadline, shut them down and put another provider in their place. In public education this is called "reconstitution"—a new principal is brought in to design a new school and is given authority to hire some or all new teachers. (A better solution would be replacement by a charter school.) Many school districts and states have policies that allow this, although it is rarely done because it is so politically difficult.

The secret is to lay down clear conditions that will trigger the first warning and the closing or reconstitution, and to require action when those conditions exist. The British now have a system, for example, in which inspection teams that find a school is "failing to give its pupils an acceptable standard of education" can designate it for "special measures." The school then has to submit an action plan for improvement to the national Department for Education and Employment. Inspectors monitor implementation of the plan and report regularly on the school's progress. Failing schools are "expected to improve and be close to providing an acceptable standard of education within two years of being deemed to need Special Measures," according to OFSTED. Between 1993 and 1997, inspection teams designated 717 schools for special measures—about 3 percent of secondary and primary schools and 8 percent of special schools. Some 55 were closed, but 143 made sufficient progress to warrant removal from special measures.

Don't let the public assume that when providers fail, the system is failing. The public schools that are most accountable for performance and most likely to be closed down are charter schools, because their charters must be renewed every five years or so. By 1999, more than two dozen charter schools in the U.S. had been closed, primarily because of internal power struggles or financial mismanagement. When this happens, the media sometimes assume the system has failed. In reality, some providers in systems of competitive choice *should* fail. If none do, either the competition is not very stiff, no one is policing the market, or both. When creating such a system, reinventors should announce in advance that they expect to shut down low-quality providers—and that this is a sign of success, not failure.

Help former monopoly providers learn how to improve and to learn from one another. When you convert to competition and choice, you may need to help former monopolies adjust to the realities of competition. When Texas converted its day-care system in the early 1990s, for example, it provided staff training scholarships, new materials, and training on marketing and financial management to providers that lost their monopolies. It also created quality criteria for providers and certified those who reached them.

In a normal competitive market, competitors will watch one another closely for innovations and then adopt those that seem to work. But when former monopolies are angry about losing market share, they often want nothing to do with their new competitors. Several studies have found that public schools are not picking up innovations pioneered by charter schools, for instance. There are many reasons for this, but two seem most prominent: public school administrators don't have the habit of making time to observe their competitors, and many resent their competitors. "Many district superintendents are angry and resentful about loss of revenue that results from students' attending the charter schools," a Massachusetts report explained. "They are therefore resistant to learning anything from them. Some are actively hostile to the charter schools."

To compensate, reinventors need to create formal forums—conferences, teacher training centers, and the like—in which competitors can swap information and learn from one another.

Don't wrap providers in red tape. Competitors in a public market will be unable to reach their potential if they are buried in red tape. Some rules are necessary, of course. But in creating systems of competitive choice, reinventors should use a formal process to eliminate unnecessary rules and to simplify administrative systems for all providers. Without this step, this tool will be akin to forcing athletes to compete when they are bound and gagged. Sadly, we have seen this done all too often in the public sector.

pp. 393–452

RESOURCES ON COMPETITIVE PUBLIC CHOICE SYSTEMS

David J. Armor and Brett M. Peiser. *Competition in Education: A Case Study of Interdistrict Choice.* Boston: Pioneer Institute, 1997. A close, honest look at the dynamics of competitive public school choice, with useful suggestions about how to best structure such systems.

Center for Education Reform Web site: www.edreform.com. A comprehensive resource on education reform, with excellent material on choice and charter schools.

Joe Nathan, ed. *Public Schools by Choice.* St. Paul, Minn.: Institute for Learning and Teaching, 1989. Still the best collections of essays we have read on public school choice.

Nancy C. Roberts and Paula J. King. *Transforming Public Policy: Dynamics of Policy Entrepreneurship and Innovation.* San Francisco: Jossey-Bass, 1996. The story of how a small group of civic activists brought public school choice to Minnesota (and thus to America), with useful lessons on political strategy and tactics.

VOUCHERS AND REIMBURSEMENT SYSTEMS

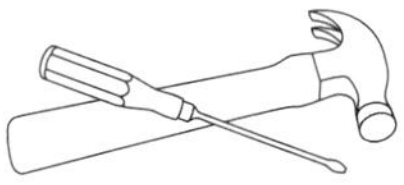

pp. 279–284

***Vouchers* give designated customers the resources to purchase services themselves, wherever they choose; *Reimbursement Programs* reimburse providers when customers choose their services.**

As Milwaukee's experience demonstrates, vouchers and reimbursement programs have enormous leverage to change public systems, because they can force public service providers to compete for their money. This very fact makes for excruciating political resistance, however. Most existing voucher and reimbursement programs, such as food stamps, housing vouchers, Medicare, and Medicaid, affect only (or primarily) private sector providers. When first introduced, such programs are generally designed to expand access to private services for low-income people, so they often are welcomed by private providers. Voucher proposals that create competition for existing public providers face a much frostier reception. When President Clinton proposed in late 1994 to allow residents of public housing to convert the funding to a voucher and use it to buy housing in the private marketplace—in part as a way to force public housing developments to compete—the idea was so controversial that even the Gingrich Republicans stonewalled it.

But in public education, voucher advocates are beginning to break through the wall. Milwaukee's program allows up to 15 percent of the district's students to use vouchers; by 1999–2000, roughly 8,500 did so. Cleveland had a similar program, with 2,900 participating students in 1998–99 (though it was still under challenge in the courts). The CEO Foundation and others fund private voucher programs in dozens of cities. And in the spring of 1999, Florida governor Jeb Bush pushed a bill through the state legislature that gives students at "failing" schools—those that fail to meet minimal state standards twice in four years—vouchers worth at least $4,000 to attend public or private schools of their choice. (It too has been challenged in the courts.)

Vouchers and reimbursement programs are, for all practical purposes, the same tool. One gives the payment to the customer; the other pays the provider after the customer has chosen that provider. Although education vouchers have passed the church-state test in the Supreme Court and reimbursement programs might not, otherwise they have the same dynamics and impact. All of the general lessons and political tips offered earlier apply to both of them.

pp. 290–302

Any service from which individuals can be excluded can theoretically be funded through vouchers or reimbursement. This leaves out police protection, fire protection, public health services, national defense, some public parks, and other "collective" services. Otherwise, vouchers and reimbursement programs can be powerful tools to create competitive choice. The decision about when to use them hinges on political realities more than anything else.

Advantages of Vouchers and Reimbursement Programs

They are administratively simple. Whereas funding systems for public competitive choice can be an administrative nightmare, vouchers are quite simple. You may have to create several classes of vouchers for different classes of customers—for example, a voucher worth $7,000 for most students, a voucher worth $15,000 for special education students, and a voucher with a negotiable value for severely handicapped students. But this is a minor complication.

They make providers more thoroughly accountable to their customers. Private institutions at risk in the marketplace are expected to expand, shrink, and die, unlike most public institutions. Since most providers in a typical voucher system are private, few people notice when one or two go under—as long as there are plenty of others still thriving. Hence providers in a voucher system are more directly at risk than are providers in most other systems of competitive public choice, which tend to protect public institutions from closure.

They tend to be less encumbered by red tape. Since many providers are private, they typically have much greater flexibility to try new things than do public providers. When public providers are included, it is easier to convince public sector leaders to give them freedom from most regulations as well, so they can compete effectively. This is less true when all competitors are public.

They can make it easier and cheaper to promote equal opportunity. With some services, it is politically acceptable to give vouchers to low-income people but not to others, so the poor enjoy the same access everyone else has. In the U.S., we do this with health care, housing, food stamps, job training, adult education, and college education. (The U.S. is now beginning to test whether this is politically possible in K–12 education; we doubt it is, due to the long-established precedent that *every child* in a community should receive the same opportunities. We suspect that once the poor are given vouchers, the middle class will quickly demand them. In Milwaukee, for example, the mayor has already proposed making every family eligible for vouchers. Universal voucher systems would, in our opinion, create less equity in education, not more.) When it is politically possible to subsidize only the poor, however, this is a far cheaper approach than creating a public choice system that subsidizes everyone.

pp. 297–300

If the voucher or reimbursement is not full payment for a service, it wastes less money. If a housing voucher is worth, say, $500 a month but most apartments cost more than that, then voucher recipients will have an incentive to shop for the best deal they can find. The same is true if a Pell Grant is worth $3,000 and most college costs are above that amount. Hence providers will have an incentive to offer the best value for the dollar, and purchasers will have an incentive to spend no more than they need to. In public choice systems, these incentives are missing. (They are also missing in voucher or reimbursement programs that don't allow providers to charge more than the voucher. There is a trade-off here between equity and efficiency.) Customers in such systems don't care how much the provider charges, because they don't pay any of it. So they often buy more expensive services than they would if they had to foot part of the bill or could keep any money they didn't spend.

Disadvantages of Vouchers and Reimbursement Programs

Voucher or reimbursement programs that are open only to the poor require eligibility checks, which can be cumbersome. To run a food stamp, Medicaid, or housing voucher program, you have to establish income and asset limits, then require people to apply and confirm whether they are telling the truth on their applications. This can be expensive. When you take shortcuts, some people will inevitably cheat, and critics will use that reality to undermine the program. In Cleveland, for example, a 1999 state auditor's report criticized the school voucher program for being lax in documenting applicants' income levels and residency.

Voucher and reimbursement programs require even more extensive efforts to regulate and police the marketplace than do other competitive choice programs. When most providers are private, fraud will usually be far more widespread than in public choice systems, because the private profit motive will encourage it. Fraud has been widespread in the food stamps program, for example—although conversion to electronic benefit transfer, using smart cards, has reduced it. By 1993, waste, fraud, and loan defaults cost federal student aid programs $3–4 billion a year. This was more than 10 percent of the Education Department's budget—enough to fund the entire Head Start program. The department's inspector general had only enough staff to audit 25 of the 7,400 schools then certified to accept Pell Grants and student loans, yet it had legal cases pending against 300 schools. The big problem was for-profit "proprietary" schools, which often enrolled students, took their Pell Grant and student loan funds, and then failed to deliver any education or training of value. The Clinton administration had to invest significant effort and resources to curb the problem, cut the number of schools eligible to participate back by 28 percent, and bring the default rate on student loans down from 22.4 to 9.6 percent by 1998.

Vouchers and reimbursement programs can be politically difficult to enact. After 20 years of fighting school vouchers, public employee unions react to the word *voucher* like a bull reacts to a red flag. If you introduce this tool, we suggest that you call it something else. For instance, a "career opportunity account" would be far easier to sell than a "job training voucher." You will still face the political hurdles we described earlier, but you may avoid instant vilification.

pp. 290–297

CUSTOMER INFORMATION SYSTEMS

***Customer Information Systems* give customers who are choosing service providers—with public resources, their own resources, or a combination—information about the quality and cost of each provider, so they can make informed decisions.**

When reinventors use competitive choice to empower customers, they must make sure that those customers have enough information to make good decisions. This kind of information generally does not exist for many services the public sector funds: education, training, child care, health care, and the like. Private businesses are trying to create it and sell it in some areas. But more often, there is simply a vacuum. Reinventors need to fill this vacuum if they want competitive choice to work.

Information can help transform a marketplace. "In 1923, only 25 percent of the New York Stock Exchange firms provided reports to their shareholders," Harvard Business School professor Regina Herzlinger points out. After the stock market crash of 1929, Congress created the Securities and Exchange Commission and gave it power to enforce "truth in securities" and regulate trading in securities.

> *Firms that trade their securities in inter-state markets must register with the SEC and file regular information reports. . . . [They] must disclose both financial and nonfinancial information in routine reports, including the firm's financial statements; management's discussion and analysis of performance; disclosure of the top executives' compensation; and evaluation of the firms' various lines of business.*

Because this information is widely available, most buyers are informed, competition over prices is stiff, and the securities market has become more and more efficient, Herzlinger explains.

Even in simpler markets, many people turn to information resources—everything from *Consumer Reports* to college guides to the *Kelly Blue Book Used Car Guide.* Information can have similar value in public sector markets. This is just beginning in public education: increasingly, states and school districts put the data they have on schools together in report cards, which they publish and post on the Web. Private companies are also jumping into the business. Though different states include different information, the range covers:

- Average test scores and annual gains in average test scores.
- SAT scores.
- Program offerings.

- Data on computer and Internet access.
- Numbers of students, student-teacher ratios, and class sizes.
- Attendance rates, dropout rates, graduation rates, promotion rates, suspension rates, and exclusion rates.
- Numbers of disciplinary incidents and incidents of violence, weapons possession, and drug possession.
- Student turnover rates (percentage of students in the school who were not there for the full year).
- Percentages of new teachers and teachers with five or fewer years of experience.
- Number of librarians and guidance counselors.
- Percentage of students who are not proficient in English.
- Percentage of students who qualify for free and reduced-price lunches.
- Racial composition.

A few jurisdictions have gone one step further and created information centers where parents can get this kind of data, plus help from experienced counselors in sorting it out.

All signs suggest that parents are hungry for this kind of information. In a 1999 national survey done by the Public Agenda Foundation, 90 percent of parents said they favored (63 percent "strongly," 27 percent "somewhat") "giving parents more information about how their schools compared with other schools in the area."

States are also beginning to assemble relevant cost and quality information for adults looking for education or training. Florida was the first state to provide this. Its Education and Training Placement Information Program captures follow-up data on employment, education, military enlistment, incarceration, and use of public assistance for graduates of every public (and many private) education, training, and job placement institution in the state. The data is available at schools, one-stop career centers, and state employment service and training offices.

The most aggressive use of this tool has come in the U.K., where the Audit Commission and other organizations publish comparative performance information on schools, hospitals and ambulance trusts, local governments, police forces, and fire services. The press, which has dubbed these "league tables," publishes the results widely. Surveys show that they are extremely popular with the public. When Tony Blair's Labor Government came to power and launched a formal consultation process to gauge the value of the Citizen's Charter, it

pp. 211–212

found that "The regular publication of performance information by local authorities, schools and hospitals was considered by many respondents to the consultation exercise to be a major success of the old Charter programme."

The government is adding performance tables for universities and teacher training institutions, as well as quality of treatment indicators for the National Health Service. They have made most of the performance information available on the World Wide Web.

The British have been particularly aggressive in publishing information about schools, where customers have a great deal of choice. The annual performance tables on schools include exam results, rates of authorized and unauthorized absences, results in pre-and post–16 vocational qualifications, and percentages of students receiving baccalaureate diplomas (the equivalent of high school plus a year of college in the U.S.). Available on the World Wide Web, the performance tables are quite readable. Newspapers publish them every year, often highlighting the best and worst schools in their area and the most improved.

p. 319

In addition to the hard data, qualitative inspections by teams of trained evaluators, which are performed at least every six years on each of 24,000 public schools in England, produce pages of data. A similar system reports on preschools that receive vouchers or other public funding.

These inspections are quite serious. Conducted by teams of three to eight people (accredited and trained by OFSTED but hired on a competitive contract basis), they last anywhere from three to ten days, depending on the size of the school. Each team is required to have one lay member, who must have no paid experience teaching or managing a school. They must report on four areas: quality, educational standards, financial management, and the spiritual, moral, social, and cultural development of students.

Parents are invited to a preinspection meeting with the team, and each inspection includes a parental survey. The inspection team leader writes a long report, which is made available at the school, and a summary is mailed to every family with children at the school. These reports include qualitative judgments, often turned into numerical scores, on all kinds of things, including "quality of teaching," "availability of quality teachers," "extracurricular provision," percentage of teachers' time spent teaching, "standards of achievement," the "leadership of the school," "efficiency and effectiveness with which resources are used," "ethos," "pupils' attitudes," and "behavior."

"The school's response to the report, known as the Action Plan, must be completed within 40 working days and also be made freely available to parents," OFSTED explains.

In the U.S., the Massachusetts Board of Education has adopted the British inspection model to evaluate its charter schools. Every five years, when a charter is up for renewal, the board hires a private company called SchoolWorks to evaluate it. Its report serves as the key piece of evidence the board will use in its renewal decision. Ted Sizer, the respected founder of the Coalition of Essential Schools, has been through the process as headmaster of a charter school. He believes it is infinitely more substantive and valuable than either school accreditation visits or the use of standardized test scores to evaluate a school.

After it was elected in 1997, the Labor Government embraced the inspection system and promised to continue improvement efforts then under way. Data from inspections would be added to the performance tables and published "in a digestible format," it said. "OFSTED will also issue annual statistical profiles of each school. They will include numerical ratings for each subject, based on inspection findings, which set the school's performance in a national context."

The government is also committed to baseline assessment at age five, so "it will be possible to measure any pupil's progress through his or her school career, and so compare that pupil with any other individual or group, whether locally or nationally." In addition, the government is developing benchmark data, so schools can compare themselves to the best performing schools with similar students.

Designing a Customer Information System: Do's and Don'ts

Get feedback from the organizations you are comparing, before finalizing your measures. Many provider organizations will find the publication of comparative information threatening. To be fair, give them ample opportunity to examine the measures you propose, critique them, and suggest others. If you work out the appropriate measures in collaboration with providers—and their customers—you will increase the credibility of your product. The British Audit Commission consults with each of 450 local councils and 50 police forces every year before finalizing its performance indicators.

p. 223

Don't compare apples to oranges. It is hardly fair to compare inner-city schools that teach low-income, disadvantaged students to suburban schools where most graduates will go on to college. Even within the inner city, there are vastly different public schools. Albert Shanker, the late president of the American Federation of Teachers, put it well in one of his monthly columns, about New York City's first school report cards:

> *What's wrong with comparing schools? Nothing, if the schools are comparable. But newspapers simply listed the schools with top scores and those with bottom scores in reading, math, SATs, etc. Some schools, like top-scoring Stuyvesant, Bronx Science and Townsend Harris, se-*

lect their students mainly by competitive examination and admit only top scorers. Other schools admit all comers. Comparing these schools is like comparing a group of athletes who have been chosen to compete in the Olympics with a group of students in a typical gym class.

To give customers the most useful context for making comparisons, it helps to ask them what kind of comparisons they value. For parents choosing a school, for example, comparisons to state and national averages are useful, but even more useful would be bar charts showing how one school stacks up, on a variety of measures, against a group of similar schools in the region. Parents want to compare schools they could actually choose.

Compare improvement rates as well as current status. Current test scores, graduation rates, customer satisfaction levels, and the like are important to customers. But the rate at which an institution is improving is also important. Two schools may look about the same when current test scores are published, but one may be losing ground while the other is improving dramatically. A school with low-income students may look far inferior on test scores to one full of affluent high achievers, but if students in the former are making dramatic gains and those in latter are not, who's to say which would be better for a particular child? "A school with a stable, nonpoor population will almost inevitably do well in terms of average score," says Peter Hutchinson, president of the Public Strategies Group (PSG). "But that doesn't mean they are progressing as rapidly as they might."

When Hutchinson served as superintendent of the Minneapolis schools, they published not only average test scores for each school but also gains. If a student was at the 60th percentile in fourth grade but moved up to the 62nd on the fifth-grade test, that was reported as a two-point gain. Rewards for schools were then built around gains, not averages. "This gives everybody a lot of information," Hutchinson explains, "but it also puts the focus on value added, where it needs to be. Because averages, as we know, are a result of many things, some of which the schools can't affect. But gains are something the schools do affect, regardless of where the students start from."

The U.K. is also piloting a method to measure student improvement rates, "to allow fairer comparison between schools with different intakes," such as suburban and inner-city schools. It compares exam results at one age level with results several years later. Each student gets a "value added" measure, which is the difference between his or her results at the second level and the median at that level for those who scored the same at the first level. These are then aggregated to give a value-added measure for each school. The government hopes to publish these comparisons for older students (age 12 and above) nationwide by the end of 2000, with younger students to follow.

In Minneapolis, comparing gains "had an interesting virtuous outcome," says Hutchinson.

> *If you had a school at which the average level of achievement was at the 35th percentile, your opportunity to improve was enormous. If you're at the 95th percentile, it's much tougher.*
>
> *I made a table of the average scores: the usual suspects were at the top, and the usual suspects were at the bottom. Then I made a ranking by gain, and the "good schools" were not necessarily at the top, and some of the so-called bad schools were in the middle. All of a sudden the so-called good schools realized that under this system they had to work harder. They couldn't take student learning for granted—which, unfortunately, happens in those schools sometimes.*

Don't let turnover of customers distort the picture. If a third of the students in a school are new every year, due to high mobility, it is unfair to compare that school to one with only 10 percent turnover. One solution is to factor out newcomers and publish test scores and the like only for students who were in the school the year before, as Minneapolis does. Another is to get data on the student in his or her previous school and use it to compare improvement rates, as the British are trying to do. (In the interim, the British are publishing a "stability measure" that shows the proportion of students who were at the school when they took their previous exams.)

If possible, factor in socioeconomic status and similar factors that make the playing field uneven. The simplest approach is to indicate the socioeconomic makeup of the school or day-care center or other program—for example, what percentage of students qualify for free or reduced-price lunches (as Minneapolis does), what percentage are not proficient in the language (as Massachusetts does), and so on. Publication of improvement rates also helps soften the impact of socioeconomic differences, though it does not eliminate it. (Advantaged students may find it easier to make rapid progress, for example.) The most sophisticated approach would be to develop a credible formula to adjust test results and similar measures for socioeconomic background and then publish both the raw comparisons and the adjusted comparisons.

In Minneapolis, Hutchinson published data that combined socioeconomic status with gains on test scores.

> *I would publish every year a scatter plot that had gains on one axis and socioeconomics along the other—using percentage of free and reduced-price lunches. You saw dots all over the place. There were some schools with lots of poor kids at the top, in terms of gains, some at the bottom, some in the middle.*

> *I'd give parents the data on free and reduced-price lunches, but I'd also show them the picture—so they could see that schools with real poor kids were performing very well, so they didn't have to accept socioeconomic makeup as an excuse for poor performance.*

Don't drown the public in data. Too many measures can confuse the public, making comparative performance data difficult to understand. "A look at school report cards from other states reveals [that this is] a common problem," the Texas Legislative Budget Board reports. "Legislators often want more data; however, at the local level, parents and community members may need less in order to get a simplified picture of school performance." The solution is to craft different versions of a report card for different audiences: a briefer version for the public, a longer one for legislators and other policymakers. The full report can then be made available to public customers who want more data, as an appendix or backup report or on the World Wide Web. The Audit Commission in the U.K. uses roughly 50 indicators for local services and 30 more for police forces, but for the public it boils each of these down to short reports containing 10 to 20 measures. Those who want the rest can find it in an appendix.

Don't display the comparisons in a way that is unfair to those being compared. There are many options. Some report cards use grades, giving organizations As, Bs, Cs, Ds, and Fs in a series of areas. Others use a style more like *Consumer Reports*, which indicates if a product is above average, average, or below average. Others, such as *U.S. News and World Report*'s ratings of American colleges, rank institutions in order.

The media and the public love rankings and grades. But the British Audit Commission decided that both of those formats would be unfair, because on some indicators the top-ranked municipality and the bottom-ranked municipality might not be that far apart—a fact rankings and grades might hide. Instead the commission chose bar graphs, which visually show how a municipality ranks but also show the spread between each one. On some indicators there is a wide gulf between best and worst; on others there is very little difference. This is generally the fairest method, in our view.

Include explanatory material rather than just numbers. Comparing performance is not cut-and-dried. There are always complicating factors, and they should be explained to the public. Perhaps the greatest is that in some cases there is no way to determine what is the "best" or "worst" performance. Some schools may invest heavily in lowering their teacher-student ratio, for example, whereas others may choose to invest instead in computers and science labs. Who is to say which is the better choice? This kind of qualification needs to be explained. Ultimately, parents should choose the school that offers what their child needs, regardless of whether it scores high in every category.

pp. 247–271

Don't rest on your laurels; keep improving your performance indicators. Comparative measurement is difficult and complex. Even a sophisticated organization like the U.K.'s Audit Commission started with some fairly crude measures, simply because that was all that was practical at first. But every year it improves them.

As you begin, the organizations you are comparing will complain bitterly that the entire exercise is unfair. They will point out what is wrong with every measure you use. The solution? Invite them to help you find better measures. When they argue that you're measuring the wrong things, ask them what the right things would be. The wonderful thing about measuring performance is that once you start, pressure from stakeholders helps you get better and better at it.

Publicize performance data widely, to maximize its impact. The point is to help customers use the information to make good choices. To reach the most people, you need to use as many channels as possible: the media; the Internet and Web; publications distributed to libraries, schools, and other public offices; information brokers; and mailings.

Don't release comparative data without briefing the media. The media will be tempted to use the data to beat up their local schools or other institutions. You cannot stop this, but you can minimize it by carefully explaining the limits of the data you present. The Audit Commission carefully explained that its indicators showed the differences between local councils, but it did not explain why those factors arose. For that, reporters would have to look further. In the first year, the commission was pleasantly surprised by the coverage. As the commission's Paul Vevers explained:

> *About 40 percent of the media coverage was relatively positive, focusing on good performance. About one-third of it was mixed, highlighting both good and bad performance. And in one-third of cases, newspapers did what councils and police forces had feared they would do and focused only on poor performance—whether the council or force merited it or not.*

Build into your system the capacity to help organizations improve their performance. In the U.K., the Audit Commission works hard to help local governments improve. It holds conferences and seminars, meets with local councils, publishes in-depth management guides profiling best practices, and issues guides that help auditors steer local authorities toward best practices. Similarly, the British system of school inspections is designed not just to report on the quality of schools but also to help them improve. This is a critical component of any information system whose ultimate purpose is improvement.

Don't forget to audit the data, just like any other form of performance measurement. If the market is truly competitive and providers face consequences, some of them will cheat. Others will make not-quite-illegal efforts to make sure they look good—prepping their students for exactly what will be on exams, putting on a special show for inspectors, and so on. This is unavoidable; it is human nature. One of the authors recently bought a new car, for example, from a dealer whose company systematically follows up every interaction with a telephone survey to measure customer satisfaction. Salesmen and service people at the dealership have learned how to coach their customers—advising them that someone will call and encouraging them to explain that everything was "excellent." To combat these perfectly normal impulses, auditors must spot-check measurement methods and data regularly.

pp. 247–271

For more information on measuring performance, see Chapter Seven.

RESOURCES ON INFORMATION SYSTEMS

United Kingdom. Audit Commission. *Local Authority Performance Indicators; Using Your Indicators; Watching Their Figures: A Guide to the Citizen's Charter Indicators; How Is Your Council Performing?* and other publications. The annual Local Authority Performance Indicators are available on the Web at www.audit-commission.gov.uk/ (click on "National Reports," then "Online Catalogue"), or from The Stationery Office Publications Centre (www.itsofficial.net), P.O. Box 276, London SW8 5DT. Phone: 0170 873 9090. Fax 0171 873 8200. The other publications are available from the Audit Commission at 1 Vincent Square, London SW1P 2PN. Phone: 0171 828 1212. Fax: 0171 976 6187.

United Kingdom. Department for Education and Employment. Performance tables on schools going back to 1994, as well as papers discussing the performance tables, the value-added pilot program, and other performance measurement issues, are available at www.dfee.gov.uk/performs.html.

United Kingdom. Office of Standards in Education (OFSTED). Information on the British inspection system, as well as all inspection reports and annual summaries of data from those inspections, are available at www.ofsted.gov.uk.

BROKERS

***Brokers* help customers find and evaluate information about different providers and choose which one would be best for them.**

When people want to buy a house, few scan the want ads. The housing market is large and complex, and most people want help navigating it. So they contact a real estate broker.

The same is true of the stock market, the commodities market, and other complex markets. Some markets for public services are complex enough that people need brokers as well. Consider adult education and job training. In most states there are dozens of different programs, but how would anyone know where to find them? The typical person looking for training in a particular field would have no idea where to look.

See *Reinventing Government* pp. 188–192

To deal with this and other problems, the Michigan Job Training Coordinating Council dreamed up a novel solution in the late 1980s: it designed a system of "Opportunity Stores" through which any citizen could get information about all education, training, and job placement services in the state. They would be small offices sprinkled throughout the state, in visible places such as main streets, malls, and community colleges. Though the effort was stopped in its tracks when Governor Jim Blanchard lost the 1990 election, his former commerce director, Doug Ross, took it with him to Washington in 1993 when he became assistant secretary of labor for employment and training. The Commerce Department created a grant program to help states create systems of one-stop career centers built on the Michigan idea. Today most states have career centers, though few resemble the original Michigan model.

About the same time, Texas created an excellent information and broker system for child care. Its Child Care Management Services program contracted with one organization in each of 27 regions to act as a broker, to help parents choose the best child care available and receive any public subsidies they qualified for. Parents could visit the brokers' offices in person or call on toll-free phone lines. This gave low-income parents an easy way to find quality child care, while giving them access to any certified provider in their region. A sophisticated information technology system matched funding programs with client eligibility categories, maintained databases of customers and providers, and reimbursed providers for care. The brokers even certified providers who met the program's quality criteria, gave them classroom materials, and provided scholarships so they could train staff.

The Texas program, a national model, won an Innovation in State and Local Government award from the Ford Foundation. But not all broker systems have to be that sophisticated. At one time Connecticut had a child care brokerage service that consisted of one person for each region of the state whom parents could call to get information about every provider certified by the state. The broker visited providers regularly to ensure that they were not breaking state rules about the number of children per child care worker and the like. Some school districts that offer public school choice also create information centers where parents can learn about the options available and get help sorting through them.

In some voucher and reimbursement programs, use of a broker is mandatory to access the public subsidy. In Texas, for example, parents had to apply for a subsidy through the broker's office, though they could do so by phone or mail. In job training, some experts believe people should be required to see a counselor before being given vouchers (or other forms of funding), so they can get good advice about which skills are in demand in the marketplace. In many areas, however, use of brokers can be purely voluntary.

Designing a System of Brokers

In designing a system of brokers, we recommend that you keep a number of pointers in mind:

The same organization does not have to provide both the information and the brokerage services. In fact, it probably makes sense to separate the two. The information system should be comprehensive and seamless, available to all. Hence one organization—or one partnership—should manage it. But brokers should be numerous and can be operated by many different organizations.

Give customers a choice of competing brokers. In brokerage services, as in most services, competitive choice will stimulate providers to do everything in their power to satisfy their customers. You can use managed competition to contract with brokers, as Texas does in its child care system and Massachusetts has for seven of its one-stop career centers. You could also use vouchers or reimbursements and let brokers compete directly for their funding by attracting more customers.

Don't let brokers also provide services that compete with those to which they refer customers. If a training or educational provider also functions as a broker, it will have an incentive to refer people to its own training or classes. It's best to avoid this conflict of interest.

Don't assume all brokers' offices should provide identical services. A comprehensive system might offer full-service brokers, satellite offices with fewer staff, and very small offices in community colleges, libraries, and government buildings where information, but not counseling, is available. This way you could locate an office near most communities but keep costs under control.

Brokers can provide some services for free while charging for others. Usually the basic functions of a broker—helping people sort through information about competing schools, day-care centers, training programs, and the like—are free to customers. But many one-stop career centers are allowed to charge for additional services, such as holding job fairs for businesses or providing extended counseling to job seekers. The advantage of this approach is that it encourages providers to get creative about meeting their customers' needs, so as to bring in more customers and more revenue. You must ensure that this does not entice brokers to let the quality of their free services lag, however, by requiring regular measurement of quality.

Information technology is often critical to the success of the system. Often, customer information systems must combine multiple funding streams for each customer. When Texas created its Child Care Management Services system, for example, it combined 14 different funding programs, which served 22 categories of eligible clients. Information systems must report on hundreds, if not thousands, of providers. And multiple brokers—some public, some private—must use the system, without much variation in the access and quality they offer customers. This level of complexity requires sophisticated information technology, which costs money. In their successful application for an Innovation in State and Local Government award, the founders of the Texas program identified the cost of such a system as one of the biggest obstacles they had encountered.

You may have to market the system. To let potential customers know about the system, you will probably have to market it. This is an unnatural act in the public sector—but in a world of choice and competition, that attitude is outdated. It would be a terrible waste to build a sophisticated information and brokerage system and then to discover that most customers don't know it exists.

Chapter 9

Customer Quality Assurance

Making Organizations Accountable for Service Quality

***Customer Quality Assurance* creates guarantees and standards of customer service, complaint systems and means of redress to make it up to customers when organizations fail to meet those standards, and customer boards, councils, and service agreements to hold organizations accountable for meeting them.**

In 1993, when Vice President Gore asked Bob Stone to be project director of his National Performance Review (NPR), one of the first people Stone recruited was an old colleague named Greg Woods. Woods, who had worked with Stone at the Defense Department, was running a high-tech company in New Mexico. But he was excited by the prospect of helping reinvent the entire federal government. They decided he should handle the "customer service" portfolio: his job would be to improve service throughout the government.

Woods immediately began contacting private companies that were legendary for their customer service, like Disney and Ritz Carlton, and pumping them for their secrets. Deputy Director John Kamensky, who had come over from the General Accounting Office (GAO), where he had drafted a report on reinvention in other countries, told Woods about the British Citizen's Charter. It required that all public organizations in the U.K. adopt customer service standards defining the levels of service they promised their customers, among other things. Intrigued, Woods invited Diana Goldsworthy from the Citizen's Charter unit to visit the NPR.

See *Banishing Bureaucracy* pp. 32–36, 192–195

Excited by what Goldsworthy told him, he called a meeting of people from federal agencies that served the most Americans: the Social Security Administration (SSA), Veterans Affairs, the U.S. Postal Service, the Internal Revenue Service, and a few others. He did a briefing on customer service standards and laid out an idea for one standard at each agency, to trigger discussion.

Woods knew that the SSA's toll-free number was important to millions of people. So he suggested that the agency promise that every citizen would get through on their first call. Only a few years old at the time, the 800 number was already the most heavily used in the world, with 60 million calls a year. But the agency was having trouble keeping up with the demand. Customer satisfaction had fallen for four years in a row, in part due to problems callers had reaching someone on the phone.

Toni Lenane, then the chief policy officer at the agency, attended the briefing. Woods remembers her reaction well: "She said, 'That's insane!'"

He asked what she meant. "She said, 'You've got to understand, currently we can't answer anywhere near 100 percent of the calls. The idea that we would invest the money to add the system and operators to do this is just not feasible.' "

But Greg Woods rarely takes no for an answer. He began talking with others at Social Security, finding allies. Larry Thompson, the acting commissioner, was receptive. Toni Lenane kept listening as well, as Woods argued that the agency could find new technologies and new methods to deal with calling volume by learning from business. When Shirley Chater, president of a women's college in Texas, was nominated to be commissioner, Lenane briefed her about Gore's and the NPR's interest in customer service. It turned out Chater had been working hard to improve customer service at her college. In her confirmation hearings, Woods remembers, "She was talking about world-class service—making it clear that customer service was something she absolutely, positively believed in."

So Woods kept pushing. He sent Lenane draft language for standards, which included his idea on the 800 number. He negotiated with Thompson and Lenane almost daily. Gore's report was scheduled to be released on September 7. As the deadline loomed, the phone conversations migrated into the late evenings. "I just hung in there," says Woods. "I was telling them, 'Well, I won't be able to include you in the book. I'll just have to take you out, and tell the VP, and we'll just go with the postal service,'" which had agreed to standards. "And finally they came through."

The Gore report prominently featured a promise from the Social Security Administration to post four performance standards in its offices.

- *You will be treated with courtesy every time you contact us.*
- *We will tell you what benefits you qualify for and give you the information you need to use our programs.*

- *We will refer you to other programs that may help you.*
- *You will reach us the first time you try on our 800 number.*

When Lenane and her colleagues managed to get complete data on the 800-number service, she says, they realized that she had been right: it *was* impossible. At the busiest times of the year in 1993, half the calls got busy signals. At the best times, 18 percent did. Every time payments went out at the beginning of the month, calls flooded the number. After weekends and holidays there were other huge "spikes." On most days, volume crested between 10 A.M. and 2 P.M., then fell off.

And the agency couldn't ask just anyone to answer the phone. Fielding questions from anxious senior citizens about their retirement checks requires knowledge, patience, and courtesy. The agency had already considered contracting the service out and decided it wouldn't work. Its phone people prided themselves on their customer service. They knew a tremendous amount. And they required significant training. Agency leaders simply didn't trust private contractors to provide the required quality of service.

So the agency put together a team and began studying its dilemma. In response to the NPR pressure, it had launched a series of new, more detailed customer surveys. When the team analyzed the new data, it was clear that Woods's instinct had been right: endless busy signals on the 800 number damaged the agency's reputation with its customers."Our data showed that access was the single biggest driver for customer satisfaction," says Lenane. "Getting through to the 800 number influenced the public's perception of our competency and knowledge and their overall satisfaction."

One of the surveys said, "From the time someone first tries to call the 800 number, it would be good service if he/she is able to get through within (blank)." The median answer was five minutes. If callers got through in two minutes, the agency could please nine out of 10 people.

"We knew we wouldn't be able to hit two minutes," says Lenane. "So we chose this median." In 1994, as Woods prepared a progress report on the customer service initiative, she negotiated to change the standard.

Woods pushed hard, telling Lenane, "You can't give ground on this, this is very visible in our report, from the vice president's office." With Gore's authority behind him, he had real leverage. "We went over and over and over it," he remembers. "Finally, we kept some things as standards and others as goals. What was essential—what I hung on to—was that they were committed in writing to someday get there."

The NPR's September 1994 report listed a series of new commitments from the Social Security Administration (SSA)—more specific this time and again featured prominently in the book. They included the following:

- *If you request a new or replacement Social Security card from one of our offices, we will mail it to you within five work days of receiving all the information we need. . . .*
- *When you make an appointment, we'll serve you within 10 minutes of the scheduled time.*
- *SSA knows that you expect world-class service in all your dealings with us. Today we are unable to meet your expectations in all areas, but we are working to change that. When we redesign our processes, you can expect that when you call our 800 number, you will get through to it within five minutes of your first try. Today we often are not able to meet this pledge. During our busiest days, you will get a busy signal much of the time.*

Almost no one familiar with the 800 number thought meeting the five-minute standard was possible. The number of calls kept rising, and Congress kept giving the agency more responsibilities. To make matters worse, downsizing was now under way, thanks to the president and Congress's agreement to cut federal employment. The agency was no longer even allowed to replace teleservice representatives (TSRs) who left. The "busy rate" was going up, not down: in fiscal 1994 the monthly low was 28.4 percent, the high 53 percent.

Yet because of their surveys, the agency's leaders knew how important access to the 800 number was to their customers. They knew the NPR was pushing for good reason. So they got to work. They led a benchmarking study the NPR did on telephone service, looking for operational changes and new technologies they could use. They considered hiring temporary employees for peak periods but decided their limited use would not justify the high cost to train them. Finally they began increasing the number of people from their Program Service Centers (PSCs), which did back-office processing of individual benefit cases, who also handled phone service when volume spiked. They knew full well that benefit processing would suffer, so at first they went slowly.

At this point, the new Republican Congress weighed in. In his budget hearings in April 1995, Congressman John E. Porter (R.-Illinois) extracted a series of performance commitments from the SSA, as part of the Government Performance and Results Act (GPRA) process. One was that 85 percent of calls to the 800 number would be answered within five minutes during fiscal 1996, and 95 percent in fiscal 1997.

Agency leaders had concluded that hitting the five-minute standard on the highest-volume days, on every call, would cost a fortune. "We had to say, the rule of common sense has to apply," says Jack McHale, deputy regional commissioner for the Philadelphia region. "Every hour [that] one of those benefit authorizers is on the telephone answering calls is an hour away from their regular work." Beneficiaries would suffer in other ways, by not having their claims processed on time. Greg Woods also agreed to the 95 percent goal.

But the fact that congressional appropriators were taking the standard seriously changed the stakes. Money talks. "We call it a Porter commitment," says Steve DeMarcos, then deputy director of the Mid-Atlantic PSC. "This is a commitment we make to Congress, where we say, we will deliver this level of service, and thereby continue to be able to receive budgetary considerations." GPRA "not only gave it teeth, but it made it a very, very clear and focused goal that everybody knew and everybody was shooting for."

Just as Porter was extracting his commitment, the agency received a huge shot in the arm. In April 1995, *Business Week* reported that Dalbar Financial Services Inc., after an independent survey of customer service over the phone, had rated the SSA's customer service the best in the country. It topped that of L.L. Bean, Federal Express, Disney World, and every other private corporation tested.

Dalbar placed calls to measure performance, explains Lenane. "We did very poorly on access but very well on competency and knowledge. And in their scoring, those were the things they valued."

This was a huge boost for those pushing for the resources necessary to meet the 95 percent standard. "It helped a great deal," says McHale.

> *While as an agency we were struggling to get the budget commitment for the TSR replacement and get the spike commitment, boy, did that get us favorable attention. That got us in the headlines. It was much easier to say afterward, "If we want to continue in our world-class status, we have to do these things."*
>
> *The employees loved it. We had a celebration. Every employee got a copy of the Dalbar letter, and of course the agency got a Hammer award [from Vice President Gore] out of that. We were able to say to employees, "Hey, we're better than Disney World, you know!" It really was a boost in morale for employees.*

Unfortunately, the access rate was still going south. In fiscal 1995, only 73.5 percent of callers got through in five minutes, the worst rate yet. The monthly busy rate went from a low of 35.5 percent to a high of 61.8 percent.

Finally, agency and administration leaders bit the bullet. First, they agreed to replace teleservice representatives when they left, despite the downsizing effort. Then they converted two Data Operations Centers (DOCs), with about 700 people, to full-time telephone work.

These two centers had low-level employees who spent their days keying information into computers. It was not clear that they could handle telephone work. "There was a reaction: 'You're going to do *what*?'" remembers Janice Warden, then the deputy commissioner for operations. The agency did have to spend more time than usual training them, but it worked. "It changed a lot of people's mind-sets about what we could do, because we found out that these people were perfectly capable of becoming teleservice representatives."

Finally, agency leaders decided to expand teleservice responsibilities to virtually every technical person who worked in a PSC, starting in January 1996. They trained 3,700 people in six large processing centers to handle calls when volume spiked—more than tripling the number of "spikers."

"We worked out a sophisticated call routing system, with the ability to quickly bring these people on during peak calling periods," says Jack McHale. "When calls fell off, they went back to their work."

This required a mammoth training program and a long effort to win the support of the union, part of the American Federation of Government Employees. The key factor was job security: automation was expected to do away with some of the processing center jobs, so shifting to telephone service saved people's jobs. Once they had won union support, Warden, Larry Thompson, and the union council president spent two months visiting the PSCs that were going to have to change.

These folks "did not do public contact work," remembers McHale, "and many of them were not at all interested early on in interviewing the public on the telephone. A lot of them resisted."

We spent "an enormous amount of time with employees, talking about the reasons we were doing it, and relating it back to the customer: customer expectations, the results of our survey," adds Warden.

Managers followed up in their own facilities. Larry Massanari, regional commissioner for the Philadelphia region, remembers those meetings. "The key is always to keep people in an agency like this one focused on customer service," he says. "Because the employees in the SSA, not surprisingly, are very much moved by serving people. And when you can put this in terms not of a number but what it means for people—who are like our parents, our brothers and sisters—then it takes on more meaning."

Meanwhile, the agency restricted leave for teleservice reps and spikers at peak times and accelerated use of overtime. It worked with employees to come up with changes in processes and rules that would improve performance. And because calls peaked after people received payments at the beginning of every month, it began staggering monthly payments for all new recipients. (Surveys had revealed that existing recipients would not take kindly to shifting away from the beginning of the month.)

The transition was hardly smooth. As the agency retrained thousands of people, customer service suffered—both in the processing centers and on the phones. November 1995 was the low point for 800–number access: only 57.2 percent of callers got through within five minutes. Then, on the first morning back to work in January 1996, as the agency put all the new spikers on to handle the post-holiday surge, AT&T's SSA 800 system crashed. Hundreds of thousands of social security recipients called in, and for several days they all got busy signals. The media gave the agency a drubbing, and agency leaders lost a lot of credibility with their employees.

But once AT&T fixed the system, the numbers began to turn around. By February the five-minute access rate was 92.1 percent, and it stayed in the 80 and 90 percent ranges for the rest of the fiscal year. In November 1996 it hit 95.9 percent, and it has stayed above 95 percent every year since. Meanwhile, customer ratings of the courtesy and knowledge of the agency's teleservice reps remained more than 95 percent positive.

It hasn't been easy. "We still really torture ourselves in terms of trying to make up for a very few days of the year [after holidays and long weekends] when you can't do 95 and five," DeMarcos told us in mid–1999. "You just can't do it on some days, and because those days come out so much lower than 95 and five—and because they're so high volume—it takes you forever to make up for them."

Agency leaders acknowledge that the improvement in 800-number service has come at the price of decreased performance in benefits processing. Many believe the agency has gone too far—that it would be much better off with a lower standard for the 800 number and faster turnaround in benefits processing. Others defend the standard, pointing to the customer surveys that prove how important access to the 800 number is to the agency's customers.

Still, achieving the goal has created real pride in the organization. "There was a lot of internal celebration" when we met "the goal in 1997 and 1998," DeMarcos remembers.

> *When you do it one year, two years, now into the third year, it really becomes a part of your culture. Internally, if you were to talk to all the people on the network . . . they know the 95 and five commitment. People know that, and that's what people work toward now. That's what drives us.*

Agency leaders also agree that it would not have happened without the service standard. Jack McHale, who was then in charge of the 800-number service, had been lobbying for many of the changes for a long time. "We had to improve, because we were so bad," he says.

But I don't think we would have stretched as far as we did. As someone who was asked what we needed to do to meet this standard, I would come up with these recommendations, and I could always lean on the standard. I could always do calculations of how short we would be. Had the standard not existed, we would have improved, but not as much.

USING SERVICE STANDARDS TO MAKE CUSTOMERS POWERFUL

The SSA story demonstrates how powerful service standards can be in driving public organizations to deliver what their customers want, when those organizations take them seriously. In September 1993, a few days after Gore presented his report, President Clinton followed through on its recommendation to issue an executive order requiring all federal agencies and departments "that provide significant services directly to the public" to identify and survey their customers, set service standards, and measure progress against them. The order proclaimed that "the standards of quality for service provided to the public shall be: Customer service equal to the best in business."

By fiscal year 1998, according to the NPR (now the National Partnership for Reinventing Government), 570 federal organizations had created 4,000 standards. But they measured performance for only 2,800 of them, and unlike the SSA's standards, the vast majority were quite vague. So in 1998 the president ordered the agencies to talk with their customers about their service and standards and to use what they learned to improve both.

Though progress has been gradual, the entire process has clearly had an impact. In a survey of federal managers conducted by the Office Of Personnel Management in 1991, only 36 percent agreed that their organizations had "service goals aimed at meeting customer expectations." When the National Performance Review asked the same question in a 1998 survey, 80 percent of supervisors agreed.

By 1998, according to the NPR:

- The National Archives and Records Administration met this standard 99 percent of the time: "Within 15 minutes of walking in, you'll have either the information or the help you need."
- The Occupational Safety and Health Administration had reduced a one-month turnaround time for responding to worker complaints to one day.
- The Bureau of Land Management had trimmed turnaround time for permits from 15 days to a few minutes.
- The U.S. Postal Service had boosted on-time (three-day) delivery of first-class mail from 79 percent in fiscal 1994 to 92 percent in fiscal 1997, though it was doing far less well on Priority Mail and Express Mail.

pp. 346–382

Every public organization can use quality assurance tools: customer service standards and guarantees, redress systems (to provide compensation to customers for failure to meet standards), complaint systems, customer service agreements, and customer councils and boards. Customer quality assurance is much like performance management, but it makes public organizations accountable to their customers, not just to their superiors in the chain of command. Like performance management, it creates less pressure—and thus slower improvement in most cases—than other approaches, such as competitive customer choice. But it works.

See Banishing Bureaucracy pp. 32–36, 192–195

In the U.K., which pioneered customer quality assurance, the Labor Party conducted an in-depth review of the Citizen's Charter in 1998, after it came to power. By then there were some 200 national charters and an estimated 10,000 local government charters, each setting service standards, most outlining complaint systems, and a few promising redress to customers if the chartered organization failed to meet a standard. The review found that although many standards "were vague, unclear and missed the issues that were most important to users," as in the United States, others were quite effective. It quoted several other positive assessments:

- "The Charter programme has provided both a stimulus and a means for organisations to raise their performance," the National Audit Office testified.
- "The Citizen's Charter is an important initiative in making public services more responsive to consumers and should be retained," added the National Consumer Council.
- "There are tangible benefits from the Charter programme which have persuaded at least some of the original sceptics," concluded Parliament's Public Service Committee. "There have indeed been real improvements, a 'change of culture' in public services."

The Labor Party pledged to continue and strengthen the program, though it made sure to remind citizens that "the Charter idea was pioneered by Labour local authorities in the 1980s." It also gave the initiative a new name, "Service First," as political parties often do when they embrace the opposition's ideas.

The basic tool of customer service standards makes so much sense that at least 15 countries have adopted it in some form, including Australia, Canada, Belgium, France, Ireland, Italy, Finland, Norway, Sweden, Portugal, Spain, Singapore, and, of course, the U.S. Some, like Australia and Canada, have done so in both national and state or provincial governments.

Survey research in Canada demonstrates why customer service standards have such appeal. The Canadian Centre for Management Development's

Citizen-Centred Service Network surveyed 2,900 Canadians in 1998. After asking about 30 different aspects of service delivery, it found that "Citizens' assessments of service quality are determined primarily by five factors: timeliness, knowledge and competence of staff, courtesy/comfort, fair treatment, and outcomes. . . . Timely services is the single strongest determinant of service quality across all services across three levels" of government. As we saw with the SSA, it is precisely these factors that service standards can improve, when used well.

Customer quality assurance has one final advantage: employees usually welcome it. Unlike managed competition and competitive choice, it is rarely threatening. Most employees genuinely want to provide excellent service.

The Key to Success: Making Customer Service Consequential

Perhaps the most important lesson learned by the pioneers of customer quality assurance is this: when you create standards, guarantees, complaint procedures, and the like, create rewards for fulfilling them and penalties for failing. As with customer choice, consequences give this approach its teeth. Service standards, complaint systems, service agreements, and customer councils will help managers and employees understand what their customers want, but consequences will give urgency to the challenge of providing it.

Consider the Social Security story. Though the SSA's leadership understood that service on its 800 number was critical to customer satisfaction, answering every call within five minutes—or even 95 percent of all calls within five minutes—seemed impossible. If Greg Woods had not used Vice President Gore's authority to cajole the agency into publishing a standard and then reported its performance every year, it would never have committed to the standard. If Representative Porter had not demanded that the SSA meet the standard or suffer budgetary consequences, the agency might never have gone to the extraordinary lengths it did to reengineer its work.

Or consider the U.K. When the Labor Government reviewed the Citizen's Charter, "Many said that, at present, the public can feel frustrated when they discover that little can be done to enforce charter targets." Without enforcement of consequences, in other words, standards pack much less punch. There are several ways to create this enforcement—all of which have been used by at least a few organizations in the U.K.

pp. 359–368

• ***Create guarantees and redress policies.*** Guarantees commit public organizations to give customers who are not satisfied—or have not been delivered the quality of services promised—either their money back or free redelivery of the services. Redress gives customers some form of compensation—financial or otherwise—if the organization fails to meet its service standards. We discuss these tools in detail later.

pp. 215–246

pp. 110–113

• ***Build service standards into your performance management system.*** The Social Security Administration holds some top managers accountable for meeting its service standards; if the organization fails, it affects their pay. Many of the U.K.'s executive agencies, which we discuss in Chapter Three, have begun to include key service standards among their annual performance targets—which also affect top management's performance bonuses.

• ***Publicize and compare performance against the standards.*** NPR's annual publication of the SSA's results was a big part of what kept it from abandoning its 800–number standards. "I think part of what helped transform them was we kept reporting on it," says Candace Kane, who succeeded Greg Woods as head of the NPR's customer service team. "They knew that they were going to be publicly humiliated if in fact they hadn't delivered what they needed to deliver."

pp. 210–214

In the U.K., the Citizen's Charter led to the publication of comparative data on local governments, schools, hospitals, and passenger rail lines. This, the government concluded after its review, "was considered by many respondents to the consultation exercise to be a major success of the old Charter programme." The Labor Government promised to expand public reporting on performance. "The key is for standards, and performance against them, to be regularly published, so that they are available to all," it said.

When there are problems with service delivery in the U.K., the published information gives the media, the government, and interest groups the facts they need to press for improvement. The performance of privatized rail lines has been disappointing, for example. Virtually every time the press or a politician calls attention to the problem, they cite the number of complaints against the rail line, the numbers of delays and cancellations, and the amount of redress money paid. The private railroads are required to provide this data by the charters they inherited from the public sector, and the government posts the information company by company on the World Wide Web. Though the railroads have at least seven-year monopoly franchises on individual lines, publishing their performance against service standards keeps significant pressure on them to improve.

• ***Create awards for meeting tough customer service standards.*** The Social Security Administration gives awards to teleservice centers for outstanding service. Vice President Gore gives out Hammer awards. The U.S. Department of Education has an "honor roll" to recognize achievement in "satisfying customers." The IRS awards a "Seal of Approval" customer service award. The Federal Emergency Management Agency (FEMA) allows employees and customers to nominate FEMA workers.

Many other organizations have done likewise. One of the most successful elements of the Citizen's Charter was its Charter Mark: a seal of approval for customer service that winners are allowed to display on their buildings, stationery, and other materials for three years. The criteria for receiving a Charter Mark are demanding, and the competition is fierce: in 1998 there were 1,202 applications, from all levels of government.

The Labor Government's review found broad support in the public sector for the Charter Mark awards. And surprisingly, 29 percent of the public was aware of them. Prime Minister Tony Blair takes the awards so seriously that he speaks at the annual ceremony.

One of the Charter Mark award's best features, in our view, is that organizations win the right to display the Charter Mark for only three years; to win again, they must continue improving their customer service. By 1999, only 18 organizations in the country had won Charter Marks three times in a row. The threat of losing a Charter Mark puts real pressure on winners. British Gas won in 1993, then saw its customer service slip after it was privatized and began downsizing. Rather than suffer the embarrassment of losing it three years later, it handed its Charter Mark back to the government—which of course attracted great publicity.

Kent County Council's Arts and Libraries won in 1992. "I think we felt much more anxious about it this time," Development Manager Maggi Waite told the *Charter News* in 1995, "because in 1992 we had nothing to lose by applying. This time our reputation was at stake. . . . The suspense in the fortnight before we received the results was awful—just like waiting for your exam results."

Customer Quality Assurance in Compliance Organizations

Some public organizations don't primarily deliver services; they enforce compliance with rules. These include police forces, court systems, corrections systems, environmental protection agencies, permitting agencies, tax collection agencies, and the like. Their activities may *include* services—such as a 911 emergency phone system for the public or free help lines for taxpayers—but their core missions are the enforcement of laws and regulations. (Occasionally, the same people are both customers and compliers. Welfare recipients, for example, are compliers with state and federal laws about who is eligible for welfare, but customers of welfare services such as monthly checks, job training, and job placement. As we discuss in Chapter Three, welfare departments should separate their compliance functions from their service functions, because the two roles conflict so much that one staff person cannot effectively play both.)

pp. 113–118

Can compliance organizations use the customer quality assurance tools? Yes, with some adjustments. Normally, their customers are not the people they deal with directly but the community at large, represented by elected officials—as we explain in the introduction to Part Three. We call the people that these organizations deal with day in and day out—taxpayers, suspected crim-

p. 274

inals, polluters, and so on—*compliers.* Compliance organizations can use quality assurance tools to improve their service to compliers, as a way to improve voluntary compliance. They can treat compliers as if they were customers. But when they do, they must balance the interests of compliers against those of their true customers. Tax collection agencies don't want to please taxpayers by letting them off the hook for taxes they owe, for example.

Many compliance organizations are now using the quality assurance approach as part of what we call "winning compliance." They have shifted some of their energies from catching noncompliers to encouraging voluntary compliance—which is the cheapest form of compliance. Quality assurance is harder to use in most compliance organizations than in service organizations, because their employees don't (and often shouldn't) think of compliers as customers. They more often see them as "deadbeats," "criminals," "polluters"—or other words we won't print. Hence it is harder to get them to buy in. "They have the enforcement mentality," says Peter Hutchinson, president of the Public Strategies Group. "Since all they see are deadbeats, day in and day out, they can't imagine treating them like valued customers."

But it can be done, and increasingly it is being done. The Public Strategies Group defines eight steps that go into winning compliance:

1. Build support for standards, if possible, by involving compliers and other key stakeholders in helping to make or even enforce the rules.

In the early 1990s, the Massachusetts Department of Environmental Protection (DEP) accomplished a sweeping reform of its permitting systems, including dramatic reductions in the time required, one-stop shopping for most permits, and reduction of the number of permits required. The crucial ingredient in its success was the inclusion of environmentalists and business leaders in a series of stakeholder groups to redesign the state's rules and processes. The first group began by doing an inventory of all 137 permits required by the state and describing the processes associated with each. This pinpointed where backlogs were occurring, where too many steps were required, and where permits were unnecessary. When business and environmental leaders agreed on solutions, the legislature was often willing to act.

The federal Occupational Safety and Health Administration went even further: it gave control over *enforcement* to large businesses that developed teams of managers and union members to perform inspections and solve problems. Workplace safety improved dramatically in those plants. The Vermont Department of Corrections even let some nonviolent offenders negotiate with community boards to define their *penalties*—and how they would make restitution to their victims and the local community. Recidivism rates fell.

pp. 489–494

2. *Focus regulations on results, not process.*

Many regulations prescribe exactly how compliers have to comply with the law, particularly in the environmental arena. They tell them what technology they must use, how it must be installed, how often it must be inspected, and so on. Often compliers know there is a better way, but the law won't let them use it. Reinventors have begun to substitute regulations that define the outcome required, but leave it up to compliers to figure out how to produce it. If a new technology will meet the goal at a lower price, they are free to use it. This not only makes it easier for them to comply, it stimulates innovation to find better and cheaper methods.

3. *Educate compliers about what is expected of them.*

When the Minnesota Department of Revenue shifted hundreds of employees from enforcement work to educating businesses about how to pay the proper amount of sales tax, it increased sales tax collections dramatically. The U.S. Customs Service similarly shifted part of its staff from inspecting goods brought into ports and airports to working with importers "so we can rely on their internal control processes," as former commissioner George Weise put it.

"Those out to break the law will continue to be apprehended," explained Dennis Murphy, then director of the Norfolk, Virginia, Customs district, "but we're moving from what you might call a 'gotcha' focus, in which we just try to catch somebody, to one of trying to make sure that the people we deal with understand what's required of them so they don't make mistakes based on ignorance, sloppy work or poor communications."

4. *Make compliance easy, by providing services that facilitate it.*

The Massachusetts DEP invited businesses planning large projects that required multiple permits to come in early in their planning process. Businesses would map out what they intended to do, and the department would help them design the project to minimize the number of permits required. This worked so well that the department decided to establish four regional service centers. It hired new staff to act as lead contacts, to shepherd businesses through the process. They and others used analytical techniques drawn from Total Quality Management (TQM) to find out who had the most permitting problems and then invited those businesses, municipalities, and consultants in early in the planning process.

Other states have since taken similar steps. California introduced "tiered permitting," replacing one-size-fits-all permits with different types based on the level of environmental risk involved. The California Environmental Protection Agency also established ten "one-stop" permitting centers around the state, to help developers get all the permits they needed for a project in one place.

5. *Establish quality guarantees, standards, and redress mechanisms for service to compliers.*

The first stakeholder group at the Massachusetts DEP recommended a money-back guarantee. Permits would have to be issued within strict time limits, and if the department missed a deadline, it would return the fee. The legislature passed the necessary legislation, and "it was the single best thing we did," then-commissioner Dan Greenbaum told us.

> *It created a dynamic like a business trying to collect a fee for a service. It provided impetus for management reforms, like a real tracking system so you would know what was happening with each permit.*
>
> *Staff told us they'd need lots more people to meet the time lines. We managed to get a few new people from budget, but then further cutbacks frustrated even that. We got like a tenth of what people thought they needed. But we met the deadlines the first year; it turned out there was a lot of slack in the system. Part of it was poor management: for example, no tracking system. And part of it was that the department had people who were environmentalists and believed that by delaying things they were protecting the environment.*

Greenbaum used a two-stage process to give the organization time to improve: after the first year, the deadlines automatically tightened by 30 percent. But over the first four years the department missed only 75 deadlines out of 14,000. Word got around about which regional and program offices were refunding the most fees. "There's a certain pride in not being the one to show up as doing the worst," said Greenbaum's successor, Thomas B. Powers.

6. *Report to the public on compliance levels, and give compliers feedback on their level of compliance.*

If taxpayers are told that they have filed incorrectly, or businesses are informed that they have violated an environmental rule, most will correct their mistakes. Even police forces use feedback to change the behavior of citizens. Captain Michael Masterson of the Madison, Wisconsin, police department describes a particularly good example.

> *Instead of going out and writing tickets in one neighborhood, we went out and set up individual speed display boards and took neighborhood residents with us. We did a little poster, a little warning notice that talked about fines for speeding. It was during the holiday, so we [gave] people a holiday greeting. But anybody that speeded, not only did the cop talk with them, but the resident talked to them too. In a very*

cordial, nonthreatening way, we said, "Look, this neighborhood is important, our children play here, they use this sidewalk, and the speed limit is 25."

They got off with a warning. We got an incredible response. The people that were stopped felt it was great that the police dealt with people in this manner. The neighborhood thought it was a great effort working with them, helping them create an awareness of the problem. And the officers thought it was great. Officers have hearts; they don't like to be laying $100 tickets on somebody around Thanksgiving and Christmas.

7. Treat compliers differently, based on their past performance, competence to comply, and motivation levels.

There is little sense in treating law-abiding citizens who have made a mistake the same as habitual lawbreakers. The police don't do it, the courts don't do it, but many compliance agencies do. Before it reengineered its sales tax process, the Minnesota Department of Revenue sent the same nasty letter to any business that missed a deadline for payment of the tax. After the reforms, it reacted very differently, based on the past performance of the business. If it had a perfect record, it sent out a very nice letter noting the missed deadline, mentioning that the check was probably already on its way, but reminding the business owner of the oversight. A series of other letters, each slightly tougher, went out to those with less than stellar records. And state revenue collectors visited habitual nonpayers—sometimes with police protection.

8. Employ a continuum of incentives and consequences for compliance.

Refunds and other forms of redress help salve the wounds inflicted by poor service, but they don't create incentives for people or businesses to comply. Governments usually use sticks, not carrots, to do this: they create stiff penalties, including fines and jail time, for failure to comply. Reinventors don't abandon the sticks, but they add carrots. The Minnesota Revenue Department announced that if you got your tax return in by a certain date, for example, you would get a refund within 48 hours. Normal turnaround was 24 days.

QUALITY ASSURANCE: OTHER LESSONS LEARNED

Because using service standards, guarantees, and redress has a lot in common with using other performance goals, we recommend Chapters Six and Seven as well as this one for guidance. Many of their lessons apply here as well. In addition, the following lessons apply to all or most of the customer quality assurance tools.

1. Involve customers in the creation of guarantees, standards, redress policies, complaint systems, and customer service agreements.

If you don't, you won't know what is important to them. When the Oregon Division of Motor Vehicles was reengineering its offices, its leaders "knew" their customers' main concern was long lines. They planned to add clerks and automate the process. But when they surveyed those customers, it turned out that their top complaint, by a wide margin, was unflattering pictures on their drivers' licenses. So they reengineered that too.

"Never assume what people want," says Steve DeMarcos at the Social Security Administration. "Find out from the customers. You can kill yourselves to do something that you find out people think is a yawner."

In both the U.S. and the U.K., many organizations have neglected this step—and paid the price with worthless, or even harmful, standards. "The place agencies have had the most trouble is the idea that they have to ask their customers what they want and whether they're getting it," says Greg Woods. "They revert to the Washington mentality: we figure it out in D.C. So they always get it wrong."

pp. 377–380, 382–388

Customer surveys are useful here, but face-to-face contact with customers is even more important. Customer councils are perhaps the best tool, though you can use many of the customer voice tools outlined later in the chapter. "It is really valuable for people to see and speak directly to their customers," says Laurie Ohmann, a Public Strategies Group partner who has helped several organizations do this. "Get the people who are charged with doing the improvements to look at people they're serving square in the face and ask the questions." You can even videotape the sessions and show them to the rest of your organization.

This not only helps generate standards that are meaningful to your customers, it helps convince your employees to take them seriously. They have to be "connected to what the customer has actually told you in the surveys and from discussions," says the SSA's Janice Warden, who now works on these issues as a deputy director of the NPR. "You have to be able to point to that, to make it credible to the entire organization." Otherwise, she says, you will run smack into this attitude: "Let's not kid ourselves. Are we doing this because it's important or because Vice President Gore told us to?"

2. Educate customers about your services, so they will have realistic notions of what is possible and will understand their own responsibilities.

If people think it should be simple for them to call the SSA's 800 number and reach a knowledgeable employee right away, they will be disappointed if they have to try for five minutes. If they know, on the other hand, that the SSA runs the world's largest toll-free service and that it gets more than 65 million calls a year, they may feel differently. So tell them. Put an explanation on a tape that plays as they wait on hold. Send one out with their monthly checks. Put signs and pamphlets in your offices.

Often, services won't work unless customers uphold their end of the deal. For example, tax agencies can't send speedy refunds if taxpayers don't fill out their returns completely and accurately. Permit offices cannot process permits rapidly if developers hide information from them. In cases like these, add customer (or complier) responsibilities to your service standards and guarantees—and publicize them.

3. Keep pressure on from outside the organization to create meaningful guarantees, standards, redress policies, and complaint systems.

As we saw at the Social Security Administration, setting meaningful standards and then fulfilling them can take almost heroic efforts. Most organizations won't do that—or will only do it until the leader who drove it moves on. So you need some external force that keeps the pressure on—forever.

In the U.S., the NPR played this role, as best it could. In the U.K., publication of performance data kept external pressure on railroads, schools, local governments, and hospitals. Another good method is a customer council or board with real power—a tool we discuss later in this chapter. Diana Goldsworthy, former deputy director of the U.K.'s Charter unit, says the British would have benefited from the presence of such a customer council:

pp. 377–380

> *The truth is that the Charter unit itself, inside the Cabinet office, is all civil servants reporting to a minister. It's very difficult for us, credibly, to present ourselves to the tabloid press as people who go and kick down doors. But that role ought to be exercised by somebody. We could have had this outside panel being the nasty guys, in the press and on the TV, saying, "I'm just going to make sure that Charter does this and Charter does that, and I've told John Major today . . ." I think it's difficult to have people who are inside the machine, if I can put it that way, also be the people who are beating your sheet to death, publicly.*

Even an elected minister or vice president cannot really do this, she points out. Imagine the media flap if Al Gore had publicly criticized Education Secretary Riley's or Labor Secretary Reich's department, and you can understand why.

4. Create an outside review process to approve guarantees, standards, redress policies, complaint systems, and the performance measurement processes associated with them.

Just as you need outside pressure, you need an external body to review and approve standards, redress policies, and the rest. Otherwise, vague standards that cannot be measured and have no means of redress attached—"We will do our best to provide timely, courteous service"— will be the norm. The review process should involve both customers (ideally through a customer council or board) and a neutral reinvention office such as the NPR or the Charter unit. In the U.K., the Labor Government has asked departments to review all charters at least once every two years, and the Cabinet Office has set up an audit system to check on the quality of charters and intervene when necessary.

pp. 377–380

When private contractors deliver public services, this is equally important. Because some private rail operators in the U.K. made their charters less uniform and harder for customers to decipher after they took over, the Cabinet Office had to force them to use a standard format. Many organizations, public and private, have quietly redefined what "on time" or "a 30-minute" wait means, as well. In the National Health Service, for instance, some clinics began to measure waiting time not when the patient arrived but when he or she first talked to the receptionist. Because this kind of fudging is inevitable—as with any kind of performance measure—an outside body also needs to review definitions, indicators, and measures to keep them honest.

p. 265

5. Publicize your standards, guarantees, redress policies, complaint systems, and results.

If people don't know about these policies, they will have far less effect than they should. For example, the U.S. Postal Service has publicized its first-class on-time delivery standards (three days within the continental U.S., one day locally) and reported quarterly on its performance. The results have generated front-page newspaper stories, creating useful urgency within top management. But the postal service has been silent about another standard: "You will receive service at post office counters within five minutes." If you look hard next time you go into a post office, you may find a tiny, 4-inch by 5-inch sign announcing the standard. But you've probably never noticed it. As a result, it is meaningless to the customer. Nor does it seem to have had any impact on employee behavior, from our observations. It is, sadly, a wasted opportunity to win over the public.

Publicizing your progress is also necessary, at times, to convince your employees that you can improve. It was only when the five-minute-access rate at the SSA began inching up that employees started to believe the goal was possible, for example.

6. Involve frontline employees in creating standards and other tools—and in figuring out how to meet them—to help them buy in.

If standards and redress policies are simply imposed on employees, few will respond to the challenge. At the SSA, says Janice Warden, "I don't think we could have done it without really engaging the employees in discussions, getting their ideas about how we could do this better. We talked with thousands of them." The commissioner made the decision to set standards, but employee input was critical in figuring out how to meet them.

The British also learned this lesson. Their review pointed out that frontline employees had "often been ignored in the past." The government's guide, *How to Draw Up a National Charter,* added, "They are the people who will have to deliver the standards in your charter, and they are often well placed to offer practical suggestions for improvements, and to identify people or organisations who should be consulted."

7. *Involve the union, if there is one.*

To improve services, you will often need to redesign work processes, change work rules, change job descriptions and classifications, and the like. Unions can block such changes. Hence it is critical to get them on board. In the SSA, this took months of discussion, but it was worth it, says Janice Warden.

8. *Empower frontline staff to make decisions.*

When organizations fail to deliver the quality of service that they have promised or customers have legitimate complaints, frontline staff need to be able to make it right, immediately. If you have to wait three weeks for management to make a decision, you will alienate your customers. Lesley Harvey at British Gas, a privatized company with a charter, remembers a customer who ordered a new oven that turned out to be defective. "I just agreed to change it," she says. "Before, I would have had to refer it to a senior manager." But "there's nothing more annoying for a customer than to be told you can't make a decision, you have to refer it upstairs. This way, the customer has more faith in you."

9. *Use standards, guarantees, complaints, and customer councils to drive redesign, reengineering, and restructuring.*

There's only so much improvement you can produce by changing attitudes and getting employees to work harder. If customer quality assurance doesn't lead to reengineering work processes and restructuring organizations, as it did at the SSA, then it won't be worth using.

Customer-driven agencies typically organize around customers' needs, not organizational functions. They create single points of contact for customers, one-stop services, and integrated work teams to handle all of a customer's needs. They use TQM and business process reengineering to redesign their work processes and organizational structures. They use internal enterprise management to get better value from their suppliers, so they can serve their customers better. Sometimes they even convert their service systems to give customers more choices—or vouchers they can use to choose their own providers.

pp. 174–182
pp. 279–322

10. Study other organizations, including private companies, to see how you might rethink, redesign, and reengineer.

Studying the best in business gets you out of your box. "We would not be where we are with the 800 number if we had not participated in benchmarking, primarily with the private sector," says Toni Lenane of the SSA. "It just opens up this whole world that you never even contemplated might be there."

11. Back up your quality assurance approach with training, mentoring, learning networks, and other support for employees.

To improve customer service, your employees will need much more than "smile training." They will need new skills: the ability to do customer surveys and focus groups; the ability to analyze, improve, and redesign work processes; the ability to build teams. You will need to support them with training, expert consultants—and if you're smart, mentoring, learning networks, and site visits.

pp. 478–486

When John Christian took over the Parks and Recreation Department in Sunnyvale, California, he sent six people to Disney's customer service training program in Anaheim: clerical, frontline, and managerial staff. When they came back, they became the Customer Action Service Team—an internal training unit for customer service. Then he took a team to the Granite Rock Corporation, a California construction company that won the Malcolm Baldridge National Quality Award in 1992, "to see what we could learn from private companies." That was so effective that he institutionalized regular "benchmarking trips" to cutting-edge parks and recreation departments as well as private corporations. The key is to send not just managers, he told us, but also professional, frontline, and clerical staff. "That's very, very powerful."

In the U.K., the Charter unit has helped build 25 "quality networks" around the country, with over 2,000 public sector members that share what they are learning. It also sponsors an annual conference and a best-practice quality forum, which brings network leaders and Cabinet Office staff together to learn from one another. There is a mentoring system, through which Charter Mark holders provide support to other organizations in their regions. And finally, the renamed Service First unit is creating a self-assessment package based on the Charter Mark criteria so that organizations that aren't ready to apply can still use the criteria to figure out what they need to do to improve their customer service.

12. Don't create a separate unit to do this; integrate customer quality assurance into your strategic and performance management systems.

If you create a separate unit to handle service guarantees and standards, redress policies, and complaint procedures, then your line operations will see these things as headquarter's agenda, not their own. They may go through the motions, to comply, but they won't build their own work around customer service. You may need a reinvention office to catalyze action, but development of standards and the like should be done by line organizations—with review by a reinvention office and customers, as we argued in lesson four. Then make sure the standards are an integral part of your strategic and performance management systems, like any other outcome goals and performance targets. Don't treat them as something separate from your performance goals.

pp. 13–59, 215–246

13. Make sure your leadership is seriously committed.

To succeed, you need commitment from your organization's leaders, their leaders, and your top civil servants. "If Shirley Chater and Larry Thompson had said to me, 'You've got to do this,' and Larry had then walked away from it, it would not have taken on the power it did," says the SSA's Janice Warden. It also helped that the vice president and president talked about service standards and the SSA's 800 number.

Then, says Warden, you have to "get the buy in from the top career executives—that layer that remains in place when the administration goes away. And you know, you do that through discussions. And there's the same credibility issue in terms of how the standards were established"—are they rooted in real customer needs?

What do you do if your organization's leader is not committed? Toni Lenane has a good answer:

> *I teach customer service at the Western Management Development Center run by the Office of Personnel Management, and what I frequently hear from agency people is, "I'm interested, but I can't get my boss to be." My advice is, find out the thing that'll make it worthwhile to them, so they'll get some kudos and some recognition. All it takes is your boss getting some success, and they'll become a believer.*

QUESTIONS PEOPLE ASK ABOUT CUSTOMER QUALITY ASSURANCE

Q: When the needs of different customers conflict, what do you do?

Often, public organizations have multiple sets of customers. Public schools, for instance, have parents, the community at large, and the future employers of graduates. Compliance organizations have both customers and compliers. Sometimes the needs of different customers conflict, and the needs of customers and compliers often conflict.

p. 274

The first step is to carefully define your primary and secondary customers and compliers. Then ask each group what they want. When their needs conflict, you can sometimes work out win-win solutions. For example, if the public wants less pollution but business wants less burdensome regulation, you can

pp. 335–337

pp. 377–380

reinvent your regulatory system, as the Massachusetts DEP did. The best method is often the one the DEP chose: create a customer or stakeholder council, which includes all major perspectives, and ask them to help you craft solutions.

Q: When more than one organization is involved in delivering the service or producing the outcome, what do you do?

Many outcomes that are important to the public involve the work of multiple organizations. Even some distinct services involve more than one organization. For example, when a public works department sweeps the streets, it usually relies on a police department to have the streets clear of parked cars. Often, this is so low on the police's priority list that it doesn't get done. The result: dirty streets and dissatisfied customers.

When customers tell you what is important to them, if it involves services from multiple agencies, bring the agencies together to develop mutual standards and policies, as well as reinforcing standards and policies. Have them report to a mutual customer council, if that is practical.

Prime Minister Tony Blair in the U.K., aware of how often this problem frustrates citizens, has made a priority of what he calls "joined-up government." "We are encouraging the development of new cross-cutting charters, which bring together information on related services," his government announced after its review of the Citizen's Charter.

pp. 380–382

When you create mutual charters—or even when you can't—another useful tool is a customer service agreement between agencies. For example, the public works department could negotiate a service agreement with the police department, specifying the level of service the police would provide in ticketing and towing illegally parked cars as well as the consequences if they failed to meet those standards.

Q: Won't guarantees, redress, and a complaints system cost too much, taking money away from investment in real customer service?

In a word, no. In fact, they will probably save your organization money. Budget offices may assume that money-back guarantees and financial redress will cost money, but if the funds come out of the organization's budget and the incentives in the budget system are right, the opposite will happen. The fear of losing money will drive managers to avoid such situations by correcting problems and improving service. This will minimize the employee time taken up with complaints and redelivery of flawed services, while maximizing value for customers. Complaints systems also look expensive until you study the realities, as the British have. "Handling complaints well saves time and resources, by ensuring complaints do not escalate up the system," the Citizen's Charter

Complaints Task Force found. Its research included a look at how much four different public services estimated it cost to deal with complaints at three levels: the front lines, the senior staff, and an external review. Not surprisingly, resolving complaints at the front lines saved enormous amounts.

THE CUSTOMER QUALITY ASSURANCE TOOLKIT

Service Standards define the levels and quality of services that public organizations commit to deliver to their customers or compliers. See below.

Quality Guarantees promise to give customers or compliers their money back or to redeliver services for free if the organization fails to meet its service standards or the customer or complier is not satisfied. See p. 359.

Redress gives customers or compliers some form of compensation—financial or otherwise—when an organization fails to meet its service standards. See p. 362.

Complaint Systems track and analyze complaints, ensure prompt responses, help organizations learn from complaints to improve their services, and hold them accountable for doing so. See p. 368.

Customer Councils and Boards are small groups of customers who meet regularly with an organization's leadership and have some power to hold it accountable for performance. See p. 377.

Customer Service Agreements are performance agreements between an organization and its customers, defining the levels and quality of service to be provided and the rewards and penalties for doing or failing to do so. See p. 380.

Customer Voice—the ability to listen to customers through surveys and other methods—is a critical competence for those using the Customer Strategy but does not have enough power to be labelled a tool. See p. 382.

SERVICE STANDARDS

pp. 331–332

Service standards are the heart of customer quality assurance. Some are very simple. Since surveys show that difficulty getting information or services over the telephone is the most common problem encountered by public sector customers, many organizations (like the SSA) have standards related to phone service. But the same research shows that people also care about much bigger things, such as the outcomes they experience. Hence other service standards focus on bigger issues: what percentage of students reads at grade level; what percentage of the community rates service "good" or "excellent"; what percentage of citizens rates the police "courteous," "respectful," or "honest."

SERVICE STANDARDS FOR ROUTINE TRANSACTIONS

The Canadian Centre for Management Development has created a national network of "service quality leaders from the federal, provincial and municipal governments," which it calls the Citizen-Centred Service Network. In 1998, it released a detailed survey of 2,900 Canadians about their perceptions of public services. One product of this research was a series of suggestions about appropriate standards for routine transactions. Although these are based on Canadians' expectations, we find them appropriate to the U.S.—and no doubt in other countries as well.

Telephone:

How many minutes is it acceptable to wait for a government representative?

- 97 percent find a 30-second wait acceptable.

What is the maximum number of people you should have to deal with?

- 85 percent find two people acceptable.

If you leave a telephone voice message at 10:00 A.M., what is an acceptable time to wait for a return call?

- 75 percent find four hours acceptable.

Counter Service:

How many minutes is it acceptable to wait in any line?

- 68 percent find five minutes acceptable.

What is the maximum number of people you should have to deal with?

- 82 percent find two people acceptable.

Mail:

What is an acceptable time to allow for a mailed reply?

- 87 percent find two weeks acceptable.

E-Mail:

If you e-mail a government office by 10:00 A.M., what is an acceptable time to wait for a reply?

- 90 percent find four hours acceptable.

You can set standards for any service. Bromley, a borough of London, created standards related to pavement, noise, and the environment, among other things. "We now promise that if you find an uneven paving stone, we'll put it right within two hours," Chief Executive Nigel Palk told us. Sunnyvale's Leisure Services unit set quality standards for virtually every piece of equipment, including a requirement for shiny seats on the play equipment, because that's what kids like. In the Minneapolis School District, the central stores and equipment unit promised 48-hour turnaround on any order of supplies. Before they did so, average turnaround had been six weeks—too slow for many orders. Teachers often had to buy supplies out of their own pockets. "So when the central stores people would show up six weeks later with the stuff, everybody was always mad at them," says Peter Hutchinson, who acted as superin-

CHARACTERISTICS OF GOOD STANDARDS

The British and Canadian governments have both published useful lists of what makes a good service standard. We have combined them and added one of our own. There are always exceptions, but in general, effective standards should be:

- *Meaningful to customers.* They should be focused on things customers care about, not things managers care about.
- *Relevant.* They should focus on those issues considered most important by customers.
- *Challenging.* They should force the organization to improve but not be completely out of reach.
- *Owned by managers and employees.* They should not be imposed without manager and employee buy-in.
- *Simple.* They should be brief, to the point, and in plain language.
- *Measurable.* You have to be able to measure them, to tell how often the organization is meeting them.
- *Monitored.* You need systems in place to measure them regularly, plus auditors to spot-check the measurements, to keep them honest.
- *Published.* After being independently validated by auditors, performance against the standards should be published and given to customers.
- *Reviewed.* Because customers' needs change, review your standards and update them when conditions or customers' needs have changed.
- *Integrated with performance management.* They should be part of the system you use to measure performance, create accountability, and foster learning.

pp. 215–246

tendent for three and a half years. After Hutchinson took away the unit's monopoly, allowing the schools to buy equipment anywhere, central stores created its 48–hour standard and offered a rebate to purchasers at the end of the year, out of any profits generated. Its business increased by 20 percent, and customer satisfaction skyrocketed.

pp. 323–330

When you want to set a stretch goal but worry that it is unattainable, you can do what the SSA ultimately did: set a two-tier or two-step goal. By saying they would answer 95 percent of all calls within five minutes, they stretched the organization but accepted the fact that on the highest-volume days they would never meet the standard. By committing to 85 percent in fiscal 1996 and 95 percent in fiscal 1997, they acknowledged the reality that it would take time to hit their stretch goal. Another option is to set one standard for most times but a different standard for the busiest periods. It's better to avoid such "loopholes," but sometimes they are necessary. When you create them, keep them small. If the SSA had used 75 instead of 95 percent, its standard would have been relatively worthless: the organization would have "succeeded" even when one of every four callers took 10 minutes to get through.

Another interesting option is to include information when you publish your standards on what the service costs. The Canadian federal government requires this. "Without relevant cost information, service users' expectations may be unrealistic and their preferences for service delivery inconsistent with what you can produce," the Treasury Board explains. "As taxpayers concerned about cost, they cannot modify their use of the service if they are unaware of service costs." To offer a concrete example, if social security recipients knew that it would cost the agency double what it spends on its 800-number service to meet the five-minute standard 100 percent of the time, they would probably be happier with the 95 percent rule. If they knew that dropping it to 90 percent would save 15 percent of the cost, they might even support that. (If you have a customer council, you can ask it to help you make such decisions.)

pp. 377–380

We would not suggest following Canada's example and making this a requirement, however. Since most organizations in the U.S. don't yet use activity-based costing, it would prevent or delay their adoption of service standards unnecessarily. It's a nice addition, but it's not a necessity.

Steps in Creating Service Standards

1. Create a plan and a timetable.
2. Define the critical success factors—the most important aspects of the service from the customer's point of view.
3. Consult your customers.

4. Analyze the survey data.
5. Draft three to five measurable standards—preferably with redress policies.
6. Review the draft standards with employees, to get their input.
7. If you need any policy changes to achieve the standards, pursue them.
8. Get feedback on the draft standards from your customers or compliers.
9. Finalize your standards (and, ideally, your redress policies), and give feedback to your employees and customers.
10. Measure your performance against the standards, and develop an improvement plan.
11. Publish your standards, and publicize them.
12. Measure performance regularly, and give rapid feedback to employees.
13. Make further service improvements that are necessary to reach your standards.
14. Review your standards every two years, because customer needs and other conditions will change.

1. Create a plan and a timetable.

To prepare your organization for service standards, there are a number of things you can do:

- Secure the commitment of top management and any elected officials whose authorization you will need.
- Pick a team or teams to produce your standards. Try to include managers, middle managers, frontline employees, and customers. You may need one team to lead the initiative, plus implementation teams dealing with different agencies or services.
- Figure out how you will consult with your customers and staff.
- Work out the time and cost that will be involved in creating and measuring service standards, and get commitments from the top to support both.
- Prepare a timetable to guide the process, so everyone knows what to expect.
- Define the services for which you want to produce standards. Remember to do this from the customer's perspective, not the organization's. You may need some standards that cross organizational (and even governmental) boundaries.
- Define the customers or compliers for each service, including both primary and secondary customers. (Remember, these may be different than the service's "users," particularly with compliance functions.) You may need different standards for different groups of customers and compliers.

pp. 274, 334–338

2. Define the critical success factors—the most important aspects of the service from the customer's point of view.

Use a variety of methods to figure out what is most important to your customers or compliers:

- Informal consultation—in waiting rooms, through customer councils, or through existing user and interest groups.
- Existing data on performance and complaints.
- Customer surveys or other market research already done.
- Examinations of similar organizations that have done this, to see what their critical success factors are.
- A walk through the system as a customer, to understand it from the customer's perspective.

The London borough of Bromley uses a "Quality Wheel" as a checklist so service teams won't miss any possible success factors. We offer a modified version of this excellent tool in Figure 9.1.

3. Consult your customers.

pp. 382–383

Now that you've done your homework, you're ready to ask good questions in a survey or focus group. Developing a good survey is not easy; the critical success factors you have defined will help you know what to ask. Professional expertise will help you make sure your sampling methods have credibility.

4. Analyze the survey data.

Sometimes the messages from customer surveys and focus groups are obvious; sometimes they are not. At the SSA, it took sophisticated analysis to reveal that timely service on the 800 number was a critical driver behind customer satisfaction for the entire agency. "We did regression analysis," says Toni Lenane, "and that's when it jumped out at us."

5. Draft three to five measurable standards—preferably with redress policies.

Armed with good data from customers, you're ready to draft standards. As we said earlier, involve staff and customers on your team. Don't draft too many standards; no service should have more standards than agency employees can easily remember. You want them focused on what is most important.

Greg Woods now runs the Education Department's Office of Student Financial Assistance, the federal government's first "performance-based organization." "If you want to create change in a large organization," he argues, "you have to have a handful—like three—simple objectives that everybody in the place understands."

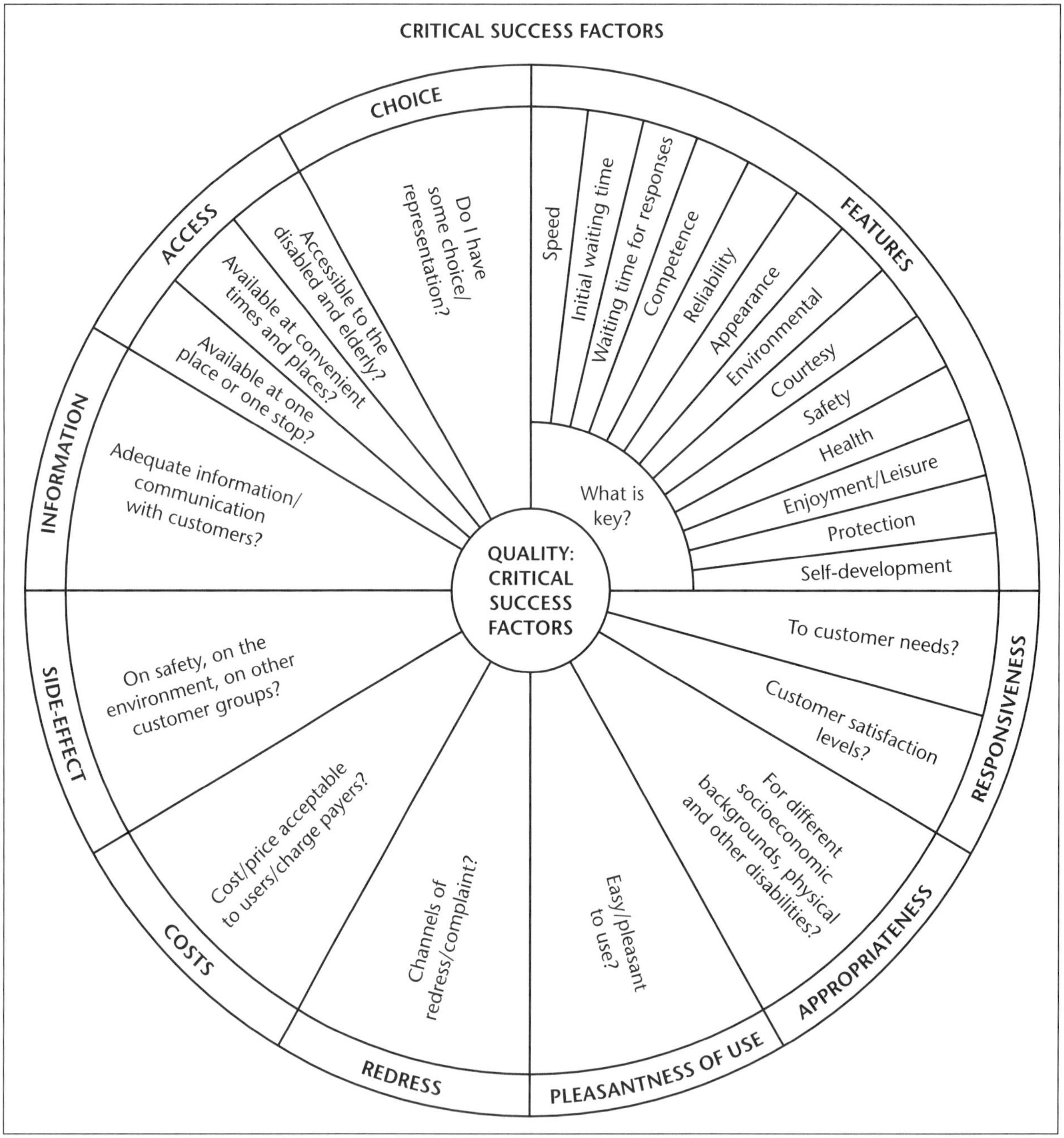

Figure 9.1. Quality Wheel

The postal service said "on-time delivery," and they measured it locally and nationally, and that drove everything. I think that's the power of customer service standards. Where the standard becomes the driver for the organization, you get dramatic change. The private sector example that I first fixed on was Federal Express—the idea that everybody in the place knew that you were supposed to get the package there by 10:30 A.M. The CEO's bonus was based on that. The entire management's bonus system was based on that, and profit, and employee satisfaction. What government doesn't have is this kind of single-mindedness about some kind of objective.

6. Review the draft standards with employees, to get their input.

Canada's Treasury Board secretariat has published a *Manager's Guide for Implementing Quality Services.* "There are no shortcuts," it warns. "The standards would not be acceptable if imposed from above or simply borrowed from elsewhere. The process itself is important, and the entire office needs to be involved."

There are many reasons to involve staff: to see if the draft standards are feasible and amend them if necessary; to learn what work process and other changes need to be made to reach them; to learn what new resources will be needed; to identify the training employees need to meet the standards; to identify other offices or units whose cooperation will be necessary to meet the standards; and most important, to secure the buy-in of all employees.

7. Pursue any policy changes needed to achieve the standards.

Sometimes you cannot provide what customers want without important changes in policy. A school district might need to change its student assignment process. A welfare office might need to change its appeals process. Policy changes like this virtually always require the approval of elected officials—or, at the least, top civil servants with policymaking jobs. If you run across policies that are in your way, do what you can to secure that approval. If you can't get it, ask for authority to run a pilot project to test the new approach.

8. Get feedback on the draft standards from your customers or compliers.

You need to see whether you've come up with standards that make sense to your customers or compliers. Is this what they care most about? Are the quality levels promised adequate? Have you missed anything important? You can use many methods for this step, from customer councils to surveys. But focus groups or councils are generally preferable to broad surveys, because they allow you to probe—to understand why one success factor is more important than another, to get recommendations for changes, and to explore ways to improve the standards.

9. Finalize your standards (and, ideally, your redress policies), and give feedback to your employees and customers.

With the input you have gathered from employees, policymakers, and customers, you can now rewrite your standards and finalize them. After you do so, tell the employees and customers you consulted what standards you have chosen and why. Employees who give you advice and then see it being ignored often become quite cynical. The same can be true of customers in councils or focus groups. They can't read your mind; employees won't know what customers told you about your draft standards, and vice versa. Neither will know what changes were rejected by policymakers. Once you explain these things, they will realize that your consultation was genuine, and they will understand and more likely embrace the final product.

10. Measure your performance against the standards, and develop an improvement plan.

If you haven't already done so, measure to see how close you are to meeting your standards. If you aren't close, it may be wise to focus on improvement before you announce your standards, or to set two-stage standards. Starting off with a dramatic failure in your customers' eyes can be motivational, but it is quite painful.

pp. 342–343

To improve, create teams to redesign processes; ask your employees for ideas; use TQM or business process reengineering if you think they will help; and figure out how new information technologies could boost your performance. Also begin training your staff.

11. Publish your standards, and publicize them.

As we said earlier, standards no one knows about are not worth much. Use every method you can imagine to educate your customers: signs in your offices, flyers in your waiting rooms, leaflets mailed with benefits, press releases and events, videos, newsletters, public service announcements on radio. Use your customer council to help; they will have more credibility with the press and public than management will. Get your union involved. Don't be passive about publicity.

12. Measure performance regularly, and give rapid feedback to employees.

Feedback on results should come monthly—or at a minimum, quarterly. "You have to make the data live and recent, so people will use it to manage," says John Kamensky, NPR deputy director. "Displaying it geographically is often important, too," because it helps people analyze it and understand how to improve their services.

The SSA gets data about its 95–5 standard daily, but data on accuracy comes in only every six months. It's produced by having quality assessment staff listen in on phone conversations, and to get enough sampling data to provide valid feedback takes six months. The agency could collect more data and report more often, but it would cost a lot more, says Larry Massanari, a regional commissioner. "It's important that you provide timely feedback, and we're not able to do that in the accuracy area," he says. "I think one of the lessons to be learned is you have to keep data in front of people. If you can't keep people in touch with the data, it's hard" to motivate them to improve.

13. Make further service improvements that are necessary to reach your standards.

If the standards are to be taken seriously by your customers, you've got to start meeting them pretty soon. The improvement process should never stop.

14. Review your standards every two years, because customer needs and other conditions will change.

You may be able to afford something now that you couldn't two years ago. The price of information technology may have plummeted. You may have new customers with slightly different needs. Or customers may have gotten so used to being served within five minutes that they want a tougher standard.

Service Standards: Do's and Don'ts

The general lessons about customer quality assurance presented earlier all apply to service standards. In addition, we offer a few more specific pointers:

pp. 332–346

Make specific, measurable commitments, not vague statements. The majority of standards we have seen are virtually worthless, because they are vague and unmeasurable. Candace Kane saw more than her share of the "We're going to be responsive to you" variety while at the NPR, she says. "You really want to get specific: 'We will resolve the problem within 24 hours.'"

Keep your standards short and to the point. British charters are often long documents that explain many things other than an organization's service standards, redress policies, and complaint systems. Many are 15-page brochures. We think this simply buries the important points, making it harder for the reader to understand just what the organization is committed to. We would prefer five-line signs in lobbies and waiting rooms. The point is to make specific commitments, not to explain everything the customer might want to know about the organization. You can use other documents for that.

The British have come at least partway toward this position; their review concluded that the charters "are often too long." Their new "how-to" guide says charters should be "simple, accessible, 'living' documents. . . . The key features of a charter are: a statement of the standards of service users can expect to receive; the arrangements for seeking a remedy should something go wrong; and brief information on the service provided (including contact numbers and addresses)." If the latter information is a paragraph or two, we agree.

The Canadians, whose documents we also find too long, seem to have learned this lesson as well. In *Service Standards: A Guide to the Initiative,* the Treasury Board Secretariat says "short, simple delivery targets will be more effective than long, convoluted ones."

Define precise terms for service commitments. Don't say "five days," say "five business days." Different interpretations of terms are inevitable when you create service standards with real, measurable commitments. When the Public Strategies Group (PSG) helped Indianapolis create service standards and redress policies, for instance, the Information Services Office created a standard about how long it would take new staff to get e-mail and Internet access. "The way they thought about it was, this became a process they could control once the employees' request for a connection made it to the Information Services in-box," says PSG's Laurie Ohmann.

> *What we learned was that the employees believed the process started as soon as they signed up to be an employee. "I start counting from today." Or at the least, "I start counting from the time I fill out the request form." The I.S. people only started counting when it got logged into their system, and the paper forms went through interoffice mail. So if they promised a two-day turnaround, they'd blown it before they ever got the form.*

Make your level of commitment very clear. Again, vagueness creeps in far too often. "We will do our best to . . ." is not going to reassure many customers. As the Canadian guide says, "'We guarantee' is better than 'We will' which is better than 'We aim to.'"

Don't use percentages in your standards, when you can avoid it. "Research shows that many people do not understand percentages," according to the British government's guide, *How to Draw Up a National Charter.* "So wherever possible you should avoid their use. For example, say 'nine out of ten' people in place of 90 percent."

Don't feel your standards have to be uniform for every unit that delivers a given service. It may be harder to meet a timeliness standard in a rural area, where people and packages have to travel long distances, than in an urban area. People may have to stand in line longer at post offices in New York City than at post offices in Montana, because lunchtime crowds in New York can be huge, no matter how many service windows you open. Let your standards vary if necessary.

Service Standards: Pitfalls to Avoid

Having too many standards. Everyone we have asked about this in our research has recommended no more than three to five standards.

Listening to your customers only at the front end. It's easy to forget that you need to listen to your customers up front, then again after you have draft standards to show them, and then again periodically to see if their needs have changed. "For me the biggest mistake in everything agencies did on customer service was not talking to their customers enough," says Candace Kane.

> *Most agencies did it as a linear process. We told them to "constantly ask your customers." What we didn't say was, "After this step, ask your customers; then do this step and ask your customers; then do this step and ask your customers." So they mostly just did it once.*

Creating expectations you can't fulfill. The last thing you want to do is to set yourself up for failure. Lorraine Chang has worked on customer service standards at Southern Pacific Railway, at the U.S. Department of Labor, and as a consultant with the Public Strategies Group. This is a classic pitfall you must avoid, she cautions. If you don't, "You discredit yourself with your customers, and then morale in the organization plummets, because you're beating yourself over the head constantly. You're widening the gap, creating more distrust."

Try not only to make sure your standards are attainable but also to help customers form realistic expectations. The private sector sometimes makes the mistake of creating expectations that are too high. The last time David Osborne bought a new car, the company he bought it from offered free coverage for all services—including oil changes—for 50,000 miles. That was impressive, but the company made one mistake. When Osborne asked how long their routine service visits and oil changes took, the salesman said "45 minutes to an hour." When it actually took 90 minutes to two hours, he was disappointed. The service was excellent—they even washed the car—but the company had created false expectations around time, which happened to be a critical success factor for this customer.

Creating perverse incentives that hurt customer satisfaction. This is perhaps the most important pitfall to avoid. "Watch out for how you set your standard up," warns the SSA's Janice Warden. "You've got to present a total picture of what the customer wants. We could have very well said 95 and five, without continuing to emphasize the courtesy and accuracy." The result could

pp. 323–330

have been teleservice representatives hanging up on customers before they were satisfied. As Warden says, "What you say is what you get."

You have to watch closely for any backfires, adds Larry Massanari. "You don't always know; only the customer begins to feel it." This is yet another reason to continue listening to the customer.

Ignoring elements of service that are critical to customers. This is a balancing act: you don't want too many measures, but you don't want to miss anything important, either. In the SSA, Massanari points out, there are three key pieces: the field offices, the benefits processing offices, and the 800 number. The agency's standards need to cover all three, which they do.

Ignoring contractors who are important parts of the supply chain. It is easy to forget to include suppliers who are critical to your performance. The SSA did, and it cost them dearly. When AT&T's 800 service crashed, it was a severe blow. "If you have a contractor involved," advises Warden, "you have to treat them as a full partner." Make them part of the team creating standards from the beginning and have them create standards for their service to you.

p. 329

RESOURCES ON SERVICE STANDARDS

Canadian Treasury Board Secretariat. *Quality & Affordable Service for Canadians: Establishing Service Standards in the Federal Government; Service Standards: A Guide to the Initiative;* and *A Guide to Costing Service Delivery for Service Standards.* Ottawa: Treasury Board of Canada Secretariat, 1996. Three useful Canadian guides, which are available for free on the Web at www.tbs-sct.gc.ca/pubpol_e.html (scroll down to "Quality Service") or on paper or diskette from the Distribution Centre: phone (613) 995–2855; fax (613) 996–0518. Available in French or English.

Erin Research Inc. *Citizens First: Summary Report and Full Report.* Ottawa: Citizen-Centred Service Network and Canadian Centre for Management Development, October 1998. Important survey research on citizens' expectations, priorities, and satisfaction with different services, including useful information about what they care about most. Available for free at www.ccmd-ccg.gc.ca/publica.publi.html (scroll down to "Service and Quality"). Phone: (613) 943 8370. Fax: (613) 995–0286. Other useful reports are available on the same web page.

National Performance Review. *Putting Customers First '97: Standards for Serving the American People.* Washington, D.C.: National Performance Review, October 1997. A summary of customer service standards and progress in the U.S. federal government, which includes learnings and links to all agencies' standards. Available for free at www.npr.gov/custserv/.

United Kingdom. Cabinet Office. *How to Draw Up a National Charter* and *How to Draw Up a Local Charter.* London: Cabinet Office, 1998. Superb nuts-and-bolts guides from the people who invented customer quality assurance in the public sector. Available for free at www.cabinet-office.gov.uk/servicefirst (click on "Best Practice," then "Best Practice Guides," then "Charters").

United Kingdom. Cabinet Office. *Service First: The New Charter Programme* and *The Citizen's Charter, A Consultation Exercise: the Government's Response.* London: Cabinet Office, 1998. In-depth reviews of the Citizen's Charter, which provide valuable lessons about what works and what doesn't. Available for free at www.cabinet-office.gov.uk/servicefirst (click on Index).

QUALITY GUARANTEES

***Quality guarantees* promise to give customers or compliers their money back or to redeliver services for free if the organization fails to meet its service standards or the customer or complier is not satisfied.**

A guarantee is the most powerful statement you can make to your customers. It also has enormous power to force your managers and employees to come up with whatever it takes to deliver. Think of the difference between Federal Express, which guarantees delivery by 10:30 A.M. the next day or your money back, and the U.S. Postal Service's express mail, which is not guaranteed and only gets there overnight two out of every three times. The former has grown rapidly for years and now controls 50 percent of the overnight business; the latter has slipped from 45 percent of the market in its early years to 6 percent.

Guarantees are common in the private sector, and they are being made more and more often in the public sector. As we said earlier, the Massachusetts DEP guarantees that it will make permit decisions on time or the fees are waived, and other states, counties, and cities have followed suit. The U.S. Census Bureau promises that if you're not happy with its products, you will get your money back.

Fox Valley Technical College, in Wisconsin, guarantees satisfaction to businesses that buy customized training from the college, or they get "the appropriate portion of the customized training redone at no additional charge." Other community colleges have created similar guarantees.

Several states and many high schools guarantee certain graduates with "certificates of employability." Typically, if an employer says a graduate has inadequate skills within the first year, the school provides free instruction to bring him or her up to par.

Sometimes new public programs use a guarantee to get over the credibility hump with their customers. In the late 1980s, the Michigan Commerce Department decided to offer a partial subsidy for 20–40 hours of general management consulting, from private consulting firms, to small businesses. It put together bulk contracts with consultants who would work for 50 percent of their normal fees, in return for a volume guarantee. More important, it offered small businesses an unconditional money back guarantee if they were not satisfied—and required the contractors to provide it! The purpose was to overcome the natural skepticism small business owners had about help from the government. Not one client asked for their money back. Customers rated its services an average of 4.5 on a 1–5 scale, with 5 being the highest rating.

pp. 174–182

Some programs use a guarantee to create a competitive advantage. When Minnesota's Department of Administration used internal enterprise management to remove the monopoly enjoyed by many of its internal support functions, the print shop, vehicle fleet, and data entry units all promised money back to other agencies if they were not satisfied. "In the printing area, it really put the focus on preventing rework, because rework became doubly expensive," says Babak Armajani, then deputy commissioner of the department.

> *In the fleet area, it had the impact of better preparation of the vehicles. Most of the dissatisfaction was from having a dirty vehicle. They actually published standards about the vehicle: that it would be clean, full of gas, everything would be in working order. They didn't have to give the money back very often—but enough that it became a major focus.*

Sometimes public leaders even negotiate guarantees with private contractors. When Indianapolis contracted with the British Airports Authority to manage its airport, the company guaranteed to lower costs for the airlines. It posted a $50 million irrevocable letter of credit to back up the guarantee.

Quality Guarantees: Do's and Don'ts

pp. 332–346, 355–358

Most of the general lessons on customer quality assurance and more specific guidance about service standards outlined earlier apply to guarantees as well. In addition, we suggest a few more pointers.

Publish a clear statement of what level of service is guaranteed. As with service standards, guarantees should be specific, to the point, and precisely defined.

Don't make guarantees hard to collect on. People are skeptical of guarantees. If they sense that they will have to jump through hoops to collect on the guarantee, you may simply increase their cynicism about government.

When you publish your guarantee, include a clear description of what the customer must do to collect on it.

Make sure your guarantee is reasonable and doable. One of the oft-cited stories about this tool concerns Domino's Pizza, which used a money-back guarantee to build one of the largest pizza chains in the world. In the 1970s, it guaranteed that if you ordered a pizza by phone, it would be there in 30 minutes. If not, it was free. Some of Domino's drivers were known to speed to meet the deadline, and the company was held liable for some of their accidents. So it kept the standard but changed to a redress approach: if the pizza is late, you get a $3.00 discount.

If you can't quite pull off a guarantee but still want to, announce that it will go into effect in 12 months. This will create the urgency in your organization to do what it takes to make the guarantee workable.

Empower your employees to make guarantees work and to make refund decisions on the spot. We've already explained why you need to empower frontline employees to make customer quality assurance work. In addition, you need to make sure they can make refund decisions. There is no better way to undercut the impression a guarantee makes than by saying to a customer who expects a refund, "I'm sorry, I'll have to check with my supervisor. We'll get back to you."

p. 342

In compliance activities, be careful that guarantees don't drive staff to cut corners in ways that undercut the outcomes you want. When the Massachusetts DEP did this, it brought compliers and customers—businesses and environmentalists—together to design its guarantee. This is a good idea, because it creates a check on any tendencies to go too far. The department also measured the percentage of permits denied, which remained at about 10 percent after the turnaround standard and money-back guarantee.

p. 335

If customer behavior is necessary to produce the outcome, specify what the customer must do to qualify for the guarantee. Some schools provide guarantees that require specific behavior by students and parents: signing weekly progress reports, missing no more than a set number of days of school and homework assignments, and the like. Some philanthropists and state governments have also used this approach, guaranteeing groups of low-income students that if they maintain at least a B average, stay in school, and stay away from drugs, their college tuition will be paid.

RESOURCE ON QUALITY GUARANTEES

Christopher Hart. *Extraordinary Guarantees.* New York: Amacom, 1993. A useful, readable book on private sector quality guarantees.

REDRESS

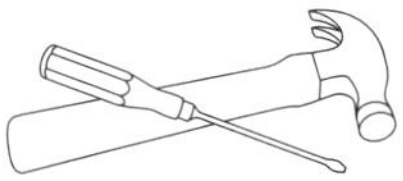

***Redress* gives customers or compliers some form of compensation—financial or otherwise—when an organization fails to meet its service standards.**

As David Osborne was preparing to write this chapter, he had an experience that brought home to him the importance of redress. He was returning from Bogota, Colombia, to Massachusetts, changing airlines in Miami. When he arrived at the American Airlines counter in Miami, they had no record of his electronic ticket. The ticket agent searched the computerized database for a few minutes and discovered the problem: for some reason, two reservations had been made, and the agent who had ticketed the first leg, from Boston to Miami, had inadvertently used the wrong one. When no one used the second reservation, the computer system automatically removed it.

The only problem was that now the plane was oversold. Osborne, who was very tired, would have to stand by for a coach seat. Frustrated, he contacted his travel agent and discovered that there was one first-class seat that had been reserved but not yet paid for. "Aha!" Osborne thought. "My ticket was purchased a week ago; I should get that seat."

Unfortunately, American's gate agents didn't see it that way. When he protested, they told him to sit down—that they would take care of him. Despite some effort, he could get no more commitment from them than this. Finally, at the last minute, he got a coach seat on the full airplane. During this entire process, which took about two hours, not one American employee apologized, much less offered to make up for the error. Osborne asked several American employees how to file a complaint, but no one knew—or cared.

You can imagine Osborne's feelings for American Airlines. Now imagine if the company had a redress policy. Any customer who got bumped from their seat or flight through the fault of the airline might get a discount on their ticket, for instance—either for that trip or the next one, whichever they preferred. This would not only mollify the passenger, it would give airline management an incentive to minimize how often such mistakes happened. And it would give employees a gracious way to apologize and make it up to the passenger, rather than simply acting defensive.

The Many Benefits of Redress Policies

Redress policies are similar to guarantees, but they offer a broader array of compensation to customers. While guarantees offer your money back or free redelivery of the services, redress policies can offer virtually anything as compensation, financial or otherwise. Typically, they are triggered automatically when an organization misses a service standard, while guarantees can be triggered that way or simply by customer dissatisfaction.

As the preceding example illustrates, redress policies have multiple benefits. First, they create satisfied customers. Indeed, market research suggests that the most loyal customers in the private sector are not those who have enjoyed years of good service but those who have experienced an incident of poor service that the company went to great lengths to put right.

Second, redress policies create incentives for service providers to get it right the first time. If they don't, they lose something valuable, like time or money.

pp. 345–346

Third, redress saves providers money, because it encourages organizations to minimize the need for rework.

Fourth, redress policies make life much easier for employees, who can now graciously apologize and do something nice to make it up to the customer, rather than stand there and take the heat.

Fifth, redress policies help organizations recover from problems even when customers don't complain. Twenty years ago, careful research in the U.S. private sector found that only 1 out of 27 people who experienced problems with service took the time to complain. Recent research in the U.K. suggests that the number may be larger in the public sector (it was 49 percent in the British survey, though it varied widely from service to service). But even in the U.K., the majority who had problems said they didn't complain. The best complaint system in the world won't help them—but automatic redress when organizations miss their standards will, because it is triggered even when people don't complain.

pp. 323–330

Finally, redress policies give organizations a constructive way to deal with the fact that they cannot always be perfect. Hitting a challenging set of service standards 100 percent of the time is impossible. As we saw with the SSA, the cost of that last 5 percent is sometimes too steep. That means some customers will be disappointed. It is far better to use redress to make it up to them than to either break the bank trying to achieve the impossible or to let 5 percent of your customers go away angry. If you do the latter, the consequences are clear: whereas the average satisfied customer tells three people about their experience, market research indicates, the average dissatisfied customer tells *nine.*

In the public sector, not every organization is in competition to attract customers. "But we're in competition for public support," Peter Hutchinson points out, "and we're losing. So ultimately, all of this is about winning the competition for public support.

> *If you want to win the competition, you have to satisfy as many people as you possibly can, and alienate as few as possible. And redress is the way you deal with the second half of the equation. Even if you're totally committed to customer service, if you ignore redress, mathematics says*

you will lose. Redress is about keeping dissatisfied customers from telling those other nine people. It's not about punishment. It's just being smart, when you can't do it right the first time. And sometimes you can't; sometimes the price of perfection is too high.

Guarantees and redress are two of the most powerful tools you have to win the competition for public support. They make service standards meaningful to customers; they give them *teeth*. Think about your own experience. Does the post office's 5-minute standard mean anything to you if you wait 10 minutes and nothing happens? No. But what if you were to get a free book of 10 stamps (worth $3.30) if you waited longer than 5 minutes? Would that convince you that the post office was serious about its service commitments?

Financial Redress

It is often hard to convince managers and budget offices to use financial redress, because they fear potential financial loss. The U.K., which pioneered the practice in the early 1990s, has experienced this problem. In 1995, the Citizen's Charter Complaints Task Force, a high-powered group drawn from both the public and private sectors, found that "managers in local offices of central Government service are cautious about offering financial compensation. The perception that the Treasury holds the purse-strings is strong." They recommended that financial redress always be included in an organization's menu of redress options.

We feel that in certain circumstances payment of financial compensation is money well spent. . . . Financial redress should be seen positively as a tangible recognition of a user's right to reasonable levels of service, providing organisations with an incentive to get things right in the future. We believe it has a powerful symbolic importance in those exceptional cases where users seek it and it is the appropriate response.

Unfortunately, the Labor Government appears to be backing away from financial redress. Virtually the only organizations forced to use it, other than the postal service and the London Underground, are privatized monopolies: the rail operators, the electric utilities, the water companies, and British Gas.

The rail companies offer a good example of the practice. The government requires them to have punctuality and reliability standards, among others. A typical set would promise, for example, that 90 percent of trains would arrive within 10 minutes of the scheduled time and 99 percent of scheduled trains would run. When a commuter line misses one of its targets over a 12-month period, riders typically get a 5 percent discount on their next season ticket.

When a line misses both targets, the discount is normally 10 percent. If any train is delayed for more than an hour, passengers get vouchers worth at least 20 percent of the price of that trip.

There are a few other examples in the U.K. In the Glasgow passport office, for example, frontline staff can offer up to £15 (about $25) to pay for a replacement set of photographs if the office loses them. Claims up to £100 pounds can be approved on the spot by the customer services manager.

In the U.S., financial redress is even more rare. When it ran the Minneapolis schools, the Public Strategies Group used it. If a school bus was late, for example, the school received a credit of $100 toward school buses for a field trip. In 1999, Cal State University at Long Beach began putting one-year "warranties" on its 700 credentialed teacher's college graduates every year. The college will send an education professor to a school district for one-on-one advice during the first year on the job if the school requests it because the teacher is having problems. The state of Georgia offers a similar plan.

The Academy of the Pacific Rim, a charter school in Boston, will turn over to another school of the parent's choosing the equivalent of the funds it would receive from the state for a child's education (roughly $7,500 in 1998) if the student fails a state standardized test in 10th or 11th grade. To qualify, parents must sign and return weekly reports on their child's progress, missing no more than three in one year, and students must miss no more than four assignments per subject per year. If teachers recommend tutoring sessions, students must attend. The school has set up a fund using donations from its founders and foundations to make the payments.

Nonfinancial Redress

Redress does not have to be financial to be effective, however. A refund, discount, voucher, or other payment not only makes a strong statement to the customer that the organization cares about satisfying them, it also creates powerful incentives for the organization to meet its standards. It's hard to top. But most people aren't looking for money when they complain about poor service.

There are an infinite number of ways to provide redress. You can make it fun: hand out chocolate, or throw a pizza party if the customers are an office or team. The Information Services Office in Indianapolis gave people things like coffee mugs and mouse pads, with an added touch: "We'll deliver it personally and tell you why we were late." Sometimes an apology is enough—or at least a very good start. For some reason, people and organizations in the public sector find it difficult to issue apologies.

Lorraine Chang urges organizations to look for redress options "that surprise and delight the customer. The best thing to do is to have a little twist of the unexpected. To have somebody show up at the door from a government agency to apologize and explain could be enough of a surprise to make it really meaningful and powerful, as opposed to getting a letter in the mail, which they might just toss."

You can even ask the complainant what form of redress he or she feels would be appropriate. Some organizations surveyed by the Citizen's Charter Complaints Task Force supported this idea—"indeed, some consider it essential, citing evidence that it puts the relationship with the service user on a positive footing, and ensures greater satisfaction with the outcome."

The task force recommended a menu of redress options, which would at minimum include:

- *An apology.*
- *An explanation.*
- *Assurance that the same thing will not happen again, backed up by action and monitoring.*
- *Action taken to put things right.*
- *Financial compensation.*

Redress Policies: Do's and Don'ts

pp. 332–346, 355–359

pp. 349–355

The general lessons about customer quality assurance all apply to redress policies, as do the "do's and don'ts" and "pitfalls to avoid" presented for service standards and guarantees. In addition, we recommend that you develop redress policies and service standards in tandem, using the steps outlined earlier. We would add just a few more pointers specifically about redress:

Make clear to your customers or compliers exactly what forms of redress are available. Just as you need to widely publicize your standards, you need to do the same for your redress policies. This is a wonderful investment: the more customers see that you offer meaningful redress, the more they will respect your organization.

Make sure the redress will be meaningful to your customers—by surveying them. If customers see your redress policy as mere window dressing, it will only feed their cynicism. If they see it as self-serving for your organization, you will have lost them. Many private companies send a voucher or discount coupon to people who have complained, for instance. But some customers who are angry enough to complain want nothing to do with the company. The last thing they want to do is use it again! So they react to the discount with understandable disdain.

Give your customers or compliers a choice of what form of redress they want, when possible. The same thing is not meaningful to every customer. When an airline bumps a passenger, for example, some are very happy to take a later flight in return for a free round-trip ticket anywhere in the country. For others, who may be traveling to events they cannot afford to miss, such an offer is unacceptable. Customer choice is a good idea even in much less dramatic situations. When David Osborne explained his idea of giving 10 free stamps to postal customers who waited in line more than five minutes, for example, his youngest daughter said, "I'd rather have 10 free lollipops." And why not?

Don't give the customer's anger time to fester; hand out your redress on the spot. When you complain, if a human being listens, acknowledges your complaint, apologizes, and presents you with redress on the spot, your anger usually dissolves. You become, if not a satisfied customer, at least a mollified customer. You leave with at least some respect for the provider. If, however, it takes three weeks for you to receive a note of apology and a discount coupon, it may only feed your anger. In the meantime, of course, you've probably told nine people about your bad experience.

Empower your frontline staff to offer redress, and give them clear guidelines and training. If you're going to hand out redress on the spot, your frontline employees have to be able to do it. (If for some reason this simply won't work, make sure each office has a customer service person who can immediately take the complaint and deliver redress.) In the Ritz-Carlton hotel chain, frontline employees are authorized to spend up to $2,000 per incident to put things right for customers. Based on experience in both the public and private sectors, the Citizen's Charter Complaints Task Force recommended "that the discretion to resolve complaints, offering immediate redress as appropriate, should be delegated as far as possible down the line."

This requires clear guidance for employees, including examples of how to respond when different things happen and which form of redress to use in which circumstances. It also requires training, with lots of role playing.

Use forms of redress that connect directly to your mission and the outcomes you want to produce for customers, if possible. A good example is the redress policy for British rail operators. The mission and desired outcomes are clear: get people there on time, every time. The central form of redress flows directly from that commitment: if your train is late, you get a discount.

pp. 364–365

Another good example is the redress policy for late school buses in Minneapolis. If bus operators harm the education process by delivering students late to school, they make it up by donating $100 in services that will help the education process. Sometimes people "just think about punishment, and we're going to hold them accountable in a hard-edged way," says Peter Hutchinson, who invented the late bus policy. "But the key to making these things successful is connecting the supplier and the redress to the outcome you're trying to produce. Then you get a powerful agreement that everybody understands and can get enthusiastic about."

p. 365

Follow up with customers and compliers to ensure that they are satisfied with the redress they received. A follow-up phone call will surprise and impress most customers. More important, if they are not satisfied, it will give you a second chance to put things right and win them back.

RESOURCE ON REDRESS POLICIES

The Citizen's Charter Complaints Task Force. *Putting Things Right.* London: Her Majesty's Stationery Office, June 1995. Though this publication only has a few pages on redress, they are excellent. See p. 377 for more information.

COMPLAINT SYSTEMS

***Complaint Systems* track and analyze complaints, ensure prompt responses, help organizations learn from complaints to improve their services, and hold them accountable for doing so.**

In their book *A Complaint Is a Gift,* Janelle Barlow and Claus Møller call complaints "the biggest bargain in market research." They tell a fascinating story about the complaints system installed by British Airways a few years after it was privatized:

> *First, [CEO Colin] Marshall installed video booths at Heathrow [airport] so that upset customers could go immediately to a video booth and sound off to Marshall himself.*
>
> *Then, to the tune of $6.7 million, BA introduced a computer system to help analyze customer preferences with the aim of keeping customers for life. The system is affectionately called Caress. . . . Before Caress, BA literally had mountains of complaint-related papers. Now they are quickly scanned into the computer, along with any relevant travel documents: tickets, baggage receipts, and boarding passes. . . .*
>
> *Caress makes suggestions as to appropriate compensation for each category of complaints, but customer relations executives can override the system if they feel something different is warranted. It used to take BA about a month to respond to complaints. Now, 80 percent of the time, BA handles complaints in only three days! BA customer surveys show an increase in satisfaction from 40 percent to 65 percent. And while satisfaction has increased, compensation given to upset passengers has actually decreased.*
>
> *Caress is also able to categorize the common complaints BA receives. Over half of them deal with seat allocation, food quality, denial of board-*

> *ing, smoking/nonsmoking conflicts, seat comfort, ticketing, delays, baggage handling, disruption of service . . . and check-in services. Now BA is attempting to proactively address these aspects of its service.*

In 1991, the Citizen's Charter required all public organizations in the U.K., at all levels of government, to create complaint systems. None that we know of rival that of British Airways. But many have made a difference. In a late 1998 survey of 5,000 people, 67 percent said public services were better at listening to complaints than they had been a few years before—up from 43 percent in 1995.

Complaint systems have a number of benefits:

They identify areas that need improvement. "Complaints should be viewed in a positive way, for each one is an opportunity to correct a problem and eliminate it forever," says Stanley Spanbauer, former president of Fox Valley Technical College. Customer surveys won't always pinpoint problems for you, because your most dissatisfied customers will have already quit using your services. And broad citizen surveys don't usually uncover the level of detail that complaints do. Complaints can tell you about frontline employees who treat customers poorly, bad handoffs between units, misguided policies, perverse incentives, even overly bureaucratic administrative systems.

"In many instances," say Barlow and Møller, "the information a company obtains through customer complaints is impossible to get through any other means."

They give you a second chance to satisfy your customers. If you respond to a complaint by solving the problem, using redress to make it up to the customer, or both, a good complaints system gives you a second chance to create a loyal customer, salvage your reputation, and halt the spread of bad reports about your service.

They support your standards and redress programs. If you encourage people to complain and make it easy for them to do so, you will have more opportunities to find out where you are failing, to offer redress, and to win back dissatisfied customers.

They remove some of the public's feeling that no one in government cares or listens to them. This perception is widespread; by aggressively courting complaints and acting on them, public institutions can overcome it.

Using Complaint Systems to Force Improvement

Some complaint systems are only a means of getting information from customers. But good ones also include action to remedy problems and rewards for doing so. Reinventors create performance targets for how complaints are to be handled: how satisfied the customer is, whether the underlying problem has been addressed, and how long it takes to acknowledge the complaint, investigate it, and resolve it. (They don't include performance measures tied to the volume of complaints, because they don't want to create any incentives to minimize the number of complaints.) In these ways, reinventors use complaint systems to build constant pressure to improve service.

Sunnyvale offers a good example. Its Parks and Recreation Department uses a computer program to track how many complaints come in and what is done to resolve them. One of the organization's performance targets is to resolve 90 percent of complaints to the customer's satisfaction. "We log the concern and give it to the best person to resolve," explains director Robert Walker. After that employee takes action,

> *We send it back to the person and say, "This is what we thought your concern was," and tell them what we did. [Then we] ask them: One, "Did we get your concern right?" Two, "Did we resolve it?" Three, "Did we do it in a courteous manner?"*
>
> *We get a lot of response to that. A lot of people say: "This is why I moved to Sunnyvale. I can't believe that a government agency would respond so quickly." We read them at meetings, use them to boost morale.*
>
> *Our goal is only 90 percent, so we have an acknowledgment from the city council that it's okay that we don't resolve all of them. Because sometimes they are just squeaky wheels that complain about everything. Or sometimes you can't figure out how to resolve it.*
>
> *In most systems, all the city manager and council would hear are the complaints; now we've got a process that gives us lots of positive feedback we can pass on, and numbers that show we've got positive resolution to 90 percent of complaints. It gives the manager and city council confidence in us.*

As Sunnyvale's experience demonstrates, complaint systems should not be isolated from performance management systems. Targets and measures related to complaint resolution should be built right into your system, and people should be rewarded for doing a good job with them. You should also use what you learn from customer complaints to set and adjust your service standards, guarantees, and redress policies—as well as the rest of your performance measures.

To make sure these systems are integrated, advises the Citizen's Charter Complaints Task Force:

- Build complaint handling into your strategic and business plans.
- Have top management and your policy board regularly review information about complaints.
- Cover information about complaints in your annual reports.
- And make complaint handling a factor in performance bonus policies.

Steps in Creating a Complaints System

1. Secure the commitment of top management, make preparations, and create a plan.

Create a team, preferably from all levels of the organization and including customers, and pick a team leader. Do a staff survey to understand current attitudes toward complaints. Use existing or new customer surveys to assess how customers view service and complaint handling. Develop a plan and timetable, and communicate it to the entire organization.

CHARACTERISTICS OF EFFECTIVE COMPLAINT SYSTEMS

An effective complaint management system should be:

- Easily accessible to customers.
- Well publicized.
- Easy to use.
- Quick to resolve complaints.
- Informative, reporting progress to people on their complaints.
- Fair, offering full and impartial investigations.
- Respectful of customers' and compliers' desires for confidentiality.
- Effective at solving problems.
- Able to provide appropriate redress.
- Used to provide information to management so services can be improved.

This list is adapted from the U.K.'s *Good Practice Guide* and Canada's *Effective Complaint Management.*

p. 377

2. *Draft a complaints policy.*

The employee-customer team should do a first draft that includes:

- Where, how, and when people can complain.
- Which complaints will be handled at the front line, which by higher-level management, which by an independent ombudsman, and which should be referred to policymaking officials, auditors, or investigators.
- A menu of redress options, and specific guidance about what authority employees have to use them.
- A policy on when follow-up calls should be made to see if the complainant is satisfied with the response.
- A policy on when to cut off response to "continual and vexatious complainants," as the British call them.
- Standards defining how many days it should take for each of these steps: to acknowledge a complaint, investigate it, provide a response, and conduct any necessary further investigation.

3. *Consult with customers and employers on the draft policy before finalizing it.*

pp. 351–352

As with service standards, consultation is important in developing complaints policies, to make sure you are delivering what customers want and what employees can actually deliver.

4. *Assign responsibility for monitoring and overseeing the complaints system.*

You need a team, unit, or individual in charge of making sure the system works as it should. They should operate or monitor the recording system, produce regular reports on the frequency and nature of complaints, identify problem areas, make sure improvements are made and measured, and evaluate the system through follow-up surveys and other methods.

5. *Develop a recording and tracking system to capture complaints and responses.*

The system should allow recording of all complaints, all communications with complainants, and all actions taken, and it should highlight areas where services appear to have the most problems, so the oversight group can intervene. Automate this process, so staff find it easy to use. And don't make it so complex that they find it a burden.

6. Create procedures for review of complaints when complainants are not satisfied with the response.

A fast, internal review should "provide a genuinely fresh look by a senior officer at a higher level in the organisation," according to the British guide *Putting Things Right.* If the internal review does not lead to resolution, the complainant should be able to appeal to an independent ombudsman. "A common theme running through our research focus groups was the lack of confidence complainants have that their problem will be taken seriously by the organisation to whom they are complaining," reports the Citizen's Charter Complaints Task Force in *Putting Things Right.*

> *Many people are concerned that there should be a "special body" or an "independent person" who could investigate complaints impartially. . . . As Fife Health Council put it to us, "Suspicions are alleviated when complainants are encouraged to seek the advice of an independent third party. It demonstrates a more open approach."*

The opportunities for review should be clearly spelled out in information given to customers, which should include contact names and phone numbers.

7. Train staff to use the system.

All staff need to know the complaints policy and what they should do when a customer complains to them. Training should not simply be about the technical side, however. As Barlow and Møller put it, you also need to "train your staff to view complaints as gifts. . . . The entire organization has to buy into the idea that effective complaint handling is the mechanism to keep dissatisfied customers from walking away." This means many employees will have to change their attitudes.

8. Develop a communications strategy to make sure all customers know how to complain.

There are myriad ways to do this. The British *Good Practice Guide* lists these options: information sheets handed out at the first contact with the customer, information sent with regular mailings, leaflets and posters, newsletters and booklets, the media, explanations and toll-free numbers in telephone directories, help desks, complaint cards that can be handed or mailed in, and signs with logos and phone numbers.

9. Institutionalize regular reports by the oversight body to senior managers, policymakers, and customers.

At a minimum, the *Good Practice Guide* counsels, reports should include the following information:

- The volume of complaints, broken down by categories.
- Performance against published standards for acknowledgment, investigation, response, and review of complaints, with comparisons to previous periods to show progress or the lack thereof.
- Analysis of the complaints, to explain contexts, highlight problem areas, and suggest which complaints are most likely to recur.
- And proposals for changes that will solve problems and keep complaints from recurring.

10. Evaluate your system, primarily by asking your customers what they think of it.

Is it easy for customers to complain? Is the process free of hassles? What percentage of the time does it lead to customer satisfaction? Use surveys, focus groups, customer panels, and other methods. Test your system by secretly filing complaints, as if you were a customer. Evaluating your system is critical. In its research in the U.K., the Citizen's Charter Complaints Task Force found that "The organisation's confidence in its complaints system and the actual perception and experience of users who complain are often at odds."

Customer Complaint Systems: Do's and Don'ts

Make it easy to complain. In most systems, people find it difficult to complain. Even after seven years of effort to create effective complaints systems in the U.K., 85 percent of citizens surveyed in 1998 agreed that "it takes a lot of determination to get something done about a complaint." You need aggressive efforts to overcome this attitude. Encourage complaints in person, by phone (toll free), by letter, by e-mail, and through your Web site. But go further: designate someone within your organization to help people make complaints and to make sure they are properly dealt with. That person should have authority to rectify any failure in complaints handling, and you should publicize his or her role to all customers or compliers. The London borough of Bexley calls these people "complainants' friends." Their job is to ensure that complaints are resolved.

Resolve complaints quickly and fairly, and keep complainants informed. When the Citizen's Charter Complaints Task Force surveyed 685 citizens about the most important factors in handling a complaint, the top priorities were "speed of response," "being kept informed," and "fair investigation."

Make extra efforts to help those who are afraid to complain. In the public sector, where people often have to deal with monopolies, many are afraid to complain for fear of retribution. Parents are afraid that principals, teachers, or coaches will take it out on their kids if they complain. Prisoners fear guards will make it tougher on them. Hospital patients and elderly residents in public housing fear worse treatment if they complain. Even in a good-government city like Sunnyvale, fear of retribution is not uncommon. When city leaders began interviewing businesspeople about permitting, remembers Bill Powers, director of community development, "One of the things we heard was people were afraid to complain, because you're complaining to the regulator who can deny you things. We didn't think we conducted business that way, but their perception was that the fear was pretty real."

There are a number of ways to combat fear of retribution. You can provide a confidential complaint channel. You can set up an independent ombudsman, with the power to intervene if the complainant later alleges retribution. You can survey people who have lodged complaints to ask if there was any retribution, then act on what they tell you. And you can identify groups of customers or compliers who appear vulnerable and rarely complain, then deliberately ask if they have complaints and reassure them that there will be no retribution. The Citizen's Charter Complaints Task Force offers a good example:

> *Lothian Regional Council's Social Work Department monitors complaints about its services. It realised that it was getting little in the way of complaints from elderly people in residential homes. The Department recognised that these users were of a generation which is, on the whole, less likely to complain but that their particular situation, being on the receiving end of care, might inhibit them further. To counteract this, the Director and other senior staff make regular personal visits to the homes to encourage users to give feedback, including complaints, on how the service works and to reassure them that they will not suffer as a result of complaining.*

Give employees the tools and authority they need to resolve complaints. "The most successful complaints handling is in services where the receiver of the complaint assumed complete ownership of it, only relinquishing this ownership when the complainant was satisfied or it became clear that the complaint should be referred to the next stage of review," the Citizen's Charter Complaints Task Force learned from its research. "We found staff that had been given such discretion were highly motivated."

To back up frontline staff, assign someone in each office to be customer service manager, make them available for immediate consultations, and give them authority to make most decisions when frontline staff are not sure what to do. Barlow and Møller also urge organizations to empower frontline staff to deviate from "marginal policies" when necessary. But, they caution, you have to make it clear which policies are inviolable.

Staff need to understand how far policies can be pushed, when exceptions simply cannot be made even if management is involved, and why the policies are there in the first place. Again, managers can create role-play situations to help coach staff as to appropriate behavior. Because front-line staff have the most direct contact with customers, and they generally know first where problems start to develop, then at staff meetings, they should be encouraged to discuss policies that need changing.

When employees do something creative but wrong to rectify a complaint, they add, never punish them. Praise their ingenuity and explain why they should make a different decision in the future.

Create communication channels that take complaints quickly and accurately from the front line to upper management. If frontline staff are not encouraged to pass information to managers, Barlow and Møller warn, complaints that cannot be handled on the front line may never make it beyond. "In fact, without open communication between front-line personnel and managers, service quality is very difficult to achieve." Forms are seldom adequate to convey the reality behind complaints, they add. "We recommend as much face-to-face reporting as possible to get some sense of customer anger or having front-line staff judge on a scale of one to five how angry the customers were." Regular meetings to discuss complaints are also useful.

Create a channel to send complaints about policy to the appropriate body. Some complainants take umbrage with policies. If a parent complains to a school principal that her daughter didn't get assigned to her first choice of school, the principal can't fix that problem with better service. Such complaints need to go straight to the superintendent and school board, who control the assignment process. If they get enough complaints about a policy, then they should review it.

Don't blame the targets of complaints. If you immediately blame employees who are the targets of complaints, you will create a culture that tries to suppress complaints. "Fix the system without rushing to blame staff," advise Barlow and Møller. "*Punish your processes, not your people.* Staff members will be more likely to pass along complaints to management if they know this is the company's approach to complaints." If you create a genuine customer quality assurance system of the kind we have been describing, staff who are the object of complaints will understand that their behavior should change. You can work with the few who don't—and if they ultimately refuse to change, let them go.

Create many ways to learn from complaints. Create a recording system, have your oversight team analyze patterns and identify problems, assign teams to solve those problems, establish regular times to discuss complaints with employees, invite customers in for focus groups, and help people learn from success stories.

RESOURCES ON COMPLAINT SYSTEMS

The Citizen's Charter Complaints Task Force. *Good Practice Guide.* London: Her Majesty's Stationery Office, June 1995. An excellent, nuts-and-bolts how-to guide. Available from the Service First Publications Line: 0345 22 32 42.

The Citizen's Charter Complaints Task Force. *Putting Things Right: Main Report.* London: Her Majesty's Stationery Office, June 1995. Another excellent source of information, somewhat duplicative of the first but with more background on research. Available from the Service First Publications Line: 0345 22 32 42.

Service First Team. *How to Deal with Complaints.* London: U.K. Cabinet Office, 1998. A more recent version of the *Good Practice Guide,* available for free on the Web at www.servicefirst.gov.uk/index/publications.htm (click on "Complaints") or from the Service First Publications Line: 0345 22 32 42.

Janelle Barlow and Claus Møller. *A Complaint Is a Gift.* San Francisco: Berrett-Koehler, 1996. An extremely useful book; though focused entirely on the private sector, it offers everything you need to know about complaint systems, from a reinventor's perspective.

Innovative and Quality Service Group. *Effective Complaint Management.* Ottawa: Treasury Board of Canada Secretariat, 1996. Though somewhat derivative of the British material, this guide is also useful. Available for free on the Web at www.tbs-sct.gc.ca/pubpol_e.html (click on "Q," then "Quality Service Guides"). Phone: (613) 995–2855. Fax: (613) 996–0518.

"Handling Citizen Complaints and Requests." In Harry P. Hatry, Louis H. Blair, Donald M. Fisk, John M Greiner, John R. Hall, Jr., and Philip S. Schaenman. *How Effective Are Your Community Services? Procedures for Measuring Their Quality.* Washington, D.C.: Urban Institute and International City and County Management Association, 1992. A useful chapter on measuring and handling complaints in local government.

CUSTOMER COUNCILS AND BOARDS

***Customer Councils and Boards* are small groups of customers who meet regularly with an organization's leadership and have some power to hold it accountable for performance.**

In the mid-1980s, reinventors in the Minnesota Department of Administration were pushing hard to improve a department known throughout state government by its initials: DOA. They had figured out how to use competition to

pp. 174–182

drive improvement, by taking away the monopolies many support functions enjoyed and making them earn their revenues from their customers. But what about functions that needed to remain monopolies, either because they were more efficient that way or because they had to offer standardized services to everyone? These included the mainframe computer unit, the statewide data and voice communications network, and the state records center, among others.

Departmental leaders decided to make the monopolies enterprise funds as well, but to call them "utilities" (as in the private sector) and regulate them to make sure they didn't abuse their monopoly power. The regulatory instrument they invented was a customer council for each utility, made up of deputy or assistant commissioners from the departments and large agencies that were their principal customers. As a department memo laying out the strategy explained, the councils had the power to advise the commissioners of finance and administration on "the types of services to be provided by the utility, service levels required, investment proposals, and rate proposals" (prices).

Babak Armajani, then deputy commissioner of administration, explains what happened when they gave customers the power to help set the utilities' prices and decide when they could invest in new technologies:

> *The telecommunications utility's council consisted of nine people. The state Department of Natural Resources (DNR) came in and said, "We want a telecommunications line that would allow for voice and data transmissions to Togo"—a tiny town in far northwest Minnesota, almost to Canada—"where we have a research facility."*
>
> *The utility costed it out and said, "Here's how it would change our rates." At that point, everybody turned to the utility manager and said, "What are you going to do about this?" He turned to them and said, "What are you going to do about it? You set the rates." So they scheduled a meeting. The big customers of the telecommunications network said to the DNR, "We don't like the idea of paying for your line to Togo, we're trying to keep our costs down." So there was a debate. And in the end, what happened was a deal was worked out, and DNR agreed to pay a lot of the cost, and the utility agreed to pay the rest. But it was negotiated between the customers, in the true fashion of a cooperative. The Finance Department and the utility really didn't get involved in deciding, yes, there should be a line to Togo, or no there shouldn't.*

This happened more and more, around different issues. "You got much tougher discussions, much stronger oversight than would have been provided otherwise," says Armajani, "because the customers knew more about this stuff and had a strong interest in keeping the rates low."

Minnesota was inventing a new tool: a customer council. Creating a board or council made up of customers—and giving it some real authority—can be a powerful way to make public organizations more accountable to their customers. It also helps ensure that improvement strategies will outlast changes in political leadership.

pp. 35–39, 518–520

Customer boards and councils are narrower than steering organizations or community governance bodies: their job is to improve service quality and outcomes for customers, not to help steer the organization or community. But if they have real power—if they are more than advisory—they make a big difference.

Some public organizations have followed Minnesota's lead and created customer boards or councils for internal support functions that retain monopolies. In the U.K., some customers sit on the boards of utilities that have been privatized. In public housing in the U.S., some resident councils advise public housing authorities. And school councils made up primarily of customers (parents, community members, and occasionally even a student or two) are becoming common.

Customer boards and councils can play a number of roles, including:

- Approving particular investments.
- Approving rates or prices.
- Commenting on outcome goals, output goals, or both.
- Commenting on CEOs' performance agreements and organizations' flexible performance agreements.
- Commissioning customer surveys and focus groups.
- Publishing performance scorecards.
- Helping write and approving organizations' service standards, performance targets, guarantees, redress policies, and customer complaint systems.

pp. 124–148

In many of these roles—such as publishing scorecards—customer councils or boards have far more credibility with citizens than an organization's management does. They can function as a source of external pressure that makes the organization take quality service seriously, as we argued earlier.

p. 340

Customer Councils and Boards: Do's and Don'ts

Don't settle for advisory status. Many local school councils have been set up without real authority. Unless they have a principal who is willing to share power because he or she believes in doing so, they often become extremely frustrated. If you ask customers to discuss real issues and offer advice, but no one takes the advice, you can end up with angry, cynical customers.

Create clear charters for customer councils and boards. Make it crystal clear what their role is and how much power they have. Otherwise, you are likely to end up with misunderstandings, conflict, frustration, and even public battles.

Train your council or board members for their roles. "You have to teach people how to be a customer board," says Armajani. They don't come in understanding their role or knowing how to play it. "This conversation [on the telecommunications council] was screwed up for three or four months until we got a facilitator to help us figure it out, because none of us knew what it meant to function like a cooperative."

Don't allow interest groups or "professional" customers on the council or board. Interest groups and professional customers—those who have become so serious about their battles with an organization that they show up at every meeting or hearing—typically bring their own narrow agendas, regardless of the public interest. Some bring conflicts of interest as well. Councils won't work well if some of their members come in with their own bones to pick.

In compliance organizations—or organizations that deliver both services and compliance—customers should be in the majority, but the council should also include some compliers. If the Environmental Protection Agency were to create a customer council, for instance, it would want the majority of its members to be normal citizens and environmentalists, but it would also want some businesspeople and state and local government representatives, representing compliers.

To keep councils and boards in touch with customer needs, rotate people on and off them. After a few years on a council or board, people will have spent so much time working with the organization that they will share its perspective as much as the customers'. At this point, it's time to replace them. The best term limits will depend on the nature of the board or council. Those that function more as governing boards will require more expertise among their members—and therefore longer terms.

CUSTOMER SERVICE AGREEMENTS

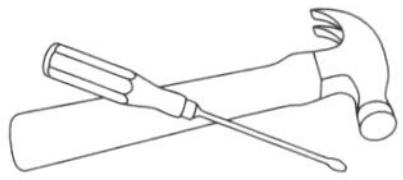

Customer Service Agreements **are performance agreements between an organization and its customers, defining the levels and quality of service to be provided and the rewards and penalties for doing or failing to do so.**

Because accountability for performance is at the heart of reinvention, reinventors use many kinds of performance agreements:

- Between a boss and subordinate.
- Between a government and a contractor (see pp. 188–210).

pp. 124–148

- Between a steering and a rowing organization.
- Between one level of government and another.
- Between customer and supplier organizations.

We call this last type of agreement a customer service agreement. Often these are between two public organizations: a line organization that serves the public and a staff organization, such as a purchasing or personnel office, that supports the line organization. But they can also be between two line organizations, between an organization and its customer board or council, or between an organization and its external customers. For instance, some public schools sign agreements with the parents of their students or even with the students themselves.

Customer service agreements include service standards and often redress, but they involve more extensive two-way negotiations and cover more issues. They can include many of the same components as flexible performance agreements: expected results, resource levels, flexibilities granted either party, special conditions, responsibilities of the customer, consequences for performance, and so on.

pp. 144–145

Why would you want to do this? "What's important about these is that they make explicit relationships between units in an organization, which are today informal, with no accountability," says Peter Hutchinson, president of the Public Strategies Group. "They allow you to have a serious conversation about the mutual expectations you hold. I think that's where the magic is: you take all this stuff that's assumed, that's underground, that you can never see—it's all built around relationships and individuals—and you make it explicit."

In organizations that are serious about reinvention, these customer service agreements have become common, simply because they make sense. Most agreements are voluntary, but top managers can also require different units to negotiate service agreements to work out problematic relationships or to figure out how to provide seamless service to the public. Negotiating them is not much different than negotiating other performance agreements, although if they are voluntary they require sincere commitment from both sides.

Pointers on Using Customer Service Agreements

pp. 124–148

Much of what we discuss in Chapter Three about flexible performance agreements applies here. In addition, here are a few more tips:

Keep them simple. People tend to make their agreements too long and elaborate, which can make them unmanageable. They don't have to focus on every dimension of the service—just on specific areas of service that the customer wants improved.

Make sure you include rewards and sanctions in the agreement. Where there are no consequences, there is no real accountability. Without consequences, when one party does not perform to expectations, nothing happens. The relationship reverts to ambiguity, and the agreement becomes a paper process with little effect on performance.

If you get creative about rewards and sanctions, you can come up with something that works. You can use financial payments, impact on a manager's performance bonus, impact on every employee's performance bonus or appraisal, redress policies, and awards.

pp. 231–237, 360–368

You can also use less formal rewards and sanctions, such as the following agreements:

- "You'll come and talk to my employees and tell them how much their work is appreciated."
- "You'll come and apologize to my employees."
- "You'll throw a Friday afternoon pizza party to thank our employees."

Use the service agreement as a living document; don't just file it away. Meet quarterly to review progress. And use the agreement's performance targets to manage: measure them regularly, reward teams for achieving them, and put teams to work to improve performance.

CUSTOMER VOICE: A CRITICAL COMPETENCE

As we argue in the introduction to Part Three, the ability to listen to your customers is a critical competence for those using the Customer Strategy. It is not a strategy or tool in and of itself, because although it is necessary, it is not sufficient to improve public organizations. Hearing what their customers want doesn't ensure that organizations will stretch themselves to provide it. But using customer quality assurance without listening to customers is impossible.

There are many different methods of listening to your customers, each of which has advantages and disadvantages. Often you will want to use multiple methods to ensure that you get both a representative picture and more detailed feedback. We list here 16 distinct methods, with the broadest forms of input (such as customer surveys) at the beginning and the most narrowly focused, in-depth forms (such as customer interviews) at the end. Think of it as a funnel, widest at the top and narrowest at the bottom.

Customer Surveys

This is perhaps the most systematic method of learning what your customers think. Surveys actually come in many varieties:

- ***Citizen surveys*** sample an entire community.
- ***Targeted customer or complier surveys*** sample a narrower slice of people who are direct users of an organization's services or objects of its compliance work.
- ***Random surveys,*** which can either be broad or targeted, ask a representative sample to get scientifically valid data. These need to be done by telephone or face to face, because mail and e-mail surveys require people to return them, which automatically makes the sample unrepresentative.
- ***Mail, e-mail, and Web site surveys*** do not provide representative samples, because those who take the time to return them typically have some bias, such as a higher-than-normal interest in the subject. They are cheap, and they can be highly suggestive. But you can never assume that they accurately reflect the views of the entire category you want to survey.
- ***Exit surveys*** ask people about a service just after they have used it. These can provide very specific feedback about a service's strengths and weaknesses. They can be representative of those who use the service, if the sample is large enough, but they are not representative of the larger universe of potential customers.

There are real limits to what even the best random surveys will tell you. If customers don't know a lot about the issues in question—particularly if those issues are somewhat technical or complex—surveys are not terribly helpful. If you don't ask about services that you don't offer but customers might want, you only get feedback on how you're doing, not on whether you're doing the right things. And even if you do ask the broader questions, few customers will be able to imagine what you might provide or how you might provide it; they simply don't know what they don't know. Finally, customer surveys don't usually tell you what customers think of your services compared with other jurisdictions' services, because they aren't always familiar with those others. Hence they rarely get you the kind of comparative information you can get from benchmarking.

Customer Panels

Customer panels are groups of customers who agree to be surveyed repeatedly and perhaps participate in focus groups, interviews, and other consultations over a period of time, to give an organization or government regular feedback. They can be as small as a dozen people or as large as 5,000, like the U.K.'s "People Panel." They help leaders and managers understand their customers' views, hear about problems when they develop, test out new ideas, get feedback on service quality, and get input on customer quality assurance tools such as standards and redress policies. Unlike customer councils and boards, however, they do not have any power to hold the sponsoring organization accountable: their only purpose is for consultation.

Customer Feedback Calls or Cards

Many organizations put customer feedback cards in their offices or hand them to customers as they enter or leave. You can also mail a card to or telephone a random sample of those you have served, asking for feedback. The Madison, Wisconsin, police department has long done this, mailing a feedback form and a note from the police chief to every 35th person its officers encounter, whether a suspect, a victim, a recipient of a speeding ticket, or someone complaining about a loud party. The forms use five-point ratings (from "excellent" to "very poor") on seven factors (concern, helpfulness, knowledge, quality of service, professional conduct, how well the police solved the problem, and whether they put the person at ease). The department uses them to rate its quality every month, and it also passes the specific forms to the officer or officers who handled each interaction, as a form of direct feedback.

See *Reinventing Government* pp. 172–173

Some organizations, such as Fox Valley Technical College, even survey customers a year or two after they were served, to see if the service yielded the desired results.

The only method here that produces a representative sample is random customer feedback calls. The others require the customer to initiate action, which automatically makes the sample nonrepresentative.

Open Days or Charrettes

When they want to get input about a service or issue from a variety of citizens without the disadvantages of holding a formal public hearing, some governments invite people to visit a set location at any time during a scheduled day to meet government staff and register their views. The Texas Performance Review (TPR) used charrettes to understand people's concerns about their public schools. These events can be relatively informal, as the TPR's were, allowing people to drop by any time, or they can be more structured, with formal presentations and discussions. They allow you to contact both users and potential users, although they don't produce representative samples. They also give you instant feedback. On the negative side, they require careful preparation, publicity, and staging to be effective.

p. 86

Written Consultations

This is an old format, which allows those concerned about an issue or service to register their views. It is typically used in the U.S. when new regulations are being drafted, though the British use it for a much wider array of purposes. The Labor Government's review of the Citizen's Charter used a written consultation exercise, for example. Though useful for hearing from organized interests, this process is not very effective if you want to hear from typical customers—who will not usually take the time to write out their views.

Test-Marketing

Occasionally public organizations pilot new services or features and then use customer interviews, focus groups, surveys, or other methods to see how people like them. Though this is more common in the private sector, it makes enormous sense.

Focus Groups

These are small groups of customers (usually under a dozen) brought together for an hour or two to discuss a particular service or issue. Typically a neutral facilitator is used to draw out the group's expectations, perceptions, and attitudes. Focus groups are quite common today. The Fund for the City of New York, a nonprofit organization dedicated to improving city government, has even used 15 focus groups from different neighborhoods to help design a scorecard to rate the quality of city services. It edited videotapes of their sessions and showed them to the agencies being discussed—another useful technique.

pp. 535–537

Meetings with User Groups and Interest Groups

User groups, interest groups, watchdog groups, and other voluntary organizations can usually give you useful feedback on services. They often represent many customers or compliers, and some carry out their own research on their members' views. Often they can help you figure out how to reach all the customers you need feedback from. However, be careful not to assume that these groups are offering representative views. Most have their own particular interests and opinions, which they are eager to share.

Telephone Help Lines and Help Desks

These are designed primarily to help customers get information and help, but like complaint systems, they can also be a source of feedback. Brisbane, Australia, a city of 950,000, has a help line citizens can call 24 hours a day and reach a human being—"on average, within 11 seconds," according to columnist Neal Peirce. That person is trained to answer questions and provide information on virtually every city activity. They can also take complaints, fill out reports on problems, or pull up a map of any property in the city and give the caller information about it. One useful technique is to have your CEO and managers staff the help line occasionally.

Customer Suggestion Forms or Boxes

Too few organizations use this tool with their customers. Fox Valley Technical College has used suggestion boxes on campus since 1990. "This can be effective if the system is carefully monitored and if there is assurance that quick action will be taken to respond to both suggestions and complaints," advises former president Stanley Spanbauer.

Customer Contact

Many managers work the front lines periodically to help them understand what customers and employees experience firsthand. Disney executives, for example, spend time wearing Goofy and Mickey Mouse costumes in their parks. Shirley Chater, former commissioner at the Social Security Administration, worked as a clerk. Others spend time talking to people in waiting rooms, or visiting with them at other times, or meeting with them to get feedback. This is extremely useful, because it is such a personal experience for the managers.

pp. 540–542

Customer Interviews

When they were reinventing the Minnesota Department of Administration in the 1980s, Babak Armajani and his colleagues required support service managers to visit their customers in other agencies. They then distributed printed reports with comments from the line agency managers throughout the department, to encourage managers to serve their customers better. When he was city manager of Salem, Oregon, Gerald Seals asked his department directors to meet with their customers and then discuss the experience at cabinet meetings. In Sunnyvale, Leisure Services had people observe a customer-provider interaction and then interview the customer immediately afterward.

In *A Complaint Is a Gift,* Barlow and Møller offer this advice: "Do not be satisfied with the first response your customers give you." They quote Granite Rock CEO Bruce Woolpert, who used customer interviews as part of the feedback process that helped his company win a Baldridge award: "If you sit with a customer long enough, eventually they will say, 'There is one thing . . .' You always want to sit long enough to hear that."

Customer Confidants

Some managers develop a relationship with a few customers they regularly call for feedback. If these customers are representative of the views of others, this can provide valuable insights that managers trust enough to act on.

Quality Inspections and "Mystery Shoppers"

"Mystery shoppers"—people who use restaurants, hotels, airlines, and other services and rate their experience—are now common in the private sector. They are used occasionally in the public sector in the U.S., but the Citizen's Charter has made them a more popular option in the U.K. The Royal Mail employs a private firm of mystery shoppers to test its customer service centers, and one of its divisions created an internal team to check its 200–odd delivery offices: to call and ask questions about services and then rate the speed with which the phone is answered; the responsiveness, courtesy, and knowledge of the person who answers; and the quality of the information given out.

Feedback from Employees

Employees who are in contact with customers every day often know what frustrates them and what they want changed. So ask them. Use formal, structured processes, from suggestion boxes to feedback forms to regular "customer feedback" meetings. Then act on what they tell you. This has the secondary benefit of building employee morale and commitment to the organization.

Walking in the Customers' Shoes

Perhaps the most intense customer feedback experience is that of being a customer oneself. Show up unannounced at offices where you are unknown and go through the system as a customer would. The experience can be eye-opening.

pp. 542–543

HOW TO CONSULT CUSTOMERS: TOP TEN TIPS

From *How to Consult Your Users: An Introductory Guide,* by the Service First team in the U.K.'s Cabinet Office.

1. Build consultation into your **regular planning** cycle and consult early. Don't wait until too late to change your plans, and do give people enough time to comment.
2. **Don't ask for views if you can't or won't do anything with them**—make clear what you can change and what you can't.
3. **Learn from others**—use experts if necessary, but don't just do something because "everyone else does." Work out what's right for your own situation.
4. Use **more than one method** of consultation.
5. **Be flexible**—think how to reach all your users (people with disabilities, people from ethnic minority groups, etc.).
6. Don't just consult your users—**ask others,** too, including your front-line staff.
7. **Be sensitive** to those you want to consult—encourage them to give honest views, e.g. by assuring confidentiality.
8. **Publicise** your consultation so that all who want to can feed in views, and so that people realise you are committed to listening to them.
9. **Report back** on what views you received and what you have done as a result.
10. **Evaluate** carefully after consulting, and learn lessons for next time.

RESOURCES ON CUSTOMER VOICE

Canadian Centre for Management Development. *Client Satisfaction Surveying: A Manager's Guide.* Ottawa: Canadian Centre for Management Development, 1998. A handbook on what kinds of survey information managers should collect, with best-practice examples from all three levels of government in Canada. Available free at www.ccmd-ccg.gc.ca/publica/publi.html (scroll down to "Service and Quality") or by e-mailing info@ccmd-ccg.gc.ca. Phone: (613) 943–8370. Fax: (613) 995–0286. Other useful reports are available on the same Web page.

Harry P. Hatry, Louis H. Blair, Donald M. Fisk, John M. Greiner, John R. Hall Jr., and Philip S. Schaenman. *How Effective Are Your Community Services? Procedures for Measuring Their Quality.* Washington, D.C.: Urban Institute and International City and County Management Association, 1992. A comprehensive guide to measuring local services that includes how-to information on a variety of customer voice methods for many services, along with sample surveys.

Harry P. Hatry, John E. Marcotte, Therese van Houten, and Carol H. Weiss. *Customer Surveys for Agency Managers: What Managers Need to Know.* Washington, D.C.: Urban Institute Press, 1998. An excellent guide on customer surveys.

United Kingdom. Cabinet Office. *How to Consult Your Users: An Introductory Guide.* London: Cabinet Office, 1998. An excellent brief guide to 16 of the methods outlined above, which is available free on the Service First Web page (www.servicefirst.gov.uk/index/publications.htm: click on "Consultation") or from the Service First Publications Line: 0345 22 32 42. Other useful reports are available on the same Web page.

Part IV

The Control Strategy

Shifting Control Away from the Top and Center

The Control Strategy changes where decision-making power lies in public organizations. It upends the bureaucratic tenets of hierarchy and centralized control and hands authority to frontline employees, organization managers, and community organizations. Leaders do this because they increasingly expect organizations to respond quickly, flexibly, and creatively to problems, opportunities, and customer needs—something that is impossible to do if everyone must wait for orders from the top. In the Information Age, success requires that those closest to a problem take initiative rather than waiting for instructions from the distant top of an organizational pyramid. People must be free to act.

But the Control Strategy is not a zero-sum game that takes power from some and gives it to others. For as the Control Strategy shifts the *locus* of control, it also shifts the *form* of control. Instead of using commands, rules, and inspections to gain compliance, reinventors develop new ways to guide the behavior of employees. Rather than trying to control what public organizations or community groups do, they try to influence what their actors want to accomplish. This is the essence of the empowerment deal: commit to producing specific results and get the power to decide how to produce those results. These deals combine several aspects of the reinventor's toolkit:

pp. 13–59

- They require decisions about what results government wants to produce—in other words, good steering.

pp. 247–271

- They require performance measurement to monitor whether those results are being achieved.

pp. 149–246

- They require consequences—rewards and sanctions—so there is accountability for performance.
- And they require empowerment, which shifts control over decisions to public employees and organizations and community-based organizations.

The Control Strategy involves three approaches. Leaders empower organizations by streamlining the many rules and regulations that central administrative offices, elected officials, and higher levels of government impose on them. They empower employees by reducing or eliminating hierarchical management and trusting them to get the job done. And they empower communities by sharing power with neighborhood organizations, public housing tenants, parents of schoolchildren, business associations, and other community-based entities.

See *Banishing Bureaucracy* pp. 236–237

All three approaches work for service, policy, and regulatory organizations. Compliance agencies can also use empowerment, within certain limits. Some controls exist to protect citizens' rights, and these cannot be modified, loosened, or dismissed. For example, police officers can have no discretion about reading Miranda rights to a suspected criminal.

In the developing world, the barriers to empowerment are formidable. In much of Asia, Latin America, Africa, and Eastern Europe, corruption is rampant, patronage is the norm, and even the courts and police are not always independent. On top of that, workforces are less educated than in the developed world.

See *Banishing Bureaucracy* pp. 238–240

Developing democracies can clearly use the Core, Consequences, and Customer Strategies—indeed, many have already embraced asset privatization, competitive contracting, and customer choice. They also need the Culture Strategy. But in these countries, leaders must decentralize control with great care. First they need to concentrate on establishing some basics: the rule of law, an independent judiciary, hiring based on merit, and financial controls, audits, and transparency. As they begin to loosen the old systems of control, they should construct new systems in their place—management information systems, systems that impose consequences, auditing systems, and systems that will prosecute corruption. When they cannot use market competition to create consequences, perhaps their best option is to grant flexibilities organization by organization, as the British Next Steps process did. Using this approach, they would grant an agency freedom from overly centralized controls only after the agency had proved its capacity to detect and control corruption, patronage, and political manipulation of employees. The freedoms could even be

pp. 110–113

granted in stages, as agencies gradually strengthened and demonstrated the effectiveness of their new control systems.

Even in the developed democracies, the Control Strategy is not easy. Many elected officials and top managers relish the control they have and are unlikely to give it up without a very good reason. Yet many are also under some pressure to produce better results. The trick is to persuade them that empowerment will do just that. In other words, strike an empowerment deal.

Chapter 10

Organizational Empowerment

Giving Managers the Power to Manage

Discourage conformity, uniformity, and centralization because they stifle innovation.

—*Principles of Excellent Installations*, U.S. Department of Defense

Organizational Empowerment **streamlines the rules, procedures, and other methods that central administrative agencies, legislatures, executives, and higher levels of government use to control government organizations, in order to help them improve their performance. It substitutes control of outcomes and outputs for control of inputs and processes.**

For 20 years, Jim Zingale was a foot soldier in the army of staffers that Florida's legislature used to keep state government under control. He wielded rules, regulations, and budget appropriations to keep the departments on a tight leash. By 1991, he had risen to a command position: head of the House appropriations staff.

"The legislature was state of the art when it came to micromanaging departments," says Bob O'Leary, a reinventor who joined the governor's office that same year.

> *They had lots of incredibly skilled staff people. They had every conceivable tool to micromanage the way the agencies ran. In some ways, they had far better ways to keep track of the agencies than the agencies had themselves.*

A year later, Zingale accepted a position as deputy director of the Department of Revenue. At the helm of an organization he had once bird-dogged, he started seeing things differently: the controls he once relished were now working against him.

Zingale and his new boss, Executive Director Larry Fuchs, wanted to improve the performance of their 3,000–employee organization. They were under pressure to increase revenue collections while reducing costs. When they looked to the private sector for advice, they found that high-performing organizations articulated the results they wanted, let managers and employees decide how to achieve these results, and provided incentives for performance. Private managers, says Zingale, "have tremendous freedom and incentives."

Unfortunately, that was not how things worked in the revenue department—or anywhere else in Florida's government. Managers had little control over departmental resources. Instead, the legislature's inflexible line-item budgets dictated how funds could be used, the state's "career service" system dictated how to use personnel, and there were practically no incentives to reward performance. Furthermore, the hierarchical structure imposed by statutes had built enormous inefficiencies into the agency.

Fuchs and Zingale realized that these systemic handcuffs prevented them from transforming the department. "We needed freedom from the normal constraints," says Fuchs.

So Zingale, the former jailer for the legislature, became a liberation activist for the imprisoned department.

THE PROBLEM WITH CENTRALIZATION

The conversion that came upon Jim Zingale is still rare among the hundreds of thousands of legislative staffers; budget, personnel, and procurement officers; inspectors; auditors; and elected officials who see their role as keeping the productive organs of government on the straight and narrow. But practically everyone else has understood for some time that the system of centralized controls that emerged and spread in the first half of the 20th century is a colossal impediment to performance.

Early in the century, government reinventors known as Progressives believed deeply in centralization. Their motives were honorable: to banish the political patronage and cronyism that riddled public service and to ensure that rapidly growing public organizations followed policies set by elected officials. They adopted an approach—"corporate management," political scientist Peter Aucoin calls it—pioneered by private businesses trying to manage their own sprawling empires. The key was administrative centralization. It made every organization of government part of a unified, corporate whole. It standardized administrative practices—in particular, budgeting, financial management, and personnel. It established central administrative agencies as keepers of the standards.

And it worked. It curbed the power of political bosses, and it embedded a set of standard operating procedures into most government organizations. But it worked with a vengeance. Handing control over day-to-day practices to central agencies—civil service commissions, budget offices, treasury departments, headquarters—takes power away from operational managers, the very people who are supposed to implement policies and produce results. This pervasive micromanagement disables those managers. They learn to follow rigid central rules rather than their own judgment about what will best produce the results elected officials want.

See *Reinventing Government* pp. 255–259

General Bill Creech, the master reinventor of the U.S. Tactical Air Command (TAC), remembers when one of his own commanders was worried about Creech's decision to get rid of at least half of the TAC's internal rules.

> *He told me, "After all, those rules are there for a reason. They are saving us from our past mistakes." My reply was "They are also saving us from our future accomplishments."*

Centralization gives managers an excuse: how can they be held accountable for results if they don't have real authority over their resources? But if managers are not responsible for results, who is? Not the central agencies; their business is to produce rules, not results. The fact is that no one in bureaucratic governments is on the hook for achieving the outcomes the people want. Is it any wonder that so few deliver them?

Perhaps the first blow against central bureaucracy was struck in the 1960s (when else?), in a most unlikely place. For nearly 50 years, Canada's federal government had been in the forefront of centralization. Right after World War I, it created a Civil Service Commission. In the 1930s it added a centralized financial management system, and by the late 1950s, says Aucoin, "the central apparatus . . . was firmly in place."

There was only minor resistance. Then in 1963, the Glassco Royal Commission on Government Organization issued recommendations that for the first time promoted decentralization of government authority. Its advice to "let the managers manage" became a rallying cry when decentralization efforts finally hit their stride—two and three decades later—in Canada, the U.K., New Zealand, Australia, and the U.S.

By the 1990s many elected officials were under pressure to produce better results while cutting costs. In the new Information Age, the price of centralization was just too high. That recognition came with many verses and voices:

- "Effective, entrepreneurial governments cast aside red tape," asserted President Clinton's National Performance Review. "They streamline their budget, personnel, and procurement systems—liberating organizations to pursue their missions."

- Create "a flexible structure within which managers can manage better and a climate that encourages, rewards and supports them," proclaimed Australia's *Diagnostic Study*.
- Make decision making as "decentralized as possible," insisted Canada's Ministerial Task Force on Program Review.

Letting managers manage means giving them control over resources so they can use them effectively and economically to achieve results. But decentralization also has a price. Managers must assume greater responsibility for deciding how to use resources. They must be accountable for their decisions. And they must agree to have their performance measured, judged, and rewarded or sanctioned.

Without this autonomy-for-accountability deal, elected officials will not—and should not—feel comfortable about reducing central controls. Thus, organizational empowerment doesn't just *let* managers manage; by tying managers' freedom to results, it also *makes* managers manage. It shifts both the *locus* of control and the *form* of control—from rules and compliance to accountability for performance.

DECONSTRUCTING THE CENTER

Before Jim Zingale joined Florida's Department of Revenue, Governor Lawton Chiles had persuaded the legislature to grant the organization some management flexibilities for one year. The pilot effort was one of Chiles's and Lieutenant Governor Buddy MacKay's first attempts to strip away central controls. "You find a really talented manager who's got the vision and you say [to lawmakers], 'Just let him try,'" explains MacKay. "When he succeeds and everybody sees he can succeed, then, by God, everybody says, 'I'm ready to do it.'"

The pilot, which also involved the Division of Worker's Compensation in the Labor Department, was successful. The department gained the flexibility to pay bonuses to 350 of its employees if they improved their performance. In some offices, productivity shot up by an estimated 34 percent. So the legislature extended the pilot by a year and then gave the same flexibility to several other departments.

As the Revenue Department continued to improve, Zingale and Fuchs won additional freedoms. In 1994, the legislature made it the first state organization to operate under a performance budgeting system, giving it flexibility to manage its budget as long as it met performance goals. In 1995, legislators allowed Fuchs to do away with the department's cumbersome structure of four divisions and 13 specialized bureaus and reorganize it around core work processes.

Over a four-year period, the department increased its collections while reducing employment (eliminating 22 percent of its management staff) and slashing operating costs. In 1995, the Federation of Tax Administrators called the department "a model of how government should function" and gave it a national Management and Organizational Initiative Award.

The Revenue Department was the "canary in the mine" that tested the atmosphere for organizational empowerment in Florida. Because legislators trusted its leaders—and because its outcomes were relatively simple to describe and measure—it was allowed to test freedoms that lawmakers might consider extending government-wide.

Reinventors like Zingale and Fuchs usually nibble away at the center's power; they break down the bureaucratic control system in small increments, because they don't have the political support to dismantle it all at once. Often they are not sure what they would put in its place. They try new tools, such as waiver policies, reinvention labs, and charter schools, to learn more about how to use management flexibility. They use these experiments to demonstrate what works and what doesn't work, and just as important, to prove that the chaos centralizers predict won't occur.

See *Banishing Bureaucracy* pp. 75–90

But nibbling away is a slow, tedious process that can wear down one's patience and stamina. When the opportunity exists, reinventors strike more boldly. In New Zealand in 1988, Labor Party leaders eliminated in one fell swoop most of the controls the State Services Commission (SSC) and Treasury Department had imposed on other departments.

In Florida, Chiles and MacKay not only went after the central budget and personnel offices, they also dismantled several departments' central headquarters. They began with the state's social welfare department, Health and Rehabilitative Services (HRS). With 45,000 employees, it was the largest state agency in America; nearly 4,500 of those positions were in the Tallahassee headquarters, distributed among eight layers of managers.

MacKay and Chiles persuaded the legislature to approve a plan to decentralize HRS into 15 community-based districts. But department officials took too long to implement the plan. So Chiles eased the department director out of the way, then assigned MacKay to run the agency for six months. The lieutenant governor demanded and received written, undated resignations from the department's senior managers to ensure their cooperation. He installed the new districts' governing bodies and administrators and gave them some authority over budgets, personnel, and planning.

"We knew we'd never get headquarters to volunteer to cut itself," says his key aide in the process, Bob O'Leary. "So everything inside the Tallahassee city limits was going to be looked at with a magnifying glass by somebody who wasn't inclined to protect it." MacKay even invited local-level HRS professionals to help him redesign the department's central office. They divested several departmental functions, axed three layers of management, eliminated 25 of the 38 senior management positions, and eliminated 2,300 positions. They gave up more than 30,000 square feet of leased office space—shipping the remaining furniture, copiers, and computers to district offices to help cut their costs. Then MacKay left the department.

One key to aggressive decentralization in Florida and New Zealand was that reinventors in those jurisdictions knew what they would use to replace the central control systems. MacKay installed community-based control and performance accountability. The New Zealanders made state-owned enterprises accountable to their customers and government departments accountable to elected officials, who contracted with them for specific, measurable outputs. According to virtually every knowledgeable observer, these changes produced significant improvements. Allen Schick, perhaps the leading American expert on public management around the globe, sums them up this way:

> *Public services are more accessible and responsive, more sensitive than in the past to the needs of citizens and clients, and much more efficient. A culture of performance has penetrated New Zealand public management. Chief executives and managers know and accept that they are judged on the performance of their organizations.*

DESIGNING A NEW CENTER

See *Banishing Bureaucracy* pp. 83–85

See *Banishing Bureaucracy* pp. 53–60

Once reinventors *deconstruct* the administrative centers of power, they find that they must *reconstruct* the center into a source of accountability and a useful partner for empowered organizations. As we reported in *Banishing Bureaucracy,* the New Zealanders gave departments control over their personnel but still had the State Services Commission appoint departments' chief executives and assess their performance. Generals Bill Creech and Michael Loh gave enormous autonomy to the 500 or so squadrons of the Tactical Air Command (renamed the Air Combat Command) but maintained a command headquarters that measured squadron performance, trained employees in Total Quality Management, and conducted annual employee surveys.

As Schick says, "Some central functions are carried out differently than they once were, and relations with line departments have changed, but it would be naive to argue that managerial freedom is incompatible with central direction."

In decentralized systems, the center has several key functions:

- ***It helps steer the system.*** Central offices like the budget and finance office, and central headquarters in large departments, are intimately involved in the steering process. They help elected officials and steering organizations create visions and outcome goals for the system, develop strategies, tie resources to those strategies through performance budgets, measure performance against outcome goals, and evaluate their strategies. We discuss this role in depth in Chapter One.

pp. 13–59

• ***It holds line organizations accountable for improving their performance.*** As part of its steering role, the center needs to oversee development of the performance measurement system that monitors organizations' improvement efforts and the accountability system that creates consequences. This should be done in collaboration with the departments and agencies that will be obliged to collect the data and use it to improve performance. But the center must be prepared to deal with organizations that are failing. In education, for example, interventions can include requiring a school improvement plan, providing technical assistance, replacing the school principal, or closing and reconstituting a school.

pp. 215–271

pp. 229–230

• ***It provides support to line organizations.*** The leaders of newly empowered organizations face challenges for which they are not necessarily prepared. The center can aid them in building capacity and improving performance. It can also provide support services: everything from training to telecommunications. Even charter schools, for example—radically independent public institutions—often turn to a school district for transportation, security services, data processing, and the like.

• ***It stimulates innovation within the system.*** The center can help spawn and spread effective improvement methods. It can support the introduction of promising innovations created outside the organization, and it can boost innovators within the system—by helping them obtain space or seed money, for instance. It can use competitive benchmarking, a tool that stimulates friendly competition among units, such as schools and squadrons, as a goad to improve performance.

pp. 210–214

Thus, there is life after death for the center, but it is a life transformed. As Gifford and Elizabeth Pinchot point out in their book *The End of Bureaucracy and the Rise of the Intelligent Organization*, the role of the new center is to create the conditions that empower others. It does not look anything like the old bureaucratic center.

One way to picture this new role is to see the new center in terms of a steering body and rowing organizations that have been uncoupled, as we discuss in Chapter Three.

pp. 105–124

EMPOWERING ORGANIZATIONS: LESSONS LEARNED

As reinventors have used various tools to get rid of unnecessary rules and refocus public organizations on results, they have learned some critical lessons about how it's done:

1. *Keep flexibility tightly linked to accountability for performance.*

Remember the empowerment deal: it's freedom *for* accountability, not freedom *before* accountability. "At each step in the evolution from centralism to decentralism there should be a balance between the freedoms granted and the accountabilities imposed," advises Graham Scott, former secretary of the treasury in New Zealand.

> *This can be thought of as a ladder in which each step balances freedom and accountability and maintains the functionality of a management system. Any step which involves imbalance between freedom and accountability is dysfunctional. The system will not work if people are held to account for things they cannot control, or if they are given freedoms without clear expectations of performance.*

All too often, reinventors focus on empowerment and let accountability go by the boards. They are prone, says General Loh, to treat empowerment as a social experiment; they "forget what the bottom line is." This is a big mistake. Without accountability for performance, the center will seldom be willing to let go, and few empowered organizations will have the urgency necessary to fight through the obstacles to improvement they will face.

2. *To remove the barriers to organizational empowerment, you need political leadership.*

See *Reinventing Government* pp. 10–11

When Bob Stone was deputy assistant secretary of defense for installations, he was having trouble getting DOD comptrollers to approve waivers to rules for military base commanders. So he went to get help from his boss, William Howard Taft IV, a political appointee.

> *When I told Taft about it, he pounded his fist on the table in a big public meeting and said, "I want all the waivers approved." I kind of gritted my teeth, because even I didn't want them all approved; only the 95 percent that were sensible. Later, one of the people I was friendly with in the comptroller's office—they were the enemy—told me, "Don't think I'm going along with this because I believe in what you're doing. I just don't want to get in trouble with Will Taft."*

Make no mistake about it: without this kind of push from elected officials and their appointees, centralizers are unlikely to relinquish their power. "I see this everywhere," says Stone, who went on to direct Vice President Gore's National Performance Review for six years.

> *The assistant administrators for personnel or finance or information technology have vested interests in the failure of such an empowered organization. If you empower an organization to make its own personnel decisions, what do you need with an assistant administrator for personnel? So these people, if they're really nice people, will just sit by and hope it will fail. But if they are ordinary human beings, they will help it fail.*

It's not easy for politicians to stay interested in public management, but it is crucial that they back up reformers in the departments. One place to start is with their own political appointees, who seldom relinquish power voluntarily. At an annual conference of federal reinvention lab leaders, Stone remembers, participants were asked to advise Vice President Gore. "Almost everything they said boiled down to one statement repeated 30 different ways: 'Don't waste time with us; we get it. Our bosses don't get it—work on them.'" One of the participants was even more direct:

pp. 449–450

> *He was angry about the political appointees who weren't supportive of reinvention. I asked him why he spared the career [civil service] people. He almost spat at me; he thought I was a pol. "If your own senior appointees don't support the program," he said, "how can you expect career people to?"*

3. *Build up organizational leaders' credibility with elected officials.*

Larry Fuchs, the former executive director of Florida's Department of Revenue, says part of his success was knowing how to work with legislators who were reluctant to give up control. To make them feel comfortable with organizational empowerment, he advises, "You have to establish unblemished personal credibility. Be the first one to reveal a problem, and make sure you're not the subject of somebody else's revelation."

In 1991, when the Chiles administration took office, the legislature was naturally skeptical about reducing central control over new department heads. But several department heads—Tom Herndon at Revenue (before Fuchs) and Frank Scruggs at the Department of Labor—had personal credibility with lawmakers, which made all the difference in the world. "Herndon could go in and say, I've been the budget director and the governor's chief of staff," explains Bob O'Leary. "Let me go to the next level. I'll put in an accountability system so you won't be uncomfortable." That pitch earned the Revenue Department new status as a management flexibility pilot.

As you work with leaders, Fuchs says, bombard them with information. "Make sure they feel comfortable about the internal workings of your organization." Use annual and quarterly reports, success stories, monthly newsletters, and anything else you can dream up.

You can get friendly lawmakers to influence their colleagues, he adds. "Find the legislators who have a genuine interest and knowledge in this, and give them the tools to educate their colleagues."

For some services, it's also important to get community leaders comfortable with organizational empowerment. When David Couper was police chief of Madison, Wisconsin, he didn't try to decentralize controls until he had won the trust of community and elected officials. "I'd been around for a while, and I think the community saw me as competent and a good police chief," he says. "They knew what I was doing, that I had a vision, that I was progressive—so when the police who resisted [changes] would go to the community, the community would say to them, 'We don't agree.'"

4. Convert the center into a champion for empowerment.

Most central controllers believe in what they're doing, and few are interested in losing their power or their jobs. Still, there are ways to recruit them to the cause of reform.

pp. 110–113

One is to pilot-test organizational empowerment and make sure the central agencies get something out of it. In the U.K., the all-powerful Treasury Department resisted organizational empowerment during the first few years of the Next Steps process. After several years, though, reluctant Treasury officials became convinced that empowerment in exchange for accountability was working; spending was not running out of control. Then *they* began to find ways to use it to save money, by forcing Next Steps agencies to eat inflation. Finally, they converted—extending management flexibilities first to agencies and then to departments as well.

At the Tactical Air Command, General Bill Creech documented the negative impact of centralized controls. "I showed [the Pentagon staff] numbers that showed we were doing worse every year, that our productivity was declining at a rate of almost 6 percent a year," says Creech. "They'd never seen numbers like that before." That made it easier to persuade the centralizers to stop micromanaging.

If you really want administrative control agencies to let go of their controls, start appointing reinventors to run them. Sometimes you may have to find these reinventors in the private sector. In the early 1990s, California officials decided to turn around their Department of General Services (DSG). In charge of the state's procurement system, it was guided by the nine-inch-thick

State Administrative Manual. The state used a headhunter agency to conduct a search. It found Peter Stamison, an executive from the aerospace and communications industries who had no government experience. "I've been a critic of government ever since I got my first paycheck," Stamison says. He quickly began to dismantle DSG's cumbersome controls.

5. *Get top managers to blow up their own central control systems at headquarters.*

George Weise, commissioner of the U.S. Customs Service, cut his HQ staff by one-third and shifted the resources to the field. Bob Stone followed a similar pattern with the office he ran in the Defense Department. "I blew up my part of headquarters," he says. "I basically took all the people in the business of checking up on compliance with silly rules and put them in charge of helping base commanders get waivers."

A rule of thumb is that you should reduce headquarters staff by at least 50 percent. But some reinventors advise going further. "You should tell them they have to do the job with no more than half of the people they have—and that each year they have to cut back even more," say Florida's Bob O'Leary.

"I think the right number [for reduction] is something greater than three-quarters of the staff," comments Stone. If you cut less than that, he explains, "people will attempt to keep doing the same things they've always done."

RESOURCES ON ORGANIZATIONAL EMPOWERMENT

Peter Block. *Stewardship: Choosing Service over Self-Interest.* San Francisco: Berrett-Koehler, 1993. Bloch critiques the rationale behind central control and offers important ideas about alternatives.

Bill Creech. *The Five Pillars of TQM: How to Make Total Quality Management Work for You.* New York: Truman Talley Books/Dutton, 1994. The inspiring and savvy tales of a master reinventor who found ways to empower his organization, the Tactical Air Command, and then reinvent it thoroughly.

Gifford and Elizabeth Pinchot. *The End of Bureaucracy and the Rise of the Intelligent Organization.* San Francisco: Berrett-Koehler, 1993. A comprehensive indictment of the command-and-control approach, with useful advice and stories, mainly from business, about empowerment.

TOOLS FOR ORGANIZATIONAL EMPOWERMENT

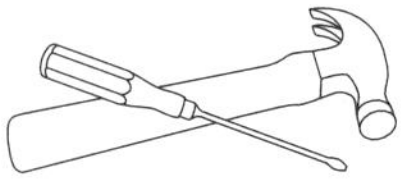

Reforming Administrative Systems gives line agencies the authority to manage their own resources within a minimal framework of mandates from and oversight by central administrative agencies. It changes budget and finance, personnel, procurement, and auditing systems to make agencies accountable for producing results rather than for simply following rules. See below.

Site-Based Management shifts control over resources and day-to-day decision making from the central office of a system, such as a school district or a national employment service, to the many frontline organizations in the system, such as schools or local employment offices. See p. 427.

Waiver Policies are a mechanism that central agencies and headquarters use to temporarily or permanently exempt organizations from rules on a case-by-case basis. See p. 430.

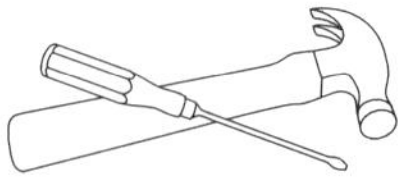

Opting Out or Chartering allows existing or new public organizations, such as charter schools, to operate outside the jurisdiction of most government control systems. See p. 434.

Reinvention Laboratories are public organizations that receive permission to break administrative rules and procedures temporarily and to experiment with new ways of improving performance. Typically they are granted waivers and protected from interference. See p. 444.

Mass Organizational Deregulation repeals many of the other internal rules and regulations created by legislatures, central agencies, and departments to dictate the behavior of public organizations. See p. 450.

REFORMING ADMINISTRATIVE SYSTEMS

After the energy crisis in the late 1970s, leaders of the police department in Madison, Wisconsin, decided to reduce fuel consumption. "The management, in its infinite wisdom, decided it was going to contribute to the cause of saving fuel by buying small police cars," recalls Michael Masterson, then a junior officer with the force. The agency replaced many traditional, larger cars with low-power subcompacts, such as Omnis and Horizons.

"Unfortunately," says Masterson, now a captain, "no one took into account those frequent times when officers had to squeeze motorists into the back seat to complete accident reports; place a combative, struggling prisoner inside; or try to guide a person incapacitated by alcohol inside for conveyance to a detoxification facility. It just didn't work."

Police officers also tampered with the small cars' engines. They "flipped the air cleaners over to make the engines sound like police cars," Masterson recalls. "Then they drove around in low gear to give them more oomph." As a result, savings from fuel economy were lost to increased maintenance and repair costs.

Unfortunately, the police car follies were not an isolated incident. Madison also issued its police officers boots for patrol. The boots were not insulated, even though Madison's winters can be severe. Managers believed that if officers had insulated boots, they would wear them off duty, wear them out more quickly, and need more frequent replacements, which would cost the city more money. Masterson remembers how he and fellow officers got around the restriction. "I was part of this and take great pride in this subterfuge. You go down [to the store] and you order the uninsulated boots, and you pay them $10 more, and they give you insulated boots." When management got wind of this, it made a new rule: all clothing had to be delivered to the police station first, so it could be inspected for compliance with the approved clothing list. Officers soon found a way around this as well: they picked up uninsulated boots at the station, returned to the store, and exchanged them and some extra money for a warmer pair.

Madison has since changed its procurement rules to give officers more say in what the city buys. But most public organizations still suffer with centralized administrative systems that take control out of managers' and employees' hands. As these examples illustrate, their effect is often counterproductive.

Bureaucratic procurement, personnel, auditing, and budget and finance systems create countless mandates for organizations. Their power shapes public organizations, work processes, and people. You can see this linked chain in Madison. When the departmental procurement system purchased subcompact cars, it affected everyday work processes, like bringing in arrested people, and it affected the morale of the department's employees—who got their revenge by tinkering with the puny engines.

Transforming Systems Instead of Gaming Them

Smart managers in government figure out how to beat bureaucratic administrative systems. They wheel and deal for special favors from the central agencies: to allow a hire or purchase that doesn't quite conform to the rules; to speed up an urgent promotion, grant, or bid. They fend off auditors by giving them too little or too much information and endlessly contesting their criticisms and interpretations. Most departments have several veterans who specialize in "working the system" to get what the agency needs, no matter what the rules say. And most central administrative agencies have staffers who play the other end of the game—helping people in agencies get around the rules.

All of this wastes precious time, money, and energy. This inefficiency is a chronic and massive problem in government.

Sometimes politicians even get dragged into the mess. In Portland, Oregon, a few years ago, the local police were trying to figure out how to get around a federal rule. They had a potbellied pig named Harley who was very good at sniffing out narcotics. They wanted to buy some more pigs and train them to sniff out guns, too. But they couldn't use federal antidrug funds to train pigs—only dogs. The bureaucratic problem went all the way to the White House, where, finally, Vice President Al Gore broke the impasse. He designated Harley an honorary dog.

The stories of Mike Masterson's insulated boots and Portland's potbellied pig highlight the enduring absurdities produced by centralized administrative systems. Instead of focusing on performance, managers spend their time maneuvering around the rules. The process wears them down, because it takes far too much energy to get little things done. They become cynical and disheartened.

See *Banishing Bureaucracy* pp. 75–90

Compare this with how managers feel in New Zealand, where reinventors released them from administrative handcuffs and began to hold them accountable for producing results.

Not long after the reforms, George Hickton became a manager in the Department of Social Welfare. He had worked for years in the private sector with Ford and Honda. When we talked with Hickton in 1994, he was general manager of the department's largest unit, Income Support Services. His 1,500 employees operated New Zealand's welfare offices.

Hickton worked for Margaret Bazeley, the department's chief executive. She had the power to hire and fire, to set salaries within broad ranges, to evaluate performance, and to negotiate performance contracts with managers like Hickton. She also worked under a performance contract, as did all department heads. Each year, she negotiated her department's expected outputs with a cabinet minister, an elected official. Then she was empowered to succeed. She controlled her agency's budget, personnel, and purchasing. In addition to giving her management autonomy, she told us, New Zealand's reforms gave her "clarity of objectives" and "accountability for performance." And she passed all three elements down to her managers.

George Hickton used the freedom Bazeley gave him to transform his organization's culture and performance. When he took over, he changed practically every member of his executive team, bringing in some new people from the outside. He invested in sprucing up the local offices and training employees in customer service. Responding to his contract with Bazeley, he focused on improving the speed with which the agency approved applications for public assistance. In 1993, it took an average of six days. One year later, it took *less* than a day. Visitors from social services agencies in other countries didn't believe the results, Hickton says. "One of them got into a car with one of my people and said, 'What's the truth?'"

George Hickton obviously relished his autonomy as a manager. New Zealand's system, he told us, provides "incredible freedoms for management." In fact, he said, it gave him more freedom than Ford or Honda ever had.

To reinvent government, you *must* do as New Zealand did and transform your administrative systems. If you don't, they will stymie change, because they have such a strong grip on the resources and incentives of public organizations and employees. Indeed, reforming administrative systems is the single most powerful tool for empowering public organizations. It is a metatool: in addition to the Control Strategy, it also uses the Consequences Strategy, to give organizations incentives and accountability for performance; the Customer Strategy, to force central agencies to pay attention to what line organizations need from them (such as insulated boots); and the Culture Strategy, to break the "comply with the rules" mind-set that keeps organizations from responding effectively to their customers.

Transforming these systems is heavy lifting at the very frontier of reinvention. Fortunately, reinventors have begun to pull it off. In the pages that follow, we sketch the many changes they are putting into place, system by system. When we describe tools discussed in other chapters, we use pointers to direct you to those more detailed discussions.

Transforming Budget and Finance Systems

In 1993, the NPR reported that "the federal books are a mess. Any business with separate, uncoordinated systems for budgeting, accounting and product sales would soon be bankrupt. But the federal government has such systems." This was not a case of American or federal exceptionalism; most governments used pretty much the same systems that the NPR condemned. Unfortunately, these systems often lead elected officials and managers to waste the public's money.

pp. 208–209

For starters, government officials and managers don't have a clue how much it costs agencies to get something done, because the accounting systems don't tell them. When employees in Indianapolis wanted to compete against private contractors for street repair work, for instance, they realized that they didn't know how much the work they performed cost the city; their financial systems were not designed to collect and report this information.

Second, public managers normally spend as much money as they can get their hands on, because budgeting systems provide disincentives for saving funds. In most public organizations, if you don't spend your entire budget, you

See Reinventing Government pp. 117–124

lose whatever you saved, and you probably get less the next year. This explains why 94 percent of senior managers in the Australia Public Service said in a 1984 survey that good financial management was "spending no more—and no less—than their budget allocation."

Indianapolis mayor Stephen Goldsmith tells a story in his book *The Twenty-First Century City* that brings the phenomenon to life:

> *We created a reward program, called the "Golden Garbage Awards," to recognize employees who uncovered such examples of waste. Dozens of examples surfaced. A parks employee identified stacks of chalk to line softball fields that had been purchased at year's end by a buyer fearful of having his annual budget reduced if he had any money left over. We had enough surplus chalk to line all the softball fields in the city for five years—even though we had switched to spray-painting the lines two years before.*

Third, public leaders don't know what they get for their money, since government budget systems don't tell them. The typical government budget counts expenditures but not results. This is like leaving a department store knowing how much you spent but not what you bought.

Thus, bureaucratic budget and finance systems create multiple problems for reinventors. They make it hard to improve steering, since steerers don't have good information about what it costs to produce results. They keep organizations from using managed competition or enterprise management, because they don't know how much it costs to produce their goods and services. And they forestall organizational and employee empowerment, because they don't give managers and employees any incentive to spend the public's money wisely, as if it were their own.

Generally, reinventors change budget, finance, and accounting systems in four ways:

1. *They introduce powerful incentives for managing and saving money.*

Quite simply, they break the traditional get-all-you-can-spend, spend-all-you-can-get mold. Instead, they reward managers for using less money while maintaining or improving service levels and quality. In Australia, Canada, the U.K., Sweden, and an increasing number of U.S. governments, departments are allowed to keep a portion of any funds they do not spend. They can "roll it over" into the next year and spend it on ways to increase productivity. This discourages wasteful year-end spending done only to avoid losing funds.

pp. 241–243

We call this tool shared savings. The British call it "unlimited end-year flexibility." Some governments let agencies keep all of what they save; others allow them to keep a percentage. In most cases, we believe, you should let organizations keep at least half of their savings, so they will have a strong enough incentive to save. You must also protect organizations from retroactive raids on their savings by legislators, who may be tempted to recapture agencies' savings or to cut future budgets of agencies that save money. Such moves quickly destroy the incentive to save.

Another tool ensures that managers will pay attention to the full cost of things. Capital charging, pioneered by New Zealand in 1991 and recently adopted by the U.K., charges departments for the cost of the capital they use for fixed assets and, sometimes, the capital they use for operations. In New Zealand, each department pays interest pegged to the cost of capital used for similar activities in the private sector. The main effect, according to Graham Scott, former head of the New Zealand Treasury Department, is that managers use assets more productively, dispose of assets they don't need, and manage debts and inventories more effectively. New Zealand also allows agencies to retain proceeds from the sale of their assets.

The Australians and British used a third tool: they reduced running (operating) cost budgets by 1 to 1.25 percent every year—an "efficiency dividend" that forced managers to find ways to boost productivity.

2. *They give managers the flexibility to manage their resources.*

The new financial systems break the habit of insisting on annual input-based budgets with innumerable, inflexible line items or accounts for practically every kind of expenditure. The best way to escape this paradigm is to give managers lump-sum operating budgets and let them figure out the most effective ways to spend the money. (*Reinventing Government* called these "mission-driven budgets.") The Australians, New Zealanders, and British all do this now, as do many state and local governments in the U.S.

See *Reinventing Government* pp. 119–124

A second, although weaker, option is to give managers more flexibility to move money between line items. The Department of Defense took this approach in its Unified Budget Test, which gave some military base commanders this authority.

Another tool for creating flexibility is the innovation fund. It allows organizations to build a pot of money out of shared savings or appropriations and use it to pay for innovations that managers support. The Air Combat Command created a $10 million fund, and several other federal organizations have similar mechanisms. Hampton, Virginia, puts 10 percent of annual shared savings into its innovation fund. In Philadelphia, an innovation fund gives agencies five-year loans that must be repaid at double the amount borrowed. Portland, Oregon, requires a three-year payback on loans from its fund. When public administration scholar Paul Light studied 26 innovative organizations in Minnesota, he found that "all but a handful . . . had an innovation investment fund of some kind."

pp. 174–182

Finally, reinventors can also give departments control over their budgets for purchasing internal services, such as printing and computer services—a tool we call internal enterprise management. In most governments, these internal services are run as monopolies. Departments must obtain goods and services from them; usually they don't even control the budgets for these purchases. Breaking up this monopoly by using internal enterprise management has saved substantial sums in Australia, New Zealand, the U.K., Minnesota, and other places. Part of the change involves giving agencies, rather than internal providers, the budgets for services they need and letting them purchase those services wherever they wish.

3. They provide better financial steering tools to elected officials and managers.

pp. 54–56

pp. 43–53

Reinventors use budgets that project revenues and costs for five to ten years rather than just one year at a time. They also use performance budgets to buy specific results rather than to pay for specified activities. Both changes help public officials improve their hand-to-eye coordination: they keep their eyes on the long-term outcomes they want, while keeping their hands on the steering wheel.

pp. 51–52

A third useful tool is biennial budgeting: drafting two-year budgets rather than the usual annual appropriations bills. This cuts the time lawmakers spend crafting budgets, giving them more time for steering and planning.

pp. 54–55

Finally, some reinventors try to make government's financial condition more visible and comprehensible to citizens. In 1994, New Zealand adopted the Fiscal Responsibility Act. In two previous elections, political parties in power had hidden the government's fiscal weaknesses during their campaigns. When the out-of-power party was elected, it discovered the real situation and had to make far more drastic spending cuts than it had promised. The new law requires full exposure of the fiscal situation in the period leading up to an election, among other things.

In the U.S., reinventors with the National Performance Review were concerned about similar problems. They recommended that the president annually release a report to the citizens, detailing "in terms that are easy to understand" the government's revenues, expenditures, investments, contingent liabilities, and financial condition.

4. They reform accounting systems to help managers do a better job.

Properly designed accounting systems expose a great deal of information about what organizations are actually doing and what they are getting for their money. This is essential for improving performance. Several basic competencies are involved.

pp. 208–209

See Reinventing Government pp. 243–246

Full cost accounting helps managers identify both the direct and the overhead costs of their programs and units. Activity-based costing helps them discover how much it costs to produce each output. Accrual accounting requires organizations to record liabilities as they occur and revenues as they are earned, rather than ignoring them until the bill or check comes in. It also requires them to depreciate capital expenditures over time, rather than treating them as an operating expense in the year they buy or build the asset. This prevents some of the perverse incentives that occur in cash accounting, which ignores the cost of deterioration in capital assets like highways, bridges, and buildings. Australia, Canada, Finland, Iceland, New Zealand, Sweden, the U.K., and the U.S. have all converted to accrual accounting. Lastly, public organizations are adopting Generally Accepted Accounting Practices (GAAP), which create more consistency and honesty in financial management and accounting practices across organizations than do other methods. Using GAAP holds governments to some basic accounting standards.

Reinventing Budget and Finance Systems

Create Incentives for Managing Money:

- Shared savings
- Capital charging
- Efficiency dividends

Give Managers Flexibility:

- Lump-sum budgets
- Line-item flexibility
- Innovation funds
- Internal enterprise management

Improve Steering:

- Performance budgets
- Long-term budget forecasting
- Biennial budgets
- Financial reports to citizens

Use Accounting to Improve Management:

- Full cost accounting
- Activity-based costing
- Accrual accounting
- Generally accepted accounting practices

Transforming Personnel Systems

In 1992, consultants from KPMG Peat Marwick evaluated the state personnel system in North Carolina, which spent nearly $4 billion a year on salaries and benefits for 212,000 employees. They found a raft of problems:

- Employees collected $30 million in annual longevity bonuses no matter how well they performed.

- Eighty-three percent of employees evaluated by managers received a rating of "exceeds expectations." Only 1 percent were identified as not meeting expectations.
- The state had 4,891 job classifications—one for every 15 workers—resulting in excessive layers of management and very small spans of control for managers.
- The state had no idea how much money it was spending on training employees, since no records on this were kept.
- Fewer than 0.1 percent of middle managers eligible for a skill development program initiated in 1988 had actually taken the course.

See *Reinventing Government* pp. 124–130

In other words, the personnel system looked like those of most bureaucratic governments: it had few incentives for performance, it was top-heavy, it gave managers little flexibility in the way they used employees, and it barely invested in developing employees' capabilities.

In half of all U.S. states, longevity pay has been a standard feature of compensation systems. Relatively few governments have effective systems for rewarding high-performing individuals or organizations. Even fewer governments have significant consequences for poor performance. North Carolina's consultants noted that managers avoided giving employees poor performance ratings because they didn't want to get involved with the state's grievance process.

pp. 216–218

Many governments have far too many job classifications. Some, like North Carolina, have thousands. Because employees are locked into their job classifications and pay grades, managers often cannot move personnel around or give people raises. They spend hundreds of useless hours haggling with personnel offices over classification issues. Virtually every personnel study in the last 10 years has recommended reducing the number of classifications. The National Commission on the State and Local Public Service, chaired by former Mississippi governor William F. Winter, concluded in 1993 that states need only a few dozen.

Finally, few governments invest significantly in training. KPMG Peat Marwick told the North Carolina legislature that Fortune 500 firms spend 3 percent of their payroll on training and the federal government spends 1 percent. Meanwhile, the two large states for which data existed at the time—Florida and New Jersey—were investing about 0.1 percent.

No wonder, then, that reinventors worldwide are transforming the standard-issue personnel or civil service system. The system needs "a complete reconstruction," say the authors of *Civil Service Reform*, published by the prestigious Brookings Institution. "In its foundations, it is slowly decaying; and in its performance, it is simply unable to continue to bear the burdens it must carry. It must be fixed, and the fix will require more than a shiny coat of new paint."

The Brookings Institution's call for radical reform echoed that of the NPR, which concluded that "we must reform virtually the entire personnel system: recruitment, hiring, classification, promotion, pay, and reward systems.

> *We must make it easier for federal managers to hire the workers they need, to reward those who do good work, and to fire those who do not. As the National Academy of Public Administration concluded in 1993: "It is not a question of whether the federal government should change how it manages its human resources. It must change."*

In New Zealand, reformers reached similar conclusions five years earlier and blew the system's foundations away—dismantling the civil service controls and letting each department manage its personnel in line with a few basic systemwide rules. Sweden and the U.K. have most of the same flexibilities. Georgia made a similar move in 1996, ending the civil service system for new employees; instead, each state agency can create its own personnel system, define job classes and pay ranges, and recruit and hire employees.

We wouldn't recommend going quite as far as Georgia has gone; we think you need to preserve prohibitions against patronage hiring and political manipulation of public employees, as New Zealand and the U.K. have done. But bit by bit, governments are revamping their personnel systems in three very important ways:

1. *They use compensation to create incentives for performance.*

pp. 215–246

They use many of the tools of performance management identified in Chapter Six, including performance contracts, performance bonuses, and gainsharing. At the same time, reinventors abolish longevity pay and routine annual increases, which are not based on performance. Thus employees can only increase their income (other than through cost-of-living adjustments) by performing well or being promoted.

pp. 478–486

With many organizations developing work teams, some reinventors are experimenting with team-based performance pay. For example, Hampton's personnel unit, which is a self-managed team, decided in 1995 that its members' raises would depend on the whole team's performance in achieving its measurable goals, not just on individuals' performance. Gainsharing is another way of rewarding teams financially, since it allows work units to keep as bonuses a portion of the savings they generate. Other organizations have begun compensating team members on the basis of the skills they have rather than their job descriptions. Skill-based pay gives employees a reason to keep building their capacities and creates mobility for employees stuck in low-level job classifications.

Personnel reformers have also invented new ways to do performance appraisals. Hampton has experimented with team-based appraisals. Other places include peer reviews as part of the process. Aggressive reinventors use a "four-way check," which solicits input from subordinates, peers, supervisors, and the employee himself or herself.

In Florida, reinventors made employees' performance a factor in determining whether they would be laid off or "bumped" into other positions during personnel reductions. (In the past, workers with the most seniority had been protected against layoffs.) Better yet, some governments have done away with bumping altogether.

2. *They give managers flexibility to shift human resources to meet the organization's changing needs, including more authority over hiring, firing, and promotions.*

The Clinton administration threw out the 10,000-page *Federal Personnel Manual* and substituted a shorter set of rules in its place. The New Zealanders and British have gone much further. In 1996, the British finished delegating all pay, pay bargaining, and civil service grading to agencies and departments. The process took two years and proceeded agency by agency. It wasn't long before organizations began making changes. For example, the 60,000–employee Inland Revenue abolished 120 traditional civil service grades and replaced them with five broad pay bands covering nearly all of the staff.

The shift from narrow to broad pay grades and job classifications is a worldwide trend, because it gives agencies much more flexibility in setting compensation, rewarding performance, and organizing work.

Reinventors are also streamlining hiring and firing processes. The latter are often so cumbersome and slow that most managers simply avoid them, choosing to put up with or transfer incompetent employees rather than try to fire them. One common reform is to simplify the appeals process for employees who are fired, so appeals do not go on endlessly. Many governments with British-style civil service systems are increasing competition for management positions by opening the door to candidates from the private sector.

Lastly, as reinventors seek more flexibility, they also are building new assistance programs for employees faced with losing their jobs due to privatization, managed competition, or other causes. As we discuss in Chapter Five, they are creating job banks, which keep some jobs vacant so dislocated workers can be moved into them; providing outplacement services; requiring private contractors to hire public employees; and providing early retirement incentives.

pp. 199–200

3. *They invest in building the capacities of public employees.*

Alan Brunacini, the fire chief of Phoenix, notes that 90 percent of his department's budget goes for personnel: "Every service that we deliver, we deliver with a real live firefighter. We are effective to the extent that our firefighters are effective. So it doesn't make a hell of a lot of sense not to invest in that workforce."

Many reinventors would agree with Brunacini's assessment. But they find that typical government personnel systems don't invest in employees. Major American corporations routinely spend four times more on training employees than the federal government does, according to the National Commission on the Public Service. But the level of investment is hardly the only issue. In 1989 the commission, chaired by Paul Volcker, issued this disapproving description of federal agencies' training practices:

> *Agencies are not sure what they should train for (short-term or long-term), who should get the lion's share of resources (entry level or senior level), when employees need additional education (once a year or more often), and whether mid-career education is of value. . . . Career paths are poorly designed, executive succession is accidental and unplanned, and real-time training for pressured managers is virtually nonexistent. At both the career and presidential levels, training is all-too-often ad hoc and self-initiated.*

Many governments are now boosting their spending on training and management development—led by Australia, which dedicates 5 percent of its payroll to training.

Reinventing Personnel Systems

Use Compensation as a Performance Incentive:	*Give Managers Flexibility to Manage Their Human Resources:*	*Invest in Capacity Building:*
• Performance management tools • Elimination of longevity pay • Team-based pay • Skill-based pay • New forms of performance appraisal • Performance criteria in personnel reductions	• Decentralized personnel authority (hiring, firing, promotions, and so on) • Simplified job classifications • Broad pay bands • Streamlined hiring and firing processes • Open-door job competition • Employee assistance programs	• Employee training • Employee and management development • Investing in employees

Transforming Procurement Systems

George Boersma chalked up 10 years running the purchasing and credit card operations of a major Detroit bank before he became Michigan's purchasing director in June 1994. He was no expert in government purchasing systems, so he had all the departments send him flowcharts of their purchasing processes. They were Byzantine: some required as many as seven or eight different people to check on and approve each purchase. "I could not look at them," says Boersma. "I decided this was ridiculous."

Then Boersma created a list of all government employees who spent at least 25 percent of their time processing and approving purchasing requests. It amounted to the equivalent of 183 full-time staffers. He tracked one $20,000 purchase: it crossed 27 desks and took 81 days—but it required just 3 hours and 15 minutes of actual work. Finally, Boersma asked how much it cost to process purchase orders. "Nobody had a clue," he says. So he figured it out. He found that the vast majority of the state's more than 100,000 purchases annually were for goods and services under $1,000. The average price of those purchases was $254. Then he took the cost of the purchasing employees (salaries, benefits, equipment, and the like), and divided it by the number of purchasing transactions. The answer: on average, it cost between $70 and $100 to make a $254 purchase. That, Boersma thought, was outrageously expensive. Sometimes the *process* cost more than the *product*!

So he found a way to cut the cost by as much as 90 percent. He offered to give purchasing cards (like credit cards) to state employees selected by their departments. The civil servants could use their cards to buy whatever they needed—no permission required—as long as it didn't cost more than $1,000. That cut out all the layers of the purchasing process, as well as all the inspectors and approvers. It didn't just save the state money, it saved the agencies an enormous amount of time.

George Boersma cut one of the Gordian knots of purchasing: the red tape created because no one trusts employees. The other big Gordian knot is the low-bid mentality. Governments have long acted as though the lowest cost is the only goal in purchasing. This is supposed to prevent corruption in bidding, but it can be a costly mistake, since low prices often mean shoddy goods and services.

The impact of bureaucratic procurement systems becomes more striking when you realize just how much purchasing governments do. By 1991, North Carolina purchased about $1 billion worth of goods and services a year. By 1993, the U.S. federal government spent more than $200 billion a year on goods and services—about $28,000 every second of every working day. Overall, government purchasing amounts to 20 percent of America's gross national product.

But there's more than money at stake in reinventing procurement. As the Madison police learned, procurement systems can be completely disempowering. Because of "Mickey Mouse rules," as Mike Masterson calls them, employees often can't get the goods and services they need to do their jobs. Sometimes they get them long after they need them. As a result, performance suffers. And no one is accountable for these failures. They just happen—*routinely*.

In response, reinventors push procurement systems to change in several ways:

1. They give managers and employees more control over purchasing decisions.

A relatively easy step is to let departments use purchase cards, as Boersma did in Michigan, the Clinton administration did in Washington, and many other states, cities, and counties are now doing. A federal government pilot begun in 1986 took off after 1994, when Congress passed a procurement reform package recommended by the NPR and President Clinton issued an executive order on purchase cards. By 1996, federal employees were making 31 percent of their acquisitions with cards—seven million purchases worth $2.9 billion. A 1994 study found that they saved an average of $54 per transaction by using cards rather than purchase orders. Do the math and federal savings were in the neighborhood of $378 million a year by 1996.

Reinventors also allow agencies to purchase more off-the-shelf commercial products rather than drawing up bid specifications and going through formal bidding processes.

In addition, many governments are raising the "purchase floors" under which simplified procurement procedures apply. This is a particularly helpful change, since most purchases involve relatively small amounts of money. In 1993, when the NPR recommended that the federal floor move from $25,000 to $100,000 (a reform Congress passed), it estimated that this would exempt nearly 50,000 transactions a year from full-scale procedures.

More generally, reinventors deregulate procurement by shifting from rigid rules and processes to general principles agencies must follow. Canada, for instance, has boiled its procurement law down to just eight pages, counting both the English and French versions. In Michigan, former chief information officer John Kost discovered that the state's cumbersome procurement system was not even required by law. "The state purchasing law required virtually none of the bureaucratic hassle that was occurring," he says. "In fact, existing law contained explicit language giving the Department of Management and Budget the authority to do whatever was in the state's best interest."

So Kost and Boersma issued purchase cards, allowed unapproved "quick purchases" for transactions under $25,000, and replaced detailed procedures with several basic principles for agencies to follow:

- The procurement outcome is more important than the process.
- Flexible purchasing processes allow the best outcomes.

- "Best value is more important than low price."
- "Time is money."
- "Invitations to bid should describe the problem, not the solution."
- Bidders should be able to propose a variety of possible solutions, not just the "right" solution.

When reinventors shift operational control of procurement to agencies, as Michigan has, some purchasing agents are no longer needed. When this happened in Minnesota, says Jeff Zlonis, a former deputy commissioner of administration, the state turned redundant purchasing agents into consultants to help agencies find the best vendors, hold down costs, and avoid purchasing pitfalls.

To speed up purchasing processes, reformers also amend protest rules to discourage vendors from making frivolous challenges. Philip Howard, author of *The Death of Common Sense,* artfully describes the way that agencies' vulnerability to protests slows purchasing down:

> *Losing vendors are actually able to sue, or "protest," when a contract is awarded to someone else. Any businessman will see immediately the paradox. Sue your would-be customer? No such legal right exists in the real world. If anyone tried it, they would never get a chance at the business again. . . .*
>
> *What this accomplishes for government is a corrosion of its bargaining power. Col. John Case, testifying recently before Congress, observed that instead of negotiating hard for taxpayers, contracting officials spend months trying to please bidders in an effort to make the bids "protest proof." The main goal—spending money wisely—gets lost in a labyrinthine exercise of process for its own sake. Soviet central planning, by comparison, seems almost crisp and efficient.*

To ensure prompt and efficient handling of protests, governments also use alternative dispute resolution: negotiation, mediation, facilitation, fact finding, and arbitration.

Another way to accelerate purchasing processes is to use catalogs with prenegotiated prices for office furniture, supplies, and other things. Basically, the government negotiates terms and conditions with vendors, then gives employees a catalog of items—or even better, puts the catalog on-line, where it can be updated daily. Managers can buy these items without bids or approvals. Usually, the vendors have also been required to guarantee fast processing of orders. In Michigan, says Boersma, "If you order something by 5 o'clock today, in 80 percent of the state you will get it delivered tomorrow. In the remaining [more remote] part of the state, delivery will be the following day."

Lastly, many governments are paying special attention to the problems of purchasing information technology (IT), a rapidly growing commodity for public buyers. Because of past problems with IT systems and eye-popping cost overruns, purchasing processes often became quite rigid and, therefore, incredibly slow. In 1993, the NPR reported that the pace of IT purchasing was causing serious problems:

> *The federal government takes, on average, more than four years to buy major information technology systems; the private sector takes 13 months. Due to rapidly changing technology, the government often buys computers that are state-of-the-art when the purchase process begins and when prices are negotiated, but which are almost obsolete when computers are delivered. The phenomenon is what one observer calls "getting a 286 at a 486 price."*

One solution is to delegate more IT purchasing authority to agencies while providing them with much more expert assistance. San Francisco opened a computer store for its agencies. It offered equipment from three vendors selected competitively, providing a wide range of choices while meeting the city's standards. The store cut the time it took to procure a personal computer from six months to about two weeks. The committee that once handled all technology purchases stepped out of that role; instead, it now oversees the system to ensure that the city's computer systems are compatible.

2. *They substitute best value purchasing for low-cost purchasing.*

Some governments, including both Canada and the U.S., have shifted their emphasis from getting the lowest bid to getting the best value. In 1993, California adopted reforms that added quality, reliability, and past vendor performance to price as important factors to consider in purchasing.

One way to identify value is to define the "full cost" or "life cycle" cost of the equipment, including the cost of disposal or recycling. This approach was introduced in Madison by elected officials. "A low purchase price means little if the equipment becomes unreliable or requires a series of expensive repairs," explains Mike Masterson. "Madison's elected leaders saw the value of looking at the total cost of a product, not just the initial price tag, and at its predicted life cycle based on how it would be used. Their aim was to minimize the total cost, not just the bid price."

Increasingly, governments are also using performance-based contracts to ensure that vendors deliver the value they have promised. In Indianapolis, for example, the company that won the right to manage the city airport guaranteed it would reduce costs by $50 million and backed up its pledge with an irrevocable letter of credit.

Another way to increase value is to create long-term partnerships with suppliers and engage them in helping improve your productivity. Michigan's Boersma put such a provision into a three-year contract with the firm that provides the state government with office supplies. The state can extend the contract by up to two years. "We told them we may extend," he explained, "provided you come to the state on an annual basis and show us how to reduce our costs by 3 percent or more."

In Canada, an innovation called Common Purpose Procurement (CPP) allows governments to select private sector partners who will work closely with them to jointly develop and manage new ways of delivering services. This process, rather than a traditional bidding process, is used "when government does not have the time, money and expertise to design and build a solution of its own," as Ontario's guide for industry suppliers explains. The Canadian federal government piloted the method, using IT purchases. New Brunswick and Ontario have implemented their own versions. "Ontario's new CPP format encourages government ministries to select partners on proven experience and expertise, project approach and management, financial stability and the ability to work in partnership where each partner shares the project's risks, investment and benefits," according to the guide.

Under CPP, an organization starts the process by asking vendors to respond to a request for proposals that describes the organization's vision or opportunity and the desired results. From the responses, the agency selects several vendors, who then compete based on the quality of their proposed business relationship, financial arrangements, project approach, and organization, as well as their capacity to partner with government. Then the agency and the highest-ranked vendor negotiate an agreement that defines initial activities and deliverables, as well as some procedures for managing the partnership. Although this procurement method is appropriate only for certain projects, it encourages innovative approaches, reduces decision-making times, and allows the public and private sectors to share risks.

3. *They build the customers' needs into the purchasing process.*

When the Madison police department bought Omnis and Horizons for its fleet, it left the customers out of the purchasing loop. No one asked those who would be driving the cars what they needed. Later, a team of employees developed ways to get the customer back into the picture. The *Purchasing Improvement Toolkit* they created explained why it was important to fully understand the end user's needs:

> *For example, one might order a dozen pairs of work gloves for a city work crew. This seems simple enough. But what is not obvious to*

City Purchasing is the relative importance of such factors as usable life, waterproofing, warmth, protection from abrasions, retention of manual dexterity, fire protection, or even color.

The team recommended that customers be involved in drawing up specifications and even in testing equipment. They called this involvement "user input." Thus when the police department purchased portable two-way radios for its officers, it insisted that the bidders provide samples for two-week trials. The police gave every bidder's radios an extensive field test before choosing the best ones.

In Minnesota, Larry Schanus at the Department of Transportation discovered that he could let people order customized equipment and still save money. Traditionally, the state had created a general specification and required every unit to buy the same product, whether that product best met their needs or not. Large manufacturers had produced lower-quality vehicles (no radios, no air conditioning, vinyl seats) to meet government specifications. Schanus learned that he could actually get much better value at the same price by promising a large number of customized purchases. He also discovered that the resale value of the nongeneric vehicles was much higher—so it reduced the life cycle cost to the state.

4. *They enhance competition between providers.*

Often governments select multiple vendors for a product, then force them to continuously compete to make sales to agencies. For instance, Michigan allows state agencies to purchase personal computers from any of three companies that meet state standards. The vendors compete for sales by periodically cutting their prices.

It is also becoming common to prequalify bidders, then pick the best ones and ask them to come up with their best proposal. This "two-step" bidding process "encourages innovation and initiative on the part of competing firms to develop new approaches, techniques, and methods in producing an item," notes Susan MacManus, a professor of public administration who specializes in procurement.

Increasingly, reinventors are also using information technology to boost purchasing competition. They create "electronic marketplaces" in which businesses and buyers enjoy rapid, computerized access to procurement information. In the most advanced systems, buyers make their purchases on-line. Canada runs an electronic marketplace in which companies list their best price every day. When President Clinton signed an executive order to create such a system for the U.S., experts predicted that average procurement times would drop from three weeks to five days.

Give Managers Control over Purchasing:

- Purchase cards
- Increased use of off-the-shelf commercial products
- Higher purchase floors
- Deregulation of purchasing processes
- Amendment of protest processes
- Simplified information technology purchasing

Build Customers' Needs into the Process:

- End-user input
- Choice and customization

Substitute Best Value for Low Cost:

- Best-value buying criteria
- Full cost or life cycle purchasing
- Long-term partnerships with suppliers
- Performance-based contracts

Enhance Competition:

- Use of multiple vendors
- Prequalification of bidders
- Electronic marketplaces

Transforming Audit Systems

In God we trust, all others we audit.

—SAYING ATTRIBUTED TO AUDITORS

When Jim Flanagan was the city auditor in Phoenix, Arizona, he met annually with a panel of city employees known as the Quality Board to get their ideas about new priorities for city government. One time, the board suggested that the city speed up inspections of blighted properties to force owners to make improvements, because people in the neighborhoods were so angry about the problem. Flanagan's auditors led the city inspectors in tackling the problem. "The inspectors were asked to redesign their own process," he says. "We went through the whole learning process with them, six months of study. It was very, very time-consuming; there were lots of angry people out there."

When the group finally designed a solution, the auditors' role as facilitators continued into the implementation phase. Then Flanagan's office helped the inspectors measure their performance. "They were able to reduce the cycle time on inspections pretty dramatically—over a 50 percent reduction, in terms of getting a case closed out," Flanagan recalls. "That became the focus of attention: getting the number down, as opposed to our issuing a report. A report probably would have been ignored."

Reinventing Procurement Systems

pp. 174–182

Another time, the Quality Board advised the city to focus on improving services to its internal customers—the agencies that depend on other agencies for vehicles, printing, and the like. So Flanagan sent Deputy City Auditor Susan Perkins to Milwaukee, which had adopted internal enterprise management. The information Perkins gathered helped Phoenix develop a pilot in this area.

In 1996, Flanagan, Perkins, and two other staffers traveled with government officials from 10 other countries to Finland and Germany to learn about organizational culture, citizen participation, alternatives to bureaucracy, and other topics.

For years Phoenix's auditors have benchmarked the city's performance against data from 10 southwestern cities of similar size. "Every time something comes up—water rates or animal control problems—one of the standard steps you go through is to check it out with the 10 cities," Flanagan explains. If his auditors find another city with better performance, "you pursue it, you figure out why it's better. We use the other cities this way; they use us this way."

Phoenix's auditors are pioneers; they are moving far beyond the auditor's traditional role as a bean-counting watchdog. They are creating new roles for themselves: facilitating work process reengineering, conducting far-flung study tours, and benchmarking performance against comparable governments. They still conduct audits, but they audit for results, instead of nitpicking about agencies' activities. And they add much more value to government than they have done in the past. "We focus on helping make change happen," Flanagan explains. "We really don't use the hammer here unless it's appropriate."

Phoenix is not alone at this frontier. Reinvention is triggering a long-overdue revolution in auditing at every level of government in the U.S., the U.K., Australia, Canada, and New Zealand. The basic trend is to do less auditing for compliance with rules and procedures, while shifting to auditing for results. "I saw a change taking place in the early 1990s in the field of auditing," Flanagan says. Increasingly, auditors recognize that if they want government to improve, they must go beyond inspecting and controlling organizations and help them change.

The Canadian auditor general's office is considered a world leader in this revolution. Auditor General Denis Desautels sketches the modern evolution of public auditing: "The emphasis of the traditional role, in the 1950s and 1960s, was on compliance with all the financial rules and regulations. The basic objective was to determine if the departments spent within their budgets for the things they were authorized." In the 1970s, he explains, some government auditors began to focus on efficiency.

> *There was a gradual movement to concern about getting value for money. And it hasn't stopped there. More recently it has evolved into concerns about effectiveness as well. In this evolution, we have also moved towards, for one thing, the notion of best practices, benchmarking, learning from what other jurisdictions are doing. And there is more emphasis on results being achieved. It is a kind of auditing that is more broad-minded. We're supporting improvements.*

Our research suggests that auditors around the world are developing four new roles:

1. They measure government's performance.

In the new world of performance management, measuring performance is absolutely critical. To do it well, you need a neutral, objective body that keeps the system honest—just as auditors do in a financial management system. The auditor's office is a perfect candidate for this function. In fact, some auditor's offices have taken the lead in introducing performance measurement. They help agencies select performance measures, prevent the adoption of vague or useless measures, monitor the process of collecting and analyzing performance data, and audit the measurement system. These tasks stretch the competencies of traditional auditor's offices, because performance measurement involves difficult technical challenges.

pp. 247–271

2. *They publish data that compares the performance of different governments.*

Performance data should not be used just by managers and elected officials. Reinventors are providing it to citizens, too. And when citizens get the information—finding out performance trends in crime control, government services, student test scores, and the like—they often pay attention. That's when politicians respond and change things. Increasingly, then, reinventors are thinking about how to get this information into citizens' hands.

A leading example is the Audit Commission in the U.K. It was launched by Margaret Thatcher's government in the early 1980s to audit local governments. But when the Citizen's Charter initiative in 1991 required some public organizations to measure their results and report them to the citizens annually, the Audit Commission took on a new role. It now gathers performance data from local authorities and publishes comparisons on 10 to 20 key measures. It does the same for police and fire brigades, which are separate from local authorities, and the national government publishes performance tables on hospitals and schools. These "league tables," as they are known, have generated enormous attention from the press.

pp. 210–214

3. *They audit competitive bids for government contracts.*

Governments that use managed competition to force improvements need someone to keep the process honest. Both public employees and private vendors will instinctively distrust the process. To build their confidence, governments must demonstrate that the playing field is level and the process is honest. This function is tailor-made for auditors.

pp. 193, 203

In Phoenix, which pioneered public-versus-private bidding, the city auditor's office has long performed the role. It audits public agencies' bids to make sure all costs have been included—all overhead and depreciated capital expenditures, for example. And if a public agency wins a bid, the auditors later check to make sure the agency is delivering the service at or below the cost it bid.

4. *They spread best practices.*

As Phoenix's Flanagan and Canada's Desautels indicate, this is the latest evolutionary phase in the history of public auditing. Because auditors often see an organization's performance problems, they can teach managers new approaches. Canada's auditor general has surveyed the world for best practices in reinvention and contrasted what it found with Canada's efforts.

In the U. K., the Audit Commission publishes studies that identify key success factors and explain how to improve management practices in police departments, fire services, transportation agencies, and other organizations. Some of these studies are guidebooks on how to solve chronic problems; others help local government agencies assess their own performance. The commission created a database of comparative information on the performance, quality, and management processes of local authorities, which they can use to benchmark their performance against best practices. The commission has also established a telephone help line for local managers, and it runs conferences that promote best practices.

In the U.S., even the inspectors general (IGs) and their staffs—widely despised by federal managers—are beginning to promote best practices. In 1994, for instance, the IG in the Air Combat Command (ACC) started helping squadrons assess their work processes. The IG started a "cross-flow" of critical information among the ACC's more than 500 squadrons, says then-commander Michael Loh.

> *They'll go to this unit, and they'll see how they are doing in their self-assessment, and then they'll just interact for a day or two. And they'll say, "You're doing great here. In fact, this becomes a new best practice for us to cross-flow to others. But in this area over here, these guys are doing this better than you."*

The box below summarizes the new roles auditors play in governments that embrace reinvention.

Reinventing Audit Systems

Measure Performance:
- Help in selection of measures
- Training in performance measurement
- Data collection monitoring
- Audits of measurement systems

Enhance Competition:
- Publication of comparative data
- Audits of competitive bids

Spread Best Practices:
- Performance audits
- Benchmarking
- Management studies and guides
- Conferences
- Consultations

RESOURCES FOR REFORMING ADMINISTRATIVE SYSTEMS

Jonathan Boston, John Martin, June Pallot, and Pat Walsh. *Public Management: The New Zealand Model.* Auckland, New Zealand: Oxford University Press, 1996. The six chapters on human resource management, financial management, and auditing describe and assess New Zealand's powerful administrative system reforms.

Albert Gore and the National Performance Review. NPR accompanying reports: *Reinventing Federal Procurement; Mission-Driven, Results-Oriented Budgeting; Improving Financial Management;* and *Reinventing Human Resource Management.* Washington, D.C.: U.S. Government Printing Office, 1993. These slim, readable reports, available at www.npr.gov/library/review.html, provide overviews of the basic ways to transform administrative control systems, at any level of government.

Charles Horngren, George Foster, and Srikant Datar. *Cost Accounting: A Managerial Emphasis.* 8th ed. Englewood Cliffs, N.J.: Prentice Hall, 1994. A good basic text on full cost accounting and activity-based costing.

Howard Husock. *Organizing Competition in Indianapolis: Mayor Stephen Goldsmith and the Quest for Lower Costs.* Cambridge, Mass.: John F. Kennedy School of Government, Harvard University, 1995. This case study about Indianapolis's work to create an activity-based costing system provides a good, concrete look at the challenge and its solutions.

Donald F. Kettl, Patricia W. Ingraham, Ronald P. Sanders, and Constance Horner. *Civil Service Reform: Building a Government That Works.* Washington: Brookings Institution Press, 1996. Focusing on the U.S. federal government, the authors describe the basic principles for "a new human resources model."

Susan A. MacManus. "Designing and Managing the Procurement Process." In *Handbook of Public Administration,* edited by James Perry. San Francisco: Jossey-Bass, 1996. An informative survey of state-of-the-art practice and innovations in procurement.

National Association of State Purchasing Officials, National Association of State Information Resource Executives, and National Association of State Directors of Administration and General Services. *Buying Smart.* 1998. A brief but meaty summary of procurement reforms in state governments; available at www.naspo.org, www.nasire.org, and www.nasdags.org.

Allen Schick. *Modern Budgeting.* Paris: Organization for Economic Development and Cooperation, 1997. A careful look at budget reforms in New Zealand, Australia, Sweden, and the U.K. Available at www.oecd.org/puma/pubs/.

SITE-BASED MANAGEMENT

***Site-Based Management* shifts control over resources and day-to-day decision making from the central office of a system, such as a school district or a national employment service, to the many frontline organizations in the system, such as schools or local employment offices.**

Site-based management is used by a wide variety of government systems to empower their organizations. In Edmonton, Canada, school superintendent Michael Strembitsky launched it in the 1970s. He started with seven schools that volunteered to receive powers long held by the central office. He rerouted 85 percent of the district's funds directly to the schools; each one got a lump-sum budget to allocate as it wished.

"There were real territorial battles" over the changes, Strembitsky says. "The central office didn't want to give up some powers." Within a year, though, he could tell the experiment was working. "People took to it like you wouldn't believe."

Within three years, Edmonton "went whole-hog." The superintendent and school board established goals in eight different areas, including student performance and employee satisfaction, and performance improved. Then they gave schools power over many internal services, through internal enterprise management. Some two decades later, the shift in control is still in place.

pp. 174–182

About the same time that Strembitsky launched his experiment, one of the largest organizations in the world, the U.S. Tactical Air Command, was also shifting central power to its "sites," hundreds of squadrons throughout the nation. Each squadron has control over its own resources and is responsible for achieving its performance standards. As *Reinventing Government* and *Banishing Bureaucracy* reported, decentralization catalyzed a remarkable turnaround in performance.

See *Banishing Bureaucracy* pp. 53–60

Britain's Employment Service has also moved power to local offices around the nation. And in Madison, Wisconsin, the police department shifted central headquarters' powers to district offices scattered among the city's neighborhoods.

These quite different organizations share a key characteristic that makes them candidates for site-based management: they have units in different places that produce similar types of results: schools produce student learning; air force squadrons produce combat-readiness; employment offices fill vacant jobs; police offices make neighborhoods safe.

Under site-based management, a site is made virtually self-sufficient. It commands the resources it needs to produce the results that are expected. As former ACC commander Michael Loh puts it: the site has to have "all its capability within it so it can do its job." In addition, as with any empowerment tool, the site is accountable for whether or not it produces the desired results.

When sites are able to manage their resources—their people, their money, and their facilities—more flexibly, they become more responsive to local conditions. "We don't get caught up in a lot of the bureaucratic shuffle and bull that takes place when you're part of the downtown station," says Captain Ted Ballesteros, who helped lead the site-based decentralization in Madison's police department. "If we want to do something quickly, we do it, as opposed to the sense downtown that you have to bounce it off all the others before you do something."

Site-Based Management: Lessons Learned

The U.S. has a 20–year history of using site-based management (SBM) in public school systems. But as the National School Boards Association reports, the reform has been "largely ineffective in raising the bar for student achievement." Why? "Schools operating under SBM often lack significant authority over budget, staffing, and instructional programming."

School boards are part of the difficulty. Some board members see school-based management as a threat to their own political power, so they limit it, override school improvement plans, or reject waiver requests. "Such acts of active and passive resistance are not at all uncommon," the association reports.

When schools do not get significant power, they tend to work on "peripheral issues, such as hall duty, campus beautification, and the assignment of parking space. This trivialization of goals and objectives represents a natural response to the limited authority and resources available to schools under SBM."

Even when the central office allows sites to have power, it is often unclear which decisions they can make. In the face of this uncertainty, people in sites are usually timid, since they worry about having the rug yanked out from under them. Or they go ahead with decision making and then get frustrated when the center does pull back the power.

Obviously, then, the most important lesson about site-based management is to give the sites real control—over their budgets, personnel, and purchasing. The second is to make it very clear where their power begins and ends. The general lessons outlined earlier also apply—along with the following:

pp. 400–403

1. To get sites focused on improvement, introduce consequences for performance.

One pillar of site-based management is a clear set of performance goals. "If expectations are not clear, no amount of delegation will make much difference," observe Peter Hutchinson and his Public Strategies Group partner Laurie Ohmann. Yet sites often plunge ahead without even a performance measurement system. When people face consequences for their performance, they pay more attention to improving it. When they can earn rewards, it makes em-

pp. 215–246

powerment feel even more worthwhile. Generally, team rewards work better than individual rewards.

2. *Help sites develop the capacity to manage their own affairs.*

Sites accustomed to having little control over their resources will not instantly know how to handle power when they get it. Yet, quite often, those implementing site-based management act as if once authority is shifted, it's up to the sites to produce.

The fact is that empowered sites need help building the capacity to manage. As the National School Boards Association says, "If SBM or any other reform strategy is going to improve student achievement, additional resources—including information, knowledge, and rewards—must be made accessible at the school site. But it will be necessary to *develop* capacity in these areas, not simply *devolve* capacity from central office to school site." People in empowered sites also have to learn how to make budget, personnel, and purchasing decisions. They need information systems, such as activity-based costing, that support their decision making. And they need help building an entrepreneurial culture, because empowerment depends on a different mind-set than bureaucratic compliance does. Finally, many site leaders need help learning how to empower their own employees and build work teams that share decision-making power.

pp. 531–609

pp. 453–488

3. *Give sites a way to get waivers of rules that restrict their flexibility.*

Central control systems have many tentacles. An individual school, for instance, must contend with rules from its school district, from state government, from the federal government, and from union contracts. So once a site has obtained some flexibility, it is still likely to bump into controls that limit its authority. A waiver policy can help the site get relief from specific controls.

pp. 430–434

4. *Don't make sites march in lockstep.*

Each site should be free to decide how it will produce the desired results. Don't make all sites try to do the same thing or proceed at the same speed. "I let each unit of production proceed at its own pace," says General Loh. To make sure he couldn't micromanage sites, he only measured their results, not their activities or inputs. "All I wanted to see was progress against performance measures."

5. *Give sites plenty of time to plan how they will function.*

Setting up self-sufficient sites is a complex undertaking. It requires thorough planning, which should involve the site's employees. Ted Ballesteros recalls how Madison's police department failed to anticipate the basic needs of the first site it established. "We originally were set up and sent down here without a unit stenographer to answer the phones," he says. "I spent six hours of the initial 12–hour days just answering the frickin' phone."

RESOURCES ON SITE-BASED MANAGEMENT

National School Boards Association. *Reinventing School-Based Management: A School Board Guide to School-Based Improvement.* Alexandria, Va.: National School Boards Association, 1999. A clear and readable analysis of what can go wrong with site-based management and how to make it work. Available at www.nsba.org/bookreports/bookreports.htm or by phone: (703) 838–6722.

WAIVER POLICIES

***Waiver Policies* are a mechanism that central agencies and headquarters use to temporarily or permanently exempt organizations from rules on a case-by-case basis.**

A waiver grants autonomy for one organization at a time; the rules in question are suspended, but they stay on the books. It can be quite narrow, covering a single rule; or broad, addressing a class of rules, like personnel matters. It may be issued to one person, a unit, an agency, or multiple agencies.

Many headquarters staffers and central agency officials deny that their rules are a serious problem. They say the controls are necessary and that their negative effect is exaggerated. When the U.S. Coast Guard set up a Model Units program, its top officers had reservations about the initiative. They felt, says Captain Ken Allington, chief of the Plans and Evaluation Division, that the Coast Guard "didn't really need a program like that because we were already doing almost everything right."

Another top official says they adopted the program as a challenge to employees:

> *One aspect of the program was, OK, put your money where your mouth is. Show us where you can be more efficient. Tell us which of these onerous regulations is keeping you from doing your job and causing you all this grief and anguish.*

Of course, *some* controls are needed. And it is true that some empowered organizations find that few of the hated rules are actually in their way. But the sheer volume of rules—and the trivial nature of many rules—shows how stifling they are. A Coast Guard unit had to get approval to allow its boats to carry nautical charts for its area only rather than for the entire Atlantic coast. The Commerce Department's Boulder Scientific Research Laboratories needed permission to eliminate a requirement that drivers have Government Motor Vehicle Operator cards to operate vehicles on the lab's grounds, even though they had normal driver's licenses already. "It was common sense," explains Paige Gilbert, a department official. But when the request went up the chain of command, "The safety officers for a couple of agencies went apoplectic."

See Reinventing Government pp. 10–11

The fact that a great many waivers are requested and granted undercuts the denials of centralizers. In 1984, when Bob Stone launched the Model Installations Program, which encouraged base commanders to request waivers, the first 15 bases generated 8,000 requests for waivers in two years; the department approved the majority of those within its power to address. Even as the Clinton administration eliminated 16,000 pages of internal regulations, reinvention labs surveyed by the GAO requested nearly 1,000 waivers in less than two years. One-third of the petitions involved agency work-process rules; the rest were aimed at personnel, procurement, and other rules.

pp. 434–450

Waivers are an essential element of several other tools for empowering organizations. Charter schools get waivers from most public school rules and regulations. Reinvention labs would make no sense without waivers.

Giving an organization waivers frees it to innovate in ways that improve its performance. Waivers also expose rules and procedures that need to be changed because they really are impediments to performance. Waivers should be used as early warning signals, telling those in charge of an organization or system which rules need to be eliminated. If leaders don't use them this way, waivers are somewhat limited in their power to create change. They aren't complete solutions to the problem of over-control; indeed, central agencies may use them as a safety valve, to let off steam that would otherwise force fundamental reform of administrative systems. After all, waivers usually help only one organization at a time, while the rule in question stands in the way of many others.

Difficulties in getting waivers are usually caused by two factors. First is the attitude of the person with the authority to issue the waiver. Usually the very people who make the rules must also give permission to break the rules, and many of them are not inclined to do so. "That's the problem we had at Defense," says Bob Stone. "If they are open-hearted and trusting, they will grant a waiver. But that's asking a lot." Somebody who wrote a safety rule because he thinks it will save lives will have a hard time changing his mind, Stone explains.

The second factor is the complexity of the waiver sought. In general, the more complex the request, the greater the difficulty in getting it granted. For example, federal personnel rules governing the use of leave time are far simpler than regulations about the use of federal funds in welfare reform. When

Oregon reinventors tried to get permission to waive the latter, they found that federal officials had to have the request reviewed by all federal stakeholders with jurisdiction over the program. The waiver had potential cost implications, which slowed things down further. And then the feds and the state had to negotiate numerous technical points. In all, it took Oregon about eight months to get federal permission to reinvest welfare savings in poverty prevention programs.

How to Increase the Flow of Waivers

Minimize the number of people who have to approve a waiver. A big problem with many waiver processes is that so many people have to say yes. In the U.S. Commerce Department, as many as 19 headquarters officials were involved in reviewing requests. "Requests for seemingly minor administrative changes triggered major bureaucratic skirmishes," says Paige Gilbert, an executive with the National Institute of Standards and Technology. This led to so many complaints that a top administrator finally allowed the department's reinvention labs to waive all internal regulations without going through the process.

Take waiver decisions out of the hands of the rule makers. When the former head of the General Services Administration, Roger Johnson, granted "reinvention charters" to two of his regional directors, he also gave them the right to unilaterally waive internal agency regulations. The Denver office used the new authority to shorten the process for selecting architects and engineers for major design projects from 12 months to 4 months. It also reorganized the workforce around service centers instead of functional specializations and allowed some agencies to negotiate their own leases for properties under 3,000 square feet.

"The beauty of the charter," says Wolfgang Zoellner, assistant regional director for the Public Buildings Service, was that "we did not have to ask the central office." He sympathizes with others who have to do so: "I spent 30 years in Washington. . . . You are asking the people who created the procedures and processes to waive them."

Although these kinds of blanket waivers can be very useful, they are not a cure-all for bureaucratic controls. For one thing, they don't cover the many rules set by central agencies, outside the department. And those agencies—the central budget, personnel, and procurement offices—will usually put up massive resistance to blanket waivers of *their* rules. Such a radical step would make elected officials very uncomfortable. After all, such broad waivers would open the door to nepotism, patronage, and many other abuses. So a blanket waiver may be appropriate and possible with departments and agencies or within small governments where people will operate on trust, but not beyond. That means reinvention labs will usually have to ask for waivers one by one, or in clusters. The challenge is to make approval easy.

The best solution is to give approval authority to a third party with a strong inclination to say yes—a high-level office near the executive in charge of reinvention, or an independent entity such as the Next Steps office in the U.K. or the National Performance Review in the U.S. This third party can of course consult with the central agencies to make sure it understands the problems that might be caused by granting a waiver. But it shouldn't be *required* to consult with anyone, since this would give those agencies the power to bog down the approval process.

Create deadlines for waiver decisions, with consequences for failure to act. Deadlines are easy to set, but that's only half the battle. The U.S. Coast Guard set a deadline of three weeks for responding to a waiver request from one of its Model Units sites. But when it took controllers much longer to act, no one did anything about it.

The trick is to enforce the deadline. One way is to have a top official keep pushing the waiver processors to get their work done, and make their performance part of their personnel evaluations. This may fall by the wayside when the top official gets too busy with other matters, however. A better answer is automatic approval if there has been no response by the deadline. NPR veteran Ronald Sanders, who has studied federal reinvention labs, would go even further. He suggests having the lab give 10 days notice before it waives an agency regulation. "Then the responsible staff office would have to convince the agency head to stop it."

Make control agencies develop lists of regulations that are ripe for waivers. It is unfair to assume that everyone in control agencies will tenaciously hang on to every single rule. Some may believe in reinvention, so it may be useful to ask them to think about which rules they would be willing to waive. They are likely to come up with something, although it may be quite modest. That's better than nothing, and it gets them thinking about what they can do to empower organizations.

Help reinventors develop and make the case for waivers. Some waiver requests involve a great deal of complexity. Although central administrators are familiar with these intricacies, most managers are not, so they are at a disadvantage in designing and arguing for waivers. "Reinvention labs need someone on their side who can do battle with the best of their bureaucratic brethren," says Sanders. One place to find this expertise is in the control agencies themselves; assign a converted expert to serve as an "angel" for the reinventors. Sanders also suggests having a high-level advocate in each department, someone "strategically placed right outside the secretary's door or perhaps right in the general counsel's office, since that is 'ground zero' for many innovations."

Automatically renew waivers unless there is an objection. This is a way to put the burden on the controllers, if waivers have a time limit.

Create an independent appeals process with override powers. If you can't issue a blanket waiver, then you need a way to review how controllers are handling waiver requests. Make their decisions subject to appeal, and conduct a periodic review of their decisions.

RESOURCES ON WAIVER POLICIES

Patricia W. Ingraham, James R. Thompson, Ronald P. Sanders, eds. *Transforming Government: Lessons from the Reinvention Laboratories.* San Francisco: Jossey-Bass, 1998. Though focused on reinvention labs, this set of essays provides valuable insight into what it takes to make waiver policies work.

OPTING OUT OR CHARTERING

Opting Out or Chartering **allows existing or new public organizations, such as charter schools, to operate outside the jurisdiction of most government control systems.**

In 1992, America's first official charter school, City Academy, opened in St. Paul, Minnesota. That was three years after reformers in the U.K. began to create the first of their "grant-maintained schools," a version of chartering that allows existing public schools to secede from their districts.

In spite of many obstacles, the charter school idea has caught on. By October 1999, some 1,684 charter schools were serving roughly 350,000 students in the U.S., in more than 32 states and the District of Columbia. And more were on the way. In California, which already had 130 charter schools, a 1998 law allowed 100 more to be added every year, with no total cap. In Milwaukee, where teacher union opposition had blocked the spread of charters, voters in April 1999 rejected all five school board candidates endorsed by the union and opened the door for more charter schools. In Colorado, Governor Bill Owens called for increased financing of charter schools so they would be funded at the same level as regular schools.

pp. 279–284

In England, one of every five secondary schools is now grant maintained. These schools have their own governing bodies, get their money directly from the national government, hire their own employees, and make their own rules.

It's not hard to understand why charter and grant-maintained schools are popular. A great many people have a passion to help children get a good education and are prepared to do something about it. They are unwilling to put up with the stifling bureaucratic controls of public education systems. Charter schools are tailor-made for them, because they allow people to escape from—opt out of—the system's rules. This "entrepreneurial approach has generally not been available to public school teachers and parents," says Joe Nathan, a former teacher and longtime leader of the charter school movement. "Teachers or parents who had ideas about new ways of organizing an entire school were out of luck."

WHEN BAD THINGS HAPPEN TO GOOD SCHOOLS

In 1993, Robert Wright, a middle school teacher in San Jose, California, wrote an op-ed piece in the *San Jose Mercury News* about his experience starting a school within his school district. What happened to him says worlds about why we need to give innovators an opportunity to get outside the district's controls.

> *Last year I started my own school and fell flat on my face.*
>
> *The staff was hand-picked, our philosophy was solid, the parents were supportive, the students loved the school and money was not a problem. But we made a fatal mistake: We created an alternative middle school within the public school system.*
>
> *We had a great idea: 1) It would be a small school that would develop its own family-like identity. 2) It would be a school of choice, not assignment. 3) Learning would be activity- based, not textbook-driven.*
>
> *The school board approved our creation when it was a nice plan on paper, but when we opened our doors we learned we could be outstanding so long as we didn't stand out. We could do whatever we wanted, so long as we didn't violate the rule of the ringing telephone.*
>
> *If somebody called an administrator to voice a compliant, that was a point against us. Substance didn't matter. The complaint that our school colors were too attractive took up just as much time as any other. The vast majority of complaints came from tenured teachers and principals.*
>
> *They complained that we would attract the best students and leave them "the dregs." They predicted that we would drain the district of scarce resources. Many complaints had little to do with us and more to do with the complainer's emotional investment in an institution that—though it couldn't provide decent pay or prestige—offered the security of inertia. It was as sad as it was strange when a teacher cornered me and blurted out screaming and crying that the existence of our school meant that what she had been doing for 25 years wasn't good enough.*

> *I had less compassion for the middle school principal who publicly cautioned parents not to enroll their children in our "risky experiment." When parents did anyway, he worked the phones in the evening persuading them to withdraw their applications. He finally got a directive from the district office prohibiting us from accepting any more of his students. So much for choice.*
>
> *I don't know if he ever gave any thought to improving his school so students would want to stay there. If the voucher initiative passes, he's going to have to.*
>
> *Since at the heart of all the complaints was a discomfort with the mere fact that we existed, we were pressured to give up, one at a time, all the elements that made up our identity as a small, separate school of choice.*
>
> *We gave up our faculty room, yearbook, school colors, budget, scheduling, staff development, recruiting—even the honor roll bumper stickers for proud parents. The reason? It made people uncomfortable. It made the phones ring.*
>
> *Before long, we were less like an actual alternative and more like a conventional school. And when that became apparent, it was used against us, too. Why have a new school if it's like all the rest?*
>
> *Finally we had to give up our name. We still could have a name, but it couldn't have "school" in it. I'm not kidding.*
>
> *I quit, along with most of the teachers who'd started the school. It's now a program that's indistinguishable from the regular school.*
>
> *The moral of our story is: If you have to get your parents' permission to run away from home, you're going to wind up in a pup-tent in the backyard.*

This tool is not just about escaping, however; it also creates accountability, because a charter is a contract in which the chartered organization pledges to achieve certain results in exchange for its freedom. "It's simple," says former Minnesota state senator Ember Reichgott-Junge, who authored the nation's first charter school law. "No results, no charter. Teachers trade away regulation for results and bureaucracy for accountability."

A charter school is a freestanding legal entity; it has its own governance board, separate financial status, and a minimum of state-imposed rules. In addition, it has a contract—a charter—with the chartering authority, which may be a state education department, a local school district, a university, or whomever else the state has authorized. "The term *charter,*" explains Nathan, "comes from the contracts given to European explorers, which specified expectations and responsibilities of both the explorer and his sponsors."

Although the most extensive use of this tool has been in elementary and secondary education, it can be applied wherever separating an organization from the rest of the system does not jeopardize its ability to perform. In Oregon, for instance, the state let part of its public university system become a more autonomous nonprofit organization. The Oregon Health Sciences University sets its own policies but still receives state funding. Every other year it must justify its use of tax dollars and request new appropriations. University president Peter Kohler says the changes have made it much easier for the university to raise capital and to establish a partnership with a local health maintenance organization. Inspired by the Oregon model, the University of Maryland at Baltimore let its hospital opt out of state regulations in late 1995. University president David J. Ramsey predicted that freedom, especially from personnel and procurement rules, could save the school millions of dollars a year.

Opting Out or Chartering: Lessons Learned

In 1994, the first charter school in Los Angeles had some 500 students—most of them dropouts with arrest records—and a board of directors that included several respected educators and businesspeople. But an outside audit discovered that the principal drove an expensive sports car leased by the school and that staff members had spent $7,000 on a secret retreat. The school lacked textbooks and supplies and was nearly $1 million in debt, including $240,000 it owed the school district for payments for anticipated students who never enrolled. When the board replaced the school's top administrators, the board president acknowledged that they were not qualified to manage such a large school.

Like their counterparts in "regular" government organizations, chartering pioneers must deal with the risk of corruption and incompetence by using audits, disciplinary processes, and other methods. But the opt-out tool comes with a set of other challenges not usually faced by mainstream government, and this is where the most lessons are being learned:

1. Take the performance of chartered organizations seriously, and hold them accountable for results.

Failure to establish performance standards is the Achilles' heel of chartering. If it's not clear what results the charter is supposed to produce, then it's hard to tell if opting out is making a difference.

In 1997, Arizona's department of education identified three dozen charter schools that had education programs bad enough to close down. The schools were allowed to continue, however, because they were not physically endangering the students or defrauding the taxpayers. The state law took a "let the market rule" approach. Its authors reasoned that the charters were primarily accountable to their customers, and if parents wanted to keep sending their kids to the schools, then that was good enough for the government. "If the education in charter schools isn't good, people leave, and the schools don't stay in business," explained Lisa Keegan, the elected superintendent of schools.

We believe this laissez-faire approach is a mistake. It misapplies the power of market forces to education, and it misses the point of chartering. There are several ways to use the powerful dynamics of markets to reinvent government. Enterprise management, which we describe in Chapter Four, forces government-run businesses to compete in the commercial marketplace for their customers and revenues. But public education is a public good, not a commercial product, because it benefits not only individual students but also the broader community. That's why it is purchased by the society, not individuals, and is required, not voluntary. That's also why we believe a chartered organization should have clear performance expectations, its performance should be measured, and if it does not deliver the expected results, its charter should be amended or withdrawn. If this is not done, charter schools will leave themselves wide open to a political backlash.

pp. 153–182

Customer satisfaction should of course be one of the expectations of a chartering authority. But in schools, parents are concerned mainly about the well-being of their own children. They may define their well-being in many ways: in terms of college-readiness, athletic opportunities, or social development, to name a few. Meanwhile, the government, on behalf of the public, is concerned mainly about the educational progress of all children. Its goal in freeing charters to experiment is to improve overall educational performance. That should be a bottom-line performance standard for any charter school.

Rather than using enterprise management to harness competitive forces in education, states that authorize charter schools are using managed competition. Charters are, in essence, three-to five-year performance contracts. They marry this approach with three others:

pp. 183–214

- Uncoupling steering and rowing, which separates the providers (schools) from the body steering the system (the school board).
- Competitive customer choice, which allows customers to choose their provider of education services, but within a system structured to achieve public goals.
- And organizational empowerment, which tests the proposition that if central administrative controls are abandoned, organizations will produce better results.

pp. 105–148
pp. 279–322

This explains why opting out or chartering is so powerful: it combines four strategies.

Some charter school authorizers have had difficulties getting clear about their standards for educational performance. They let charters get away with vague goals rather than requiring measurable improvements in student achievement. In California, for example, a 1999 study of 17 charter schools found that because there were no student assessment processes at the state level, charter schools were "more likely to be held fiscally than academically accountable." In contrast, Massachusetts uses rigorous three-day evaluations, built on the British model, to review each charter school every five years. The charter spells out expected results, and the evaluation reports on the school's performance in achieving them. The state board of education uses the evaluation, as well as test scores and other evidence, to decide whether to renew the charter.

p. 306

Authorizers must also be prepared to monitor performance. In the rush to set up charters, this is sometimes overlooked. In Michigan, for instance, one university put nearly 30 charter schools into operation before it hired any oversight staff.

2. *Give several bodies the power to charter, so that no one entity can choke off the escape route.*

Opting out is usually viewed as a hostile act by the entity from which the charter organization is trying to escape. School districts fear that charter schools will take away their students and, therefore, their per-pupil financial support. "Many school boards regard these schools as competition," explains Joe Nathan. "If you give people with power the opportunity to decide what kind of competition they will face, they don't want competition."

Cordia Booth, a school teacher, ran into a brick wall when she asked the Denver school district to approve her charter proposal. First the district, which had budget problems, rejected the plan, along with 11 other charter efforts. When the state board of education ordered it to take another look, it rejected Booth's charter again. Finally the state board ordered it to approve the charter and make sure the school opened the next school year.

If we wanted to ensure choice and competition in the software industry, we wouldn't dream of letting Microsoft decide who gets to start a software company. Letting a school board decide who gets to start a charter school amounts to the same thing.

To prevent school districts from closing down the opt-out route, you should also let other entities that are completely independent of the district issue charters. In Michigan, for instance, state universities can and do charter schools. In many states, the state department or board of education can also issue charters.

In California, county boards of supervisors can approve charters if school boards turn them down—but they are not independent enough, as it turns out. Elected school board members, district administrators, and teachers' unions have enough political clout to intimidate them at times.

As you spread the power to charter, be careful what incentives and disincentives you create for authorizing charter schools. In Arizona, for instance, school districts can make money when they charter schools. In one case, teachers looking for a quick charter gave a school district at a distant Indian reservation 3 percent of their revenues in exchange for their charter. The transaction was legal, but it was hardly the basis for the future accountability one should expect from a charter school.

3. Make the competence of charter entrepreneurs a standard for obtaining a charter.

School charter entrepreneurs run the gamut from employees, such as public school teachers and administrators, to customers, such as parents and businesses, to alternative organizations, such as museums, private schools, and even a teachers' union. In England, the process for converting a school to grant-maintained status starts when a majority of the parents at a school vote for the idea.

But the "due diligence" applied in assessing a charter proposal should include a careful look beyond the entrepreneurial spirit of the charter sponsors. Their competence and credibility as managers of a charter enterprise matters, too. Do they have a reasonable plan that is clear about goals and performance standards? Do they have the expertise to implement the plan?

Make sure the charter team has some business and financial expertise, since chartered organizations are independent businesses. "Many charter-school organizers are long on educational expertise but short on business skills," cautions a report by the Kennedy School of Government. "As with any start-up enterprise, this lack of management savvy can lead schools into trouble."

4. Keep the rules to a bare minimum.

Approving a charter should be close to granting a blanket waiver from central controls. Like any experimental effort, a charter school should still be expected to adhere to certain basic standards, such as following regular health and safety practices, not charging tuition or permitting religious instruction, and undergoing regular third-party audits. Like other institutions that opt out, it should still be subject to broader laws dealing with equal opportunity, due process, and the like. But it should be exempt from most of the system's internal regulations.

Although this may seem obvious, it's not that simple to put into practice. In Arizona, for instance, state lawmakers did not impose on charter schools the antinepotism rules that apply to school districts—and then had to deal with cases of nepotism. The state also let charters own property they purchased with public funds, so they would be able to borrow funds to build or renovate facilities. But when a charter school went bankrupt, the state had no legal position to try to recover equipment that had been purchased with taxpayer dollars.

Charters or opt-outs should not be subject to existing union contracts. A charter school should have the right to establish its own contracts, and its employees should have the right to organize and bargain collectively. But bargaining units in charter schools should be kept separate from the district's bargaining unit. Otherwise, charter schools' hands will be tied by the contract's rules regarding pay, benefits, work hours, and work rules.

5. *Avoid erecting inadvertent barriers to chartering or opting out.*

In Colorado, state law allowed districts to give charters less per-pupil funding than regular schools received. In some states, funding levels are equal for charter elementary schools, middle schools, and high schools, even though high schools are more expensive to operate. Few states fund start-up costs for charter schools, as we discuss in the next lesson. Reinventors should systematically weed out all such barriers.

6. *Help chartered organizations get started.*

Charter schools face the same problems as any start-up organization. Their biggest difficulties tend to be locating facilities and finding start-up capital, since they usually receive no public money until they open. That's why the U.S. federal government, some state governments, private foundations, and corporations are providing start-up grants to charter schools. The U.K.'s government does this as well; a transitional grant covers the early costs of a grant-maintained school, such as hiring a financial manager, setting up a payroll, and buying equipment. The government also provides grants for capital projects.

Charter schools have several problems locating facilities. One is a lack of vacant buildings that meet basic standards for providing education service. Another is local opposition to charter schools; some opponents put pressure on building owners to keep them from renting or selling to charter schools. A third is the cost of buying and renovating facilities. Because few states provide up-front funding for facilities, charters have to raise private funds or borrow what they need to secure and upgrade facilities. However, private financial institutions usually regard charter schools as risky propositions. Charters are new public organizations with no financial track record, and they have only three to five years before they must seek renewal—much less than the term of a typical building loan.

In *Paying for the Charter Schoolhouse,* the Charter Friends National Network identifies several ways to address financing problems:

- Governments can increase public funds going to charter schools to cover the cost of facilities. Several states offer charter schools funds beyond their operating revenues to pay for facilities.
- Governments can allow charter schools to use tax-exempt financing, which cuts the cost of borrowing. Two states already allow bonding authorities to issue tax-exempt bonds for charter schools.
- Governments can fund low-interest loan pools for charter schools. The Chicago Public Schools set aside $2 million for such lending.
- Governments can encourage property owners to provide facilities. They can offer tax credits to those who donate facilities to charters, or allow employers to reserve school seats for children of their employees if they invest in charter facilities.
- Governments can establish real estate trusts to acquire potential school properties and lease them to charter schools, as recommended by the Education Commission of the States.

7. *Be prepared for failures.*

There's no guarantee that every organization working outside the administrative control system will succeed. Some charter schools fail to deliver good student performance. Others have financial difficulties. A few falter due to malfeasance or corruption. So advocates of opting-out efforts should anticipate disappointment. Unfortunately, few of them do. "We expect some charter schools to fail, possibly even within the next few months," analysts at the Hudson Institute reported in 1996. "Yet we have not found a single state with a well-formed plan for dealing with these contingencies." The Hudson researchers suggest the development of monitoring systems to provide early warnings that charters are in trouble and a technical assistance capacity to help charters avert disaster.

RESOURCES ON CHARTERING

Center for Education Reform Web site: edreform.com. A comprehensive source on education reform, it includes exhaustive, up-to-date information on charter schools, as well as summaries of state laws, key studies of charter school performance and impact, and guides and workbooks for those starting charter schools. Scroll down to the index and click on "Charter Schools."

Charter Friends National Network. Established in 1997 as a project of the Center for Policy Studies in St. Paul, Minnesota, the network helps start and strengthen state-level resource centers that support charter schools. It offers publications, conferences, and grants. Contact the network at www.charterfriends.org, (651) 649–5479, or 1745 University Avenue, Suite 110, St. Paul, Minn. 55104.

Chester E. Finn Jr., Bruno V. Manno, and Gregg Vanourek. *Charter Schools in Action: Renewing Public Education.* Princeton, N.J.: Princeton University Press, 2000). A spirited but balanced account of charter schools nationwide, including a vision of how public education would work if every school in a district or region were a charter school.

Keith A. Halpern and Eliza R. Culbertson. *Blueprint for Change: Charter Schools, A Handbook for Action.* Washington, D.C.: Democratic Leadership Council, 1995. A brief guide to charter school legislation and tactics, available from the DLC at (202) 546–0007 or 600 Pennsylvania Avenue, S.E., Washington, D.C. 20003.

Bryan C. Hassel. *The Charter School Challenge: Avoiding the Pitfalls, Fulfilling the Promise.* Washington, D.C.: Brookings Institution Press, 1999. A new overview of charter schools and laws that looks specifically at Colorado, Georgia, Massachusetts, and Michigan and offers recommendations to enhance charter schools' autonomy, give them more resources, and help district-run schools learn from their success.

Joe Nathan. *Charter Schools: Creating Hope and Opportunity for American Education.* San Francisco: Jossey-Bass, 1996. A leader of the charter school movement, Nathan offers a readable explanation of the concept, stories from the front lines of charter schools, and excellent advice about how to create charter schools. Nathan runs the Center for School Change at the University of Minnesota's Humphrey Institute. Phone: (612) 625–3506.

REINVENTION LABORATORIES

Reinvention Laboratories **are public organizations that receive permission to break administrative rules and procedures temporarily and to experiment with new ways of improving performance. Typically they are granted waivers and protected from interference.**

If you want to start a revolution, build 100 fires and fan the flames.

—Bob Stone, former Energizer in Chief, National Performance Review

A reinvention lab is a small patch of temporarily liberated ground in the battlefield over control in government. It is an experiment in decontrol, often carried out at the front lines. A tool for bottom-up empowerment, reinvention labs turn loose selected organizations without having to free everyone.

In 1993, at Bob Stone's suggestion, Vice President Al Gore made reinvention labs a key tool of the National Performance Review (NPR). He asked cabinet members and heads of major independent agencies each to designate several units or programs to be reinvention labs. "Pick a few places where we can immediately unshackle our workers so they can reengineer their work processes to fully accomplish their missions—places where we can fully delegate authority and responsibility, replace regulations with incentives, and measure our success by customer satisfaction," Gore said. By 1999, more than 300 federal reinvention labs were in operation.

In Gore's model, there are no rules about creating reinvention labs; no central agency runs the process. Instead, each department determines its own criteria for labs and its own rules for how labs should function. "Each lab is unique," says Jeffrey Goldstein, an NPR staffer who surveyed the labs. "They are born out of different reasons to tackle different things. Each of them faces different issues and conditions." Some previous efforts, such as the U.S. Coast Guard's Model Units and the U.S. Forest Service's pilots in the 1980s, have included only a few handpicked sites. Gore, by contrast, sought to light a great many fires of change.

See *Banishing Bureaucracy* pp. 203–211

Benefits of Being a Reinvention Lab

Although being designated a reinvention lab does not usually mean a unit receives extra money, it does bring other benefits:

It gives innovative leaders the running room they need to move existing improvement efforts forward. John Haines, director of the Debt Collection Service in the U.S. Department of Education, had long wanted to change the budgeting methods used in his office. When Gore asked departments to create labs, Haines rushed to respond. "I got something to the department before they knew what was going on," he recalls. "It was on the fast track, and we were the only game in town."

For Richard Kelly, in the Office of Regulatory Analysis and Development at the U.S. Department of Agriculture (USDA), Gore's initiative was just the opening he needed. "We were active before the call came," he says. "We had people reading, and we were tracking the formation of NPR. We had our proposal on the assistant secretary's desk at the same time the people from the White House called to say, 'What are you doing about reinvention?'" Kelly used reinvention lab status to cut the time it took the USDA to review regulations generated by its offices.

It gets the organization's reinvention juices flowing. Becoming a reinvention lab "emboldens your own people to think creatively and to want to meet the higher expectations," says Doug Ross, a former assistant secretary in the U.S. Department of Labor. A U.S. Commerce Department reinvention lab in Boulder, Colorado, sparked unprecedented employee participation in trying to improve performance, for example. "This place is traditionally apathetic; [employees] don't want any part of the administrative stuff," noted Paige Gilbert, an executive with the National Institute of Standards and Technology. To her surprise, the reinvention lab generated 300 ideas, and 90 employees volunteered for task forces to implement them.

It eases the difficulty of obtaining waivers. Being a reinvention lab "gives us visibility and support for central office waivers," says Adelaide De Falco, from the New York regional office of the Veterans Administration. "It makes it easier to get the green light." Some federal departments gave their labs blanket waivers for all department regulations; others did not. Lab status did not mean, however, that the rules of central administrative agencies, such as the Office of Management and Budget, were automatically waived. In a survey conducted by the GAO, staffers in reinvention labs reported that waivers were still difficult to obtain from central agencies. (For solutions to *that* problem, see pp. 432–434.)

It shields innovators from bureaucratic opposition and other dangers. When you are recognized as a reinvention lab, it is riskier for managers in your own bureaucracy—or legislators or central agencies—to thwart your experiments. Bob Stone recalls how reinvention lab status protected one federal employee who worked in a two-person office in Mississippi.

> *One night, someone broke into the office and stole their two laptops. So he calls procurement and they say, "You know you can't get that equipment right away. Fill out a requisition form and wait." Instead, he went to a local computer store and ordered two laptops. Then he had a rubber stamp made that said, "Purchased in accordance with*

Al Gore's reinventing government program." He stamped the bill and sent it to the procurement office. One of our people [at the National Performance Review] found out about this and we made a fuss over this guy.

Several years later, Stone ran into someone from the same agency.

I told him about the story and said I always wondered if it had been made up. He said, "No, it wasn't." I said I was afraid the guy had been fired for what he did. He said, "No, but he probably would have been if you hadn't made a hero out of him. Once you did that, we couldn't touch him."

Doug Ross says the reinvention lab label may help a unit secure its funding. "When you're in the budget development process," he explains, "it's difficult for the central budget office to cut something that's just been designated as a learning center for the government."

Lab status can protect you from political risks as well. "It gives you some additional standing in Congress, because you're not forced to defend the status quo," Ross says. "You can claim to be an active part of making government work, rather than a part of the problem."

It increases opportunities to build cross-sector and cross-agency partnerships. "By virtue of their visibility," says the NPR's Goldstein, "reinvention labs seem to have lots of opportunities for partnerships with state and local government, academia, industry, and with each other."

These benefits are quite important to innovators at lower levels of organizations. "When we were first asked to set up a lab," recalls one federal employee, "we all laughed at Gore's memo—'Take away all the rules,' etc. Now I can't imagine going back."

Reinvention Labs: Pitfalls to Avoid

Reinvention labs don't always succeed. Some use their freedom in ways that don't accomplish much; others shoot themselves in the foot early on and don't recover. Here are a number of other potential pitfalls:

Revenge of the bureaucracy. Relief from central controls is "the lifeblood of reinvention labs," says Ronald Sanders, but "headquarters staffs are clogging their arteries. Many labs must fight through layers of bureaucracy to get waivers from even the most innocuous administrative rules within their own organizations, as well as those spawned by central agencies." If bureaucratic controllers are allowed to block or punish labs' efforts, reinventors will eventually lose heart.

pp. 432–434

This is perhaps the worst thing that can go wrong, because it crushes the hopes of employees and stymies change. Paige Gilbert says one of her colleagues compared their group to flies trapped in a jar:

> *At first, they want desperately to get out and will bump against the lid. After a few weeks of beating themselves up, when the lid is removed, the flies don't try to get out again. It was the same with us: there was so much frustration initially that people gave up.*

Overshooting the mark. Freedom can go to a reinventor's head. Some labs file numerous requests for waivers, only to find they don't really need them all. Joe Thompson's veterans office in New York started out by submitting 140 requests, then boiled it down to the 31 that made sense. The lab in Boulder, Colorado, started out with a great many unfocused ideas or trivial requests for waivers. A Coast Guard commander's first request for a waiver was prompted by his anger over a botched moving job; he got the waiver, but he never used it. These exaggerated actions are a mistake. They anger the very controllers whose cooperation is needed, and they make reinvention lab leaders look like they don't know what they're doing.

Bottling up the reinventors. The great value of reinvention labs is that they unleash innovations. Yet many government officials are timid about doing this; they authorize a handful of labs, call them pilots, and announce that "when we learn what works, we'll do more." Sometime this ends well—with Bob Stone's Model Installations Program, for instance. All too often, however, it just ends: there is no "more." Al Gore understood that the power of labs was in their proliferation, in freeing tens of thousands of federal employees to innovate and improve performance. But even his effort, which gave departments the authority to create as many labs as they wanted, was regarded by some as too constraining, since departmental brass were sometimes reluctant to use the authority. "There needs to be an easier way to become a reinvention lab," said Ronald Sanders. "There are lots of reinvention wannabes out there, and they shouldn't be kept bottled up. . . . The executive branch needs a nice, simple, fast way of giving them reinvention licenses."

See *Reinventing Government* pp. 10–11

Silence of the labs. Lab participants may be reluctant to share their stories and what they've learned, because of the risk of repercussions. "Many reinvention labs are clandestine," says Sanders. Some labs don't tell superiors exactly what they're doing, because they don't want to be stopped. The problem with silence is that it doesn't help other labs learn, and it doesn't build the case for more systemic changes. The NPR has tried to stimulate communications by organizing annual conferences, attended by Vice President Gore and other top officials, as well as an on-line information clearinghouse.

STARTING A REINVENTION LAB: A CHECKLIST

Do you have your leadership's buy in? A lab "just isn't going to work if your leadership isn't totally and enthusiastically supportive, all the way through the management chain," says Jeff Goldstein, who worked with many labs in the Defense Department. Getting your leadership's buy in means more than just getting top managers to say yes to the idea. "I see an awful lot of labs where the leadership commitment is real," Goldstein says. "I also see some where the words are there, but the actions may not be."

pp. 247–271

Do you know how you will measure your lab's progress? One important measure of success is customer satisfaction. Other measures might assess changes in the lab's effectiveness, efficiency, and employee morale.

Do you have a plan for capturing lessons you learn? A reinvention laboratory is valuable in part because of what it learns about what works. Unless you dedicate time and resources to capturing the learning, the lessons will quickly be lost. You should then identify ways to share your learning with others—particularly headquarters and central control agencies, which have the power to eliminate or change rules that have been waived.

Reinvention Laboratories: Lessons Learned

1. Labs need "top cover."

A reinvention lab needs an "angel" to help it overcome the resistance of headquarters staff and central agencies. This should be either the top person in the organization—a director, secretary, city or county manager, or the like—or someone who is perceived to be acting on behalf of the top person. The advocate should help the labs get regulatory relief and shield them from threats. He or she must remain highly visible in support of the labs—sending clear signals that the labs' work is critical to the department's future and that barriers to the labs will not be tolerated. Vice President Gore and the National Performance Review offer one model: the reinvention office helped the labs, using the power and prestige of the vice president. Within a large department, however, it also helps to have a reinvention office closely linked to the director or secretary.

2. Don't leave the controllers in control.

When the Coast Guard set up its early version of reinvention labs, the Model Unit Program, it designed a special process for the approval of waivers. Only the headquarters chief of staff could say no; everyone else could only approve or comment negatively on the request. And each waiver had to be handled within three weeks. The idea was to ensure that the approval process would be easy and efficient, but it didn't work out that way. The waiver request had to "travel up the usual chain of command," says Susan Rosegrant, who studied the program for the Kennedy School of Government. It went "to the district office, where it would circulate among the district staff and appropriate program managers, and then on to headquarters, where it would be reviewed by the branch staff, more program managers, the resource director, and, finally, the chief of staff." In short, it had to run the gauntlet of controllers, usually at least a dozen of them.

Only 3 of the first 19 requests made it through in three weeks; most took nearly twice as long. With later requests, processing took an average of more than 10 weeks. But that wasn't the only problem. Of 28 waiver requests submitted during the program, the controllers recommended killing 18. The chief of staff, with the ultimate power to decide, denied 13 of the 28. So nearly half of the time that commanders submitted requests, they were wasting their energy. And more than two-thirds of the time that the controllers objected to a request, they won. It's little wonder that this process had a chilling effect on the units. With the chances of getting a waiver about 50–50 and a strong likelihood that it would be opposed every step of the way, reinventors grew reluctant to take on the system. "People really don't want to put their careers on the line over some silly little issue," explains Commander Ron Frazier.

The Coast Guard had the right intention—to design the waiver process so that it would be easy and efficient. But it gave controllers far too much power to hamper the process. That's what controllers will do, if you give them the chance. The solution is to take the waiver decision out of their hands, as we explained earlier.

p. 432

3. *Keep labs focused on achieving the mission and improving customer service.*

Reinvention labs have a strong drive to try new things, to innovate. What they come up with will be all over the map. So it is critical that they always keep their purpose in mind. If they lose track of their mission and customers, they will not use the flexibility they have as a lab to improve their performance in ways that matter. To ensure that this doesn't happen, a reinvention lab should articulate a clear vision of what it is trying to accomplish for the organization and its customers, with goals and objectives linked to the organization's. It should do this at the outset and periodically check on progress.

4. *Reward the labs for success.*

It would be easy to think that for members of reinvention labs "innovation is its own reward." To a large extent this is true; the chance to try out new ideas

pp. 215–246

and to escape from stifling rules and regulations is important. But why stop there? You can use performance management to introduce incentives—bonuses, gainsharing, shared savings, and awards. Vice President Al Gore does this by awarding symbolic Hammer Awards to high-performing reinvention labs, for example.

RESOURCES ON REINVENTION LABORATORIES

Patricia W. Ingraham, James R. Thompson, and Ronald P. Sanders, eds. *Transforming Government: Lessons from the Reinvention Laboratories.* San Francisco: Jossey-Bass, 1998. Chock full of stories from federal reinvention labs, this set of essays provides valuable insight into what it takes to make reinvention labs work.

MASS ORGANIZATIONAL DEREGULATION

Mass Organizational Deregulation **repeals many of the other internal rules and regulations created by legislatures, central agencies, and departments to dictate the behavior of public organizations.**

Some elected officials relish the opportunity to slaughter government's rules. In 1993, President Clinton ordered federal departments to eliminate half of their internal regulations within three years. In 1995, Michigan governor John Engler pushed for repeal of the state's school code, the 172 pages of state government rules and regulations that controlled school districts. That same year, Florida's governor, Lawton Chiles, proposed repealing half of the state's 28,750 rules. At a press conference, the governor wore a back brace so he could hoist into camera view the many pounds of state publications containing rules and regulations he wanted to eliminate.

Some government managers also catch the deregulation fever. When General Bill Creech ran the 115,000–person Tactical Air Command, he realized that administrative rules were preventing him from empowering frontline employees.

> *I called in working-level groups from operations, maintenance, supply, and the various other field activities. I then put them in a room with all the regulations that pertained to their activities and told them to get rid of at least half of them—and even more if they thought appropriate. It was a labor of love.*

Mass deregulation thins out the thick regulatory "underbrush" that builds up over the years and becomes a frustrating thorn in the side of organizations.

Clearing this brush, says Bob O'Leary, a former Chiles appointee, helps reinventors get at rules that really are in the way. "By getting all the nonsense out of the code, you get to the point where you can focus in on the issues and what really needs to be changed."

In Florida, O'Leary explains, the process of banishing rules *en masse* went through three phases. "We called the first phase 'Cleaning Out the Garage and the Closets.' Departments identified rules that didn't need to be on the books anymore, that didn't apply anymore, or were just a rewrite of a statute." Some agencies found that 30 percent of the rules were "junk," he says. So they started asking the legislature to repeal them.

The second phase, nicknamed "Squeezing the Accordion," involved cleaning up and consolidating rules and rewriting them into plain English. A benefit of the effort, says O'Leary, was that it forced agencies to ask why the rules were written the way they were; that effort led to new candidates for elimination.

The last phase, which went unnamed, involved tackling the more important rules that were still causing problems.

Mass Organizational Deregulation: Lessons Learned

1. A big push from the chief executive is critical.

Governor Engler said he wanted to repeal the entire school code. Governor Chiles, President Clinton, and General Creech said they wanted to gut half the regulations. These targets may sound arbitrary and aggressive, but setting such targets is important, because it takes a major, sustained effort to cut a path through a vast thicket of rules. By so visibly going out on a limb, the chief executive signals to everyone—department heads, central agencies, employees, legislators—that he expects the effort to be made and sustained. That helps keep up the pressure when the process bogs down.

2. Publicize early successes.

In response to President Clinton's call for mass deregulation, the U.S. Department of Labor eliminated a requirement that employees fill out daily time cards. This reduced the organization's paperwork by 14,000 documents every two weeks. When you get rid of a rule with this much impact, you should celebrate. Publicize it, and give the deregulators an award. This helps keep up the momentum behind the effort.

3. To ease resistance to mass deregulation, establish legislative-executive cooperation at the outset.

pp. 61–104

Getting rid of some rules can be almost as difficult as clearing the decks of government programs or assets. Interests that benefit from the rules resist the effort. They influence legislators, who are usually already concerned that eliminating rules will let public organizations run amuck.

Governor Engler's assault on the school code produced considerable anxiety in school districts and some resistance in the legislature. Although his party controlled the legislature, lawmakers took nearly a year before finally approving a revision—not a repeal—of the code. They chopped out numerous sections of the code, but they also added significant new requirements.

The lesson is that it takes cooperation between the legislative and executive branches to get rid of external rules—that is, rules that govern citizens, businesses, communities, and others outside the bureaucracy. Elected executives should get legislative buy-in at the outset of the process, rather than assume that lawmakers will go along with whatever they come up with. One way to forge this collaboration is to establish an independent commission, jointly appointed by the executive and legislature, to fashion a package of rules for abolition. Another useful step is to require the legislature to vote yes or no on the entire package of rules, not on one rule at a time. The U.S. Congress has successfully used this method to overcome lawmaker resistance to closing military bases, as we detail in Chapter Two.

pp. 68–69

4. *Save some energy for the end game.*

In any mass deregulation exercise, some rules will be tougher to eliminate than others because they have the backing of central agencies, special interests, or legislators. It's important, then, not to stop the process once you've gotten rid of the easy rules. Resist the tendency to declare victory just because you've eliminated hundreds or thousands of rules. Bear down on the really important ones that are left.

5. *Be vigilant: prevent regulations from creeping back into place.*

After his mass deregulation effort, General Creech found that he had to stay alert for recidivism. "If commanders at lower levels added any rules, a copy came to my office for my personal attention," he recalls. "If I detected even a hint of CYA in the rule, or thought it patently unnecessary, I picked up the phone and reasoned with the rule writer."

Creech recognized that the top manager in an empowered organization should not micromanage. But fighting recentralization was an exception. "Normally I practiced a hands-off style," he says. "But I found that you have to work hard *at keeping organizations decentralized.*"

Chapter 11

Employee Empowerment

Giving Frontline Employees the Power to Improve Results

***Employee Empowerment* pushes decision-making authority down to frontline government employees, who instead of waiting for orders take responsibility for using the organization's resources to achieve results.**

Virgil Lee Bolden had been laying water pipes for the city of Fort Lauderdale for about 30 years when he heard he would be transferred and retrained for a different job in city government. The city commission wanted to outsource his work to private contractors. "They said the pipe-laying crew wasn't productive," Bolden recalls. "After all these years, I had to move. I felt everybody was kicking me around."

A few days later, the president of Bolden's union, Cathy Dunn, convinced management to listen to the crew's ideas for improving the unit's efficiency. The employees delivered a simple message: the problem isn't us, it's the system. They described the way management's design of their work prevented them from working full-time, and they suggested some changes."The managers added on to our list," says Bolden. "The department director said he was with us, the city manager—they seemed to listen to us."

The meeting persuaded Mike Bailey, manager of distribution and collection, to reexamine the decision to contract out pipe-laying. He checked what it cost the city crew to lay a foot of water pipe, on average, and compared it with prices charged by private contractors. What he found shocked him. "It was costing us $68–$74 a foot; contracting was $82," says Bailey. Earlier estimates had understated the contractor's costs. "We looked at that and said, 'It's a bad idea to let good pipers go.'"

At that point, "The guys said, 'Wait a minute, we still have a lot of good ideas about how to make it cheaper for you.'" The employees said they weren't spending enough of the work week actually laying pipe. They lost time at the beginning of the day because they had to report to the administration building before going to the job site. So the rule was changed to allow them to report directly to work sites. To further increase time on task, they suggested longer days; a four-day, 40–hour work week became the norm. They began storing equipment on site, having the police keep an eye on it, rather than hauling it back to the city's equipment facilities.

So many of these changes were "no-brainers," says Bailey, that he asked the crew foreman why they hadn't been made long ago. "The foreman said, 'That's the way your predecessor said to do it. That's the way we've always done it.'"

Once the changes were made, says Bailey, productivity soared. The cost of laying pipe dropped to about $38 a foot, more than a 50 percent reduction. In the first six months after the changes, the crew laid 15,000 feet of pipe—more than double the amount laid in any previous *year.* They weren't working harder, just smarter. "They didn't work any overtime," says Bailey, "but there was a certain amount of motivation. They were saying, 'These are our ideas and we don't want them to flop.'"

"The city manager says we have saved him over $4 million," says Bolden. "We did beat the system. Everybody cooperated with us, and we were able to show we could produce."

Virgil Bolden is not alone among public employees in wanting to improve his performance, in being prevented from doing so by a management system that expected him to do as he was told, and in substantially boosting productivity once he was unshackled from the system's constraints. Indeed, stories like Bolden's are the new norm in governments where reinventors are using employee empowerment to unleash energy and creativity.

PASSING THE POWER DOWN

See *Banishing Bureaucracy* pp. 224–227

When governments empower their *organizations,* the power goes straight to their heads—to the people who run them. To get better results, those managers need to turn around and empower their employees. There is no guarantee that they will; indeed, without pressure to do so, many empowered managers will simply grasp the reins more tightly. In *Banishing Bureaucracy* we discussed several ways to get them to pass the power down:

- You can create rewards for empowering their employees.
- You can create a unit close to the executive, like the National Performance Review or the President's Management Council, that will keep pushing agency directors to decentralize authority.

- You can teach managers the benefits of letting go.
- And if they still can't let go, you can let *them* go.

When top management does pass the power down, they typically give employees authority to make decisions in three areas:

• ***Management of personnel.*** Employees can be allowed to set schedules for work, training, and vacations; establish worker assignments and set job performance standards; conduct employee performance appraisals and administer discipline; hire new workers; and determine sick leave, substance abuse, and sexual harassment policies. In Fort Lauderdale, for example, employees joined managers in revamping sick leave policies for public safety (911) dispatchers, reducing sick leave by 1,329 hours in one year. In Portland, Maine, a similar labor-management team developed a new performance appraisal system, and employees in Seattle helped revise the system for progressive discipline.

• ***Redesign of work processes.*** Employees can be encouraged to identify problems with work processes and then investigate their causes, select and test solutions, change the processes, and monitor the results. Businesses began implementing systematic process improvement decades ago, using continuous incremental improvements, Total Quality Management, radical redesign, business process reengineering, and other methods. These powerful methods are now wielded by public sector organizations too.

• ***General management functions.*** Employees can take on planning, budgeting, communicating with suppliers, and problem solving in general. For example, in Indianapolis, where government employees compete with private vendors for work, they develop budgets and work plans for their bids.

To implement these changes, reinventors must dismantle bureaucratic systems that are based on constraining employees rather than trusting them. They must get managers to change their authoritarian ways. They must establish clear performance targets for employees and invest in employees' ability to make good decisions. And they must measure employee performance and reward it.

pp. 214–271

Breaking Down the System of Employee Control

Empowering employees is not only about cheering them on or being nicer to them. It is about giving them real power. To do that, you must dismantle bureaucratic controls that keep workers in their place. Reinventors target several control mechanisms in particular:

• ***Highly centralized organizational structures.*** Most bureaucratic organizations keep their various subunits at the mercy of a central office, which sets the rules and hands out the resources. Top managers run the place by establishing one-size-fits-all controls for the units.

• ***Excessive layers of management.*** Government has become the Grand Canyon of organizational design: it has more strata than anyone can fathom. And it keeps on adding to them. The trend occurs in most governments, but it has been especially pronounced in the U.S. federal government.

These management layers are a drag on the system. They increase the time it takes to get things decided and done, they constrict the flow of information, and they constrain employee initiative. Having too many management layers kills innovation, because it takes a chain of yeses to approve a decision and only one no to kill it. Management layers have the same effect as resistors on an electrical circuit, says John Scully, a former manager at NASA and the National Performance Review: the greater the number of resistors, the less electricity reaches its destination.

• ***Rigid job classifications and functional "silos."*** Government entities typically organize their work processes, jobs, and units by functional specialties. Work is designed as an assembly line, in which the "product" moves from worker to worker, each of whom performs a special task. The workers are segregated into units based on their special function. By amassing the specialists into these units, organization designers hoped to achieve efficiencies of scale.

Unfortunately, functionalism often breeds inefficiency. One reason is that performing the organization's work requires many handoffs between functional units; these consume enormous amounts of time and money. When the Social Security Administration (SSA) analyzed its work design, it found that the average claim from a disabled American was touched by 26 workers over 155 days; appeals added 17 workers and 585 days.

Functional silos strip workers of control. Employees follow procedures established by management, rather than deciding for themselves how to perform their work. They also place the interests of their units above those of their organization's customers and colleagues. At SSA's disability unit, the same analysis found, "Nobody . . . felt very responsible for the end result." The watchword of many a functional unit is, "That's not my job."

• ***Written rules.*** Bureaucracies thrive on rules. Many organizations magnify the problem by creating more rules than they are required to. The National Performance Review found that federal departments often interpreted legislation in a more restrictive manner than necessary. For example, after they were given purchasing authority for items up to $25,000, many kept lower limits. Many organizations don't even realize how many rules they've created. They routinely blame someone else—lawmakers, central headquarters, budget offices—for all their rules, when much of the problem is homegrown.

• ***Inflexible labor-management contracts and grievance processes.*** Since 1983, roughly 1.2 million public employees in the U.S. have become union members. The increase means that about 38 percent of all government workers are unionized—more than triple the penetration of private employment. Typically, these unions are engaged in a constant tug-of-war with management. The struggle seldom gets as nasty as some conflicts in the private sector, partly because most public employee unions are prohibited from striking. Still, government unions and managers tend to negotiate contracts with very detailed and rigid working conditions. "The contract is the Holy Grail," says Cathy Dunn, president of AFSCME Local 532 in Fort Lauderdale.

Breaking down this array of control mechanisms—centralized structures, management layers, job classifications, functional silos, rules, labor contracts, and grievance processes—is no simple task. They have been a part of bureaucratic government for a long time and are embedded in the culture of public organizations. Many people, including public employees themselves, assume that government needs lots of inspectors to check up on workers, lots of rules to keep workers in line, and lots of managers to make sure workers know what to do. They are conditioned to accept control from above.

Managing in a New Way

Mike Bailey, the manager who unleashed Fort Lauderdale's pipe layers, began his career in government as an engineer. He says he first learned how to manage by watching other managers. "Having seen my predecessors, I assumed that management was a lot of decision making, a lot of instruction giving, a lot of telling people what you wanted them to do. I felt it would be a very, very busy position; you would be always involved in day-to-day operations."

Then Bailey was promoted to run a division in public works, with about 140 employees. He discovered that everything he had learned about how to manage was wrong.

The people who reported to him expected him to tell them what to do. "They would always be in here asking me, 'What do you want me to do? How do you want me to do it?'" Bailey says. "I discovered I didn't know how to answer the questions. I didn't know enough about how the day-to-day operation worked."

Bailey says he "took a stab" at answering employees' questions, but it didn't work. "They would say, 'That's not going to work because of this and this.' And they were right." That's when Bailey realized that his role should not be to command the troops but to clear the way for them to use *their* skills and knowledge. He began to let the pipe layers manage their own work. For instance, he let them set their own vacation schedule. They decided to have everyone take vacation at the same time, shutting the operation down for two weeks a year. That was better for employees than having to spread vacations throughout the year; everyone could take off during Florida's unbearably hot summers. And it was good for productivity, because during the rest of the year work crews would be at necessary staffing levels.

Bailey says he had little trouble letting go of power because he was just getting started as a manager; he didn't have to break any bad habits. But it has taken some doing to get his division's mid-level managers to let go.

> *The way I've tried to convince them that this is a good thing is to show them how much easier it is for the managers. Before, the employees would not make a decision without asking. And if someone screwed up, they wouldn't take responsibility. That's pretty stressful [for managers].*

The stresses fade when managers empower employees, says Bailey. "Life is easier, because these guys are trying to run themselves now." Under this approach, the foreman of the pipe-laying crew is not in charge of the workers anymore. But he still has important work to do: getting permits from the county, expediting the delivery of equipment, purchasing new equipment, planning the pipe-laying projects with the city's engineers.

In Fort Lauderdale, Bailey has become a symbol of a new management style. He is sometimes asked by Scott Milinski, the city's employee relations director, to talk with other managers about it. "I feel guilty that I'm being praised," Bailey says. "It's almost like I pushed away a lot of work and everybody's praising me for it."

Mike Bailey is unusual; for most managers, the shift to employee empowerment is a difficult change. "The emphasis is moving from the manager as a controller to the manager as leader," explain Sue Vardon and Karen Morley, reinventors in the state of South Australia.

> *The new manager will be a leader, a coach, a teambuilder. People who make things happen will be encouraged. People who work out ways to stop things happening will be identified, appraised and helped to change. Managers will provide the model for their staff for the new public sector: respect for customers and staff.*

Empowering managers must act more as coordinators than as bosses. "In a traditional organization, managers function as the hub for information," observes Robert Bacal, a management consultant and author of *Performance Management*. "In the empowered organization, information flows in many directions. Managers need to be able to create structures of coordination so that decisions made by individual staff members do not adversely affect the work of others."

Most managers have trouble letting go of power. Some like wielding control. Their professional identity has become wrapped up with being in command. What will they do if not that? Will they still have a job with the organization? Others are afraid to let go because they believe that they—not employees—will be on the hook if things go wrong. "Who is the city manager going to call when there's a problem?" a department head might ask. "The employees who are supposed to be responsible—or me? I bet it will be me."

Still other managers just don't know how to change their ways—or are threatened by the very idea of change. To help managers make the transition, you can do a few simple things:

- ***Be clear about what you mean by "new management."*** Most descriptions of new management competencies include concepts like visionary leadership, team building, coaching, facilitation, and the like. Managers need concrete examples of what these behaviors look like in real workplace situations.
- ***Assure managers that they have a place in the organization.*** Managers (and nearly everyone else) will resist and undermine changes that threaten their livelihood. It is crucial to let managers know that the organization still needs them, but for different purposes.
- ***At the outset, give all managers opportunities to develop and use new competencies; don't write off any of them.*** "Avoid blaming those who don't immediately embrace the planned change," advises Mike Masterson, from the Madison, Wisconsin, police department. "They are not whiners or naysayers—they are good workers with legitimate questions. Their early fears will often be exaggerated and eventually disappear with time."
- ***Use incentives to motivate managers to make the transition.*** For example, make success at adopting new management methods a part of managers' performance appraisals. You can even let their own employees rate them on how well they are making the change.
- ***Invest in your managers.*** Make an explicit, significant commitment to helping managers develop new skills. This can involve an ongoing training program (in-house or purchased, say, from a business school or consultant), as well as a variety of other learning experiences, including job rotations, mentoring, and coaching.

Giving Employees a Stake

It isn't enough for managers to let go of power; employees have to accept it, too. Usually, they won't accept it right off the bat. Faced with a manager who says, "I want to empower you," the typical employee first thinks, "Is this for real?" If persuaded that the offer is sincere, the employee responds by thinking (and perhaps saying), "What's in it for me?" This response may startle a would-be emancipator, but it is basic human nature. "If leaders cannot answer that question to the satisfaction of their employees, the chance for successful change is nil," say David Couper, the former police chief of Madison, Wisconsin, and his coauthor Sabine Lobitz.

Although empowerment shifts control to employees, it also gives them new responsibilities and new accountability for their performance—reasons to pause before accepting. Do they want more control if it also means their performance will be measured and judged?

Many managers make the mistake of assuming "that all it will take to empower staff is to invite them in, much like one would invite a houseguest into the house," says Bacal.

> *Keep in mind that staff who have worked in a more traditional hierarchical structure have developed some level of comfort with the status quo. We all get used to our work environments and tend to resist change. It is even possible that some staff will not want more responsibility—they prefer the more predictable arrangement where the boss makes most major decisions and tells them what to do.*

For some employees, getting more control is its own reward. They may be excited about being able to make changes that matter to them or about working in teams with peers rather than under constant management supervision. Other employees may seek more tangible incentives for taking charge: pay increases and bonuses, for example. The keys to winning them over are much like those for helping managers let go of power:

- ***Communicate and consult with them.*** Employees need to be clear about why empowerment is occurring and how it will meet the purpose and goals of the organization. They should have substantial input into how the organization will proceed with employee empowerment. And they must have some time and many opportunities to adapt.
- ***Give them information.*** No one can make good decisions without good information. An organization committed to empowering employees must ensure that they have access to all the relevant information. You need a "well-thought-out and effective way of moving information around the organization," says Bacal.
- ***Invest in them.*** Most employees have little experience in making the kinds of decisions—personnel management, work process improvement, and general management—that empowerment gives to them. Usually, their skills at this work are underdeveloped. That's why Bacal says that "empowerment without skill building or knowledge development is a setup for failure." The empowering organization must make sure employees have a chance to succeed when they get decision-making authority.
- ***Reward them.*** This point is a simple one: you get what you pay for, whether the currency is money or recognition. Use the many tools of performance management to reward employees for taking on new responsibilities.

pp. 215–246

Getting the Most Out of the Tools

The five tools for employee empowerment that we describe in the following pages are more powerful when used together. Each can stand alone, but if you use them in isolation, don't expect to get much bang from them. If you just organize work teams, for instance, that will help improve employee morale and productivity a bit. But unless you also delayer management and break up functional silos, the teams won't have much decision-making authority, and they won't create dramatically better performance. Similarly, if you start an employee suggestion program, it will receive many more good ideas for improvement if employees have been empowered through delayering, work teams, and labor-management partnerships.

Bill Creech, reinventor of the U.S. Tactical Air Command and author of *The Five Pillars of TQM*, repeatedly makes this point: if you leave functional silos and multiple layers of management in the way, you will be telling people they are empowered without giving them real power over important decisions. As Creech puts it, you must "build a decentralized structure" that supports teams:

> *Eliminate unnecessary layers. Tear down all of the functional walls. Recast the rules. Streamline the paperwork. Shorten the cycle times. Maintain coherence and control with incentive, not authoritarianism.*

THE EMPLOYEE EMPOWERMENT TOOLKIT

Delayering Management eliminates management positions and even entire management classifications dedicated to supervising, checking up on, or otherwise controlling employees. See p.462.

Breaking Up Functional Silos eliminates units, work processes, and job classifications based on functional specialization, substituting instead teams that combine more roles. See p. 463.

Labor-Management Partnerships institutionalize power sharing between organizations' management and unions to address a wide array of workplace issues and work processes. See p. 466.

Work Teams are groups of employees who share a specific goal they cannot attain without coordinating their activities and who hold themselves mutually accountable. See p. 478.

Employee Suggestion Programs encourage employees to provide suggestions for improving performance, saving money, and eliminating unnecessary rules and practices. See p. 487.

DELAYERING MANAGEMENT

Delayering flattens an agency's management hierarchy and reduces its overhead costs. But it must be done very deliberately. Too often, top managers choose an arbitrary number—say, a 15 percent cut in management positions. We recommend that you instead assess your organization's mission, priorities, and needs and *then* determine your real management needs.

Managers also make the mistake of assuming that delayering will automatically redistribute power to employees. In reality, control may concentrate instead in the hands of remaining managers. "A short, fat elephant is still an elephant," says Bill Creech. "It's only marginally more nimble!" Thus the success of delayering depends on also using other tools—such as work teams and labor-management partnerships—to ensure employee empowerment.

One indicator of excessive layering is a low span of managerial control, or a low manager-to-employee ratio. In 1993, the National Performance Review found the average span of control in the federal government was one manager for every seven employees (1:7). That's much lower than in most private businesses. In Oregon, when the Department of Transportation eliminated management layers, cutting out 200 positions, it boosted the average manager's span of control from 1:6 to almost 1:12.

TO FIND USELESS MANAGEMENT LAYERS, LOOK FOR . . .

- Work units with spans of control that are too narrow.
- Line employees that lack the authority to provide responsive service to customers.
- Managers, assistants, or deputies with duplicate responsibilities.
- Headquarters, regional, and district offices that perform the same functions.
- Managers who act as "pass-through" mechanisms and not as decision makers.
- High-level executives and policymakers who micromanage operations.

—From the National Performance Review report
Transforming Organizational Structures

There are a number of elements critical to the success of delayering:

Eliminate the positions. Until you formally get rid of the jobs, no one will believe it's going to happen. Set a date when the positions will come out of the budget and off the organization chart. And when you've made the decision, communicate it clearly to the people who will be affected. Don't waffle about whether or not it will happen. If you do, managers may try to generate pressure to reverse the decision. And they won't use the time they have left to find new jobs.

Give people enough advance notice so they have time to find another job. How much time is enough? Sometimes, personnel contracts specify how much notice must be given. If not, it's a judgment call. If you offer too much notice, managers may not feel any immediate pressure to start working on the problem; the event is too far away in the future. You also run the risk that they will perform little of the organization's work during the remaining months. If you offer too little notice, managers won't have the time it takes to find new work. We recommend two to four months, depending on the circumstances.

Help the managers develop an exit route. In Florida in 1993, Governor Lawton Chiles and Lieutenant Governor Buddy MacKay decided to wipe out three layers of managers in the Department of Health and Rehabilitative Services. Included on the hit list were 25 of the department's 38 senior managers. Under a provision in the state constitution, Chiles assigned MacKay to run the department temporarily. MacKay created "Job Changer Teams" to help dislocated managers find other positions in state government. Because managers knew their jobs would be eliminated in 60 days, they were very interested in working with the teams, says Bob O'Leary, then a special assistant to the lieutenant governor.

See *Banishing Bureaucracy* pp. 132–135

Florida's commitment to help displaced managers find jobs was not unusual. In *Banishing Bureaucracy* we urged reinventors to protect employees from the threat of unemployment, unless they could not afford to because of a fiscal crisis. The best way to do this is to make a no-layoff pledge, which means that managers will be retrained and transferred into other government jobs. Some organizations create a "job bank" by holding a certain number of vacancies open, to be filled by those whose jobs have been eliminated. Others offer managers early retirement and severance packages or career counseling and outplacement services.

pp. 199–200

BREAKING UP FUNCTIONAL SILOS

Breaking Up Functional Silos **eliminates units, work processes, and job classifications based on functional specialization, substituting instead teams that combine more roles.**

Until 1994, the federal government's veterans benefits office in New York City was a classic example of organization by functional silos. The process for determining applicants' eligibility for benefits was broken down into seven broad steps and many substeps. Different specialists performed different steps—file clerks, correspondence clerks, claims development clerks, claims examiners, senior adjudicators, ratings specialists (who examined the medical evidence for disability claims), supervisors, and section chiefs.

"The system was based on Taylorism," says Joe Thompson, then the regional office director, now undersecretary for benefits of the Department of Veterans Affairs. "The underlying premise was that the best way to do a job is to break it down into its smallest tasks, then write a procedure for that task so nobody can vary from it." As many as 20 people might handle a single claim. When one completed a task, he would hand the applicant's documentation to the person in charge of the next task.

The different job classifications required different skills and came with different salaries. Many of these differences couldn't be justified, according to Veronica Wales, the office's personnel director. "We place people in these circles and squares even though we have a hard time explaining the distinctions."

The office took an average of 264 days to process a compensation claim. That was nearly two months longer than the national average for veterans offices, five months longer than the national target for performance, and six months longer than the system's customers said would satisfy them.

The veterans felt that the process was designed to meet the needs of the organization's bureaucracy "rather than to provide service to them," as Thompson put it. He knew this from personal experience: after two years in Vietnam, he had spent 32 days in a veterans hospital, then applied for disability benefits. "You realize the person you're speaking to on the phone couldn't really help you; they had to get back to you," he remembers. "They weren't in a position to really answer your question; it took a long time to get the decision made." He had also come up through the VA ranks, beginning as a claims examiner, so he knew firsthand how "isolating and mind-numbing" the system was for employees.

When Thompson asked managers and employees to figure out how to improve their chronically poor performance, they ended up blaming the office's functional organization. The handoffs between specialists were wasting time and producing errors. And the divisions didn't help one another—even though they shared the same work process and customers. "There were times I was afraid to go to Adjudication and ask for something, because they'd bark at you," says Bill Golding, a services division manager.

In short, the specialists worried only about performing their task in the process. They took as long as they wanted, and they didn't worry about how well the next step would be performed. The functional divisions blamed one another for any problems, and needless to say, few people focused on meeting the customers' needs.

Thompson's study team concluded that it had to dismantle the functional silos. It merged the services and adjudication divisions into a single unit to handle claims from start to finish, then broke the unit into self-directed work teams. It collapsed the many specialized jobs into just two general jobs: case technician and case manager. (It also eliminated a job called "file searcher," created so someone would look full-time for lost files.) Members of each self-directed team were cross-trained so they could perform multiple tasks in the claims process. All learned how to start the application process.

Then Thompson tied employee compensation to workers' skills and performance rather than their job descriptions. "This encourages people to do all they can, to bring to the workplace a range of skills that are not in the job description but are developed in the community, family, and church," observes Wales. The old system, she adds, "values the piece of paper [the job description] more than the person."

The new "case management" model gave customers one person they could rely on to process their claim. Applicants now get to know the people working on their claims, notes Bruce Westin. "If a customer has a question, they know who to call or see. They don't have to start educating the service provider from the beginning again." Workers on a team also have a stake in the same outcome. "If we're all on the same team, it makes us accountable for results," says Bob Dolan, a codirector of the consolidated unit. "The winner is the customer."

Breaking down the functional silos improved performance measurably. Processing time declined significantly in the beta unit that Thompson used to pioneer the new design. The office cut the time it took to answer applicants' phone calls, and it reduced the amount of time applicants had to wait when they came to the office for interviews. With the performance improvements in hand, Thompson spread the changes to the entire office. They quickly reduced the backlog of pending cases by more than a third and cut customers' average waiting time from 30 minutes to 3. In 1996 the National Performance Review noted that the office "now serves customers so fast that they do not need a waiting room anymore. In fact, they are turning it into a museum of VA memorabilia."

There are several key elements involved in breaking up functional silos:

- ***Redesign work processes.*** Use business process reengineering and other methods to break out of the assembly-line model of work.
- ***Redesign jobs.*** Replace narrow job descriptions and classifications with multiple-skill jobs. Define roles and desired results, rather than jobs. Some employees will resist this, but you can't give in to them. In the New York veterans office, opposition came from the elite "ratings specialists," a highly trained classification that decided the legitimacy of claims and how much money beneficiaries should receive. They resisted Thompson's shift to a team-based operation, because they would lose their elite status in the organization's

pp. 411–415

"food chain." When Thompson went ahead anyway, some of the 20 specialists retired or quit; only nine of them were still with the organization two years later.

- ***Redesign management structures.*** Delayer and consolidate management positions, and replace functional units with work teams in which employees share performance goals.

pp. 462–463, 478–486

- ***Redesign the workplace and its symbols.*** Break down physical barriers between units and between people. Relocate (and rename) units so that they are together. Let them "own" their space.

RESOURCES ON BREAKING UP FUNCTIONAL SILOS

Bill Creech. *The Five Pillars of TQM: How to Make Total Quality Management Work for You.* New York: Dutton, 1994. The masterful reinventor of the U.S. Tactical Air Command provides powerful advice and compelling stories about breaking down silos and shifting to a team-based organization.

Michael Hammer and James Champy. *Reengineering the Corporation: A Manifesto for Business Revolution.* New York: HarperCollins, 1993. This classic on redesigning work processes includes a wide range of insights about why and how to break up silos.

Russ Linden. *Seamless Government: A Practical Guide to Re-engineering in the Public Sector.* San Francisco: Jossey-Bass, 1994. Linden, a management consultant, uses numerous stories from public agencies to illuminate the importance of and methods for redesigning functions.

LABOR-MANAGEMENT PARTNERSHIPS

***Labor-Management Partnerships* institutionalize power sharing between organizations' management and unions to address a wide array of workplace issues and work processes.**

> *Labor and management are committed to revolutionary changes in the way we do business.*
>
> —Mission statement of the City of Fort Lauderdale Cooperative Association of Labor and Management

Partnerships between public employee unions and government managers are often born out of crises.

Cathy Dunn, president of an American Federation of State, County, and Municipal Employees (AFSCME) local in Fort Lauderdale, remembers when layoffs hit her members hard in 1993. "The union had 1,300 employees then. By 1995 we were 930," she says.

> *We lost some through attrition, some through contracting out. I sat with my members for weeks, telling them, "You no longer have a job." At the end of that, I said, "I will never do this again."*

When Scott Milinski, the city's director of employee relations, suggested to Dunn that they explore creating a labor-management partnership, she agreed. "We went into it thinking it was a way of opening communications," she says, "so that when the next layoff comes, we'll be able to deal with it better."

In Portland, Maine, the people desperate for a new labor-management relationship were government managers. The public works department had been under fire for several years; it was the target of most of the customer complaints the city received. The city council and city manager believed the agency was inefficient and poorly managed. By 1993 there was serious talk of outsourcing most of its work or laying off many of its employees. Then the department got a chance to redeem itself—by proving it could build a minor league baseball stadium on an impossibly tight schedule and budget. Project managers realized from the outset that they needed the cooperation of AFSCME Local 41 to get the workplace flexibilities they needed. They wanted, for instance, to handpick workers for the project, not just rely on job classifications or seniority; to schedule work hours around the clock; to give people assignments outside of their job classifications; and to hold down costs by using compensatory time instead of overtime pay. These practices would have violated the city's labor contract, so the managers negotiated a special agreement with the union.

In Seattle, fear of job losses drove the 30 unions that represented city workers to come together in a rare collaboration to develop a partnership with management. "We were faced with the specter of contracting out. It was a threat to all of us," says Kathleen Oglesby, staff representative for the local AFSCME union.

Sometimes labor-management partnerships arise not from crisis but from conviction. A union leader or a top manager decides that there just has to be an alternative to the persistent conflicts that characterize traditional labor-management relations.

In 1991, for example, the 39,000–member Ohio Civil Service Employees Association (OCSEA) proposed during tough contract negotiations that a joint labor-management committee study and make recommendations about productivity, quality, the quality of work life, and the quality of union-management relationships. The idea was advanced by Paul Goldberg, OCSEA's executive director. Clearly, he wanted to protect union jobs. "If the taxpayers think government is broke, something's going to change one way or the other," Goldberg says. "So our best prophylactic strategy is to make sure we're doing things right, efficiently, effectively, with high-quality outcomes." This, Goldberg explains, reduces pressure "to get rid of government or to [introduce] privatization and subcontracting."

But Goldberg also wanted workers to have more influence over the design of work, which was controlled by management. "Unions have been filing grievances and negotiating contracts—with little measurable effect on the systems and processes of work," he says. "It seemed like it was time to try measures which might help to fix the system, rather than the blame." To gain more influence, the union and its members would have to embrace a more collaborative approach, Goldberg believed. "Most workers' paradigm of the labor-management relationship is that the union kicks management's ass." His proposal, which became part of the contract agreement, meant the union would "have to move away from what we have traditionally regarded as the attributes and values of . . . the trade union personality—the kick-ass negotiator, the rough-and-tumble fighter."

Goldberg is not alone in coming to the conclusion that the decades-old labor-management paradigm has to change. In Phoenix in 1978, Fire Chief Alan Brunacini and the president of Firefighters Local 493, Pat Cantelme, decided to end decades of labor-management conflict. They initiated annual planning retreats, during which managers and union leaders jointly decide how to address problems and improve service. The personal trust between them was evident when we talked with them, and they were developing joint committees and project teams to ensure that the partnership did not just depend on their relationship. Because of the trust and problem-solving ability they had built, they have not had to use arbitration since the mid-1980s.

At the heart of a labor-management partnership is a negotiated shift in power. Managers share their control over the workplace, their "management rights." In exchange, the unions help management define and address some of the organization's problems. They may give up some contractual rights obtained through bargaining—by changing work schedules or compensation arrangements, for instance. Or they may use their knowledge and experience to increase efficiency, the way Fort Lauderdale's pipe-laying crew did. In all cases, the two sides collaborate in ways that create benefits for each of them—a "win-win" outcome. As Paul Goldberg observes, the most important outcome for government managers and unions is to produce better results for a public that is dissatisfied and angry.

pp. 453–454

The partnership does not replace the traditional mechanisms that labor and management use: collective bargaining, contracts, and accepted ways for administering contracts, such as grievance procedures. Rather, it is a "parallel system of collaboration," as Warner Woodworth and Christopher Meek put it in *Labor-Management Partnerships*. As they point out, a partnership is more than just a way of reducing friction between union leaders and managers to ease contract negotiations and reduce grievances. And it involves more than just opening up communications between the two sides.

For labor and management to share responsibility and credit for making changes, they must share decision making. There is no alternative.

Obviously, this makes labor-management partnerships challenging, to say the least. Like cats and dogs, labor and management have the habit of conflict in their blood. Yet, in an increasing number of public organizations, union leaders and top managers are making love, not war.

One reason is that labor is not going to go away. As we said earlier, organized labor is gaining influence in government, at least in the U.S. And in surveys, the vast majority of the nation's seven million public union members say they want to keep the union in place. If you've got to live with unions, some managers figure, you might as well learn how to work with them.

A second reason is that in today's economic and political environment, neither labor nor management can afford to continue the usual pattern of intense conflict around contract negotiations and a steady state of grievances and other skirmishes the rest of the time. Instead, they must focus on improving performance. In 1994, a committee of the AFL-CIO recognized this fact of life. It called on unions "to take the initiative in stimulating, sustaining and institutionalizing a new system of work organization based upon full and equal labor-management partnerships."

Like most of the legacy of bureaucratic government, the old adversarial labor-management system is outdated. In the future, government will have fewer managers and more empowered workers. More and more managers are struggling to transform their organizations; to succeed, they need employees' cooperation. More and more public employees, who are increasingly highly educated, want to have a say in workplace decisions; to get this, they need managers' cooperation.

No wonder that in 1996, a U.S. Labor Department task force found in government "a growing realization that labor and management are in the same boat. . . . From school house to fire house, a growing number of state and local governments are forming cooperative workplace partnerships in an effort to transform their public agencies into flexible, customer-responsive organizations better equipped to serve citizens."

The Structure of Labor-Management Partnerships

Since shared decision making is the ultimate goal of these partnerships, they are built on a foundation of joint representation in decision-making processes. Labor and management usually have an equal number of seats (or votes) in labor-management committees. Beyond these basics, the structure is tailored to local circumstances. "There isn't any one perfect model," says Toni Riley Jones, education and training coordinator for the Federal Mediation and Conciliation Service.

In many places, a government-wide joint steering committee is established to oversee the partnership process. The labor side will typically include union presidents and other officers as well as rank-and-file employees. The management side will usually include the top executive or deputy, the labor relations negotiator, and department heads. In Seattle, the management caucus includes three city council members and a deputy mayor. This was done, explains AFSCME's Kathleen Oglesby, so that the council and mayor's office would speak with the same voice to the unions. "We needed a forum in which they talked to each other so they could figure out how they wanted to talk to us."

A typical steering committee will charter projects, which also are jointly run. And, as it matures, it will establish permanent, joint standing committees that deal with specific recurring topics, such as performance appraisals. Pushing the partnership's work down into the ranks—engaging supervisors and rank-and-file employees—is a crucial development, says Al Bilik, president of the AFL-CIO's Public Employee Department. "You need participation at the lowest level of the organization, where the workers are."

A government-wide steering committee is useful because it can tackle problems within the administrative systems, which are government-wide, not the terrain of a single department. "You need to be able to fix specific problems and also the systemic problems, like purchasing, that get in the way of employees," notes Geni Giannotti, then management cochair of Detroit's labor-management committee.

Having a government-wide committee also helps to ensure the continuity of the partnership effort, says Bilik. Even if a city manager or union president is replaced, there's an institutional structure for successors to use.

However, not all governments that pursue partnership have turned to the steering committee format. Portland, Maine, has kept committees at the department level, which has worked well for about a decade.

What Labor-Management Partnerships Do

Whatever the structure of these partnerships, they all focus on improving communication and building trust. They serve as early warning systems so that small problems don't become big troubles. Former Seattle deputy mayor Bruce Brooks says his city's Labor-Management Steering Committee, which he cochairs, allows him "to hear things before they become virulent—so we can work through it sooner rather than later." This is only possible, he adds, when labor and management members use the committee as "a place [where] we can talk with each other candidly."

Sometimes, partnerships deal with problems that are too explosive for the contract bargaining process. In Peoria, Illinois, for instance, city government managers and unions agreed to take health care off the bargaining table because costs were out of control. Instead, they tackled the issue through a joint labor-management committee, which developed a cost-saving solution that did not lead to the usual disputes and arbitration.

Most partnerships address a wide range of problems in the personnel area. The concerns may be social, such as substance abuse and sexual harassment by employees and managers. Or they may involve the nitty-gritty elements of personnel systems: job classifications, job performance standards, performance appraisal, employee discipline, and the like.

Two of the most important personnel changes involve grievance processes and training. Many partnerships work on modifying or even replacing the cumbersome, conflict-oriented grievance process; as alternatives, they often turn to mediation and conflict resolution. This clearly benefits managers, the target of time-consuming grievances. But it can also help unions be more responsive to their members' problems. Often, unions find their energies tied up in grievance proceedings. In Ohio, for instance, the OCSEA had more than 3,800 cases awaiting formal arbitration in 1988. Yet only a tiny minority of employees used this service, which consumed the bulk of the union's resources. Partnerships routinely use the reduction in grievances as an indicator of their success. After the Clinton administration called in 1993 for labor-management partnerships in every federal organization, many agencies began using alternative dispute resolution rather than grievances. In 1994 and 1995, the number of unfair labor practice filings with the Federal Labor Relations Authority dropped 28 percent. One air force base avoided $2 million in litigation costs by using dispute resolution processes.

Many partnerships also become effective advocates for more and better training for workers, especially entry-level employees. Training helps employees improve their performance, so managers win, and it helps employees gain career mobility, so they win too.

For some managers, gaining the union's insight into specific personnel problems has an unexpected effect. Nadeen Daniels, Portland's assistant city manager, says that partnering has changed her attitude toward some difficult employees she wanted to fire.

> *I can sit down with the union, and they say, "This guy has five kids, or an alcohol problem. You can't do this to him five years out from retirement." All of a sudden, it makes me realize that this is a human being. I can move him somewhere else, act humanely.*

Another function of most partnerships is to redesign work processes. The first project tackled by Fort Lauderdale's partnership—called the Cooperative

Association of Labor and Management (CALM)—provides an example. Local residents and tourists were dissatisfied with the way the city cleaned up its renowned beaches. The underlying problem was typical of government: no one was really accountable for getting the job done right. Five departments had some responsibility; each had a specific assignment and worked in isolation from the others. For example, one department's workers picked up plant debris on the beach but left other types of litter for other crews. This, CALM concluded, gave "the public the perception that the beach maintenance and clean up is never 'finished.' . . . The citizen assumes that the employees did not properly do their job."

CALM recommended that one department, not five, be put in charge of beach cleaning. To increase the time employees actually spent cleaning the beaches, it suggested that they report to the beach for work, not to their department's offices, and store their equipment at the beach rather than hauling it back and forth from city facilities.

The recommendations worked. The work crews "have the beach cleaned by 10 A.M.," Dunn testified. Customer surveys gave them a 9.5 rating [on a scale of 1–10], which "made the employees feel really great."

In Ohio, state government's labor-management partnership is attacking work processes on a large scale. Since 1993, it has unleashed tens of thousands of state employees to make improvements in every nook and cranny of state government. Nearly 50,000 workers have attended three-day training sessions on using quality management methods. And more than 1,000 teams of employees have undertaken specific improvements—often with nice payoffs:

- A team in mental health saved $1.5 million in the treatment of schizophrenia patients while improving the treatments' success rate.
- Another team streamlined the process for preparing and approving travel expense reports, saving $510,000 annually.
- The "Jam Busters" in Toledo's worker's compensation office wiped out a backlog of 50,000 pieces of mail and saved $94,000 a year by eliminating overtime and two temporary positions.

Finally, some partnerships tackle the problem of helping public organizations compete successfully with the private sector. In Fort Lauderdale, CALM helped employees cut costs $1.3 million to compete successfully against private bidders to run the city jail. With a consultant's help, wastewater treatment plant employees developed a five-year plan to close their "competitive gap" with private plant operators. In Portland, Maine, after the labor-management collaboration successfully built the baseball stadium, it went on to create a "construction company" to bid against private companies for city work.

As labor-management partnerships mature, they can become a powerful tool for reinvention. In Fort Lauderdale, for instance, CALM has come to see itself as an instigator of reinvention. "Our mission statement started off as promoting cooperation," says Milinski, the city employee relations director. "After a year and a half, we changed it. Now, it's to make revolutionary changes in the way city government does its business—to totally reinvent government."

Developing Labor-Management Partnerships: Lessons Learned

It takes two to do the labor-management tango. Both union and management must be ready to try something new. Labor leaders must be willing to deal with management's real concerns, including changing the contract if necessary. If they're not open to the possibility, they can't become partners. The same goes for managers: if they're not ready to address labor's concerns with management rights, then they're not ready either.

What if only one side is ready? How do you get a reluctant partner to step up? Sometimes it's just not possible. But you can't know until you try. Bob Tobias, former president of the National Treasury Employees Union, spent years battling managers of the U.S. Internal Revenue Service on behalf of his union members. But in 1987 he got an unexpected call from IRS commissioner Larry Gibbs. The agency was under fire, and its senior staff wanted to empower employees to make big changes.

"Gibbs said, 'I'm not going to be here forever. I need your help to push change from the bottom up,'" Tobias recalls. In spite of their history of disputes, Tobias agreed to start several experiments using Total Quality Management. Within a few years, the effort grew into hundreds of labor-management collaborations throughout the agency.

Sometimes you can pick someone on the other side to cultivate. In Ohio, union leader Paul Goldberg looked for ways to bring along the Republican governor, George Voinovich. "Paul found a partner in Voinovich, a very unlikely one," says the AFL-CIO's Bilik. "He found him and cultivated him. Without necessarily going to bed with each other, they moved on to a cooperative level."

Once the dancing has begun, there are some basic lessons to follow to build the partnership:

1. *Build trust between union and management leaders.*

Without trust, there can be no partnership. Trust building is slow work, in part because labor and management usually have a history of bad relations. At the outset, unions are likely to suspect that management wants a partnership just so it can secure contract givebacks. And managers will suppose that labor is looking for more benefits without having to give up anything. In other words, both sides will probably think and act as though they are still adversaries.

pp. 575–581

To start to dissolve this mind-set, many fledgling partnerships use a facilitated retreat, with equal representation from labor and management. These sessions usually include team-building exercises that allow the participants to get to know one another as people and to learn about one another's perspectives. Because they are private settings, there's a chance for greater candor.

Ohio's efforts to build a partnership stumbled early on because union leaders felt they were not being treated as equals. Governor Voinovich's top managers didn't "understand what we meant by partnership," says OCSEA's Goldberg. "They thought, we'll let the union know what we're going to do, so they can get their members lined up." In early 1993, Goldberg joined the governor for a special training session in quality management at a Xerox facility. During the meeting, he complained about the way the unions were being treated.

"Most of the cabinet folks started snickering," he recalls. "You know, 'There goes Goldberg again.'" But Xerox officials emphasized how valuable their union had been in implementing quality management. That caught Voinovich's attention.

"The governor raised his hand," says Goldberg. "And when he was called on, he said, 'I think we've been going about this all wrong.'" Soon after that, Voinovich created a steering committee with five union leaders and five agency heads. Nothing could happen unless both sides agreed.

In Fort Lauderdale, it took nearly a year for labor and management to hammer out a statement of philosophy in which they articulated new shared principles. They agreed, for instance, that "the focus of our efforts should be on our customers." And they committed to working in teams that were willing "to take risks, to be innovative."

As participants in a partnership build a sense of trust and win-win thinking becomes the norm, the two sides gradually shed their conflict orientation. Sometimes you can't even tell them apart, says Denis Morse, president of Local 740 of the International Association of Fire Fighters in Portland, Maine. He tells the story of a reception he attended with labor and management partners from five cities: "I tried to pick out the labor and management people. You really couldn't tell; they see themselves as a team."

2. *Guarantee that no layoffs will result from partnership activities.*

Management can help labor leaders buy in by guaranteeing that no union member will lose employment or even pay levels because of efficiencies gained through the partnership's work. This allows union leaders to tell their members that cooperation won't exact economic penalties—an important message to secure the rank and file's blessing. It gives unions "the confidence that they're not being sandbagged," says Bilik.

In Ohio, adds Goldberg, "our people had to be assured that this was not just a device to use their intellects and then discard them like old typewriters." In response, Governor Voinovich wrote into the labor contract a pledge that partnership-driven improvements would not lead to workforce reductions.

There are many ways to absorb surplus workers when innovation eliminates their positions.

pp. 199–200

3. *Train participants in critical skills, such as conflict resolution.*

To become good partners, labor and management must learn how to solve problems and resolve conflicts together. This does not come naturally, especially after years of tension. Traditional negotiating tends to lock negotiators into the positions they take. It puts their egos on the line, diminishes the value of personal relations between the sides, and rarely acknowledges that both parties may be right.

To change their ways, budding partners need training—and they should go through that training together. For instance, they can learn how to achieve consensus without compromising. This involves techniques for identifying solutions and outcomes they might not have considered and for contemplating their own behavior while encouraging empathy for and acceptance of others. It also involves mastering the discipline of listening to others.

In Portland, where management and labor collaborated to build the baseball park, they invented a unique way to resolve conflicts that arose. As the Labor Department task force reported:

> *Whenever there was a problem, the dispute was dealt with by taking what became known as "the walk to center field." That's where individuals involved immediately met to attempt to resolve their conflicts. This method worked: the deputy director of the division was jointly empowered to make on-the-spot decisions to keep the project—and the teamwork—moving along.*

4. *Get the right people on your joint decision-making body.*

"You have to have the right kind of people on these committees," says Fort Lauderdale's Milinski—people who are committed to the process of partnership building. Some managers and union officials won't be committed—and may become an obstacle. If they do, get them off the committee. Others start out enthusiastically but then stop attending sessions, because it's not a priority or they don't have a tolerance for the slow work of relationship building. CALM has a simple rule for dealing with this, says Milinski: "After three absences, we assume you've quit. I've replaced department heads."

When you create a partnership decision-making body, you must be clear about its purpose, scope, and ground rules. We suggest you adopt a formal charter that spells these things out. Although decision making is the body's ultimate function, it can begin with advisory or fact-finding roles. It can cover the entire government, a single department, or just one work unit. Everyone on the body should take part in orientation and training—about the purpose of the group, its ground rules, how to resolve conflicts, and so on.

It's usually helpful to let a neutral facilitator run the body's initial meetings. Cincinnati found that an outsider's guidance was essential, says Frank Hotze, Cincinnati's chief negotiator and a member of its labor-management committee: "We needed someone to kick us, to keep us on track, to bring us back to the track sometimes."

5. *Establish ground rules for joint decision making.*

Any group needs shared understandings about which behaviors are acceptable and which are not. Many of these norms are obvious: respect other members of the group, tell the truth, start and end meetings on time, distribute agendas ahead of time, keep minutes, and so on. In labor-management partnerships, in particular, several other ground rules are helpful:

- All decisions require a consensus of the members, so that labor and management move together in sync.
- All members are equal—a reflection of the joint ownership that labor and management have.
- What is said in the meeting stays in the meeting. This makes it easier for participants to be candid at partnership sessions.
- The group speaks with one voice to the media. In Seattle, for instance, the cochairs of the labor-management committee serve as official spokespersons for the committee. Other members must consult with them before making any public statements regarding the partnership.

6. *Leave the attorneys at home.*

The lawyers that labor and management use to negotiate with each other are well trained for adversarial situations, but they often don't know how to handle efforts at collaboration. Their style of attacking, seeking advantage, and then compromising can get in the way of building a cooperative relationship.

7. *Start with some small projects.*

Veterans of labor-management partnerships consistently advise those beginning them to start with small steps. That way, new efforts can build relationships and trust between management and labor, without having a great deal at stake. You can start with more than one project. No matter how many you launch, make sure they can be accomplished in the short run, no more than three to six months. This lets you rack up some early successes, building the confidence of participants.

8. *Help managers and union leaders change their roles.*

In more and more cases, creative union leaders are focusing on service improvement efforts rather than on settling grievances. "Their roles are changing," says Jonathan Brock, the Labor Department task force's executive director. "For many, it makes their jobs more interesting."

The task force reported that in Massachusetts, for instance, leaders of a union representing state highway maintenance workers (SEIU, Local 285) have taken responsibility for organizing and managing highway jobs. It found that union officers "have de-emphasized their role as 'grievance handlers' in favor of becoming 'motivators' who urge employees to work smarter to save their jobs. They act as liaisons between workers and management in sharing concerns and solving service problems, including those that might develop because of poor managers or inefficient management policies or systems."

Managers also must change their roles, as we described earlier in this chapter.

pp. 457–459

9. *Ride out the bumps in the road.*

Being partners does not mean you will agree on everything. Labor and management will still argue strenuously when it comes to negotiating labor contracts that set wages, benefits, and other conditions of employment. This is inevitable when the pie is being cut up. But partners learn to fight with each other in ways that don't put the partnership itself at risk. When they hit a bump in the road, they don't let go of the collaboration they've built.

In Ohio, OCSEA opposed Voinovich when he sought reelection in 1994. He won easily, and the labor-management partnership continued. When union and management negotiated a new contract in 1997, both sides went back to the tough language and behavior of adversaries. "You don't give up all your weapons" when you are in a labor-management partnership, noted union executive Goldberg.

It was a "crazy season," acknowledges Steve Wall, the governor's point man for the quality management initiative. But he and Goldberg were confident that once the contract was settled, they could get back to collaborating. As Goldberg put it, "The bargaining pain passes."

RESOURCES ON LABOR-MANAGEMENT PARTNERSHIPS

AFL-CIO. *Excellence in Public Service: Case Studies in Labor-Management Innovation.* Washington, D.C.: Public Employee Department, AFL-CIO. Describes more than a score of case studies of public sector unions involved in workplace change, from improving service delivery to redesigning personnel systems. Available from the AFL-CIO at 815 16th Street, N.W., Washington D.C. 20006.

State and Local Government Labor-Management Committee. This committee, which was created by more than 20 public employee unions and government management organizations, such as the International City/County Management Association and the National Association of Counties, is supported by a Ford Foundation grant to develop a national labor-management program for the public sector. A good source of information, training, and referrals to experts. Phone: (202) 393–2820. Address: 1925 K St., N.W., Suite 402, Washington, D.C. 20006.

U.S. Secretary of Labor. Task Force on Excellence in State and Local Government Through Labor-Management Cooperation. *Working Together for Public Service.* Washington: U.S. Government Printing Office, May 1996. An excellent study of the whys and hows of government labor-management partnerships. Contains useful lessons and success stories.

Warner Woodworth and Christopher Meek. *Creating Labor-Management Partnerships.* Reading, Mass.: Addison-Wesley, 1995. A thorough analysis of the history and challenges of labor-management partnering, with lots of good advice and examples.

WORK TEAMS

***Work Teams* are groups of employees who share a specific goal they cannot attain without coordinating their activities and who hold themselves mutually accountable.**

The word *team,* which comes from Old English, originally referred to animals yoked together. Two animals could handle a heavier load than a single creature could—if they pulled in the same direction.

A team "is not just any group working together," explain management consultants Jon R. Katzenbach and Douglas K. Smith. "Committees, councils and task forces are not necessarily teams. Groups do not become teams simply because that's what someone calls them." A group is a team when its members share common goals, need one another to act and succeed, and are accountable for producing the same results.

Many government managers turned to team building after seeing the success that businesses achieved by using teams. Companies reported productivity improvements, better quality control, reduced absenteeism, and lower employee turnover. The team is becoming the "basic unit of empowerment," say Gifford and Elizabeth Pinchot in *The End of Bureaucracy and the Rise of the Intelligent Organization.* Team members pool their complementary skills. They tap into the potential of the many, not just that of the individual. They make a collective effort to achieve a common goal.

Teams can perform most tasks in an organization: temporary special projects; the permanent, day-to-day activities necessary to provide services or accomplish regulatory tasks; or even top management. In the U.S. Forest Service, a three-person leadership team ran the 300-employee Eastern Region office for seven years, beginning in the mid-1980s. Even though one of them had been appointed to run the office, the trio used consensus to set their goals and shared a single performance evaluation.

See Banishing Bureaucracy pp. 203–211

Organizations often create temporary teams to work on a project or a specific problem. For instance, "continuous improvement" teams are the hallmark of quality management initiatives. The team identifies what it wants to improve—for example, how long a work process takes or how much it costs. It analyzes the process and identifies possible improvements to test. It selects an improvement, implements it, and studies the effect. Then, usually, it disbands. (Sometimes improvement teams move on to other problems.) This can be very effective for accomplishing the given task, but typically it has limited impact on the rest of the organization, where bureaucratic controls remain intact.

However, establishing *permanent* teams often has a transforming effect on the whole organization. It requires supervisors and other managers to radically change their roles and behaviors: to shift from commanding the troops to supporting teams. It also forces fundamental changes in the traditional personnel system. Because job classifications, compensation schemes, and performance evaluations are tailored to the individual employee, they don't work for teams.

Some teams are "self-directed": members take full responsibility for managing their own work. In place of a supervisor there is a team leader, who facilitates the team's work, develops its members' skills, gathers and provides the team with information, and generally negotiates for the team with the rest of the organization. The team leader works for the team, which makes the decisions.

Austin, Texas, stopped supervising street-repair crews and let them manage their own work in the early 1990s. City manager Camille Barnett turned them loose after training them in Total Quality Management, so they could develop their own work process improvements. They created team mission statements and ways to score the quality of their work. They developed and coordinated schedules for the various paving functions: tearing out concrete, replacing curbs, sealing cracks, seal-coat resurfacing, and hot asphalt overlay. And they redesigned their work methods and equipment.

Productivity soared: crews that had laid 28 tons of asphalt an hour boosted their rate to 100. The quality of street surfaces jumped. Citizen complaints about the paving process dwindled. And the morale of city work crews improved.

How to Build Teams: Lessons Learned

You build teams in government the same way as in business—but it's harder to do. One reason is that public agencies typically face less pressure than do businesses to improve their performance; thus, leaders have fewer incentives to embrace team building. Another is the reluctance of government to upend its personnel system. Overcoming this barrier is absolutely critical.

In addition, public officials must deal with the fact that, at the outset at least, the process consumes a great deal of employees' time—with little immediate improvement in performance. It may also create intense tensions in and between employees as they proceed through the team-building process. Experts say that teams go through their own evolution, a developmental process with four distinct stages:

The Four Stages of Team Building

In this stage . . .	*Team members . . .*
1. *Forming*	"Cautiously explore the boundaries of acceptable group behavior." They feel excitement, anticipation, pride in being chosen, suspicion, and anxiety. They are still quite distracted from the team's work.
2. *Storming*	"Begin to realize the project is different and more difficult than they imagined, becoming testy, blameful, or overzealous." They are impatient and resist the need to collaborate with one another. They are defensive and they argue.
3. *Norming*	"Accept the team, team ground rules (or 'norms'), their roles in the team, and the individuality of fellow members." They express criticism constructively, confide in one another, and openly discuss the team's dynamics. A sense of team cohesion grows.
4. *Performing*	"Have discovered and accepted each other's strengths and weaknesses." They have insights into personal and group processes. They have developed a close attachment to the team. "The team is now an effective, cohesive unit." They start getting a lot of work done.

Source: Adapted from Peter R. Scholtes, *The Team Handbook* (Madison, Wisc.: Joiner Associates, 1988), pp. 64–67.

The team-building process usually starts in a small part of the organization—not across the board. The organization needs to gain experience at making the transition, and it needs some "local" successes to motivate others to try.

1. *Clearly identify the team's purpose and goals.*

A team needs a charter, which spells out why it exists and what is expected of it—in concrete, measurable, uplifting terms. Teams that are unclear about these things will get nothing done. A team's objectives should challenge team members—by stretching the limits of past performance, creating urgency, or providing the opportunity to excel.

Losing sight of the team's goal is the greatest danger to a team's effectiveness, according to Carl Larson and Frank LaFasto, authors of *TeamWork*. A team may become unfocused for many reasons. Its individual members' goals may take priority over the team's goals; it may loose the sense that its work is significant or urgent; it may have too many competing goals; or it may become distracted by other organizational issues. Unless teams have specific performance objectives and time lines for performance, they will falter.

Creating teams just for the sake of creating them—a common mistake—guarantees there will be problems. The Oregon Department of Transportation (ODOT) learned this the hard way, says former ODOT director Don Forbes. It started building teams without having concrete tasks for them to do. "Teams were floundering for a while, because they had no particular focus," Forbes says. When the agency finally introduced performance measures for teams, it helped them get on track.

2. *Be clear about how much autonomy the team has.*

A team's *charter* should spell out its limits. What are the "givens" that it must accept? What can it decide without permission? Otherwise, the team may go beyond the unspoken boundaries. Or it may waste time trying to figure out whether or not it can make a particular decision.

A team charter should address at least the following elements:

- In which decisions does the team have a role?
- What decision-making role does the team have? Final say? Advisory?
- With whom must the team work?
- What will be indicators of the team's success in fulfilling its decision-making role?

3. *Help your managers learn a new style of management.*

In Hampton, Virginia, when the professional staff in the human resource department became a self-directed team in 1986, department head Tharon

CLARIFYING A TEAM'S AUTHORITY

Joann Neuroth, a consultant in organizational change, has identified a set of questions that help teams become clear about their authority to make a decision. A team should ask itself which of the following it has been convened to do:

- Listen to someone else's decision.
- Ask questions about a decision.
- Advise about how to implement a decision.
- Suggest and evaluate alternatives to a tentative decision.
- Investigate and help frame the problem to best solve it.
- Make the decision within specified limits.
- Take full responsibility for making the decision, communicating it, and dealing with the consequences of the decision.

Greene found she had to stop managing them. "If you're the boss," she says, "you have to go in your office, close the door, leave them alone, and not get into constant micromanaging.

> *Some folks have more trouble than others trusting employees to do the right thing. Managers need to realize that it's the employees' job to do things right and the manager's job to make sure they're doing the right things. The manager in a team setting is in the best position to step back and see the big picture; the team is best able to deal with the realities of making things work day-to-day.*

4. Ensure that team members all face similar consequences for the team's results.

"In an effective team," write the Pinchots, "everyone shares a common fate. If a commitment is made, all share responsibility for it. If things go well, all win; if things go poorly, all lose." Sharing a common fate helps team members pull together. It also makes it possible for them to police themselves, to set and enforce behavioral norms as peers rather than using a supervisor to do so. And it keeps teams focused on their performance.

Failure to attach consequences to a team's work makes it likely that team building will fail. "If management fails to pay persistent attention to the link between teams and performance, the organization becomes convinced that 'this year we are doing team,'" explain Katzenbach and Smith. To address this

pp. 215–246

problem, reinventors can use performance management—introducing performance bonuses, awards, gainsharing, and the like.

5. *Provide teams with support and recognition.*

Teams need to believe that the organization's top managers have a long-term commitment to team building. The best way to build this belief is for high-level managers themselves to model teamwork. That gives employees confidence that it is not just a fad—that their bosses know how difficult it is to do.

Teams also need other kinds of support. They often have trouble accessing the information they require, because managers won't share it with them. Or they have difficulty tapping into the knowledge of other people in the organization who are busy and won't set aside time to help them. To break down these and other barriers, organizations often assign a *champion* or *sponsor* to help the team get what it needs. The champion should have significant standing in the organization and the visible blessing of top management.

Organization leaders must also celebrate the team's work. Providing visible recognition may seem hokey, and after a few efforts it may feel repetitious, but it helps sustain the team's momentum through what team-building expert Peter Scholtes calls the "roller coaster of highs and lows" that every team experiences. Providing a team with too much recognition is a far better sin than failing to recognize it at all.

6. *Invest in developing key team-based competencies.*

Don't assume that employees will know how to be effective team members. They usually won't. Under the bureaucratic model, workers get little experience teaming in the workplace. Their attitudes, skills, and knowledge are geared to job specialization and to being controlled by supervisors. They need help developing the collective competencies of teaming, such as:

- **Group processes.** Team members must learn how to think, act, and make decisions *together.* They have to learn to communicate openly with one another, to trust one another, to listen to and probe one another's thinking. They must select from among the different ways to make decisions—by consensus, by majority vote, by delegation. In general, teams must consciously evolve group norms, which means members must participate in self-assessment, discussion, and reflection. They must learn how to set high standards for their performance and how to hold one another to those standards.
- **Problem solving.** Teams must learn how to improve their work. In the past, managers decided which improvements to make; now the team does. To do this effectively, team members must learn about the system or

> processes they control. Individuals typically know only their own piece of the process: "I do this step, when . . ." It is rare for anyone to know the way the whole process works; teams need to develop this knowledge. They also need to learn how to plan: deciding what needs to be done, how it will be done, who will do it, when it must be done. And they must learn effective ways to create improvements: defining the problem, brainstorming causes of the problem, gathering data about performance, analyzing the data, identifying possible solutions, selecting solutions, planning implementation, and monitoring results.

If teams are left on their own to manage their group processes and problem-solving competencies, they often run into trouble. One reason is that this learning takes time that teams are reluctant to give. Because they are under pressure to produce, teams shortchange the time needed to grow as a team. Even if they are encouraged to spend time learning, they feel vulnerable to criticism that they are spending too much time at it. As a result, teams will tend to underinvest in themselves.

A second reason is that mastering these team competencies is very difficult. It involves more than just picking up some new techniques. It also requires "unlearning" old assumptions, routines, and habits—which is very hard for people to do by themselves. Old patterns of thinking and acting often are invisible to us; when they are exposed, we may feel embarrassed or threatened and become defensive. It usually takes a skilled outsider to help a team work through these challenges.

One way to more effectively develop team-based capabilities is to hire a trainer or consultant to support teams in the early stages of their development. Larger organizations sometimes decide to create a permanent position to do this. When they do, they should temper the instinct to hand the assignment to their personnel administrators. These people usually know very little about team building; they know how to run bureaucracies. Don't give them the task unless they are deeply committed to employee empowerment. It's easy to test their commitment: make them lead the charge by practicing teaming in their own units.

In Hampton, Virginia, Tharon Greene, the city's human resources director, turned her unit into the city government's guinea pig for teaming. This gave her staff credibility when they preached teaming to other agencies and said they knew how to help.

Fox Valley Technical College, in Appleton, Wisconsin, assigned the team-building function to a special unit, the Quality Academy, rather than to its personnel office. The academy offered a curriculum that included courses in team basics, roles and responsibilities, mission, linkages to other teams, customer focus, planning, problem-solving tools, and consensus building tools.

HOW DO TEAMS MAKE DECISIONS?

Teams usually are not *democracies,* although they sometimes resort to taking a vote to make decisions. More often, though, teams decide by *consensus:* everyone has to agree on a decision, or at least be able to live with it.

If consensus is not reached, teams may postpone the decision and ask a subgroup or outsiders to rethink the problem and try to develop a solution. If accord remains elusive and the decision is fundamental to the team's survival, a number of things may happen. Sometimes, teams resort to majority voting to reach a decision. Or they replace a member who is not in concert with the rest of the team. If the team cannot come to a resolution, a manager may step in and force a decision by threatening to take control away from the team.

Delegation is another important decision-making mechanism. Teams may authorize one or more of their members to make certain decisions—perhaps after consulting with their teammates.

7. *Invest in new technical skills for team members through cross-training.*

Being a team member often requires employees to take on multiple jobs. "In all the successful teams we've encountered," Katzenbach and Smith say, "not one had all the needed skills at the outset." Thus, training people in other job skills is important. This helps teaming, and it increases an employee's potential for job mobility. It often makes employees' jobs more satisfying as well.

8. *Change the organizational systems and structure to support teams.*

Team building only succeeds when the organization becomes a hospitable environment for teams. If you build teams but do not change your systems and structures in ways that give sufficient power to teams, you will not reap the benefits of employee empowerment. As we've discussed, you must reduce the number of management layers and functional silos. You must move more decisions to the front lines. And you must change basic work processes, assumptions about supervision, and compensation, performance measurement, and training systems.

But that's only the beginning. An organization's information and communication systems must become more open, supporting a free flow of data to all levels. Hiring processes must take into account the need for employees who know how to work in teams. (Some organizations let teams hire their new members.) Teams may also take responsibility for employee appraisal, using a "peer review" process. Shifting to teams can have significant implications for labor-management relations and union contracts, as well.

9. *Build your initial teams with volunteers.*

The difficulties of getting through the stages of team development will test employees' commitment to the process. They are more likely to stick it out if they start it of their own accord. But as organizations gain experience, they learn how to ease the passage's stresses, and they build up successes they can point to. At that point, requiring people to work in teams is likely to provoke less resistance.

10. Keep your teams small, and give them time.

Teams should have no more than 15 or so members. Any more than that is likely to complicate logistics (such as setting up meetings), dilute the frequency and intensity of interactions that team members need, and result in unproductive group behaviors, such as a herd instinct or pack mentality. Finally, team builders must recognize that it takes time for a team to gel, to build the collaborative relationships that will become its strength.

COMBINED ACTIONS THAT MAKE TEAMS SUCCESSFUL

Trust them	after training them
Empower them	with wide latitude
Aim them	with objectives & goals
Measure them	for feedback & comparison
Support them	with backing & resources

—from Bill Creech, *The Five Pillars of TQM*

RESOURCES ON BUILDING TEAMS

Jon R. Katzenbach and Douglas K. Smith. *The Wisdom of Teams: Creating the High-Performance Organization.* New York: HarperBusiness, 1994. A classic on team building, with insightful analysis and advice.

Kimball Fisher. *Leading Self-Directed Work Teams: A Guide to Developing New Team Leadership Skills.* New York: McGraw-Hill, 1993. Very useful, easy-to-use advice about how to lead self-directed work teams, based on many examples from the private sector and the author's personal experience.

Gifford and Elizabeth Pinchot. *The End of Bureaucracy & the Rise of the Intelligent Organization.* San Francisco: Berrett-Koehler, 1993). See Chapter Ten, "Liberated Teams." The Pinchots are articulate advocates of employee empowerment and, in particular, of using teams.

Peter R. Scholtes. *The Team Handbook.* Madison, Wisc.: Joiner Associates, 1988. One of the best practical guides to team building and Total Quality Management, this handbook has been used by many organizations.

EMPLOYEE SUGGESTION PROGRAMS

***Employee Suggestion Programs* encourage employees to provide suggestions for improving performance, saving money, and eliminating unnecessary rules and practices.**

Opening the door for employee suggestions is relatively easy. In fact, it's too easy. Some top managers simply announce that they want input and then wait for ideas to roll in. Suggestions may arrive, and someone may do something about a few of them. But before long, the process usually peters out, because it doesn't build credibility with employees. They can see that it doesn't lead to much change.

To be successful, an employee suggestion program must meet two standards for credibility:

- Employees must believe that managers really want suggestions.
- Suggestions that are made must lead to change.

These are not easy hurdles. In most organizations, managers have not previously wanted employee suggestions about how to organize work. So employees are likely to greet management's call for suggestions with justifiable skepticism.

To address this credibility problem, the U.S. Social Security Administration issued its call for suggestions in the name of both the organization's top managers and its union leaders. Together they asked their 66,000 employees to identify barriers that prevented them from achieving world-class service and ways to overcome those barriers. They received 17,000 suggestions.

See *Banishing Bureaucracy* pp. 208–211

In the U.S. Forest Service's regional office in Milwaukee, Regional Supervisor Butch Marita boosted his suggestion program's credibility with his visible, boisterous embrace of employee ideas. His office implemented 70 percent of the employee suggestions in his first four years—and employees responded by increasing the number they submitted *50-fold.*

You can gather many employee suggestions without having to launch a full-scale, ongoing program. For example, you can run a limited-time suggestion campaign. You can even concentrate efforts into one day. When the Office of Human Resources and Administration in the U.S. Department of Energy held an "Idea Day," it generated 2,000 ideas for providing better service; 1,400 of them were implemented.

Some organizations offer employees cash awards for coming up with suggestions that are implemented. Others give prizes, or give employees 10 percent of the savings their ideas generate.

Performance incentives can work, but they still leave open the possibility that most suggestions will never be used. For employees, dropping an idea into a suggestion box is like playing the lottery: if the chance of winning is too low, their desire to play the game decreases. In contrast, when employees see their ideas having impact, it stimulates a greater willingness to come up with suggestions. Organizations with successful employee suggestion programs, say the authors of *Improvement Driven Government,* "have a 'yes' bias and accept up to 90 percent of employee ideas."

Many organizations take too long to decide whether to act on suggestions. Ideas have to work their way up the lengthy hierarchical ladder, and at any point, someone may raise concerns that require yet more people to get involved. Deadlines help. Butch Marita announced that any employee suggestion that did not involve changing law or official policy would be automatically approved in 30 days unless it had been specifically disapproved. Other organizations put employees—not just managers—onto a panel that reviews suggestions, to increase the pressure to make a decision.

It's also important to keep track of employee ideas and what happens to them. This helps ensure that they don't get lost in the system, and it generates performance data about how a suggestion program is working. Monitor the number of suggestions made in a unit, the percentage that are implemented, how long it takes, how many employees participate, and so on.

Chapter 12

Community Empowerment

Giving Communities the Power to Solve Their Own Problems

Community Empowerment **shifts control over government decisions and responsibilities to community-based entities, such as neighborhood organizations, public housing tenants, or business associations, by creating power-sharing arrangements between them and government.**

When Linda Stein moved from New York City to Newbury, an idyllic small town in Vermont, she figured she'd seen the last of crime. During the past few years, though, she has spent one evening a month in Newbury's social hall deciding how to deal with local lawbreakers.

Stein and other community volunteers meet regularly with adult nonviolent offenders (often drunk drivers) to decide how they should repair the damage they have done to the community. One month, they talked with someone who had driven off without paying for gas he had pumped. "We had him interview the gas station owner to find out how the crime had affected him," Stein says. Then he paid for the gas and wrote an essay about the crime's effects on other people and the potential effect on his life if he were to repeat the crime.

About 30 miles east of Newbury, in Barre, Richard Jenny spends his Wednesday mornings this way. He and several other members of the community reparative board, as the volunteer groups are called, handle two or three cases in a sitting. One, which Jenny calls "the banged-up cow story," involved a young man who, while drunk, drove into a cow that a farmer was taking across a road. The driver was cited by the police, and the farmer presented a claim for payment.

"When the offender came before us," says Jenny, "we asked him what he thought about trying to make amends to the farmer. He felt the [farmer's] claim was outrageous and that the accident was partly the farmer's fault." The offender didn't seem very flexible about his position, so one of the board members asked if he'd be willing to go with him to talk to the farmer. The meeting occurred several days later, Jenny says, in the farmer's barn—in front of the cow. When the farmer stated his case, he pointed out the injury and said that, as a result, the cow had to be hand-milked, which cost extra money. Because the cow was no longer economically feasible to retain, the farmer would have to sell it; and because it was injured, it was less valuable.

Then, says Jenny, the farmer and the offender talked with the community member about the situation. "They talked about how much the farmer was losing in this. Then they negotiated what would be reasonable for the young man, who didn't have a very good job, to pay."

Over in Bennington, Vermont, a college town, Ron Cohen remembers an intense case tackled by the board he joined in 1996. A teenage girl with an underage-drinking offense came before the group. When given an opportunity to speak, she was unresponsive, Cohen says.

> *There were probably lots of reasons for this. Most of us were over 40 years old, and we must have looked like 80 to her. All but one of us were men. She was embarrassed and her response sounded surly.*

One of the board members, a father of two daughters, pointed a finger at the girl and insisted that she look at board members when she spoke to them. When he pressed the matter and kept pointing his finger at her, she broke into tears. After the girl left the room so the board could discuss what it wanted to do, Cohen complained angrily that she had been mistreated. The board talked about this for a while. When the girl rejoined the meeting, the finger-pointing board member apologized to her, and the board and the offender reached an agreement on her restitution. When the board ended its meeting, the girl was sitting in a hallway waiting to see someone in another office. Cohen remembers what happened next:

> *There was one woman on the board, a retired kindergarten teacher. She went up to the girl and said, "How are you doing?" The kid just nodded her head. Then the woman said, "You look like you could use a hug." The kid looked up and all of a sudden she just broke—and they hugged each other. And as the rest of us left, we said good luck to her.*

Ron Cohen, Linda Stein, Richard Jenny, and hundreds of other volunteers serving on community reparative boards in every county of Vermont are not cops or lawyers or judges or jury members. Cohen is a college professor. Members of his board have included an insurance agent, an artist, a bartender, and a retired motel owner. They are not part of state or local government, yet they are wielding government's power to determine what will happen to criminal offenders. They are part of a radical experiment in criminal justice, launched in 1994, to shift government's power back into the hands of community members. "This is democracy; this is people solving their community's problems," says John Perry, one of the Vermont corrections officials who launched the effort. "I get choked up watching the boards work."

By early 1999, Vermont's reparative boards had seen more than 3,000 low-risk adult offenders who had committed the sorts of petty crimes that make up most of the workload for police, prosecutors, courts, and prisons. These low-level crimes are on citizens' minds because they wreck a community's quality of life, says Perry.

> *People care about shoplifting, vandalism, disorderly conduct, noise at . . . parties, and kids speeding on their streets—because those things happen thousands of times. You worry about murder if that happens in your town. But if there are loud parties every damned Friday night and nothing gets done about it, first you get angry, then you start getting afraid, and then you demand that legislators get tough on crime.*

The offenders had been sentenced by a court, after pleading guilty to their crimes. Then, with the offender's approval, the sentence had been suspended, so the offender could work out a "reparative contract" with a community board. This step is a big departure from the traditional model of criminal justice in the U.S. Under the centuries-old "retributive" model, crime is viewed as a wrong against the government. Justice is adversarial—the state versus the offender. Once the state has established guilt, its method of evening the scales of justice is to punish the offender, to exact retribution by taking away something of value, such as the offender's freedom or money. In contrast, the reparative model used in Vermont sees the *community* as another victim; it achieves justice by having the offender repair the damage.

Vermont started using this model because the retributive model wasn't working well enough. In 1991, the state's prisons were extremely overcrowded. One of every four sentenced criminals was on the streets, because there was no prison space for them—the highest percentage in the country. The crime rate was down, and arrests and convictions had not increased. But the incarceration rate—the percentage of convictions leading to a prison sentence—was up substantially. More people were being sent to jail, with longer sentences, because legislators had responded to public fear of crime by passing tougher laws.

This put impossible pressures on the corrections system. Because it didn't have enough prison space, it became known as a "revolving door." Yet citizens didn't want new prisons built in their communities, and the governor's budget office said too much money was already going to corrections. In short, the public couldn't afford the retribution its elected officials demanded.

Furthermore, sending petty criminals to prison didn't work. When offenders got out, state records showed, they were more likely to commit another crime than if they had been put on probation in the community.

Faced with these problems, corrections officials started looking for alternatives to prison for offenders who were not real risks to commit serious crimes. They used a series of focus groups and then a scientific survey to ask the public what it thought. The results were a surprise, say John Perry and John Gorczyk, the state corrections commissioner.

> *They did not want vengeance. They wanted what everyone wants from their children when they violate the contract each family has. They wanted a learning experience to occur.*

Vermonters said they wanted nonviolent offenders to be held accountable for their crimes, but not by being sent to prison. Instead, offenders should acknowledge their crime, say they were sorry and mean it, and repair the damage they had done. And, a report on the findings said, Vermonters wanted to participate in the process:

> *They want IN on the decision-making because they think they can help do a better job. They think the criminal justice system isn't paying much attention to minor crime. They think we ignore the crime that most immediately impacts their lives. . . . They don't want that crime ignored, and they are willing to spend time and effort to deal with it, if we let them.*

In response, the corrections department started the first community reparative boards. In every case they handle, board members and the offender must agree, in a written contract, how the offender will repair the damage he or she did to the victim and the community. Making a contract usually involves several steps: first, victims get to tell their story and say what they need to be restored; next, offenders are encouraged to take responsibility for what they did and to understand that their conduct hurt the community's well-being; finally, offenders participate in a discussion to decide how to make things right.

This is quite different from the typical sentencing process, in which the offender speaks through an attorney. "In the traditional process," note Vermont corrections officials, "the offender can continue to deny the reality of his offense . . . and continue to see himself as the victim of the system. With the reparative board, however, he has to talk about the offense, and when a whole group of his neighbors just doesn't buy his bill of goods, he has to begin to acknowledge the reality of his offense, and at least begin to recognize his responsibility."

Through the boards, Perry says, "the community gets to face its citizens—both the victims and the offenders—and understand the dynamic of crime on an individual level." He describes the potential power of the process:

> *The community gets an apology, an acknowledgment of a violation of the rules, and a recognition on the part of the offender that he belongs to the social contract. The offender gets to sign the social contract and gets to make amends for his crime. He gets to add value to the community and, more important, he gets to demonstrate that he* **can** *add value. As a result, the offender is seen as a positive force. And the community gets to embrace the victim and the offender as members of the society, rather than as pariahs.*

By 1999, every court in Vermont was using reparative boards as an alternative to sentencing. There were 41 boards. Early concerns about the program had faded. Originally, criminal justice professionals were skeptical, according to Gorczyk and Perry. "The fundamental criticism of all of these justice professionals was egocentric—how could untrained, mere citizens do the complicated job of justice?" But after four years of experience, "These criticisms have largely been muted." In 1998, the program not only earned a budget increase, it also won a prestigious Innovations in American Government award from the Ford Foundation.

The reparative boards are clearly having positive effects. In 85 percent of their cases, according to corrections officials, the offender has reached a contract with the board and then fulfilled it. (In the rest, a contract could not be reached or the offender failed to fulfill the contract; either way, offenders were returned to court for sentencing.) When the department followed up with 154 offenders who had completed the process, it found they had an 8.2 percent recidivism rate after six months, compared to an 11.6 percent rate for those on regular probation. The program also relieves the crunch in the prison system. Based on historical patterns, Perry estimates, as many as half of the offenders sent to the boards might have ended up in prison.

In responses to surveys, about 90 percent of the offenders have expressed satisfaction about the reparative experience. Board members also report that the experience is a positive one for themselves and their communities. "For me, it's personally fulfilling," says Richard Jenny. "It involves working with people, the offenders, so many of whom seem to be young and uneducated, from backgrounds with psychological and social impoverishment."

In some communities, the boards have become far more involved than corrections officials expected. One board negotiated with the local prosecutor to get him to send drunk driving cases to them. It also recruited local businesses to hire offenders so they could pay their restitution. Several boards have created panels to help victims and mentoring processes for offenders after they fulfill their contracts.

Serving on a board changes the way you think about crime in your community, says Jenny. "It hammers home the fact that people who end up in our courts tend to be the people at the bottom of the social hierarchy. This is painfully evident."

"The experience gives board members a better understanding of things in their community," adds Ron Cohen. He tells the story of a local woman who was guilty of about $4,000 in welfare fraud. When the board asked her what had happened, Cohen recalls, she said she had three children, one of whom had a chronic illness; she needed very expensive medicine and decided to get the money even though it wasn't legal.

"Then," says Cohen, "she looked at us and said, 'What would you have done?' We looked at each other and said we would have done the same thing. That really affected people's thinking about who was in front of them and why they might have done what they did."

The bottom line for Linda Stein is that the reparative process is building her community. "It helps make offenders more a part of the community," she explains.

> *I would like to think that offenders who go through the program and succeed feel some caring from the community. And there's actual physical work that has been done for the community; the offenders give back to the community. This makes Newbury a better place to live.*

CHANGING THE BALANCE OF POWER

See *Reinventing Government* pp. 49–75 and *Banishing Bureaucracy* pp. 229–235

Community empowerment radically undermines the exclusive control of elected officials and government managers over public decisions. It is a great American tradition that is being increasingly applied to government services: education, low-income housing, community planning, neighborhood development, economic development, business district improvements, and human services. Indeed, a 1999 poll found that 68 percent of adults in the U.S. believed the best way to solve America's problems was for "individuals within their communities [to] take responsibility for themselves"—more than triple the number who thought "government must come up with solutions."

Community policing, through which police officers work with communities to help them solve the problems that underlie crime, has spread across the country. So has neighborhood-based planning, which engages residents in designing their own communities. When Robert Bobb was city manager of Richmond, Virginia, he wanted to give citizens more input into how public services were delivered to their neighborhoods. So he divided the city into nine planning districts, where city staff and neighborhood leaders met monthly to discuss priorities and solve problems. In 1999, Seattle began to spend $24 million to implement plans developed by people in 37 neighborhoods. Nationally, more than 200 community-government partnerships have been created to provide neighborhood-based services for families in distress. In some American cities and in other nations—Great Britain and New Zealand, in particular—reinventors have aggressively used community empowerment to break bureaucratic control over public schools.

The spark for community empowerment usually arises from the community itself, from an earnest desire to pitch in where the public sector has failed. In Savannah, Georgia, for example, the city's main approaches to poor neighborhoods—policing and human service agencies—were having little effect. So business leaders got involved. Together with the heads of nonprofit agencies, they targeted the poorest neighborhood for an unprecedented improvement drive. The civic leaders joined with government officials to obtain a $10 million foundation grant and then created an umbrella organization, the Youth Futures Authority (YFA).

The YFA asked neighborhood residents to help design a family resource center, then found an abandoned Catholic high school to house it. "Day and night, the center pulses with activity," wrote an observer in 1997.

> *In a drug-abuse prevention program, middle school kids are studying the Nguzo Saba, African life principles to help them resist the lure of the streets, while next door the old school gym is being renovated to give them a positive alternative to the streets. . . . At the Kid's Cafe, volunteers are getting ready to serve more than 100 youngsters their daily hot meal.*

In Indianapolis, help for government came from the presidents of seven inner-city neighborhood groups. They met with Mayor Steve Goldsmith in a church basement and told him they wanted to join the fight against crime. "Juanita Smith, who represented one of the very toughest neighborhoods, presented me with a contract to sign," the mayor recalls.

> *Remarkably, the contract offered by Juanita not only demanded more patrols and tougher judges but also accepted more responsibilities as*

well. The contract spelled out specific actions that she and her neighbors would undertake—photographing drug dealers, recording customers' license plates, and picketing problematic landlords—to support the police. These leaders wanted to work with officers to develop specific plans for reducing crime. They asked the city to live up to its responsibility, and they were willing to play an important role in that endeavor.

Like employee and organizational empowerment, the two other approaches of the Control Strategy, community empowerment breaks the grip of government hierarchies and administrative control agencies. But it is far more radical, because it shifts control to those *outside* government. Instead of redistributing power within government's ranks, it hands power to community-based entities.

Community empowerment should not be mistaken for community *development* or community *building*, which are ways to improve the well-being of communities and usually involve much more than reinventing government. Nor should community empowerment be confused with merely boosting public participation in government decision making; it goes far beyond the notion of increasing a community's access to government decision makers. It actually gives control of government resources, programs, processes, or institutions to a community.

Alti Rodal and Nick Mulder, veteran Canadian public administrators, note that there is a continuum of government control. At one end of the continuum, they say, "The government organization is influenced by outside input but retains control." This is not community empowerment. At the other end of the spectrum, "authority and responsibility" belong to nongovernment entities. Community empowerment sometimes takes this form—when public agencies sell or give an asset, such as a public housing development or an unused school building, to a community group, for instance. Most of the time, though, community empowerment occurs in the middle of the continuum, where government *shares* authority, responsibility, investment, and risks with community-based entities.

Reinventors use community empowerment to shift government's steering or rowing functions—or both—into community hands. In the case of Vermont's reparative boards, it is rowing: the government sets the broad policies for reparative justice, and the boards implement them by making sentencing contracts with offenders. In other cases, empowered community entities take on steering functions, setting the direction, policies, and budgets for such typical government functions as welfare services and education.

BUREAUCRACY VERSUS COMMUNITY

When Vermont asked its citizens how well they thought the state corrections department was doing, only 37 percent rated its performance as fair or good. In the eyes of department leaders, this was a sobering indictment. It forced them to rethink their purpose, according to Gorczyk and Perry:

> *What wasn't on the traditional corrections list of purposes . . . was what the public wanted. Not prison and probation, but justice. Not singular answers to complex problems, but solutions. Not punishment, but repair of damage. Not retribution, but restoration with value added. Not isolation and banishment, but involvement.*
>
> *We realized that our product line was inadequate. Focusing on the offender for the past 200 years, we had forgotten that our customers weren't interested in our methods, and they [wanted] different outcomes than those produced by the adversarial justice system. . . .*
>
> *The public was interested in . . . quality of life, cooperation, value added, and empowerment.*

The alienation between Vermont's citizens and its corrections department was hardly unique. As John Gardner, chairman of the National Civic League, puts it: "Too many Americans feel hopelessly separated from the centers of decision, hopelessly jerked around by circumstances they cannot even understand, much less combat."

In many communities, people have begun to *demand* some control. One of the most dramatic examples occurred in the late 1980s in Chicago, where a coalition of parents, community activists, and business leaders went to war with the school board and the teachers' union. The school district was one of the worst in the nation. Nearly half of the students who entered the city's 18 most economically disadvantaged high schools eventually dropped out, and half of those who did graduate were reading below the ninth-grade level. Yet no one was doing anything about it. Parents and community activists were fed up, so when another teacher strike began—the ninth in 18 years—they took their anger into the streets and the state legislature. During several years of fierce politicking, community groups and business leaders negotiated a law that moved a significant amount of the school board's power, including the authority to hire and fire school principals, to governing councils elected by neighborhood residents at each of the system's nearly 600 schools.

How did it come to this, to communities versus their government bureaucracies? The fact is that for most of this century we have designed into government a strict limit on the role of communities in governance. John Clayton Thomas, a professor of public administration, traces this history in his book

Public Participation in Public Decisions. Around the turn of the century, Thomas explains, civic reformers tried to minimize political interference in the management of government. They limited public participation to voting in elections or lobbying elected officials. The people's elected representatives were to enact laws that assigned tasks to professional administrators who would report back to them. Reformers thought administration should be insulated from political involvement. They were right about this, but many of them also pushed community members out of government as well—by building public bureaucracies and monopolies that took control of decision making and service delivery.

Several other trends contributed to this separation of government and community. The rise of a large, industrialized, urban society meant that communities, which are typically organized informally and on a small scale, could not cope with emerging problems. At the same time, a "professional ethos" took over social work, policing, education, and other occupations. This was particularly true in education, write professor Tony Bryk and his colleagues:

> *The ties of local school professionals to their communities eventually weakened. Instead, school-based professionals increasingly looked to their central office superiors for guidance. In this process, parents' interests and concerns were subordinated to the expertise of educational professionals. Principles of public participation and local flexibility had been exchanged for established routine, centralized authority, and professional control.*

New technologies also increased the separation. Police officers walked neighborhood beats until cars and radios gave them an alternative. With the new technologies, they could respond more rapidly to reports of crimes. But because they mainly responded to crimes, they developed a limited perspective about the communities in which they worked. Officers, says Mayor Goldsmith, "left their cars only to make arrests, thus making most of their experiences in high-crime areas difficult and adversarial." As a result, "Many officers began to assume the worst of all residents in troubled neighborhoods, and often behaved accordingly."

The Progressive Era model of public administration came under attack in the 1960s. As Thomas explains, critics characterized it "as the enemy of the disadvantaged, servants of the elite rather than of the 'public,' who were sometimes willing to pursue whatever nefarious strategy was necessary to repel the demands of the disadvantaged." This criticism remains alive today. Many protests against government plans and actions involve people, often the poor and minorities, who feel their concerns have been ignored. They seek new ways of making decisions that reflect a wide range of community perspectives, not just those of professionals.

Mayors, governors, city managers, and department heads have begun to push for community empowerment from the other end, because they believe it will produce better outcomes. Vermont's corrections officials expected community boards to do a better job than the courts and prisons. The boards would reduce fear of crime: as community members dealt personally with offenders and victims, they would understand more about crime than if they read about it in the newspapers or watched it on television news. By negotiating reparative contracts with offenders, they would learn what could really be done to repair a crime's effects and to prevent its recurrence. Boards would also reduce recidivism rates, because the process would encourage both a sense of shame and of social belonging among offenders. Finally, the boards would build a stronger sense of connection within the community, which crime tends to erode. These ambitious hopes are already being realized.

See *Reinventing Government* pp. 66–70

Community empowerment achieves powerful effects for several reasons, as *Reinventing Government* discussed. For example:

Communities understand their problems in ways that service professionals simply cannot. "The real experts are in the neighborhoods that experience the problems," explains Robert Woodson, president of the National Center for Neighborhood Enterprise. A community's "indigenous knowledge" may take forms a public bureaucracy could never comprehend. In St. Louis, for instance, the Caring Communities program relies on cultural and spiritual resources as an important factor in its efforts to rebuild poor, drug-infested African American neighborhoods. "The program is grounded in Afrocentricity," reports author Lisbeth Schorr, "emphasizing the history and contributions of African-Americans, and using Swahili principles."

In Durham, North Carolina, Parks and Recreation Director Carl Washington heard Arthur Lee West, a former gang member and Black Panther, speak at a church about his program to keep young men out of trouble. He offered West the free use of a gymnasium and cosponsored the group—because he recognized that "no government agency has been able to match West's success in gaining the attention and interest of the hardest-to-reach teens."

Communities can be more creative and flexible than large service bureaucracies can. Bureaucracies are guided by rules and procedures. Community groups also have rules, but they are guided by the desire to produce results. Vermont's reparative boards have only a handful of rules: they cannot unilaterally punish offenders, restrict their freedom, or prescribe treatment for them. Otherwise, they have room for creativity in repairing the damage done to their communities and crime victims.

"The process is very personalized," says Richard Jenny. "There's no cookie-cutter. Contracts emerge out of the situation when we collectively, with the offender and victim, work on it."

The flexibility leads to a great deal of variation in what the boards decide. Two offenders who commit the same crime, may—probably will—end up with very different reparative contracts. This variation is a stark contrast to efforts in traditional justice systems to be "fair" to offenders by ensuring that similar crimes receive similar punishment. "Variation is what we want," declares John Perry.

> *We do not want uniformity. Identical justice is not necessarily equal justice. The worst thing that justice can be is a cookie-cutter. We're trying to define an incredible range of human behaviors, consequences, and situations. One petty theft is* **not** *the same as another. The point isn't to be fair to the offender. The point is, what does the community want?*

Communities enforce standards of behavior more effectively than bureaucracies or service professionals do. Community members often respond better to their peers than to government employees. As the Heritage Foundation's Stuart Butler observes, tenants are willing to accept from their peers in a resident corporation tough rules that they would reject if they came from city hall. And many public entities simply can't enforce standards of behavior; the political process won't let them, because one group or another always objects.

When communities have a stake in decision making, they are more willing to accept the results. It's basic human nature: the more say you have over what happens, the more you are willing to accept it. When a community group has been part of a planning process, for example, it is much more likely to buy into the planning decisions—and therefore less likely to raise obstacles to implementing plans.

Community empowerment produces spillover benefits. When community groups start to exercise power, it's not just the decisions they make that matter. The very process of making decisions can have a positive impact on the community, because it builds "social capital"—strengthened relationships and involvement in civic affairs. For instance, a 1998 study in New York City found that when some public housing residents became owners of their buildings, they also began to support one another's families during times of crisis and to help one another find jobs and education.

What Is a Community?

Vermont's Ron Cohen and Richard Jenny live in towns with 10,000 residents; Linda Stein's rustic Newbury is much smaller. So it is fairly easy to say what their "community" is; it's the town, a self-contained geographic and political entity. This is the usual way of identifying a community, but there are others. In large cities, for instance, different neighborhoods are distinct communities even though they don't have formal political standing. In Chicago, reinventors organized community empowerment around the student "catchment" districts of individual public schools. In rural areas, a community may be the area within a common environmental boundary, such as a watershed.

It took a while for corrections officials in Vermont to discover which community they would empower.

"We didn't know what 'community' meant when we started the reparative boards," John Perry recalls. They assumed the boards should be organized at the county level, but it didn't turn out that way. "The boards in practice discovered the county was too much territory to cover." Some of the first boards started breaking up in response to *their* sense of what their community was. In Chelsea, a town of fewer than 1,000 souls, board members decided that they couldn't hear a case from Randolph, a slightly larger town some 15 miles away, because the offender "wasn't from here." So a board member from Randolph started a new board there.

"We didn't define community," says Perry. "We let it define itself."

Not all communities are based on location, like towns. They can be based on shared interests: a group of businesses, professionals, or nonprofit service providers, or even a government program's customers or compliers. Several years ago, for instance, the federal agency for workplace safety, the Occupational Safety and Health Administration (OSHA), realized it would take 87 years for its inspectors to visit every worksite in the U.S. So OSHA experimented in Maine with turning the inspection over to employers and labor unions. Injury rates dropped 35 percent.

When the city of Santa Fe, New Mexico, adopted a plan for affordable housing, it turned to nine local nonprofit organizations. They created the Santa Fe Affordable Housing Roundtable, which has wide latitude to design and implement programs. In British Columbia, the provincial social services agency handed over the design and administration of a new program to assist families in caring for severely disabled children to the children's parents, charitable organizations, and community representatives. In Florida, Governor Chiles and the state legislature dissolved the state's Department of Commerce and gave responsibility for economic development to Florida's business community, working in partnership with government.

However you define community, *don't* define it as "local elected officials." Handing power to a mayor or county officials does not put it into the hands of community groups.

Holding Communities Accountable

Vermont's community reparative boards have a great deal of discretion in how they operate, says Perry.

> *The parameters we set were focused on the positive outcomes we wanted to achieve: Restore and make the victim whole. Make amends to the community. Learn about the impact of the crime. Learn ways to avoid reoffending. These are in three-inch letters on the boards' walls. They can do anything they want to get there.*

So different boards work quite differently. Some conduct meetings that are quite informal; others hold no-nonsense, just-the-facts sessions. Some boards ask the offender to leave after hearing from him or her, so they can discuss in private their ideas about a reparative contract. Others talk about it in front of the offender. Some boards make decisions by consensus and rotate the chair for every meeting; others don't.

When the corrections department has tried to impose more order on the process, boards have sometimes refused to go along. "Whenever we try to get too specific, the boards rebel," says Perry. "As soon as we start treating them like state employees, they say no." At one point the department developed a lengthy training manual for board members. "It was about 500 pages thick," Perry recalls. "The boards protested; it's now about 20 pages long."

Still, the boards are accountable for their performance. The commissioner of the corrections department appoints all board members, and if they fail to respect the department's parameters, he may revoke the appointments. This has happened several times, says Perry—mainly when a board member focused on just punishing offenders instead of getting them to repair the damage they caused.

This is a form of *administrative* accountability. Essentially, board members have a contract with the department to follow the basic guidelines, and the department has full discretion to judge how well they are doing. Such accountability is usually built into a tool we call an empowerment agreement.

pp. 514–518

Community groups can also be held *politically* accountable, although this is fairly rare. In Chicago, the hundreds of Local School Councils (LSCs) that have gained significant authority over each school are accountable to voters, not school district administrators or even school district board members. Some 6,000 LSC members are elected every two years by residents in the school council's neighborhood.

Community entities can also be held accountable through any of the Consequences Strategy approaches: enterprise management, managed competition, or performance management. And these methods can be augmented by the Customer Strategy approaches.

pp. 149–246, 273–388

The keys to holding empowered community groups accountable for their performance are much the same as those for empowered government organizations and employees:

They must have clear goals and parameters from the outset. Community groups must be clear about what they are trying to accomplish and what authority they have. The Youth Futures Authority in Savannah, for instance, focuses on reducing the school dropout rate, preventing teen pregnancies, improving students' academic performance, and increasing the number of youths who go to college.

Community groups must also know where the lines are drawn when it comes to their authority. These outcomes and boundaries should be spelled out in writing as power is shifted to the community.

pp. 247–271

They must measure their performance and make the results public. Without performance data, community groups cannot tell how well they are doing, and neither can anyone else. Such data is a fundamental element of accountability, no matter which approach you are using. Sharing information about results also helps promote even more community involvement, because it allows people to see that community-based efforts can have a real impact on their problems.

Making Government Community-Friendly

Vermont's community reparative boards depend on the state department of corrections for essential services. The agency doesn't tell the boards what to do, but it does provide them with training, administrative support, advice, and performance evaluation.

Early on, corrections officials realized that their agency wasn't ready for this radically new role. So "we essentially blew up the organization," says John Perry, the planning director. They created a unit for reparative services and staffed it with employees who volunteered. "We let the staff choose where they would go, to focus on what they wanted to do," explains Perry. "So the people we got were the experimenters, the risk takers, the entrepreneurs."

More recently, the department has been exploring ways to devolve to local communities its authority over the boards and its supportive role. "Our experience has been that the towns really want to take this over," says Perry. "What they do not want is a pig in a poke or to get left holding the bag." So the department has asked the legislature to give funding for the boards to the towns, not the department. (How often have you seen state bureaucracies do *that*?)

In its evolution from launching an experimental program to potentially devolving ownership to local government, the Department of Corrections has been reacting to a fundamental reality: when you empower community groups, you must further reinvent government so that it can do its part in the new power-sharing arrangement. Handing power to communities and then having them interact with public agencies that behave bureaucratically is a recipe for disaster.

Many reinventors understand this but still struggle to find a solution. They tend to tinker with the structure of government. In Indianapolis, Mayor Goldsmith divided the city into nine "townships" and assigned an administrator—a "mini mayor"—to each one to learn what the neighborhoods needed and to deliver it. In Hampton, Virginia, then–city manager Bob O'Neill created the Department of Neighborhood Services to help neighborhood groups gain access to city government's resources. But both efforts—one a decentralized structure, the other a centralized one—found it difficult to get the *rest* of the bureaucracy to respond to the neighborhoods; most departments continued with business as usual.

See *Banishing Bureaucracy* pp. 21–48

These and similar experiences elsewhere reinforce the central lesson of *Banishing Bureaucracy:* to accomplish significant change in bureaucratic behavior, you must change the purpose, accountability, incentives, controls, and culture of government organizations. When you change only the structure, you usually don't get much leverage. Establishing a department for neighborhoods in Hampton did not significantly increase the incentives for other agencies to respond to neighborhoods' needs, for example. Such structural changes can even have a negative impact: when an agency or administrator is designated as the "neighborhood connection," other agencies and administrators often feel they are off the hook.

In short, to create community-friendly government, you must use the five strategies, not simply redraw government's organizational chart. Specifically, you might:

pp. 215–246

- Give some departments specific performance goals related to the condition of the community, with consequences.

pp. 323–388

- Have some agencies treat community groups as customers, measuring their satisfaction with services and establishing service standards, guarantees, and redress policies.

pp. 174–182

- Give community groups control of public funds that they can use to purchase services from city departments. (For ideas about how to design this, see internal enterprise management.)

pp. 232–237

- Offer performance bonuses to managers and employees who partner well with communities.

pp. 531–609

- Use the Culture Strategy tools to help public employees understand the importance of community groups.

A particularly pervasive barrier to community empowerment is the way government is organized into functional silos that separate public employees and funds into narrow, specialized categories. This is compounded by the federal and state levels, which routinely use categorical funding streams to channel money to the local level. The silos make it nearly impossible to mount comprehensive efforts to deal with a community's problems. Instead, each agency and its administrators focus on their niche. No one is responsible for thinking about the whole picture—or even for collaborating with other agencies.

To overcome this separation, reinventors in Louisville, Kentucky, and San Diego County, California, began training professionals who dealt with community problems together. They "have found it very productive to train social workers, police officers, nurses, teachers, mental health workers, probation officers, community liaison workers, and others together, rather than separately," according to the Center for the Study of Social Policy. "The aim is to develop a common perspective on helping families and a common set of core skills within a neighborhood delivery system."

Many communities discover the limits of categorization when they tackle crime problems. It became obvious to Indianapolis mayor Goldsmith that even when police and community residents worked together, they needed the help of other agencies to clean up drug-infested neighborhoods. City attorneys helped the city seize dozens of abandoned properties, while the public health and fire departments wrote citations for nuisances that violated city ordinances and the city demolished dilapidated buildings and gave sound structures to community organizations. "In the first two years of the project," Goldsmith says, "more than a hundred nuisance sites were corrected or conveyed to not-for-profit development corporations." Accomplishing this required a great deal of coordination among the agencies—the typical method of dealing with categorization. Coordination is necessary, but it is often an unnatural act between unconsenting partners. Unless it is combined with reinvention strategies, it will rarely be enough to make governments more responsive to empowered communities.

Building a Community's Capacity

In Vermont, members of community reparative boards are not simply thrown into the fray. The first members were trained for their new task by participating in mock board meetings. "One of us [from the corrections department] would play the offenders," says John Perry, "and the board would try to figure out what to do. Some of our probation officers know all of the tricks, how to hustle you." Since those early days, the orientation process has evolved. Now new board members can observe board meetings, read materials about reparative justice, and talk with the state's coordinator for their board. In addition, they must participate in 15 hours of training within their first six months. "Board members participate in role-playing exercises and other activities designed to develop good communications skills in their interactions with offenders, victims, and other board members," says David Karp, a sociologist who studies the boards. Ongoing board members must participate in seven hours of training each year.

As Vermont found, it's important to prepare community members for empowerment. A number of cities—including Hampton, Dayton, and Indianapolis—have set up institutes or colleges to educate and train neighborhood residents (and city employees) for empowerment. Indianapolis created the Neighborhood Empowerment Initiative, funded by three national foundations, to provide neighborhood associations with training, technical assistance, and workshops to learn how to work with one another and local government. The city also set up the Neighborhood Resource Center, located in a building donated by a local hospital. Run by a board of community activists, it holds workshops and classes for citizens and neighborhood associations and acts as an information clearinghouse on programs and initiatives in the neighborhoods. In its first three years, the center helped create 80 new neighborhood and homeowner associations.

"Building capacity in these ways is a great idea," says Ted Staton, city manager of East Lansing, Michigan. "But you should make sure that there's a place for people after they finish training—an advisory board, a commission, whatever, where they can use what they've learned."

Often, communities need extensive technical assistance to help strengthen community organizations so that they can take and use power. In Canada, for instance, tenant groups get technical assistance before a housing co-op is created and for five years after occupancy. In the U.S., public housing residents often get technical assistance before their resident management corporations take over management of their developments.

Information is another element of capacity building. Charlotte, North Carolina, created detailed profiles of its 73 inner-city neighborhoods. Information of this sort can become the basis for performance indicators to measure the impact city agencies and community organizations are having on neighborhoods.

Information about the various tools community groups can use is also valuable. Seattle maintains and publicizes an index of more than 50 tools for community groups, including a primer for designing effective community participation, a planning guide for parks and open space, a guide to zoning, a video about designing city streets, and a handbook on neighborhood planning.

When reinventors build community capacity, they must walk a fine line between providing too little support and providing too much. If you do too much, you're likely to hobble the community by creating dependence on your support. But if you keep your hands off, the community may flounder.

Former president Jimmy Carter erred on the side of providing too little direction when he launched the Atlanta Project, designed to rebuild the city's decaying neighborhoods in time for the 1996 Olympics. Carter emphasized a bottom-up approach: "I have seen so many programs designed by brilliant people," he said, "and they have all failed because we didn't allow the people to whom the programs were directed to decide." But after five years, there was not much to show for the effort, reports Lisbeth Schorr. "The Atlanta Project may have overlearned one valuable lesson to the exclusion of several other, equally important ones," she writes in *Common Purpose.* "Leery of dictating to those they intended to help, the project leaders leaned far over backward in providing only a blank slate and a process—and no substantive guidance."

However you develop a community's capacity, it is important to ensure that it does not get tied up in bureaucratic red tape from government's central administrative agencies. You still need safeguards such as audits and investigations. But if you handcuff community groups with ironclad rules and regulations, you will diminish the advantages of empowering them in the first place.

COMMUNITY EMPOWERMENT: OTHER LESSONS LEARNED

Empowering communities involves two steps: shifting power from government to the community, then organizing at the community level to use the power effectively. As we've seen, accomplishing this reinvention two-step requires both partners to learn new dancing skills. Governments must reinvent themselves to play new roles as coaches, listeners, and responsive partners. Community entities must learn how to produce results. Like public organizations, they should get clear about their purposes, face consequences for performance, be accountable to their customers, empower their employees, and create entrepreneurial cultures focused on continuous improvement.

As governments and community entities undertake these challenging tasks—often working in tandem—they can benefit from the lessons learned by those already on the path to community empowerment.

1. Public officials who want to empower communities must build trust first.

Usually, public officials have to take the first steps to overcome the pervasive distrust between government and communities. This is because *they* hold the power that must be shared. To begin with, they have to decide to trust the community. "Government has a lot to learn," says Vermont's John Perry. "We think the communities don't trust us, when in fact we don't trust them."

Officials also have to stop assuming that all the public wants from government is results. Citizens do want results, but often they want to be involved in producing the results. That's what Vermont officials found. When city commissioners in Battle Creek, Michigan, conducted a poll and newsletter survey and held 10 focus groups, they discovered the same thing: residents wanted local government to actively solve community problems, but they wanted it to be more a convener than a doer. Residents wanted teamwork between citizens and community organizations.

Public officials also need to say clearly that they want a new relationship with the community. But the key to building trust is not words; it is deeds. And the deeds must respond to real community desires. In Indianapolis, Mayor Goldsmith learned this the hard way. He was visiting the Fountain Square neighborhood on the city's southeast side to announce new infrastructure investments. "I was greeted by children picketing the press conference and carrying signs demanding a new neighborhood park," he recalls. "The children complained that they had no place to play; their mothers told me of syringes lying in plain sight on the streets and open drainage holes as big as craters."

The mayor asked one of the demonstration leaders, Estelle Parsons, what she wanted.

> *More police and a new playground, she said without missing a beat. She proceeded to tell me precisely where the playground could go. I told Estelle the city would have a park and a playground on the spot she identified within ninety days. When Estelle and I cut the ribbon on that park ninety days later, everyone was amazed—including me. Gradually, we began to build trust between City Hall and the neighborhoods.*

It's not enough to build a community's trust in government *leaders,* however. At some point, citizens must believe that ordinary public employees will respond to their needs, too. In Minneapolis in 1990, for instance, three government agencies launched the Community Action and Resource Exchange (CARE) program to involve citizens in dealing with drug problems in their neighborhoods. The residents of the first neighborhood they targeted were skeptical initially, said Jay Clark, director of the Jordan Area Community Council: "They thought the city people were a bunch of lazy farts." But when the city started listening to their complaints and responding—closing down crack houses and curbing gang activity—the residents' attitudes changed. "When citizens found they could come with a complaint and it would be handled soon, they'd be impressed," said Jim Haugen, a police officer involved with CARE. "They got the impression that they could actually talk to the city and we would listen." Clark described how the residents saw it: "The city people have changed."

Getting public employees to give power to communities can be difficult. Police unions sometimes block changes in deployment necessary to implement community policing, for example. And many professionals resist community empowerment because they are skeptical that community organizations or volunteers can do the job. Reinventors must overcome this resistance, using other reinvention strategies to pull and push public employees through the changes that community empowerment requires.

pp. 504–505

2. *Information is a powerful stimulus for community empowerment.*

In the late 1980s, Don Mendonsa, the city manager of Savannah, asked the school superintendent for data on school dropouts by race, gender, and grade. Mendonsa was worried about juvenile crime; large numbers of idle teenagers were hanging out downtown, not in school and not working. At first, the superintendent refused to provide the data, saying it was privileged information that had never been released before. When the city manager insisted, the data showed that of 16,270 students in grades six to twelve, 21 percent had failed, over one-third were at least a grade behind, nearly a third had missed 16 or more days of school, and 13 percent dropped out every year.

When the data became public, it caused an uproar. The school superintendent resigned, and community members and city officials put together an initiative to turn things around. The key energizer was information, says Mendonsa: "If we had not aired our dirty linen in public, showing these astounding failure rates, I'm not sure we would have had as much support from the public as we've gotten."

The information in Savannah was powerful because it contained disturbing news. In other communities, a "community scorecard," which presents data on a range of indicators, is used to prod the citizenry and government into action. Such a system "can present great motivation for community self-improvement," says Con Hogan, head of Vermont's human services agency. In 1993, he addressed the Rotary Club in Bennington. "Usually they are twenty minute, two point speeches and they are over and done with," he says.

pp. 30–35

> *However, this particular day I took down two charts. The first chart was the good news chart. I showed them the early stages of what looked to be the beginning of a very strong trend curve in the reduction of child abuse in Vermont. A couple of people in the audience at that point spontaneously applauded, and I was a little taken aback. I*

guess I hadn't thought through how fundamental this issue is to many people.

And then, I showed them the bad news chart. The chart showed that even though the news around the state of Vermont is good, the same can't be said for Bennington. In fact, in an environment where overall child abuse rates were going down, theirs was going up. A minute later, I had normally calm businesspeople very upset. They demanded to know why it was happening in their community, where it was better, why it was improving in other areas, and what they could do about it. I am pleased to report that since then, child abuse rates in Bennington have declined significantly, almost to the level of the state's improving rate.

3. *Community empowerment requires patience and early successes.*

It can take years for community entities to work well as decision makers and doers, especially when they must work closely with government agencies. Vermont's reparative program, first piloted in 1994, took four years before it started handling a substantial level of cases. As a result, reinventors often find they have to "go slow to go fast." They must take the time to build trust, relationships, knowledge, and skills, so they can create the capacity to move more quickly later. Indeed, not taking the time up front may only waste time later.

Thus, some reinventors prefer to phase in community empowerment. Missouri launched its Caring Communities effort—a partnership of parents, community leaders, school staff, and state agencies—in 1989 in one school. Five months later, it launched a second project, in a rural area. By 1995, it was spending $24 million to expand Caring Communities to 50 sites. While expanding the program, the state simplified procedures, changed budgeting and financing practices, and gave more and more power to local leaders.

Other public leaders have to give the empowered community organization time to "shake out"—to test itself, adapt, and improve. Savannah's Youth Futures Authority had a rocky start before it became a successful model. Early on it had to adjust its mission. Then it failed to develop a partnership with the city's school system.

Starting small and slowly runs the risk of leaving the public and the politicians unsatisfied, of course. They may lose patience or interest before community empowerment has demonstrated its effectiveness.

There are at least two solutions to this dilemma: first, manage the expectations of the community, so people understand that the payoff is long-term; and second, deliver some short-term victories. Reinventors should make sure that they get some easy wins, such as shutting down a crack house or solving a truancy problem, even as they begin building the community's capacity.

4. *Empower your public employees to help prepare them to work with empowered community groups.*

Working in an environment where you share decision-making power is quite different from working in one where you hold all the cards. And working with community groups is often messier and less predictable than working within government bureaucracies is. Employees must learn to listen to the community without becoming defensive when its members vent their frustrations. They must learn to listen to many voices, some of which conflict. They must learn to respond in ways that enlist the community's energies, rather than relying solely on the government. They must learn to be patient with the often tedious process of building buy-in throughout a community. Most essential, they must fully embrace the philosophy that underpins community empowerment—the belief that communities can and should solve some of their own problems.

pp. 453–488

In addition to training and education, a powerful way to help public employees adapt to community empowerment is to empower *them.* To help employees learn how to collaborate with communities, get them into the habit of collaborating inside their organizations.

5. *Don't just empower "the usual suspects."*

Everyone has some idea of who "the community" is, and usually these ideas don't include people or groups who have not been visibly active. So it's likely that government officials and even civic leaders will overlook the possibility of shifting power to nontraditional players in the community: small business owners, youth, or the poor, for instance. This is a mistake. As one study puts it, empowerment "is not about a small number of community leaders sitting around a table and making decisions for the larger community."

Compounding the problem is the fact that most communities already have organizations that have grown up in response to local needs. Some represent the grass roots, but others don't. Usually, though, reaching beyond the usual suspects is less a question of whom to avoid and more a matter of figuring out how to engage people and organizations that are not typically on the list. There are many ways of doing this:

- Reach out to grassroots community entities: churches, small businesses, service and fraternal organizations, and neighborhood associations, among others.
- Target specific outreach strategies for different constituencies—senior citizens, young people, renters, gays.
- Provide sufficient funding to ensure that parties with fewer resources or less time are able to participate.

- Use bilingual materials and public service advertisements to publicize opportunities for involvement, and use interpreters at meetings if necessary.
- Design meetings and other processes to overcome barriers to participation. For example, holding meetings in central locations near mass transit lines helps people who don't have cars. Providing free or low-cost child care helps people with young children.
- Train and employ community members to conduct outreach efforts to their neighbors. Lisbeth Schorr reports that neighborhood residents in Baltimore were trained and paid to participate in the design of new community-based programs:

> *Some could reach out to young mothers. Others knew the streets and could relate to the long-term unemployed and the drug culture. One advocate was a high school dropout who proved particularly valuable in encouraging young people to stay in school. All had been unemployed at the time they were hired. Some were struggling with drug problems or hampered by criminal records. Most lacked the self-confidence to take the necessary steps for their own advancement. Yet each was able to connect to a particular place, culture, or subgroup within the neighborhood.*

6. Build accountability into community organizations to protect them from criticism.

Reinventors should anticipate that community empowerment will draw fire from skeptics or opponents. Particularly if the partnership is a new organization, people in existing entities may fear losing some of their authority and status. Public employees or their unions may attack community organizations for mishandling resources or not being accountable. That's why analysts at the Center for the Study of Social Policy emphasize that empowered community entities "must 'bend over backwards' to demonstrate [their] accountability for operations, expenditures, services, and results." They warn against delay in creating accountability:

> *The usual excuse given for ignoring accountability issues is that this issue can be addressed only after governance entities have built their basic capacities for planning and implementing programs. According to this logic, accountability is important after many other responsibilities of local governance are under way.*
>
> *In fact, the opposite seems to be true: unless a climate of accountability is established immediately with regard to local governance en-*

tities, they run the risk of repeating the mistakes (and having the lack of impact) of the existing system. Furthermore, establishing up-front accountability for local governance entities may be essential to garner necessary public, political and financial support.

7. *Beware of creating a bureaucratic wolf in community clothing.*

Government's tendency to bureaucratize everything dies slowly. John Perry finds that some of his colleagues keep insisting that the community reparative boards operate in a more orderly fashion. "From the bureaucrats, I hear, 'We have to do some procedures.' The boards say, 'Get off our backs; we know what we're doing.'" This tug-of-war is natural during an empowerment process, but it's usually a mistake to give in to the bureaucratic impulse. Public officials must consciously resist the tempting sense of control and order that bureaucracy offers. They must recognize that variation is an advantage of community control, because one size does not fit all. The point of empowerment is to create entrepreneurial, community-based entities that will produce better results than government bureaucracies do.

RESOURCES ON COMMUNITY EMPOWERMENT

Clint Bolick. *Transformation: The Promise and Politics of Empowerment.* Oakland, Calif.: Institute for Contemporary Studies Press, 1998. In a fast-paced argument for community empowerment across a wide spectrum of government services, Bolick provides telling anecdotes and an array of policy ideas.

National Center for Neighborhood Enterprise. The nerve center of a national movement to empower tenants of public housing to manage and own their own developments, NCNE provides information and technical assistance on empowerment of poor communities. Contact them at 1367 Connecticut Ave., N.W., Washington DC 20036. Phone: (202) 331–1103.

John G. Perry and John F. Gorczyk. "Restructuring Corrections: Using Market Research in Vermont." *Corrections Management Quarterly,* 1997, *1*(3), 26–35. Provides background on Vermont's community reparative boards and the paradigm-shifting philosophy of reparative justice.

William R. Potapchuk, Jarle Crocker, and William H. Schechter Jr. *Systems Reform and Local Government: Improving Outcomes for Children, Families, and Neighborhoods.* Washington, D.C.: Program for Community Problem Solving, February 1997. This relatively brief paper provides an overview of reinvention in local governments, with a focus on the community empowerment approach.

Program for Community Problem Solving. Established in 1988 and cosponsored by the National League of Cities, the American Chamber of Commerce Executives, the International City/County Management Association, the International Downtown Association, and the National Civic League, this organization offers training, presentations, technical assistance, coaching, facilitation, information, and publications about collaborative approaches for communities. Based in Washington, D.C. Phone: (202) 783–2961.

Lisbeth B. Schorr. *Common Purpose.* New York: Anchor Books, 1997. Focusing mainly on how to strengthen families and neighborhoods, Schorr provides a rich compendium of community-based change efforts. Chapter Three, "Taming Bureaucracies to Support What Works," lays out a strong case for community empowerment.

TOOLS FOR COMMUNITY EMPOWERMENT

Empowerment Agreements create a power-sharing understanding between a government agency and an empowered community group, specifying the responsibilities of both parties. See below.

Community Governance Bodies are community-based steering organizations with the authority to make decisions and take on responsibilities once handled by government organizations. See p. 518.

Collaborative Planning gives community entities decision-making authority in the planning of community and public projects and regulations. See p. 520.

Community-Based Funding provides revenues to empowered community groups, either directly from government revenues or through the power to generate their own funds. See p. 527.

EMPOWERMENT AGREEMENTS

In Boston in 1989, a pregnant white woman, Carol Stuart, was murdered. Her husband told police that a young black male had committed the crime. What happened next outraged the city's African American community. "The Boston police descended on inner-city neighborhoods in their search," report Harvard sociologists Orlando Patterson and Christopher Winthrop. "The police tactics in the Stuart investigation, along with the stop-and-frisk policies of the Citywide Anti-Crime Unit," led to protests about rights violations.

It turned out that the husband had committed the murder. But out of the tensions created during the initial search for a suspect emerged a partnership between the police and community leaders, particularly a group of black ministers known as the Ten-Point Coalition. "This partnership is key to explaining why Boston has been successful in reducing crime," say Patterson and Winthrop, noting that the city's homicide rate fell 77 percent between 1990 and 1999. The key to the partnership, they continue, has been a set of principles that bind the government and community together in mutual responsibility.

One principle spells out the responsibility of the community partners to help police identify the small percentage of youths who are causing most of the crime. Another makes it clear that if police behave badly, they will be punished. A third states that community leaders will have an informal say in decisions to arrest certain teenagers, such as those with no prior offenses.

Shared principles such as those laid out in Boston are one element of empowerment agreements between organizations and community entities. They define the basic commitments each party is willing to make to behave in new ways. Other elements include the following:

- ***The measurable results the community and government partners hope to produce.*** In Portland, Oregon, for instance, the police, citizens, neighborhood groups, and businesses negotiate and sign a written agreement that lists the goals of their community policing effort in particular parts of the city, as well as specific actions the partners and police will take.
- ***The specific authority that government is shifting to the community.*** In Georgia, state government shifted the authority to allocate some social service funds to Savannah's Youth Futures Authority.
- ***The ways that government agencies and community groups will collaborate.*** In Dane County, Wisconsin, the agreement defines how teams of community members, police officers, public health nurses, social workers, and school staff will team up in neighborhoods to improve the health of children.
- ***The consequences that either partner faces for the quality of their performance.*** When a public housing authority gives tenants who have organized a resident management corporation the right to operate their own housing development, for instance, the contract often spells out performance goals, incentives, and penalties. If the corporation fails to keep performance up to the standards, it loses the right to run the development. This should go both ways, however. If the public housing authority fails to meet its standards—for police protection, its contribution to maintenance, or financial support—it should face penalties, too.

These empowerment agreements should be in writing, and they should be public. They may take many forms: contracts, protocols for collaboration, memoranda of understanding, or co-investment agreements. They are similar to the flexible performance agreements (FPAs) described in Chapter Three, and many of the lessons learned about FPAs will help you design more effective community empowerment agreements.

pp. 125–136

By negotiating empowerment agreements, community and government leaders get an opportunity to assess each other's intentions and commitments. This helps build understanding and trust. By spelling out who does what—and the reciprocal commitments among the parties—such agreements set the stage for the community to use its new power. And by specifying consequences for performance, they give each partner recourse if something goes wrong.

Empowerment Agreements: Other Lessons Learned

1. *Maintain the community's independence from government.*

Even when they are accountable to public officials, empowered communities must have an autonomous voice and be free to take independent positions. They should not become just an arm of the government, for this would compromise their ability to work effectively in the community.

2. *Focus on realistic goals.*

After establishing principles, the most important aspects of an empowerment agreement are the shared goals that the community and government adopt. These should come before any decisions about strategies or actions. It's important to be candid about what can and cannot be accomplished by the community organization. Setting goals too high will put too much pressure on the community and lead to disappointment when the goals are not achieved. Think about making incremental progress—not gigantic (and unrealistic) leaps. For instance, the goal of completely eradicating open-air drug sales in a neighborhood is probably unrealistic, whereas the goal of cutting the rate in half may not be.

The national goals for academic achievement by the year 2000 that U.S. governors set in the late 1980s were completely unrealistic, as many school districts are finding. The Illinois legislature compounded the problem by setting them as five-year goals for every school in Chicago. This may have played well as political rhetoric, but "as a timetable for institutional change in a major urban school district with more than 400,000 students and 25,000 teachers, it is simply not realistic," note the authors of a comprehensive study of Chicago school reform.

3. *Build in administrative flexibility.*

Lisbeth Schorr, in her book *Common Purpose,* tells a story of a typical elected official's reaction to the idea of variation in community initiatives:

My presentation was to follow a film on the family support centers recently established in Kentucky. The film emphasized the significant variation in design and operations in each of the seven centers shown. Before I could begin to speak, the lieutenant governor [of Illinois] interrupted to ask whether I supported the local variation that the film seemed to be promoting. When I indicated—to his horror—that I did, he said, "Now look here, we have one hundred and two counties in Illinois; surely you're not saying that the State of Illinois should fund one hundred and two family support centers, each of which would look different from the others? That would be an administrative nightmare!"

Of course, it would only be a nightmare to those who focus on control and order rather than results. As Schorr points out, family support centers are "more likely to accomplish their purpose if they [are] shaped by local communities to reflect local needs and strengths."

Empowerment agreements must recognize that flexibility is an essential part of sharing power with communities. Imposing government's bureaucratic administrative systems—for budgeting, procurement, and personnel—on community groups will only diminish their chances of producing the desired results. That doesn't mean anything goes, but it does mean that public officials should encourage entrepreneurial approaches that help community entities produce results, rather than controlling how they produce them.

Vermont's Success by Six initiative took this approach. State government challenged local communities to develop comprehensive strategies to reduce infant mortality and promote healthy development of children in the first three years of life. "Communities were encouraged to develop their own approach to achieving these results, rather than following any one service model," reports the Center for the Study of Social Policy. "Vermont communities and state agency officials believe that the resulting local plans were more creative, more rooted in local conditions, and more cost-effective than if the state had tried to mandate one or two strategies that every community must use." North Carolina's huge Smart Start initiative, created by Governor Jim Hunt to help ensure that every child was ready for school, used the same approach.

4. *Use performance incentives.*

Creating consequences for performance stimulates government agencies to improve their performance—and it can do the same for community entities. Governments can use managed competition with community-based organizations, and they can use many of the performance management tools outlined in Chapter Six. Maryland's state government, for instance, offers financial incentives to its Local Management Boards (LMBs)—collaborative

pp. 183–214, 215–246

community-government groups that provide services to children and families—if they produce predetermined outcomes and spend less money than state agencies would have. LMBs can use their earned incentives to pay for comprehensive services. In Baltimore, the LMB used incentives it earned to finance parent support groups, beds in the Salvation Army shelter, and school projects.

RESOURCE ON EMPOWERMENT AGREEMENTS

Center for the Study of Social Policy. *Creating a Community Agenda: How Governance Partnerships Can Improve Results for Children, Youth, and Families.* Washington, D.C.: Center for the Study of Social Policy, February 23, 1998. An excellent first step toward a curriculum on this and other aspects of community empowerment, this document is based on research from a number of community-government partnerships and is aimed squarely at practitioners.

COMMUNITY GOVERNANCE BODIES

***Community Governance Bodies* are community-based steering organizations with the authority to make decisions and take on responsibilities once handled by government organizations.**

When community entities make decisions about what social services a neighborhood should receive, what outcomes government agencies should focus on achieving, or which plan to use to improve environmental conditions, they are steering. They are community-based versions of the steering organizations we described in Chapter One. They set goals, choose strategies, and measure performance against goals. They may also conduct research and analysis, convene community leaders, develop a vision for the community, coordinate the work of diverse organizations, and use contracts, charters, vouchers, performance agreements, and other means to direct the work of rowing organizations. To distinguish them from government-driven steering organizations, we call them community governance bodies.

pp. 35–39

There is no standard model for what a community governance body looks like or how it should operate. However, a great many of Chapter One's lessons learned and do's and don'ts apply, particularly the following:

- Strong governance bodies should have control over significant resources.
- Steering organizations should steer resources, not manage them.
- Don't tie governance bodies' hands with categorical funding.
- Don't promise too much too soon.

Using Community Governance Bodies: Other Lessons Learned

Some additional lessons apply specifically to community governance bodies:

1. Get many different hands on the steering wheel.

A key issue for community governance bodies is the makeup of their boards. When the Center for the Study of Social Policy studied such organizations in the human services field, it found that they tended to have governing boards of 15 to 30 people, with a mix of community advocates, local residents, businesspeople, and elected officials from the city, county, and school districts. In other words, they were a mosaic of a community's many stakeholders.

As we said earlier in the chapter, there are many techniques for ensuring that community empowerment includes more than "the usual suspects" in a community. In addition, governance bodies should reexamine their membership periodically to see if it is still broadly representative of the community.

pp. 511–512

Some governance bodies include government officials as members of their boards. Others, such as Kansas City's Local Investment Commission (LINC), which oversees the local office of the state Department of Social Services, are citizen-only boards. (LINC allows elected officials to participate as ex-officio members of the board and has an advisory cabinet of officials from public agencies.) In our view, local context should determine whether or not elected officials are part of the governance body. However, as we said in Chapter One, it is important to keep providers—from the private or public sectors—off steering boards, since they have potential conflicts of interest in setting direction.

p. 39

2. Ensure that steering decisions affect the use of resources.

Steering—setting direction—is meaningful only if it affects the way resources are used. So there must be a clear link between steering and spending. One way to ensure this is to give the governance body the power to set budgets for public funds—or at least veto power over the budgets in question. A less radical method is to build consideration of the governance body's recommendations into the government's process for setting budget priorities. Whatever the method of control, reinventors should use performance budgeting for funds that are influenced or controlled by communities, so that there will be a direct tie between budget levels and results.

pp. 43–53

Community governance bodies should also seek to affect other spending in the community: by foundations, corporations, and nonprofit organizations. After all, community governance is not just about public institutions; it is about leading all community institutions and members to solve problems and meet community needs.

3. Uncouple steering and rowing.

pp. 113–118

As we explain in Chapter Three, separating the steering and rowing functions in government has important positive effects. The most significant one for a steering body is that instead of having to do the rowing itself, it gains the flexibility to select from a wide range of service delivery options. In addition, its decisions won't be influenced by its interests as a provider, and it will be easier to hold providers accountable for their performance.

4. Monitor the performance of rowing organizations—and hold them accountable.

Without data about performance, steering bodies can't steer very well. They cannot tell what is working and what is not, and they cannot hold anyone accountable for their performance. So governing bodies must build a mandate to track performance into their relationship with rowing organizations. In Maryland, Local Management Boards that develop community-based services for children and families look at performance data every month. "The impact of having these data on a continuous basis has been remarkable," reports one observer. "Board members can spot when program implementation is not being effective and immediately change course or refine their programmatic initiatives and policy strategies."

RESOURCE ON COMMUNITY GOVERNANCE BODIES

Center for the Study of Social Policy. *Creating a Community Agenda: How Governance Partnerships Can Improve Results for Children, Youth, and Families.* Washington, D.C.: Center for the Study of Social Policy, February 23, 1998. An excellent first step toward a curriculum on this and other aspects of community empowerment.

COLLABORATIVE PLANNING

Collaborative Planning **gives community entities decision-making authority in the planning of community and public projects and regulations.**

In 1992, the Chicago Transit Authority considered shutting down the Lake Street "El," one line of its famous elevated rail system. A region-wide coalition of 200 community groups—churches, businesses, transit riders, neighborhood councils, and the like—rose up in noisy opposition. Meeting in church basements, the activists held six planning workshops for community members. Since the transit authority contended that ridership on the line was too low to merit further public investment, they focused on showing how a rejuvenated line could be a shot in the arm for the neighborhoods it traversed. To model this transit-driven community development strategy, they used the workshops to redesign the Pulaski Street station.

"The meetings allowed people in the communities to say what a revitalized train station and community would look like for them," says Scott Bernstein, president of the Center for Neighborhood Technology, one of the opposition leaders.

> *They said they wanted it safe, walkable, with multifamily housing. They said they didn't want a station that was just a platform with stairways up and down. They wanted it to be a building that was a 24-hour-a-day mixed-use facility. Out of these meetings, we developed principles that everyone signed on to.*

Architects used the principles to create a new design for the Pulaski station, which the community coalition unveiled in July 1993. About 10 days later, the transit authority dropped its plan to kill the Green Line and pledged to invest some $300 million in renovating it. "The city did a remarkable about-face," says Bernstein. "They took dollars from other projects and put them into rebuilding this line."

Bernstein and his fellow Chicago activists had unprecedented leverage to back up their demands. A clause in a 1991 federal statute, the Intermodal Surface Transportation Efficiency Act (ISTEA), required state, regional, and local public agencies to involve the public in deciding how to spend federal transportation dollars. The community was advocating for the preservation and maintenance of existing government transportation assets, which was one of the federal government's priorities. Ignoring the community's opposition to shutting down the Green Line could have put federal funding at risk.

ISTEA ended the days when departments of transportation could impose their priorities on communities. The law required "early and continuing involvement of the public" and encouraged cooperation in planning and consensus building. It created an opportunity for communities to demand access to decision making. ISTEA, says Pittsburgh regional planner Bob Kochanowski, "changes the rules, moves the competition into a new stadium, drafts new players, and even invites the spectators onto the field."

The Collaborative Alternative

For decades, government planners have had a typical way of making plans; they decide what should be done, announce their plan, and then defend it from attack. "Decide-announce-defend," some critics call it. Before ISTEA, for instance, transportation planning was usually about "telling and selling"—tell the public the plan, then sell the public on it.

These traditional processes often produce persistent opposition, divide the community into warring factions, and make citizens cynical about government, observe Bill Potapchuk and Caroline Polk, advocates of collaborative planning. "Local politics," they add, "is often characterized by traditionally powerful organizations proposing major projects, proposals which then become mired in controversy as they provide convenient targets for newly organized and ongoing citizen and activist groups. Such conflicts often drag on for years, productive outcomes stymied by lawsuits and a 'winner take all' approach."

The alternative is to try collaborative planning, which cures the "We're the government, you're not" syndrome by giving citizens and community groups a share of the decision-making power. In traditional planning processes, citizens are invited to attend hearings where they may comment on plans, and a specific period is set aside for gathering comments. The views offered on these occasions may influence government decision makers—especially if 1,000 people show up to express them. But a public hearing is a process "owned" by the government, and it is rarely a dialogue. When controversial issues are on the agenda, it usually becomes an invitation for people to yell louder, to get angrier, to emphasize their disagreements—all to get the attention of government decision makers. In contrast, collaborative planning is an invitation to the people with a stake in the outcome of the planning—community groups, interested individuals, and government officials—to come together and jointly make decisions.

Collaborative planning is being used by all levels of government to develop all manner of plans. In cities such as Hampton and Richmond, Virginia, Indianapolis, Charlotte, and Seattle, city government is collaborating with neighborhood groups to develop city and neighborhood plans. The federal government required collaborative planning by communities applying for empowerment zone status. Some regulatory agencies, such as the Environmental Protection Agency, use collaborative planning to avoid problems with controversial rules they are developing. In a process called negotiated rule making, or "reg-neg," they bring stakeholders together to work out aspects of draft regulations that have the potential to create conflict among them. "By consulting with the parties," say Potapchuk and Polk, "agencies using reg-neg have been able to substantially reduce their litigation and other costs associated with rule promulgation."

In general, collaborative planning increases stakeholder and community acceptance of plans, because people have had a hand in making the plan. This boosts the chance that plans will be implemented, since the possibility of lawsuits and other delaying tactics by opponents is reduced. Hence a collaborative planning process may take longer and cost more than a traditional planning process does, but it can save a community time and money in the long run.

Collaborative plans are often better plans, too, because they are informed by the diverse experiences and knowledge of the many stakeholders involved.

The very process of collaborative planning also creates other benefits, such as healing or preventing rifts in the community. It may even increase a community's collaborative capacity, by building trust, strong relationships, and people with collaborative skills. This can help solve or even prevent problems in the future, saving time and money in the process.

BARRIERS TO CONSENSUS BUILDING

An excellent guidebook on community decision making, *Involving Citizens in Community Decision Making*, describes some of the attitudes that are barriers to effective consensus building:

"Someone has to lose." "The truth is, when people have to work together over time, if you 'win' at the expense of someone else losing, all you've done is plant the seeds for the next conflict. Resentment builds. People want to get back at you. . . . The premise behind collaborative problem solving is that it is possible to come up with a solution that meets everybody's needs. There may not need to be any losers."

"If we've got the votes, we've got the power." "After an election, groups may gloat over the fact that they've got a one-vote majority on a city council or county commission. Their glee may be short-lived. The truth is that when governing bodies are badly divided, they often vote on issues only to find that in actuality they haven't the power to make their decision happen. . . . One-vote victories often bog down in a quagmire of challenges and new requirements."

"Building a consensus takes too long." "You can make a decision fast by majority vote, but you may never be able to implement the decision. Or the cost of implementation may be so high that you'll wish you never got involved. There's little doubt that it takes longer to build a consensus before making a decision. The cost of *making* the decision will be higher. But the costs *resulting from* the decision may be much lower."

Elements of Collaborative Planning

Collaborative planning is not a highly predictable process. It can take days or years, depending on what is being decided and who is involved in making decisions. It can cost very little or hundreds of thousands of dollars. Yet some steps are common to collaborative planning in most situations:

1. Identify the stakeholders and invite their participation.

In most communities, stakeholders fall into three categories, notes Bill Potapchuk, a veteran of collaborative planning processes:

- People who are formally responsible for making the decision.
- People affected by or concerned about the potential outcome.
- People who can block or ensure a potential outcome, such as city council members, newspaper publishers, or watchdog organizations.

To be an inclusive process, collaborative planning should draw broadly from these three categories; everyone who wants to participate should have an opportunity.

There are many techniques for getting stakeholders informed and involved. Some communities survey residents to identify their concerns. (Some of these pay residents, rather than a company, to conduct the surveys, so they get engaged in the process.) Some communities use town hall meetings, which can be televised. Some do formal outreach to community-based organizations and churches. Others use the media to publicize the process, including public service announcements and cutout coupons to elicit responses.

2. Secure agreement among participants about the planning process that will be used.

This is crucial, because the point of collaborative planning is to create satisfaction with the *process* of planning as well as with the *content* of the plan. From the outset, the participants must agree on what is fair as far as the process goes. This may require some give-and-take. To get things going, government officials may want to propose a process, but they must be ready to modify or even abandon it in the face of community desires.

In other words, share power right from the beginning by designing the process together. This will help strengthen relationships at the early stages of the process, which will pay off later when disputes must be resolved. It is easy to deride this as "planning to plan," and some stakeholders will urge that you "get on with the planning." But this would be a mistake, because the planning process must be subject to the approval of the participants. Do not proceed without it.

3. Plan together.

For planning to be collaborative, all participants must share the same information. They must share basic understandings and definitions. They must work together on problems, then identify the options and select which ones they will pursue. During this process, the stakeholders should engage in face-to-face dialogue, negotiation, and problem solving.

To facilitate this, you should offer stakeholders many ways of becoming involved in the process and getting information: by serving on committees, attending meetings, providing written feedback, and the like.

4. *Make decisions by consensus.*

This is the heart of community empowerment in planning. A plan is not a plan until all the stakeholders agree that it is. If the process gets stuck or falls apart because a consensus cannot be achieved, use a facilitator or mediator to get things moving again. If that doesn't work, the fallback alternatives include going with a super-majority of the group, approving those items for which there is consensus and holding back the others, or even issuing a minority report. Another method, which might be called a "default agreement," was used by one county working on new ordinances. At the beginning of the consensus-building process, says Bill Potapchuk, a written draft of the new ordinances was presented and the stakeholders agreed that if they failed to reach a consensus, that draft would be automatically adopted.

Collaborative Planning: Lessons Learned

pp. 511–512

As we have explained concerning community empowerment in general, it is critical to go beyond rounding up the usual suspects when developing a community-based planning process. Diversity improves the quality of the dialogue and helps develop broad community buy-in. In addition, some lessons apply specifically to collaborative planning processes:

1. *Build capacity in your community to conduct collaborative planning.*

In most communities, few people know how to design and manage collaborative planning processes. So when a community decides to use collaborative planning, it tends to look for an out-of-town expert. That's not the first place to look, says one of those experts. Instead, check out the local possibilities. "If the choice is between using a consultant like me to run a planning process," says Bill Potapchuk of the Program for Community Problem Solving, "or finding someone at the community college or somewhere else local, that's a no-brainer." Use the local.

Potapchuk is not trying to put himself out of business; he just recognizes that communities should think about collaborative planning as a community competence—an ability that will be needed not just once for one planning process but over and over again. "The question is how to strategically embed this capacity in your community," he explains.

If there is no capacity in your community, then hook up consultants with local people who want to learn how the work is done. They can develop their skills by serving as apprentices to the process. They won't become instant experts, since collaborative planning is a complex skill. But they will get a real-world taste of it, which can be supplemented with training and coaching.

2. *Invest in developing the collaboration skills of government planners.*

Most government planners have little familiarity with collaborative planning processes, yet they are essential participants in them. They may be called on to play different roles: designing entire planning processes, facilitating meetings, resolving conflicts, or negotiating on behalf of the government's interests.

You can turn to others in government to develop these skills as well. You may want to develop a cross-functional team: a group of individuals with complementary skills—such as facilitation, process design, and conflict resolution—who work together. This may even break down some of the categorical boundaries that often stymie cooperation within government.

3. *Don't try to solve tough, controversial issues right away.*

Every community has its hot-button issues, concerns that are divisive and explosive. They have to be tackled sooner or later, but if you are just launching collaborative planning, later is better. "Immediate controversial issues tend to overshadow longer-term planning," observes Mutsumi Mizuno of the Environmental Action Foundation. It's more important to build early momentum for the planning process than to tackle tougher issues and risk getting bogged down.

4. *Fund community groups to provide planning services.*

Governments are increasingly turning to community groups to manage collaborative planning exercises. Oakland, California, awarded a community development corporation, the Spanish-Speaking Unity Council (SSUC), $185,000 to plan the redevelopment of a Bay Area Rapid Transit station. SSUC met with community leaders and held a design symposium on a Saturday to give community members a chance to express their ideas.

If the community group has good local connections and credibility, it may be able to generate significant community participation. This can go wrong, however, if the community group tries to advance its own agenda rather than facilitate the community's dialogue or if it fails to draw many different stakeholders into the process.

RESOURCES ON COLLABORATIVE PLANNING

William R. Potapchuk and Caroline G. Polk. *Building the Collaborative Community.* Washington, D.C.: National Institute for Dispute Resolution, 1994. An excellent description of various collaborative planning and dispute resolution cases and the basic principles of using this tool.

Program for Community Problem Solving. Established in 1988 and cosponsored by the National League of Cities, the American Chamber of Commerce Executives, the International City/County Management Association, the International Downtown Association, and the National Civic League, this organization offers training, presentations, technical assistance, coaching, facilitation, information, and publications about collaborative approaches for communities. Based in Washington, D.C. Phone: (202) 783–2961. Address: 915 15th St., N.W., Suite 600, Washington DC 20005.

Urban Land Institute. *Pulling Together: A Planning and Development Consensus-Building Manual.* Washington, D.C.: Urban Land Institute, 1994. ULI Catalogue No. P90. A detailed workbook, focused mainly on building community participation in processes.

COMMUNITY-BASED FUNDING

Community-Based Funding **provides revenues to empowered community groups, either directly from government revenues or through the power to generate their own funds.**

All too often in community empowerment, the community gets the power but not the purse. "One of the most common failures in governance is allowing a 'disconnect' between the fiscal strategy and the program strategy," note analysts at the Center for the Study of Social Policy. Many community-based organizations find that funding is their Achilles' heel. They constantly scramble to assemble sufficient revenues from a patchwork of sources: federal, state, and local government grants or contracts; grants and loans from foundations or community-minded corporations and philanthropists; and capital raised from the community itself. For some empowered entities this may not be a big barrier, if they require only small amounts of money or do not intend to stay in business for many years. But those tackling long-term community issues need a more secure funding base.

In 1967, Robert F. Kennedy, then a senator from New York, helped launch a community development organization for the Bedford-Stuyvesant neighborhood of Brooklyn. This entity was the first prototype for the community development corporation (CDC), which rehabilitates and builds housing; provides social services, job training, and adult education; and invests in business development and commercial real estate—all in low-income neighborhoods and communities. By the 1990s, there were more than 2,000 CDCs operating nationwide; they had developed more than 320,000 units of affordable housing.

Like most empowered community entities, CDCs generate their funds from a variety of sources. Grants from foundations played a major role in developing the early CDCs and in starting up many more; in the 1960s and 1970s the Ford Foundation invested more than $100 million to develop them. CDCs also make money in the private marketplace—from renters of housing units and from businesses repaying loans. The New Community Corporation in Newark, New Jersey, runs six for-profit businesses, rents 2,500 apartments, and employs more than 1,000 people, for example. CDCs receive funds from government agencies that contract with them to provide services. And finally, the federal government's tax credit for investment in low-income housing development has stimulated the flow of billions of dollars into CDC projects.

Thus, community development corporations demonstrate four ways that empowered community organizations can be funded:

- By grants from philanthropic sources.
- By revenues from their businesses (an approach more and more are using).
- By contracts or grants from government.
- By private investors lured by government incentives.

A fifth method is for government to grant the community entity the power to tax. Many cities and states, for instance, give business owners the right to tax themselves (in addition to paying existing taxes) to raise money to spruce up their business districts, through business improvement districts. In 1998, Missouri went a step further, approving a law that allows community organizations to create "community improvement districts" that can impose and collect taxes to provide services or pay for capital improvements. The local government must approve the creation of the district.

Using a taxing district can generate a more secure revenue stream. In East Lansing, Michigan, merchants in the downtown were having trouble competing against big shopping centers that had been built in the suburbs. "Our merchants' group raised about $13,000 in their best year to market the downtown stores," says Jim van Ravensway, the city planner. "The malls have $500,000 budgets and marketing staff. It's just no comparison." So the city took advantage of a state statute to create a downtown management board of businesses. The nine-member board collects a special assessment against downtown property owners, which amounts to about $60,000 a year, to spend on marketing the stores. "That's not a lot, but it's a fourfold leap," van Ravensway points out. Most businesses pay the assessment (unless the property owner doesn't pass the charge on to them), whereas no more than 20 percent of them contributed voluntarily in the past.

Community-Based Funding: Lessons Learned

1. It doesn't always require a lot of money to fuel the empowerment engine.

A little money can go a long way. In Baltimore, the city took $20,000 it received from a Ford Foundation award and used it to provide $500 grants for community development projects designed by inner-city residents. Other communities, such as Indianapolis and Multnomah County, Oregon, have also tried these mini-grant programs to get many small projects done. They help build enthusiasm for empowerment, and they strengthen the relationship between government and the community. The key is to avoid bureaucratizing the program; attach minimal strings and paperwork to the small grants.

Still, if you want to accomplish big things through community empowerment, it will take larger amounts of money. And quite realistically, such money is hard for community groups to come by.

2. *Transform government budgeting to make it community-friendly.*

As we emphasized earlier, governments must change to become better partners for empowered community entities. This is especially true of their budgeting systems, which typically use categorical funding streams that earmark separate funds for distinct purposes. Narrow line item budgets make it hard to assemble funding for broad-based efforts to solve community problems.

In Iowa, the state created "decategorization boards" to solve this problem. These boards of county and community leaders develop plans to help at-risk children. The state, meanwhile, acts as a banker for each board. It pools together different departments' funds and then disburses money to the counties to implement the boards' plans. This allows the local planners to escape from the categorical imperatives in the state budget. In addition, "decat boards" are allowed to carry their unspent funds across fiscal years.

3. *Tap into and build indigenous resources.*

Communities can raise donations from individuals or community organizations, such as block clubs, parent groups, churches, synagogues, and civic organizations. Most community-based organizations are old hands at this sort of fund-raising.

One type of community-based organization, the community foundation, raises money so it can provide funding to other community-based organizations. The number of community foundations in the U.S. has grown to more than 500; they hold more than $20 billion in assets. Most of the money they attract from local philanthropists goes into their endowments, which are invested in perpetuity; they use the income from these investments to make grants. "A community endowment works much like a permanent collective savings account where the specified community determines how to distribute the earned interest," explains Janet Topolsky, associate director of the Aspen Institute's Community Strategies Group.

Although community foundations traditionally get their money from wealthy individuals, some of these philanthropies mobilize even the poorest of communities to generate endowment funds. In sparsely populated Daniels

County in northeast Montana, communities raised an astonishing $1 million for a community endowment. It was an intense effort, Topolsky reports:

> *The fundraising effort itself has required a comprehensive countywide education effort about endowments, using the newspaper, the radio, public forums, and one-on-one meetings. . . . Fundraising efforts are bringing people out of the woodwork and building community peer pressure and social capital, as "paper a-thon" contributors or radiothon listeners challenge fellow community members who attended a certain high school or who have a spare bale of hay to "put your asset where your community is." Children's piggy bank donations and teenagers' yard work and babysitting pledges or help at community gatherings are as highly valued as the larger gifts made by trust benefactors, giving these younger residents both pride and stature in the community.*

4. *Look for "hidden" funds.*

Money already allocated but not put to use is another potential source of funding for community entities. In 1999, the Corporation for Enterprise Development (CFED), a "think-and-do tank" focused on economic development, reported that hundreds of millions of dollars in investment capital for local and state economic development were going unused. The money is held by what CFED calls "revolving loan funds," which are public, quasi-public, private, or community-based financial institutions that make loans to local businesses that cannot attract traditional financing. "There's a significant amount of underutilized capital in these institutions," says Andrea Levere, CFED's vice president. "In Minnesota, for example, we found $202 million in capital—and $91 million just sitting around." Other examples of "hidden funds" that community groups may be able to get permission to tap include the unclaimed property funds held by governments for people they can't find, unclaimed bank accounts, and sales of assets seized from criminals, such as drug dealers' cars and yachts.

RESOURCE ON COMMUNITY-BASED FUNDING

The Corporation for Enterprise Development (CFED). A nonprofit organization, CFED focuses primarily on "asset-building" strategies for low-income and distressed communities. It is a seedbed of many innovative policies and ideas about community-based economic development. Its 1999 publication *Ideas in Development* describes many of these ideas. Contact CFED at 777 North Capital Street, N.E., Suite 410, Washington DC 20002. Phone: (202) 408–9788. Web: www.cfed.org.

Part V

The Culture Strategy

Developing an Entrepreneurial Culture

An organization's culture is a social reality that signals to employees what they should do, feel, and think. It is a set of behavioral, emotional, and psychological frameworks that members adopt and perpetuate, often unconsciously. It is "the way we do things around here."

Bureaucratic culture—the tendency to avoid risks and responsibility, blame others for problems, follow the rules, settle for less than high-quality results, and resist change— takes hold in government organizations for several reasons:

- They are organized as command-and-control hierarchies in which managers are supposed to do the thinking and workers are supposed to follow orders.
- They treat people like cogs in a machine—paid to perform highly defined jobs and nothing more, expected to leave their dreams and imagination at home.
- Their members must defend themselves from the incessant demands and hostile scrutiny of elected officials and interest groups—by acting ignorant or obsequious.
- Their leaders worry mostly about their budgets and status rather than about improving their performance, because they face little pressure from customers or competitors.

In *Banishing Bureaucracy,* we argued that the most powerful way to change this culture was to use the other four strategies for reinventing government. Clarifying the purpose of public organizations helps them focus on goals instead of rules. Creating consequences for performance makes them focus on producing better results. Making them more accountable to their customers forces them to deliver results their customers value. And shifting the locus and form of control empowers organizations, employees, and sometimes communities to take responsibility for producing results.

Unfortunately, these strategies are rarely sufficient. Bureaucratic culture is difficult to overcome because it is deeply embedded in the habits, hearts, and minds of employees. It fights back. Some people comply with change but don't embrace it. Others avoid it or openly resist it. Sometimes the culture changes, but not fast enough. At other times it changes, but not in the ways leaders intended. All of this has led experienced reinventors to conclude that they need a strategy that seeks to reshape the culture consciously and deliberately—in specific, intended ways.

See *Banishing Bureaucracy* pp. 262–265

This is slow work. There is no quick way to change a culture, because it is retail work: the conversion process occurs person by person. There are also many factors that shape a culture, from tradition to incentive systems to the organization's external environment. These factors create the basic assumptions that employees hold about their organization. They define its cultural paradigm—the lens through which people perceive reality.

The paradigm of entrepreneurial organizations is very different from the paradigm of bureaucratic organizations. Employees assume that they should improve the organization's efficiency and results, think about and change the way things are done, work together on solving problems and coming up with innovations, and respond flexibly and quickly to feedback from customers. They feel a strong connection to the organization's purpose. They welcome change as an opportunity, not a threat.

See *Banishing Bureaucracy* pp. 265–268

To build an entrepreneurial culture, you must change people's bureaucratic paradigms. This involves getting people to let go of their assumptions, introducing them to new assumptions, earning their trust, and providing safety nets so they will take the risk of using the new assumptions. We recommend that you read about the process of shifting paradigms in *Banishing Bureaucracy.*

We have defined three approaches for doing this:

- *Changing habits* creates new experiences for people that challenge their paradigms. Changing what employees do at work confronts them with new problems that cannot be solved by using career-long habits. They must find new ways of acting.

- *Touching hearts* shifts the emotional commitments of public employees—their hopes, dreams, and expectations for themselves, their organization, and one another. They break out of their deeply felt attachment to bureaucratic status, or their resentment of authority, or their investment in being a victim.
- *Winning minds* helps employees develop new understandings—conscious, rational "mental models"—about where the organization needs to go and how to get there.

See *Banishing Bureaucracy* pp. 278–293

Reinventors use a great many tools to implement these approaches, as you will see in the chapters that follow. Whichever ones you choose, be aware of the dozen fundamental lessons about leading cultural change that we explained in *Banishing Bureaucracy:*

1. *Involve the employees.* Woo them, reward them, entertain them—whatever it takes to get them to try new things.
2. *Walk the talk.* Leaders must model the behavior they want; if they don't, the new paradigm will have no credibility.
3. *Make yourself visible.* Get out of the front office and mix with your employees.
4. *Make a clear break with the past.* Send an unmistakable signal that you are initiating culture change.
5. *Unleash—but harness—the pioneers.* Channel their energy in constructive directions.
6. *Get a quick shot of new blood.* Bring in new managers who already carry the new culture. Then continue the transfusion every time you hire someone new.
7. *Drive out fear, but don't tolerate resistance.* Give employees lots of information and rewards. But if someone repeatedly undermines the change process, remove them.
8. *Sell success.* Constantly call attention to the new behavior you're looking for, and reward it. But don't make the new culture politically correct.
9. *Communicate, communicate, communicate.* You cannot communicate enough with employees. If they don't know what your change strategy is, they are more likely to feel threatened by it.
10. *Bridge the fault lines in the organization.* Help people reach across dividing lines.

pp. 404–426

11. *Change administrative systems that reinforce a bureaucratic culture.* These control systems send powerful signals that undercut a leader's signals about cultural change. Sooner or later you must reform these systems.
12. *Be patient.* Commit for the long haul, because it takes five to 10 years to transform a bureaucratic culture. Don't let the bureaucracy wait you out.

Chapter 13

Changing Habits

Creating a New Culture by Introducing New Experiences

Habits are like a cable. We weave a strand of it every day and soon it cannot be broken.

HORACE MANN

Changing Habits immerses employees in new experiences—altering what they do, where they do it, and with whom they do it—to push them to let go of old behaviors and develop new ones.

When Doug Ross went to Washington in 1993 to head the U.S. Employment and Training Administration (ETA), he was convinced that the 1,800-employee organization did not treat its customers very well. ETA's Employment Service funds and oversees the nation's unemployment offices, where millions of people go each year to obtain unemployment benefits, job counseling, or job openings. "My own sense was that many of the customers regarded it as an unpleasant experience," Ross says.

Ross didn't expect the agency's senior civil servants to agree with him. "There was a general feeling that we did a reasonable job of dealing with the people who come to us because they lost their jobs," he says. In any case, "I had no special credibility as a leader coming in from the outside." So he hired a respected polling firm, Yankelovich Partners, to find out what customers of the employment service thought about the agency. It organized a series of meetings in which small groups of customers—blue-collar workers, white-collar workers, and small business owners who used the service to find new workers—talked candidly about their recent experiences with employment service offices in Maryland. Ross took his top managers to the sessions, to listen from behind a one-way mirror.

They caught an earful—for hours. "These people said they were treated like numbers, not people," remembers Carolyn Golding, a longtime deputy assistant secretary. "That was the most devastating thing I had ever heard. They said they weren't called by their names, they were called 'Next.'"

"What came across actually stunned some of the civil servants," Ross says. They couldn't believe how angry their customers were about how they were treated at unemployment offices. In one of the groups, Ross recalls, a customer declared, "I hate this place [the unemployment office] and if you gave me a chance, the first thing I would do is privatize it!" Another unemployed worker complained that government workers "talk down to you like they know better. I want to be treated as a customer!"

When a blue-collar group in Baltimore said that going to the Employment Service was as frustrating as visiting a motor vehicle bureau, "That immediately hit the ETA professionals," says Ross. "It was something they dreaded having to do, too."

Yankelovich later summarized the customers' dissatisfaction this way:

> *Workers feel they are treated as second class citizens, given inaccurate information about prospects for employment and provided with little guidance that can help them find a job. . . . Workers feel that the staff is poorly trained and unmotivated to provide customer service. There are also complaints that the service is impersonal—there is a lack of interest in the individual.*

The experience of listening to her customers affected Golding viscerally.

> *It was like being fed rocket fuel. It reenergized me. One of the reasons I'm in this business is because I believe these programs can help people to help themselves. But if you're not treating them like people, then you're missing a basic building block. You're not even in the game.*

Other managers reacted similarly, says Ross. "When they heard people say they hated us, it had an emotional impact. It made people feel bad, because most of them—even the relatively cynical ones—wanted to believe that they were doing some good, that their work had some benefit for somebody."

During the hour-and-a-half drive back to the office, Golding and a colleague talked about what they had experienced. When they returned, she says, they immediately started sharing the experience with people in the agency and in state governments, which operate unemployment offices. "I asked them what they were doing to find out how people view their services," Golding says. The answers were disappointing: mainly, administrators looked at follow-up forms that some customers filled out and mailed in.

"It was nothing like the vivid experience I had gone through," says Golding. "Seeing it firsthand was much more powerful than reading about it."

Golding threw herself into Ross's struggle to reinvent ETA's programs. She found that other managers who attended the focus groups were also more receptive to change. Ross showed video clips of the focus groups to ETA employees who had not been there. "The visual impact [of the video] had a long-lasting impact," says Lorraine Chang, who ran the agency's reinvention office.

> *You can talk forever about being customer-focused and listening to the customer, but it is important to actually be struck in the face by the image—either in person or on video—of who the customer really is. The customer focus groups were one of the first key steps in getting the organization to begin seeing the world differently.*

Golding and her colleagues put in long hours negotiating with ETA managers, state and local governments, and public employee unions over their proposed reforms. During these mind-numbing discussions, the focus group experience became a touchstone for them. They doggedly steered discussions back to the issue of customer service. "Bureaucracy is like water on a stone; it does wear you down after a while," says Golding. "You really need something to hang on to that is worth fighting for. That's what the customer experiences gave us."

Listening to customers tear your organization down is an intense experience for practically anyone. You leave your comfortable paradigm and enter theirs. You see the world through their eyes. You become totally immersed—for a short while, at least—in a new, challenging, and disturbing experience. And if that experience is powerful enough, you change your feelings, your ideas, and your behavior.

As we said in *Banishing Bureaucracy*, immersing people in new experiences is the most powerful of the three Culture Strategy approaches. It reopens their hearts and minds and changes habitual ways of thinking.

Sometimes the first step is simply to expose habits that exist but typically go unrecognized. In East Lansing, Michigan, a team of managers volunteered to help develop a strategy to change the city government's culture. Their initial target was City Manager Ted Staton's Tuesday morning staff meeting—a ritual whose cultural implications had gone unexamined. Nancy Moylan, a district court administrator, describes one of the habits she had observed during 14 years under the previous city manager:

> *It used to be that everyone had assigned seats. Certain people sat at the conference room table; they were the players. Others sat in smaller chairs along the walls. The first time I attended a meeting, I took the seat closest to the door. Suddenly everyone in the room just stopped. I thought I had done something bad. Someone said, "You can't sit there, that's the city manager's chair." They showed me where my predecessor had sat.*

Years later, Moylan says, chairs were still "owned" by specific managers—including her. After she had missed several meetings once, the police chief told her that he had been sitting in her seat, but she could have it back. The seating arrangement, of course, reflected the power structure in the organization.

The culture change volunteers decided to stage a skit spoofing the meeting's habits. They wrote a script and held the "meeting" at the usual time. The volunteer who played the city manager came late, as always. No one started the meeting until he arrived. He passed out the meeting agenda, which no one had seen beforehand. Some managers sat in chairs against the walls rather than in empty seats at the table. Some walked in late, talking to other late arrivers as though the meeting had not yet begun. And when it came time for participants to contribute to the meeting—to offer news or advice—all of them "passed."

The skit's message: no one, except the city manager, felt a stake in the meeting. As a result of this exposure, the staff made changes. It moved the meeting to a bigger room so everyone could sit at the table. Each meeting had a new chairperson. Agendas were sent out ahead of time. And discussion—rather than "passing"—occurred.

Still, says Moylan, the power of habit dies hard. "Somehow, at the staff meetings, I find myself sitting in the same corner."

After people become aware of their habits, they need reasons and opportunities to change them. This is the purpose of many of the tools reinventors use to help public organizations escape the gravitational forces of bureaucratic habits. Basically, these tools immerse public employees in new experiences that pose new problems that cannot be solved by using career-long habits. For instance, listening to customers complain about the Employment Service created a dissonance that was hard for Carolyn Golding and other administrators to ignore. The experience challenged them to find new ways of acting.

THE ELEMENTS OF EXPERIENTIAL CULTURE CHANGE

These tools fall into a number of categories. Most of them help with the front end of culture change: jarring loose existing paradigms and helping people let go. Perhaps the most effective way to do this is to give people encounters with their customers, as Doug Ross did. Tools here include meeting the customers and walking in the customer's shoes.

A second alternative is to help employees experience new roles, by giving them encounters with other jobs, other organizations, and other people. Tools here include job rotation, internships, and externships.

Once people begin to let go, you need to coax them into trying new behaviors. Several tools, including institutional sponsors and contests, play this role.

The final two categories not only work on the front end of culture change, they also help move people all the way through the process. Hence they contain the most powerful experiential tools. The first is what Bob Filipczak, an editor of *Training* magazine, calls critical mass events. These tools, which involve many or all of the members of an organization in a new experience, are "used most often to do things such as change business strategies, develop a mission or vision about where the company is headed in the next century, or foster a more participative environment," he explains. "In some cases, critical mass events are used as ways to kick off other popular initiatives like committing to total quality management, starting self-directed work teams, or reengineering the organization."

Some critical mass events, including future-search conferences, have been used for decades. Others, such as large-scale, real-time strategic planning, are more recent inventions. Some are more ad hoc events: hands-on organizational experiences such as the three-day "energy mobilization" that St. Paul mayor George Latimer led in 1979.

The final category is the most profound and permanent step you can take to give people different experiences: redesign their work. As we have argued, when people do new things, they begin to think new thoughts and feel new emotions. Redesigning their work is the best way to change their culture for good.

TOOLS FOR CHANGING HABITS

Meeting the Customers—through focus groups, conversations, or frontline work—exposes employees to the people their work is designed to help. See p. 540.

Walking in the Customer's Shoes asks employees to go through their own system as customers so that they can experience it from the customer's point of view. See p. 542.

Job Rotation exposes employees to different jobs in an organization. They move through various jobs, taking full responsibility for the work and staying in each position long enough to learn its intricacies. See p. 543.

Externships and Internships allow an organization's members to work in other organizations for a stint—from six months to several years, usually—or bring outsiders in for a similar period. See p. 545.

Institutional Sponsors establish a formal process that attracts, supports, protects, and celebrates innovative behaviors in public organizations. See p. 545.

Contests promote behaviors reinventors want to see in their organizations. See p. 548.

Large-Scale, Real-Time Strategic Planning immerses most, if not all, of an organization's employees in an intensive multiday retreat, during which they identify necessary organizational changes and commit to implementing them. See p. 549.

Hands-On Organizational Experiences are less formally structured learning events in which hundreds of employees share new experiences that build the culture leaders want. See p. 553.

Redesigning Work, whether by reengineering business processes, reforming administrative systems, or introducing new technology, permanently changes employees' experiences. See p. 554.

MEETING THE CUSTOMERS

When Doug Ross took his managers to see focus groups of employees, he exposed them to a profound new experience, which shook their paradigms. Ross also had his employees meet with customers face-to-face, to discuss their needs and how satisfied they were with the service they received in employment centers.

Other organizations have employees work the front lines to meet customers. When Kathryn Roberts took the helm at the Minnesota Zoo, a state organization, she found that most of her employees looked at the zoo's customers as a nuisance. "At least to some degree, our animal care staff believed that this zoo was a place for animals, and the public kind of bugged 'em," she says. Because of the public, "They had to do some of their work behind the scenes, or at times that weren't so convenient for them." They didn't like it when she told them, "'I want you to feed the gibbons their watermelon when the public is here, not at 8:00 A.M. when it's convenient for you.'"

The Public Strategies Group, which Roberts hired to help her develop a strategy to change the zoo's culture, suggested that she have employees greet the public on the way in and out of the zoo. They would welcome people, hand out maps, explain any special events scheduled for that day, and answer questions. As people left, they would hand them customer feedback cards, talk with them about their visit, and invite them to return.

When Roberts required this, she ran into real resistance from some employees. "Plumbers and carpenters and others said to us, 'I wasn't hired to do this; you hired me to put in the plumbing lines,'" remembers Connie Braziel, director of operations for the zoo. "So we had our talks about how things change."

But many enjoyed the experience. "When they came out from behind the scenes for the first time and had to interact with customers, I think many of them were flabbergasted, listening to our customers describe what was important to them," says Roberts.

One employee, a union steward, fought the requirement tooth and nail. After he finally had to do his turn, he wrote the zoo management a letter:

> *I must admit, I approached the scheduled confrontation determined to role-play my way thru. I think that as an employee I sometimes see our guests as a reflection of my specific tasks; i.e., as a janitor assigned to outside trash collection, "They" were just rude people who filled up the cans with trash, and tossed diapers onto the parking lot, etc. I know that sounds awful but it was part of my attitude that was changed after my first three hours as a Greeter!*
>
> *I stood my ground. They were coming in packs of four and five—adult people; little people—all with looks of anticipation. Children whose eyes seemed to grow wider as they neared the entrance. They excited me. I found myself saying "Welcome to the Zoo! Thanks for coming! Have a great day!" without thinking about it. . . .*
>
> *And then it happened. Someone asked me if there were picnic areas inside the Zoo. As you know, I have been on the Zoo grounds since before the Zoo opened. I have enjoyed many hours of gawking at the wonders, etc., but I do not like to picnic and therefore did not know where the picnic grounds were for sure. I took a guess and replied affirmatively hoping they would not ask me, "Where?" That stung! I had other stings too numerous to mention here. . . .*
>
> *Perhaps I can sum this up as follows: The experience was very educational and positively affected my attitude. In response to my enhanced appreciation of the Zoo and my role as an employee, I shall: visit the Zoo as a Visitor; learn more about the presentations; become familiar with the many programs offered and prepare myself for the next opportunity to thank our guests for coming to a great Zoo!*

This employee went back and began encouraging his colleagues to spend more time as greeters.

Roberts and Braziel believe the greeters program, now voluntary, has nudged the culture in the right direction. "Remarkably, to me, some of these animal care staff have come forward and are presenting ideas to make their animals more available to the public," says Roberts. "We would never, ever have had that five years ago. So when you hear that, you think, okay, all that work was worthwhile."

WALKING IN THE CUSTOMER'S SHOES

Walking in the Customer's Shoes **asks employees to go through their own system as customers so that they can experience it from the customer's point of view.**

David Couper, a former police chief of Madison, Wisconsin, always remembered a story about the Dutch police. Most of their command staff had been imprisoned by the Germans during World War II. "They had this empathy for people who were put into prison," he says. "And that's why for years, until the jail got filled up, we used to take our recruit class and say, 'Sometime during your training you will be picked up and put in jail overnight, because you need to know what that's like.'"

Though it is rarely used in the public sector, this tool is a powerful way to get people to understand the needs of their customers. Many businesses use it. In their 1990 book *Excellence in Government: Total Quality Management in the 1990s,* David K. Carr and Ian D. Littman describe an example involving employees of the Defense Industrial Supply Center.

> *Every weekend, supply specialists join active and reserve Navy personnel in an exercise at sea. They learn what teamwork means to ship operations and how the materials they supply can make a difference.*
>
> *"When civilians see the rigors of life at sea, they're shocked," notes a Naval reserve officer who helps coordinate the program. "They develop a real appreciation of their customer's setting—and maybe the customer's mood when he's making a request."*

The Institute for Educational Leadership used a shoes-of-the-customer experiment with a group of welfare policy experts, state legislators, members of Congress, and their staffs. In 1995, in an effort to influence welfare reform, the institute's Margaret Dunkle had the group apply for benefits. Posing as the Hernandez family, they visited a special room set aside for the experiment. In the room were an AFDC and Medicaid benefits analyst, an employment and training specialist, an IRS expert on earned-income tax credits, a school nurse-practitioner, a child care coordinator, a city housing assistant, and local health department workers. Dunkle described what happened in *Education Week:*

> *None of the Ph.D.s, lawyers, elected officials, administrators, or assorted policy wonks participating in the exercise could deal competently with the mounds of paperwork that would face the barely literate Hernandez family.*
>
> *Just about everyone participating in the exercise lied, cheated, or purposely withheld information. It seemed like the only sensible thing to do. When faced with the reality of the current system, members of Congress as well as senior staff members who draft or administer programs distorted or conveniently "forgot" such bottom-line facts as the work history of Carlos and Yolanda, Carlos's income, or the specifics about Alicia (who was not a documented U.S. citizen).*

Not even the most sophisticated legislators were familiar with the 20 different programs for which the Hernandez family could apply. None of them could handle the 800 pages of forms and explanatory material—a *condensed version*—Dunkle had put together for the exercise. State legislators, shocked to discover how much of the complexity their own states had created, suddenly realized how much work they would have to do before they could make a block grant system work. "Having survived the experience as the Hernandez family, one seasoned congressional staff aide wryly expressed surprise that there were so few shootings in welfare offices," Dunkle reports. "Others left the exercise saying 'surely we can do better.'"

pp. 540–542

To get maximum impact from both the shoes-of-the-customer and the meeting-the-customers tools, we recommend that you facilitate employee discussions of the experience afterward, in small groups. The facilitator should push employees to discuss how their behavior should change, based on what they have learned, and how the organization and its work processes should change. Some people will figure these things out for themselves, but others will need help.

It is also important that those who have the power to force change, such as middle and senior managers, participate. Most employees already know how service could be improved, but they have long since given up telling management, because nothing ever happens.

JOB ROTATION

***Job Rotation* exposes employees to different jobs in an organization. They move through various jobs, taking full responsibility for the work and staying in each position long enough to learn its intricacies.**

Job rotation forces people outside their normal boxes. They have different tasks, colleagues, and customers. Usually, this kind of experience challenges and invigorates them—and changes their habits.

Bill Creech, who reinvented the Tactical Air Command, required his wing leaders to periodically "immerse themselves totally, with no distracting influences, in the hour-to-hour frontline work activity for enough time to see all the victories and vexations going on there." When they were done, they had to write to Creech about their insights and recommendations.

Madison Police Chief David Couper spent a month every year working the front lines as a beat cop. When Mike Ramsey became director of general services in Visalia, California, he spent every Thursday for the first few months working on the garbage trucks and with the auto mechanics—starting at 4:00 A.M.

In the U.K., the Employment Service's London and southeast regional office rotated its senior staff into a local office to provide services to customers for two weeks. "The frontline staff were terrified because they thought the managers were going to make such a mess of it," says Diana Goldsworthy, then deputy director of the Cabinet Office's Next Steps Team. So the staff made sure that one clerical officer stayed behind to coach the novice bosses, while the real experts were away.

Martin Raff, who directed the regional office, reported that the experience motivated managers to improve customer service. "For example, they picked up one long-standing customer and local office gripe about the complexity of the forms for registering and claiming for unemployment pay, for the first time," he says. The job rotation also had great symbolic value: it "dramatically raised the profile of improving customer service in the region," and it heightened employee respect for the management team.

Some places rotate staff for much longer periods. In Canada, when the Edmonton school district decentralized control to nearly 200 individual schools, it created an assistant superintendent job in the central office that is filled by rotating school principals. Their assignment: help the other principals improve their schools. In this way, principals get a chance to play a new role as a coach, and at the same time they get a kind of sabbatical during which they can concentrate on learning new things.

Because there are limits to how many people can experience job rotation, reinventors also use interagency task forces, project teams, partnerships with other agencies and businesses, site visits, and quality councils to help employees get outside their boxes and interact with people from different parts of the organization.

All of this allows employees to gain a broader perspective about the organization—to develop new understandings about and sympathy for others. And it gives them an opportunity to hone new skills and gain new knowledge. It is like pumping fresh air through an organization, cleaning out its cobwebs and stimulating its brain cells.

EXTERNSHIPS AND INTERNSHIPS

Externships and Internships **allow an organization's members to work in other organizations for a stint—from six months to several years, usually—or bring outsiders in for a similar period.**

This tool plunges public employees into completely new organizational environments. In some cases the organization serves as the "host"; in others it is the "dispatcher." Either way, the experience can be habit-breaking.

When employees venture into the unfamiliar territory beyond their job and unit borders, their experiences can shatter their paradigms. Often it is as if they have entered a foreign culture. Their awareness that the social rules are different leads them to question things they have always taken for granted.

Because an internship or externship is temporary, participants tend to compare the new culture to their culture back home and draw lessons for use when they return. Because the assignment is long enough and involves performing real work in an unfamiliar setting, participants must let go of old habits and develop new ones.

Many quality or reinvention teams are staffed, at least in part, by civil servants doing externships of anywhere from six months to several years with the team. In the U. K., the Efficiency Unit, the Next Steps Team, and the Citizen's Charter team were all staffed this way. In the U.S., the Federal Quality Institute and the National Performance Review also got most of their people this way. The U.S. federal government allows civil servants to work in other agencies, in state or local governments, or in quasi-governmental operations such as the National Academy of Public Administration for up to four years.

But use of this tool need not be limited to public servants. In the U.K., for example, civil servants sometimes spend time in the private sector on externships, and businesspeople sometimes spend several years working in government. The U.K. also brings in many interns from other nations.

When Ted Gaebler was city manager of Visalia, California, he liked to bring local businesspeople who were between jobs into city government for a few months, to expose his employees to their way of thinking.

Since externships cannot be used with large numbers of people, managers use the tool mainly to develop employees with clear leadership potential. They are very selective about who gets to go off on an externship.

INSTITUTIONAL SPONSORS

Institutional Sponsors **establish a formal process that attracts, supports, protects, and celebrates innovative behaviors in public organizations.**

In most governments, the risks of innovating outweigh the rewards. By creating institutional sponsors for innovation—people and programs that encourage and protect the innovators—reinventors can change this balance dramatically. This tool encourages people to try new behaviors and offers them assistance: expertise, political muscle, and, occasionally, resources. It gets top management to pay attention to innovations, and it insulates innovators from attacks.

Leaders can use this tool to target a broad range of habits for change. Michigan's Department of Commerce used an internal "business incubator" to turn loose civil servants with promising ideas for new customer services. They received seed budgets, advice, and the visible blessing of top management.

An institutional sponsor can also operate systemwide. In 1985, Minnesota governor Rudy Perpich created a 22-member public-private steering committee to sponsor teams of government employees with innovative ideas. This initiative, called Strive Toward Excellence in Performance (STEP), was highlighted in *Reinventing Government.* The STEP board invited teams to submit proposals, then picked the best ones and offered them support and protection. As *Reinventing Government* explained:

See Reinventing Government pp. 271–275

> *The STEP seal of approval did four things. It gave people permission to innovate. It offered them technical assistance. It forced their bosses to sit up and listen. And it gave them protection when the inevitable flak hit.*

To help the innovators, STEP advisors held conferences, consultations, seminars, and training sessions on relevant topics: performance measurement, marketing services, and managing service quality.

In 1993, Florida governor Lawton Chiles initiated a similar effort to lure public innovators. Later adopted by the legislature and named the Innovation Investment Program, the effort attracted 163 proposals in its first two years. It funded 38 of the projects, at a cost of $11.8 million. The state estimated that the first 22 projects generated a total of $19 million in cost avoidance, productivity gains, and new revenues.

Institutional Sponsors: Do's And Don'ts

Have top leaders play the sponsoring role. In Minnesota, Governor Perpich cochaired the STEP board, which also included corporate leaders and public union officials. In Michigan's Commerce Department, a top deputy sponsored the in-house incubator. Having top leaders play the sponsoring role makes it much easier to ward off attacks from managers, central agencies, and elected officials.

Invite everyone to participate. Managers don't have a monopoly on good ideas, so make sure frontline employees feel sponsored, too. At least one-third of Minnesota's STEP innovators were line employees, not managers.

Be very clear about which behaviors you are sponsoring. In Michigan, potential innovators had to demonstrate a customer orientation. In Minnesota, proposals had to exemplify at least one of six behaviors: closer contact with the customer, employee participation, decentralization of authority, public-private-academic partnerships, state-of-the-art productivity improvement techniques, or performance measurement.

Assure innovators that they will be held harmless. Guarantee innovators they will not lose their budgets if they improve productivity, nor suffer negative consequences if they fail.

Emphasize long-term results, not short-term fixes. The idea is to promote new behaviors, not just to cut budgets. Give people time to change their habits.

pp. 564–566

Celebrate the innovations. The Minnesota Business Partnership created an annual award for STEP innovators.

Evaluate the effectiveness of the institutional sponsor. There is no simple formula for sponsoring innovations; organizations have to learn how to do it. STEP redesigned itself several times in its first years of existence.

Don't make it bureaucratic. Don't insist on detailed initial proposals from employees. Let them keep it short; if it looks promising, have them flesh it out and refine it. Good ideas come before good plans.

Don't make submission of projects mandatory. Keep it voluntary. Look for innovators driven by a desire to change, not by the feeling that they must comply.

Don't just turn innovators loose—support them. Employees with good ideas don't necessarily have the knowledge and skills needed to implement them. They will face barriers within their own agencies. Set up a technical assistance team to help them, and encourage the innovators to call on the high-level sponsor for political clout when they need it.

RESOURCES ON CREATING INSTITUTIONAL SPONSORS

Sandra J. Hale. "Reinventing Government the Minnesota Way." *Public Productivity and Management Review,* 15, no. 2 (winter 1991). A good summary of the STEP program.

Sandra J. Hale and Mary M. Williams, eds. *Managing Change: A Guide to Producing Innovation from Within.* Washington, D.C.: The Urban Institute, 1989. This excellent how-to book was written by STEP staff. It is distributed by the University Press of America, Lanham, Md.

CONTESTS

Contests promote behaviors reinventors want to see in their organizations.

Because contests often get many people energized, leaders use them to give employees a reason to try out new behaviors. The most widespread use of this tool is the competitive award program. For example, U.S. federal agencies may compete for a set of quality awards determined annually. They must submit a detailed application and undergo extensive auditing to qualify. Ohio, Texas, Arizona, and other states have created similar awards.

General Creech used this tool repeatedly in the Tactical Air Command (TAC). A classic example was his "Top Wheels" contest. Creech believed that TAC was not maintaining its vehicles properly, which increased repair and replacement costs. So he made sure every vehicle had an "owner," then gave those owners a reason to take pride in their vehicle. "He said the same kind of pride you get from taking care of a fighter plane can be gotten by taking care of a garbage truck," remembers Doug Farbrother, a former Defense Department manager who moved on to the National Performance Review. "The prize was for good looks, and of course that meant people spent a lot of their own time, making sure things looked and ran well."

Creech explains how it worked:

> *Every six months the wing commanders would have a "rollby." We used to have "flybys" in the Air Force. What we did in the rollby was everybody was on parade. They could show their truck or sedan or pickup or whatever it was. . . . We also had someone writing down numbers of vehicles that looked shabby, and they went straight to the paint barn. We didn't criticize anybody; it was all positive. We had awards and best-maintained-fleet by squadron and all that.*

Some contests are informal, but still very real. Robbie Stokes, Bromley's director of leisure services and a Charter Mark winner, has every unit compete to come up with the best ideas for the next year's service plan. "I think it's important to have competition," he says. "It's like sports—the great fun you can have on a tennis court, while you're competing. That's the kind of fun we want people to have at work."

To create contests that change the culture, you need to:

- ***Determine what success looks like.*** You need some way of picking the winners, some criteria for judging success.
- ***Ensure a fair process for judging entries.*** Minnesota's STEP program used a public-private panel to make final decisions.

pp. 453–488

- ***Give public employees the autonomy to try new behaviors.*** Unless employees and organizations have the freedom to try new things, the competition will be a sham.
- ***Support competitors who want to learn how to get better.*** Contests can be powerful learning experiences—for winners and losers. In the Air Combat Command, units with relatively low performance in particular areas are encouraged to learn from the high performers.

LARGE-SCALE, REAL-TIME STRATEGIC PLANNING

Large-Scale, Real-Time Strategic Planning **immerses most, if not all, of an organization's employees in an intensive multiday retreat, during which they identify necessary organizational changes and commit to implementing them.**

Imagine a gathering of hundreds, even thousands, of employees in a government agency to figure out how to change the organization. To accomplish this task, they stay together for three days.

The first day, they work in small groups, getting to know one another and openly discussing the condition of the agency—focusing on its warts and identifying its most pressing problems. The organization's leaders describe their strategy for the agency's future. Customers and stakeholders share their perspectives about what the organization must do for them.

The second day, the employees first hear from and question people in another organization that is further ahead in the process of changing. Then members of each of the agency's units make wish lists of changes they want other units to make to better meet customers' needs. Each unit receives this massive feedback and—with coaching that helps them overcome their defensiveness—prepares responses, including commitments to do things differently in the future. They announce their commitments to the whole group of employees. As they do so, something in the room changes. The information exchanged is not new, but the behavior—blame-free and change-oriented—certainly is.

Following this exercise, employees discuss the unwritten rules—the norms or givens—that guide behavior in the organization: "never disagree with the boss in front of others," or "don't pass on bad news, because they always shoot the messenger." Then they identify and announce the norms that *must* change if each unit in the organization is to live up to the commitments it has made. They also define the new norms that should take their place. They are describing the kind of organization they want to have.

At this point, the organization's leaders again describe their strategy for the future. They tie the strategy to what they have heard during the gathering.

They identify those parts of the strategy that are open for revision and explain why some parts are not. Then employees discuss in small groups what they agree and disagree with in the strategy and what changes they would make. Each group recommends changes, and the entire group then votes for the recommendations with which they agree.

That evening, the organization's leaders meet to review the voting. They incorporate many of the employees' ideas into a final strategy they will present to the large group the next day.

The third and final day begins with employees hearing—and judging—the leaders' revised strategy. Then they begin to translate that strategy into action. They generate ideas by using a technique called "preferred futuring." They imagine that it is two years into the future and the organization has done well in implementing its strategy. Then they envision what is happening inside this organization-to-be: what people are doing, saying, and feeling. This generates an outpouring of ideas for each part of the strategy, which they write down and post.

Teams assemble to sort through the ideas for each portion of the strategy. They brainstorm about what the organization must do differently to advance the strategy, and then they agree on a specific plan of action. The many action plans are posted so employees can vote for those that are most promising and identify those that are not feasible or are off track. Through this prioritization process, a common direction for the organization emerges.

The next step puts employees back into small groups, but this time in their own organizational units. They identify and commit to ways that they will work differently—with one another and with other units—when they get back home. Each unit reports its "back-home plan" to the entire group of employees.

Finally, the organization's leaders summarize and reflect on the progress made during the three-day session, the lessons learned and agreements reached. They emphasize the work that lies ahead—plans that must be made, actions that must be taken. The event—exhausting and exhilarating—is over.

p. 553

We have described this tool at length because it is so remarkable. (Our description is based on an excellent book by Robert W. Jacobs, *Real Time Strategic Change.*) As implausible as this may seem to government leaders, it enables organizations to involve huge numbers of employees in rapidly deciding on change strategies and plans. In the U.K., the 40,000–member Employment Service has used the tool repeatedly. In the U.S., users include METRO, the 4,000–employee agency responsible for water pollution control and public transportation in the Seattle area; the New York City public hospital system; NASA's Lyndon B. Johnson Space Center; Sedgwick County, Kansas; and the

St. Lawrence-Lewis Board of Cooperative Educational Services in upstate New York.

Martin Raff, a former regional director in the U.K. Employment Service, first used the tool with 600 employees from a local area office. Brought together to create a strategic plan, they could "hear from each other and hear from other stakeholders including customers, Government Ministers, the ES Chief Executive and others," Raff explained.

> *They could then use all this data to discuss together their vision of a more successful future and the best way forward, including the immediate next steps following the meeting. We found that the whole system perspective that people received, mostly for the first time, the fact that everyone listened to each other, and that the leaders were prepared to modify their views to take account of those at the meeting, generated great commitment to the plan. People also had a clear understanding of the plan, and the vision behind it, because they had contributed to its formation.*

Raff also used real-time strategic planning in the Birmingham area office, traditionally the region's worst performer. That session triggered an increase in the area's performance the very next month—a trend that continued for three years. Then he took it to the Staffordshire area office, where he wanted to break down the "command-and-control" organizational culture. Next he used it at the regional level to help middle and senior managers develop new ways of leading the organization.

The Employment Service's central office became intrigued by what Raff was doing. CEO Michael Fogden decided to bring 850 senior managers together for two days to develop a strategy for changing the agency. At the end of the first day, Fogden and his leadership team modified the strategy they had outlined earlier in the day. The next day they presented the changes to the group. After further feedback and revisions, the managers agreed to the strategy and developed back-home action plans.

"The event had a noticeable effect on the behaviours of senior management afterwards," according to Raff. "Working groups were set up to look at how head office and the regions (previously suspicious of and blaming each other) could work together on new programs and some administrative issues."

The impact of these large-scale events depends greatly on follow-up by leaders. "It is best to capitalize on the energy for change that has been unleashed in the process by having leaders make a few quick and especially meaningful changes immediately after the event," advises Jacobs. "Publicizing these decisions and actions widely reinforces people's beliefs that this time, change is for real."

Leaders of large organizations that cannot fit all of their employees into a single large-scale event use "diffusion events" to spread the effects throughout their ranks. These additional mass meetings usually last two days and are held with divisions or teams in the organization. They build on the information generated at the first event. Some organizations use a cascade approach to diffusion: the first event involves top leadership, and then follow-up sessions bring in more and more levels of the organization.

Changing Habits in Real Time

Large-scale, real-time strategic planning was invented by Dannemiller Tyson Associates, organizational change consultants located in Ann Arbor, Michigan. A genuine innovation, it bundles together a set of familiar techniques for organizational development into a powerful experience that changes behaviors. (It also changes hearts and minds, but because it creates such a powerful experience, we have chosen to discuss it in this chapter.)

"The real time strategic change technology creates an opportunity for people to break down arthritic blockages and develop enduring ways of working together," writes Jacobs. It creates a variety of habit-breaking experiences:

- ***Employees set aside daily work routines to work on the unfamiliar.*** Participants leave their usual tasks behind and work instead on the big picture. This new work involves the unfamiliar tasks of processing and analyzing enormous amounts of feedback.
- ***Employees listen to customers and stakeholders.*** There is no better reality check to help people see beyond the walls of their organization.
- ***Employees leave their bureaucratic cubbyholes and work with strangers and enemies in the organization.*** During the meeting, participants must work extensively with colleagues outside their units.
- ***Employees openly and constructively discuss ideas for organizational change.*** Rather than keeping ideas to themselves or talking just in the bathrooms and hallways, participants share their ideas openly. They engage in face-to-face group dialogues, not monologues. They learn how to raise concerns about other people and units without provoking defensiveness. And they learn how to respond to concerns raised about them without being defensive. As METRO executive director Dick Sandraas puts it, they learn "how to dissent with each other productively."
- ***Employees take personal responsibility for making change happen.*** They make commitments to one another. They don't hide behind rules, bosses, or other excuses. They realize they "have a unique opportunity to influence

the future course of the organization," writes Jacobs. "You viscerally come to understand the meaning of a fundamental principle underlying the real time strategic change technology: 'If it is to be, it is up to me.'"

• ***Employees envision a successful future for the organization and what it takes to get there, rather than just focusing on problems.*** There is a world of difference in these approaches, as Jacobs points out.

> *The vast majority of organizations attack all problems by trying to isolate them and solve them. . . . Done well, problem solving ensures you will not have your current problems pestering you anymore. However [this] is different from working out the future you prefer, then taking steps to achieve it.*

RESOURCES ON REAL-TIME STRATEGIC CHANGE

Robert W. Jacobs. *Real-Time Strategic Change: How to Involve an Entire Organization in Fast and Far-Reaching Change.* San Francisco: Berrett-Koehler, 1994. An exciting, enormously useful book that walks the reader through this tool in depth.

Bob Filipczak. "Critical Mass: Putting Whole-Systems Thinking into Practice." *Training* (September 1995). A good review of various ways of organizing large-scale meetings for organizations.

HANDS-ON ORGANIZATIONAL EXPERIENCES

Hands-On Organizational Experiences **are less formally structured learning events in which hundreds of employees share new experiences that build the culture leaders want.**

In December 1979, St. Paul deputy mayor Dick Broeker sat down to watch a videotape on the energy crisis. As Broeker remembers it, the speaker said, "When you think about it, whether you run a soap factory or a city, all you've got is people and money." All Broeker had was people, no money. So he dreamed up a new way to use his people: a three-day "energy mobilization," in which *every city employee* would go door to door, handing out information about saving energy, giving people weatherization kits, and asking them to fill out a survey about their energy use. He and staff member Alice Murphy put together a 100-member team and designed the 3,000-employee operation, which reached 100,000 homes. "The city attorney said we couldn't do it, because somebody'd get raped or bit by a dog," Broeker remembers. "But we said, 'Well, it's the one thing we can do, so we're going to do it.'"

> *This was a real new experience. I remember when they all got together for the big party afterwards. The place was packed. Almost everybody came. We gave away a vacation to Hawaii that was won by a perfect employee, who had given all these hours. There was a real sense of community in that place—you could just tell everybody felt like they had built a barn together.*
>
> *There was an editorial cartoon with Mayor Latimer wearing a Russian cap leading 3,000 employees out. I think there was a real sense of team, because everybody was stripped of rank for those three days. Everybody was shoulder to shoulder with Latimer—he spent the three days out in the field. There were no check-ups on the employees. We spent no time at all policing the system. It was done like you would do it if you didn't have all the rules and regulations; it was done for a purpose. I can't help but believe that that sent a real powerful message. There was a period when you could really feel the employees drop their cynicism and skepticism about this mayor.*

St. Paul's energy mobilization was a classic example of a hands-on experience that changed the organization's culture. Ted Gaebler had a similar experience in Visalia, with an annual city fair employees put on for the citizens. While not formally structured as learning events, these experiences can have a huge impact on an organization's culture.

REDESIGNING WORK

***Redesigning Work*, whether by reengineering business processes, reforming administrative systems, or introducing new technology, permanently changes employees' experiences.**

pp. 463–465

When the New York City regional Veterans Affairs office reengineered its work processes, it shifted people from rote jobs in which they performed one function repeatedly to teams that handled all aspects of processing a customer's application. Once people began handling customers face-to-face and performing the many tasks necessary to serve them, their attitudes changed. "I went up there when about a third of the operation had been converted to teams, rather than this assembly line process," says Doug Farbrother, then with Vice President Gore's reinvention team.

I talked to people who were working on teams, and people who were working the old way. The old people called their job "the hump," because it was just this burden you carried through your life, having to get up in the morning and go to the hump. But the people on the teams were just wildly enthusiastic about what they were doing. They kept talking about helping the veterans. And I think all [Regional Director] Joe Thompson did was change the work they did every day.

See Banishing Bureaucracy pp. 281–283

Another common way to redesign work is to introduce new technology. Consider the Crookston campus of the University of Minnesota, which in 1993 gave every student and faculty member a laptop computer. As we explained in *Banishing Bureaucracy,* this was a small, two-year agricultural school that the president of the University of Minnesota wanted to close down. "They called this Moo U," says Peter Hutchinson, whose Public Strategies Group helped the school develop its survival plan.

Chancellor Don Sargeant decided to turn Crookston into a four-year school with a technology focus. The laptops became his principal tool. "The really interesting part of the story is what happens to the faculty when they realize this is actually going to occur—that this madman chancellor is actually going to make this happen," says Hutchinson.

All the kids will have computers. What are they gonna do? What they did, they spent the whole summer learning about computers and trying to find ways to integrate them into their classes. So when the kids show up, the faculty is basically about a week ahead of the students. It's like the customers are chasing you all year, and you're running as fast as you can. That's got to change the culture.

Sargeant says that when he first decided to do this, 20 percent of the faculty were excited, 20 percent were hostile, and 60 percent were on the fence. The first thing he did was to set up small work groups. He didn't use the traditional faculty committees, because they were too slow.

I listed 1,000 things that needed to be done between February and September, broke them up, asked two or three students and two or three faculty to take each group, and asked them to get these things done. I said, "You don't have to check with me. Just get it done."

Professors were not accustomed to working with students on teams, but there was so much to do that many of them dived in.

Once the computers arrived, "The first change I noticed was, there were at least three, four, five problems everybody faced every day.

> *They absolutely had to respond to a whole bunch of new situations on a daily basis. When you start to do that, you really do change your behavior—rather than being so critical, standing back and criticizing things, they had to ask themselves, "How can we solve this?" And then they would ask for help—which is very hard for most professors to do.*

Pretty soon the fence sitters became supporters, and a culture of continuous learning and improvement began to emerge. On a survey taken after about two years, more than 80 percent of the faculty said the ubiquitous computers had "encouraged work on interactive learning tools," nearly 80 percent said the computers had stimulated changes in their teaching approaches and class materials, and nearly 60 percent said they had helped the faculty become better teachers.

"I think more and more they are willing to rethink what they're doing, what their objectives are, why their course exists, and [whether there is] a different way to do it," says Sargeant.

Faculty have also changed the way they look at students. Many now clamor to hire students, to help put courses on the World Wide Web and make other technological strides. More important, Sargeant says, "They look at the education process differently—more at students as being responsible for part of it, rather than just passive."

Many schools, at all levels, face the dilemma of how to get their faculty to embrace computer technology. Crookston did it by giving their customers computers. It changed the daily *experience* of faculty members, forever. Suddenly every student they faced, every day, had a computer on his or her lap. They had little choice but to respond. New work and new experiences created a new culture.

Chapter 14

Touching Hearts

Developing a New Covenant Within Your Organization

***Touching Hearts* helps employees create new emotional bonds—covenants with one another and with the organization. These heartfelt commitments shape people's attitudes and beliefs and change their behaviors.**

When General Bill Creech took over the Tactical Air Command (TAC) in 1978, he was determined to change its culture from the bottom up. He wanted a culture focused on quality, teamwork, and performance. He quickly began refurbishing the shabby buildings and equipment he found throughout the TAC: repainting, putting carpets in offices, upgrading the maintenance shops and equipment, and so on. *"Quality begets quality,"* he later wrote. "And one cannot justifiably expect employees to appreciate quality, think quality, and produce quality if top management shows by its actions that it is indifferent to it."

During his journeys from one TAC base to another, Creech ran across a beat-up old office chair used by a maintenance supervisor responsible for more than 100 people and hundreds of millions of dollars of resources. "One of its four casters was missing, stuffing was coming out, and its general appearance was atrocious," he recalls. "In using that chair, he was making a graphic statement regarding the quality standard he expected."

Creech took the chair back to his headquarters at Langley Air Force Base and put it in his conference room, for the chief logistician—the man responsible for equipment. "It became my symbol of the way we had been neglecting our people, their attitude, and the quality mind-set," he said. "Everyone got the message."

Indeed, when we did a video on Creech's organization 15 years later, people were still talking about his chair. But by then the legend had grown. Major Carl Williamson, deputy director for quality education, told it this way:

> *The chair was a beat-up kind of chair, very small, and had a brick under one of the legs. [Creech] asked the young man, "Have you tried to get a chair? Do you have another chair?" He said, "Well, yes, sir, we've requisitioned that, but you know, it's going to take a lot of time for it to get out here."*
>
> *[Creech] took the chair, he had the chair flown back to Langley. So he flew himself back to Langley and walked into our senior logistician and said, "Can I have your chair?" Now we're talking about a beautiful, plush chair here. He took that chair, he flew it out to the young airman, and took the chair with the brick under it and gave it to the senior officer and said, "And when you fix the system that supports the people, then you can get yourself a chair."*

As Creech says, "Such symbols can be very useful in making sure everyone understands that there is a new approach to carrying out the business."

When the late Martin Raff ran the West Midlands Employment Service in the U.K., he wanted to remove the physical and psychological barriers that separated managers from their teams. He started by removing the walls between managers' offices.

> *I took the lead by moving out of my office into the open-plan area, in which about 40 other people on my floor worked, and took down the walls of what had been my office. It was very tough for about six weeks, and I longed for the quiet seclusion of my office. After that, I quickly began to feel comfortable in the open plan. . . .*
>
> *Nobody copied me initially. One manager said, "I've worked all my life to get my own office, and I'm blowed if I'm going to give this up for the sake of some theory." . . . I never actually* **ordered** *anyone to move out—but I had a strategy for getting people out.*

Raff gathered a group of middle managers whom he knew were pioneers. He asked them to consider moving out of their offices en masse.

> *To my astonishment, they reported back to me that it was* ***impossible*** *for managers of Job Centers to be in open plan. They argued that they needed privacy for seeing people, taking telephone calls and reading confidential files, and that the staff would not like managers to be with them all the time.*

After Raff applied what he calls "considerable moral pressure," they agreed to try it for six weeks. "Within a fortnight," he reports, "most of them said that they liked being out, and *none* went back after six weeks." During the next two years, Raff took down the walls of managers' offices throughout the organization. The change, he says, helped "to create belief that radical change in the way we worked was possible and *was* going to happen."

Using a beat-up chair as a symbol of what has to change and taking down walls that separate managers and employees are two examples of the many ways reinventors can change their organization's culture. They help change the *emotional commitments* of public employees: their hopes and dreams, their expectations, their commitments to one another.

As we explained in *Banishing Bureaucracy,* organizational cultures are rooted in emotional commitments, many of which are barely even conscious. In bureaucratic cultures, many people are emotionally committed to their status in the organization's hierarchy. Others are committed to holding deep resentments—toward management, toward unions, toward politicians.

To create an entrepreneurial culture, you must get employees to commit to new things: taking personal responsibility for the health of their organizations, performing well for their customers, teaming up with their colleagues, and the like.

FIFTY WAYS TO LEAVE YOUR CULTURE

There are many ways to touch hearts. We are aware of at least five basic elements in the process of building new emotional commitments:

- Dislodging old emotional commitments through experience.
- Creating new emotional touchstones to guide behavior.
- Staging events that embody new emotional commitments.
- Reinventing the work environment to build new commitments.
- Using bonding events to create new emotional commitments.

pp. 537–539

The first element is the one we discussed in Chapter Thirteen: dislodging the old emotional commitments by creating new experiences that help people let go and begin to change.

The second method is creating touchstones—symbols and stories—that give people guideposts to help them make changes and emotional anchors once they have embraced the new culture. Some touchstones are primarily emotional: they give people a gut sense of the new values and norms you are trying to create. Others are more rational: they give people a set of concepts, articulated in things like mission statements and codes of values, that they can use to figure out what behavior is consistent with the new culture. We cover the latter in Chapter Fifteen; here we focus on two types of emotional touchstones: symbols and stories.

The third method is to stage events and activities—celebrations, honors ceremonies, and rituals—that embody the new emotional commitments you want people to make. Symbols and stories signal the culture you want, and celebrations and rituals reinforce it. They actively fortify people when they begin to embrace the new paradigm, by recognizing and cheering on their efforts. They proclaim to everyone in the organization: *This is the kind of behavior we want!*

The fourth is to reinvent your work environment to communicate the values and attitudes you want in the organization. This helps answer what Bill Creech calls one of the four great management questions: "What's in it for me?" Because concrete investments offer unmistakable proof of your values, they make it much easier for people to commit to change. Symbols, stories, celebrations, and rituals are all effective—but only if you back them up with action. If management's actions contradict these signals, then employees will tune them out. As Ralph Waldo Emerson once wrote, "What you do thunders so loudly, I cannot hear what you say to the contrary."

Finally, the fifth course is to build new emotional bonds between people around the values and commitments you want, through bonding events and truth-telling activities. This is a powerful way to solidify the new beginnings you are asking people to make. This is what a covenant is all about: as Webster's says, it is a "solemn and binding agreement." When your people make that kind of agreement with one another, they are forging the new culture.

There are many, many tools you can use to win people's hearts. We have written about those we have encountered frequently, but there must be 50 more that people have invented—or will invent. Don't let our list limit your imagination. The important thing is to understand the basic elements in touching hearts, then invent whatever tools will work best in your organization.

RESOURCES ON TOUCHING HEARTS

William Bridges. *Transitions: Making Sense of Life's Changes* and *Managing Transitions: Making the Most of Change.* Reading, Mass.: Addison-Wesley, 1980 and 1991. These two books are superb guides to helping people make cultural transitions.

James M. Kouzes and Barry Z. Posner. *The Leadership Challenge: How to Keep Getting Extraordinary Things Done in Organizations.* San Francisco: Jossey-Bass, 1995. One of the better books on leadership; includes two useful chapters on "Encouraging the Heart."

Harrison Owen. *Leadership Is.* Potomac, Md.:Abbott Publishing, 1990. A brilliant little book on leadership that includes, among other gems, a useful chapter on "Growing Spirit Through Collective Storytelling."

TOOLS FOR TOUCHING HEARTS

Creating New Symbols and Stories communicates at a gut level the culture you want to build. They become cultural artifacts: anchors that help bind employees together around common values, expectations, hopes, and dreams. See p. 562.

Celebrating Success creates regular and spontaneous events that honor the achievements of individuals, teams, and the organization as a whole. See p. 564.

Honoring Failure turns innovations that fail into opportunities to improve performance and promote innovation—not occasions to blame and punish. See p. 566.

New Rituals are special events that embody and reinforce the new culture. Repeated regularly, they give people new touchstones. When they are participatory, they also draw people in, helping them make the emotional commitments required by the new culture. See p. 569.

Investing in the Workplace upgrades the quality of the standard-issue working environment, which demonstrates a commitment to public employees. See p. 571.

Redesigning the Workplace reinforces the emotional commitments you want, such as a sense of teamwork or a commitment to customer service. See p. 572.

Investing in Employees shows workers that management is serious about the changes it advocates, because it is investing in the employees' capacity to make those changes. See p. 574.

Bonding Events develop powerful new relationships among groups of employees, based on trust, collaboration, and taking shared responsibility for producing results. See p. 575.

Sending Valentines is a group exercise in which employees tell other work units what they would like them to do differently. It helps them speak the truth to one another without getting hung up in workplace rivalries and antagonisms—and to change their commitments to one another. See p. 581.

CREATING NEW SYMBOLS AND STORIES

Almost anything can take on the power of a cultural symbol. When Peter Hutchinson stepped into the role of Minneapolis school superintendent, he found a large magnetic board hanging in the school board's meeting room. The district had been implementing site-based management, but in a very top-down manner. The central office had required schools to do a great deal of planning before giving them any autonomy, and the magnetic board depicted the results. "It had a line down the middle with the site-based schools on one side and the nondesignated schools on the other," says Hutchinson. "This magnetic board was a symbol of the dominance of the central office." Hutchinson took it down and declared all schools to be site-based from that moment on. The fate of the magnetic board became a powerful symbol of his new approach.

Bob Stone, former director of Vice President Gore's reinventing government team, the National Partnership for Reinventing Government, has long been a master of symbolism. When he first met with Gore to discuss reinvention, he took along one of his most potent symbols: a steam trap. A device used in steam heating systems, it takes condensation out of the steam lines. When we first met Stone, at the Pentagon, he showed us one and told us about it:

> *When it leaks, it leaks $50 a week worth of steam. The lesson is, when it leaks, replace it quick. But it takes us a year to replace it, because we have a system that wants to make sure we get the very best buy on this $100 item, and maybe by waiting a year we can buy the item for $2 less. In the meantime, we've lost $3,000 worth of steam.*

Stone used the steam trap to explain the idiocy of government's centralized systems. Before the meeting with Gore, he told his two companions that they would know the meeting had been a success if Gore asked to keep the steam trap. Sure enough, he did—and it became the first in a succession of symbols Stone supplied to help the vice president communicate his message of radical reinvention. Perhaps the most famous was the ashtray Gore smashed on the David Letterman show, to illustrate the absurdity of federal procurement specifications. In nine pages, the draft specifications detailed exactly the size and shape federal ashtrays were to be, including the fact that when struck in a particular fashion, they should shatter into no more than 35 pieces, each at least a quarter of an inch thick.

Sometimes organizations adopt symbols that remind them of the culture they are trying to build. Babak Armajani, CEO of the Public Strategies Group, tells one such story:

> *We did a lot of work with the Roseville, Minnesota, schools. We were having trouble getting people to think of continuous improvement, in-*

stead of searching for "the right way" to manage. One day we were having one of these meetings, where different teams were reporting about what they did. A team of janitors said, "We want to show you the turtle."

They were having enormous problems with the machines you drop into swimming pools that motor around and clean the pools, which are called turtles. Lowering these things in and out of the pools, they were getting banged up and broken, so they had these high repair costs. So they designed this little cart to carry the machine and lower it in. It lowered repairs, lowered their injuries, and lowered their workman's compensation costs. All of a sudden everybody got it—that's what continuous improvement was all about. So the turtle became their symbol of continuous improvement—they did turtle chains and turtle this and turtle that.

Stories are a similarly potent currency of culture. Over the water coolers and coffee pots, in the hallways and bathrooms, and at lunch, we tell stories about our organizations. They travel the organizational grapevine with remarkable speed and impact. In telling them, members of an organization share their unspoken assumptions and beliefs about the organization.

Leaders must generate and tell *new* stories to develop a new culture. Bob Stone and his team constantly told stories—many of them illustrated with the kind of symbols we have been discussing. In Visalia, Ted Gaebler constantly told stories about the entrepreneurial behavior of his staff: the third-level employee who bought an Olympic pool for half price because he wrote a $60,000 check on the spot; the recreation director who built restrooms for the softball teams and made a profit doing it, by tacking on a concession stand; the police officers who pioneered a lease-purchase program for squad cars that was copied by two dozen cities.

See *Reinventing Government* pp. 2–5

See *Banishing Bureaucracy* pp. 116–117

Leaders often need stories to build their credibility. In Indianapolis, union members still tell the story of Transportation Director Mitch Roob's laying off 18 supervisors so the workers' bid to keep their work would have a shot. In Sunnyvale, people tell the story of a department head who faked his performance data because he didn't believe in the city's performance measurement system—and who was fired as a result. These stories are about leaders proving they are serious about change.

In telling stories, don't ignore the grapevine in favor of official communications methods such as newsletters and memos. When Babak Armajani was an executive in the Minnesota Department of Administration, he and others realized that "if you told 20 people in the organization something, word would quickly get out to everyone." So they formally convened those 20 people every time they wanted to get the word out, and they called it "the grapevine."

CELEBRATING SUCCESS

***Celebrating Success* creates regular and spontaneous events that honor the achievements of individuals, teams, and the organization as a whole.**

pp. 463–465

In New York City in early 1993, a team of about 20 employees in the Veterans Administration (VA) regional office assembled in Training Room B. They had been there many times before, to reengineer the organization's process for ruling on veterans' claims for benefits.But this meeting was special: Joe Thompson, the regional office director, was treating the team to lunch. Thompson had decided to implement their new process design throughout the agency, and he wanted to celebrate. He announced that each team member had earned an extra eight hours of leave and a $200 bonus. Later, he took them to Washington, where they received a Hammer Award from Vice President Gore.

Celebrating success makes people feel good about their work, their colleagues, and themselves. More important, it reinforces the values and mission of the organization. Celebrating the behavior you want to see is one of the easiest, most effective ways to get people to buy into a new culture at an emotional level.

Many leaders are unaware of the power of celebration. They may think celebrating is unnecessary—it should be enough just to know you have succeeded. They may already be focusing on the next challenge. Or celebrating may make them feel uncomfortable, because they don't know how to give or receive praise.

But celebrations are powerful ways to influence behavior. They give employees special moments they can share. They stimulate a deep-rooted commitment to organizational goals, because they help create a sense of belonging and acceptance. Showcasing successes "generates a sense among everybody that you can make a difference and that there's a structure that supports your good ideas," says Colonel Dick Frishkorn, former director of quality for the Air Combat Command.

In short, celebrating success helps develop an emotional covenant that shapes behavior.

Most public organizations don't know how to throw a party. And even if they do, they worry about being criticized by elected officials or the media. So the first rule is to celebrate unabashedly. Have fun, and don't be defensive about it. When Alan Krause was a deputy in the New York City welfare department, he held staff celebrations in classy restaurants, staged fashion shows, even hired rap groups to perform songs about reducing error rates.

Another rule is to be clear about what you're celebrating. To celebrate *success,* you must define what success is—for the organization, teams, or individuals. It should be closely related to the organization's mission, goals, and values. For example, managers, union representatives, and employees of the 6,000–

employee Internal Revenue Service center in Ogden, Utah, decided to celebrate their "champions"—people who exemplified a customer orientation, innovation, and dedication. Phoenix annually honors city employees who implement innovative ideas or take extraordinary actions.

In both places, employees decide who wins these awards—an excellent way to make sure employees buy in emotionally. Some organizations use on-the-spot awards, in which peers can honor one another without going through nominations and selections. Peer awards create powerful emotional bonds among employees. (For more on performance awards, see Chapter Six.)

pp. 231–232

Celebrations don't have to be planned; they can be spontaneous, like Joe Thompson's luncheon. But it helps to establish a more formal, ongoing process as well. One reason is that this allows lots of employees to get involved—and to be recognized. From 1987 to 1991, the Ogden IRS office honored more than 1,400 champions. Eighty-seven of them had their names engraved on a "quality champion" board in the hallway of the center's main building.

Making celebrations a fixture also helps deal with political and media scrutiny. It says to elected officials and journalists, "When we perform well, we celebrate—just like you do when you win elections or break big stories."

When you can, it makes sense to invite your stakeholders and customers. In particular, get the "big cheeses" there: the mayor, the governor, CEOs, union leaders. Their presence builds interest in the event and makes the celebration even more meaningful to workers. And it insulates the organization from attack.

Do's and Don'ts of Celebrating Success

Spread the honors. Keep the process of identifying success from getting too clubby; don't let any clique hog the awards.

Let the public in on your success. Phoenix broadcasts its annual ceremony over the city's cable TV channel. Sandra Hale, former commission of administration in Minnesota, worked tirelessly to generate newspaper and television coverage of celebrations. She called her campaign "exposing good government." "If the public hears only criticisms of your agency, there is nothing to bank against," Hale explains. "One of my reasons for wanting to get out the positive messages . . . was to develop the kind of relationships that would help us in the tough times."

Defend yourself against people who attack you for celebrating. When the state treasurer in Minnesota criticized Hale's use of $10,000 for an employee recognition day and dinner, Hale shot back: "What would they have preferred we use [to motivate employees]? Whips?" She repeated this everywhere. It sent a strong message to her organization—and to politicians who liked to take potshots.

Don't just look for "home runs," or extraordinary successes. Find the smaller successes and celebrate them, too. They offer employees a more believable model of what they, too, can accomplish.

Don't celebrate just individual accomplishment. Team and organization-wide accomplishments are as important as individual accomplishments—even more so.

RECOGNIZING EMPLOYEES: PITFALLS TO AVOID

- Nominating processes that take too much of the nominators' time.
- Having too many different kinds of awards.
- Awards that lack clear standards.
- Giving people in more visible jobs more of the recognition.
- Favoritism in making awards.
- Elitist celebrations that exclude people.

HONORING FAILURE

Honoring Failure **turns innovations that fail into opportunities to improve performance and promote innovation—not occasions to blame and punish.**

Government organizations are extremists when it comes to failure. At one extreme, they ignore it; pretending it didn't happen seems to make it so. At the other, they punish the people who try something new and fail. The sum of both extremes is a "no mistakes" organizational culture of blaming and fear, cover-ups and snow jobs. This discourages employees' creativity, preventing innovation and improvement.

Yet an innovative, entrepreneurial organization will always have failures, simply because its members are trying new things. This is widely recognized in the private sector. "Tolerance for failure is a very specific part of the excellent company culture—and that lesson comes directly from the top," wrote Peters and Waterman in *In Search of Excellence.* "Champions have to make lots of tries and consequently suffer some failures or the organization won't learn."

The same is true in the public sector. When the Ford Foundation and Harvard's Kennedy School of Government launched their Innovation in American Government Awards, in the mid-1980s, one of the first things they learned was that the winners experimented constantly. Just as in any other field, they made progress through trial and error, and they learned from their errors. Few of the winning innovations emerged full-blown from innovators' minds.

New York City's School District Four, which pioneered public school choice, provides a perfect case in point. Its leaders tried new schools, grew the ones that succeeded, and shut down the ones that failed. As Seymour Fliegel said in his book *Miracle in East Harlem*, "The District Four experience suggests that in order to build a network of good schools, one also has to be willing to fail."

pp. 225–226

One response to failure phobia is to create a performance management system that can distinguish between honest mistakes and behavior that requires sanctions. Another important antidote—albeit a tough one for many leaders to swallow—is to honor those who try new things and fail. This tool honors risk taking by signaling an understanding that, as Peter Drucker once said, "Innovative ideas are like frog's eggs: of a thousand hatched, only one or two survive to maturity." The eggs that don't make it are honorable failures.

This is initially a leader's tool, because only leaders can change the "no mistakes" tone and create safety for employees. How they deal with failures—other people's and their own—matters greatly.

There are many ways to communicate that your organization values innovation, even when it fails. Here are a few:

Celebrate honorable failures. Ted Gaebler created the best example we know when he served as city manager of Visalia, California. At the suggestion of two of his department heads, he created an award for the year's most spectacular failure. One year he even won it himself, when he suggested at the annual corporate report meeting—without checking with his city council and with television cameras rolling—that the city distribute its surplus in the form of "dividends" for its shareholders, the citizens.

You don't have to use a formal award. In the late 1980s, in Michigan, Doug Ross encouraged a particularly entrepreneurial staffer, Geri Larkin, to create a new program to support start-up companies. After a year and a half, it became clear that it was not working. Larkin recommended closing it down. Ross decided she was a hero: she had tried something for which she had a passion and that fit the department's mission, she had documented the results, and she had told the truth about them. So at a departmental gathering, Ross recognized her and told her story.

Honor your free spirits. Another method is to give awards to the free spirits in the organization for breaking the mold and pushing their innovations. The Albuquerque office of the U.S. Immigration and Naturalization Service gives a Giraffe Award to people who "stick out their necks." The Department of Veterans Affairs gives out Scissors Awards to employees who cut red tape and improve efficiency.

Declare an amnesty. Stephen Cohen and Ronald Brand, authors of *Total Quality Management in Government*, recommend an organization-wide "amnesty" that signals that employees will not be punished for reporting that performance is poor. The amnesty encourages employees to "tell management the truth" about what is working and what is not.

Hand out forgiveness coupons. Dan Beard, former commissioner of the U.S. Department of Interior's Bureau of Reclamation, issued forgiveness coupons to his senior managers. They read: "It is easier to get forgiveness . . . than permission." Managers could cash them in when they made mistakes.

Protect your employees from punishment. It's not enough to permit or celebrate honest mistakes; it's even more important to protect employees from punishment. Butch Marita, a former regional leader of the Forest Service, understood that fending off vengeful Washington staffers was part of his job. Often, when Washington headquarters wanted him to punish an employee who had goofed up, he just ignored them. Typically, the pressure went away.

The economist John Kenneth Galbraith perfected this technique when he was director of the U.S. Strategic Bombing Survey in Europe, at the end of World War II. Gifford Pinchot III tells the story in his book *Intrapreneuring:*

> *Under his care were a few unruly mavericks whom he could count on to succeed at any task too tough for the military system. Unfortunately, these doers of the impossible had little respect for the system and were always in trouble. Galbraith received stacks of complaints urging him to discipline them.*
>
> *Galbraith knew that bearing down on them was out of the question, but he had to do something about the avalanche of complaints. He hit upon this solution: each time he received another complaint he would lift up his desk blotter, slip the complaint underneath, and forget about it. Soon the inevitable follow-up call would come: "Major Stuffed Shirt here, have you done anything about that impertinent So and So?" Galbraith would respond, "Funny you should mention that. I have your memo right in front of me on my desk. Rest assured I am handling it as it should be handled."*

Prepare the politicians for failure. One of the biggest fears in government is that failures will be made public—drawing ridicule or punishment from elected officials and the media. In a hostile environment, public officials ask, how can organizations be honest about their mistakes? When little that government does can be kept confidential, how do you engage in self-criticism that surfaces problems?

There are no easy answers to this. Cohen and Brand advise organizations undertaking quality-based improvement projects to limit how much self-criticism they put into writing. Another tactic is to package reports on mistakes together with reports on successes. When you have the politicians in to celebrate success, also acknowledge some failures in front of them. Even better, bring the politicians into the organization's change process and educate them about the fact that there will be failures as well as successes. If they develop some ownership of the changes, they will be more tolerant of failures.

Sometimes, you can announce mistakes before they happen. In the 1980s, Doug Ross created the first state government youth corps in Michigan. He anticipated that starting up the program in just two months—signing up 40,000 youths and putting them to work—would lead to problems. So he publicized a toll-free telephone number—inviting the public to let him know if they saw youth corps workers loafing or causing problems. When the calls came, Ross welcomed them. He did not have to defend the program, just improve it.

Reinvent the role of the auditors. Often it is not the politicians people fear but the auditors. When Vice President Gore began holding "town meetings" at federal departments in 1993, he found the employees' most bitter complaints were reserved for the inspectors general and their staffs, who stifled innovation by investigating every time someone deviated from the rules and regulations, regardless of their motives or results. Many leaders of the 300 reinvention labs that sprung up over the next few years were careful not to report in detail on what they were doing, for fear of the auditors. The solution, which Gore and his reformers have worked hard to achieve, is to reinvent the role of the auditors.

pp. 422–425

NEW RITUALS

***New Rituals* are special events that embody and reinforce the new culture. Repeated regularly, they give people new touchstones. When they are participatory, they also draw people in, helping them make the emotional commitments required by the new culture.**

The 1,000-member Phoenix Fire Department uses many rituals to shape its members' emotional commitments. One of the most important occurs when Chief Alan Brunacini hands a small red booklet, *The Phoenix Fire Department Way*, to new hires. It is the agency's Bible. On the cover is a space for the new firefighter's name. Inside are the commitments a Phoenix firefighter must make.

Like novices entering a religious order, the new firefighters commit publicly to follow "the way." It is all part of winning their hearts. "We deal with people very personally—intensely," says Brunacini.

> *We hold their hand. We tell them they're going to be okay, they're going to survive. Those are very primitive things, but they are very socializing. We put our hands on people.*

Like many organizations, the U.S. Defense Department's Defense Reutilization and Marketing Service has an annual meeting of its 100 or so top managers, to align the organization around the same vision and to plan strategy. When Captain Don Hempson ran the organization, two of the top brass—a different two each time—would appear at a key dinner dressed as "Reut Rabbit" and "Bucks-a-Billion Bunny." No one could tell who was under the costumes, but it didn't take them long to figure it out. The ritual, corny as it was, reinforced the sense of play Hempson wanted to create in an otherwise formal military organization. It also helped create a sense of family and teamwork within a world that was normally very hierarchical.

Not all rituals have to be participatory to be effective. In Minneapolis, Superintendent Peter Hutchinson appeared on the school district's cable television channel every weekday evening at 6 o'clock to read books to children. He started the ritual to communicate the enormous priority the district placed on improving student reading. "I probably read 100 books," he says.

Rituals sometimes mark organizational passages: endings, beginnings, even wanderings in between. The induction of Phoenix firefighters marks a beginning. In the late 1980s, the Minnesota Department of Revenue used a ritual to mark an ending.

The department was about to move to a new, much nicer office building. But many employees were grumpy about the disruption. They worried about being across the river, away from the restaurants. They worried about having to walk too far to catch their buses. They fretted about losing their current offices—even though the new building was a palace compared to their old one.

Finally, one of the managers got tired of all the complaints. He announced that they were going to have a "funeral" for the old building. He and others built a wooden coffin and got permission from the fire department to light a bonfire under it. They promoted the funeral throughout the department.

"We said, 'Bring symbols of the old Revenue Department and burn them,'" remembers Babak Armajani, then deputy director. "Then we're going to move across the river, and we don't want to hear any more about the move.'"

Employees responded enthusiastically.

> *People brought all kinds of stuff: memos, dead rats, furniture, you name it. It was a cold afternoon. People stood in line and threw stuff in. We burned it up, and everybody cheered. After that, there was no more bitching. People started saying, "When are we going to move?"*

You can make rituals out of almost anything: graduation and award ceremonies, annual meetings, homecoming ceremonies, holiday parties, speeches, even collective bargaining exercises. The key is the content: if possible, involve employees in something that helps them let go of the old culture or embrace the new.

INVESTING IN THE WORKPLACE

***Investing in the Workplace* upgrades the quality of the standard-issue working environment, which demonstrates a commitment to public employees.**

John Glenn tells an apocryphal story about orbiting the earth the first time. As he rode in the tiny space capsule, he says, it was a great comfort to know that everything keeping him aloft had been purchased from the lowest bidder.

In truth, NASA does not always buy from the lowest bidder. But many other public organizations do. The rule, for less exotic employers, is all too often, "Invest as little as possible in the quality of the government workplace."

"When I took over TAC, the appearance and upkeep of the aircraft in that huge fleet could most charitably be described as *shabby*," remembers Bill Creech. "In fact, in my first swing around TAC's many bases nationwide, I found lots of *eyesores* which had no place in an outfit that ever hoped to be proud and professional."

The problem is not limited to American governments. When Derek Volker became director of the Australian Social Services Department, he took one look at the carpeting in its hundreds of welfare offices and knew he had to do something about it. "It was a horrible *bluey* color that immediately stained once somebody dropped something on it," he says. "It was stained, looked horrible—but very, very good-wearing stuff. So it would last for five years, with all the stains all over the place, and with cigarette holes in it." He quickly replaced it with pastel-colored carpets that created a more cheerful atmosphere.

Employees read management's indifference to workplace quality as a signal that they, the workers, are not valued. This affects their attitude, reducing their sense of commitment to the organization and producing a culture of low expectations. Leaders like Volker and Creech make upgrading the workplace a central part of their culture change strategies. Creech was a fanatic on the subject: he had virtually every building in TAC repainted, he gave the mechanics new uniforms and cleaned up their facilities, and he launched programs with names like "Proud Look" to refurbish every part of the organization. (The joke was that if you stood on a corner at a TAC base for too long, you'd get painted brown.)

To change the pattern of chronic, debilitating underinvestment, public organizations must take a number of steps:

Figure out which changes will make the most difference to employees. Just as with customers, you can't assume you know until you ask. For some employees, it's not the office that matters the most. As we describe in Chapter

Ten, in the 1980s, the city of Madison, Wisconsin, bought new cars for its police department. The city was concerned about costs and saving fuel, so it bought small, fuel-efficient vehicles: Omnis and Horizons. But their engines were weak and they were too small for transporting arrestees or drunks. The officers hated them. "Nobody had asked the officers how they wanted their *offices* to look," says Michael Masterson, a captain in the department.

Find the money you need to invest in workplace quality. Figure out where you can save money, or what you're spending money on that you can abandon. "We funded [workplace investments] out of our many savings elsewhere, as our family of quality programs took hold," Creech says.

One way to reduce costs is to have employees do much of the work. When Creech had all TAC facilities repainted, TAC workers did the job. Creech joined the crew that painted his headquarters—generating a powerful story for the organizational grapevine. (They still call the color TAC used "Creech brown.") To hold costs down, he often had facilities refurbished and renovated rather than replaced. He even opened what he called "self-help stores," where employees could pick up wallpaper, paint, building materials, tools, brushes, and the like for free.

> *I had another rule: if the government paid for a new thing, I tried to have a 2–3 percent self-help component. Say I'm building a new squadron building; I complete it 98 percent, but I don't finish off the pilot briefing room and so on—and I give them the materials to finish it. So they own it. . . . Invariably when I would go into a building they would show me what they had done, not what the government had done for them.*

pp. 241–243

Another way to find money is to use shared savings: allow employees to keep budget savings they achieve and invest them in improving workplace quality.

pp. 415–422

Make government purchasing systems more employee-friendly. Adding fresh paint and changing carpeting doesn't take care of the systemic causes of underinvestment. You have to tackle the procurement process, which usually values low cost over quality and ignores what employees want. The Madison police built employee satisfaction into bidding specifications for new cars, police radios, winter boots, guns, and other equipment. When officers were given a voice in selecting their cars, says Masterson, their purchases consistently came in under budget while satisfying employees.

REDESIGNING THE WORKPLACE

Redesigning the Workplace **reinforces the emotional commitments you want, such as a sense of teamwork or a commitment to customer service.**

Derek Volker didn't just replace the carpets in his welfare offices. He also had the television sets in the waiting rooms moved. Usually the TVs were hung from the ceiling so clients could watch them and the service counter at the same time. In one office, however, the staff couldn't hang the set from the ceiling, so they put it on the wall across from the counter. Then they turned all the seats in the room around to face the TV.

"The tension in this office, which was a fairly difficult one, just dropped completely," says Volker. Clients "weren't worried about what was going on at the counter," he explains. "They were concentrating on the TV." This reduced the pressure on employees enormously. So Volker told all welfare offices to move their televisions onto the wall opposite from the service counters.

In Volker's case, redesign was a simple, almost accidental change. In other cases, it is a profound, well-thought-out restructuring of the basic relationships in the organization. Consider the story of Martin Raff and the U.K. Employment Service we told at the beginning of this chapter. By taking managers out of their offices and putting them in with their employees, Raff proved to employees how deep his commitment was to a less hierarchical, more teamwork-oriented organization. When managers go so far as to give up their offices, they earn enormous credibility for the new culture.

pp. 558–559

Minnesota's Department of Revenue conducted a major reengineering project in the early 1990s that required enormous cultural changes. Some supervisors who got excited about the new culture decided to attack the stress levels among employees who sat all day, wearing little rubber tips on their fingers, processing tax returns. First they created a "stress room," where employees could go at any time and listen to music. Management backed it completely. "We just said, 'Our supervisors will worry about it if people disappear,'" says Babak Armajani. Next they hired a full-time industrial nurse to deal with medical complaints. Then they turned one employee into a full-time "stress reliever."

"Among other things, she would carry a boom box with her, and every so often she'd walk into the processing room and tell everybody to stop working," remembers Armajani. "Then she'd turn on the boom box and lead them in five or 10 minutes of aerobics. People loved it, and it led to much higher productivity."

Finally the stress reliever convinced Armajani to turn a room in the basement into a gym. "We got sick leave way down, much lower than the rest of state government," he says. "We got an incredible return on those investments."

If you want to be sure to get employee buy-in, go one step further and give them control over workplace design. Quit telling them what they can do with office plants and coffee makers and the like. And if you have the courage, invite them to redesign their offices or shops.

Madison, Wisconsin, did this with its Experimental Police District, set up in 1991. The 38 volunteers who staffed it designed their own station, a one-story house renovated around an open-space plan. A three-year evaluation of the district by the National Institute of Justice found increased satisfaction with working conditions and increased interaction among employees.

INVESTING IN EMPLOYEES

***Investing in Employees* shows workers that management is serious about the changes it advocates, because it is investing in the employees' capacity to make those changes.**

See *Banishing Bureaucracy* pp. 239–298

To change your culture, we argued in *Banishing Bureaucracy,* you have to convince people to let go of their old paradigms, cope with the confusion they experience, and finally embrace a new paradigm—a new set of assumptions that revolve around customer service, innovation, continuous improvement, empowerment, and results. You are asking them to trust you enough to let go of the safety of their old paradigm.

Most employees will do this very reluctantly. They have heard their leaders talk about change for years. They have watched department heads get excited about searching for excellence, producing total quality, reinventing government, and reengineering processes. They know everything there is to know about fads. By now, they could be from Missouri, because their attitude is "show me."

If you really want the culture to change, in other words, you have to offer proof. One of the best ways to do this is to put your money where your mouth is: invest in helping employees develop the new skills and values they will need to succeed in the new culture.

Sunnyvale, California, offers a good example. Its culture is one of hard work and an intense focus on bottom-line results. It produces high stress levels. Yet most employees have fully embraced that culture. Why? In large part because Sunnyvale is willing to invest in them.

Union president Loren Wiser feels good about working for Sunnyvale, he says, even though "people are really pushed to the limit, and they don't get a lot of strokes around here." When we asked him the best thing the city had done in his 20 years to improve morale and performance, he talked about its training courses. Any employee can take any course for free—in management skills, customer service, even writing skills. "I've really benefited from this organization," he said. "I've taken a lot of training, and it's really helped me. I've had some really positive experiences—and it's that way for a lot of people."

But investing in employees means much more than training. The seminal study on what motivates employees identified seven factors, in the following order of importance: achievement, recognition, challenge, interest, responsibility, advancement, and salary and benefits.

Investing in employees means investing in all these things. To give employees greater opportunities for challenge, achievement, and advancement, you will need what is often known as an employee development program. In

Visalia, Ted Gaebler asked for volunteers to create the program, then trained them. They set up training courses, did career counseling, and even did internal consulting. Because it was run entirely by employees, the program helped staff members get out of their boxes and stretch themselves. It both facilitated and symbolized an important piece of Visalia's culture: the fact that good employees could move up very quickly.

Carol Cairns was a police officer when she volunteered to help create the employee development program. She ended up as the city's human resources director. And she was not alone: Gaebler also plucked his risk manager, his municipal services director, and his general services director from the police department. At the airport, he promoted the secretary to manage the place.

Every employee in Visalia knew these stories. It meant an enormous amount to them that employees who worked hard and showed an entrepreneurial bent could rise quickly to the top of the organization. This opportunity to rise as far as your talents can take you—this very real commitment to job mobility for employees—is one of the best ways we know to get *everyone* in the organization, from the top managers to the most junior secretaries, to commit to the new culture and give their all.

"Promotions are the lifeblood of an organization and have tremendous symbolic as well as actual impact," says David Couper, former chief of police in Madison. "Who gets promoted sends a louder message than any words from management. It sends a strong message throughout the organization as to the direction of the department and the values of top management."

In 1986, when Couper first surveyed his employees, the promotion process was their biggest concern. Given that feedback, he created a quality leadership council, made up of nine volunteers, to advise him and his management team on implementation of quality principles department-wide. It took on the issue of promotions as its first challenge. Led by a sergeant, it looked at public and private promotion processes and listened to people in the department. It then recommended an eight-step process for all promotions except to captain—including creation of a "quality leadership academy" that anyone applying for a promotion would have to attend. This meant Couper could no longer decide who would move up, but he signed on. "The chief gave up a tremendous amount of his discretion, his power," says Captain Mike Masterson.

BONDING EVENTS

***Bonding Events* develop powerful new relationships among groups of employees, based on trust, collaboration, and taking shared responsibility for producing results.**

On a Saturday morning in 1989, Peter Plastrik found himself sitting in a conference room with about 20 other employees of the Michigan Department of

Commerce. His heart was pounding and he felt very nervous. He didn't like what was happening, and he wasn't sure what was going to happen next. Looking around the room, he could tell that many of his colleagues—maybe all of them—felt the same way.

They were guinea pigs, a group that had volunteered to start addressing racial problems in the agency. Months earlier, a leadership team had identified relations between black and white employees as a critical issue that needed attention. Black employees felt they were subject to various forms of discrimination. Plastrik (who is white) and others had arrived that morning to work with a facilitator, C. T. Vivian, a minister and legend of the civil rights movement. No one knew what to expect, although word had gone around that Vivian's style was "confrontational."

An hour into the meeting, Plastrik would have said that "confrontational" was an understatement. He felt verbally assaulted by the aging, wiry black man. Even humiliated. Years later, he remembered the painful feeling, although not all the details. Vivian had subjected the white members of the group to harsh questioning. Were they racist? No? How could they say that? How did they know? What did they really know about black people and their condition in America? Where did they get their ideas about black people? He had thundered at them for what seemed like hours. They were winners in a society that victimized blacks. They only knew blacks as stereotypes. Vivian seemed to have an endless stream of angry accusations and tricky questions.

Occasionally, Vivian turned to the blacks in the room for affirmation of his views. They seemed unsure about how to react, but they did not deny what he said. "The level of intensity was pretty much set for everybody—black folks as well as white folks," recalls Willard Walker, the agency's personnel director (who is African American). "It was total exposure, even for those of us not directly challenged in any way except to sit through it and watch C. T.'s process. I didn't like watching the pain; it was not nice."

Several people, including a black man, walked out of the meeting and did not return.

When the group broke for lunch, Plastrik was seriously depressed. He dreaded going back in for more punishment. He considered leaving, but did not. Over the food, no one talked much. After a while, they filed back into the meeting room. The chairs were arranged in a horseshoe, and Plastrik sat at one of the ends.

When everyone was seated, Vivian came over and stood in front of Plastrik and asked him to stand up. When he did, Vivian took his hands and held them. He looked Plastrik in the eyes and said softly, "I ask you to reconcile with me." Plastrik did not understand. Vivian explained briefly that he wanted Plastrik to forgive him for the morning's treatment—that it had all been done to make

Plastrik feel just a small bit of the oppression that is a daily burden for blacks in America and that is unknown to most whites.

When Plastrik told Vivian that they were reconciled, Vivian moved on to the next person in the same manner, then worked his way around the room. The tone of the meeting changed miraculously. Everyone talked about the experience and their feelings. The awful pressure in Plastrik's chest eased.

The meeting proved to be a breakthrough. It led to a prolonged, often intense and candid dialogue between black and white employees about their racial relations. "Those who sat through it were the better for it," says Walker.

> *We felt a responsibility to put the relationships among us back together again. That was the strength of the whole thing. We all felt the pain—but we did a decent job of talking about it after C. T. left. We didn't try to pretend it didn't happen. The strength of the experience was when we tried to set up communications after C. T. left. We carried the dialogue forward.*

The participants developed and implemented a plan to improve racial relations. "The trust, discussion, and dialogue that were built enabled us," Walker says. They got the agency to commit to new strategies for minority recruiting, promotions, and mentoring. And leaders invited all other employees to attend Vivian's training, if they wanted to.

"Those people heard stories about what had happened," Walker says. "There was peer pressure on them to go, too. They thought, 'If I don't do this, I may not be viewed the way I want to be viewed by my colleagues.'"

The retreat with C. T. Vivian built bonds that were still powerful half a dozen years later. "The results of that experience are still with many of us," Walker notes. "It still sustains our relationships. You can tell by the way we greet each other and continue to come to each other when things are going wrong."

The Power of Bonding Events

A bonding event is a way of jump-starting or hastening the process of building emotional bonds in an organization. Not all of them are emotional battlefields. In Chapter Thirteen we discussed "critical mass events" such as large-scale, real-time strategic planning. These are bonding events, too. They bring employees together to work on the organization's direction. Some—but not all—of that work involves making new emotional connections.

pp. 549–553

Bonding events do not even have to involve the organization's work: you can take employees off to do other work that builds new emotional bonds. For example, Xerox has had teams of employees spend a day building a house for poor people in their community. Its leaders think this is valuable because employees get to build something of value, the company communicates its commitment to helping others, and the employees bond with one another during the work.

The most valuable bonding events happen when you put real time, energy, and care into them. Not every bonding event has to involve the tension and drama that C. T. Vivian provided—but they do have to create emotional risks, to get the participants to make significant new emotional commitments.

The Michigan Commerce Department experience illustrates several key elements of successful bonding events:

They overcome the workplace taboo against showing and dealing with emotions. Most employees leave their emotions at the door when they get to work. "We spend years and years editing our emotions at work—for very good reasons," observes John Johnson, a longtime organizational development consultant.

> *If we show them, we get into trouble. People can get demoted, fired sometimes, or shunned by others. So the work setting is essentially nonemotional. Usually, it is not an intimate community.*

Bringing emotions out into the open and working with them is not easy and often risky, but it is absolutely necessary. "If you want people to join together, then they must begin to buy into the dreams and deep commitments of the person next to them," says Johnson.

They overcome the lack of trust, respect, and acceptance that divide people in most organizations. "Trust glues people together," says Steve Kaagan, a consultant, professor of leadership development, and former Vermont commissioner of education. "If there isn't mutual trust, there's no lubrication for bonding."

During bonding events, group members build trust by learning to respect and accept one another. "Trust is built by consistently respecting other people's fundamental humanity," explains Kaagan.

> *During the process, you uncover people's individual gifts, honor them, and use them. It's amazing to see. You've worked with each other for years, and you know so little of each others' gifts. Suddenly, you're in a group that knows what you can bring to the table, that appreciates each others' gifts. That's key to creating a sense of belonging.*

They build a strong sense of personal responsibility for shared goals and efforts. After their encounter with C. T. Vivian, each of the Commerce Department participants wanted to work on the problem of bridging racial relationships in the agency. They had different ideas and feelings about what should be done, but they took responsibility for making something happen together. "When this happens," says Kaagan, "you get tremendous emotional energy."

The ABCs of Bonding Events

John Johnson describes the process of bonding as a "journey you take with other people, a direction you go in together." A bonding event "quickens the process." It gets individuals "to experience each other in moments of substantial challenge and stepped-up emotions. They experience handling each other's emotions and helping each other take on the challenge and survive." There are many ways to make this happen. Johnson has taken groups on canoe trips for several days in the Boundary Waters of Minnesota. He has also had groups do gourmet cooking for one another at his home. Some organizations, such as Outward Bound, specialize in creating bonding experiences for teams. They take groups sailing, mountain climbing, or hiking together for a week or two.

The key to a bonding event is to challenge people in ways that open up and change their hearts. First, people must get away from work for a prolonged period. When the Michigan Commerce Department decided to take a leadership group off for a breakthrough retreat, its consultants said four days would be required. This seemed excessive to Plastrik, who was designing the event. But as it turned out, every minute of the four days was necessary.

Second, you must create an emotionally safe environment in which people can try out new ways of relating to one another. "People need practice at this," says Kaagan. "Building new emotional bonds doesn't happen naturally in organizations; you have to try it out and see the outcomes." Usually, a trained facilitator is needed to make the bonding environment safe and to keep it that way. "No greater wounding can take place than to have this emotional opening up followed by repression," says Kaagan. "Everyone in an organization can give you chapter and verse about this happening: 'I tried it once, I opened up, and later someone came in and stepped on my face, and I haven't said a word since.'" The facilitator makes sure this doesn't happen.

Obviously, the boss must be on board. The leader's behavior during a bonding event is crucial. Is he receptive to or defensive about what is said? Is she willing to examine and change her behaviors? Every move the leader makes will be interpreted by others in the group. These signals can build trust or destroy any hope of building trust.

Third, you must create structured challenges for the group that remove barriers between members and give them compelling opportunities to work together. This, too, usually requires the help of consultants skilled at designing group dynamics. Good facilitators have an enormous kit of group exercises that can be used to design the bonding event. Some challenge participants' perceptions of one another and of themselves. Others require participants to solve problems that force them to work in new ways with their colleagues.

Fourth, you must be ready for what can happen when the lid comes off. Often people vent their anger, resentments, or anxieties. David Couper, the former police chief in Madison, Wisconsin, remembers the anger that spewed out when he first met with employees to find out how they thought the department should change: "It was like dealing with a foster child, an adopted child, saying, 'I'm going to be bad to see if you really love me or not, Dad.'"

Venting is natural in people who have kept their emotions tightly reined for years. "People need an opportunity to vent at authority," Kaagan says. "They need some kind of escape valve, a chance to get things off their chests. Once that's done, you can get on with the real business."

A key part of the real business is to get people to overcome their fear of voicing concerns about the organization and about other members of the group. "People need air time, they want to be heard," says Kaagan. They need help naming dangerous issues such as racial or gender discrimination and then discussing them.

Just as important, they must learn to listen to one another. "People also want to know that they were heard. It means a lot to them when others hear the content of what they're saying, then can play it back to them, and take responsibility to build on what they said, not just go off in their own direction."

As participants build trust during bonding events, they begin to see one another in a different light. They learn to be more accepting of one another, instead of assuming the worst motivations on the part of others. They realize that other people can change. And—slowly—they learn to take responsibility for the health of the group, not just for their own well-being. Participants stop waiting for someone else to take act; they stop being bystanders.

"The process creates a different relationship between the I and the we," says Kaagan.

> *Every I is joining to form a we. People start feeling a collective responsibility. You can see it in their words and bodies. They start to attack tasks together. Nobody sits back. You can feel the excitement.*

Finally, you must organize the follow-up. The event accelerates the journey, as John Johnson says, but it is not the entire journey. Before people leave the event, they should make commitments about what they will do together when they get back to the organization. There is always the risk that nothing will happen because of the distractions of the daily grind. The group needs to anticipate this problem and figure out how it will keep its momentum going.

RESOURCE ON BONDING EVENTS

Stephen S. Kaagan. *Leadership Games: Experiential Learning for Organizational Development.* New York: Sage Publications, 1998. Kaagan gives readers 25 useful exercises to employ in bonding events.

SENDING VALENTINES

***Sending Valentines* is a group exercise in which employees tell other work units what they would like them to do differently. It helps them speak the truth to one another without getting hung up in workplace rivalries and antagonisms—and to change their commitments to one another.**

This tool, described by Robert Jacobs in *Real Time Strategic Change,* breaks down barriers between people in an organization and builds powerful commitments among them.

At a meeting, people in each unit in the agency create wish lists of changes they want other units to make. As Jacobs explains, these "valentines" list the things others need the unit to do differently in the future so that the entire organization can better meet its customers' needs. For example, line employees might tell the procurement office they need supplies when they order them—not six months later. They might tell the maintenance shop they need their vehicles fixed right the first time. Participants sign and post their valentines on a wall under the name of the appropriate department.

Then the departments read the valentines they have received. This is the first tricky step in the exercise, because most units will react defensively. Typically, a consultant coaches participants in how to prepare non-defensive responses and how to deal with other people's defensiveness. Jacobs describes what often happens next:

> *You pass the Valentine sheets around and read them, vent your frustrations and note who sent which Valentines. . . . It's not easy for people to make the shift from blaming others to taking responsibility for your function's contribution to the problems plaguing the entire organization. . . . You finally break through. It is at this point that the message becomes very clear. The only way to bring about significant change across the organization is for everybody—including you—to make it happen, to start* **doing** *things differently.*

As a result, units begin to commit to some of the changes the valentines requested.

The process offered employees in Sedgwick County, Kansas, "an opportunity to say things to each other that often wouldn't be said otherwise," says Jerry Harrison, an assistant county manager.

> *The way it plays out it's not a "gotcha." Instead it's more like "Let me help you so you can help me. . . ." People really didn't realize the impact they had on other departments, but when they kept getting the same messages from all over the county it became easier to see these themes and became harder to ignore them all. . . . The messages are so clear that something clicks and you see the world differently.*

And that is what culture change is all about.

RESOURCES FOR SENDING VALENTINES

p. 553

Robert W. Jacobs. *Real Time Strategic Change.* San Francisco: Berrett-Koehler, 1994. We recommend Jacobs' excellent book in Chapter 13. The section on sending valentines is on pp. 84–85.

Chapter 15

Winning Minds

Changing Employees' Mental Models

***Winning Minds* forges among employees a common understanding of the organization's purpose, roles, goals, values, beliefs, and situation. Together, employees create new mental models of where the organization needs to go and how to get there.**

In Madison, Wisconsin, in the mid-1980s, the chief of police started talking with his top managers about changing the organization's way of doing business. Chief David Couper drafted a document called "Quality Leadership," in which he spelled out the major principles of a new management style. Further discussion with his management team led to the development of 12 principles for supervisors and managers, many of them derived from Edward Deming's 14 points for quality management.

Within a few years, Couper embedded the principles firmly into the organization's consciousness by requiring police officers to attend a two-week course on quality leadership to qualify for promotion. His police officers learned specific values for leading people in the agency because their career advancement depended on it.

Values and beliefs are ideas about how things should be or are. Quite often the words *value* and *belief* are used interchangeably, although they mean different things. A value is a statement about desired behavior. You can value innovation, telling the truth, teamwork, or compliance with rules. A belief is a statement about how you think the world works. For example, many teachers believe that "all children can learn."

Our values and beliefs come from our parents, our religions, our schools, our peers, people we admire, and our culture, notes Charlotte Roberts, a consultant with Innovation Associates. "Many go back to childhood; we take on others as adults." For all practical purposes, values and beliefs lead to the same

MADISON'S 12 QUALITY PRINCIPLES

1. Improve systems and examine processes before blaming people.
2. Have a customer orientation and focus toward employees and citizens.
3. Believe that the best way to improve the quality of work or service is to ask the employees who are doing the work how and listen to their responses.
4. Be committed to the problem-solving process; use it and let data, not emotions, drive decisions.
5. Be a facilitator and coach. Develop an open atmosphere that encourages providing and accepting feedback.
6. Encourage creativity through risk taking, and be tolerant of honest mistakes.
7. Avoid top-down, power-oriented decision making whenever possible.
8. Manage based on the behavior of the 95 percent of employees who do not cause problems, not on the 5 percent who do. Deal with that 5 percent promptly and fairly.
9. Believe in, foster, and support teamwork.
10. Through teamwork, develop with employees agreed-upon goals and a plan to achieve them.
11. Seek employees' input before you make key decisions.
12. Strive to develop mutual respect and trust among employees; drive out fear.

place: to behavior. As James Kouzes and Barry Posner say in *The Leadership Challenge*:

> *Values help us determine what to do and what not to do. They're the deep-seated, pervasive standards that influence every aspect of our lives: our moral judgments, our responses to others, our commitments to personal and organizational goals. Values set the parameters for the hundreds of decisions we make every day.*

Most public sector organizations have strong bureaucratic values: obedience to authority, compliance with rules and procedures, and deference to hierarchy. These values are built into the design of bureaucratic control systems. Although they may clash with some people's personal values, they have great power throughout the public sector. People take them to be givens, like the air they breathe. They adapt to them. Bureaucratic values stimulate and reinforce a host of behaviors—waiting for the boss's orders, avoiding risks, ignoring the benefits of collaboration.

In Madison and in many other places around the globe, reinventors have worked aggressively to instill new values and beliefs, because they hold the key to changing organizational culture.

THE POWER OF GOVERNING IDEAS

See *Banishing Bureaucracy* pp. 262–277

Values and beliefs are two of an organization's "governing ideas," the compelling concepts that guide its behavior. Others include the organization's mission; its vision; its assumptions, or "givens"; even its language. As we explained in *Banishing Bureaucracy*, governing ideas have power because they become part of people's "mental models." Everyone has mental models—their understanding of how the world works. Through these inner models, we perceive and make sense out of reality.

To change an organization's governing ideas, you must change its members' mental models—one by one. This involves a process of inquiry, discovery, and reflection. Sometimes the shift takes a long time, particularly if many people are involved. But for individuals, if often occurs suddenly—as if the scales have fallen from their eyes.

Consider the experience of Bob Stone at the Office of the Secretary of Defense (OSD). When he was appointed deputy assistant secretary of defense for installations in 1981, Stone says, "I was a believer in centralized management."

> *I'm not sure that I thought very much about centralization versus decentralization; I just thought that if you were in trouble, you added more management, more controls, more briefings. So I got the deputy secretary of defense, Frank Carlucci, to direct my boss to design and evaluate a central command that would own and operate all military bases.*

This would move all military bases and depots into one organization, where Stone and his staff thought they could introduce more professional management and economies of scale. But it flew in the face of what General Bill Creech was preaching and practicing in the air force. "The services hated it," Stone recalls.

> *The air force went really ballistic. So they hijacked me. My predecessor had badgered the air force into setting up a mini version of what I was trying to do in San Antonio, Texas, because it has four major air force bases and one major army base. I wanted to visit San Antonio and see how it worked. So the air force offered to fly me down there. And I was really surprised by that, because they weren't really trying to help me at all.*

When Stone boarded the plane at Andrews Air Force Base, his escort, Colonel Bud Ahern, informed him that they had to make a stop at Langley Air Force Base in Virginia, headquarters of Creech's Tactical Air Command. When they got to Langley, the plane developed mechanical problems. So Ahern suggested they have a look around. Creech was away, but Ahern ushered Stone into the office of his vice commander, Lieutenant General John Piotrowski. And Piotrowski proceeded to give Stone what he later came to know as "the Creech briefing." Complete with charts and graphs, it showed the TAC's decline through the 1970s, then its abrupt turnaround after Creech arrived and began decentralizing the command, breaking up functional silos, giving the pilots and mechanics ownership of their planes, empowering them to make their own decisions, and comparing squadron performance. Piotrowski described Creech's philosophy of empowering teams and holding them accountable for results, Stone recalls, "in almost magical terms."

See *Banishing Bureaucracy* pp. 53–56

> *He said, "We believe in having pilots with red scarves flying airplanes with red tails, maintained by mechanics with red caps." Creech had the red squadron, the blue squadron, the green squadron, and so on. Piotrowski also showed me the numbers. The safety record was up, flying hours were up, average hours to fix a broken airplane were down. You looked at their data—hours between accidents tripled, time to get a part from supply into a plane down from four hours to 11 minutes—it was just obvious they were on to something. I was just sold. I saw the future, and it worked.*

Stone experienced a classic paradigm shift.

> *I just saw that it was right. It was a gestalt. I've had experiences in engineering: I once made a discovery that was very important in a very, very narrow and specialized field of heat exchanger design. In its world it was important. And it just hit me in the face. I was working, and suddenly there it was. I showed it to my boss, and he was amazed by it, and then pretty soon we couldn't understand how we could not have always known it, because it was so obvious. That's the sort of feeling I got.*

Stone returned to the Pentagon and told his deputy, Doug Farbrother, who was conducting the study to justify their centralized installation command, what he had found.

> *And he started yelling at me. He said, "Mechanics in red caps and pilots in red scarves—have you lost your mind?" He was quite angry.*

> *But Creech did a frontal assault on Doug. He invited Doug down to Langley, or summoned him, as I think Doug put it.*

Like Stone, Farbrother was a scientist by background and a centralizer by habit. "My training is as a mathematician," he says.

> *I was an operations research person when I first came to the Pentagon—which is all about mathematical modeling. So I was very much dependent on analytical solutions and numerical analysis. And I had never had a job outside of Washington, so all of my natural thinking, plus the people I was surrounded with at headquarters, led me to be an advocate of central control and economies of scale. We had also been rewarded for being tough on our subordinates. What we were famous for, both Bob and me, at OSD, was coming up with clever reasons for why what the services wanted in their budgets was nonsense.*

Farbrother had just been to England and Germany to look at their centralized installation commands.

> *In both countries I saw the same thing: When I talked with the people from PSA or STOV [the British and German installation commands], they talked in theoretical terms about the advantages of this kind of organization, but had no numbers to prove that things were cheaper or more efficient. When I talked with the military commanders who were being supported by them, their jaws would redden and their faces tighten and they would spit as they spoke about the support they were getting from these organizations. One cornered me in a hanger and stabbed me in the chest and said, "Don't do this to my American friends."*

Still, Farbrother gave little credence to the base commanders' views. "I'm sure it was a classic example of evidence being right under my nose, and me not being able to take it in," he says. But Stone had given him Tom Peters and Robert Waterman's *In Search of Excellence,* which he happened to read on the way down to Langley to see Creech. And it had begun to open his mind.

Farbrother had been told that Creech "was the most powerful general in the air force—the only reason he wasn't chief of staff was because he didn't want to be in Washington; politics wasn't his game. So I was intimidated before I got there."

> *Creech, while he's not a large man, or charismatic, is meticulous in his appearance and bearing. And I showed up in my usual slovenly attire.*

> *It was an intimidating experience, walking down there and going into his presence. And the first thing he said to me was, "You've got the dumbest damned idea I've ever heard."*
>
> *So here I am, feeling like a punk kid in the presence of the most powerful general in the air force. He's spending all his time trying to convince me my idea was the dumbest thing that ever came around. And he had a briefing that really would move an analyst. He called it his slippery slope briefing. It was a series of trend charts showing the years before he took over and the years since. It was a V-shape.*
>
> *He had gone to lengths to explain why it wasn't other factors—was it more money; well no it wasn't. Was it more training for pilots; well, no, it wasn't. They all showed that in the years he had been there, he had doubled TAC's capability to fly and fight, without adding resources.*
>
> *He said, "The key is pride. Pride is the fuel of human accomplishment, so you've got to give people something to be proud of." And that's why he was such a nut on great-looking buildings and grounds, and had the airmen fix them up themselves. And he used competition—breaking up what he called "communist maintenance" into three units and having them compete.*
>
> *In that one and a half hours, I had a humbling emotional experience, and some convincing charts shown to me. It changed the way I looked at everything. I heard years later the words* paradigm shift, *and I think that's what happened. I could see all this evidence that I couldn't see before. And I understood why numerical analysis is so lacking, in a way I couldn't see before.*

See *Reinventing Government* pp. 132–135

p. 431

Stone and Farbrother proceeded to kill the centralized installation command and began spreading the gospel according to Creech. They took their staff off on retreat and together crafted a values statement called "The Principles of Excellent Installations," which they circulated in every way they could dream up, worldwide. They collared influential people and dragged them down to Langley for the briefing and tour. They addressed every military group or class they could find. They eliminated thousands of pages of regulations and set up a "Model Installations Program" and a "Unified Budget Test" to give base commanders the flexibility they needed to improve their operations. In other words, they did everything they could to spread the new paradigm they had learned from Creech.

We have told this story at length because it illustrates almost all five elements we have found in the process of shifting mental models:

1. Opening minds by dislodging old mental models.
2. Introducing new mental models.
3. Collectively building new mental models.
4. Creating new touchstones.
5. Spreading new mental models through teaching.

Creech and Piotrowski used performance data to pry open Stone's and Farbrother's minds—the first step in the process of conversion. Often, new experiences do the trick, but as Farbrother's experience in Europe showed, someone with a strong paradigm will ignore or deny the validity of contradictory experience. For some people, rational processes such as briefings or benchmarking data are necessary.

Creech and Piotrowski didn't just open Stone's and Farbrother's minds, however; they then laid out a new mental model, the second element. As Stone says, "It was numbers, and they really hung on a picture, which is this pilots in red scarves, flying airplanes with red tails, maintained by mechanics with red hats. I not only had the data, but here's the theory: these guys are all one team with one product." There are many tools one can use to introduce new models, from briefings and courses to learning groups and site visits.

The third element is probably the most important part of converting an organization: a collaborative process to create new mental models. This is what Stone and Farbrother did when they took their staff off to write a values statement. It can also be done through the collective creation of mission and vision statements or through critical mass events, like large scale, real-time strategic planning.

pp. 549–553

This step is so important because an organization's culture changes when its members change their minds *together.* It is not enough for a few leaders to change their mental models—the rest of the organization must, too. Leaders must learn how to bring their members together so that many minds will be working on the organization's challenges, not just a few.

As you create new shared mental models, often you will want to codify them in ways that provide new touchstones for everyone in the organization. Mission, vision, and values statements play this role after they are written—although this role is not as important as the one they play in shaping the collective culture as employees help create them. Many leaders also create new language, as a way of providing new touchstones. This is because the very words we use are inextricably linked to our mental models. Unless we change what they mean—or better yet, use new words—we cannot communicate about new ideas.

Finally, most successful leaders of culture change do not stop at creating the new governing ideas. They work hard to *spread* them, through tools such as in-house schoolhouses and orientation of new members.

The point is not to unfold these five elements in order. Changing culture is a process of person-by-person conversion. Different people will change at different times, for different reasons. So you need to keep using these and other tools continuously.

Often one tool will perform several functions. When Stone and Farbrother made their site visits to Langley, for instance, Creech and Piotrowski both opened their minds and introduced them to new mental models. Learning groups can do the same thing.

Whatever tools you use, there are two fundamental instructions to keep in mind. First, you must get employees genuinely involved in changing their minds; you can't really do it to them. The point is to create mental *commitment* to new ideas, not just *compliance* with them. Second, the new governing ideas must be connected to behaviors. It isn't enough to simply espouse the ideas; they must be lived. To help along the process of turning thought into action, reinventors should use the tools of the Consequences Strategy to reward the behaviors they want.

pp. 149–246

RESOURCES ON WINNING MINDS

Joel Arthur Barker. *Paradigms: The Business of Discovering the Future.* New York: HarperBusiness, 1992. The seminal work on shifting paradigms.

James M. Kouzes and Barry Z. Posner. *The Leadership Challenge.* San Francisco: Jossey-Bass, 1995. A good book on leading cultural change, with useful treatments of visioning, values, rewarding new behavior, and many other topics.

Peter Senge, Charlotte Roberts, Richard B. Ross, Bryan J. Smith, and Art Kleiner. *The Fifth Discipline Fieldbook: Strategies and Tools for Building a Learning Organization.* New York: Doubleday, 1994. A tool book that amplifies the basic ideas of Senge's *The Fifth Discipline.* It contains an entire section on changing mental models.

Douglas K. Smith. *Taking Charge of Change: 10 Principles for Managing People and Performance.* Reading, Mass.: Addison-Wesley, 1996. Contains useful insights on changing an organization's mental models.

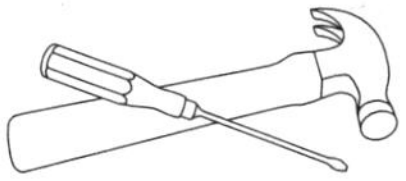

TOOLS FOR WINNING MINDS

Benchmarking Performance compares the performance of different organizations, in this case to dislodge outdated mental models by undermining faith in the old ways of doing business. See below.

Learning Groups and Site Visits change employees' minds by helping them learn new things together. The groups undertake disciplined study processes and site visits—identifying what they want to learn, who they will learn with, and what they will do with what they learn. See p. 592.

Creating a Sense of Mission develops a widely shared understanding of an organization's basic purpose. It captures this understanding in a brief statement that serves as a beacon for the organization, guiding its people's decisions. See p. 596.

Building Shared Vision develops a "picture in words" of the future that employees seek to create through the organization—their collective image of what the organization is there to accomplish. See p. 599.

Articulating Organizational Values, Beliefs, and Principles allows organizations to create and adopt nonbureaucratic standards for behavior that guide their members' actions in the workplace. See p. 602.

Using New Language replaces the language of bureaucracy—its phrases, metaphors, and vocabulary—with a language that reinforces more entrepreneurial assumptions and ideas. See p. 606.

In-House Schoolhouses educate and train change agents to become carriers of the new culture. See p. 608.

Orienting New Members teaches incoming employees the organization's mission, vision, and values—the basic mental models that are shared throughout the agency. See p. 609.

BENCHMARKING PERFORMANCE

When Bill Creech and John Piotrowski converted Stone and Farbrother, their best weapon was data. Several years earlier, when Creech took the helm at the TAC, he quickly began setting up decentralized models, measuring their performance, and comparing it to the rest of the TAC. He used this data to undermine the mental models of Defense Department officials who supported the centralized approach he was trying to change. The data showed huge variations between the performance of different wings that performed the same functions. The centralizers, who assumed that as long as the resources and training were the same, performance would be about the same, couldn't explain it. "That attracted lots of attention throughout the nationwide organization," Creech reports. "Everyone was scratching their heads, trying to explain it. . . . The old conditioning began crumbling."

pp. 210–214

Benchmarking has many forms and functions, and one of those functions is to undermine old mental models. It's hard to defend current practices when data proves they are inferior to the alternatives. Phoenix, which was named one of the two best-managed cities in the world a few years ago by Germany's Bertelsmann Foundation, has for years benchmarked against 10 other southwestern cities, including Dallas, Houston, Albuquerque, and San Diego. Whenever they want to improve a city service, the auditor's office or department heads check to see how it compares to the same service in the other cities. They do it so often that many units have begun to do it themselves, just to keep track of where they stand and how they could improve. It is one of many tools that make Phoenix's city government a learning organization.

RESOURCE ON BENCHMARKING PERFORMANCE

Patricia Keehley, Steven Medline, Sue MacBride, and Laura Longmire. *Benchmarking for Best Practices in the Public Sector.* San Francisco: Jossey-Bass, 1997. A useful guide to performance benchmarking in the public sector.

LEARNING GROUPS AND SITE VISITS

***Learning Groups and Site Visits* change employees' minds by helping them learn new things together. The groups undertake disciplined study processes and site visits—identifying what they want to learn, who they will learn with, and what they will do with what they learn.**

In the U.K., the West Midlands office of the Employment Service often sends employees on site visits. In 1992, four employees traveled across America for nine days, studying how public agencies and businesses were using Total Quality Management (TQM) to improve their performance. They met with nine organizations and logged more than 6,000 miles in the air—in the U.S. alone. Already in their third year of implementing TQM, they needed to learn more than they could in the U.K., where it was not in wide use in the public sector. During one visit, they unexpectedly learned about another tool—large-scale, real-time strategic planning—that became an important part of their change effort.

pp. 549–553

Every year, the City of Charlotte, North Carolina, takes up to 100 community leaders to another city for a site visit. They focus on a problem or opportunity they face in Charlotte, and they visit a city that has dealt with it successfully. They take business leaders, city government managers, community leaders, and elected officials from the city, county, and school district. The bonding they do while traveling together is one of the site visit's most important benefits, says former mayor John Belk. "You get to know people much better," he explains. "You get everybody talking the same language."

In the London borough of Bromley, Robbie Stokes, the director of leisure services, uses site visits *within his agency* to help employees percolate ideas. "We have 'away days,' in which people will visit other areas, where they will present what they're doing," he says. Library staffs visit recreation programs; landscape specialists visit libraries. During the visits, "People will start asking, 'Why can't we do that in our area?'"

Hampton, Virginia, sends "venture teams" to other cities that are on the cutting edge. Phoenix, Arizona, has a study tour budget, so it can send a team on a site visit whenever it needs to. Palm Springs, California, set up a regular "Palm Springs Pirates" group, which visited a new place every month and stole as many good ideas as it could.

Taking people to see something for themselves is always more powerful than telling them about it or having them read about it. People are not only exposed to new concepts, they *experience* those concepts in action. They talk to leaders, employees, customers, and stakeholders. They get a visceral feel for the new reality. As Jim Flanagan says about Phoenix's study tours, "Lots of times when you read it, it's one thing—but when you go there, it's another."

According to Bob Stone, General Creech's ideas "jumped species" to the army because General Carl Vuono, then commander of the army's Training and Doctrine Command, next door to Langley, Creech's headquarters, wondered why so many people who visited his command stayed over at Langley. The reason was Creech's fanatical commitment to quality facilities and quality equipment. The guest quarters at Langley were immaculate, the best in the military. Vuono finally drove over to see for himself. "He got a tour," says Stone, "and he became a believer."

When Stone became director of Vice President Gore's National Performance Review, he fought hard to make sure Gore's first trip was to Langley. "It was wonderful," he remembers.

> *General Loh had an awful lot of charts that he briefed Gore on. I was afraid Gore was going to be irritated, but he was really captured by them. And then they walked around, and Gore and his staff talked to young pilots and mechanics. I think he was there a total of maybe three*

and a half hours. He started talking about it a lot. When we had our reinventing government summit with corporate CEOs, he insisted on having Mike Loh there. He wanted Loh to be the last person to speak in the last session of the day, because he wanted to punctuate the day with the Air Combat Command, which he saw as an example of government working well.

Stone believes the site visit is the single best way to convert people. "It's showing people examples of success," he says.

Group site visits have several benefits. First, they expose people to new ideas and, sometimes, to whole new paradigms. Second, they give people an opportunity to analyze and discuss what they are learning—and its relevance for their organization—as they are learning it. And third, they help people bond as a team. Done well, a site visit not only gives people powerful images of alternative futures they could create, it also gives them the emotional bonds necessary to take on the job.

Sometimes leaders use site visits to teach their employees about the challenges they face rather than about models of success. Doug Ross took his top managers at the U.S. Employment and Training Administration (ETA) to world-class companies to see firsthand the kind of skills ETA's customers—unemployed workers—would need to get good jobs.

The success of site visits depends on selecting the right place to visit, selecting the right team, and preparing the team and visit. When 100 people from Charlotte visit another city, for example, an enormous amount of preparation is necessary. "You can't afford to have that many people go and then screw it up," says Belk.

Debriefing is also critical. It gives team members a chance to figure out just what they have learned and what they could apply back home—and to begin making plans to do so.

Site visits are time-consuming and expensive; fortunately, they are not the only way to introduce groups to new ideas. Joann Neuroth used a learning group to bring TQM to the Michigan Commerce Department. She led a team of 18 employees, who met for one hour a week for many months to learn the tools of TQM and group facilitation. They read and discussed articles and books, tried small projects, and received training. As a result, she and some of her group became the quality champions who convinced much of the organization to try TQM.

The U.K.'s Inland Revenue Department uses what it calls "action learning" courses for senior managers. Each course starts by bringing roughly 20 managers together from different places in the organization, for three days. Led by a consultant, they use the Myers-Briggs assessment tool to profile their work styles, then discuss their strengths, weaknesses, and the like. Then comes the "action" part: they break into groups of six, which meet monthly to discuss books, videos, and ideas. Each group defines a research project focused on some challenge facing the organization.

Steve Banyard, who described this tool to us, was in a group that studied cultural change in large, dispersed organizations. They visited large private companies, especially those that had been recently privatized, to find out what they had done to change their cultures.

"The point is to study it, but not too academically—very much with a bias for action," says Banyard. Part of the "idea is to take these people who are specialized, like engineers, and give them a broader focus—to get them to look at what we do and why. It usually leads to a more participatory leadership style."

Tips for Learning Groups and Site Visits

Make it clear that the organization is willing to invest in the learning group—and expects a return on its investment. Organizations should give learning groups permission to work together during paid time, to signal that the learning is valued.

Define clear deliverables for each learning group. Organizations must be clear that the group is not, as Neuroth puts it, "just out to entertain itself." It should have clear deliverables—new knowledge that other members of the organization want. Many organizations ask learning groups to write reports for the rest of the employees. That's a good idea, but it's even better to ask them to make presentations to top management and other employees (using "brown bag" lunches, for example). This puts pressure on the group to get very clear about what it has learned.

Study something that is likely to transform your thinking. Don't go on fishing expeditions. Figure out what you really want to learn—what might help you improve your services or reinvent your organization.

Learn things you can put to use. Neuroth advises that groups focus on learning things that would change their own practices. All too often, she cautions, they learn interesting things but then conclude that "no one in the organization will let us do it."

Ensure diverse participation in study groups. Neuroth's group drew volunteers from many different units in the department. The West Midlands team included the regional director, a local office manager, a quality facilitator, and an employee with frontline experience. This kind of diversity enhances a group's learning, since different people bring different perspectives and skills to the study process. It also increases the group's credibility with the rest of the organization.

Be disciplined about your course of study. Learning about something that is important to the organization is worth doing well. Plan carefully how you will go about it. Spend time mapping out your agenda—identifying topics, resources, and methods for learning.

CREATING A SENSE OF MISSION

Creating a Sense of Mission **develops a widely shared understanding of an organization's basic purpose. It captures this understanding in a brief statement that serves as a beacon for the organization, guiding its people's decisions.**

When Doug Ross became head of the U.S. Education and Training Administration (ETA), he asked most employees he met what their mission was.

> *Most of them described their individual jobs to me. They had no sense of what the organization was supposed to make happen on the outside. They were not connected to their customers' needs. They existed solely within their walls.*

Unfortunately, the ETA was more the norm than the exception; tunnel vision is pervasive in public organizations. It is a legacy of the bureaucratic model, which assumes that workers need only know their jobs, while managers worry about higher-order concerns.

Lack of knowledge is hardly the only problem, however. As we discuss in Chapter Three, many government agencies receive ambiguous, confusing, or conflicting missions from elected officials. Hence it is difficult for anyone to pinpoint their real mission. And even when leaders try to clarify the mission, employees often don't internalize what they are told. If they are handed the mission from on high and expected to memorize and repeat it back, they usually don't make it their own. They may learn to *espouse* it, but not to *embrace* it.

pp. 108–110

The main vehicle for creating a shared sense of mission is to develop a mission statement—new language that conveys the organization's purpose. Although the words are important, it is the process of creating them that makes the difference. You can hang an eloquent statement on the walls and even print it on employees' business cards, without getting employees to use it as their own. To do that, you must involve them in creating, testing, and using it.

There are several keys to tapping the full power of a mission statement:

Focus only on what is most important. Many authors and practitioners have taken a crack at explaining the purpose of a mission statement. Peter Drucker writes simply that "a mission statement has to focus on what the institution really tries to do."

Make it brief. "It must be succinct enough that people can hold it in their minds," says Joann Neuroth. If you can keep it under 20 words, do it.

Make it inspiring. What can be memorized must also be worth remembering. "It's got to really excite you. It has to have some passion in it," says Neuroth.

Make sure it provides guidance to employees. "It must be specific enough that you can steer by it—figuring out which things to do and which not to do," says Neuroth. To illustrate the point, she tells a story from a Michigan school district.

During a workshop in the fall of 1993, teachers in the Lakeview schools decided that one purpose of their organization was to help students become "thoughtful learners." Those two words grabbed their attention. Ensuring that students thoughtfully steered their own learning "was a goal worth achieving. It excited them; it lit them up," says Neuroth.

And it provided guidance. "They said, if we *really* thought that was what mattered, almost everything we do in schools would have to change." On the spot, they started thinking about their work as if the mission did matter. The curriculum would have to change; so would student assessment practices. Teachers couldn't just cover the material in textbooks; they would need new instructional practices.

Involve employees in crafting the statement. When General Michael Loh wanted to create a new mission statement for the 150,000–employee Air Combat Command, he took his top 90 officers on a three-day retreat. "I wanted to come out of there with a shared common mission, and I wanted our

MISSION STATEMENTS: PITFALLS TO AVOID

- ***Plain-vanilla statements.*** If it's uninspiring, if it doesn't differentiate the organization from others, if it has become what Drucker calls "a hero sandwich of good intentions," don't use it.
- ***Statements that are too global.*** If it's too general and vague—if just about any decisions or actions could fit the mission—it won't provide useful guidance.
- ***Statements that are too narrow.*** If some employees cannot see themselves and their work in the mission statement, it will make them feel unimportant and unneeded.
- ***Statements that are too wordy.*** If it's too long, if it fails to boil the mission down to its essence, no one will remember it.

people to create it," Loh says. Before they convened, Loh asked participants to send him their versions of the new mission. His staff synthesized them into 16 different statements. At the retreat, Loh broke the participants into four groups and gave each of them all of the statements. "You can use these, or you can throw them away and come up with your own," he told them, "but each group should come up with a mission statement." As the groups worked on the task, each boiled their ideas down into one statement. Then they discussed the final four as a whole group. Overnight, Loh took the four statements and synthesized them into a single statement. He took this back to the officers:

> *I said, "Okay, here's a version that I think captures what we think all of you wanted." They kind of tinkered with that a little bit, and then I said, "I want to take one more step. This is 90 percent [completed], but take it back to your people and show it to them and see if you get any people saying 'bullshit.'"*

After getting some feedback from the units, Loh adopted the statement:

Air Combat Command—Our Mission

Air Combat Command professionals
providing the world's best combat air forces
delivering rapid, decisive airpower
anytime, anywhere

A top-down process like this can work, as long as employees get a real opportunity to provide feedback. But in smaller organizations, you can let the employees write the mission statement themselves.

This is what the Michigan Department of Commerce did in 1989. Its leaders asked a group of employees—professionals and secretaries, veterans and relative newcomers—to tackle the assignment. Initially, employees were bewildered by the task. Finally a manager asked them, "What is the one word that, if it were true about our department, would make you feel really good about working here?" That broke the logjam: there were many responses, including *community, flexibility, innovation.* Gradually the team warmed to the task and began drafting a statement. Then it invited other employees to join in. After several months, the group brought a draft back to the top managers, who liked it and said they would market it to the rest of the organization. But the rank-and-file team insisted that *it* wanted to lead the process of getting feedback, because it would have more credibility with the organization.

The team met with individual units to share the statement, answer questions, and listen to suggested changes. Then they surveyed the organization, asking people to rate several features of the statement—its clarity and accuracy, for instance—on a scale of 1 to 5. Before conducting the survey, they decided that if at least two-thirds of the employees rated the statement a 4 or a 5, it would be adopted. They did, and it was. At an all-employee ceremony several weeks later, the team distributed T-shirts with the new mission statement printed on the back:

> *We support and promote an economic development environment that increases business investment, job creation and retention, and the state's overall economic competitiveness. We do so to improve the standard of living and quality of life for the people of Michigan.*

Use your mission statement in day-to-day management. You want it present in the *minds* of your people—not just in their line of sight, on the walls. The best way to make sure this happens is to use the mission statement to drive the development of organizational goals, indicators, and plans.

Periodically revisit the mission statement. Ask your organization if it still reflects the basic purpose and motivates employees. If not, have them update it. Treating the mission statement as a living document keeps employees engaged with the question of organizational purpose.

BUILDING SHARED VISION

***Building Shared Vision* develops a "picture in words" of the future that employees seek to create through the organization—their collective image of what the organization is there to accomplish.**

Some leaders are famous for their visions, their sense of direction for their community. Thomas Jefferson, Abraham Lincoln, Franklin Roosevelt, and Martin Luther King Jr. come to mind. They painted pictures of what America—and the world—should become. Other politicians, such as former President George Bush, became famous for not having any compelling vision.

Expecting our government leaders to have a vision of the future is nothing new. But the notion that a public *organization* should have a vision is. In the bureaucratic paradigm, it doesn't matter whether an organization's employees share a sense of direction or not. To do their jobs, they need only know the organization's rules and procedures. Thus, most public employees are never invited to dream about what their organization might accomplish or become.

"A vision is a mental picture of what tomorrow will look like," explain James Kouzes and Barry Posner in *The Leadership Challenge.* Visioning creates concrete images of what the organization will look like, be doing, and accomplish some span of years ahead.

James Eason, mayor of Hampton, Virginia, points out that many athletes try to improve their performance by "picturing the successful completion of moves they want to make." A golfer pictures the shot she wants to make; a basketball player pictures the free throw going in. Organizations do the same thing, collectively, when they build shared visions.

A vision is an ideal and an aspiration, not a prediction. Why is this beneficial? One reason is that shared vision inspires people. The idea of achieving something worthwhile motivates them.

A second reason is that vision disturbs the status quo. The picture of an organization's desired future stands in contrast to the organization's current reality. People see the gap and—as long as the distance does not seem impossible to bridge—begin working to close it.

A third reason to build shared vision is that it gives focus to people's energies. When people share a vision, they align their diverse activities to achieve a common future. When an organization's energies are focused in this way, it is much more likely to achieve its goals.

How to Build Shared Vision

In many organizations, a leader provides the vision. He or she goes off somewhere to think and write down the vision, then comes back and tells everyone what it is. The problem with "telling the vision," as consultant Bryan Smith notes in *The Fifth Discipline Fieldbook,* is that it rarely becomes deeply shared by the organization's members.

Many leaders go beyond merely telling the vision, Smith adds. They also negotiate, sell, and test their vision with employees. They invite people to raise concerns about their vision or even to offer amendments. Or they consult with people about what they like and don't like about the vision and then revise it accordingly. In these ways, leaders build broader buy-in for their visions. But there is a much more powerful way for a leader to build a truly shared vision: start the visioning process with the employees, not the leader. Co-create a shared vision.

Co-creating a vision is an enormously challenging process, particularly for leaders who assume that their role is to *provide* the vision. They must shift their paradigm of leadership to one in which leaders *help* organizations develop collective visions that speak deeply to their members. The process is also quite challenging for employees, because it is often unlike anything they have been asked to do before.

The process begins by asking employees to articulate their deepest desires for their own future. What do they dream of achieving? What do they want, and why? What, in other words, is their personal vision? This matters because, as Senge explains, "If people don't have their own vision, all they can do is sign up for someone else's. The result is compliance, never commitment."

When groups of people do this work, they usually find that they share many of the same personal aspirations: happiness, having good families and communities, making a difference in the world, and so on.

In the next step, employees build their shared personal visions into a vision for the organization. To do this, they must first develop key information about the organization. They must be clear about the organization's mission. They must know key trends that may influence the organization's fate. They must study the organization's past and its future. And they must have some awareness of alternative ways of organizing to accomplish their work. Otherwise, their imaginations will be limited by the bureaucratic paradigm they have experienced.

Given this information, employees begin to picture a future organization that will be true to its mission *and* will help employees realize their common personal visions. Integrating personal visions with organizational vision is neither simple nor quick, but it is crucial. "When a shared vision starts with personal vision, the organization becomes a tool for people's self-realization, rather than a machine they're subjected to," says Smith. "Only then can they wholeheartedly participate in guiding its direction."

Out of this process emerge concrete pictures of the organization's desired future. These images should answer questions like the following: How does the organization produce value for its customers and stakeholders? What is its unique contribution to the world? What is the impact of its work? What does the organization look like? What do its people do? How are decisions made? What incentives are in place?

At this point, the emerging vision should be put on paper. The task is to imagine that it is some time in the future—perhaps 5 or 10 years forward—and the organization you desire has in fact been created. Now write a description of it. Then write a short summary or even a slogan that captures the future organization's essence. (For example, Hampton's vision is to become "the most livable city in Virginia.") The full vision statement should appeal broadly to the organization's many stakeholders, and it should keep people focused on the future. Test it with stakeholders, then embrace it publicly as an organization.

See *Banishing Bureaucracy* pp. 248–249

Finally, *use it.* Decide how you will measure progress toward the vision and how you intend to make that progress.

Other Tips for Building Shared Vision

Make sure the vision is relevant to people throughout the organization. Employees must be able to see themselves participating in and benefiting from the future organization.

Tell the truth about the organization's current reality. "Anything less than the truth can destroy credibility," warns Bryan Smith. If, for instance, leaders try to squelch negative information about the organization's situation, employees will conclude that they are not serious about the exercise.

Paint concrete details, but not too many. Don't write a full-scale novel, just enough detail to give people a motivating picture.

Honor the organization's past. Show employees how the vision builds on the organization's history or why it must depart dramatically from the past. If you don't, they may feel that the vision demeans their current work and performance.

Link the visioning process with the development of organizational mission and values, if those don't exist. A vision does not stand in isolation. It can't be created without knowing the organization's mission. And it calls into question what the organization's values are—what standards should guide behavior. "A vision not consistent with values that people live by day by day will not only fail to inspire genuine enthusiasm," Peter Senge warns, "it will often foster outright cynicism."

RESOURCES ON VISIONING

John P. Kotter. *Leading Change.* Boston: Harvard Business School Press, 1996. One of the best books on leading organizational transformation, this contains two excellent chapters on creating and communicating organizational vision.

Peter M. Senge. *The Fifth Discipline: The Art and Practice of the Learning Organization.* New York: Doubleday, 1990. Chapter 11 is a masterful account of the art of visioning and its value to organizations.

Peter Senge, Charlotte Roberts, Richard B. Ross, Bryan J. Smith, and Art Kleiner. *The Fifth Discipline Fieldbook: Strategies and Tools for Building a Learning Organization.* New York: Doubleday, 1994. A tool book that amplifies the basic ideas of *The Fifth Discipline.* It contains many exercises and tips for vision building.

ARTICULATING ORGANIZATIONAL VALUES, BELIEFS, AND PRINCIPLES

***Articulating Organizational Values, Beliefs, and Principles* allows organizations to create and adopt nonbureaucratic standards for behavior that guide their members' actions in the workplace.**

In the late 1980s, Don Forbes, then head of Oregon's state highway division, called the state police in to investigate what he suspected was unethical behavior. The investigation led to the indictment of almost 20 low-level employees and managers for petty theft. The experience was traumatic enough that the organization's leaders began looking for ways to rebuild the culture around a commitment to common values.

In 1991, Forbes was promoted to director of the entire Department of Transportation. He decided to define the organization's values and train all employees in how to use those values as guideposts when making decisions. He called the initiative "Pride in Public Service," and it became one of the four pillars of his philosophy of "shared leadership," along with performance management, team-based management, and an employee development program.

"As teams are out there having to make more decisions, people have to have skills to deal with that," Forbes told us. "Otherwise, you have chaos." One of those skills is knowing what is permissible and what is not. "In the absence of that values guidance, you could have teams out there making what they think are very good decisions, but [those decisions] could get us in very serious trouble, because they didn't consider the legal context or whatever."

Forbes hired a consultant, who helped the organization put together "a fairly straightforward decision-making model and an acronym that goes with it, as a memory device for people. We came up with Decision PLUS":

> ***P** is for policies*
> ***L** is for legal*
> ***U** is for a universal set of ethical principles*
> ***S** is for self*

The organization trained all employees to ask themselves if their decisions were consistent with departmental policies, with the law, and with a list of key ethical principles such as honesty, integrity, fairness, excellence, and accountability. If a decision passed those tests, Forbes says, then the final question was, "Does it pass the butterfly test? That is, do you feel good about it yourself?"

Forbes says this approach has penetrated at least through the organization's management: "I've found now, after some reinforcing, that whenever we get together, once a month, someone will say, 'I was looking at this, but it didn't pass my PLUS test, so I didn't go with it.'"

Craig Holt, who ran Forbes's Office of Productivity Services, goes further:

> *Pride in Public Service is our backbone. I used to think measurement was; now I think values are. They're the golden thread that you can hang everything on. Because enabling the mission is about making decisions and carrying those forth. And values are all about enabling people to make the decisions. If you know all the values of the organization, then you know you won't get fired for making the decision. So it allows you to move real quickly and not spend a whole lot of time wondering about the ramifications.*

When organizations align their collective values with their members' values, they experience a significant payoff. Citing their 15 years of research involving thousands of public and private sector managers, Kouzes and Posner identify the following impact that shared values can have:

- *They foster strong feelings of personal effectiveness.*
- *They promote high levels of company loyalty.*
- *They facilitate consensus about key organizational goals and stakeholders.*
- *They encourage ethical behavior.*
- *They promote strong norms about working hard and caring.*
- *They reduce levels of job stress and tension.*
- *They foster pride in the company.*
- *They facilitate understandings about job expectations.*
- *They foster teamwork and esprit de corps.*

Making Values, Beliefs, and Principles Effective

Creating an organization's statement of values or principles has to start with its leaders, but it cannot end there. Employees must have a chance to participate—to think about, discover, discuss, test, and refine these values, beliefs, and principles. This is a lesson that Kouzes and Posner learned the hard way:

> *Many senior executives have taken the shared values message to mean that they should go off on a week-long retreat to formulate a corporate credo, then return home and announce it to constituents. We confess to having once been advocates of this exercise. Experience has taught us, however, that no matter how extensive top management's support of shared values is, leaders can't impose their values on organizational members. Consensus about values is more difficult to achieve than clarity, and without consensus it's hard to get consistent implementation of values throughout an organization. Leaders must be proactive in involving people in the process of creating shared values.*

In their book *The Reengineering Revolution,* Michael Hammer and Steven Stanton describe what happens to most values statements created by management alone:

> *First, management distributes a memorandum communicating the new values. When this goes the way of all memos, the next phase centers on*

> *plastering large posters and wall banners everywhere. In the terminal phase, the values statement is printed on wallet-size laminated cards that are distributed to everybody in the organization. . . .*
>
> *We have a collection of these cards, which we have gathered in our travels over the years. They represent a touching affirmation of management's belief in the power of cliches to alter and modify behavior. . . .*
>
> *Sometimes, at our seminars, we take out our laminated cards and read these bits of wisdom aloud. The response is always the same—gales of laughter from the audience. And when we ask the attendees why they are laughing, once again the response is uniform: "They are so empty." "It's all mush." "They don't mean anything."*
>
> *These are very serious indictments, but it is also notable what people are* **not** *saying. Nobody is saying that these values are wrong. Quite the contrary, the thematic consistency suggests that their authors are onto something. In fact, customer focus, teamwork, personal responsibility, speed, innovation and the like are* **exactly** *the values required. . . . No, the little laminated cards are not wrong. . . . The problem is actually much worse. The weakness is, as our attendees recognize, that's all they are—laminated cards. The noble principles printed on them are empty words, backed by nothing whatsoever.*

How do leaders go beyond the laminated card stage? There are a number of critical steps:

Get employees to articulate and discuss their own personal values and beliefs. As with vision, people who are unclear about their personal values are not likely to feel a strong commitment to any organizational values.

Have employees identify which personal values and beliefs they share broadly. Usually some common values will be readily apparent.

Identify the key behaviors that the shared values or principles imply. This is where the rubber meets the road. Employees must articulate which kinds of behaviors are now valued and which they want to see disappear.

Assess how well the organization follows its values and beliefs. Ask employees to what degree actual behavior in the organization reflects the shared values and behaviors they desire. Use this assessment to make people conscious of the key behaviors that need to be improved and as a benchmark for measuring progress. You can do this as part of a broader organizational assessment.

Identify important organizational barriers to real adoption of the shared values. Sometimes individual managers undermine the shared values because they don't walk their talk. Sometimes the organization's administrative control systems undermine them: budgeting, personnel, procurement, and auditing. Unless you are able to change these managers' behaviors (or remove them) and change the offending administrative control systems, all your work on values will be in vain. In fact, it will be worse than useless, because it will create cynicism about your motivations and sincerity.

pp. 404–426

Reinforce the values. Some organizations use rewards to promote their values—celebrating the desired behaviors. Others, like the Oregon Department of Transportation, train their people in how to make decisions in line with the organization's values. The Madison Police Department requires such training for promotion.

pp. 583–584

Connect values and behaviors to real consequences. If people can get away with behaving in ways that violate the organization's shared values, then articulating these values will make little difference.

Don't forget about the customers and stakeholders when you articulate values. Some organizations just look inward, at how employees should treat one another, when they think about their values. This is a mistake. It ignores values like customer service, which can transform an organization's mental models.

RESOURCE ON ARTICULATING VALUES AND BELIEFS

James M. Kouzes and Barry Z. Posner. *The Leadership Challenge.* San Francisco: Jossey-Bass, 1995. A good book on leading change, with an excellent chapter on values.

USING NEW LANGUAGE

***Using New Language* replaces the language of bureaucracy—its phrases, metaphors, and vocabulary—with a language that reinforces more entrepreneurial assumptions and ideas.**

Many organizations find that working with new ideas requires them to develop new language, because the very words they use are inextricably linked to their mental models. As Ted Gaebler once said, "Our words will think our thoughts for us, so we've got to change our words."

When Doug Ross became director of the Michigan Department of Commerce in 1984, the state's economy was in terrible shape. The collapse of the auto industry had triggered prolonged double-digit unemployment. To Ross, economic development was an exciting, noble calling, a challenge that required risk taking and innovation on the part of government. But the Commerce Department he inherited was a classic bureaucracy. Like most public employees,

Ross says, the department's workers had "a bit of an inferiority complex." They thought of themselves as bureaucrats.

One way to change people's mental models, Ross thought, was through their language—the words they used to describe their world. He decided to invent a new language for the department. "We needed some analogies, to help us figure out which behaviors were important," he remembers. "That's when we came up with the metaphor of Michigan economically being an industrial park." Using this image, Ross told the organization that its role was to manage the "industrial park" on behalf of its stockholders, the citizens.

> *This made it clear that we weren't the ones that created economic value; that we didn't run the businesses in the park. Our responsibility was to make sure that the occupancy rate in the park was high enough [and] that it was filled with good-paying jobs so that residents who also lived in the park could be gainfully employed.*

As the metaphor took hold, it led to new thinking. "It quickly became clear that we had very specific customers: current tenants of the park and prospective tenants. And therefore, to succeed, we had to become very customer focused." The department came to see itself as a supplier to businesses; it redesigned its offices "to look more like other businesses that served our customers." It adopted a slogan—"Our customers are our reason for being"—and put it up on the wall, in huge letters, in the place where people entered the department. It consulted with private development firms to find out how they kept real industrial parks full.

Ted Gaebler used language in exactly the same way when he was city manager of Visalia, California. He wanted people to think more like entrepreneurs than bureaucrats, to ask themselves, "If this were my money, would I spend it this way?" So he talked about the city as a corporation, himself as its CEO, and the council as its board of directors. He used terms like *product lines, profit centers, business reports,* and *annual corporate report.* "It was important to talk a different language—very important," he says. "You've got to get yourself rid of the tar baby of bureaucratic words and images—get that stuff off of you—before you get more entrepreneurial behavior."

Total Quality Management and performance management often have a similar impact. People start talking about *customers* and *value-added work* and *outcomes* and *outputs*.

Tips for Using New Language

Don't impose new language; help the organization develop it. As with any new approach, people will buy into new language far faster if they help develop it themselves. Leaders often need to catalyze this process, but they should seize on and reinforce new words and phrases that employees come up with. They can even devote group sessions, such as parts of retreats, to mutual explorations of new language.

Change the titles people use. In Region 9 of the U.S. Forest Service, employees signed their letters and memos with their team name. The Michigan Commerce Department changed the name it uses to refer to staff members who work with businesses from "industrial agents" to "account representatives."

Use slogans and mottoes. Just a few well-chosen words can convey deep meaning. In the U.K.'s Employment Service, former chief executive Michael Fogden explained, "We have a phrase: 'We own the business now.' Not the bureaucrats or the ministers. It's our business. We actually made a video called 'It's Our Business.'"

Change the organization's visual language. In 1985, the government of Bromley, a London suburb, created a new visual image for itself. The old image "used a lot of symbols like the coat of arms, which our customers said gave us an old-fashioned and bureaucratic look," public officials explained. So they had a new corporate logo designed—a bright green brush stroke they call "the Bromley splash."

Publish a glossary or owner's manual. The Surrey County Council in England gave employees a glossary about managing change that included 44 unfamiliar words and terms. It included definitions of terms such as *accountable, business plan, customers, mission statement, proactive, strategic direction, values,* and *vision.*

Name the beast. The flip side of this tool is using new language to put names on facets of the organizational culture that people are afraid to discuss. For example, in many organizations distrust is rampant, but most employees consider it too dangerous to discuss, at least with management. Fear is another common taboo, racism a third. When leaders bring taboo subjects like these out into the open, they can make it safe to confront them. Once people begin talking about these things, they lose some of their power and become far easier to change. It is a basic principle of psychology that a person can't change an aspect of their personality unless they first recognize it and accept it. The same is true of organizations.

pp. 575–581

IN-HOUSE SCHOOLHOUSES

***In-House Schoolhouses* educate and train change agents to become carriers of the new culture.**

Many organizations train their employees, even if only slightly. But only a few organizations train them to become cultural change agents. This is the purpose of the "in-house schoolhouse." It is a transformational tool. It does more than provide professional development or job skills training, although both are important. It reorients employees' thinking about the organization and its work—and prepares them to spread the gospel.

One of the most impressive examples we know is the Quality Center at the Air Combat Command (ACC). The ACC school has trained thousands of change agents in TQM and leadership. In 1995, for example, more than 600 senior officers attended two courses: a one-day immersion in the organization's leadership philosophy and a two-day session to learn the team approach to quality improvement. A much smaller number of employees spent a week in "train the trainer" classes designed to help them conduct quality training throughout the organization. At least 85 people performed this training function. After they took the courses, they returned to their units and conducted courses.

The in-house schoolhouse was a crucial part of General Michael Loh's effort to change the ACC culture. "We're talking about 150,000 people out there," he said. "You don't do this overnight."

Smaller organizations also create this kind of capacity. The city government in Madison, Wisconsin, ran a series of courses intended, among other things, to make quality improvement principles and practices a part of daily work life for its employees. Although many courses involved basic skill building, others taught the organization's values and quality principles and methods.

ORIENTING NEW MEMBERS

***Orienting New Members* teaches incoming employees the organization's mission, vision, and values—the basic mental models that are shared throughout the agency.**

In bureaucratic organizations, new employees usually receive some sort of orientation to familiarize them with their job and its duties. Sometimes they get an employee handbook that lays out the organization's rules. But the organization usually makes no effort to familiarize the employee with its governing ideas—its mission, vision, and values.

In entrepreneurial organizations, governing ideas are crucial touchstones for employees new and old. Organizations such as the Phoenix Fire Department, the Sunnyvale city government, and the U.S. Forest Service invest heavily in preparing incoming employees to fit in with the culture they are entering. Some organizations use a formal orientation process—for instance, a day of training on the organization's thinking. Others assign mentors to show new employees the practical and mental ropes of their new workplace. As Chapter Fourteen describes, Phoenix's fire department turns its orientation into a formal ritual.

p. 569

The best time to shape an employee's mental models is on his or her first day. This is probably the best investment you can make in culture building. Given normal attrition rates of 5–10 percent a year, every seven years you bring in close to half of your employees.

Appendix

General Resources

Throughout this book, we have included resource boxes to point you to other books, reports, Web sites, and similar resources on particular tools. Here we would like to call your attention to several more comprehensive resources on reinvention.

The Public Strategies Group

David Osborne is a managing partner of the Public Strategies Group (PSG), one of the nation's foremost consulting firms specializing in reinvention. Made up of experienced public sector practitioners, it is led by CEO Babak Armajani, coauthor of *Breaking Through Bureaucracy.* PSG has worked with clients throughout the nation and the world: local governments, state agencies, federal agencies, school districts, and special districts. In addition to hands-on consulting, the firm offers speaking, seminars, and workshops on a variety of topics related to reinvention, and it produces workbooks and other products for use by practitioners. PSG also operates a network of other consulting firms with expertise in various aspects of reinvention, called the **Reinventing Government Network**.

Address:	275 E. 4th St., Suite 710 St. Paul, MN 55101
Phone:	(651) 223–8371
Fax:	(651) 292–1482
E-mail:	reinvent@psgrp.com
Web sites:	www.psgrp.com; www.ReinventGov.com

The Reinventing Government Workbook

In 1998, Jossey-Bass Publishers brought out a workbook designed to introduce frontline employees to the basic ideas of reinventing government. Authored by David Osborne and Victor Colón Rivera, it includes segments on each of the 10 principles outlined in *Reinventing Government,* by David Osborne and Ted Gaebler. To order, contact Jossey-Bass Publishers.

Address:	350 Sansome St. San Francisco, CA 94104
Phone:	(800) 956 7739
Fax:	(800) 605 2665
Web site:	www.josseybass.com

The Reinventing Government Video

David Osborne and Ted Gaebler have produced a one-hour video designed to introduce people to the basic ideas of reinventing government and help them grasp its potential. Done in documentary fashion, it intersperses insights from Osborne and Gaebler with four stories of fundamental reinvention: the Air Combat Command, competitive contracting in Indianapolis, public school choice in Minnesota, and tenant management at the Cabrini Green public housing development in Chicago. The video is available from Video Publishing House.

Address:	930 North National Parkway Schaumburg, IL 60173–9921
Phone:	(800) 824–8889 (708) 517–9744
Fax:	(708) 517–8752

National Partnership for Reinventing Goverment (NPR) Resource Guide

In October 1996 the NPR published a resource guide for reinventors, *Reaching Public Goals: Managing Government for Results,* chock full of useful organizations, publications, periodicals, and Web sites. Four years later, it is still useful. You can find it on-line, at www.npr.gov/library/review.html (scroll down to "Background Papers and Other Reports").

Web Sites on Reinvention

Over the past five years, many Web pages have been created to offer information on reinvention and related topics. We have cited some of them in our resource boxes and endnotes. Our favorite comprehensive Web pages are the following:

The Public Strategies Group: www.ReinventGov.com.
Our own web site is our favorite place for reinventors to gather on the web. It features additional material that builds on this book; previews of future books; answers to your questions from the most experienced practitioners in the field; links to other organizations and web pages involved in reinvention; articles by David Osborne, Peter Plastrik, and other PSG thought leaders; and on-line diagnostic and "how-to" tools that will help you apply the strategies, approaches, and tools in this book.

The Public Innovator Learning Network: www.Alliance.napawash.org.
Full of hundreds of brief case studies, the Learning Network Web site is a good place to start any search for information you need to help you reinvent. Whether you want to know how to measure performance or how to listen to your customers, you will find brief essays, case studies, bibliographies, and links to more information, all available free of charge. You can also jump with the click of a mouse into other useful databases, such as those of the National Partnership for Reinventing Government, *Governing* magazine, and *Government Executive* magazine.

The National Partnership for Reinventing Government: www.npr.gov.
Since it was formed by Vice President Gore in 1993 (as the National Performance Review), the NPR has posted a series of useful reports and other information on the Web. You can find past NPR reports, surveys, press releases, as well as long lists of resources on reinvention.

The Oregon Progress Board: www.econ.state.or.us/OPB.
The Progress Board's "Website Sampler" is a comprehensive list of other useful Web sites on reinvention, to which you can link with the click of a mouse. In addition, it has information on Oregon's pioneering Benchmarks effort, which we described in Chapter One.

pp. 13–18

The British Service First Initiative: www.servicefirst.gov.uk.
The British government has put an enormous amount of useful information on the Web, including many practical how-to guides for managers. The best place to begin to access this network of information is on the Service First (formerly the Citizen's Charter) Web site. It also includes a list of other useful Web sites around the world.

The New Zealand State Services Commission: www.ssc.govt.nz.
New Zealand's State Services Commission has published a series of extremely valuable reports on the status of reinvention there, as well as discussion papers looking at key challenges New Zealand still faces.

The Canadian Treasury Board Secretariat: www.tbs-sct.gc.ca.
The Treasury Board secretariat's Web site includes a number of subsections devoted to public sector reform that include how-to guides, reports, papers, and links to other sites. For a good starting point, click on "Policies and Publications."

The Australian Department of Finance and Administration (DOFA): www.dofa.gov.au.
Similarly, DOFA's Web site includes subsections on public sector reform. Try www.dofa.gov.au/scripts/services2.asp?Id=239 for discussion papers and reports.

The Organization For Economic Cooperation and Development's Public Management Service (PUMA); www.oecd.org/puma/pubs; and www.oecd.org/puma/online.htm.
PUMA's Web site has a variety of papers on public sector reform in OECD countries, many of them available on-line, as well as links to national Web sites of interest.

Notes

All quotations that are not attributed in the text or in these endnotes are from interviews with the authors or their associates. Only in cases where there might be some confusion about the source of a quotation have we indicated in a note that it came from an interview.

Introduction

P. 5 "Canada's national government . . . since 1950": Interview with Peter DeVries, director of the Fiscal Policy Division of The Canadian Department of Finance.

P. 5 "Twenty-seven American states . . . public school choice": "Choice of Schools: State Actions," *Clearinghouse Notes,* June 1999 (newsletter of the Education Commission of the States).

P. 5 "In the U.S., nearly 1,700 charter schools . . . school year": "CER Charter School Numbers Are In," *About Charter Schools,* www.edreform/charters.htm (Web site of the Center for Education Reform), 1999.

P. 5 "In England, 20 percent . . . in the U.S." Office for Standards in Education (OFSTED), *Secondary Education 1993–97: A Review of Secondary Schools in England* (London: The Stationery Office, 1998), ch. 1: available at www.ofsted.gov.uk/ (click on "Publications," then "OFSTED Publications 1996–2000").

P. 5 "Every state in the U. S. . . . measure performance": *Budget Processes in the States* (Washington, D.C.: National Association of State Budget Officers, October 1999).

P. 5 "In a 1997 survey . . . their citizens": Barry M. Feldman, "Reinventing Local Government: Beyond Rhetoric to Action," in *The Municipal Yearbook 1999*

(Washington, D.C.: International City/County Management Association, 1999), pp. 20, 24.

P. 5 "... surveys show that public confidence ... begun to rebound": "Americans Gain a Small Measure of Confidence in Government," *The Washington Post*, March 24, 1997; and *Findings from a Research Project About Attitudes Toward Government* (Washington, D.C.: Council for Excellence in Government, 1997).

P. 9 Roger Douglas quotes: Roger Douglas, "The Politics of Successful Structural Reform," unpublished manuscript, pp. 40, 42.

Chapter One

P. 13 "As Governor Barbara Roberts ... with $130 million": Interviews with Michael Marsh, former budget director for Governor Roberts, and presentation by Governor Roberts at advisory board meeting of Alliance for Redesigning Government, Denver, May 27, 1994.

P. 13 "Employment in the state's lumber ... 55,000 in 1982": Governor Neil Goldschmidt, *Oregon Shines: An Economic Strategy for the Pacific Century—Summary* (Salem: Oregon Economic Development Department, May 1989), p. 4.

P. 13 "By 1987, state wages ... below it": Ibid., p. 6.

P. 13 "They called for ... several decades'": Ibid., p. iv.

P. 15 "Governor Goldschmidt's successor ... consistent with the Benchmarks": Interviews with Governor Roberts and Michael Marsh, former budget director; presentation by Governor Roberts at advisory board meeting of Alliance for Redesigning Government, Denver, May 27, 1994; and Governor Barbara Roberts, *Urgent Benchmarks and the 1993 Legislature: Opportunities for Progress* (Salem: Office of the Governor, February 1993).

P. 15 "So the Department of Economic Development ... a brief action plan": Interviews with Director Bill Scott and Duncan Wyse, former executive director of the Oregon Progress Board.

P. 15 "When the State Police ... their basic assumptions": Interviews with Major Lee Erickson, Duncan Wyse, Michael Marsh.

P. 16 "Outside state government ... funding decisions": Oregon Progress Board, *Oregon Shines II: Updating Oregon's Strategic Plan, A Report to the People of Oregon* (Salem: Oregon Progress Board, January 21, 1997), p. 24.

P. 16 "Six counties ... steering organizations": Interviews with Jeffrey Tryens, Oregon Progress Board executive director, and Beverly Stein, Multnomah County executive.

P. 16 "With a combination ... 81 percent by 1997": *Oregon Baby Shots Survey, 1997 Preliminary Results: Descriptive Analysis* (Salem: Oregon Health Division Immunization Program, 1999). Based on a random survey of 18-to 36–month-olds in 1997, eighty-one percent had all required immunizations and 87 percent had almost all; 77 percent of two-year-olds had all immunizations. Lorraine Duncan of the state immunization program explained to the authors, through e-mail, that Oregon and the federal Centers for Disease Control both define two-year-olds as up to 36 months, for this purpose.

P. 19 Gary Hamel quotation: Gary Hamel, "Strategy as Revolution," *Harvard Business Review* (July-August 1996), p. 71.

P. 19 "He and others argue . . . real strategic thinking": See, for example, Henry Mintzberg, *The Rise and Fall of Strategic Planning* (New York: Free Press, 1994).

P. 19 State Services Commission quotation: *Strategic Management in the Public Service: A Review of the Implementation of Key Result Areas 1994–1997, Stakeholders' Perspectives* (Wellington, New Zealand: State Services Commission, 1997), p. 4.

P. 20 Graham Scott quotation: Graham Scott, *Public Management in New Zealand: Lessons and Challenges* (Wellington, New Zealand: Daphne Brasell Associates, forthcoming).

P. 21 Linda Loomis Shelly quotation: Katherine Barrett and Richard Greene, "Why Good Programs Die," *Governing* (July 1998), p. 68.

P. 22 Michael Marsh quotation: Duncan Wyse and Michael Marsh, "The State of Oregon: Setting Measurable Standards for Progress" (presentation at conference at LBJ School, Austin, Texas, 1993), p. 55.

P. 24 Tryens quotations: Jeffrey Tryens, "Aligning Government Priorities with Societal Hopes and Expectations: Oregon's Strategic Planning Model" (testimony before U.S. House of Representatives Committee on Government Reform and Oversight, Subcommittee on Government Management, Information and Technology, October 31, 1997), pp. 9–10; provided by Oregon Progress Board.

Pp. 26–27 *Oregon Shines* quotations: Ibid., pp. 18–19.

P. 27 Harrison Owen quotation: Harrison Owen, *Leadership Is* (Potomac, Md.: Abbott Publishing, 1990), p. 61.

P. 28 John Kotter quotation: John Kotter, *Leading Change* (Boston: Harvard Business School Press, 1996), p. 81.

P. 28 *The Path to Prosperity* quotations: *The Path to Prosperity* (Lansing: Task Force for a Long-Term Economic Strategy for Michigan, 1984), pp. 44–56.

Pp. 28–29 Chrislip and Larson quotation: David D. Chrislip and Carl E. Larson, *Collaborative Leadership: How Citizens and Civic Leaders Can Make a Difference* (San Francisco: Jossey-Bass, 1994), p. 84.

P. 29 Goals for Dallas example: Robert B. Bradley, "Goals for Dallas," in *Anticipatory Democracy: People in the Politics of the Future,* ed. Clement Bezold (New York: Vintage Books, 1978), p. 73.

P. 29 Phoenix Futures Forum example: Chrislip and Larson, *Collaborative Leadership,* pp. 41, 85, 111, 122.

P. 29 Tom Peters quotation: Tom Peters, *Thriving on Chaos: Handbook for a Management Revolution* (New York: Knopf, 1988), p. 403.

P. 31 Beverly Stein quotation: Ed Finkel, "Feds Join Oregon's Reinventing Pioneers," *The Public Innovator* 18 (December 15, 1994), p. 2 (published by the National Academy of Public Administration's Alliance for Redesigning Government, in Washington, D.C.; available at www.Alliance.napawash.org).

P. 31 National goals for war on drugs: See *Performance Measures of Effectiveness* (Washington, D.C.: Office of National Drug Control Strategy, 1998).

P. 31 "Typical examples": From *Strategic Result Areas for the Public Sector, 1997–2000* (Wellington, New Zealand: Department of the Prime Minister and Cabinet, June 1997), available at www.ssc.govt.nz/Documents/SRA_complete.htm.

P. 31 "Lacking any requirement . . . outcomes": Hon. Paul East, Minister of State Services, "Opening Address: Lifting the Game From Outputs to Outcomes," in *Lifting the Game from Outputs to Outcomes: Proceedings, Public Service Senior Management Conference* (Wellington, New Zealand: State Services Commission, 1998), pp. 7–13, available on the Web at www.ssc.govt.nz; and interviews with current and former government officials.

P. 32 Allen Schick quotation: Allen Schick, *The Spirit of Reform* (Wellington, New Zealand: State Services Commission, 1996), "Strategic Capacity" chapter, p. 12; available at www.ssc.govt.nz/spirit/Strategic.asp?MenuID=52.

P. 33 "In 1997 . . . realistic levels": See Oregon Progress Board, *Oregon Shines II.*

P. 33 "Vermont even televises . . . indicators": Cornelius D. Hogan, "Accountability in an Age of Federal Devolution and Emerging Community Partnerships On Behalf of the Well-Being of Children, Families, and Communities" (unpublished manuscript, provided by Hogan, secretary of the Vermont Agency of Human Services), pp. 11–12.

P. 37 "The Oregon legislature created the Commission on Children and Families . . . system": Interviews with Beverly Stein, former state legislative sponsor of the commission; Lynn Fallin, executive director of the commission; and Jim Clay, director of the Multnomah County Commission on Children and Families.

P. 37 "The Massachusetts legislature created the Mass Jobs Council . . . spending": Personal experience; David Osborne was a member of the council from 1991 to 1998.

P. 37 "Many counties in Oregon . . . effective": Interview with Suzanne Riles, staff professional with Public Safety Coordinating Council in Multnomah County.

P. 38 John Carver quotations: John Carver, *Boards That Make a Difference* (San Francisco: Jossey-Bass, 1990), pp. 202–203.

P. 39 "Iowa invented 'decategorization boards' to allow pooling of state funds": Bill Rust, "Decat in the Hat: Iowa's Successful First Step Toward Devolving Resources, Responsibility, and Accountability for Child and Family Outcomes," *Advocasey* 1, no. 1 (Spring 1999), pp. 4–12.

P. 39 *Oregon Shines II* quotation: Oregon Progress Board, *Oregon Shines II,* p. 71.

P. 40 "As Henry Mintzberg explains . . . actually works": See Mintzberg, *The Rise and Fall of Strategic Planning,* pp. 296–297.

P. 40 Henry Mintzberg quotations: Mintzberg, *The Rise and Fall of Strategic Planning,* pp. 109–110, 288–289, 209.

P. 40 Organization for Economic Cooperation and Development quotation: PUMA (Public Management Service), *Building Policy Coherence: Tools and Tensions* (Paris: Organization for Economic Cooperation and Development, 1996), p. 10.

P. 41 Mintzberg quotation ("Hard information . . . is unreliable") and subsequent point: Mintzberg, *The Rise and Fall of Strategic Planning,* pp. 259–264, 329.

P. 44 "By 1997, fifteen states . . . departments": *Performance-Based Program Budgeting in Context* (Tallahassee, Fla: Office of Program Policy Analysis and Government Accountability, April 1977), p. 13.

P. 44 "Agencies are required . . . each strategy": *Instructions for Preparing and Submitting Agency Strategic Plans: Fiscal Years 1999–2003* (Austin, Tex.: Governor's Office of Budget and Planning and Legislative Budget Board, January 1998).

P. 46 "In a 1998 survey of state legislators . . . report": *Interim Report of the Senate Finance Subcommittee on Articles II and VIII Agencies on the Performance-Based Budgeting Process,* report to Senate Finance Committee, June 1, 1998.

P. 46 "Allen Schick . . . benefit": Interview with Allen Schick.

P. 49 "When Minnesota began . . . what to measure": Jeffrey Itell, "Where Are They Now? Performance Measurement Pioneers Offer Lessons from the Long, Hard Road," *The New Public Innovator* 92 (May-June 1998), p. 12.

P. 50 U.S. General Accounting Office study: *Performance Budgeting: State Experiences and Implications for the Federal Government,* GAO/AFMD–93–41 (Washington, D.C.: General Accounting Office, 1993), p. 4.

P. 51 "When the GAO studied . . . doing so": Ibid., p. 6.

P. 51 "Sweden made the same mistake": Allen Schick, *Modern Budgeting* (Paris: Organization for Economic Development and Cooperation, 1998), p. 108.

P. 52 "Arizona has adopted . . . total appropriations": Foundation for State Legislatures and National Conference of State Legislatures, *Fundamentals of Sound State Budgeting Practices* (Denver, Colo.: National Conference of State Legislatures, 1995), p. 30.

P. 52 "In Minnesota, managers worried . . . with detail": Ronald K. Snell, "Reinventing Government—Not Easy, But Possible," *State Legislatures* (February 1998), p. 37.

P. 52 "Arizona's budget includes . . . published separately": *A Guide to Developing and Using Performance Measures in Results-Based Budgeting* (Washington, D.C.: The Finance Project, May 1997), pp. 26–27.

P. 53 Representative Junell quotation: Karen Carter, "Performance Budgets: Here by Popular Demand," *State Legislatures* (December 1994), p. 25.

P. 54 OECD quotations: PUMA (Public Management Service), *Budgeting for the Future* (Paris: Organization for Economic Cooperation and Development, 1997), p. 5.

P. 55 Ruth Richardson quotation: Ibid., p. 19.

P. 55 "After years of struggling . . . in 1998": Prime Minister Jenny Shipley, "Getting New Zealand Right," presentation on Web site www.executive.govt.nz/minister/ (click on Shipley) 1998.

P. 55 "In Florida, budget staff . . . can be made": Interview with John Turcotte, director of Florida's Office of Program Policy Analysis and Government Accountability.

P. 55 "In New Zealand . . . its forecasts": PUMA, *Budgeting for the Future,* p. 23.

Pp. 55–56 OECD quotation: Ibid., p. 12.

P. 56 "When the U.K. . . . non-inflation-adjusted figures": Ibid., pp. 5–6.

Chapter Two

P. 61 Armey quotation: Elizabeth Drew, *Showdown: The Struggle Between the Gingrich Congress and the Clinton White House* (New York: Simon & Schuster, 1996), p. 259.

P. 61 "Gingrich and his lieutenants . . . Congress": about budget recission, see *Congressional Quarterly Almanac: 104th Congress, 1st Session, 1995* (Washington, D.C.: Congressional Quarterly, Inc.), p. 11–96.

P. 62 "Targets included . . . in New York City": "No Winners in Budget Showdown," in *Congressional Quarterly Almanac: 104th Congress, 1st Session, 1995* (Washington, D.C.: Congressional Quarterly, Inc.), p. 2–46.

P. 62 "They planned to kill . . . breaks for business": David Frum, *What's Right: The New Conservative Majority and the Remaking of America* (New York: Basic Books, 1996), pp. 30–31.

P. 62 "Gingrich had even dreamed up . . . like the Berlin Wall": Nancy Gibbs and Michael Duffy, "Fall of the House of Newt," *Time* (November 16, 1998), p. 45.

P. 62 Frum quotation: Frum, *What's Right,* p. 99.

P. 62 GOP leader quotation: Drew, *Showdown,* p. 263.

P. 62 Gingrich quotation: Newt Gingrich, *Lessons Learned the Hard Way: A Personal Report* (New York: HarperCollins, 1998), pp. 55–56.

P. 63 "What had started . . . as one analyst put it": "104th Congress Ushers in New Era of GOP Rule," *Congressional Quarterly Almanac: 104th Congress, 1st Session, 1995* (Washington, D.C.: Congressional Quarterly, Inc.), p. 1–11.

P. 63 "It set up a federal tea-taster . . . $1.2 billion": From August 17, 1993, draft of National Performance Review manuscript.

P. 64 "In 1993, President Clinton's . . . be eliminated": Vice President Al Gore, *From Red Tape to Results: Creating a Government That Works Better and Costs Less* (Washington, D.C.: National Performance Review, 1993), p. 98.

P. 64 Gingrich quotation: "104th Congress Ushers in New Era of GOP Rule," *Congressional Quarterly Almanac: 104th Congress, 1st Session, 1995* (Washington, D.C.: Congressional Quarterly, Inc.), p. 1–21.

P. 65 "In Texas in 1991 . . . no position to resist": Texas Office of the Comptroller, "The Texas Performance Review: Breaking the Mold," in *Special Financial Report* (Austin: Texas Office of the Comptroller, July 1991).

P. 66 ". . . that's why Gingrich installed . . . seniority system": Drew, *Showdown,* p. 36.

P. 66 "At one point during negotiations . . . bill to advance": *Congressional Quarterly Almanac: 104th Congress, 1st Session, 1995* (Washington, D.C.: Congressional Quarterly, Inc.), p. 11–102.

P. 66 Frum quotation: Frum, *What's Right,* p. 31.

P. 66 Douglas quotations: Roger Douglas, "The Politics of Successful Structural Reform" (unpublished manuscript).

P. 68 "That summer, it approved plans . . . 20 years": "Base Closures Enter Final Phase," *Congressional Quarterly Almanac: 104th Congress, 1st Session, 1995* (Washington, D.C.: Congressional Quarterly, Inc.), pp. 9–19.

P. 68 "According to a 1999 report . . . within two years": Elizabeth Becker, "Administration to Urge Congress to Close More Military Bases," *New York Times,* January 26, 1999.

P. 68 "But base closing . . . bipartisan majority in Congress": "Base Closures Enter Final Phase," *Congressional Quarterly Almanac: 104th Congress, 1st Session, 1995* (Washington, D.C.: Congressional Quarterly, Inc.), pp. 9–22.

P. 69 "It initially added 29 bases . . . possible closure": Ibid., p. 9–20.

P. 69 ". . . and ultimately agreed with . . . proposed list": Ibid., p. 9–22.

P. 69 "But rather than reject the entire list . . . those states": Ibid.

P. 70 Douglas quotations: Douglas, "The Politics of Successful Structural Reform."

P. 70 Sharp quotation: John Sharp, "Restructuring the Public Sector to Deliver More for Less" (testimony before the Joint Economic Committee of the U.S. Congress, Washington, D.C., March 4, 1992), p. 6.

Pp. 70–71 Gingrich quotation: Drew, *Showdown,* p. 276.

P. 71 Douglas quotation: Douglas, "The Politics of Successful Structural Reform."

P. 71 Clinton quotation: Al Gore, *Creating a Government That Works Better and Costs Less: Status Report* (Washington, D.C.: U.S. Government Printing Office, 1994), p. 8.

P. 72 Kost quotation: Kost, *New Approaches to Public Management* (Washington, D.C.: The Brookings Institution, 1996), p. 21.

P. 73 "The eight criteria used . . .environmental impacts": "Base Closures Enter Final Phase," *Congressional Quarterly Almanac: 104th Congress, 1st Session, 1995* (Washington, D.C.: Congressional Quarterly, Inc.), pp. 9–19.

P. 73 "The Texas Sunset Advisory Commission . . . statutory objectives": *Guide to The Texas Sunset Process* (Austin, Tx.: Sunset Advisory Commission, 1999), p. 3 (available at www.sunset.state.tx.us; click on "Sunset Guide").

P. 73 " . . . called PERM, because . . . or modified": Kost, *New Approaches to Public Management,* pp. 19–21.

P. 76 Sharp quotation: John Sharp, "Restructuring the Public Sector to Deliver More for Less," p. 6.

P. 76 "The management team at the NPR . . . and the public": Personal experience; David Osborne was a member of that management team.

P. 77 "For instance, when the Canadian government . . . transitional funding": Minister of Transport, *Transport Canada's New Direction and the 1995 Budget* (Ottawa: Transport Canada, 1995), p. 27.

P. 78 "On February 27, 1995 . . . top to bottom'": Paul Martin, *Budget Speech* (Ottawa: Department of Finance, Canada, February 27, 1995), pp. 6–7.

P. 78 "Their first priority . . . gross domestic product": Canada Department of Finance, *Budget Plan: Including Supplementary Information and Notices of Ways and Means Motions* (Ottawa: Minister of Supply and Services, Canada, 1996), p. 136.

P. 78 "Previous Canadian governments had . . . in eight years": Richard Paton, "Reinventing Government Through Program Review: The Canadian Experience," overheads for presentation.

P. 78 "While failing to tame . . . indiscriminately": From "1994–95: The Year in Review," fax from Privy Council Office, p. 19.

P. 79 "... what they called a Program Review ... federal department": Canada Department of Finance, *Budget Plan,* p. 32.

P. 79 "The first phase of the review ... $2.2 billion in potential savings": Privy Council Office, *Program Review: User Guide* (Ottawa: Minister of Supply and Services, Canada, 1996), p. 9.

P. 79 "Overall, the Liberals shrunk ... of GDP": Interview with Peter DeVries, director of fiscal policy division of the Canadian Department of Finance.

P. 79 "Economic programs such as corporate ... dwindling pie": Privy Council Office, *Getting Government Right: A Progress Report* (Ottawa: Government of Canada, March 7, 1996).

P. 79 "Perhaps the most radical ... grain transport": Privy Council Office, *Getting Government Right,* p. 10; Minister of Transport, *Canada's New Direction and the 1995 Budget: Toward an Integrated and Affordable National Transportation System* (Ottawa: Ministry of Transport, February 28, 1995).

P. 80 "Canada's Deck-Clearing Criteria" box: Privy Council Office, *Getting Government Right,* p. 30.

P. 81 "Indianapolis created a Regulatory ... unneeded rules": Stephen Goldsmith, *The Twenty-First Century City: Resurrecting Urban America* (Washington, D.C.: Regnery Publishing, 1997), p. 87.

P. 81 "In California, Governor Pete Wilson's ... 3,100 regulations for abolition": California Office of the Governor, *Competitive Government: Highlights* (Sacramento: California Office of the Governor, 1997).

P. 81 "New York Governor George Pataki ... two years of reviews": "Reg Thermometer Rising," *Reg Watch* 2, no. 3 (Summer/Fall 1997). *Reg Watch* is a newsletter published by the New York State Governor's Office of Regulatory Reform; for more see www.state.ny.us/gorr.

P. 84 "This nonrandom method ... insiders": Based on observation by David Osborne, who helped manage the first National Performance Review process.

P. 87 Weaver quotation: R. Kent Weaver, "Reinventing Government or Rearranging the Deck Chairs? The Politics of Institutional Reform in the 1990s," in *New Ideas, Better Government,* ed. Patrick Weller and Glyn Davis (Brisbane: Allen & Unwin, 1996), pp. 263–282.

P. 88 "Two central organizations ... it is thorough": *Guidance on Agency Reviews* (London: Cabinet Office, December 1995), p. 6.

P. 88 "In their first five years ... a dozen organizations": Personal communication from Jeremy Cowper, then head of the Next Steps Team, September 6, 1996.

P. 88 "The state of Arizona created ... with the legislature": Ed Finkel, "Raising Arizona's Program Performance," *The Public Innovator,* no. 44/45 (January 18, 1996), pp. 1–3.

P. 91 Springer quotation: Ibid.

P. 93 "By 1995, some 100 ... $445 billion": Robert W. Poole Jr., "A Federal Privatization Agenda" (testimony to Senate Budget Committee, June 29, 1995) (Los Angeles: Reason Foundation, 1995); and Reason Foundation, *Privatization 1994* (Los Angeles: Reason Foundation, 1994), p. 43.

P. 93 "Though Latin American and Asian . . . economic activity": E. S. Savas, "Privatization in Post-Socialist Countries," *Public Administration Review* 52, no. 6 (November-December 1992), p. 573.

P. 93 "Sales have included anything . . . and dams": Wilbur L. Ross Jr., "Privatization: An Important Tool for Government" (unpublished manuscript). Also see Poole, "A Federal Privatization Agenda."

P. 93 "In December 1994 . . . toll road": The Reason Foundation, *Privatization 1995* (Los Angeles: Reason Foundation, 1995), p. 32.

P. 93 "In 1995, New York City . . . television stations": The Reason Foundation, *Privatization 1996* (Los Angeles: Reason Foundation, 1996), p. 8.

P. 93 "In 1997, the U.S. . . . public asset in the U.S.": Martha M. Hamilton, "U.S. Agrees to Sell Calif. Oil Reserve," *Washington Post,* May 22, 1997, p. E3.

P. 93 "And in 1998 . . . frontier of privatization": Charles Fleming, "Water Business Is Hot as More Cities Decide to Tap Private Sector," *The Wall Street Journal*, November 9, 1998, A1, A15.

P. 94 "The sale may be to . . . users or customers": Savas, "Privatization in Post-Socialist Countries," pp. 573–581.

P. 94 Thatcher quotation: Margaret Thatcher, *The Downing Street Years, 1987–1990* (New York: HaperPerennial, 1995) p. 677.

P. 94 Ross quotation: Ross, "Privatization," p. 1.

P. 94 "In the early 1990s, for instance . . . unpaved roads": Mary Shirley, "Privatization: Misconceptions, Glib Answers, and Lessons 1992" (presentation to the Carnegie Council on Ethics and International Affairs, New York, March 20, 1992).

P. 95 "According to Per Westerberg . . . competitive": Per Westerberg, "From Confusion Economics to a Market Economy: The Only Way for Sweden" (presentation to the Carnegie Council on Ethics and International Affairs, New York, April 6, 1992).

P. 95 Bell quotation: Geoffrey Bell, "Privatization in a Capital-Short World" (presentation to the Carnegie Council on Ethics and International Affairs, New York, June 28, 1991).

P. 95 "In 1986 . . . British Gas": Treasury Department, *Privatisation—Sharing the UK Experience* (London: Her Majesty's Treasury), p. 14.

P. 95 ". . . such as British Airways . . . world-class airline": Ross, "Privatization"; Treasury Department, *Privatisation—Sharing the UK Experience.*

P. 95 "An authoritative study by the World Bank . . . by 30 percent": Mary Shirley, "Privatization: Misconceptions, Glib Answers, and Lessons."

P. 96 "When Germany's Treuhandstalt . . . was assassinated": Steven Cohen and William Eimicke, *Tools for Innovators: Creative Strategies for Managing Public Sector Organizations* (San Francisco: Jossey-Bass, 1998), pp. 195, 112.

P. 96 Pomeroy quotation: Brian W. Pomeroy, "An Assessment of Privatization in the U.K.: Mistakes, Successes, and Future Prospects" (presentation to the Carnegie Council on Ethics and International Affairs, New York, September 20, 1991), p. 4.

P. 97 "Another option is to sell only the profitable . . . Ross": Ross, "Privatization," p. 8.

P. 97 Shirley quotation: Shirley, "Privatization: Misconceptions, Glib Answers, and Lessons," p. 3.

P. 97 "The British, for instance, split National Bus . . . bus operators": Treasury Department, *Privatisation—Sharing the U.K. Experience,* p. 5.

P. 98 "When the British sold Rolls Royce . . . national defense": Ibid., p. 10.

P. 98 Ross quotation: Ross, "Privatization," p. 5.

P. 98 "Other ways for the government . . . if the government so desires": Ibid.

P. 98 "The British did this several times by letting employees . . . private companies": Savas, "Privatization in Post-Socialist Countries," and Treasury Department, *Privatisation—Sharing the U.K. Experience,* p. 12.

P. 98 Poole quotation: Poole, "A Federal Privatization Agenda," p. 5.

P. 99 "The first U.S. agency to try this . . . was eliminated": Ronald P. Sanders and James Thompson, "Live Long and Prosper: How One Former Federal Organization Is Adjusting to Life After Government," *Government Executive* (April 1997), pp. 50–53.

P. 100 "When Canada set up . . . lost interest in the process": Donald J. Savoie, *Thatcher, Reagan, Mulroney: In Search of a New Bureaucracy* (Pittsburgh: University of Pittsburgh Press, 1994), p. 167.

P. 100 Ross quotation: Ross, "Privatization," p. 5.

P. 100 "And as Ross points out . . . they benefit": Ross, "Privatization."

P. 100 "But so did customer complaints . . . 88 percent": David Norris, "Gravy Train Is Derailed," *Daily Mail,* September 12, 1998.

P. 100 "Under fire, newly private railway operators . . . service capacity": Charles Batchelor, "Strategic Rail Authority to Be Prescott's Main Line of Attack," *Financial Times,* September 12, 1998.

P. 101 "Mexico has had serious problems . . . on the brink of bankruptcy": Anthony DePalma, "Mexico's Garage Sale: In a Third Round of Privatization, Will a Nation Learn from Mistakes?" *New York Times,* June 2, 1995, pp. C1, C5.

P. 102 "In 1997, the government announced . . . two of the bridges": Sam Dillon, "Mexico's Privately Run Highways Prove a Costly Failure," *New York Times,* August 23, 1997.

P. 102 "In 1994, for example, Australia's national . . . preservation as airports": The Reason Foundation, *Privatization 1995* (Los Angeles: Reason Foundation, 1995), p. 37.

P. 102 "Austin, Texas, leased its hospital . . . 30 years": Richard L. Treadwell, *Privatizing Public Hospitals: Strategic Options in an Era of Industry-Wide Consolidation* (Los Angeles: Reason Public Policy Institute, August 1998).

P. 102 "The state-appointed directors . . . spending on operations": Ibid., pp. 26–27.

Pp. 102–103 "In Australia, for example, the government of the state of Victoria . . . owned and operated prisons": The Reason Foundation, *Privatization 1997* (Los Angeles: Reason Foundation, 1997), p. 50.

P. 103 "California leased the right of way . . . on the freeway": Governor Pete Wilson, *Competitive Government: A Plan for Less Bureaucracy, More Results* (Sacramento: California Governor's Office, April 1996), p. 42.

P. 103 "In the United Kingdom, the Private Finance Initiative . . . wanted built": Adrian Montague, *The United Kingdom's Private Finance Initiative,* presentation on May 21, 1999, in Boston.

P. 103 "A PFI contract . . . and operations": *The Government's Response to the Treasury Committee's Sixth Report, 1995–96 Session: The Private Finance Initiative* (HC 146), p. viii.

P. 103 "This method has been used . . . and schools": H.M. Treasury, *The Private Finance Initiative* (London: Treasury Department), www.hm-treasury.gov.uk/pub/html/econbf/eb09/2pfi.html.

P. 103 Montague quotation: Montague, *The United Kingdom's Private Finance Initiative.*

P. 103 "In addition, they only get . . . specified levels": H.M. Treasury, *The Private Finance Initiative.*

P. 103 "Treasury was so enamored . . . PFI potential": H.M. Treasury, *PFI: Guidelines for Smoothing the Procurement Process* (London: Treasury Department,1996), www.hm-treasury.gov.uk/pub/html/finance/1996/pfi_0496.html.

P. 104 Montague quotation: Montague, *The United Kingdom's Private Finance Initiative.*

Chapter Three

P. 105 "The U.S. Federal Aviation Administration ... every year": Federal Aviation Administration Air Traffic Services web page, www.faa.gov.ats/; and related pages.

P. 105 "It regulates an aviation industry . . . GDP": National Civil Aviation Review Commission, *Avoiding Aviation Gridlock and Reducing the Accident Rate: A Consensus for Change* (Washington, D.C.: Federal Aviation Administration, December 1997), p. 10. (The page numbers cited from this publication are from its on-line version, at www.faa.gov/NCARC/reports/pepele.htm.)

P. 105 "While other nations import . . . its ancient computers": Ibid., p. 17.

Pp. 105–106 "'Antiquated backup systems . . . 40 percent'": Ibid., pp. 17, 11–13.

P. 106 "'The FAA is unique . . . responsibility'": Ibid., p. 13.

P. 106 "Until 1996 . . . reported": Ibid. (quotation p. 13).

P. 106 Aviation Safety Commission quotation: *Aviation Safety Commission: Final Report and Recommendations* (Washington, D.C.: U.S. Government Printing Office, 1988), p. 25.

P. 107 Clinton Oster Jr. quotations: Clinton V. Oster Jr., "Air Traffic Control Reorganization and Aviation Safety: Ending Self-Regulation at the FAA" (paper presented at a Transportation Research Forum annual meeting, San Antonio, Texas, October 18, 1996), p. 3.

P. 107 "In 1993, the National Commission . . . same separation": National Commission to Ensure a Strong Competitive Airline Industry, *Final Report* (Washington, D.C.: U.S. Government Printing Office, August 1993).

P. 107 "Later that year . . . clearer purpose": Al Gore, *From Red Tape to Results: Creating a Government That Works Better and Costs Less* (Washington, D.C.: National Performance Review, 1993), p. 61.

P. 108 "Under Gore's scheme . . . for performance": *Background Paper: Creating Performance-Based Organizations* (Washington, D.C.: National Performance Review, October 1996).

P. 108 Mineta Commission quotation: National Civil Aviation Review Commission, *Avoiding Aviation Gridlock,* p. 25.

P. 109 "Since it formed . . . endangered species": National Performance Review, *Agency for International Development: Accompanying Report of the National Performance Review, Office of the Vice President* (Washington, D.C.: U.S. Government Printing Office, 1993), pp. 5–10.

P. 109 General Accounting Office quotation: *Foreign Assistance Economic Issues,* GAO/OGC–93–25TR (Washington, D.C.: General Accounting Office, December 1992), p. 8.

P. 110 Peter Drucker quotation: Peter F. Drucker, *The Age of Discontinuity* (New York: Harper Torchbooks, 1978), p. 233.

P. 110 Efficiency Unit report: Kate Jenkins, Karen Caines, and Andrew Jackson, *Improving Management in Government: The Next Steps* (London: Her Majesty's Stationery Office, 1988).

P. 111 "It came first because . . . launched": Interview with Ron Oliver.

P. 111 A. P. Brown quotation: House of Commons, Committee of Public Accounts, *The Vehicle Inspectorate: Progress as the First Executive Agency,* Session 1992–93 (London: Her Majesty's Stationery Office, 1993), pp. 23, 7.

P. 112 Vehicle Inspectorate flexibilities: Interview and personal communications with Ron Oliver.

P. 112 "They worked with . . . four basic goals": National Audit Office, *The Vehicle Inspectorate: Progress as the First Executive Agency—Report by the Comptroller and Auditor General* (London: Her Majesty's Stationery Office, 1992), p. 22.

P. 112 "They removed a tier . . . the management structure": Ibid.; and *Improving Management in Government: The Next Steps Agencies, Review 1991,* Cm. 1760 (London: Her Majesty's Stationery Office, 1991), p. 67.

P. 112 "They devolved more responsibility . . . decision making": National Audit Office, *The Vehicle Inspectorate,* pp. 23–24.

P. 112 "They competitively bid out . . . number of services": *Next Steps Review: 1993,* Cm. 2430 (London, Her Majesty's Stationery Office, 1993), p. 122; *Next Steps Review 1994,* Cm. 2750 (London, Her Majesty's Stationery Office, 1993), p. 118.

P. 112 "And after the department merged . . . over four years": 1991 figure of 1950 staff members: *The Next Steps Agencies, Review 1991,* p. 67; 1995 figure of 1556 staff members: *The Vehicle Inspectorate: An Evaluation of Performance From 1 August 1988 to 31 March 1995* (London: Department of Transport, November 1996), p. 5.

P. 112 "The department set aggressive targets . . . first eight years": *The Vehicle Inspectorate: An Evaluation of Performance,* 1996, p. 13; and "Vehicle Inspectorate," in *Next Steps Report 1997* (www.official-documents.co.uk/document/cm38/3889/doe156.htm, March 12, 1998), p. 1.

P. 112 "These results were audited . . . National Audit Office": *The Vehicle Inspectorate: An Evaluation of Performance,* 1996, p. 16.

P. 112 "During the agency's . . . a year": *The Next Steps Agencies, Review 1991,* p. 67; and *The Next Steps Agencies: Review 1992,* Cm. 2111 (London: Her Majesty's Stationery Office, 1992), p. 92.

P. 112 "On the quality front . . . increased staff training": See Next Steps annual reviews cited earlier, plus National Audit Office, *The Vehicle Inspectorate,* p. 25.

Pp. 112–113 "By 1991 . . . had grown worse": Ibid., p. 13.

P. 113 "Oliver and his agency went on . . . development of the inspectorate": *Next Steps Review: 1993,* p. 122; *Next Steps Review 1994,* p. 118; *The Vehicle Inspectorate: An Evaluation of Performance,* 1996, p. 19; and Rt. Hon. John Prescott MP, "Secretary of State for the Environment, Transport & the Regions," in *Next Steps Report 1997*, p. 4.

P. 116 William Waldegrave quotation: William Waldegrave, *Public Service and the Future: Reforming Britain's Bureaucracies* (London: Conservative Political Centre, 1993), p. 17.

P. 117 "In 1999, the Education Commission . . . school boards to consider": National Commission on Governing America's Schools, *Governing America's Schools: Changing the Rules* (Denver: Education Commission of the States, 1999).

P. 117 Waldegrave quotation: Ibid.

P. 117 Allen Schick quotation: Allen Schick, *The Spirit of Reform* (Wellington, New Zealand: State Services Commission, 1996), "Accounting for Results" chapter, p. 3.

P. 117 William Eggers quotation: William Eggers, "The Wonder Down Under," *Government Executive* (March 1997), pp. 38–39.

Pp. 118–119 Price Waterhouse survey quotation: *Executive Agencies: A Briefing for New Ministers* (London: Price Waterhouse, Nov. 1996), p. 11.

P. 119 Allen Schick quotation: Allen Schick, *Modern Budgeting* (Paris: Organization for Economic Development and Cooperation, 1998), p. 83.

P. 121 Allen Schick quotation: Schick, *The Spirit of Reform,* "Organizational Capacity" chapter, pp. 4–5.

P. 121 Sweden's problems: Schick, *Modern Budgeting,* pp. 105–106.

P. 121 Quotation from British government paper: *The Civil Service: Continuity and Change,* Cm. 2627 (London: Her Majesty's Stationery Office, July 1994), p. 22.

P. 121 1994 survey of agency executives: *Executive Agencies: Survey Report 1994* (London: Price Waterhouse, 1994), p. 20.

P. 122 Department of the Environment, Transport, and the Regions review: see "The DVO Report" (an extract from the report of the DVO Steering Group to DETR Ministers) (London: Department of the Environment, Transport, and the Regions Press Office, February 1, 1999).

P. 122 "It recommended . . . change across the area'": "Note to Editors" (provided by DETR Press Office with news release "Serving the Motorist Better: Whitty Launches New Agency"), February 1, 1999.

P. 122 "Meanwhile, the Labor Government . . . productivity": *Public Services for the Future: Modernisation, Reform, Accountability,* Cm. 4181 (London: The Stationery Office, July 1998).

P. 122 "The government promised . . . are met'": "Agency Performance and Efficiency," in *Next Steps Report 1998,* Cm. 4273 (London: The Stationery Office, March 1999).

P. 123 "When Canada copied . . . direct consequences": *Special Operating Agencies: Taking Stock* (Ottawa: Auditor General of Canada, May 1994), p. 44.

Pp. 123–124 "In contrast, Canada . . . all SOAs": Ibid., p. 54.

P. 124 Parliament quotation ("'the single most successful . . .'"): *Next Steps: Briefing Notes* (London: Office of Public Service, February 26, 1996), p. 6.

P. 124 "Meanwhile, the province of Manitoba . . . not far behind": *Special Operating Agencies* (Winnipeg: Government of Manitoba).

P. 124 "The Netherlands also copied . . . in 1997": A. Sorber, "Developing and Using Performance Measurement: The Netherlands Experience," in *Performance Management in Government: Contemporary Illustrations,* ed. PUMA (Paris: Organization for Economic Cooperation and Development, 1996), pp. 93–106; personal communication from Peter Matwijiw, Department of Treasury and Finance, Australian state of Victoria.

Pp. 124–125 "The Swedes . . . six-year terms": Yvonne Fortin, "Autonomy, Responsibility and Control: The Case of Central Government Agencies in Sweden," in *Performance Management in Government: Contemporary Illustrations,* pp. 33–44.

P. 125 "Richmond, Virginia . . . in 1998": Personal experience; David Osborne worked with Richmond on this effort as a consultant.

P. 125 "In Canada, Winnipeg and Toronto . . . modeled after SOAs": *Special Operating Agencies.*

P. 125 "Beginning in 1993, for example, Catawba County . . . their performance targets": Jeffrey Itell, "Where Are They Now?" *New Public Innovator* 92 (May-June 1998), pp. 11–17.

P. 131 "'Throughout the study . . . influenced its evolution'": *Special Operating Agencies: Taking Stock,* p. 50.

P. 131 "In the U.K., Thatcher . . . from their departments": Patricia Greer, *Transforming Central Government: The Next Steps Initiative* (Philadelphia: Open University Press, 1994), p. 47.

P. 131 "'Many participants felt . . . conflicted'": *Special Operating Agencies: Taking Stock,* p. 50.

P. 132 "But in the U.K. . . . in a 1993 survey": *Executive Agencies: Survey Report 1994* (London: Price Waterhouse), p. 8.

P. 133 Quote from the permanent secretary in the Department of Social Security: Greer, *Transforming Central Government,* p. 39.

P. 135 "In 1995, a cantilevered deck . . . killing 14 people": Jonathon Boston et al., *Public Management: The New Zealand Model* (Auckland, New Zealand: Oxford University Press, 1996), p. 323.

P. 135 "In the U.K. . . . both 1994 and 1995": *Next Steps Review 1995,* Cm. 3164 (London: Her Majesty's Stationery Office, February 1996), p. 106.

P. 135 National Performance Review quotation: Gore, *From Red Tape to Results,* p. 34.

P. 136 "As the Canadian evaluation put it . . . make the difference'": *Special Operating Agencies: Taking Stock,* p. 43.

P. 136 "This shift toward . . . betrayal": See, for example, *Survey Report: Executive Agencies* (London: Price Waterhouse, March 1993), p. 12.

P. 138 "New Zealand has confronted this problem . . . ownership interests": Alex Matheson, Gerald Scanlan, and Ross Tanner, *Strategic Management in Government: Extending the Reform Model in New Zealand* (Wellington, New Zealand: State Services Commission, November 1996), p. 10.

P. 139 "This problem . . . and Sweden": Joan Spice, *Management Reform in Four Countries* (Ottawa: MAB-MIAC Task Force on Management Improvement, November 1992), p. 16; and Sylvie Trosa, *Next Steps: Moving On* (London: Office of Public Service and Science, February 1994), pp. 39–42.

P. 139 "In the United Kingdom, for example . . . formulation": *Executive Agencies: A Briefing for New Ministers* (London: Price Waterhouse, November 1996), p. 5.

P. 139 "'One of the risks . . . information management": Judith Johnson, Katrina Casey, and Tony Crewdson, "Team Synergy: Inter-agency Cooperation—Information Management," in *Lifting the Game from Outputs to Outcomes: Proceedings, Public Service Senior Management Conference* (Wellington, New Zealand: State Services Commission, 1998), pp. 60–64. Available at www.ssc.govt.nz.

P. 141 "A British government review of best practices . . . from managers'": Next Steps Team, *The Strategic Management of Agencies: Models for Management* (London: Her Majesty's Stationery Office, September 1995), p. 40.

P. 142 "As Price Waterhouse advised . . . need to intervene'": *Executive Agencies: A Briefing for New Ministers,* p. 8.

Chapter Four

P. 154 "And it's why the FSS . . . with its contractors": Lisa Corbin, "Smart Shopping," *Government Executive* (October 1996), pp. 41–44.

P. 155 "When the FSS was thrown into the marketplace. . . . Annual sales were $13 billion": Ibid.

Pp. 155–156 "Before Sunnyvale's leisure services unit . . . millions of dollars": Personal communications from Tom Lewcock, former city manager, and Robert Walker, parks and recreation director.

P. 157 Douglas quotation ("information systems . . . producing"): Roger Douglas, *Unfinished Business* (Auckland, New Zealand: Random House, 1993), p. 177.

P. 157 Anderson quotation: Robert Anderson, "The Establishment and Control of State-Owned Enterprises: The New Zealand Experience" (presentation to National Administrative Bureau of State Owned Property, May 15–19, 1990, in Shenzhen, China), p. 18.

p. 157 Douglas quotation ("'The authority delegated . . . '"): Douglas, *Unfinished Business,* p. 177.

P. 158 Douglas quotation ("Their 'status and personal advancement . . .'"): Ibid., p. 176.

P. 158 Douglas quotation ("Over the years . . ."): Ibid.

P. 159 ". . . —with $56 billion in revenue in 1996— . . .": Peter Passell, "Battered By Its Rivals: Competition at Every Turn Has Post Office on the Run," *New York Times,* May 15, 1997, p. D1.

P. 159 "In 1970, package deliveries . . . overnight delivery market": Ibid.

P. 159 "In 1996, it went after a larger portion. . . volume by 20 percent": Kenneth N. Gilpin, "Advertising," *New York Times*, November 15, 1996.

P. 160 World Bank study quotation: Mary M. Shirley, "Getting Bureaucrats Out of Business: Obstacles in State Enterprise Reform," article downloaded from Internet, based on World Bank, *Bureaucrats in Business: The Economics and Politics of Government Ownership* (New York: Oxford University Press, 1995).

P. 161 "When Karen Sorber and Ronald Straight published an analysis . . . the worst obstacles": Karen D. Sorber and Ronald L. Straight, "Franchising the Procurement Function: Competitive Contracting Offices" (paper presented at American Society for Public Administration 56th annual conference, July 1995).

P. 161 Australian Finance Department quotation: Task Force on Management Improvement, *The Australian Public Service Reformed: An Evaluation of a Decade of Management Reform* (Canberra: Australian Government Publishing Service, 1992), p. 279.

P. 161 Goldsmith quotation: Stephen Goldsmith, *The Twenty-First Century City: Resurrecting Urban America* (Washington, D.C.: Regnery Publishing, 1997), p. 40.

P. 162 Barzelay quotation: Michael Barzelay, "Introducing Marketplace Dynamics in Minnesota State Government (A)" (case study prepared for the John F. Kennedy School of Government, Harvard University, 1988), pp. 9–10.

P. 163 Armajani quotation: Ibid., p. 3.

P. 164 "In the mid-1980s . . . and ran a savings bank": Richard Prebble, "How to Privatise Postal Services: Lessons from New Zealand" (lecture to the Canada Post Privatization Conference, Toronto, June 1989).

P. 165 "For example, it created an SOE to run . . . identity and culture": Anderson, "The Establishment and Control of State-Owned Enterprises."

P. 166 "Until February 8, 1988, local post offices . . . if they met an indispensable social need": Prebble, "How to Privatize Postal Services."

P. 166 Prebble quotation: Ibid.

Pp. 166–167 "Within a year, the postal service was . . . next-day delivery service": Ibid.

P. 167 "It improved on-time delivery. . . the national treasury": Office of the Auditor General of Canada, *Toward Better Governance: Public Service Reform in New Zealand (1984–94) and Its Relevance to Canada* (Ottawa: Minister of Supply and Services, 1995).

P. 167 "In similar fashion . . . six weeks to two days": Ibid.

P. 167 Douglas quotation ("'The gains in efficiency . . .'"): Douglas, *Unfinished Business*, pp. 179–180.

p. 167 Douglas quotation ("'Quality outcomes start . . .'"): Roger Douglas, "National Policymakers' Experience—New Zealand" (address to the World Bank Conference on Privatization, Washington, D.C., June 11–13, 1990), p. 11.

P. 167 "In Australia, government businesses . . . significantly as well": Task Force on Management Improvement, *The Australian Public Service Reformed*, p. 322.

P. 168 Douglas quotations ("'All hell broke loose . . . difficult decisions'"): Douglas, *Unfinished Business*, pp. 189–192.

P. 168 Michael Morris quotation: Ibid., p. 191.

P. 168 Douglas quotation ("'are under significantly less . . .'"): Ibid., p. 183.

Pp. 175–178 Minnesota internal enterprise management: This material is drawn from Barzelay, "Introducing Marketplace Dynamics in Minnesota State Government (A);" Michael Barzelay and Babak Armajani, *Breaking Through Bureaucracy* (Berkeley, Ca.: University of California Press, 1992); and interviews with Babak Armajani and Jeff Zlonis, former Department of Administration deputy commissioners.

P. 178 "In 1996, the selected agencies launched . . . accounting services": William Jackson, "Agencies Enter Systems Services Market via Franchise Fund Test," *Government Computer News* (August 5, 1996).

P. 178 "About a year later . . . the private firms": Rajiv Chandrasekaran, "When the Government Hires the Government," *Washington Post,* May 22, 1997, p. A1.

P. 179 Armajani quotation: Michael Barzelay and Babak J. Armajani, "Managing State Government Operations: Changing Visions of Staff Agencies," *Journal of Policy Analysis and Management* 9, no. 3 (1990), pp. 326–327.

P. 179 "As Australian reinventors put it . . . consumption patterns'": Task Force on Management Improvement, *The Australian Public Service Reformed,* p. 270.

P. 179 "When Minnesota made telecommunications a utility . . . 50 percent": Barzelay and Armajani, "Managing State Government Operations," p. 326.

Chapter Five

P. 184 "In April 1997 . . . publicly managed wastewater facilities": EMA Services, Inc., "City of East Lansing: Selecting the EMA/FTC&H Team Will Provide a Plan for Most Cost-Effective Plant Operations" (handout from presentation to City of East Lansing, March 19, 1997). Using as many as 120 wastewater treatment assessments, EMA had previously found that the average public operation faced a 24 percent gap.

P. 184 "During the next five months . . . training and performance incentives": City of East Lansing, *Request for Proposal and Statement of Qualifications: Wastewater Treatment Plant Optimization Study,* December 1996. The EMS review cost no more than $57,780, about 2 percent of the wastewater treatment plant's annual operating budget.

P. 185 "Finally came the news . . . eliminating 8 of the 26 jobs": EMA Services, Inc., "Plant Optimization Study: Report and Workplan" (study submitted to City of East Lansing, September 16, 1997).

P. 185 "When the council approved the plan . . . attrition and retirement": East Lansing City Council, *Resolution to Accept the Wastewater Treatment Plant Optimization Study and Six Year Implementation Plan,* October 2, 1997.

P. 186 Goldsmith quotation: Stephen Goldsmith, "Competition, Strategies, and Restructuring," *Construction Business Review* 6, no. 4 (1996), pp. 56–61.

P. 186 Jensen quotation: Ron Jensen, *Managed Competition: A Tool for Achieving Excellence in Government* (Washington, D.C. Alliance for Redesigning Government, 1995); available at www.Alliance.napawash.org.

P. 188 "Between 1987 and 1995 . . . food services at public facilities": Reason Foundation, *Privatization 1995* (Los Angeles: Reason Foundation, 1995), p.2.

P. 188 "Taylorsville, Utah, an edge city . . . shared with another government": Dennis D. Wellendorf, Michael T. Eversden, and Thomas F. Olsen, *Sarpy County Efficiency Study* (Omaha: Constitutional Heritage Institute, September 1997), p. 18.

P. 188 "Similar growth in outsourcing . . . state and federal levels": Council of State Governments, *State Trends & Forecasts* 2, no. 2 (November 1993). Nor was the pattern likely to change. For instance, most state auditors, budget directors, and comptrollers surveyed by the council predicted further increases in contracting out.

P. 188 "By 1991, outsourcing accounted . . .Australia's federal outlays": Task Force on Management Improvement, *The Australian Public Service Reformed: An Evaluation of a Decade of Management Reform* (Canberra: Australian Government Publishing Service, 1992), p. 295.

p. 188 "And Wyoming, Arizona, . . . contractors' hands": Penelope Lemov, "The Rocky Road to Privatizing Welfare," *Governing* (July 1997), pp. 36–37.

P. 189 Council of State Governments quotation: Council of State Governments, *State Trends & Forecasts*, p. 26.

P. 189 "State administrators told the council . . . high-quality services": Ibid.

P. 189 Sturgess quotation: Gary L. Sturgess, "The Decline and Fall of the Industrial State," in *New Ideas, Better Government*, ed. Patrick Weller and Glyn Davis (St. Leonards, Australia: Allen & Unwin, 1996), p. 36.

P. 189 "Indianapolis mayor Steve Goldsmith declares . . . competitively bid": Interview in *Government Technology* (July 1995).

P. 190 Council of State Governments quotation: Council of State Governments, *State Trends & Forecasts*, p. 32.

P. 191 "For instance, the former commissioner . . . to collect current taxes": Robert D. Hershey, Jr., "G.O.P. Wants I.R.S. to Use Bill Collectors," *New York Times*, September 26, 1995, p. D8.

P. 194 "*The Government's Guide to Market Testing* . . . during the contract": United Kingdom, Efficiency Unit, *The Government's Guide to Market Testing* (London: Her Majesty's Stationery Office, 1993), pp. 52–54.

P. 194 *Government's Guide* quotation ("'Unless suppliers . . .'"): Ibid., p. 60.

Pp. 194–195 "For example, the Oxfordshire County . . . other counties": British Audit Commission, *Realising the Benefits of Competition: The Client Role for Contracted Services* (London: Her Majesty's Stationery Office, 1993), p. 38.

P. 195 "In 1986, Brian Mulroney's . . . the government quietly dropped it": Donald Savoie, *Thatcher, Reagan, Mulroney: In Search of a New Bureaucracy* (Pittsburgh and London: University of Pittsburgh Press, 1994), pp. 155–157.

P. 196 Goldsmith quotation: Stephen Goldsmith, *Moving Municipal Services into the Marketplace* (New York: Carnegie Council on Ethics and International Affairs, 1992), p. 3.

P. 197 "This is the method the British . . .managing the contract": United Kingdom, Efficiency Unit, *The Government's Guide to Market Testing*.

P. 199 "As the British Efficiency Unit . . . prices may fall": Ibid., p. 20.

P. 199 British Audit Commission quotation: British Audit Commission, *Realising the Benefits of Competition*, p. 37.

Pp. 199–200 "A U.S. Department of Labor study in 1989 . . . and 7 percent retired": Governor Pete Wilson, *Competitive Government: A Plan for Less Bureaucracy, More Results* (Sacramento: California Governor's Office, April 1996), p. 29. This publication cited *The Long-Term Employment Implications of Privatization,* NCEP, March 1989.

Pp. 200–201 "A third reason . . . advice to policymakers": The British government sometimes does this. See United Kingdom, Efficiency Unit, *The Government's Guide to Market Testing,* p. 13.

P. 201 "In Indianapolis, government bidders won . . . launched managed competition": Jon Jeter, "A Winning Combination in Indianapolis," *Washington Post,* September 21, 1997.

P. 201 "When the Australian . . . won 16 times": Interview with Paul Goshler, Australian Department of Defense.

P. 201 "In Phoenix . . . 56 contests": Jim Flanagan and Susan Perkins, "Public/Private Competition in the City of Phoenix, Arizona," *Government Finance Review* (June 1995), pp. 7–12.

P. 201 "And in the U.K. . . . subsequent rounds": *Next Steps Review: 1995,* Cm. 3164 (London: Her Majesty's Stationery Office, 1996), p. v. The 20–25 percent figure applies to the U.K., where savings averaged 21 percent in the early rounds, as well as Phoenix, Indianapolis, and other places that have used this tool.

P. 201 Fantauzzo quotation: William D. Eggers and John O'Leary, *Revolution at the Roots: Making Our Government Smaller, Better, and Closer to Home* (New York: Free Press, 1995), p. 11.

Pp. 202–203 Goldsmith quotation: Mayor Stephen Goldsmith, "More Bang for Tax Buck," *The Indianapolis News;* July 21, 1992 (letter to editor).

P. 205 Jensen quotation: Ron Jensen, *Managed Competition.*

P. 206 "The British did this with compulsory . . . competition for each one": *Competing for Quality: Buying Better Public Services,* Cm 1730 (London: Her Majesty's Stationery Office, November 1991), pp. 24–25.

Pp. 208–209 Howard Husock case study: Howard Husock, *Organizing Competition in Indianapolis: Mayor Stephen Goldsmith and the Quest for Lower Costs* (Cambridge, Mass.: John F. Kennedy School of Government, Harvard University, 1995).

P. 211 Creech quotations: Bill Creech, *The Five Pillars of TQM: How to Make Total Quality Management Work for You* (New York: Truman Talley Books/Dutton, 1994), p. 473.

P. 211 "In Australia . . . 12 services in eight states": See Steering Committee for the Review of Commonwealth/State Service Provision, *Report on Government Services 1998,* vols. 1 and 2 (Melbourne: Industry Commission, 1998). The Web page for the Industry Commission is www.indcom.gov.au/

P. 211 Thompson quotation: In Anjetta McQueen, "US Children Not Reaching Education Goals, Panel Says," *Washington Post,* December 3, 1999, p. A3.

Pp. 211–212 "In the U.K. . . . publication of the first *Performance Indicators*": Personal communication from Paul Vevers, Audit Commission. The data is published a year after each local council collects it, so the worst-performing councils knew they had problems a year before the first publication.

P. 212 Foster quotation: Quoted in Philip Johnston, "Councils Shamed into Doing Better," *The Daily Telegraph,* March 21, 1996, p. 6.

Chapter Six

Pp. 215–216 King County information: From interviews and Wastewater Treatment Division reports, summary sheets, and handbook.

P. 217 "Typically, civil servants . . . which depend on their performance": Charles A. Pounian and Jeffrey J. Fuller, "Compensating Public Employees," in *Handbook of Public Administration,* 2nd ed., ed. James L. Perry (San Francisco: Jossey-Bass, 1996), pp. 405–423.

P. 217 "In the first year of Australia's bonus program . . . officials got a bonus": Department of Industrial Relations and Department of Finance, "Joint PSC, DIR, and DOF Memorandum to Agencies on Performance Appraisal and Performance-Based Pay" April 27, 1994, p. 4.

P. 217 "This was also the norm . . . spread merit pay increases equally": Donald Savoie, *Thatcher, Reagan, Mulroney: In Search of a New Bureaucracy* (Pittsburgh: University of Pittsburgh Press, 1994), p. 296–297.

P. 217 Behn quotation: Robert D. Behn, "Measuring Performance Against the 80–30 Syndrome," *Governing* (June 1993), p. 70.

P. 217 Creech quotation: Bill Creech, *The Five Pillars of TQM: How to Make Total Quality Management Work for You* (New York: Truman Talley Books/Dutton, 1994), p. 435.

P. 221 Creech quotation ("'Many of his disciples . . .'"): Ibid., p. 479.

P. 223 "In the U.K., for example . . . reviews the annual targets": United Kingdom, Her Majesty's Treasury, *Executive Agencies: A Guide to Setting Targets and Measuring Performance* (London: Her Majesty's Stationery Office, 1992), p. 25–26.

P. 224 "For example, schools and school districts . . . according to *Education Week*": "Keeping Tabs on Quality: Part III," in *Quality Counts* (Washington, D.C.: Education Week, 1997). Available at www.edweek.org/sreports/qc97/intros/cover3.htm

P. 225 Vaughan quotation: Roger J. Vaughan, "Is It Working? Measuring the Performance of Public Programs," *The Entrepreneurial Economy Review* published by the Corporation for Enterprise Development in Washington, D.C. (July-August 1989), p. 3.

P. 225 Rogers quotation: From Patricia Rogers's contribution to the on-line dialogue "Evaltalk," October 19, 1997.

P. 225 "In January 1998, an internal audit . . . entire affair as a scandal": David E. Rosenbaum, "Audit Confirms Abusive I.R.S. Practices," *New York Times,* January 14, 1998, p. A13.

Pp. 225–226 Sylvie Trosa quotation: Sylvie Trosa, "The Australian Connection: Outputs and Outcomes Australian Style—The Importance of Stakeholder Management, Outcome Measurement and Information," in *Lifting the Game from Outputs to Outcomes: Proceedings, Public Service Senior Management Conference* (Wellington, New Zealand: State Services Commission, 1998), pp. 7–13. Available at www.ssc.govt.nz.

P. 226 Jerome Winston quotation: From Jerome Winston's contribution to the on-line dialogue "Evaltalk," October 21, 1997.

P. 227 "In Houston several years ago . . . Paige said": Kevin Bushweller, "Show Us the Money," *The American School Board Journal* (June 1997), p. 16.

P. 228 World Bank quotation: In Reason Foundation, *Privatization 1996* (Los Angeles: Reason Foundation), p. 10.

P. 228 "In Kentucky, where the state . . . professional pride": Steven Drummond, "Bonuses Weren't Prime Reason Schools Worked to Improve, Study in Ky. Says," *Education Week* (April 2, 1997), p. 7.

P. 228 "One year, Kimberly Gonzalez . . . I wanted to know why'": Mark Andrejevic, "Five Lansing-Area Schools Get High Marks from State," *The Lansing State Journal,* April 20, 1995, p. 1A.

P. 229 Hornbeck quotation: Bushweller, "Show Us the Money," *The American School Board Journal.*

P. 229 "In 1996, for example, Chicago's school board . . . it could close the schools": Don Terry, "One Fifth of Schools Put on Probation in Chicago," *New York Times,* October 1, 1996, p. A8.

P. 229 "In the mid-1990s . . . measurable improvements": Drummond, "Bonuses Weren't Prime Reason . . . ," p. 7.

P. 229 "By 1996, neither showed improvement in student test scores": Arthur Allen, "Newark Postcard: Whacked," *The New Republic* (April 29, 1996), pp. 12–14.

P. 231 Behn quotation: Behn, "Measuring Performance Against the 80–30 Syndrome," p. 70.

P. 232 "In 1984, South Carolina began . . . new equipment or materials": Carolyn Kelley and Allan Odden, "Reinventing Teacher Compensation Systems," *CPRE Finance Briefs* (New Brunswick, N.J.: Consortium for Policy Research in Education, Rutgers University, September 1995), p. 3.

P. 233 "By 1995, ten state governments . . . pay to performance": *Workforce Policies: State Activities and Innovations* (Washington, D.C.: National Association of State Budget Offices, 1995), p. 43.

P. 233 Harry Hatry study: Harry P. Hatry, John M. Greiner, and Brenda G. Ashford, *Issues and Case Studies in Teacher Incentive Plans,* 2nd ed. (Washington, D.C.: Urban Institute Press, 1994), p. 239.

P. 233 "In 1995 Kentucky handed out $26 million . . . in their schools": Kelley and Odden, "Reinventing Teacher Compensation Systems," p. 2.

Pp. 233–234 "Since 1990, Dallas teachers and principals . . . other staff members": Kelley and Odden, "Reinventing Teacher Compensation Systems," p. 5.

P. 234 "And more than a dozen British . . . each staff member": *Survey Report: Executive Agencies* (London: Price Waterhouse, March 1993), p. 14.

P. 234 "A few government . . . extraordinary merit": See, for example, Al Gore, *Common Sense Government: The Third Report of the National Performance Review* (Washington, D.C.: National Performance Review, 1995), pp. 64–65.

P. 234 "In the first month alone . . . increase in output": David Osborne, "Raise Taxes? Slash Services? Is There Another Choice?" *Governing* 5, no. 6 (March 1992), p. 55. Statistics provided by the Florida Division of Worker's Compensation.

P. 236 “We agree with Robert Behn . . . a bad idea”: Behn, “Measuring Performance Against the 80–30 Syndrome.”

P. 237 “In Indianapolis, garbage collectors . . . in the previous year”: R. Joseph Gelarden, “Trash Haulers Get Cash for Saving Money for City,” *Indianapolis Star,* March 18, 1995.

P. 238 “In New York City . . . three workers per truck to two”: Personal communication from Barbara Cohn, Fund for the City of New York.

P. 239 “. . . workers in the U.S. Air Force PACER SHARE project received 50 percent”: Office of Personnel Management, “Proposed Demonstration Project: Pacer Share: A Federal Productivity Enhancement Program; Notice of Final Approval,” *Federal Register* (November 20, 1987).

P. 240 “Research about gainsharing confirms . . . increased productivity”: Spencer Graves Associates, *Compensation Systems and Other Human Resources Policies to Promote Quality and Productivity Improvement,* Report 91–4 (San Jose, Calif.: Spencer Graves Associates, 1991).

P. 241 Fleming quotation: Al Gore, *From Red Tape to Results: Creating a Government that Works Better and Costs Less* (Washington, D.C.: National Performance Review, 1993), p. 18.

P. 244 “The U.S. General Accounting Office . . . the success of their agencies’ ”: U.S. General Accounting Office, *Managing for Results: Experiences Abroad Suggest Insights for Federal Management Reforms* (Washington, D.C.: U.S. General Accounting Office, May 1995), p. 39.

P. 244 “By 1995, only six of the 33 . . . as chief executives”: Jonathon Boston et al., *Public Management: The New Zealand Model* (Auckland, New Zealand: Oxford University Press, 1996), p. 107.

P. 244 Barnes information and quotation: Bill Graves, “Putting Pay on the Line,” *The School Administrator* (February 1995), p. 13.

Chapter Seven

P. 247 Goethe quotation: Quoted in Roger J. Vaughan, “Is It Working? Measuring the Performance of Public Programs,” *The Entrepreneurial Economy Review* (July-August 1989). Published by the Corporation for Enterprise Development, Washington, D.C.

P. 248 Behn quotation: Robert Behn, *Bottom-Line Government* (Durham, N.C.: The Governors Center at Duke University, 1994), p. 12.

P. 249 “In early 1994, twenty-one federal agencies . . . Management and Budget”, *Toward Useful Performance Measurement: Lessons Learned from Initial Pilot Performance Plans Prepared Under the Government Performance and Results Act* (Washington, D.C.: National Academy of Public Administration, November 1994).

P. 249 “When they submitted their plans . . . trying to understand it”: Ibid.

P. 249 Kettl quotation: Donald F. Kettl, “Measuring Performance When There Is No Bottom Line” (paper prepared for a conference of the New Zealand Politics Research Group, Victoria University of Wellington, July 8, 1994).

Pp. 253–254 British Treasury’s quality measures (in box): United Kingdom, Her Majesty’s Treasury: *Executive Agencies: A Guide to Setting Targets and Measuring Performance* (London: Her Majesty’s Stationery Office, 1992), pp. 13–16.

P. 259 "Most of the U.S. GPRA . . . their missions": *Toward Useful Performance Measurement.*

P. 259 "In Australia, a review of performance reporting . . . little data on outcomes": Task Force on Management Improvement, *The Australian Public Service Reformed: An Evaluation of a Decade of Management Reform* (Canberra: Australian Government Printing Service, 1992), pp. 351–359.

P. 259 "The same thing happened in the U.K.": See, for instance, Sylvie Trosa, *Next Steps: Moving On* (London: Office of Public Service and Science, February 1994).

P. 261 Atlantic Richfield officials quotation: Project USA, *Performance Measurement: Report on a Survey of Private Sector Performance Measures* (Washington, D.C.: U.S. Department of the Treasury, January 1993), p. D–1.

P. 261 "Based on the experience of executive agencies . . . any particular unit": United Kingdom, Next Steps Team, *The Strategic Management of Agencies: Models for Management* (London: Her Majesty's Stationery Office, 1995), p. 40.

P. 261 British Treasury quotation: United Kingdom, Her Majesty's Treasury, *Executive Agencies: A Guide to Setting Targets and Measuring Performance,* p. 34.

P. 262 U.S. Treasury quotation: Financial Management Service, *Performance Measurement Guide* (Washington, D.C.: U.S. Department of the Treasury, November 1993), p. 32.

P. 262 Sylvie Trosa quotation: Trosa, *Next Steps: Moving On,* p. 13.

P. 264 Boeing quotation: Project USA, *Performance Measurement: Report on a Survey of Private Sector Performance Measures,* p. D–1.

P. 266 NAPA quotation: *Toward Useful Performance Measurement.*

P. 267 Portland annual report: Interviews with Audit Director Richard Tracy.

P. 269 "Checking Your Organization's Progress" box: Adapted from Craig Holt, "Review of the Performance Measurement Program Strategy," internal memo, Oregon Department of Transportation, March 31, 1995.

Chapter Eight

P. 279 "With 209 schools . . . have not": *1997–98 Accountability Report* (Milwaukee: Milwaukee Public Schools, December 1998), p. 14; 12th largest: John Gardner, "How School Choice Helps Public Education" (unpublished article, 1997), p. 2.

P. 279 Howard Fuller quotation: Howard Fuller, *Strategy for Change: Superintendent's Report to the Board of School Directors* (Milwaukee: Milwaukee Public Schools, August 6, 1991), pp. 1, 7.

P. 280 "The principals . . . bureaucratic loophole": David Ruenzel, "A Choice in the Matter," *Education Week* 15, no. 4 (September 27, 1995), p. 27.

P. 280 "In desperation . . . the state gave districts per pupil": For descriptions of the political battle for vouchers and the early voucher program, see John O. Norquist, "A Ticket to Better Schools," *Reader's Digest* (July 1993), pp. 65–70; and George A. Mitchell, *The Milwaukee Parental Choice Program* (Milwaukee: Wisconsin Policy Research Institute, November 1992). The dollar figure is from John S. Gardner, "The Milwaukee, Wisconsin, School Choice Experience," memo to Virginia legislators, February 7, 2000.

P. 280 "The voucher program was small enough . . . attracted enormous publicity": Mitchell, *The Milwaukee Parental Choice Program,* p. 3.

P. 280 "Williams's idea . . . compensation for it": Derrick Z. Jackson, "The Corruption of School Choice," *Boston Globe,* October 28, 1998.

P. 280 Polly Williams quotation: Ruenzel, "A Choice in the Matter," p. 26.

Pp. 280–281 Howard Fuller proposals: Fuller, *Strategy for Change.*

P. 281 "Over the next three years . . . the union erupted": Personal communications with John Gardner, Howard Fuller, and David Riemer, director of administration under Milwaukee mayor John Norquist.

P. 281 "Two weeks later . . . blocking his reform efforts": Associated Press, "Milwaukee School Superintendent is Resigning," *New York Times,* May 20, 1995.

P. 281 "That spring, however . . . the eligibility list": See, for example, Ruenzel, "A Choice in the Matter."

P. 281 "Suddenly the district stood to lose . . . $785 million budget": *Report to the Community* (Milwaukee: Milwaukee Public Schools, December 1998), p. 21.

Pp. 281–282 List of Milwaukee School Board actions: Gardner, "How School Choice Helps Public Education," and personal communications with John Gardner.

Pp. 282–283 "In March 1996 . . . revolutionary reform has all but died'": Ibid.

P. 283 "The three managed . . . charter schools in Milwaukee": Interviews with John Gardner, Bruce Thompson, and David Riemer.

P. 283 "The union gave up . . . favorable to the reformers": Interviews and personal communications with John Gardner, Bruce Thompson, and David Riemer.

P. 284 *Milwaukee Journal Sentinel* quotation: "In MPS Races, Reform Finishes First," *Milwaukee Journal Sentinel,* April 8, 1999.

P. 284 "The new board quickly . . . sweep away the old system'": Interviews and personal communications with John Gardner, Bruce Thompson, and David Riemer.

P. 284 Kolderie quotation: Ted Kolderie, "The States Will Have to Withdraw the Exclusive Franchise," *Newsletter of the Public Services Redesign Project,* 1990. Published by the Center for Policy Studies, St. Paul, Minn.

P. 285 Gardner quotations: Gardner, "How School Choice Helps Public Education," pp. 9, 10, 13.

Pp. 285–286 Pioneer Institute study: David J. Armor and Brett M. Peiser, *Competition in Education: A Case Study of Interdistrict Choice* (Boston: Pioneer Institute, 1997).

Pp. 286–287 Rofes study: Eric Rofes, *How Are School Districts Responding to Charter Laws and Charter Schools*? (Berkeley: Policy Analysis for California Education, University of California-Berkeley, April 1998).

P. 287 "Schools can opt out . . . secondary schools)": United Kingdom, Office for Standards in Education (OFSTED), *Secondary Education 1993–97: A Review of Secondary Schools in England* (London: Her Majesty's Stationery Office, 1998), ch. 1; available at www.official-documents.co.uk/document/ofsted/seced/review.htm.

P. 287 "No one can prove . . . from reform)": Ibid.

P. 287 "Since the reforms began . . . roughly 50 percent": United Kingdom, Office for Standards in Education (OFSTED), *The Annual Report of Her Majesty's Chief Inspector of Schools: Standards and Quality in Education 1997/98* (London: Her Majesty's Stationery Office, 1999), paragraph 161; available at www.official-documents.co.uk/ (click on "Publications," then "Inspection Findings").

P. 287 "Student participation in higher education . . . in 1997–1998": Data provided by U.K. Department for Education and Employment.

P. 288 OFSTED quotation: United Kingdom, OFSTED, *The Annual Report of Her Majesty's Chief Inspector of Schools 1997/98,* Commentary pp. 1–7.

P. 289 Consolidated Chemical Dependency Treatment Fund: Minnesota Department of Human Services, preliminary application for Innovations in American Government Award, 1993, p. 2; obtained from awards program at John F. Kennedy School of Government.

P. 290 "Also in Minnesota . . . if they had to compete": Sandford Borins, *Innovating with Integrity: How Local Heroes Are Transforming American Government* (Washington, D.C.: Georgetown University Press, 1998), pp. 175–176.

P. 290 The dozen transitions to competitive choice that we studied are the following: District 4 schools in East Harlem (see David Osborne and Ted Gaebler, *Reinventing Government* [Reading, Mass.: Addison-Wesley, 1992], pp. 5–8, 103–104); Minnesota schools (see *Reinventing Government,* pp. 96–104 and David Osborne and Peter Plastrik, *Banishing Bureaucracy: The Five Strategies for Reinventing Government* [Reading, Mass.: Addison-Wesley, 1997], pp. 157–174); Milwaukee schools (see this book, pp. 279–285); Massachusetts schools (see this book, pp. 285–286); charter schools nationally (see this book, pp. 286–287, 443); U.K. schools (see *Banishing Bureaucracy,* pp. 174–175, and this book, pp. 287–288); Michigan's Human Investment System (see *Reinventing Government,* pp. 186–192); One-Stop Career Centers in Massachusetts; Minnesota's Department of Administration (see *Reinventing Government,* pp. 90–92, and this book, pp. 175–182;) Minnesota's Consolidated Chemical Dependency Treatment Fund (see this book, p. 289); Texas's Child Care Management Services Program (see this book, p. 320); and New Zealand's reforms (see *Banishing Bureaucracy* pp. 75–90, 174).

P. 291 Norquist quote: Norquist, "A Ticket to Better Schools," p. 65.

P. 291 Michael Joyce quote: Peter Applebome, "Milwaukee Forces Debate on Vouchers," *New York Times,* September 1, 1995, p. A12.

P. 291 John Gardner quote: Curtis Lawrence, "John Gardner's Style Has Rocked the Boat at MPS," *Milwaukee Journal Sentinel,* August 11, 1996.

P. 292 Consolidated Chemical Dependency Treatment Fund quotations: Minnesota Department of Human Services, semifinalist application, p. 13.

P. 292 Peterson study: Paul Peterson and Jay Greene, "Race Relations, Vouchers, and Central-City Schools," in *The Taubman Center Report* (Cambridge, Mass.: John F. Kennedy School of Government, Harvard University, 1998), pp. 10–12; and Jay P. Greene, Paul E. Peterson, and Jiangtao Du, "Effectiveness of School Choice: The Milwaukee Experiment, *Education and Urban Society* (February 1999), pp. 190–213.

P. 293 "State hospitals and their unions . . . develop the final legislation": Minnesota Department of Human Services, semifinalist application, pp. 7, 9.

P. 294 "When the Perpich administration . . . take on that battle": Ibid., pp. 9, 13.

P. 294 "When Texas converted . . . training in marketing techniques": Borins, *Innovating with Integrity,* p. 176.

P. 295 Roger Douglas quote: Roger Douglas, "The Politics of Successful Structural Reform" (unpublished manuscript), p. 20.

P. 295 Roberts and King quote: Nancy C. Roberts and Paula J. King, *Transforming Public Policy: Dynamics of Policy Entrepreneurship and Innovation* (San Francisco: Jossey-Bass, 1996), p. 189.

P. 296 "This is one of the basic rules . . . Minnesota reformers": Ibid., p. 100.

P. 296 Douglas quote: Douglas, "The Politics of Successful Structural Reform," p. 6.

P. 298 Michael Alves quotation: Edith Rasell and Richard Rothstein, eds., *School Choice: Examining the Evidence* (Washington, D.C.: Economic Policy Institute, 1993), p. 137.

P. 301 "Within four years . . . public school population": Charles Mahtesian, "Charter Schools Learn a Few Lessons," *Governing* (January 1998), p. 23.

P. 301 "According to *The Wall Street Journal* . . . generate excess state aid": Steve Stecklow, "Start-Up Lessons: Arizona Takes the Lead in Charter Schools—For Better or Worse," *Wall Street Journal,* December 24, 1996, pp. A1, A4.

P. 303 Michael Alves quotation: Rasell and Rothstein, eds., *School Choice,* p. 136.

P. 303 "In addition, the evidence . . . education and income": See, for example, Douglas Willms and Frank H. Echols, "The Scottish Experience of Parental School Choice," in *School Choice: Examining the Evidence,* p. 63.

P. 305 "The biggest obstacle": Keith A. Halpern and Eliza R. Culbertson, *Blueprint for Change: Charter Schools, A Handbook for Action* (Washington, D.C.: Democratic Leadership Council, 1994), p. 12.

P. 305 "In many statewide interdistrict . . . win back market share": Armor and Peiser, *Competition in Education,* p. 48.

P. 305 "Not surprisingly, they did nothing to respond": Ibid., pp. 106–107, 144.

P. 305 Jerri O'Brien-Cass quotation: In Michael Winerip, "Schools for Sale," *New York Times Magazine,* June 14, 1998, p. 45.

P. 305 OFSTED quotation: United Kingdom, Office of Standards in Education, *OFSTED, Secondary Education 1993–97,* ch. 2, p. 6.

P. 306 "The British now have a system . . . according to OFSTED": United Kingdom, Office of Standards in Education, "Inspections," www.ofsted.gov.uk/about/inspect.htm, 1999.

P. 306 "Between 1993 and 1997 . . . special measures": United Kingdom, Office of Standards in Education, *The Annual Report 1997/98,* paragraph 222.

P. 306 "By 1999, more than two dozen . . . financial mismanagement": Dave DeSchryver, "Part II: The Closures, the Opportunity for Accountability," in *Charter Schools: A Progress Report* (Washington, D.C.: Center for Education Reform, February 1999), available at www.edreform.com/.

P. 306 "When Texas converted . . . reached them": Texas Department of Human Services, semifinalist application, Innovations in State and Local Government Awards Program, 1993; obtained from awards program at John F. Kennedy School of Government.

P. 307 "Several studies have found . . . many resent their competitors": See, for instance, Eric Rofes, *How Are School Districts Responding to Charter Laws and Charter Schools*? pp. 2, 14.

P. 307 Massachusetts report: A legislatively mandated study conducted by Rosenblum Brigham Associates, quoted in Bill Rust, "Promises to Keep," *Advocasey* 1, no. 1 (Spring 1999), p. 23.

P. 308 "Cleveland has a similar program . . . in 1998–99": Jeff Archer, "Policies of Cleveland Voucher Program Faulted," *Education Week* (January 20, 1999), p. 3.

P. 308 "Any service from which . . . vouchers or reimbursement": E. S. Savas, *Privatization: The Key to Better Government* (Chatham, N.J.: Chatham House, 1987), p. 279.

P. 310 "In Cleveland, for example . . . income levels and residency": Archer, "Policies of Cleveland Voucher Program Faulted," p. 3.

P. 310 "By 1993, waste, fraud, and loan defaults . . . education or training of value": Michael Winerip, "Billions for School Are Lost in Fraud, Waste and Abuse," *New York Times,* February 2, 1994, pp. A1–D20; and Michael Winerip, "Overhauling School Grants: Much Debate but Little Gain," *New York Times,* February 4, 1994, pp. A1–A16.

P. 310 "The Clinton administration . . . 9.6 percent by 1998": U.S. Department of Education, Office of Student Financial Assistance, *IPOS: The Gatekeeper* (Washington, D.C.: U.S. Department of Education, February 1999); and U.S. Department of Education, Office of Student Financial Assistance, *Results of Recertification 1993–1997* (U.S. Department of Education, April 1999).

P. 311 Herzlinger quotation: Regina E. Herzlinger, *Protection of the Health Care Consumer: The "Truth" Agency* (Washington, D.C.: Progressive Policy Institute, March 1999), pp. 13–14.

P. 312 "In a 1999 national survey . . . other schools in the area": Ann Bradley, "Parents Express Scant Interest in Helping Govern Schools," *Education Week* (March 24, 1999), p. 5.

P. 312 "Florida was the first state . . . and training offices": Anthony P. Carnevale and Neal C. Johnson, "Focus on Results," *Government Technology* (October 1998), p. 18.

P. 313 Labor Government quote: United Kingdom, Cabinet Office, *Service First: The New Charter Programme* (London: Cabinet Office, 1998), paragraphs 3.16 and 3.17; available at www.servicefirst.gov.uk/ (click on "Index").

P. 313 "The Labor government is adding . . . National Health Service": United Kingdom, *The Citizen's Charter-Five Years On* (London: Her Majesty's Stationery Office, September 1996), pp. ix, 32.

P. 313 "In addition to the hard data . . . cultural development of students": United Kingdom, Office of Standards in Education, "Background Briefing on OFSTED," 1999, and "Inspections," www.ofsted.gov.uk/about/inspect.htm.

P. 313 "Parents are invited . . . 'behavior' ": United Kingdom, Office of Standards in Education, *Secondary Education 1993–97,* ch. 1.

P. 313 " 'The school's response . . . OFSTED explains' ": United Kingdom, Office of Standards in Education, "Inspections."

P. 314 "Ted Sizer . . . to evaluate a school": personal communications with Ted Sizer, May 1999.

P. 314 "After it was elected in 1997 . . . with similar students": United Kingdom, Department for Education and Employment, *Excellence in Schools* (London: Her Majesty's Stationery Office, July 1997), pp. 25, 31, 32.

P. 314 "The British Audit Commission . . . finalizing its performance indicators": Paul Vevers, presentation from 1995 conference at LBJ School, University of Texas, Austin, p. 3. Vevers, associate director for audit support at the Audit Commission, provided the presentation to the authors.

Pp. 314–315 Albert Shanker quotation: Albert Shanker, "Reporting on Schools," *The New Republic* (April 17, 1995). (Published as a paid advertisement.)

P. 315 "The U.K. is also piloting a method . . . measure for each school": See www.dfee.gov.uk/performance/vap_98/docC.htm.

P. 316 "(In the interim . . . took their previous exams)": Ibid.

P. 317 Texas Legislative Budget Board quotations: Legislative Budget Board, "Staff Performance Report: Report Card on the Texas Public School Accountability System," from www.lbb.state.tx.us/spr75.nsf, 1998.

P. 318 Vevers quotation: Vevers, presentation from 1995 conference at LBJ School.

P. 320 "About the same time, Texas created . . . so they could train staff": Texas Department of Human Services, semifinalist application.

P. 322 "Often, customer information systems . . . eligible clients": Pat Wong, site visit report for Innovations in State and Local Government Awards Program, 1993.

P. 322 "In their successful application . . . they had encountered": Texas Department of Human Services, semifinalist application.

Chapter Nine

P. 324 "Only a few years old . . . 60 million calls a year": Interviews with Jack McHale, deputy regional commissioner for the Philadelphia region of the Social Security Administration, and Steve DeMarco, acting director, Mid-Atlantic Program Service Center.

P. 324 "Customer satisfaction had fallen . . . reaching someone on the phone'": Al Gore, *From Red Tape to Results: Creating a Government That Works Better and Costs Less* (Washington, D.C.: National Performance Review, 1993), p. 46.

Pp. 324–325 "The Gore report prominently featured . . . *on our 800 number*": Ibid.

P. 325 "At the busiest times . . . 18 percent did": Data on busy rates and access rates from October 1992 through March 1999 provided to the authors by Steve DeMarco, acting director, Mid-Atlantic Program Service Center.

P. 325 "The agency had already . . . quality of service": Interview with Larry Massanari, regional commissioner for the Philadelphia region.

P. 325 "One of the surveys said . . . 10 people": Interview with and written communication from Toni Lenane, May 21, 1999.

P. 325 "The NPR's September 1994 report . . . *busy signal much of the time*": President Bill Clinton and Vice President Al Gore, *Putting Customers First: Standards for Serving the American People* (Washington, D.C.: National Performance Review, 1994), p. 14.

P. 326 "Almost no one . . . standard was possible": Interviews with current and former Social Security Administration officials Toni Lenane, Janice Warden, Larry Massanari, and Steve DeMarco.

P. 326 "The 'busy rate' was going up, not down . . . 53 percent": Data on busy rates and access rates from October 1992 through March 1999 provided by Steve DeMarco.

P. 326 "So they got to work. . . they went slowly": Interviews with current and former Social Security Administration officials Toni Lenane, Janice Warden, Larry Massanari, Jack McHale, Steve DeMarco, and Jean Venable.

P. 326 "In his budget hearings . . . fiscal 1997": Ibid.

P. 327 "Greg Woods also agreed to the 95 percent goal": Interviews with Greg Woods.

P. 327 Dalbar Financial Services rating: President Bill Clinton and Vice President Al Gore, *Putting Customers First '95: Standards for Serving the American People* (Washington, D.C.: National Performance Review, 1995), p. 7.

P. 327 "In fiscal 1995 . . . 61.8 percent": U.S. Social Security Administration, *Social Security: Report to Our Customers* SSA 05–10617 (Washington, D.C.: Social Security Administration, September 1996), p. 3. Data on busy rates and access rates from October 1992 through March 1999 provided by Steve DeMarco. The two sources conflict slightly: the published report says 72.5 percent of callers got through in five minutes in fiscal year 1995. According to Toni Lenane, 73.5 percent is the correct figure.

P. 328 "They trained 3,700 . . . of 'spikers'": Interview with Toni Lenane.

P. 328 "This required . . . have to change": Interviews with current or former SSA officials Janice Warden, Jack McHale, Steve DeMarco, and Larry Massanari.

P. 328 "Meanwhile, the agency restricted . . . from the beginning of the month.)": Interviews with current and former Social Security Administration officials Toni Lenane, Janice Warden, Larry Massanari, Jack McHale, Steve DeMarco, and Jean Venable.

P. 329 "November 1995 was the low point. . . all got busy signals": Data on busy rates and access rates from October 1992 through March 1999 provided by Steve DeMarco; information on the 800 system crash from interviews with Janice Warden, Greg Woods, Jack McHale, and Steve DeMarco.

P. 329 "By February . . . every year since": Data on busy rates and access rates from October 1992 through March 1999 provided by Steve DeMarco.

P. 329 "Meanwhile customer ratings . . . 95 percent positive": U.S. Social Security Administration, *Social Security: Report to Our Customers* and "SSA—A High Impact Agency," *Social Security Online*, www.ssa.gov/agencygoals.html; and interviews with Jack McHale and Janice Warden.

P. 329 "Agency leaders acknowledge . . . the agency's customers": Interviews with current and former Social Security Administration officials Toni Lenane, Janice Warden, Jack McHale, and Steve DeMarco.

P. 330 President Clinton's executive order: See Clinton and Gore, *Putting Customers First* (1994), p. 5.

P. 330 "By fiscal year 1998 . . . quite vague": President Bill Clinton and Vice President Al Gore, *Putting Customers First '97: Standards for Serving the American People* (Washington, D.C.: National Performance Review, October 1997), pp. 2–3. Available at www.npr.gov.

P. 330 1991 OPM survey and 1998 NPR survey: Personal communications from NPR deputy director John Kamensky.

P. 330 "By 1998, according to the NPR . . . Priority Mail and Express Mail": Clinton and Gore, *Putting Customers First '97.*

P. 331 "By then there were some 200 . . . quite effective": United Kingdom, Cabinet Office, *Service First: The New Charter Programme*, paragraphs 2.3, 4.5, 4.8.

P. 331 National Audit Office quote: Ibid., paragraph 2.1

P. 331 National Consumer Council quote: United Kingdom, Cabinet Office, "The Citizen's Charter Performance to Date," in *The Citizen's Charter, A Consultation Exercise: The Government's Response* (London: Cabinet Office, 1998), p. 1.

P. 331 Public Service Committee quote: United Kingdom, Cabinet Office, *Service First,* paragraph 2.2.

P. 331 "The Labor Party pledged . . . opposition's ideas": Ibid. Quote is in the foreword by David Clark, then chancellor of the Duchy of Lancaster (the minister in charge of public service reform).

P. 331 "The basic tool . . . or provincial governments": *The Citizen's Charter-Five Years On* (London: Her Majesty's Stationery Office, September 1996), p. 5; Kirsi Kuuttiniemi and Petri Virtanen, *Citizen's Charters and Compensation Mechanisms* (Helsinki: Finland Ministry of Finance, 1998); and Australian Department of Finance and Administration, "Client Service Standards and Other Quality Initiatives," www.dofa.gov.au/pubs/pig/reform/reform09.htm.

P. 332 Citizen-Centred Service Network survey: Erin Research Inc., *Citizens First: Summary Report* (Ottawa: Canadian Centre for Management Development, 1998), pp. 2, 5.

P. 332 "When the Labor government reviewed the Citizen's Charter . . . enforce charter targets'": United Kingdom, Cabinet Office, *The Citizen's Charter, A Consultation Exercise,* ch. 2, p. 3.

P. 333 "This, the government concluded . . . old Charter programme'": United Kingdom, Cabinet Office, *Service First,* paragraph 3.16.

P. 333 "'The key is for standards . . . it said": United Kingdom, Cabinet Office, *The Citizen's Charter, A Consultation Exercise,* p. 4.

P. 333 "The Social Security . . . FEMA workers": Clinton and Gore, *Putting Customers First '97,* p. 12.

P. 334 ". . . in 1998 there were 1202 applications": United Kingdom, Cabinet Office, *Service First: The New Charter Programme (Summary)* (London, Cabinet Office, 1999). (A two-page summary provided to the authors.)

P. 334 "The Labor government's review . . . of them": United Kingdom, Cabinet Office, *Service First,* chs. 2, 6.

P. 334 "By 1999, only 18 organizations . . . three times in a row": Prime Minister Tony Blair, "Modernising Public Services," speech at Charter Mark Awards, Central Hall, Westminster, January 26, 1999; available at www.servicefirst.gov.uk/1999/mark/pmspeech.htm.

P. 334 "British Gas won in 1993 . . . attracted great publicity": Personal communications from Eugenie Turton, former director of the Citizen's Charter Unit, and Gloria Craig, deputy director of Service First Unit.

P. 334 Maggi White quote: "In the Hot Seat," *Charter News* (Autumn 1995), p. 7. *Charter News* was published by the Citizen's Charter Unit in the U.K. Office of Public Service.

P. 335 Massachusetts Department of Environmental Protection story: Interviews with Dan Greenbaum, former commissioner of the organization.

P. 336 "When the Minnesota Department of Revenue . . . dramatically": Interviews with former department officials Connie Nelson and Babak Armajani.

P. 336 Weise and Murphy quotes: A.L. Singleton, "Custom Tailoring: The Remaking of a Bureaucracy," *Government Executive* (July 1995), pp. 30–34.

P. 336 Massachusetts DEP story: Interviews with Dan Greenbaum, former commissioner.

P. 336 "California introduced 'tiered permitting' . . . in one place": Governor Pete Wilson, *Competitive Government: A Plan for Less Bureaucracy, More Results* (Sacramento: California Governor's Office, April 1966), pp. 48–50.

P. 337 "Greenbaum used a two-stage process . . . Thomas B. Powers": Interviews with Dan Greenbaum, former commissioner; and Ed Finkel, "Permits On Time, Or Money Back," *The Public Innovator* 24 (March 16, 1995): pp. 1–3 (published by the National Academy of Public Administration's Alliance for Redesigning Government, available at www.Alliance.napawash.org).

P. 338 "Before it reengineered . . . police protection": Interview with former deputy commissioner Babak Armajani.

P. 338 "The Minnesota Revenue Department announced . . . 24 days": Ibid.

P. 339 "When the Oregon Division of Motor Vehicles . . . reengineered that too": Clinton and Gore, *Putting Customers First* (1994), p. 8.

P. 341 "In the U.K., the Labor government . . . intervene when necessary": United Kingdom, Cabinet Office, *The Citizen's Charter, A Consultation Exercise,* ch. 2, and *Service First,* paragraphs 4.11 and 4.12.

P. 341 "Because some private rail . . . a standard format": "Panel Call for Public Services to Be More Responsive," *Results from the People's Panel* 2 (January 1999), p. 11; available at www.servicefirst.gov.uk/1999/panel/2ndwave/summary2.htm.

P. 342 "Their review pointed out . . . 'in the past'": United Kingdom, Cabinet Office, *Service First,* 1998, paragraph 2.3.

P. 342 "The government's guide . . . should be consulted": United Kingdom, Cabinet Office, *How to Draw Up a National Charter* (London: Cabinet Office, 1998), paragraph 3.4; available at www.cabinet-office.gov.uk/servicefirst/1998/natguide/bk31toc.htm.

P. 342 Lesley Harvey quote: "Promises," *Charter News* 1 (November 1993).

P. 343 "In the U.K. the Charter unit . . . learn from one another": United Kingdom, Cabinet Office, *The Citizen's Charter, A Consultation Exercise,* ch. 5.

P. 343 "There is a mentoring system . . . to improve customer service": United Kingdom, Cabinet Office, *Service First,* paragraphs 6.18, 6.21.

P. 345 "Prime Minister Tony Blair . . . review of the Citizen's Charter": United Kingdom, Cabinet Office, *The Citizen's Charter, A Consultation Exercise,* ch. 4.

Pp. 345–346 "'Handling complaints well' . . . enormous amounts": Citizen's Charter Complaints Task Force, *Putting Things Right* (London: Her Majesty's Stationery Office, 1995), pp. 26, 44.

P. 346 "Since surveys show . . . outcomes they experience": Erin Research Inc., *Citizens First: Summary Report,* p. 8. This survey research, done in Canada, concluded that "Telephone problems are the most common barrier. Forty percent of all respondents reported one or more phone-related problems."

P. 347 "Service Standards for Routine Transactions" box: Erin Research Inc., *Citizens First,* p. 12.

P. 348 "Sunnyvale's Leisure Services unit . . . that's what kids like": Interviews with Robert Walker, director of parks and recreation.

P. 348 "Characteristics of Good Standards" box: For the British and Canadian lists, see United Kingdom, Cabinet Office, *Service First,* paragraph 4.9; and Charles Malé, *Service Standards: A Guide to the Initiative* (Ottawa: Treasury Board Secretariat, 1996), pp. 4–5. See the resource list on pp. 358–359 to find how to obtain these documents.

P. 349 Treasury Board quote: Malé, *Service Standards,* p. 23.

P. 353 "'There are no shortcuts . . . needs to be involved'": Canadian Treasury Board, *Manager's Guide for Implementing Quality Services* (Ottawa: Treasury Board Secretariat, 1996), pp. 20–21.

P. 355 "The SSA gets data . . . six months": Interview with Larry Massanari, regional commissioner, Philadelphia region.

P. 355 "The British have come . . . 'often too long'": United Kingdom, Cabinet Office, *Service First,* paragraph 4.2.

Pp. 355–356 "Their new 'how-to' guide . . . contact numbers and addresses).'": United Kingdom, Cabinet Office, *How to Draw Up a National Charter,* paragraphs 1.1 and 2.1.

P. 356 Treasury Board Secretariat quotation: Malé, *Service Standards,* p. 22.

P. 356 "As the Canadian guide says": Ibid., p. 23.

P. 356 "'Research shows . . . 90 percent'": United Kingdom, Cabinet Office, *How to Draw Up a National Charter,* paragraph 4.8.

P. 359 "Think of the difference . . . 6 percent": Frederick W. Smith, "Competing with the Postal Service," *CATO Policy Report* 21, no. 2 (March/April 1999), pp. 1, 10–12.

P. 359 "The U.S. Census Bureau . . . get your money back": Clinton and Gore, *Putting Customers First '97,* p. 4.

P. 359 Fox Valley Technical College quote: Policy reprinted in Stanley J. Spanbauer, *A Quality System for Education* (Milwaukee: ASQC Quality Press, 1992), p. 12.

P. 359 "Typically, if an employer . . . up to par": See, for instance, Jerry Thomas, "High School Gives Warranties," *Boston Globe,* June 1, 1991.

P. 360 Michigan Commerce Department example: From personal experience; Peter Plastrik was a top official in the department at the time.

P. 360 "When Indianapolis contracted . . . back up the guarantee": Gordon St. Angelo and Michael Wells, "IAA Managed Competition Committee Recommendation," August 23, 1995, memorandum from St. Angelo, committee chairman, and Wells to members of the Indianapolis Airports Authority Board.

P. 361 Domino's Pizza story: Janelle Barlow and Claus Møller, *A Complaint Is a Gift* (San Francisco: Berrett-Koehler, 1996), p. 67.

P. 361 "The department also. . . money-back guarantee": Finkel, "Permits On Time, or Money Back," *The Public Innovator* 24.

P. 363 "Twenty years ago . . . took the time to complain": Technical Assistance Research Programs Inc., *Consumer Complaint-Handling in America: Final Report* (Washington, D.C.: White House Office of Consumer Affairs, 1980).

P. 363 "Recent research in the U.K . . . said they didn't complain": Citizen's Charter Complaints Task Force, *Putting Things Right,* p. 14.

P. 363 "If you do the latter . . . customer tells *nine*": Barlow and Møller, *A Complaint Is a Gift,* p. 38. They rely on research on the private sector by Technical Assistance Research Programs, Inc. The number may be different in the public sector.

P. 364 Citizen's Charter Complaints Task Force quotations: Citizen's Charter Complaints Task Force, *Putting Things Right,* pp. 23, 40–41.

P. 364 "Unfortunately, the Labor government . . . and British Gas": Ibid., p. 23; and *The Citizen's Charter—Five Years On* (London: Her Majesty's Stationery Office, September 1996), p. 37.

Pp. 364–365 "The rail companies offer . . . at least 20 percent of the price of that trip": See Osborne and Plastrik, *Banishing Bureaucracy: The Five Strategies for Reinventing Government* (Reading, Mass.: Addison-Wesley, 1997), p. 35. Standards have remained fairly stable since the rail lines were franchised to private operators, according to the Service First Unit in the U.K. Cabinet Office.

P. 365 "In the Glasgow Passport Office, for example . . . customer services manager": Citizen's Charter Complaints Task Force, *Good Practice Guide* (London: Her Majesty's Stationery Office, June 1995), p. 11.

P. 365 When it ran the Minneapolis schools . . . field trip": Interviews with Peter Hutchinson, PSG president, who served as superintendent of schools in Minneapolis under the PSG contract.

P. 365 In 1999, Cal State University. . . . a similar plan": Julie Blair, "Warranty Pledges Help for Struggling Teacher Graduates," *Education Week* (March 3, 1999), p. 5.

P. 365 "The Academy of the Pacific Rim . . . make the payments": Charles A. Radin, "Charter School Offers a Guarantee," *Boston Globe,* April 7, 1998.

P. 365 "The Information Services office in Indianapolis . . . why we were late'": Interview with Laurie Ohmann, PSG partner who consulted with Indianapolis.

P. 366 Citizen's Charter Complaints Task Force quotation: Citizen's Charter Complaints Task Force, *Putting Things Right,* p. 22.

P. 366 Menu of redress options: Ibid., pp. 39–40.

P. 367 "In the Ritz-Carlton hotel chain . . . put things right for customers": Barlow and Møller, *A Complaint Is a Gift,* p. 174.

P. 367 Citizen's Charter Complaints Task Force quotation: Citizen's Charter Complaints Task Force, *Putting Things Right,* p. 42.

Pp. 368–369 British Airways story from Barlow and Møller: *A Complaint Is a Gift,* pp. 17–18.

P. 369 "In 1991, the Citizen's Charter . . . complaint systems": *The Citizen's Charter: Raising the Standard* (London: Her Majesty's Stationery Office, 1991).

P. 369 "In a late 1998 survey . . . 43 percent in 1995": 1998 data—"Panel Call for Public Services to Be More Responsive," p. 4; 1995 data—Citizen's Charter Complaints Task Force, *Putting Things Right,* p. 14.

P. 369 Spanbauer quotation: Spanbauer, *A Quality System for Education,* p. 45.

P. 369 Barlow and Møller quote: Barlow and Møller, *A Complaint Is a Gift,* p. 22.

P. 371 "To make sure these systems are integrated . . . performance bonus policies": Citizen's Charter Complaints Task Force, *Putting Things Right,* p. 43.

P. 373 "A fast internal review . . .": Citizen's Charter Complaints Task Force, *Putting Things Right,* pp. 47–50.

P. 373 "'A common theme . . . *more open approach*'": Ibid., pp. 28, 35.

P. 373 "As Barlow and Møller put it . . .": Barlow and Møller, *A Complaint Is a Gift,* p. 148.

Pp. 373–374 British *Good Practice Guide* advice: Citizen's Charter Complaints Task Force, *Good Practice Guide,* pp. 4–5, 25.

P. 374 Complaints Task Force quote: Citizen's Charter Complaints Task Force, *Putting Things Right,* p. 13.

P. 374 "Even after seven years . . . done about a complaint": "Panel Call for Public Services to Be More Responsive," p. 4.

P. 374 Borough of Bexley example: Citizen's Charter Complaints Task Force, *Good Practice Guide,* p. 8.

P. 374 "When the Citizen's Charter . . . 'fair investigation'": Ibid., p. 18.

P. 375 "Lothian Regional Council's . . . :" Citizen's Charter Complaints Task Force, *If Things Go Wrong . . . Access to Complaint Systems* (London: Cabinet Office, June 1994), p. 12.

P. 375 "'The most successful . . . highly motivated'": Citizen's Charter Complaints Task Force, *Putting Things Right,* p. 24.

Pp. 375–376 Quotation on "marginal policies": Barlow and Møller, *A Complaint Is a Gift,* pp. 170–173.

P. 376 "'In fact, without open . . . are also useful'": Ibid., pp. 161–162.

P. 376 "'Fix the system . . . approach to complaints'": Ibid., p. 91.

P. 378 "But what about functions . . . 'and rate proposals' ": Department of Administration, "A Strategy for Funding and Managing DOA Activities," reprinted in Michael Barzelay and Babak Armajani, *Breaking Through Bureaucracy* (Berkeley: University of California Press, 1992), pp. 137–160. (Quote p. 150.)

P. 384 "Some organizations . . . desired results": David Osborne and Ted Gaebler, *Reinventing Government* (Reading, Mass.: Addison-Wesley, 1992), p. 171.

P. 385 "The Fund for the City of New York . . . another useful technique": Personal communication from Barbara Cohn, Fund for City of New York.

P. 385 "Brisbane, Australia . . . columnist Neal Pierce": Neal Peirce, "City Service—In 11 Seconds," syndicated column sent to authors by e-mail, March 21, 1999.

Pp. 385–386 "Fox Valley Technical College . . . former president Stanley Spanbauer": Spanbauer, *A Quality System for Education,* pp. 43–44.

P. 386 "When they were reinventing . . . customers better": Michael Barzelay and Babak J. Armajani, "Managing State Government Operations: Changing Visions of Staff Agencies," *Journal of Policy Analysis and Management* 9, no. 3 (1990), pp. 322–323.

P. 386 "When he was city manager of Salem, Oregon . . . cabinet meetings": Gerald Seals, *Taming City Hall: Rightsizing for Results* (San Francisco: Institute for Contemporary Studies Press, 1995), p. 59.

P. 386 Barlow and Møller quote: Barlow and Møller, *A Complaint Is a Gift,* p. 150.

Pp. 386–387 "The Royal Mail . . .given out": "Going Undercover," *Charter News* 4 (January 1994), p. 11.

Chapter Ten

P. 393 Department of Defense quotation (epigraph): U.S. Department of Defense, *Principles of Excellent Installations,* handout.

P. 394 "Their motives were honorable . . . elected officials": Peter Aucoin, *The New Public Management: Canada in Comparative Perspective* (Montreal: Institute for Research on Public Policy, 1995), pp. 99–107.

P. 395 Creech quotation: Bill Creech, *The Five Pillars of TQM: How to Make Total Quality Management Work for You* (New York: Dutton, 1994), p. 315.

P. 395 "For nearly 50 years . . . firmly in place" and Aucoin quotation: Aucoin, *The New Public Management,* p. 100.

P. 395 "Its advice to 'let the managers manage'": Ibid., pp 101–102.

Pp. 395–396 National Performance Review quotation: Al Gore, *From Red Tape to Results: Creating a Government That Works Better and Costs Less: Report of the National Performance Review* (Washington, D.C.: U.S. Government Printing Office, 1993), p. 6.

P. 396 *Diagnostic Study* quotation: Quoted in Task Force on Management Improvement, *The Australian Public Service Reformed: An Evaluation of a Decade of Management Reform* (Canberra: Australian Government Publishing Service, 1992), p. 90.

P. 396 Ministerial Task Force quotation: Aucoin, *The New Public Management,* p. 128.

P. 396 "The department gained the flexibility . . . 34 percent": State of Florida, Office of the Governor, *The Quiet Revolution: Victories for the People, 1991–1992* (Tallahassee, Fla.: Office of the Governor, 1992), p. 20.

P. 397 "In 1995, the Federation of Tax Administrators . . . Management and Organizational Initiative Award": Interviews with Larry Fuchs and Jim Zingle.

P. 398 "They divested several departmental functions . . . help cut their costs": Buddy MacKay, *Report to the Governor: HRS Redevelopment: The State of the Agency,* handout, July 15, 1993, pp. 8, 13.

P. 398 Schick quotation ("Public services are more accessible . . ."): Allen Schick, *The Spirit of Reform: Managing the New Zealand State Sector in a Time of Change* (Wellington, New Zealand: State Services Commission, 1996), chapter 8. Available at www.ssc.govt.nz/Documents/Reform12.htm.

P. 398 Schick quotation ("Some central functions are . . ."): Ibid.

P. 400 Scott quotation: Graham C. Scott, *Government Reform in New Zealand,* (International Monetary Fund Occasional Paper No. 140 (Washington, D.C.: 1996).

Pp. 402–403 "In the early 1990s . . . DSG's cumbersome controls": Tod Newcombe, "Culture Shock: Agency Forsakes Control for Customer Satisfaction," *Technology Trends,* annual supplement to *Government Technology,* 1998.

P. 403 "George Weise, commissioner . . . to the field": John Kamensky, "The Best Kept Secret in Government: How the NPR Translated Theory into Practice," in *Transforming Government: Lessons from the Reinvention Laboratories,* ed. Patricia W. Ingraham, James R. Thompson, and Ronald P. Sanders (San Francisco: Jossey-Bass, 1998), p. 70.

P. 406 "In Portland, Oregon . . . only dogs": Al Gore, *Common Sense Government: Works Better and Costs Less: Third Report of the National Performance Review.* (Washington, D.C.: U.S. Government Printing Office, 1995), p. 34.

P. 407 National Performance Review quotation: Al Gore, *Improving Financial Management: Accompanying Report of the National Performance Review* (Washington. D.C.: U.S. Government Printing Office, September 1993), p. 1.

P. 408 "This explains why 94 percent . . . budget allocation": Task Force on Management Improvement, *The Australian Public Service Reformed: An Evaluation of a Decade of Management Reform* (Canberra: Australian Government Publishing Service, 1992), p. 256.

P. 408 Goldsmith quotation: Stephen Goldsmith, *The Twenty-First Century City: Resurrecting Urban America* (Washington, D.C.: Regnery Publishing, 1997), p. 60.

P. 409 "The main effect . . . manage debts and inventories more effectively": Scott, *Government Reform in New Zealand.*

P. 409 "New Zealand also allows agencies . . . sale of their assets": Office of the Auditor General of Canada, *Toward Better Governance: Public Service Reform in New Zealand (1984–94) and Its Relevance to Canada* (Ottawa: Office of the Auditor General of Canada, 1995).

P. 409 "In Philadelphia, an innovation fund . . . double the amount borrowed": Al Gore, *Improving Financial Management,* pp. 45–49.

P. 410 Paul Light quotation: Paul C. Light, *Sustaining Innovation: Creating Nonprofit and Government Organizations That Innovate Naturally* (San Francisco: Jossey-Bass, 1998), p. 115.

P. 410 "In the U.S., reinventors with the National Performance Review were concerned . . . and financial condition": Al Gore, *Improving Financial Management,* p. 60.

P. 411 "Australia, Canada, Finland . . . accrual accounting": Public Management Service (PUMA) "Accrual Accounting and Budgeting in the Public Sector," *Focus,* no. 12 (March 1999), p. 4 (published by the Organization for Economic Cooperation and Development, Paris).

Pp. 411–412 "In 1992, consultants from KPMG Peat Marwick . . . taken the course": KPMG Peat Marwick, "Performance Audit of Personnel Systems" (report to the North Carolina General Assembly Government Performance Audit Committee, December 1992).

P. 412 "In half of the states, longevity pay . . . compensation systems": KPMG Peat Marwick, *Performance Audit of Personnel Systems,* p. 3.40, citing survey by National Association of State Personnel Executives.

P. 412 "The National Commission . . . few dozen": National Commission on the State and Local Service, *Hard Truths/Tough Choices: An Agenda for State and Local Reform* (Albany, N.Y.: Nelson A. Rockefeller Institute of Government, 1993), p. 27.

P. 412 "KPMG Peat Marwick told the North Carolina legislature . . . invested about 0.1 percent": KPMG Peat Marwick, *Performance Audit of Personnel Systems,* pp. 3.79–3.80.

P. 412 *Civil Service Reform* quotation: Donald F. Kettl, Patricia W. Ingraham, Ronald P. Sanders, and Constance Horner, *Civil Service Reform: Building a Government That Works* (Washington: Brookings Institution Press, 1996), pp. 3–6.

P. 413 NPR quotation: Gore, *Creating a Government That Works Better and Costs Less,* p. 22.

P. 413 "Sweden and the U.K. have most of the same flexibilities": Allen Schick, *Modern Budgeting* (Paris: Organization for Economic Development and Cooperation, 1998), pp. 35–38.

P. 413 "Georgia made a similar move . . . and hire employees": Robert D. Behn, "Ending Civil Service as We Know It," *Governing* (November 1996), p. 86.

P. 414 "In 1996, the British finished delegating . . . agency by agency": Next Steps Team, *Next Steps: Briefing Note* (London: Office of Public Service, February 26, 1996), p. 5.

P. 415 "Major American corporations routinely spend . . . 'self-initiated'": *Leadership for America: Rebuilding the Public Service.* (Washington, D.C.: National Commission on the Public Service, 1989), quoted in Al Gore, *Reinventing Human Resource Management: Accompanying Report of the National Performance Review* (Washington, D.C.: U.S. Government Printing Office, 1993), p. 43.

P. 415 ". . . led by Australia, which dedicates 5 percent of its payroll to training": Donald F. Kettl, *Reinventing Government? Appraising the National Performance Review* (Washington, D. C.: Brookings Institution, 1994), p. 20.

P. 416 "He tracked one $20,000 purchase . . . 15 minutes of actual work": John Kost, presentation to Governor's Conference on Accountability and Citizens' Services, Baton Rouge, La., September 24, 1997.

P. 416 "North Carolina purchased about $1 billion . . . a year": KPMG Peat Marwick, *Performance Audit of Purchasing Activities,* report to the North Carolina General Assembly Government Performance Audit Committee, December 1992, p. 2.1.

P. 416 "The U. S. federal government spent . . . every working day": Al Gore, *Reinventing Federal Procurement: Accompanying Report of the National Performance Review* (Washington, D.C.: U.S. Government Printing Office, 1993) p. 2.

P. 417 "By 1996, federal employees . . . rather than purchase orders": Anne Laurent, "Sudden Impact," *Government Executive* (September 1997), pp. 31–36.

P. 417 "In 1993, when the NPR recommended . . . full-scale procedures": Gore, *Reinventing Federal Procurement,* p. 28.

P. 417 John Kost quotation: John Kost, *New Approaches to Public Management: The Case of Michigan* (Washington, D.C.: Brookings Institution, 1996), p. 32.

Pp. 417–418 List of "basic principles for agencies to follow": Ibid.

P. 418 Philip Howard quotation: Philip K. Howard, "Ketchup and the Absurdity of Government Contracting," *Washington Times,* November 21, 1995, p. A15.

P. 418 "To ensure prompt and efficient handling . . . and arbitration": MacManus, "Designing and Managing the Procurement Process," pp. 602–603.

P. 419 NPR quotation: Gore, *Creating a Government That Works Better and Costs Less,* p. 29.

P. 419 "San Francisco opened a computer store . . . are compatible": Brian Miller, "Governments Pilot New Procurement Models," *Technology Trends,* annual supplement to *Government Technology,* 1996.

P. 419 Mike Masterson quotation: Michael F. Masterson, "Buying Radios Is Adding Quality to Madison's City Government," *Quality Progress* (January 1995), p. 50.

P. 420 Ontario guide for industry suppliers quotations: *Ontario's Modified Common Purpose Procurement Format: A Guide for Information Industries Suppliers* (Ontario: Government of Ontario, Management Board Secretariat, February 1996).

P. 420 "Under CPP, an organization starts . . . managing the partnership": Ibid.

P. 421 MacManus quotation: MacManus, "Designing and Managing the Procurement Process," p. 596.

P. 428 National School Boards Association quotations: Darrel W. Drury, *Reinventing School-Based Management: A School Board Guide to School-Based Improvement* (Alexandria, Va.: National School Boards Association, n.d.). Available from the association's Web site: www.nsba.org.

P. 429 National School Boards Association quotation: Ibid., p. 5.

P. 430 Allington quotation: Susan Rosegrant, *The Coast Guard's Model Unit Program: Testing the Waters of Change* (Cambridge, Mass.: John F. Kennedy School of Government, Harvard University, 1993), p.3.

P. 430 Another top official quotation: Ibid., p. 4.

Pp. 430–431 "A Coast Guard unit had to get approval . . . entire Atlantic coast": Ibid., p. 1.

P. 431 Gilbert quotation: James Thompson, "Eureka," *Government Executive* (June 1995), pp. 32.

P. 431 "In 1984, when Bob Stone launched . . . its power to address": Susan Rosegrant, *The Coast Guard's Model Unit Program,* pp. 2–3.

P. 431 "Even while the Clinton administration eliminated . . . and other rules": U.S. General Accounting Office, *Management Reform: Status of Agency Reinvention Lab Efforts* (Washington, D.C.: General Accounting Office, March 1996), p. 38.

Pp. 431–432 "When Oregon reinventors tried to get permission . . . poverty-prevention programs": Christina H. Macy, *The Oregon Option: A Federal-State-Local Partnership for Better Results* (Baltimore: Annie E. Casey Foundation), p. 12.

P. 432 "In the U.S. Commerce Department . . . reviewing requests": U.S. General Accounting Office, *Management Reform,* p. 85.

P. 432 Gilbert quotation: Thompson, "Eureka," p. 32.

P. 432 "This led to so many complaints . . . the process": Ibid., p. 33.

P. 432 "When the former head of the General Services Administration . . . internal agency regulations": Ronald P. Sanders, "Heroes of the Revolution," in *Transforming Government: Lessons from the Reinvention Laboratories,* ed. Patricia W. Ingraham, James R. Thompson, and Ronald P. Sanders (San Francisco: Jossey-Bass, 1998), p. 40.

P. 432 "The Denver office used . . . 3,000 square feet" and Zoellner quotation: Thompson, "Eureka," p. 34.

P. 433 "The U.S. Coast Guard set a deadline . . . no one did anything about it": Rosegrant, *The Coast Guard's Model Unit Program,* p.4.

P. 433 Sanders quotations: Ronald P. Sanders, "Reinvention: Back to the Future," *Government Executive* (December 1996).

P. 434 "By October 1999 . . . District of Columbia": "About Charter Schools," Center for Education Reform Web site: www.edreform.com/charters.htm.

P. 434 "In California, which already had . . . with no total cap": Neal R. Peirce, "Charter Schools: Competition at Work," obtained on-line from *Washington Post* Writers Group, August 30, 1998.

P. 434 "In Milwaukee, where teacher union opposition . . . for more charter schools": Kerry A. White, "Milwaukee Voters Reject Union-Backed Candidates," *Education Week* (April 14, 1999), p. 3.

P. 434 "In Colorado, Governor Bill Owens . . . as regular schools": Mark Walsh, "Owens Wants to Spend More on Colorado Charter Schools," *Education Week* (January 27, 1999), p. 12.

P. 434 "In England, one of every five secondary schools is now grant maintained": United Kingdom, Office for Standards in Education, *Secondary Education 1993–97: A Review of Secondary Schools in England* (London: Her Majesty's Stationery Office, 1998), ch. 1, p. 1, available at www.ofsted.gov.uk.

P. 435 Nathan quotation: Joe Nathan, *Charter Schools: Creating Hope and Opportunity for American Education* (San Francisco: Jossey-Bass, 1996), p. 17.

P. 436 Robert Wright article: Robert Wright, "When Bad Things Happen to Good Schools," *San Jose Mercury News,* October 11, 1993.

P. 436 Reichgott-Junge quotation: Senator Ember Reichgott-Junge, address to Democratic Leadership Conference, New Orleans, May 1, 1992.

Pp. 436–437 Nathan quotation: Nathan, *Charter Schools,* p. xiv.

P. 437 "The Oregon Health Sciences University . . . its poor fiscal performance": David Folkenflik, "UMAB Heads Ponder Split from System," *Baltimore Sun,* December 11, 1995, pp. B1–2.

P. 437 "In 1994, the first charter school in . . . manage such a large school": Amy Pile, "Audits Cast Shadow on Charter School's Future," *Los Angeles Times,* November 28, 1994, A1, A2.

Pp. 437–438 "In 1997, Arizona's department of education identified . . . elected superintendent of schools": Thomas Toch, "Education Bazaar," *U.S. News and World Report* (April 27, 1998), p. 44.

P. 439 "In California, for example . . . academically accountable": "Charter Schools Fall Short of Expectations," *The American School Board Journal* (February 1999).

P. 439 "In Michigan, for instance, . . . any oversight staff": Toch, "Education Bazaar."

P. 439 Nathan quotation: Pat Burson, "Charter Schools Say Let Us Do It Our Way," *Saint Paul Pioneer Press,* July 13, 1995, pp. 1D, 8D.

P. 439 "Cordia Booth, a school teacher . . . the next school year": David Hill, "Charter Champion," *Education Week* (October 4, 1995), pp. 23–29.

P. 440 "In one case, teachers looking . . . for their charter": Steve Stecklow, "Arizona Takes the Lead in Charter Schools—For Better or Worse," *Wall Street Journal,* December 24, 1996, p. 1.

P. 440 Kennedy School of Government quotation: Bryan Hassel, "The Politics of Charter Schools," *Taubman Center Annual Report* (Cambridge, Mass.: A. Alfred Taubman Center for State and Local Government, John F. Kennedy School of Government, Harvard University, 1996), p. 9.

P. 441 "In Arizona, for instance, state lawmakers . . . cases of nepotism": Toch, "Education Bazaar."

P. 441 "But when a charter school went bankrupt . . . with taxpayer dollars": Stecklow, "Arizona Takes the Lead in Charter Schools—For Better or Worse."

P. 441 "The U.K.'s government . . . grants for capital projects": United Kingdom, Department for Education, *Grant-Maintained Schools: Funding Worksheet 1995–96* (London: Crown, 1995).

P. 441 "One is a lack of vacant buildings . . . providing education service": Charter Friends National Network, *Paying for the Charter Schoolhouse: Policy Options for Charter School Facilities Financing* (St. Paul, Minnesota: Charter Friends National Network, 1999), p. 1.

P. 441 "Another is local opposition . . . selling to charter schools": Kate Zernike, "Charter Schools Sometimes Forced to Fight for Space," *Boston Globe,* June 10, 1996, p. 20.

P. 442 Charter Friends National Network's list of ways to address financing problems: Charter Friends National Network, *Paying for the Charter Schoolhouse.*

P. 442 Education Commission of the States recommendation: *Governing America's Schools: Changing the Rules* (Denver: Education Commission of the States, 1999), p. 30. Available at www.ecs.org.

P. 442 Hudson Institute quotation: Chester E. Finn, Louann A. Bierlein, and Bruno V. Manno, *Charter Schools in Action: A First Look* (Washington, D.C.: Hudson Institute, January 1996), p. 8.

P. 442 "The Hudson researchers . . . avert disaster": Ibid.

P. 444 Stone quotation (epigraph): Thompson, "Eureka," p. 31.

P. 444 Gore quotation: Ibid.

Pp. 444–445 John Haines quotation: Thompson, "Eureka," p. 32.

P. 445 Richard Kelly quotation: Ibid., p. 31.

P. 445 "Kelly used reinvention lab status . . . by its office": Ibid.

P. 445 "A U.S. Commerce Department . . . task forces to implement them" Ibid., p. 32.

P. 445 "In a survey conducted by the GAO . . . from central agencies": U.S. General Accounting Office, *Management Reform,* p. 3.

P. 447 Federal employee quotation: Ronald Sanders and James Thompson, "The Reinvention Revolution," *Government Executive* (March 1996), p. 4A.

P. 447 Sanders quotation: Sanders, "Reinvention: Back to the Future."

P. 447 Gilbert quotation: Thompson, "Eureka," p. 33.

P. 447 "The lab in Boulder, Colorado, . . . trivial requests for waivers": U.S. General Accounting Office, *Management Reform,* pp. 137–141.

P. 447 "A Coast Guard commander's first . . . but never used it": Rosegrant, *The Coast Guard's Model Unit Program,* p. 1.

P. 448 Sanders quotation ("There needs to be . . . "): Sanders, "Reinvention: Back to the Future."

P. 449 "Only 3 of the first . . . denied 13 of the 28": Rosegrant, *The Coast Guard's Model Unit Program,* pp. 2, 4.

P. 449 Frazier quotation: Ibid., p. 4.

P. 450 "In 1995, Michigan Governor John Engler . . . controlled school districts": Joan Richardson, "School Code Package Offers More Freedom," *Detroit Free Press,* November 2, 1995, pp. 1B, 3B.

P. 450 Creech quotation: Bill Creech, *The Five Pillars of TQM,* p. 314.

P. 452 "Governor Engler's assault on . . . added significant new requirements": Richardson, "School Code Package Offers More Freedom."

P. 452 Creech quotation: Creech, *The Five Pillars of TQM,* pp. 314–315.

Chapter Eleven

Pp. 453–454 Virgil Lee Bolden story and quotes: The story of Fort Lauderdale's water pipe crew is based in part on presentations by Virgil Lee Bolden and Cathy Dunn at a November 17–19, 1996, meeting in Fort Lauderdale of the Cities Action Clinic, sponsored by the State and Local Government Labor-Management Committee.

P. 455 "In Fort Lauderdale, for example . . . for progressive discipline": From City of Fort Lauderdale Cooperative Association of Labor and Management materials updating labor-management committees activities, part of background materials for Cities Action Clinic meeting, November 17–19, 1996.

P. 456 "The trend . . . has been especially pronounced in the U.S. federal government": According to Paul Light, author of *Thickening Government: Federal Hierarchy and the Diffusion of Accountability* (Washington, D.C.: Brookings Institution, 1995), the U.S. federal government got taller and wider after 1960. Management layers doubled to 32.

P. 456 "Management layers have the same effect . . . its destination": John Scully, unpublished, untitled manuscript.

P. 456 "For instance, when the Social Security Administration (SSA) analyzed . . . and 585 days": Al Gore, *Creating a Government That Works Better and Costs Less: Status Report, September 1994* (Washington, D.C.: U.S. Government Printing Office, 1994), pp. 29–30.

P. 456 Assessment of SSA disability claims quotation: Ibid., p. 30.

P. 456 "The National Performance Review found that . . . kept lower limits": Al Gore, *Transforming Organizational Structures: Accompanying Report of the National Performance Review* (Washington, D.C.: U.S. Government Printing Office, 1993).

P. 458 Vardon and Morley quotation: Sue Vardon and Karen Morley, "What Are the Skills and Attributes of a New Public Manager?" presentation to Fulbright Symposium on Public Sector Reform, June 23–24, 1994, Brisbane, Australia, pp. 14, 22.

P. 458 Bacal quotation: Quoted on the Web site of the City of Grande Prairie, Alberta, Canada (www.city.grande-prairie.ab.ca/self_emp.htm), from articles in Robert Bacal's newsletter *The Public Sector Manager.* Many of these articles are posted on Bacal's Web site: www.work911.com.

P. 459 Couper and Lobitz quotation: David C. Couper and Sabine H. Lobitz, *Quality Policing: The Madison Experience* (Washington, D.C.: Police Executive Research Forum, 1991), pp. 87–88.

P. 460 Bacal quotations ("Many mangers make the mistake . . . is a setup for failure'"): Quoted on the Web site of the City of Grande Prairie, Alberta, Canada (www.city.grande-prairie.ab.ca/self_emp.htm), from articles in Robert Bacal's newsletter *The Public Sector Manager.* See www.work911.com.

P. 461 Creech quotation ("As Creech puts it . . . 'not authoritarianism'"): Bill Creech, *The Five Pillars of TQM: How to Make Total Quality Management Work for You* (New York: Dutton, 1994), p. 528.

P. 462 Creech quotation: ("A short, fat elephant . . . nimble"): Ibid.

P. 462 "In 1993, the National Performance Review found . . . most private businesses": Al Gore, *From Red Tape to Results: Creating a Government That Works Better and Costs Less* (Washington, D.C.: National Performance Review, 1993), pp. 70–71.

P. 462 "In Oregon, when the Department of Transportation . . . almost 1:12": Interview with Don Forbes, then director of the department.

P. 462 "To Find Useless Management Layers, Look For . . ." box: Based on Gore, *Transforming Organizational Structures*, p. 10.

P. 464 Joe Thompson story and quotations: Interviews with Joe Thompson.

P. 465 "They quickly redirect . . . 30 minutes to 3": Al Gore, *Creating a Government That Works Better and Costs Less: Status Report* (Washington, D.C.: U.S. Government Printing Office, 1994), p. 4.

P. 465 National Performance Review quotation: Al Gore, *The Best Kept Secret in Government: A Report to President Bill Clinton* (Washington, D.C.: U.S. Government Printing Office, 1996), p. 30.

P. 466 Cooperative Association of Labor and Management quotation (epigraph): City of Fort Lauderdale, "A Calm Model for Successful Labor/Management Partnerships," *Quality Cities* (September 1995), p. 11.

P. 467 Oglesby quotation: Oglesby spoke during presentations at the November 17–19, 1996, meeting of the Cities Action Clinic.

P. 467 "In 1991, for example, the 39,000-member. . . union-management relationships": Esther Scott, with Linda Kaboolian and Howard Husock, *Shifting the Labor Relations Paradigm: Union-Management Partnership in Ohio State Government* (Cambridge, Mass: John F. Kennedy School of Government, Harvard University, 1996). A case study revised by Linda Kaboolian, written by Esther Scott, researched by Howard Husock.

P. 468 Goldberg quotations: Ibid., pp. 6, 7.

P. 468 "Because of the trust . . . since the mid-1980s": U.S. Secretary of Labor's Task Force on Excellence in State and Local Government Through Labor-Management Cooperation, *Working Together for Public Service* (Washington: U.S. Government Printing Office, May 1996). Updated February 7, 2000, through personal communication with Kathi Holmes, fire chief's assistant.

Pp. 468–469 Woodworth and Keek quotation: Warner Woodworth and Christopher Meek, *Creating Labor-Management Partnership* (Reading, Mass.: Addison-Wesley, 1995), p. 29.

P. 469 "And in surveys, the vast majority . . . keep the union in place": U.S. Secretary of Labor's Task Force on Excellence in State and Local Government Through Labor-Management Cooperation, *Working Together for Public Service,* p. 52.

P. 469 AFL-CIO committee quotation: ALF-CIO Committee on the Evolution of Work, *The New American Workplace: A Labor Perspective* (Washington, D.C.: AFL-CIO, February 1994), p. 2.

P. 469 "More and more public employees . . . they need managers' cooperation": U.S. Secretary of Labor's Task Force on Excellence in State and Local Government Through Labor-Management Cooperation, *Working Together for Public Service,* p. 51.

P. 469 U.S. Labor Department task force quotation: Ibid., pp. 6, 13–14.

P. 471 "In Peoria, Illinois, for instance . . . the usual disputes and arbitration": Ibid., p. 4.

P. 471 "In Ohio, for instance . . . the bulk of the union's resources": Esther Scott et al., *Shifting the Labor Relations Paradigm,* p. 3.

P. 471 "After the Clinton administration . . . rather than grievances: Cathie M. Lane, "Bittersweet Partnerships," *Government Executive* (February 1996), pp. 41–43.

P. 471 "In 1994 and 1995 . . . dispute resolution processes": David Hornestay, "Partnership Pays," *Government Executive* (February 1996), p. 43.

P. 472 CALM quotation: Fort Lauderdale Cooperative Association of Labor and Management, report on beach maintenance project, from background materials for Cities Action Clinic meeting, November 17–19, 1996, Fort Lauderdale.

P. 472 Examples of specific improvements undertaken by more than 1,000 teams of employees: Ohio Office of Quality Services, *Process Improvement Teams' Re-*

sults Booklet, version 1 (Columbus: Ohio Office of Quality Services, January 29, 1996), and *Process Improvement Team Results Book,* 2nd ed. (Columbus: Ohio Office of Quality Services, August 1996).

P. 474 "They agreed, for instance . . . to be innovative'": Cooperative Association of Labor and Management, *Philosophy,* handout at Cities Action Clinic meeting, November 17–19, 1996.

P. 475 Labor Department task force quotation: U.S. Secretary of Labor's Task Force on Excellence in State and Local Government Through Labor-Management Cooperation, *Working Together for Public Service,* p. 58.

P. 477 "The task force reported that in Massachusetts . . . management policies or systems": U.S. Secretary of Labor's Task Force on Excellence in State and Local Government Through Labor-Management Cooperation, *Working Together for Public Service,* p. 21.

P. 478 Katzenbach and Smith quotation: Jon R. Katzenbach and Douglas K. Smith, "The Discipline of Teams," *Harvard Business Review* (March-April 1993), p. 112.

P. 479 Pinchots' quotation: Gifford and Elizabeth Pinchot, *The End of Bureaucracy and the Rise of the Intelligent Organization* (San Francisco: Berrett-Koehler, 1993), p. 194.

P. 480 Austin, Texas example: From interviews with Austin Department of Public Works and Transportation managers and their street repair crews.

P. 482 Tharon Greene quotation: E-mail from Tharon Greene to the authors, June 2, 1999.

P. 482 Pinchots' quotation: Gifford and Elizabeth Pinchot, *The End of Bureaucracy and the Rise of the Intelligent Organization,* p. 206–207.

P. 482 Katzenbach and Smith quotation: Katzenbach and Smith, "The Discipline of Teams," p. 117.

P. 485 Katzenbach and Smith quotation: Katzenbach and Smith, "The Discipline of Teams," p. 115.

P. 486 "Combined Actions That Make Teams Successful" box: Bill Creech, *The Five Pillars of TQM,* p. 459.

P. 487 "When the Office of Human Resources and Administration . . . 1,400 of them were implemented": U.S. Forest Service, Eastern Region Office, *Creativity Fringes* (Milwaukee, Wisc.: U.S. Forest Service, Eastern Region Office, September 1995), p. 3.

P. 488 Authors of *Improvement Driven Government* quotation: David K. Carr, Ian D. Littman, and John K. Condon, *Improvement Driven Government: Public Service for the 21st Century* (Washington, D.C.: Coopers & Lybrand, 1995), p. 453.

P. 488 "It's also important to keep track . . . and so on": Ibid., p. 458.

Chapter Twelve

P. 491 "Cohen is a college professor . . . retired motel owner": Ron Cohen, "Method and Practice in Understanding Procedural Justice: Some Suggested Developments for the Future" (presentation at the Seventh International Conference of the International Society for Justice Research, Denver, May 28–31, 1998), p. 5.

P. 492 "Yet citizens didn't want . . . going to corrections": John G. Perry and John F. Gorczyk, "Restructuring Corrections: Using Market Research in Vermont," *Corrections Management Quarterly* 1, no. 3 (1997), pp. 26–35.

P. 492 "When offenders got out . . . in the community": Ibid., p. 31.

P. 492 "The results were a surprise . . . commissioner": Ibid., p. 29

P. 492 Perry and Gorczyk quotations: John F. Gorczyk and John G. Perry, "The Negative Economics of Control" (unpublished manuscript, October 1, 1997).

Pp. 492–493 Vermont corrections officials quotation: Walther and Perry, *The Vermont Reparative Probation Program* (Montpelier, Vt.: Department of Corrections, July 18, 1997), p. 26.

P. 493 "By 1999, every court in Vermont . . . 41 boards": David R. Karp, "The Offender/Community Relationship: An Evolution with the Vermont Reparative Boards" (unpublished manuscript, January 27, 1999).

P. 493 Gorczyk and Perry quotation: Vermont Reparative Probation Program, semifinalist application for the Innovations in American Government 1998 Award Program, April 14, 1998.

P. 493 "In 1998, the program . . . in the country": Vermont Department of Corrections, *Vermont Reparative Probation: Fact Sheet* (Montpelier, Vt.: Department of Corrections, n.d.).

P. 493 "In 85 percent of their cases . . . then fulfilled it": Ibid.

P. 493 "When the department followed up . . . regular probation": Vermont Reparative Probation Program, semifinalist application, p. 8.

P. 494 "In some communities . . . fulfill their contracts": Walther and Perry, *The Vermont Reparative Probation Program,* p. 34.

P. 494 "Indeed, a 1999 poll . . . come up with solutions'": Mark Penn, "The Community Consensus," *Blueprint: Ideas for a New Century* (Washington, D.C.: Democratic Leadership Council, Spring 1999), p. 52.

P. 495 "When Robert Bobb was city manager . . . and solve problems": Curtis Johnson, "Renewing Community," *Governing* (July 1995), p. 56.

P. 495 "In 1999, Seattle . . . living in 37 neighborhoods": Seattle Neighborhood Planning Office, *Neighborhood Focus: The Newsletter of the Neighborhood Planning Office* 13 (February 1999), p. 2.

P. 495 "Nationally, more than 200 community-government partnerships . . . families in distress": Center for the Study of Social Policy, *Creating a Community Agenda: How Governance Partnerships Can Improve Results for Children, Youth, and Families* (Washington, D.C.: Center for the Study of Social Policy, February 23, 1998).

P. 495 "In Savannah, Georgia . . . Youth Futures Authority (YFA)": Joan Walsh, *Stories of Renewal: Community Building and the Future of Urban America* (New York: Rockefeller Foundation, January 1997), pp. 2–5.

P. 495 Observer in 1997 quotation: Ibid., p. 2.

Pp. 495–496 Goldsmith quotation: Steve Goldsmith, *The Twenty-First Century City: Resurrecting Urban America* (Washington, D.C.: Regnery Publishing, 1997), pp. 149–150.

P. 496 "Alti Rodal and Nick Mulder . . . community-based entities": Alti Rodal and Nick Mulder, "Partnerships, Devolution and Power-Sharing: Issues and Implications for Management," *Optimum: The Journal of Public Sector Management* 24, no. 3 (Winter 1993), p. 28.

P. 497 "When Vermont asked its citizens . . . fair or good": Perry and Gorczyk, "Restructuring Corrections: Using Market Research in Vermont," *Corrections Management: Quarterly* 1, no. 3 (1997), pp. 26–35.

P. 497 Gorczyk and Perry quotation: Ibid., pp. 29–30.

P. 497 Gardner quotation: John W. Gardner, "We Need to Strike A Spark . . . ," *Governing* (July 1995), p. 53.

P. 497 "Nearly half of the students . . . below the ninth-grade level": Steering Community Consortium on Chicago School Research, *A View from the Elementary Schools: The State of Reform in Chicago* (Chicago: Steering Community Consortium on Chicago School Research, July 1993), p. 1.

P. 498 Bryk and colleagues quotation: Anthony S. Bryk, Penny Bender Sebring, David Kerbow, Sharon Rollow, and John Q. Easton, *Charting Chicago School Reform: Democratic Localism as a Lever for Change* (Boulder, Colo.: Westview Press, 1998), p. 16.

P. 498 Goldsmith quotations: Goldsmith, *The Twenty-First Century City,* pp. 132, 133.

P. 498 Thomas quotation: John Clayton Thomas, *Public Participation in Public Decisions: New Skills and Strategies for Public Managers* (San Francisco: Jossey-Bass, 1995), p. 19.

P. 499 Woodson quotation: Quoted in Rochelle Watson, "Robert Woodson's Conservative Prescription for Change," *Ethnic Newswatch* (January 31, 1995); cited in Clint Bolick, *Transformation: The Promise and Politics of Empowerment* (Oakland, Calif.: Institute for Contemporary Studies, 1998), p. 10.

P. 499 Schorr quotation: Lisbeth B. Schorr, *Common Purpose* (New York: Anchor Books, 1997), p. 99.

P. 499 "In Durham, North Carolina . . . hardest-to-reach teens'": Bolick, *Transformation,* p. 109.

P. 500 "As the Heritage Foundation's Stuart Butler observes . . . reject from city hall": Ibid., p. 119.

P. 500 "For instance, a 1998 study . . . jobs and education": Susan Saegert and Gary Winkel, "Social Capital and the Revitalization of New York City's Distressed Inner-City Housing," *Housing Policy Debate* 9, no. 1 (1998), p. 48. (Published by the Fannie Mae Foundation.)

P. 501 "Some of the first boards started . . . new board there": Vermont Reparative Probation Program, semi-finalist application.

P. 501 "Several years ago, for instance . . . every worksite in the U.S.": National Performance Review, "The New OSHA: Getting a GRIP on Workplace Injuries, Illnesses, and Deaths," *Reinvention Roundtable* 1.3, no. 2 (Winter 1996–97), p. 6. (Published by the National Performance Review, Washington, D.C.)

P. 501 "Injury rates dropped 35 percent": John Kamensky, "The Best-Kept Secret in Government," in *Transforming Government: Lessons from the Reinvention Laboratories,* ed. Patricia W. Ingraham, James R. Thompson, and Ronald P. Sanders (San Francisco: Jossey-Bass, 1998), p. 71.

P. 501 "In British Columbia . . . and community representatives": Rodal and Mulder, "Partnerships, Devolution and Power-Sharing," p. 48.

P. 501 "In Florida, Governor Chiles . . . in partnership with government": Enterprise Florida, *Annual Report: 1995–1996* (Tallahassee: Enterprise Florida, 1996).

P. 503 "The Youth Futures Authority . . . go to college": Center for the Study of Social Policy, *Creating a Community Agenda,* p. 7.

P. 505 Center for the Study of Social Policy quotation: Center for the Study of Social Policy, *Creating a Community Agenda,* p. 36.

P. 505 "It became obvious to Indianapolis Mayor Goldsmith . . . not-for-profit development corporations'": Goldsmith, *The Twenty-First Century City,* p. 139.

P. 506 Karp quotation: Karp, "The Offender/Community Relationship."

P. 506 "Indianapolis created a Neighborhood Empowerment Initiative . . . initiatives in the neighborhoods": William R. Potapchuk, Jarle Crocker, and William H. Schechter Jr., *Systems Reform and Local Government: Improving Outcomes for Children, Families, and Neighborhoods* (Washington, D.C.: Program for Community Problem Solving, February 1997), pp. 38–39 (working paper).

P. 506 "Since 1994, the center has helped . . . associations": Goldsmith, *The Twenty-First Century City,* p. 160.

P. 506 "In Canada, for instance . . . years after occupancy": Saegert and Winkel, "Social Capital and the Revitalization of New York City's Distressed Inner-City Housing," p. 52

Pp. 506–507 "Seattle maintains and publicizes . . . neighborhood planning": Seattle Office of Neighborhood Planning, *Toolbox Index* (Seattle: Office of Neighborhood Planning). Available from the office at 600 Fourth Ave., Room 200, Seattle WA 98104–1826.

P. 507 Carter quotation: Schorr, *Common Purpose,* p. 345.

P. 507 Schorr quotation: Ibid.

P. 508 "When city commissioners in Battle Creek . . . community organizations": Potapchuk, Crocker, and Schechter, *Systems Reform and Local Government*, p. 28.

P. 508 Goldsmith quotation: Goldsmith, *The Twenty-First Century City,* p. 158

P. 509 "In Minneapolis in 1990 . . . a bunch of lazy farts'": David A. Plotz, *Community Problem Solving Case Summaries, Volume III* (Washington, D.C., Program for Community Problem Solving, 1991), p. 5.

Pp. 508–509 Haugen quotation: Ibid., p. 4.

P. 509 Clark quotation: Ibid., p. 5.

P. 509 "In the late 1980s, Don Mendonsa . . . and not working": Center for the Study of Social Policy, *Creating a Community Agenda*, p. 72.

P. 509 "When the data became public . . . turn things around": Ibid, p. 73.

P. 509 Mendonsa quotation: Schorr, *Common Purpose,* p. 339.

Pp. 509–510 Hogan quotation: Cornelius Hogan, "Accountability in an Era of Federal Devolution and Emerging Community Partnerships on Behalf of the Wellbeing of Children, Families, and Communities" (unpublished manuscript), p. 9.

P. 510 "Missouri launched its Caring Communities . . . local leaders": Schorr, *Common Purpose,* p. 96–97.

P. 511 Study quotation: Center for the Study of Social Policy, *Creating a Community Agenda,* p. 9.

P. 512 Schorr quotation: Schorr, *Common Purpose,* p. 323.

Pp. 512–513 Center for the Study of Social Policy quotations: Center for the Study of Social Policy, *Creating a Community Agenda,* p. 54; and *Toward New Forms of Local Governance* (Washington, D.C.: Center for the Study of Social Policy, 1996) , p. 33.

Pp. 514–515 "In Boston in 1989, a pregnant white woman . . . such as those with no prior offenses": Orlando Patterson and Christopher Winthrop, "Boston's Police Solution," *New York Times,* March 3, 1999, p. A23.

P. 515 "In Portland, Oregon, for instance . . . police will take": Potapchuk, Crocker, and Schechter, *Systems Reform and Local Government,* p. 31.

P. 515 "In Dane County, Wisconsin . . . the health of children": Potapchuk, Crocker, and Schechter, *Systems Reform and Local Government,* p. 21.

P. 516 Study of Chicago school reform quotation: Bryk and others, *Charting Chicago School Reform,* pp. 31–32.

P. 517 Schorr quotations: Schorr, *Common Purpose,* p. 78.

P. 517 Center for the Study of Social Policy quotation: Center for the Study of Social Policy, *Toward New Forms of Local Governance,* pp. 21–22.

Pp. 517–518 "Maryland's state government . . . and school projects": Ibid., p. 32.

P. 519 "When the Center for the Study of Social Policy . . . city, county, and school districts": Center for the Study of Social Policy, *Creating a Community Agenda,* p. 5.

P. 519 "Others, such as Kansas City's Local Investment Commission . . . officials from public agencies": Ibid., p. 22.

P. 520 Observer quotation: Ibid., pp. 35–36.

P. 520 "In 1992 the Chicago Transit Authority . . . rose up in noisy opposition": Laura Olsen, *Transit-Oriented Communities* (Washington, D.C.: Mobility Partners, n.d.), pp. 17–25. The Mobility Partners Program is an initiative of the U.S. Environmental Protection Agency's Office of Policy and the Surface Transportation Policy Project.

P. 520 "Meeting in church basements . . . Pulaski Street Station": Ibid., pp. 18–19.

P. 521 "About 10 days later . . . $300 million in renovating it": Ibid., pp. 21–22.

P. 521 ISTEA quotation: U.S. Department of Transportation, *Working Together on Transportation Planning: An Approach to Collaborative Decision Making* (Washington, D.C.: U.S. Department of Transportation, May 1995), p. 9. (Report No. FTA-DC–26–6013–95–1.)

P. 521 Kochanowski quotation: Ibid., p. 8.

P. 521 "Before ISTEA . . . then sell the public on it": Ibid., p. 20.

P. 522 Potapchuk and Polk quotation ("'Local politics . . . '"): Potapchuk and Polk, *Building the Collaborative Community,* p. 5.

P. 522 Potapchuk and Polk quotation ("'By consulting with the parties . . .'"): Ibid., p. 18.

P. 523 Barriers to Consensus Building box quotations: James Creighton, *Involving Citizens in Community Decision Making: A Guidebook* (Washington, D.C.: Program for Community Problem Solving, 1992), pp. 60–62.

P. 523 Elements of collaborative planning: adapted from Potapchuk and Polk, *Building the Collaborative Community,* p. 12.

P. 526 Mizuno quotation: U.S. Department of Transportation, *Transportation, Environmental Justice, and Social Equity Conference Proceedings* (Washington, D.C.: U.S. Department of Transportation, Federal Transit Administration), p. 28.

P. 526 "Oakland, California awarded . . . a chance to express their ideas": Olsen, *Transit-Oriented Communities,* pp. 31–32.

P. 527 Center for the Study of Social Policy analysts quotation: Center for the Study of Social Policy, *Creating a Community Agenda,* p. 45.

P. 527 "By the 1990s, there were . . . affordable housing": Schorr, *Common Purpose,* pp. 316–319.

P. 528 "The New Community Corporation . . . 1,000 people, for example": Ibid.

P. 528 "In 1998, Missouri went . . . creation of the district": See the Web site for the Missouri state legislature: www.house.state.mo.us/bills98/ (click on "Biltxt98," then "Truly98," then "HB1636.HTM.".

Pp. 528–529 "In Baltimore, the city . . . designed by inner-city residents": Borins, *Innovating with Integrity,* p. 223.

P. 529 "The number of community foundations . . . $20 billion in assets": Janet Topolsky, "Community Endowments for Community Futures," in *Ideas in Development* (Washington, D.C.; Corporation for Enterprise Development, 1999), p. 33.

Pp. 529–530 "In sparsely populated . . . community endowment": Interview with Sid Armstrong, executive director of the Montana Community Foundation.

P. 530 Topolsky quotations: Topolsky, "Community Endowments for Community Futures," pp. 32, 34.

P. 530 Corporation for Enterprise Development report: Kent Marcoux and Andrea Levere, "Creating Our Own Capital Markets: A Development Finance Strategy," in *Ideas in Development,* p. 56.

Chapter Thirteen

P. 536 "Another unemployed worker . . . a customer!": Morley Winograd and Dudley Buffa, *Taking Control: Politics in the Information Age* (New York: Henry Holt, 1996), p. 203.

P. 536 Yankelovich quotation: Yankelovich Partners and Jobs for the Future, "Summary of Focused Groups" (report for the U.S. Department of Labor, June 4, 1993).

P. 539 Filipczak quotation: Bob Filipczak, "Critical Mass: Putting Whole Systems Thinking into Practice," *Training* (September 1995), p. 34.

P. 542 Carr and Littman quotation: David K. Carr and Ian D. Littman, *Excellence in Government: Total Quality Management in the 1990s* (Arlington, Va.: Coopers & Lybrand, 1990), pp. 39–40.

Pp. 542–543 Dunkle quotation: Margaret Dunkle, "A Bottom-Up Look at Welfare Reform: What Happens When Policymakers Apply for Assistance from the Programs They Created?" *Education Week* 15, no. 13 (November 29, 1995).

P. 544 Bill Creech quotation: Bill Creech, *The Five Pillars of TQM: How to Make Total Quality Management Work for You* (New York: Dutton, 1994), p. 383.

P. 546 "Later adopted by the legislature . . . productivity gains, and new revenues": Florida Department of Management Services, Innovation Investment Program status reports, fiscal years 1993–1994 and 1994–1995 (Tallahassee: Florida Department of Management Services, 1994 and 1995).

P. 550 "In the United Kingdom . . . used the tool repeatedly": Julie Beedon, "Joining Forces for Strategic Change," *People Management* (October 5, 1995).

Pp. 550–551 "In the U.S., users include . . . in upstate New York": Robert W. Jacobs, *Real Time Strategic Change* (San Francisco: Berrett-Koehler, 1994).

P. 551 Raff quotations: Personal communication from Martin Raff, February 16, 1996.

Pp. 551–552 Jacobs quotation: Jacobs, *Real Time Strategic Change,* p. 167.

P. 552 Sandraas quotation: Ibid., p. 95.

Pp. 552–553 Jacobs quotations: Ibid., pp. 103, 111–112.

P. 556 "On a survey taken after about two years . . . faculty become better teachers": Donald Sargeant, Richard Heydinger, and Tom Jorgens, "A Notebook Computer for Everyone: The University of Minnesota Crookston's Technology Strategy," in *Mobilizing for Transformation: How Campuses Are Preparing for the Information Age,* New Directions for Institutional Research, no. 94, ed. Donald M. Norris and James L. Morrison (San Francisco: Jossey-Bass, 1997), pp. 47–56.

Chapter Fourteen

P. 557 Creech quotation ("'*Quality begets quality . . .*'"): Bill Creech, *The Five Pillars of TQM: How to Make Total Quality Management Work for You* (New York: Dutton, 1994), p. 171.

P. 558 Creech quotation ("'Such symbols can be . . .'"): Ibid., p. 172.

Pp. 558–559 Raff quotations: Martin Raff, *Leading Transformation* (Salisbury, England: British Deming Society, 1995), p. 13.

P. 560 Emerson quotation: quoted in Al Gore, *From Red Tape to Results: Creating a Government That Works Better and Costs Less* (Washington, D.C.: National Performance Review, 1993), p. 72.

P. 562 Stone's story: See David Osborne and Ted Gaebler, *Reinventing Government* (Reading, Mass.: Addison-Wesley, 1992), p. 10.

P. 565 Hale quotation ("'If the public hears . . . '"): Sandra J. Hale, "The Minnesota Approach to Revitalizing Government," in *Lessons for Florida: The Minnesota Approach to Revitalizing Government,* ed. Florida Center for Public Management (Tallahassee: Florida State University, 1992), p. 8.

P. 565 Hale quotation ("'What would they have preferred . . . '"): Quoted in Kim Ode, "She Strives to Make System a Pleasant Surprise," *Minneapolis Star Tribune,* Oct. 20, 1987, p. 1C.

P. 566 Peters and Waterman quotation: Tom Peters and Robert Waterman, *In Search of Excellence: Lessons from America's Best-Run Companies* (New York: Warner Books, 1982, p. 223.

P. 566 "When the Ford Foundation . . . full-blown from innovators' minds": Fred Jordan, *Innovating America* (New York: Ford Foundation, 1990), pp. 117–118.

P. 567 Fliegel quotation: Seymour Fliegel, *Miracle in East Harlem: The Fight for Choice in Public Education* (New York: Times Books, 1993), p. 126.

P. 567 Drucker quotation: Peter F. Drucker, "The Innovative Organization," in *The Frontiers of Management* (New York: E. P. Dutton, 1986), p. 261.

P. 568 Galbraith quotation: Quoted in Gifford Pinchot III, *Intrapreneuring* (New York: Harper & Row, 1985), pp. 146–147.

P. 572 Creech quotations: Creech, *The Five Pillars of TQM,* pp. 171, 173.

Pp. 573–574 "A three-year evaluation . . . interaction among employees": Mary Ann Wyckoff and Wesley G. Skogan, *Community Policing in Madison: Quality from the Inside, Out: Executive Summary* (Washington, D.C.: National Institute of Justice, 1993).

P. 574 "The seminal study on what motivates employees . . . salary and benefits": Frederick Herzberg, *Work and the Nature of Man* (New York: World Publishing, 1966.)

P. 575 Couper quotation: David C. Couper and Sabine H. Lobitz, *Quality Policing: The Madison Experience* (Washington, D.C.: Police Executive Research Forum, 1991), p. 62.

P. 581 Jacobs quotation: Jacobs, *Real Time Strategic Change,* p. 84.

P. 582 Harrison quotation: Ibid., p. 85

Chapter Fifteen

P. 583 Roberts quotation: Charlotte Roberts, "Checklist for Personal Values," in Peter M. Senge et al., *The Fifth Discipline Fieldbook* (New York: Doubleday, 1994), p. 209.

P. 584 Kouzes and Posner quotation: James M. Kouzes and Barry Z. Posner, *The Leadership Challenge: How to Keep Getting Extraordinary Things Done in Organizations* (San Francisco: Jossey-Bass, 1995), p. 212.

P. 592 Creech quotation: Bill Creech, *The Five Pillars of TQM: How to Make Total Quality Management Work for You* (New York: Dutton, 1994), p. 128.

P. 596 Drucker quotation: Peter F. Drucker, *Managing the Non-Profit Organization: Principles and Practices* (New York: HarperBusiness, 1992), p. 4.

P. 599 Kouzes and Posner quotation: Kouzes and Posner, *The Leadership Challenge,* p. 111.

P. 600 Senge quotation: Peter M. Senge, *The Fifth Discipline: The Art and Practice of the Learning Organization* (New York: Doubleday, 1990), p. 211.

P. 601 Smith quotation ("When a shared vision starts . . ."): Bryan Smith, "Building Shared Vision: How to Begin," in Senge et al., *The Fifth Discipline Fieldbook,* p. 323.

P. 601 Smith quotation ("'Anything less than the truth . . . '"): Ibid., p. 316.

P. 602 Senge quotation: Senge, *The Fifth Discipline,* p. 223.

P. 604 Kouzes and Posner quotations: Kouzes and Posner, *The Leadership Challenge,* pp. 213, 217.

Pp. 604–605 Hammer and Stanton quotation: Michael Hammer and Steven Stanton, *The Reengineering Handbook: A Revolution* (New York: HarperBusiness, 1995), pp. 161–163.

P. 609 "The city government in Madison . . . of daily work life": City of Madison Organizational Development and Training Office, *Training Opportunities: 1993* (Madison, Wisc.: Organizational Development and Training Office, 1993).

About the Authors

David Osborne is the author or coauthor of three other books on government reform: *Laboratories of Democracy* (1988), *Reinventing Government* (1992), and *Banishing Bureaucracy* (1997). A managing partner of the Public Strategies Group, a consulting firm, Osborne has worked with governments at every level—local, state, federal, and foreign—to help them develop strategies to improve their performance. In 1993 he served as a senior adviser to Vice President Al Gore, providing intellectual guidance to Gore's National Performance Review and serving as chief author of its 1993 report. He is also a founder and former board chairman of the Alliance for Redesigning Government, a fellow of the National Academy of Public Administration, a fellow at the Progressive Policy Institute, and a member of the Education Commission of the States' National Commission on Governing America's Schools.

Peter Plastrik is a coauthor of *Banishing Bureaucracy*, as well as the author of many articles and columns about reinventing government, community development, and economic development. He has served as chief deputy of the Michigan Department of Commerce, president of the Michigan Strategic Fund, and chief of staff of the Michigan Partnership for New Education, an education reform initiative. He now consults primarily for foundations and nonprofit organizations.

Visit www.ReinventGov.com for more information and tools that build on those in this book.

Index

B

D

E

H

I

J

K

P

Q

R

T

U

Grateful acknowledgment is made to the following for permission to reprint previously published material:

Berrett-Koehler: From *A Complaint Is a Gift.* Copyright © 1996 by Janelle Barlow and Claus Moller. Berrett-Koehler Publishers, Inc., San Francisco, CA. All rights reserved. 1/800–929–2929.

Berrett-Koehler: From *The End of Bureaucracy and the Rise of the Intelligent Organization.* Copyright © 1993 by Gifford and Elizabeth Pinchot, Berrett-Koehler Publishers, Inc., San Francisco, CA. All rights reserved. 1/800–929–2929.

Doubleday: From *Common Purpose* by Lisbeth B. Schorr. Copyright © 1997 by Lisbeth Bamberger Schorr. Used by permission of Doubleday, a division of Random House, Inc. Additional reprint rights granted by permission of Russell & Volkening as agents for the author.

Dutton: From *The Five Pillars of TQM: How to Make Total Quality Management Work for You* by Bill Creech. Copyright © 1994 by Bill Creech. Used by permission of the author.

Free Press: From *The Rise and Fall of Strategic Planning* by Henry Mintzberg. Reprinted with the permission of The Free Press, a division of Simon & Schuster. Copyright © 1994 by Henry Mintzberg. Additional reprint rights granted by permission of Pearson Education Limited.

Regnery Publishing: From *The Twenty-First Century City: Resurrecting Urban America* by Steven Goldsmith. Copyright © 1997 by Regnery Publishing, Inc. All rights reserved. Reprinted by special permission of Regnery Publishing, Inc., Washington, DC.

Simon & Schuster: From *Showdown* by Elizabeth Drew. Reprinted with the permission of Simon & Schuster. Copyright © 1996 by Elizabeth Drew. Afterword Copyright © 1997 by Elizabeth Drew. Additional reprint rights granted by permission of Sterling Lord Literistic, Inc.